BRITISH HISTORICAL MEDALS OF THE 17TH CENTURY

MEDALLISTS, BOOKS, AUTHORS, COLLECTORS, BOOK-SELLERS & ANTIQUARIES

"'George Vertue, portrait of himself.' A richly symbolic drawing in pen and ink with black and [red] chalk, ca. 1713. Inserted in his note-book (B.M. Add. MS. 21,211)." Image © Trustees of the British Museum.

The antiquary John Nichols, in his *Literary Anecdotes…*, comments:

> *The notebooks kept by the engraver George Vertue on the work of his artist contemporaries and predecessors are one of the most significant sources of information for the history of British art. In this self-portrait Vertue surrounds himself with symbols of patronage.*

(Continued on page viii)

BRITISH HISTORICAL MEDALS OF THE 17TH CENTURY

MEDALLISTS, BOOKS, AUTHORS, COLLECTORS, BOOK-SELLERS & ANTIQUARIES

Jerome J. Platt & Arleen Kay Platt

SPINK

LONDON

ESTABLISHED 1666

BRITISH HISTORICAL MEDALS OF THE 17TH CENTURY:

MEDALLISTS, BOOKS, AUTHORS, COLLECTORS BOOK-SELLERS & ANTIQUARIES

A Companion Volume to:

The English Civil Wars: Medals, Historical Commentary & Personalities (*Vols. 1 & 2*)

Published by Spink & Son Ltd.
69 Southampton Row
Bloomsbury
London WC1B 4ET

Library Of Congress Cataloging-in-Publication Data
Platt, Jerome J.
Arleen Kay Platt
British Historical Medals of the 17th Century:
Medallists, Books, Authors, Collectors, Book-sellers & Antiquaries
A Companion Volume to:
The English Civil War: Medals, Historical Commentary & Personalities (vols. 1 & 2)

ISBN: 978-1-907427-48-0

Includes bibliographic references and index
1. Medals. 2. Numismatics. 3. Great Britain—History. 4. Medallists. 5. 17th century. 6. Historical medals. 7. Commemorative medals. 8. Military medals. 9. Authors and Books on medals. 10. Collectors and Collections. 11. Medallic art. 12. Antiquaries & Chronographers. 12. Booksellers and Printsellers—Great Britain. 13. Collectors and collections.

The illustration appearing on the title page is from George Vertue's *Description of the Works of the Ingenious Delineator and Engraver Wenceslaus Hollar, Disposed into Classes of Different Sorts; with some Account of His Life*, London. Printed for William Bathloe, at his Circulating Library in the Strand, near Exeter Exchange. 2nd ed., 1759. The bust is of Thomas Howard, earl of Arundel and Surrey, after Van Dyck. Hollar came to Arundel's attention in 1636 during the latter's tour of Europe, and was taken on as a draftsman and illustrator. Hollar then travelled with Arundel during the remainder of his tour and returned to England with him, remaining a member of the earl's household until Arundel's death in 1646. The image portrays Arundel in front of a pyramid with some of the art treasures that he collected as well as Holler's instruments. Note the badge or medal worn on a chain by Howard. Image © Trustees of the British Museum.

Table of Contents

Preface

Authors & Published Works Associated with British Medals of the 17th Century

Louis Jobert (1637-1719) & Obadiah Walker (1616–1699) 3
La Science des Médailles... (1693),
The Knowledge of Medals... (1715)
Charles Patin (1633-1693) 9
Introduction to the History of Medals (1683)
John Evelyn (1620-1706) 13
Numismata: A Discourse of Medals (1697)
Joseph Addison (1672-1719) 27
Dialogues upon the Usefulness of Ancient Medals (1721)
George Vertue (1684-1756) 33
Medals, Coins, Great-Seals... of Thomas Simon (1753; 1780)
David Jennings (1691-1762) 45
An Introduction to the Science of Medals (1764)
Thomas Snelling (1712-1773) 49
Thirty-Three Plates of English Medals (1776)
Pierre (Peter) Duby (1721-1782) 58
Des Pieces Obsidionales et de Nécessité (1785)
John Pinkerton (1758-1826) 61
The Medallic History of England (title varies; 1790, 1802, 1831, ?)
Henry Henfrey (1852-1881) 81
Numismata Cromwelliana (1877)
Mr. Taylor Combe (1774-1826) & Dr. Charles Combe (1744-1817) 85
Edward Hawkins (1780-1867) 87
Augustus W. Franks (1826-1897) 91
Herbert A. Grueber (1846-1927) 96
Medallic Illustrations of the History of Great Britain and Ireland, to the Death of George II (1885; 1969) 97
Herbert Gruber's Medallic Illustrations of the History of Great Britain and Ireland ('The Plates') (1904-11; 1979) 101
Helen Farquhar (1869-1953) 105
On Tudor and Stuart Coins and Medals (1909-1915)
Other Published Works on 17th century Medals: A Brief Review of the Literature 109

Medallists Associated with 17th Century British Medals

Nicholas Hilliard (ca. 1542?–1619) 115
Charles Anthony, (fl. 1599-1615) 119
van Abeele, Pieter (1608-ca. 1677 or 1684?) 123
Christoph[er] Adolfszoon (fl. 1666-1676) 125

Pierre Regnier (ca. 1577-after 1640) 127
Nicholas Briot (1579?-1646?) 131
Simon de Passe (ca. 1595-1647) 139
Claude Warin (Varin) (1606/07?-1654; fl. 1630–1654) 143
Jean Warin (Varin) (1604/6?-1672, fl. 1629-1672) 145
Thomas Rawlins (1620?-1670; fl. 1641-1670) 149
Peter (Pierre) Blondeau (16??-1672; fl. ca. 1636-1664) 159
Heinrich Reitz the Younger (1622?-1692?; fl. 1636-1649) 167
Abraham Simon (1622?-1692?) 171
Thomas Simon (1623 OR 1623?-1665) 181
Jean Petitot (1607/8-1691) & Pierre Bordier (1676-1763) 193
John Roettier[s] & Family (1631-1703) 199
George Bower[s] (fl. 1664–1689; d. 1690?) 207
Jan Smeltzing (1656 - 1693) 209
John Croker (1670–1741) 211

❖

Later Medallists Associated with 17th c. British Medals

Jean Dassier (1676-1763) 215
_____ 'Stuart' (fl. 1740-1780?) 221
James 'Athenian' Stuart (1713-1788) 225
John Kirk (1724?-1776/8?) 229

❖

Eminent Collectors and Collections of 17th c. British Medals

The Royal Collections of Princes James & Charles 237
Samuel Pepys (1633-1703) 243
Ralph Thoresby (1658-1725) 247
Sir Hans Sloane (1660-1753) 251
Dr. Richard Mead (1673-1754) 253
Edward Harley, 2nd earl of Oxford (1689–1741) 259
Sir Hugh Percy, 1st Duke of Northumberland (1715-1786)
& Elizabeth, his duchess (1716-1776) 264
Horatio Walpole, 4th earl of Orford (1717 –1797) 267
Dr. William Hunter (1718-1783) 275
The Rev. Mr. Richard Southgate (1729-1795) 279
Thomas Dimsdale (1758-1823) 283
Thomas Thomas (?-1843) 285
Samuel Tyssen (1756-1800) 289
Edward Solly, (1776-1844) 295
Sir Joseph Banks, Bart. (1743-1820) 297
Sarah Sophia Banks (1744-1818) 299
W. Matthew Young (1771-1838) 301
Marmaduke Trattle (1751-1831) 303
Surgeon-Major J. W. Fleming (?-1877) 307
Sir Richard Tangye (1833-1906) 309
Hyman Montagu (1844-1895) 313
John G. Murdoch (1830-1902) 319

R. W. Cochran-Patrick (1842-1897) 323
Greta Heckett (1899-1976) 327
'A Collection of British Historical Medals' (1889) 329
The 'Papillon Collection' (1998) 333
'An Important Collection of British Historical Medals' (2003) 335
The Christopher Foley Collection of English medals (2014) 337

Antiquaries, Chroniclers, Engravers, Printers, Book- & Print-sellers

Josiah Ricraft (d. 1688) 341
Edward Hyde, earl of Clarendon (1609-1674) 345
Martin Folkes (1690–1754) 349
Rev. Andrew Coltée Ducarel (1713-1785) 351
Francis Perry (fl. 1750-1765; d. 1765) 355
Thomas Hollis (1720-1774) 361
Rev. James Granger (1723-1776) 367
John Thane (1747/48?-1818) 375
James Caulfield (1764-1826) 383
The Bowyers & Nichols Families
William Bowyer the Elder (1663-1737) 387
William Bowyer the Younger (1699-1777) 389
The Nichols Family
John Nichols (1745-1826) 391
John Bowyer Nichols (1779-1863) 393
John Gough Nichols (1806-1873) 394
Richard Gouth (1735-1809) 397

Bibliography

Index

The Rev. Granger on his 'Singular Book'

To the Honourable Horace Walpole

Sir,

This singular book, which has been the employment of my leisure hours for several years of my life, will, doubtless, be numbered among my idlenesses, perhaps my weaknesses; but, I hope, never amongst my sins. The performance falls far short of my own expectation; I wish, Sir, it may, in any degree, answer yours. I was not sufficiently informed of my ignorance when I undertook it: like one walking in a fog, I fancied I saw it at a distance, when I was surrounded with it. The work, with all its defects, has afforded me much amusement, and not a little labour: the pleasure of writing resembles that of travelling; many delightful scenes present themselves on the road; but there are also objects to create disgust, and it is attended with languor and fatigue.

However well-meant my poor endeavours may be, I do not expect to escape censure. To this I shall very patiently submit. All the favour that I desire from the reader is, that he will judge with the same candor with which I have written. I have attempted to act the part of an humble author; but have no kind of anxiety for fame...

— Rev. James Granger, the dedication to *A Biographical History of England*..., 3rd ed., 1779, vol. i.

(Continued from page ii)

The National Portrait Gallery further comments:

> ***The miniature which he holds in his left hand is of his friend and patron Edward Harley, 2nd Earl of Oxford. His right hand rests on his own engraving of Shakespeare and a bust of Charles I, a royal patron of a previous age, is visible to the right. In the bottom right corner a Latin motto, 'Honour nourishes the arts', is probably an appeal to Frederick, Prince of Wales, another connoisseur of the arts.***

A letter referencing this drawing appeared in the April 1810, issue of *The Gentleman's Magazine* (p. 313). It was dated March 27 and signed 'S. W.' The date attributed to the drawing, 1741, would appear to be that of the print made by Maxim Gauci (1776-1854) and published by Anthony Molteno (ca. 1784-1845):

> ***...Mr. Stevenson of Norwich possesses a spirited head, merely a profile, of Mr. Vertue...also a half-length, octavo size, by himself, 1741, slight, but well touched in chalk, holding a miniature of the Earl of Oxford, sitting in a library, before a table, on which are prints, coins, and medals, palate and pencils, engraving tools, &c. Charles the First's bust over the chimney-piece, and in a little ornamental compartment "Honor alit artes..."***

Preface

The Long History of Commemorative Medals

A 4TH CENTURY GOLD MEDALLION FROM TICINUM (TODAY'S PAVIA) IN ITALY, THIS EXAMPLE OF A MEDAL COMMEMORATING MILITARY SUCCESS ILLUSTRATES THE LONG TRADITION OF ISSUING MEDALS WITH SUCH THEMES.* THIS MEDAL BEARS ON THE OBVERSE A BUST OF THE EMPEROR CONSTANTINE I ('CONSTANTINE THE GREAT,' A.D. 272-337) WEARING A HELMET AND ARMOR, AND ON THE REVERSE TWO WINGED AND DRAPED VICTORIES (NIKES) HOLDING A SHIELD WITH AN INSCRIPTION CELEBRATING THE 'JOYFUL VICTORIES OF OUR EMPERORS.' THE BRITISH MUSEUM DATES THIS MEDAL AS CONTEMPORANEOUS TO THE DEDICATION OF THE TRIUMPHAL ARCH ERECTED TO COMMEMORATE CONSTANTINE'S VICTORY OVER HIS RIVAL MAXENTIUS (A.D. 315). THE MEDAL WAS LIKELY ISSUED TO CELEBRATE HIS MANY VICTORIES IN CIVIL WARS AS WELL AS IN WARS AGAINST THE FRANKS, ALAMANNI, VISIGOTHS AND SARMATIANS. THIS EXAMPLE WAS ACQUIRED BY THE BRITISH MUSEUM IN 1896 AS A PURCHASE FROM ROLLIN & FEUARDENT, A DEALER IN COINS, GEMS AND ANTIQUITIES IN PARIS AND LONDON. IT WAS FORMERLY IN THE COLLECTION OF HYMAN MONTAGU (*SEE PP. 312-317*). IMAGE © TRUSTEES OF THE BRITISH MUSEUM.

*APART FROM COMMEMORATIVE MEDALS, BY THE 1ST CENTURY A.D., AND PERHAPS AS EARLY AS THE 1ST CENTURY B.C., THE ROMAN ARMY POSSESSED A FORMAL, COMPLEX, RANK-RELATED SYSTEM OF MILITARY REWARDS AND DECORATIONS WHICH HAS BEEN LIKENED TO THAT WHICH EXISTED IN THE 20TH CENTURY BRITISH ARMY. MAXFIELD PRESENTS THE EVIDENCE FOR THE EXISTENCE OF SUCH AWARDS, AS WELL AS HER CONCLUSIONS CONCERNING THEIR ORIGINS, ORGANIZATION AND DISTRIBUTION. THE READER IS REFERRED TO HER WORK FOR MORE INFORMATION (MAXFIELD, V. A., *MILITARY DECORATIONS OF THE ROMAN ARMY*. BERKELEY: UNIV. OF CALIFORNIA PRESS, 1981).

§

THE BRITISH MUSEUM, IN THE OVERVIEW OF ITS 2002 EXHIBITION, '*REFLECTIONS OF GLORY: THE MEDALLIC ART OF 16TH CENTURY ITALY*,' SUCCINCTLY SUMMARIZES THE 'MODERN' HISTORY OF THE COMMEMORATIVE MEDAL:

> *THE FIRST MEDALS WERE MADE IN ITALY IN THE 1430S. ONE HUNDRED YEARS LATER THE ITALIAN MEDAL WAS FIRMLY ESTABLISHED, WITH PRINCES, CLERICS, ANTIQUARIES, MERCHANTS AND MANY OTHERS USING THE MEDIUM TO SIGNIFY PERSONAL WORTH. BEING PORTABLE AND DURABLE, MEDALS WERE RECOGNISED AS HIGHLY EFFECTIVE WAYS OF CONVEYING A MESSAGE TO CONTEMPORARIES, AND ALSO TO POSTERITY. IMAGES AND INSCRIPTIONS WERE CAREFULLY CHOSEN TO INDICATE THE VIRTUES AND EVENTS WITH WHICH THOSE REPRESENTED ON THE MEDALS WISHED TO BE ASSOCIATED.*

—http://www.britishmuseum.org/whats_on/past_exhibitions/2002/archive_reflections_of_glory.aspx

PREFACE

AS ATTRACTIVE as historical or commemorative medals are in their own right and as telling as they are by their designs and inscriptions of the persons or events they honor (or, in some cases, vilify or deride), they also tell us much more. By means of words, design and allegory, they tell us of their age, of their makers, of the purpose for which they were made, the manner in which they were made and the 'story' their maker wished to communicate. This volume presents the published works on 17th c. British medals that appeared in the late 17th through late 19th centuries as well as brief biographies of the authors. It also surveys the medallists who created the medals, the major collectors of the medals, some of whom built great collections that we know of through auction catalogues,[1] and finally, the antiquaries and chroniclers who wrote on the period, or who were otherwise associated with these works.

This work is intended as a companion volume to *The English Civil Wars: Medals, Historical Commentary and Personalities*.[2] The approach taken by the authors has been one of organizing the notes and observations they made during four decades of collecting in order to inform themselves of the historical context(s) within which 17th century medals and military rewards could best be understood. Their primary interest has always been in 'the story behind the medal.' The authors' view is that this story is not limited to the persons or events the medal was intended to commemorate and that to fully understand the significance of a particular medal the story should also include information about those persons who created the medals, studied and wrote about them, and where possible, collected them. A brief introduction to these individuals, some of whose names may not be at the forefront of every collector's consciousness—their biographies, written works, visages where available, characters, and personalities—is what the reader should expect to encounter in this volume.

The reader will of course immediately note that although the word 'medal' was in the titles of some early works (e.g., Louis Jobert'*s La Science des Médailles...,* 1693, or David Jennings' *An Introduction to the Science of Medals,* 1764), these books dealt with coins and not medals in the modern sense of these terms. Their inclusion in this volume reflects the present authors' view that for a full appreciation of British 17th c. medals it is necessary to understand numismatic history and literature in general in addition to those works dealing primarily or exclusively with medals, as we know them. To this end, the authors have included figures who were involved in the publication of a number of the classic works on the subject of numismatics. Thus, some personages included in this book may at first glance appear to have only a tangential relationship to 17th century *British medals*. In a number of cases, for such writers as Charles Patin, Louis Jobert, and Pierre (Peter) Duby, this reflects the present authors' interest in illustrating the development and eventual partial separation of interest in medals from coins, to which the former term was also applied. In other cases, for collectors such as Sir Martin Folkes and the Rev. Richard Southgate, who were only peripherally involved in medal collecting as an adjunct to coin collecting, it reflects the present authors' desire to present examples of how medals were represented in such collections.

The final grouping of personalities is those antiquaries, chroniclers, illustrators, printers and booksellers of the 17th through 19th centuries associated with British medals. Some of these individuals, such as the members of the Bowyer-Nichols publishing family and the engraver Francis Perry, are known to students of 17th century numismatics through their relationships to the 'Snel-

---

[1] Auctions of collections containing large numbers of 17th c. British medals are covered up to the present.

[2] Platt, J. J. & Platt, A. K. (2013). *The English Civil Wars: Medals, Historical Commentary, and Personalities*, London: Spink (2 vols.).

ling/Pinkerton plates'—two of the four editions of John Pinkerton's work were printed by the Nichols family while Francis Perry was involved in the original preparation of the plates which appeared in Thomas Snelling's predecessor volume. Others, such as Edward Hyde Clarendon and Josiah Ricraft, are included because their writings constitute part of our knowledge of the tumultuous events of mid-17th century Britain. As the present authors carried out the research for their earlier work on Civil War medals, they could not help but also become fascinated by the works, lives and personalities of authors of histories both of that period and of the 18th and 19th centuries as well as by the mediums through which history has been preserved—books, prints and paintings—in addition to medals. This led to many diversions from the path of completing their work on English Civil War medals, but resulted in much pleasure. The same was true for the collectors of 17th c. medals—for the authors, as collectors themselves, wished to learn of their earlier fellow collectors. For the authors, the entire panoply of persons connected with early medal collecting provided an enrichment of the tapestry of medal collecting since that time. Thus, this work is offered to the reader not only as a means of introduction to medallists associated with 17th century British medals, but also as an introduction to other persons through whose written works and collections readers, collectors and non-collectors alike, can expand their appreciation and understanding of these 'pieces of history.'

Numismatic literature on British medals has a clear lineage, beginning with John Evelyn's *Numismata: A Discourse of Medals...*, which appeared in 1697. With respect to subsequent works initially appearing in English, a full half-century after *Numismata...* was published, George Vertue's *Medals, Coins, Great-Seals...of Thomas Simon* appeared in 1753. Thomas Snelling's *Thirty-Three Plates of English Medals* was published in 1776 and a second edition of Vertue's book prepared by Richard Gouth appeared in 1780. Four subsequent versions of Snelling's *Thirty-three Plates...* volume, entitled *The Medallic History of England* or some variant, followed between 1790 and 1831, with at least the first volume having been edited by John Pinkerton.

The early works on numismatics which became available in England initially appeared in languages other than English, e.g., Charles Patin's *Introduction á L'histoire par la Connoissance des Médailles* appeared in 1665, and Jobert's *La Science des Médailles* appeared in 1693. Pierre (Peter) Duby's posthumous work *Des Pieces Obsidionales et de Nécessité* appeared in 1785.[3] While the books by Jobert and Duby were written in French and initially published in France and Holland, and only later translated into English, both influenced British coin and medal collectors by generally expanding interest in numismatic collecting in Britain. As noted above, these works, which were almost exclusively concerned with coins, used the terms coin and medal interchangeably. Even as medal collecting became differentiated from coin collecting, coins were usually the primary collecting interest for the majority of early collectors, with medal collecting a secondary interest. This is certainly true of the majority of those individuals we have labeled 'the eminent collectors.'

In reviewing the numismatic and historical literature of the 17th through 19th centuries, the authors have also come to greatly appreciate the world of the antiquaries, chroniclers, printers, & booksellers associated with books on medals or the histories that the authors consulted in preparing their earlier work on English Civil War medals. It was thus decided that knowledge of these individuals and their work might also be of value to others interested in antiquarian works on medals of this period. It is the authors' fervent hope that the reader will come away from reading this volume with an appreciation of the richness of person, time and place that medals of the 17th through 19th centuries reflect in terms of those individuals who have been associated with their creation and manufacture, as well as with collecting and studying them.

[3] Jobert's work dealt with the collecting of coins while Duby's work focused on coins, tokens and medals issued by besieged cities.

Initially the authors began research for this work and the earlier two volumes of *The English Civil Wars: Medals, Historical Commentary and Personages* for their own personal use by assembling information from the usual sources, i.e., books, journals, and other printed material. As has been previously noted, this took place over a period of decades. At a certain point, the need arose to personally visit and examine medals and books in the major institutional collections in which they now reside. When a decision was made to collate and expand this information into publishable form, the emphasis was on the medals and the personages and historical events associated with them. The results of this research were presented in *The English Civil Wars*. Originally, it had been intended that the earlier work would incorporate much of the material that appears here. It simply was not possible, however, to do so as it soon became clear that material primarily associated with authors, medallists, antiquaries, chroniclers, publishers and book-printers and sellers required a separate exposition.

Numerous persons and institutions have assisted the authors in collecting the information and illustrations needed in the preparation of this book. It is always difficult to prepare such a list and ensure that everyone who deserves credit receives it, but we will attempt to do so. Those who facilitated our research and tolerated our repeated visits and queries fall into several categories. First are those scholars, faculty and curatorial staff members at the institutions we visited—the British Museum's Department of Coins and Medals, the Department of Coins and Medals of the Fitzwilliam Museum, Cambridge, the Heberden Coin Room of the Ashmolean Museum, Oxford, the Victoria and Albert Museum, the Coins and Medals Collection of the Hunterian Museum, Glasgow, the Museum of London, the National Museums of Scotland, and most recently, the University of South Carolina's Irvin Department of Rare Books and Special Collections. A second group consists of those individuals at auction houses and specialist dealers who shared their expertise and/or images of medals and other material with us, including, but not limited to, Baldwin's Auctions, Classical Numismatic Group, Dix Noonan Webb, Morton & Eden, Noble Numismatics (Australia), Spink & Son, Tim Millett Historical Medals and Works of Art and Woolley & Wallis, Auctioneers. Thanks are also due to Ben Weiss for providing images of medals in his collection.

The specific individuals who assisted us in the preparation of this volume form a third group, and many stand out in our recollections. Their names appear here in alphabetical order: Martin Allen, Benjamin Alsop, the late Mark Blackburn, Lucy Cullen, Nimrod Dix, Daniel Fearon, John Goldsmith, Mary Hinton, Nick Holmes, Henry Kim, Janet Larkin, Tim Millett, James Morton, the late Graham Pollard, Luke Syson and Chris Webb. Some may not remember us as visitors, but we remember them and their assistance, of which we can say that we were, and still are, most appreciative. There are also those persons and organizations that have generously granted permission to reprint illustrations from their collections—these sources are credited in the relevant illustration legends. Illustrations without an attribution may safely be assumed to have come from the authors' own collection.

Finally, a word about the plan for, and final arrangement of, this book. First, with respect to chronological issues, the initial intent of the authors was to cover the entire series of British medals of the 17th century, but it was decided to end the survey (with some very few exceptions) with the year 1688 as the 'Glorious Revolution' provided a natural breaking point. Secondly, the reader will find that personages within sections (i.e., authors, medallists, collectors, etc.) are presented in roughly chronological order, taking into account dates of both birth and death, as well as years of productivity. Hopefully, this will not lead to the confusion that it has sometimes caused the authors. Third, a number of 18th and 19th c. medallists [e.g., Jean Dassier (1676-1763), the engraver 'Stuart' (*fl.* 1740-1780?), James 'Athenian' Stuart (1713-1788), John Kirk (1724?-1776/8?), and Amédée Durand (1789-1873)] are included because of an association, in some manner, with 17th c. medals.

Fourth, the reader will note that a modest number of the illustrations in this volume (fewer than ten percent) appeared previously in *The English Civil Wars: Medals, Commentary and Personalities*. The inclusion of these illustrations was intended to save the reader the necessity of consulting either the earlier work or the volume of plates for *Medallic Illustrations*. In some cases, better images than those used previously became available, and they were included for that reason. Illustrations of medals are accompanied by reference to entries for the specific medal in Hawkins, Franks & Grueber's *Medallic Illustrations...* (M.I., vols. I and II), the accompanying volume of Grueber's illustrative plates (M.I.Ill), Eimer's *British Commemorative Medals* ('Eimer,' 2010 ed.) or the present authors' previous work, *The English Civil Wars...* ('Platt,' 2013). Where these sources do not completely illustrate the point, other sources have been used. Fifth, this work is not intended to be a complete record of those collections including 17th century commemorative medals that have appeared at auction—there inevitably being collections that have not been included. A line had to be drawn somewhere, and a guiding principle was the extent to which the inclusion of an individual collection would illustrate some aspect of collecting. Sixth, as was the case in the authors' earlier work on English Civil War medals, to impart the flavor of the persons and times, and where material is clearly not directly concerned with the 17th-early 19th c. medals themselves but nonetheless is important in understanding this period, the authors have included information on some additional contemporary persons. Finally, while every effort has been taken to ensure accuracy in attributing illustrations, the possibility exists that we may have missed or erred in crediting an individual or organization. If this has occurred, the authors offer their sincere apologies. In the final analysis, the authors must and do assume responsibility for any errors of either omission or commission which appear within this work.

Jerome J Platt & Arleen Kay Platt
Charleston, South Carolina
January, 2017

Medal, Medallion. [*medialle* Fr. from *μέταλλογ*, metal, Gr.] A medal denotes a piece of metal in the shape of a coin, such as was either circulated as current money among the ancients, or struck on any particular occasion, in order to transmit to posterity the portrait of some great person, or the memory of some illustrious action. Scaliger derives the word *medal* from the Arabic *methalin*—a sort of coin with a human head upon it. But the opinion of Vossius is more generally received, who derives it, as we have done, from the Greek *μ έταλλογ*, of which substance medals are commonly made...

—J. Elmes, *A General and Bibliographical Dictionary of the Fine Arts*. 1826 Ed.

§

med-al. Etymology: Middle French *médaille*, from Old Italian *medaglia* coin worth half a denarius, medal, from (assumed) Vulgar Latin *medalis* half, alteration of Late Latin *medialis* middle, from Latin *medius*...circa 1578...a piece of metal often resembling a coin and having a stamped design that is issued to commemorate a person or event or awarded for excellence or achievement.

—*Merriam-Webster's Collegiate Dictionary & Thesaurus*, Version 2.5, 2000.

A mid-17th-century View of London

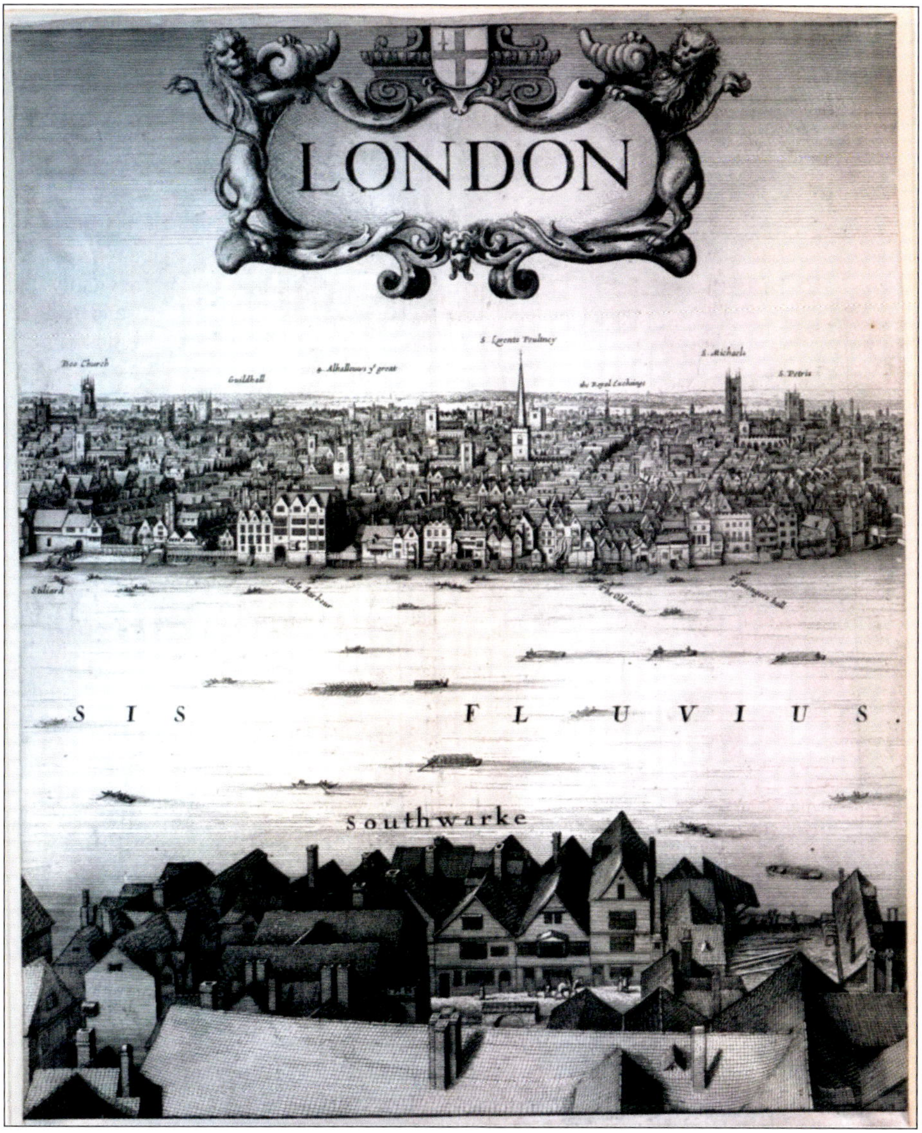

Wenceslaus Hollar's *Long View of London*, the fourth of seven panels,* provides a view of the City of London, Bow Street to St. Peter's, from a perspective overlooking Southwark on the south bank of the Thames, ca. 1647. While in Antwerp, Hollar prepared this etching from his own sketches and the earlier (1616) panoramic etching by the Dutch draftsman and map-maker Claes Jansz. Visscher (1587–1652). The view is from the tower of St Saviour's in Southwark (now the Cathedral and Collegiate Church of St. Saviour and St. Mary Overie). Several structures on the north bank are identified. these include the Old Swan stairs, Fishmonger's Hall, Guildhall, the Royal Exchange and a number of churches. This section has a street scene complete with pedestrians, a horse and a dog on the south bank. Hollar also drew views of London and Westminster in 1666, showing the city 'before and after' the Great Fire of 1666 (*see p. 353*). Image © Trustees of the British Museum, acc./reg. no 1864,0813.331.

*Actually etched on six plates, with the two end panels being etched on a single plate and requiring division.

The Medalet Struck by Augustus W. Franks, Antiquarian, Scholar, Collector and long-time Keeper at the British Museum

I may mention that in 1884 [Franks] had a medalet struck, with his crest and motto on the obverse and his name and family arms on the reverse, which he gave to his more intimate friends as a kind of numismatic memorial...

—Franks' obituary in the *Numismatic Chronicle and Journal of the Numismatic Society*, 1897, 3rd series. vol. xvii, p. 24.

§

Collecting is an hereditary disease, and I fear incurable.

—A. W. Franks, *The Apology of my Life*, in Caygill & Cherry, Appendix 1, p. 324.

Authors & Published Works Associated With British Historical Medals of the 17th Century

AN EARLY 18TH C. ENGRAVING OF TWO NUMISMATISTS SEATED BEFORE A CABINET EXAMINING COINS OR MEDALS. NOTE THE EMPTY SLOTS FOR THE TRAYS. FROM THE 4TH EDITION OF JOBERT'S *LA SCIENCE DES MÉDAILLES, ANTIQUES ET MODERNES…*, *PUBLISHED IN* 1717.

NOTHING can be pleasanter than to see a circle of...virtuosos about a cabinet of medals, descanting upon the value, rarity, and authenticalness [sic] of the several pieces that lie before them (R. Hurd, ed., *Works of Addison,* 1811, vol. i, p. 340).

Louis Jobert

(1637-1719)

(& Obadiah Walker)

(1616–1699)

LOUIS JOBERT, Jesuit priest, antiquary, and professor of rhetoric, was the author of *La Science des Médailles, Antiques et Modernes,* first published in 1693. Although concerned with coins and not medals, this work elicited a good deal of interest in both France and England in the early years of the 18th century, and both reflected and, in turn, contributed to the increasing popularity of coin and medal collecting in England. This interest in numismatics is evidenced by the sheer number of editions of this work, in various languages, which soon appeared. It also contributed to the developing view of numismatics as a science.

There appear to have been *at least* five French language editions of Jobert's work:

(1) 1692, Paris: Louis Lucas.

(2) 1693, Amsterdam: George Gallet; *also* Paris: chez la veuve Marbre-Cramoisy.[4]

(3) 1715, 3rd ed., 'Paris: Jean Boudot (two vols.).

(4) 1717, Amsterdam: Aux dépens de la Compagnie.

(5) 1739, 4th ed., Paris: de la Bastie; also at Paris by deBure (2 vols.).

The work was also translated into other languages. The first Italian edition appeared in 1728 (Venice: Lorenzo Baseggio)[5] while a Dutch language edition appeared in that same year (Amsterdam: Joh. Artnold Langerack and translated by J. Alençon). The first English language edition, published in London in 1697 by Wm. Rogers, and entitled *Instructions for those who apply themselves to the Study of Medals*, was translated by the antiquary Roger Gale.[6]

A very similar work to Jobert's but in English by Obadiah Walker,[7] *The Knowledge of Medals,* was published in 1697 (London: Wm. Rogers)[8] and a second edition in 1715 by E. Curll[9] and Thomas Caldecott.

---

[4] FRANCOISE MARBRE-CRAMOISY (née LOIR), king's printer, bookseller, and director of the 'Royal Printing Louvre' (until 1691). The daughter of a Parisian goldsmith, she was the widow of SÉBASTIEN MARBRE-CRAMOISY whom she had married in 1670.

[5] *La scienza delle medaglie antiche e moderne.* (Opera tradotta dal linguaggio Francese nell'Italiano da Selvaggio Canturani). Another Italian edition, *La scienza delle medaglie. Nuova edizione con annotazioni storiche e critiche* (Venice), translated by POMPEO BERTI, appeared in 1756.

[6] ROGER GALE (1672–1744) MP, diplomat, antiquarian, coin collector, and frequent contributor to JOHN NICHOLS' *Literary Anecdotes*.

[7] OBADIAH WALKER (1616–1699), a Royalist adherent whose mother was a cousin of Samuel Pepys, was dismissed by Parliament in 1648 from his position as fellow and tutor at University College, Oxford. Reinstated at Oxford at the Restoration, in 1676 Walker became master of his old college. With the accession of King James II in 1688, Walker converted to Catholicism, which he openly practiced. In 1687, Walker became very involved in James II's quarrels with the fellows of Magdalen College over the latter's order to elect a Catholic as their president, a conflict which eventually resulted in the king ejecting the fellows and replacing them with Catholic supporters. Following James' flight from England, and before Walker could join him in France, he was charged with having changed his religion and other offenses and imprisoned. Acquitted in 1690, he survived on the charity of friends and likely also the proceeds of activities such as the translation of *The Knowledge of Medals*.

[8] The engraved plate on page 2 was the frontispiece in at least the 1715 and 1717 editions of Jobert's work. The prominence in the plate of a massive cabinet suggests the popularity of coin and medal collecting at the time.

[9] This apparently pirated edition of *The Knowledge of Medals*... has been referred to as "Curll's 'second edition'" by Guthrie (2012). *See also* E. Straus' *The Unspeakable Curll* (London: Chapman and Hall, 1927).

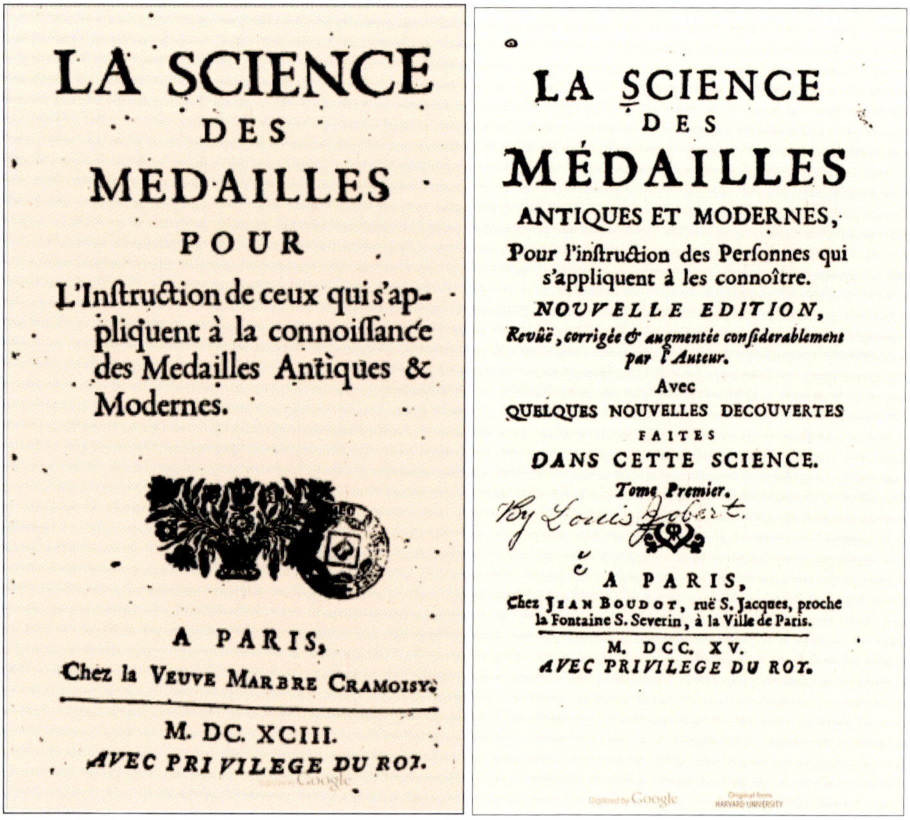
LA SCIENCE
DES
MEDAILLES
POUR
L'Inſtruction de ceux qui s'appliquent à la connoiſſance des Medailles Antiques & Modernes.
A PARIS,
Chez la Veuve Marbre Cramoisy.
M. DC. XCIII.
AVEC PRIVILEGE DU ROY.

LA SCIENCE
DES
MÉDAILLES
ANTIQUES ET MODERNES,
Pour l'inſtruction des Perſonnes qui s'appliquent à les connoître.
NOUVELLE EDITION,
Revûë, corrigée & augmentée conſiderablement par l'Auteur.
Avec
QUELQUES NOUVELLES DECOUVERTES
FAITES
DANS CETTE SCIENCE.
Tome Premier.
By Louis Jobert.
A PARIS,
Chez Jean Boudot, ruë S. Jacques, proche la Fontaine S. Severin, à la Ville de Paris.
M. DCC. XV.
AVEC PRIVILEGE DU ROY.

THE TITLE PAGES OF *(LEFT)* THE FIRST EDITION OF JOBERT'S WORK *LA SCIENCE DES MÉDAILLES...*, PUBLISHED IN 1693, AND (*RIGHT*) VOL. 2 OF THE THIRD EDITION (1715). IMAGES BY GOOGLE.

In a *Numismatic Circular* article which appeared in 1895, the Rev. A. W. Hands commented:

> The earliest work in English on this subject appears to be a 12mo published in London 1692, by O. W. (Obadiah Walker), but out of 360 pages not 60 are really concerned with the coinage. The same writer probably translated the French work of Jobert in 1695....In 1715 appeared a small volume, 4" x 6 ½", 12°, called "The Knowledge of Medals" "written by a Nobleman of France. Made English by an eminent Hand". It is sometimes to be picked up on second hand bookstalls for sixpence, and contains a great deal of information somewhat quaintly expressed. The writer of these lines believes this little work "The Knowledge of Medals " to be the translation of Jobert's work by the O. W. above mentioned, although it is strange that he should use the expression "an eminent" and "of himself"[10](p. 1285).

While the first English language edition of Jobert's book appeared in 1697, with the translation attributed to Roger Gale,[11] another English language edition of Jobert's work appeared in 1715.

---

[10] Hands, Rev. A. W. (1895). Chats on Roman Coins with Young Collectors. *Numismatic Circular*. vol. iii, pp. 1283-1288.

[11] Clapinson, M., 'Roger Gale.' *ODNB* (2013).

This second, unauthorized, edition[12] contained an appended critique by Samuel Addison[13] entitled:

> *The knowledge of medals: or, instructions for those who apply themselves to the study of medals, both ancient and modern...Written by a nobleman of France. Made English by an eminent hand. The second edition. To which is added, an essay concerning the error in distributing modern medals by Joseph Addison, Esq.*[14]

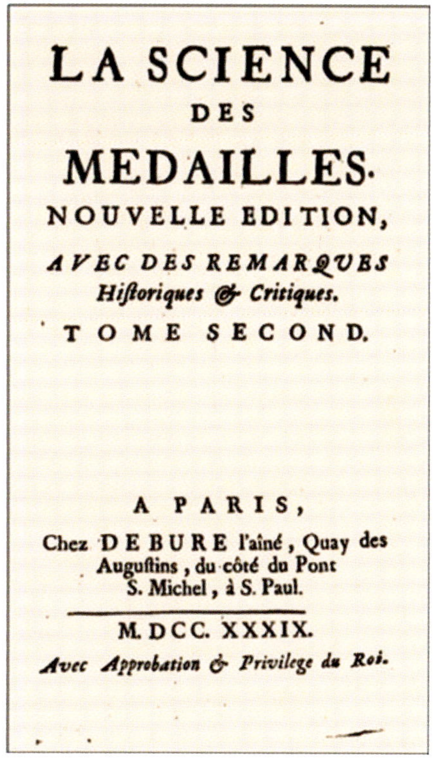
LA SCIENCE
DES
MEDAILLES.
NOUVELLE EDITION,
AVEC DES REMARQUES Historiques & Critiques.
TOME SECOND.
A PARIS,
Chez DE BURE l'aîné, Quay des Auguſtins, du côté du Pont S. Michel, à S. Paul.
M. DCC. XXXIX.
Avec Approbation & Privilege du Roi.

THE TITLE PAGE OF VOLUME 2 OF THE FOURTH EDITION (1739) OF *JOBERT'S LA SCIENCE DES MÉDAILLES.* IMAGE BY GOOGLE.

The British Museum's copy of the 1715 English language version states on the front endpaper:

> This Treatise is said on the Title page to have been written by a Nobleman of France; this is a mistake, the Author was Father Jobert, a Jesuit who published it in 1692. This translation is by Obadiah Walker.

John Pinkerton,[15] a prominent, if somewhat disreputable figure associated with the late 18th c. interest in medals in Britain, commented on what he thought of Jobert's work:

> In the very year that Jobert published his book, one, something similar, first appeared in the English language. It's title is, "The Greek and Roman History illustrated by Coins and Medals, representing their Religions, Rites, &c. &c. By O. W. (Obadiah Walker) "London, 1692." 12 mo. The work answers to the title in one respect; that, of 360 pages, not 60 are medallic; the rest are all made up of Roman antiquities and history: but how it illustrates Greek history cannot be discovered. It's plan is so very confused and bad, and the whole work so feeble, that it is no wonder that it never had any success. In 1695 a translation of Jobert's work appeared, entitled, "The Knowledge of Medals," which is ascribed to Walker.[16]

---

[12] 2nd English ed. London: Printed for E. Curll, at the Dial and Bible [over against Catherine-street in the Strand]; and T. Caldecott, at the Sun, 1715.

[13] *See this vol., pp. 26 ff.*

[14] This essay was also pirated, in this case from *The Guardian*, where it had appeared as issue no. 96 (July 1, 1773). *The Guardian* evolved from *The Tatler*, founded in 1709 by JOSEPH ADDISON'S university friend RICHARD STEELE (1672-1729). *The Tatler* was a magazine published thrice weekly, to which Addison very soon began contributing essays. The stated purpose of *The Tatler* was to:

> ...expose the false Arts of Life, to pull off the disguises of Cunning, Vanity, and Affectation, and to recommend a general Simplicity in our Dress, our discourse, and our Behavior (1710, vol. i, dedication).

When political complications arose, Steele ceased publication of *The Tatler* and in 1711 began a new daily publication, *The Spectator*, which was followed in short order by *The Guardian* in 1713; this publication continued through the end of 1714. During the brief lifespan of *The Guardian*, Addison contributed just under one-third of its essays.

[15] *See this vol., pp. 59 ff.*

[16] J. Pinkerton (1789). *An Essay on Medals, especially those of Greece, Rome, and Britain.* London, vol. i, pp. vii-viii.

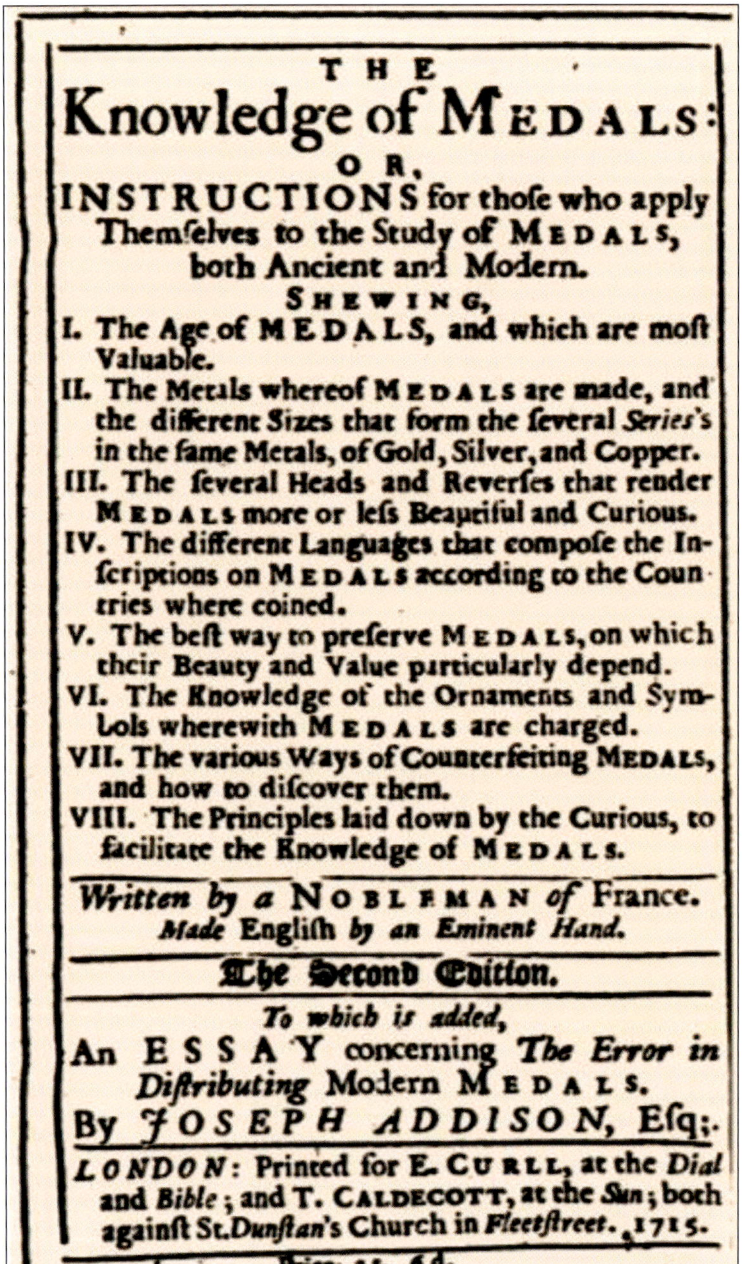

THE

Knowledge of MEDALS:

OR,

INSTRUCTIONS for thoſe who apply Themſelves to the Study of MEDALS, both Ancient and Modern.

SHEWING,

I. The Age of MEDALS, and which are moſt Valuable.

II. The Metals whereof MEDALS are made, and the different Sizes that form the ſeveral *Series*'s in the ſame Metals, of Gold, Silver, and Copper.

III. The ſeveral Heads and Reverſes that render MEDALS more or leſs Beautiful and Curious.

IV. The different Languages that compoſe the Inſcriptions on MEDALS according to the Countries where coined.

V. The beſt way to preſerve MEDALS, on which their Beauty and Value particularly depend.

VI. The Knowledge of the Ornaments and Symbols wherewith MEDALS are charged.

VII. The various Ways of Counterfeiting MEDALS, and how to diſcover them.

VIII. The Principles laid down by the Curious, to facilitate the Knowledge of MEDALS.

Written by a NOBLEMAN *of* France.
Made Engliſh *by an Eminent Hand.*

The Second Edition.

To which is added,
An ESSAY concerning *The Error in Diſtributing* Modern MEDALS.
By *JOSEPH ADDISON*, Eſq;.

LONDON: Printed for E. CURLL, at the *Dial* and *Bible*; and T. CALDECOTT, at the *Sun*; both againſt St. *Dunſtan*'s Church in *Fleetſtreet*. 1715.

Price 2s. 6d.

THE TITLE PAGE FROM THE SECOND ENGLISH EDITION OF *THE KNOWLEDGE OF MEDALS* (1715), TRANSLATED FROM THE FRENCH BY OBADIAH WALKER WITH AN ESSAY BY JOSEPH ADDISON. THIS EDITION HAS BEEN LABELED "A PIRACY" BY GUTHRIE (IN CLARK AND ERSKINE-HILL, 2012, P. 95), WHO ALSO NOTED THAT THE ESSAY BY ADDISON HAD BEEN PILFERED FROM *THE GUARDIAN* (1773, NO. 96).

John Pinkerton further accused Jobert of borrowing from Charles Patin's *Introductio ad Historiam Numismatum* (*Introduction to the History of Medals)* which had first been published in France in 1683:

> Notwithstanding the high merit of this Work, and it's vast success, in 1692 Pere Jobert presented to the public his Science des Medailles; a title surely the most impudent that ever stood at the head of any book. Patin had modestly called his an Introduction to the science; but Jobert's was the science itself; and the book corresponds to the title, being every way worthy of a Jesuit, and replete with the most glaring plagiarism from Patin, whom he does not mention above once. But such is the preference of impudence over modesty that his book effectually supplanted that of Patin, and has stood it's ground ever since, passing thro many editions, and being translated into most languages. Every bookseller will tell us, that literature is a lottery; and the observation was never more verified than in this instance.[17]

It would appear that Pinkerton would later modulate his publicly stated opinion of Jobert. This passage from the 1789 edition of *An Essay on Medals* should be compared with the later revised one from the 1808 edition which appears below on page 10.

"THE PIAZZA IN COVENTGARDEN"

AN ETCHING BY WENCESLAUS HOLLAR, CA. 1647, WITH A VIEW FROM THE MARKET IN COVENT GARDEN IN THE DIRECTION OF ST PAUL'S CHURCH. IMAGE © TRUSTEES OF THE BRITISH MUSEUM.

[17] *An Essay on Medals…,* 1789 ed., vol. i, pp. v-vi.

THESAURUS
NUMISMATUM.

E MUSÆO

CAROLI PATINI
Doctoris Medici Parisiensis.

SUMPTIBUS AUTORIS.
M. DC. LXXII.

Thesaurus numismatum e musaeo Caroli Patini (1672). Amsterdam: Sumptibus autoris.* According to Stouraiti, this work was actually a catalogue of a cabinet of coins owned by Pietro Morosini, a Venetian senator. Although Patin took credit for the publication, it was prepared by Morosini before he bequeathed the collection to Venice and after the collection had been ordered and indexed by the Cretan scholar Nicolò Bon (1635-1712).

*Self-published.

Charles Patin

(1633-1693)

THE son of Guy Patin, a prominent Paris physician, Charles Patin was a French physician who is equally well known today for his numismatic works. Initially trained as a lawyer, Patin then chose to study medicine. In the end, Patin accumulated quite a résumé—academic physician (anatomy, surgery and practice), lawyer, archeologist, and numismatist. Both during his lifetime and to the present day, he achieved equal, if not greater, recognition for his numismatic work.

In 1668, Charles Patin was forced to flee France, having been sentenced to the galleys in absentia for possession of banned books. Apparently he had been sent to Holland by a member of the French royal family to buy up all copies of a potboiler—*Les Amours du Palais Royal*—however, instead of burning them, he brought them back to France to sell. This was to become a repeated offence over the next few years,[18] resulting in the need for Patin to flee France.

After sojourns in Frankfurt and Heidelberg, Patin settled at the University of Padua where he was to become chair of medicine and then surgery. Elected to membership in L'Accademia dei Ricovrati[19] not long afterwards, his wife and his two daughters were also elected to membership. Fontijn suggests that Patin's intention was to promote the status of his own family, and in doing so, to impress the French king sufficiently that he would allow the Patin family to return to France.[20] However, this hope was never fulfilled. Charles Patin died in Padua in 1693.

CHARLES PATIN, 17TH C. FRENCH LAWYER, PHYSICIAN AND NUMISMATIST. AN ENGRAVED PORTRAIT (CA. 1663-1693) BY ANTOINE MASSON (1636-1700). IMAGE © TRUSTEES OF THE BRITISH MUSEUM.

[18] Packard (*Annals of Medical History*, 1922, vol. iv, p. 226) suggests that the reason for this was not profit, but rather 'compulsive bibliophilia.' The rumor also existed that Patin had become involved romantically with one of the King's favorites.

[19] The Accademia Galileiana, or 'Galilean Academy,' in Padua—the society now known as the Accademia Galileiana di Scienze, Lettere ed Arti in Padova.

[20] Fontijn, C. (2006). *Desperate Measures: The Life and Music of Antonia Padoani Bembo*. Oxford: Oxford Univ. Press.

John Pinkerton, in the 1808 edition of his 'Essay on Medals,' commented thusly on Patin's published work:

...[I]n 1665 Charles Patin, son of the celebrated Guy Patin, physician to the French king, and a very skilful medallist, published his *History of Medals, or Introduction to that Science.*[21] This treatise, of which the last edition, 1695, is, in my opinion, much superior to the work of Jobert, next to be mentioned, ran through many editions, and was translated into all the languages of Europe.

Notwithstanding the high merit of [Patin's] work, in 1692 Pere Jobert presented to the public his *Science des Medailles.* It is proper to observe, that the first edition of Jobert is the best of those published by himself; for that of 1715, which he published in two volumes, is only swelled with impertinence, and the crude reveries of Pere Hardouin,[22] whom the author wished to flatter. The edition of 1739 is doubtless the very best; but this we owe to the editor, and not to the author; and even of this edition the second volume is a mere "farrago of useless lumber."

—J. Pinkerton, *An Essay on Medals...*, 1808 ed. vol. i, pp. vii-viii.

CAROLI PATINI, Equit.
D. Marci, Doct. Med. Parif. & in
Acad. Patav. Med. Prof.

INTRODUCTIO
AD
HISTORIAM
NUMISMATUM.

Antehâc Gallicè bis edita; Nunc Latinè
versa, & novis accessionibus
locupletata.

AMSTELÆDAMI,
Apud HENR. WETSTENIUM,
cIↄ Iↄc LXXXIII.

The title page of the Dutch edition of Charles Patin's numismatic work *Introductio ad Historiam...*, published in 1683. Although Patin wrote over 40 learned works, he is perhaps best remembered for his numismatic writing. In addition to *Introductio ad Historiam...*, these included *Introduction a l'histoire par la connoissance des médailles* (1665), *Thesaurus Numismatum* (1672), *Practica delle Medaglie* (1673) and *Histoire des médailles ou introduction à la connaissance de cette science* (1695). Image by Google.

[21] C. Patini [sic] (1683). *Introductio ad Historiam Numismatum...* Amsterdam: A. H. Wetstenium (2 vols.).

[22] Jean Hardouin (1646-1729), controversial Jesuit priest and prolific theologian, philosopher and student of ancient numismatics, who criticized not only the writings of his peers, but also questioned the authenticity of classical authors and early Christian literature.

Three Illustrations from:
Thesaurus numismatum e musaeo Caroli Patini

Three chapter head illustrations from Patin's 1672 work. Such attractive illustrations have largely disappeared from modern works.

JOHN EVELYN, DIARIST AND AUTHOR OF THE FIRST PUBLISHED WORK DEVOTED TO ENGLISH MEDALS. FROM AN OLD ENGRAVING (C. 1650) BY JOHN SWAINE, AFTER THE 1650 PAINTING BY ROBERT NANTEUIL (1623?-1678).[23] FROM JOHN THANE'S *BRITISH AUTOGRAPHY*..., 1788, VOL. 2.

[23] ROBERT NANTEUIL (1623?-1678) was 'designer and engraver of the cabinet' to Louis XIV. His work is known for its precise engraving and what were thought by his subjects and other engravers to be excellent likenesses of his subjects. JOHN SWAINE (1775-1860), like many of the engravers of the late 17th and early 18th centuries, worked primarily on antiquarian subjects, and is known for his having created excellent facsimiles of old portraits.

John Evelyn

(1620–1706)

JOHN EVELYN, the author of the first work on British medals, *Numismata, a Discourse of Medals, Antient [*sic*] and Modern,* was the second son of Richard and Eleanor Evelyn. He was born in 1620 at Wotton House in Surrey into a wealthy family originally from Evelin in Normandy. The family wealth was earned from the production of gunpowder at Long Ditton and Godstone, Surrey, during Queen Elizabeth I's reign. Richard Evelyn was a humble man and like his son after him, refused honors. In fact, Richard's refusal of a knighthood resulted in the imposition of a fine. Later, however, he accepted an appointment to the office of High Sheriff of Surrey.

A PORTRAIT OF JOHN EVELYN AT AGE 28 BY ROBERT WALKER, CA. 1648. IMAGE © NATIONAL PORTRAIT GALLERY, LONDON. THE NPG COMMENTS THAT EVELYN NOTED IN HIS *DIARY* THAT HE WAS ORIGINALLY PORTRAYED HOLDING A MEDAL OR MINIATURE OF HIS WIFE, MARY BROWNE, IN HIS HAND AND THAT THIS PORTRAIT WAS TO ACCOMPANY A TREATISE ON MARRIAGE WHICH HE HAD PREPARED FOR HER. THE SKULL WAS PAINTED IN LATER IN HIS LIFE.

Although John's father wished him to be educated at Eton, rumors reached his grandmother, with whom he was living at the time, that Eton had such strict discipline that it frightened both John and his grandmother; as a result, he remained at Lewes School. This was a decision Evelyn appears to have regretted throughout his life. He was further educated at Balliol College, Oxford and by 1631 he had begun his diary. According to his modern editors, however, he started the diary, which he continued to keep for sixty-six years,[24] in a:

> ...blank almanac, as he had seen his father do, but the Diary which we possess could not have been commenced until a much later period of his life, although the events of these early years are related in it. [25]

Evelyn was a Royalist but aside from a brief stint of *three days* in active service when he joined the Royalist retreat from Brentford on November 12, 1642, he was not a participant in any man-

---

[24] C. P. Hill (1988). *Who's Who in Stuart Britain*, p. 283.

[25] W. Bray, *Diary of John Evelyn*, 1906 ed., vol. i, pp. xviii, xix. Bray does not elaborate on his reasons for believing this.

ner. He was with the Royalist Army until November 15 and when he found the army was advancing to Gloucester, he rationalized that further service:

> ...would have left both me and my brothers expos'd to ruine, without any advantage to his Majestie.[26]

Evelyn then deserted, traveling instead to Wotten. Charles Carlton comments that:

> ...when on coming down from Oxford he volunteered to join the king's army. The drunkenness, swearing and fornication of the soldiery upset him so much that he retreated quite literally to cultivate his garden [at his country estate]. When England became too dangerous even for that harmless hobby, Evelyn fled to the continent...[27]

Evelyn's only apparent contribution to his king and the Royalist cause was:

> ...his 'black menage horse and furniture' [sent] by a friend to the King, who was then at Oxford.[28]

Following his short-lived service, Evelyn chose to escape the Civil War by traveling in Europe. Later, he was to write:

> I went by Epsom to Wotton, saluting Sr Rob. Cook and my sister Glanvill; the country was now much molested by souldiers, who tooke away gentlemen's horses for the service of the State as then call'd.
>
> [Then on the] 12th. [Set] out for Paris, taking post at Gravesend, and so that night to Canterbury, where being surpriz'd by the souldiers, and having only an antiquated passe, with some fortunate dexterity I got cleare of them, tho' not without extraordinary hazard, having before counterfeited one with successe, it being so difficult to procure one of the Rebells without entering into oaths, which I never would do. At Dover, money to the searchers and officers was as authentiq as the hand and seale of Bradshaw[29] himselfe, where I had not so much as my trunk open'd.[30]

On June 27, 1647, just before concluding four years of travel abroad, Evelyn married Mary, daughter of his good friend Sir Richard Browne, ambassador to France, in Paris. However, because of her age—she was twelve—he left her in the "...care of an excellent lady and prudent mother."[31]

Since Evelyn's primary fame results from his work as a diarist, one could speculate that he would have made a major contribution as a historian of the war. Unfortunately, his absence from England during the Civil War deprives the modern reader of his astute observations for the events of this period that might have been entered in his diary.

On September 3, 1658, the day of Oliver Cromwell's death, Evelyn wrote in his diary:

> Died that arch rebell Oliver Cromwell, call'd Protector."[32]

Then on October 22, he wrote of the funeral:

> ...but it was the joyfullest funeral I ever saw, for there were none that cried but dogs, which the soldiers hooted away with a barbarous noise, drinking and taking tobacco in the streetes as they went.[33]

---

[26] Bray, vol. i, p. 39.

[27] C. Carlton, *Going to the Wars, The Experience of the English Civil Wars...*, p. 9. This was ...with the King's permission to go on the Grand Tour (ibid. p. 293). Carlton further comments that JOHN EVELYN was "loathe to choose sides" (p. 293), which may just be another sign of Evelyn's fear of making a commitment for which he might have been held to account.

[28] Bray, vol. i, p xxii.

[29] JOHN BRADSHAW, a Parliamentarian officer and one of the regicides. At this time, president of the Council of State.

[30] Bray, *Diaries*, vol. ii, pp. 17-18. Entry for July 25, 1650.

[31] Ibid. vol. i, pp. xxix, 296. JOHN and MARY EVELYN had eight children, but four sons died in infancy, and of the three sons who lived to adulthood, two preceded their parents in death. Only one daughter outlived her parents.

[32] Ibid. vol. ii, p. 103.

On July 4, 1665, the plague was raging in London, and those residents who could afford it abandoned their homes and fled to the country. Margaret Verney noted in her diary that:

> ...[John] Evelyn, going to the City on business, was 'environ'd with multitudes of poor pestiferous creatures begging alms, the shops universally shut up, a dreadful prospect'[34]. [On July 8th Evelyn wrote] 'Died this week in London 4000 [adding on the 15th] There perished this week 5000...[35]

To which he appended on August 28 and Sept. 7, respectively:

> The contagion still increasing and growing now all about us, I sent my Wife and whole family (two or three necessary servants excepted) to my brother's at Wotton, being resolved to stay at my house myselfe and to looke after my charge, trusting in the providence and goodnesse of God.
>
> Came home, there perishing neere 10,000 poore creatures weekly; however, I went all along the Citty and suburbs from Kent Streete to St. James's, a dismal passage, and dangerous to see so many coffines expos'd in the streetes, now thin of people; the shops shut up, and all in mourneful silence, not knowing whose turn might be next. I went to ye Duke of Albermarle for a pest-ship, to wait on our infected men, who were not a few.[36]

Mary Evelyn (née Browne, 1636-1709). This stipple engraving, dated 1818, is by Henry Hoppner Meyer (1782?-1847). It is after the oil painting by Robert Nanteuil (1623?-1678), the artist who also painted the well-known portrait of John Evelyn which appears on page 12. The original portrait by Nanteuil was likely painted in 1650.

Now well into the Restoration, Charles II demonstrated, as had his father before him, a high regard for Evelyn.[37] Thus, with the plague still raging, Evelyn found employment when Charles II appointed him a commissioner for the care of sick and wounded seamen and the care and treatment of prisoners taken in the Dutch Wars. Although this was nominally a paid position, most of Evelyn's expenses were paid from his own pocket. He was to be commended by the king for carrying out his duties despite the dangers of contracting the plague.[38]

By late November, the plague had receded, in London at least, and on March 15, Evelyn wrote:

> Our parish was now more infected with the plague than ever, and so was all the countrie about tho' almost quite ceas'd at London.[39]

Unfortunately, although Evelyn's diary was his most important legacy, it gives us little insight into his character and personality, aside from the inferences one can make from his description of events involving himself and his pious and self-righteous devotion to religious matters. In this regard, Latham commented:

---

33 Bray, ibid. vol. ii, pp. 104-105.
34 Margaret Verney, *Memoirs of the Verney Family*, vol. iv, p. 120.
35 Bray, ibid. vol. ii, p. 186.
36 Ibid. vol. ii, pp. 186-187.
37 A surprising view, given Evelyn's lack of contribution to the Royalist war effort, and indeed, total absence from England.
38 Ibid. vol. i, p. xvi.
39 Ibid. vol. ii, pp. 193-194.

Compared with Pepys's [diary] it is stilted, impersonal and unevocative.[40]

Evelyn had a keen interest in gardens and horticulture, architecture, and the environment, as well as numismatics. He was a relatively eclectic writer, as evidenced by his published piece titled *Fumifugium,* in which he wrote of the foul air and smoke in London and suggested ways to eliminate it.[41]

Evelyn had been a habitué of museum collections on the Continent as well as those of friends and acquaintances. He sought to replicate these collections, although in a modest manner, being restricted by the somewhat limited size of his purse. His 'curiosity cabinet,' absent its contents, has survived and now resides in the Geffrye Museum, London.[42]

'JOHN EVELYN'S BOOKPLATE FROM THE COLLECTION OF AUGUSTUS W. FRANK' (FROM: HOWE, *FRANKS BEQUEST...OF BRITISH AND AMERICAN BOOK PLATES,* 1908).

Like many of his contemporaries, Evelyn was an avid collector of coins and medals. This is evident in a letter to Samuel Pepys in which he commented that:

> ...men curious of books & antiquities have ever had medals in such estimation, & rendered them a most necessary furniture to their libraries, because by them we are not onely [sic] inform'd whose real image & superscription they beare, but have discovered to us, in their reverses, what heroical exploits they perform'd...[43]

After sending his manuscript for *Numismata...,* the first work on medals in the English language, to the printer, Benjamin Tooke, Evelyn found that Tooke had made many errors despite the fact that he had asked him to take extra precautions in the supervision of the typesetting.[44] Thus, he wanted Tooke to place the following sentence in the preface:

> Finding [this work] so miserably deformed through the confident undertakers.[45]

Tooke, obviously very concerned that this should not happen, said that:

> It will really hinder the sale of the book, and do you no more service than the list of errata does alone sufficiently do.[46]

Ultimately, Evelyn was "...induced to expunge it by the advice of Dr. Bentley." Upon publication of this book, it was given a less than stellar review by numismatic scholars, as well as by Horace Walpole, who quite correctly complained that:

---

[40] R. Latham, *The Diary of Samuel Pepys 2000, Companion,* vol. x, p. 123.

[41] Bray, *Diary...,* vol. i, p. cviii. Evelyn suggested that, in place of coal, the burning of wood would be less harmful to the lungs and that the burning of lime for use in construction and brewing, two of the industrial practices which greatly added to pollution, be relocated outside of London.

[42] Such cabinets were a common possession among gentlemen of the 17th and 18th centuries, and Evelyn likely made good use of his, for as Pearce & Arnold (2000) comment on p. 38:

> ...Evelyn spent a good part of his life either looking at the collections of others, or amassing his own.

[43] Bray, *Diary,* vol. iii, p. 439.

[44] *The complete letter appears, below, on p. 21.*

[45] Bray, ibid. vol. i, p. lxxix.

[46] Ibid. vol. i, p. lxxx.

> I turned to the Index, and to my greater surprise found almost every thing but what I wanted...[47]

In addition, that:

> ...little or nothing is said of our medallists, the names of the gravers being very generally omitted.[48]

ʃʃʃ

On January 27, 1705/06, Evelyn wrote in his diary:

> My indisposition increasing, I was exceeding ill this whole week.[49]

John Evelyn died on February 27, 1706, at 86 years of age. His wife Mary lived only three more years, dying at the age of seventy-four. They are both buried in the Evelyn Chapel in St John's Church, Wotton.[50] Of five sons and three daughters, only one daughter, Susanna, survived her parents. She married William Draper, Esq. of Adscomb.[51]

MRS. GODOLPHIN (MARGARET BLAGGE, 1652-1678), WIFE OF SIDNEY, 1ST EARL OF GODOLPHIN (1645-1712). AN ENGRAVING (CA. 1888) BY W. HUMPHREYS AFTER THE PAINTING BY MATTHEW DIXON (FL. 1671-1710). *DNB* STATES THAT "SHE BECAME STRONGLY ATTACHED TO [EVELYN, AND] GAVE HIM A DECLARATION OF 'INVIOLABLE FRIENDSHIP' IN WRITING...AND EVER AFTERWARDS CONSIDERED HERSELF AS HIS 'ADOPTED DAUGHTER'" (1890, VOL. 42, P. 21). EVELYN'S ATTACHMENT TO HER WAS APPARENTLY OF NO LESSER INTENSITY.

In summary, Evelyn lived through and wrote in his diary of the major events of the second half of the 17th century. During this time, he witnessed the deaths of Charles I and Oliver Cromwell, the Great Plague of London, as well as the Great Fire that engulfed London in 1666. It must be recognized that Evelyn, like Samuel Pepys, left a detailed diary, both diarists providing the modern reader with detail about daily life in England in the latter half of the 17th century. Evelyn's diary covers the years 1641–1706, although it was not published until 1818. Pepys' (1633-1703) diary covers the years 1660-1669, when he was forced to abandon it because of failing eyesight. It was published in part in 1825, and was only published in full in the 1980s. Evelyn and Pepys, besides sharing a long and close friendship, also were senior civil servants in the reign of Charles II. Evelyn was a major planner in the rebuilding of London after the Great Fire and in the reconstruction of St. Paul's Cathedral by Christopher Wren. Pepys rose from clerk to Secretary of the Admiralty, a role in which he helped build the Royal Navy to its preeminence. Both men were also involved in founding the Royal Society and were devoted bibliophiles.

---

[47] Ibid.

[48] Ibid. pp. lxxix-lxxx.

[49] Ibid. vol. i., p. 172.

[50] A modern writer, GUY DE LA BÉDOYÈRE, has reported that in addition to JOHN EVELYN'S books now preserved in the British Library Museum, pieces of his furniture can be found at the Victoria and Albert Museum and the Geffrye Museum, Bethnal Green. Sadly, however, de la Bédoyère reports that:

> The monument to [Evelyn's] son Richard and his daughter Mary is still on the wall of the church of St. Nicholas, Deptford. His own tomb is no longer accessible as the private Evelyn chapel in Wotton church has been closed ever since the extraordinary break-in in 1992. Evelyn's, and his wife's, tombs were broken into and their skulls removed. No-one knows why or how, and the event remains a tragic mystery (*See de la Bédoyère's website at www.romanbritain.freeserve.co.uk*).

[51] Bray, Ibid. vol. i, pp. xcvii-xcviii.

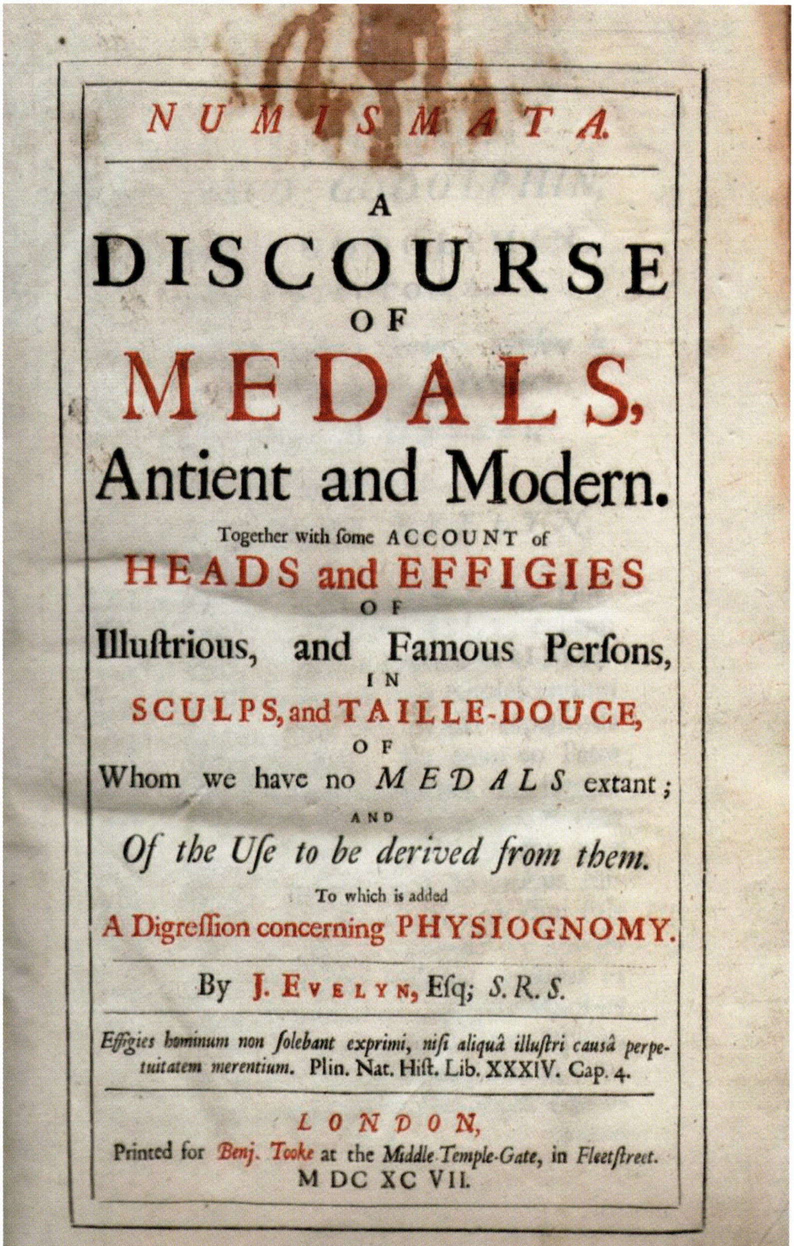

NUMISMATA.

A
DISCOURSE
OF
MEDALS,
Antient and Modern.
Together with some ACCOUNT of
HEADS and EFFIGIES
OF
Illustrious, and Famous Persons,
IN
SCULPS, and TAILLE-DOUCE,
OF
Whom we have no *MEDALS* extant;
AND
Of the Use to be derived from them.
To which is added
A Digression concerning PHYSIOGNOMY.

By J. EVELYN, Esq; *S. R. S.*

Effigies hominum non solebant exprimi, nisi aliquâ illustri causâ perpetuitatem merentium. Plin. Nat. Hist. Lib. XXXIV. Cap. 4.

LONDON,
Printed for *Benj. Tooke* at the *Middle-Temple-Gate*, in *Fleetstreet*.
M DC XC VII.

THE TITLE PAGE TO JOHN EVELYN'S *NUMISMATA...*, 1697, THE FIRST PUBLISHED WORK ON ENGLISH MEDALS. KNOWN BEST FOR HIS DIARIES, EVELYN (1620-1706) WAS 77 YEARS OF AGE WHEN *NUMISMATA* WAS PUBLISHED. A FREQUENT WRITER OF ROYALIST TRACTS, HE WAS HIGHLY CRITICAL OF DISSIPATION AND CORRUPTION IN PUBLIC LIFE, PARTICULARLY IN THE RESTORATION COURT. EVELYN ALSO AUTHORED WORKS ON ARCHITECTURE AND ART. 'TAILLE-DOUCE' REFERS TO THE PROCESS OF LINE ENGRAVING ON COPPER PLATE.

John Evelyn's
NUMISMATA: A DISCOURSE OF MEDALS
(1697)

THE first published work on British historical medals is John Evelyn's *NUMISMATA: A Discourse of Medals, Antient* [sic] *and Modern...,* which appeared in 1697, the breathtakingly full title of which appears on the title page. In the title for the first chapter of *Numismata*, Evelyn makes clear what his intended coverage is:

> ...*Medals*, whether for *Money*, or to preserve the Memory of Worthy Actions; their *Antiquity*, *Materials*, *Size*, *Model*, &c.

The volume also touches on such subjects as:

> Instructions how to Collect, and Procure such *Medals* as are *Antique*, and *Rare*; and to Distinguish the *True* from the *False*, for the prevention of Frauds and Impostures (Chapter VI).

THE ILLUSTRATION FROM EVELYN, *NUMISMATA...*, **(1697, P. 171, PL. XCIII)** OF THE MEDAL CELEBRATING JOHN LILBURNE'S ACQUITTAL ON CHARGES OF HAVING FALSELY ACCUSED CROMWELL AND IRETON OF TREASON **(1649, M.I.I 385/3, M.I.ILL XXXIV/21, PLATT & PLATT II/202/A).** LILBURNE, A CONTENTIOUS MAN WHO SEEMED TO HAVE OPPOSED OR OFFENDED ALL MAJOR FIGURES BEFORE, DURING AND AFTER THE CIVIL WAR, IS ONE OF THE MOST INTERESTING CHARACTERS OF THE TIME.

The subject of this chapter, if updated to the present, would doubtless be of use to 21st century collectors. Evelyn's coverage begins with antiquity, and if it is not comprehensive, he is the first to admit it with a disclaimer to that effect in the preface. Subsequent authors, in their critiques, have noted that his volume, like George Vertue's *Medals, Coins, Great Seals...of Thomas Simon,* the next work on British medals, the first edition of which appeared in 1753, contains a large number of errors. Examples of errors in *Numismata...* include incorrect or incomplete inscriptions and unlabelled and unexplained illustrations. Evelyn's errors were the subject of a scathing review by John Pinkerton in the first edition of *An Essay on Medals*, published in 1784:

> **The size is folio, and the plan and writing are likewise in folio. That gentleman's style is so very uncouth and unintelligible, that, while he wrote upon every thing, he ought to have written about the black art only; but in his work *he outdoes his former out-doings*; for it is impossible for any one to know his meaning if he did not know it before.** None of his observations are new, but all tacitly taken from Vico, Le Pois, Patin, and Jobert. The plates of English medals are of little use, now that those of Snelling have appeared. Even they would have been better understood, had he not added explanations. There is, in the British Museum, a copy of this work, corrected by the author, with an original letter prefixed, complaining that the printer had utterly mangled and spoiled his work, so that it is necessary to give corrections. The corrections are for the worse (pp. viii-ix).[52]

Numismata..., covers British medals and coins from Edward III to 1688.[53] It contains 97 illustra-

---

[52] The sentence in **bold type** was deleted from the later editions.

[53] Evelyn acknowledges medals "struck since the late signal *Revolution*" (p. 156) of 1688, but takes note of their having been published in *Histoire Metalique de Guillaume III. Published, and very Artistly Ingraven and Historically Illustrated by N. Chevalier, in Folio[sic],* Amsterdam, 1692.

tions by John Savage.[54] A number of medals of the Civil War and Interregnum periods proper are illustrated, from the 'Coronation of Charles I' medal of 1626 (Evelyn, p. 104, M.I.I 243/10, M.I.ILL pl. XX/1, *see text box, right*) through 'John Lilburne's Acquittal' in 1649 (Evelyn, p. 171, Fig. 1, M.I.I 386/4, M.I.ILL XXXIV/21).

AN ILLUSTRATION, FROM EVELYN'S *NUMISMATA...* (P. 104, PL. XXIV) OF THE MEDAL COMMEMORATING THE CORONATION OF CHARLES I, 1626, BY NICHOLAS BRIOT (M.I.I 243/10, M.I.ILL XX/1). THE *REV.* DESIGN WOULD APPEAR TO BE SYMBOLIC OF THE NEW KING'S INTENT TO CONTINUE HIS OTHERWISE PEACEFUL FATHER'S MILITARY ADVENTURES IN THE UNITED PROVINCES AND BOHEMIA.

While Evelyn's *Numismata* has been recognized since its publication as containing numerous errors, such errors should be considered within the context of the comment by Keynes that:

> Evelyn's curiosity was unquenchable, and he was already an old man when he began in 1692 to collect notes for a work on medals. He had found that little had been written on the subject in English, and, animated by a commendable regard for portraits and portraiture, sought in his *Numismata, A Discourse of Medals* to remedy this defect...He intended that his book should be worthy of its subject, and his letter to Tooke[55] illustrates well his solicitude for every aspect of its make-up...*Numismata* is a handsome folio, and the engravings of medals are excellently done. But a pleasant appearance cannot compensate in a work of this kind for faulty scholarship and typography.[56]

Numismata... was printed three times, and each of the three printings is identifiable by errors. For example, the first printing repeats the incorrect duplicate placement of plate LXXIX instead of the correct plate LXXXI while THE second printing contains the correct plate LXXXI pasted over the incorrect plate on page 156. There are other errors as well. The third printing is printed correctly.[57]

> IN fine, a most excellent person he is, and must be allowed a little for a little [sic] conceitedness; but he may well be so, being a man so much above others.
>
> —Pepys, commenting about John Evelyn. In Lord Braybrooke (ed.), *[Pepys'] Diary...*, November 1665.

[54] This is the only mention of JOHN SAVAGE, who is presumed to be the person of that name (*fl.* 1690-1700), who was an engraver and bookseller in London. E.g., 'Sold by J. Savage at the Golden Head at the Old Bailey.' *DNB* notes that he:

> ...executed a few portraits, which, although of little artistic merit, are valuable as records of interesting persons of his day... (1897 ed., vol. I, p. 339).

[55] BENJAMIN TOOKE, his publisher. The full text of the letter is reproduced below.

[56] G. Keynes. *John Evelyn: A Study in Bibliophily...* (1968, 2nd ed.), p. 230.

[57] C. E. Dekesel (2003), *Bibliotheca Nummaria: A Bibliography of 17th Century Numismatic Books*, vol. iii, p. 917. Manville, in his valuable *Numismatic Guide to...Printed Books* (2005, p. 38) further describes how to differentiate the three printings. Interestingly, Manville (2005) notes that one of the British Library's copies is a signed presentation copy to SIR HANS SLOANE with a letter and notes in JOHN EVELYN'S hand (p. 18).

JOHN EVELYN'S INSTRUCTIONS TO THE PRINTER
FOR
NUMISMATA: A DISCOURSE OF MEDALS, ANTIENT AND MODERN...,

To Mr. Benjamin Tooke (Printer).[58]

Mr. Tooke,

Tarde, sed tandem.[59] At last I send you the copy you have so long expected; never the worse, I hope, for coming no sooner. I wish it may answer the paines I have taken in compiling: for it would amount to the value of many Medals. I was indeede unwilling it should scape from me without something more than an ordinary treatise. It will therefore require a more than ordinary supervisor. You tell me, such a one you have; if not, pray make use of the poore man I directed to you, who is also acquainted w^ith my hand, & will be ready to assist you. There being aboundance of writers on this subject in all other polite European languages, & but one very short & partial one in ours, will I hope render this the more acceptable, & give ferment to the curious. I expect attaques from some peevish quarter, in this angry age, but so it make for y^r interest, & satisfy equitable judges, I shall not be much concern'd.

The Medals which are here sent you, pray take care of, & deliver but one by one to y^r graver, nor supply him with any other till he returnes you that he is graving with the plate. You'l find I have mark'd the paper, wherein you must keepe the plates, and apply to the pages as directed, by which you'l avoid mistakes, easily fallen into without some such method. Such as you are to have from the Earle of Clarendon, Dr. Plot,[60] &c. I will take care to procure you by the time these are dispatch'd. As for the graving, so the contours and outlines be well design'd, I am not solicitous for the hatching (as they call it), since we have laudable examples of the other in Gruter, Spanheim, & other excellent authors. Mr White if he have leisure, will be y^r best man; & for the volume, I should think a thin moderat folio, with a faire letter most desireable. As for the title, epistle, & preface, I shall provide you in good time, & as I see cause; onely I pray take special care of the insertions & paragraphs which I have marked [: when all this is finish'd, I propose a very accurate index.[61] This being all at present, I wish you good successe, and am,

Y^r &c.......

Wotton, 2 June, 1694.

[58] Bray, *Diary...*, vol. iii, pp. 478-479.

[59] 'Too late, but finally.'

[60] Presumably 'the learned' ROBERT PLOT, D. D. (1640-1696), a naturalist and Oxford University's first professor of chemistry and first keeper of the Ashmolean Museum.

[61] This was also Walpole's complaint, however, as previously noted, the result was less than satisfactory:

> I turned to the Index, and to my greater surprise found almost everything but what I wanted (Evelyn, *Diary*, 1879 ed., vol. I, p. lxxiii). *See also Walpole's comment, this volume, p. 24.*

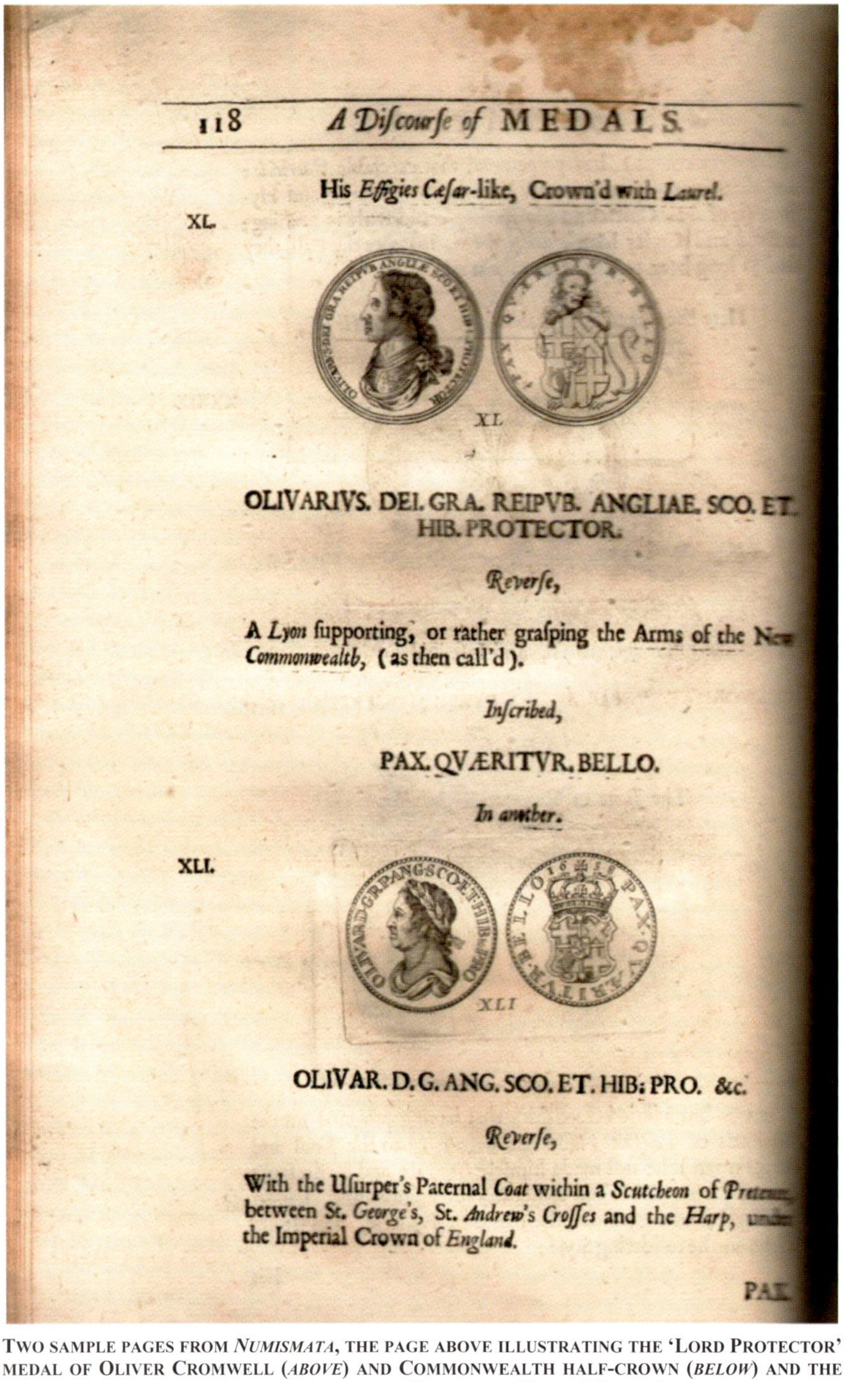

118 *A Discourse of* MEDALS.

His *Effigies Cæsar*-like, Crown'd with *Laurel.*

XL.

XL

OLIVARIVS. DEI. GRA. REIPVB. ANGLIAE. SCO. ET. HIB. PROTECTOR.

Reverse,

A *Lyon* supporting, or rather grasping the Arms of the New *Commonwealth*, (as then call'd).

Inscribed,

PAX. QVÆRITVR. BELLO.

In another.

XLI.

XLI

OLIVAR. D. G. ANG. SCO. ET. HIB. PRO. &c.

Reverse,

With the Usurper's Paternal *Coat* within a *Scutcheon* of *Pretence*, between St. *George's*, St. *Andrew's Crosses* and the *Harp*, under the Imperial Crown of *England*.

PAX.

TWO SAMPLE PAGES FROM *NUMISMATA*, THE PAGE ABOVE ILLUSTRATING THE 'LORD PROTECTOR' MEDAL OF OLIVER CROMWELL (*ABOVE*) AND COMMONWEALTH HALF-CROWN (*BELOW*) AND THE ONE ON THE FOLLOWING PAGE, THE SO-CALLED CROMWELL 'DEATH MEDAL.'

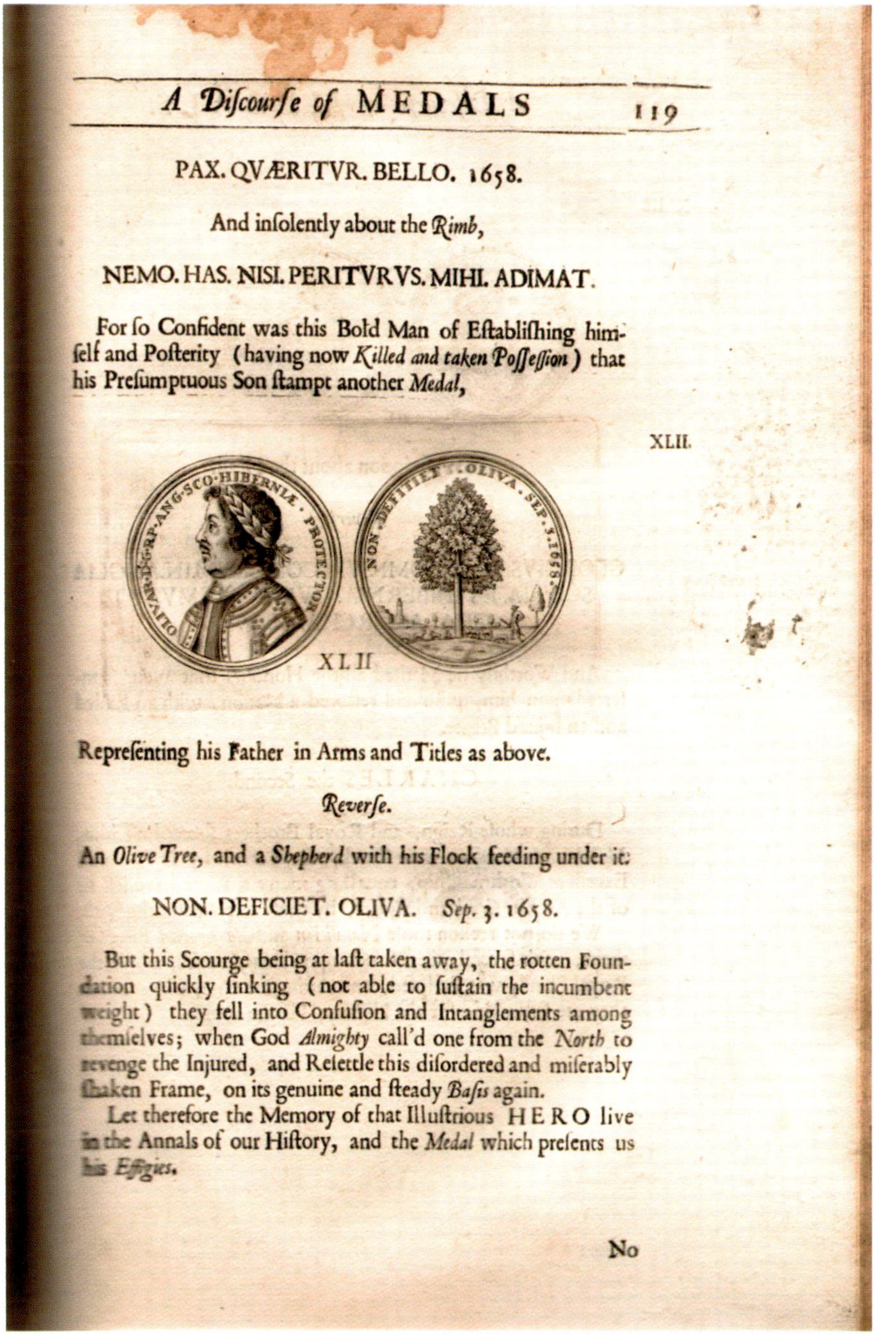

A *Diſcourſe of* MEDALS 119

PAX. QVÆRITVR. BELLO. 1658.

And inſolently about the *Rimb*,

NEMO. HAS. NISI. PERITVRVS. MIHI. ADIMAT.

For ſo Confident was this Bold Man of Eſtabliſhing himſelf and Poſterity (having now *Killed and taken Poſſeſſion*) that his Preſumptuous Son ſtampt another *Medal*,

XLII.

XLII

Repreſenting his Father in Arms and Titles as above.

Reverſe.

An *Olive Tree*, and a *Shepherd* with his Flock feeding under it:

NON. DEFICIET. OLIVA. *Sep.* 3. 1658.

But this Scourge being at laſt taken away, the rotten Foundation quickly ſinking (not able to ſuſtain the incumbent weight) they fell into Confuſion and Intanglements among themſelves; when God *Almighty* call'd one from the *North* to revenge the Injured, and Reſettle this diſordered and miſerably ſhaken Frame, on its genuine and ſteady *Baſis* again.

Let therefore the Memory of that Illuſtrious HERO live in the Annals of our Hiſtory, and the *Medal* which preſents us his *Effigies*.

No

PAGE 119 OF EVELYN'S NUMISMATA, *A DISCOURSE OF MEDALS* (1697). THE BRIEF SNIPPET OF TEXT SHOWN HERE WILL PROVIDE THE READER WITH THE FLAVOR OF EVELYN'S COMMENTARY.

Historical Commentary on John Evelyn

John Evelyn, in a letter dated August 12, 1689, to his friend and correspondent Samuel Pepys, a fellow collector, discusses the subject of 'medals.' The following are passages from that letter, and as is the case with other numismatic comment of the period, these would seem to be as applicable to medals as to coins:

...men curious of books & antiquities have ever had medals in such estimation, & rendered them a most necessary furniture to their libraries, because by them we are not only inform'd whose real image & superscription they beare, but have discovered to us, in their reverses, what heroical exploits they perform'd; ...till...others raised it out of the dust, & restor'd that noble art, by their owne and other learned men consulting & comparing the reverses of medals & medallions: besides what they farther contribute to the elucidation of many passages in historic, chronologic, & geography. So as I do not see how Mr. Pepys's library can be long without this necessary adjunct...But, Sir, I am sensible I have quite tir'd you by this time with medals, & therefore I will say nothing concerning those observations in the filing, sharpness, & due extanic vernish, & other markes, necessary to be critically skill'd in to prevent the being cheated & impos'd upon by copies & counterfeits for antique & original...Mr. Ashmole, our common friend, had collected all the antient & modern coines of this kingdome, which were very rare, together with seuerall medalls of our British, Saxon, & other Kings vpon occasion of births, coronations, marriages, & other solemnities. I know not whether they escap'd the burning of his study at the Middle Temple...In the meane time, the curious of this sort of erudition (I meane of medalls) were formerly, & I believe at present, very few in England....That greate lover of antiquity Thomas [Howard, 21st] Earle of Arundel had a very rich collection as well of medalls as other intaglios, belonging to the cabinet he purchased of Daniel Nice at the cost of ten thousand pounds, which with innumerable other rarities, have been scatter'd & squander'd away by his Countesse when she got that treasure to Amsterdam, whilst my Lord was in Italy, where he died...The same fate befell a noble collection of medals belonging to the then curious Sr Simon Fanshaw of Ware-park...

—Excerpted from W. Bray (1819), *Memoirs…&…Diary…*, 2nd ed., vol. ii, pp. 240-241.

§

I was in hopes of completing this article by having recourse to Mr. Evelyn's Discourses *on Medals*, but was extremely disappointed to find that in a folio volume, in which he has given the plates and inscriptions of a regular series of our medals, he takes not the least notice of the gravers. I should not have expected that a virtuoso so knowing would have contented himself with descriptions of the persons represented, he who had it in his inclination, and generally in his power, to inform posterity of almost everything they would wish to learn. Had Mr. Evelyn never regretted his ignorance of the names of the workmen of those inimitable medals of the Seleucidae, of the fair coins of Augustus, and of the denarii of the other Roman emperors?...Why did he think posterity would not be as curious to learn who were the medallists of Char. II., James I., Mary I.? He has omitted all names of gravers except in two or three of the plates, and even there says not a word of the artist. For instance, in a medal of Char. I..., under the king's bust are the letters N. R. F. I cannot discover who this N. R. was (fn.: Unless it was Norbert Rotier [sic], who arrived in the reign of Charles II. In that case, the medal in question must have been executed after the Restoration.)

—H. Walpole, *Anecdotes of Painting in England,* 1879 ed., p. 133.

§

Thomas Rawlins was a graver of the mint about this time; perhaps he had a brother who worked in partnership with him. I was so surprised at this omission, that I concluded Mr. Evelyn must have treated of the gravers in some other part of the work. I turned to the index, and to my greater surprise found almost everything but what I wanted. In the single letter N, which contains but twenty-six articles, are [some] subjects, which I believe would puzzle any man to guess how they found their way into a discourse on medals...In short, Mr. Evelyn, who loved to know, was too fond of telling the world all he knew. His virtue, industry, ingenuity, and learning were remarkable; one wishes he had written with a little more judgment—or perhaps it is not my interest to wish so; it would be more prudent to shelter under his authority any part of this work that is not much to the purpose.

—H. Walpole, ibid. pp. 133-134.

§

In 1697 a Mr Evelyn published the 'Numismata', a book compiled from the works of Patin, Jobert, and others.[62]

—A. W. Hands, Rev. (1895), 'Chats on Roman Coins with Young Collectors.' *Numismatic Circular,* vol. iii, pp. 1285.

[62] An interesting perspective on Evelyn's work.

The First Medal(s) made in Britain?

•Antecedents of 17th c. English Medallic Art•

Medal design and manufacture came relatively late to Britain, which lagged behind the Continent in these arts. The two medals illustrated above, believed to be the first medals both designed and manufactured in Britain, have much more in common with medieval design, as seen on coinage of the period, than with the influence of the Renaissance as seen in the design of Italian portrait medals of the mid-15th century onwards.

This medal, which commemorates Henry VIII as 'Supreme Head of the Church,' thus legitimizing his authority, is dated 1545. It is struck in gold and is 54 mm. in size (M.I.i 47/44, acc./reg. no. M.6802, ex Edward Hawkins collection). Only four examples of this medal are known—another in gold and two in silver—making it extremely rare. Although the records are scanty, it is attributed to Henry Basse (*or* Bayse). Appointed 'chief graver' in 1544, Basse remained in this position until his retirement in 1549 due to ill health. M.I.i translates the obverse inscription as: 'Henry VIII, King of England, France and Ireland, defender of the faith, and under Christ, the supreme head on earth of the Church of England and Ireland.' The same inscription, in Hebrew and Greek, appears on the reverse, reflecting the three languages of the Bible.

Another medal in the same style is the coronation medal of Edward VI (dated 1546, struck in gold, 60 mm., M.I.i 53/1, acc./reg. no. G3,EM.1, ex George III collection). G. F. Hill was of the opinion that Basse was 'responsible wholly' for the medal of Henry VIII and 'at least [responsible] for the design' of the Edward VI medal (1920, p. 152). Silver examples of the original medal exist as do later (18th c.) copies. M.I.i notes that this medal was cast or 'struck with only a gentle pressure upon cast metal' and 'more or less' chased, while the 18th c. copies were cast and highly chased. Both images © Trustees of the British Museum *(q.v. this vol., p. 364).*

AN INTERESTING DRAWING ENTITLED:

CHARACTERS WHO FREQUENTED BUTTON'S COFFEE HOUSE ABOUT THE YEAR 1730. FROM THE ORIGINAL DRAWING BY WILLIAM HOGARTH IN THE COLLECTION OF SAM. IRELAND.

THIS ETCHING AND AQUATINT DRAWING APPEARS FACING P. 31 OF SAMUEL IRELAND'S GRAPHIC ILLUSTRATIONS OF *HOGARTH*, VOL. I, 1794. FURTHER PUBLICATION DETAILS ARE GIVEN AS 'MARCH 1, 1786, BY W. DICKINSON, NO. 158, NEW BOND ST.' THE ACTUAL DATING OF THE DRAWING ITSELF IS 1786 AND IT IS AFTER ONE FORMERLY ATTRIBUTED TO THE ARTIST AND SATIRIST WILLIAM HOGARTH (1697-1764). IN THIS DEPICTION, FOLKES IS SHOWN EXAMINING WHAT APPEARS TO BE A WATCH, OR POSSIBLY A MEDAL, CONTAINED WITHIN A WATCHCASE. WHAT IS PARTICULARLY INTERESTING ARE THE NOTATIONS ABOVE THE HEADS OF THE TWO SUBJECTS IDENTIFYING HOGARTH AND FOLKES. THE REVERSE ALSO CONTAINS THE ANNOTATION 'MARTIN FOLKES./ADDISON/35.'[63] THE DRAWING EXISTS IN THREE STATES IN THE BRITISH MUSEUM COLLECTION, THIS APPARENTLY BEING THE FINAL ONE. IMAGE © TRUSTEES OF THE BRITISH MUSEUM.

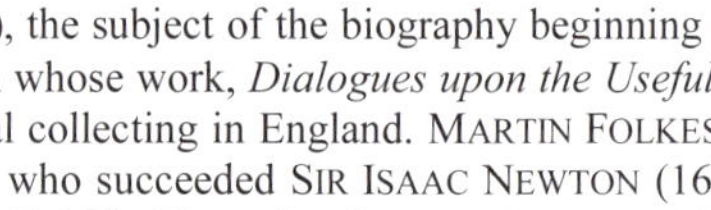

[63] JOSEPH ADDISON (1672-1719), the subject of the biography beginning on the facing page, was an essayist, poet, playwright and politician whose work, *Dialogues upon the Usefulness of Ancient Medals,* contributed to popularizing coin and medal collecting in England. MARTIN FOLKES (1690-1754) was an antiquary, numismatist, and mathematician who succeeded SIR ISAAC NEWTON (1643–1727) as president of the Royal Society (*See this vol., pages 348-350*). The artist, SAMUEL IRELAND (1744-1800), was a printseller, collector, author and self-taught engraver.

Joseph Addison

(1672-1719)

CLASSICIST, essayist, poet, playwright and politician, Joseph Addison was born in Milton, Wiltshire, to a Royalist clergyman and his wife. He was educated at Charterhouse School and Queen's College, Oxford.

Addison's poem, *The Campaign*, commemorating the Battle of Blenheim (1704), first brought him to the attention of the Whig party, which was responsible for his initial appointment as an undersecretary of state and his subsequent positions in the government. Elected to Parliament, he held a seat in that body until his death. During this time, he continued his output of plays. He is perhaps best known for his authorship of the play, *Cato: A Tragedy,* which explored such themes as liberty vs. tyranny, republicanism vs. monarchism and logic vs. emotion. Performed for George Washington and his officers during the Continental Army's encampment at Valley Forge, *Cato*… has been said to be an ideological contribution to the American Revolution. Addison extensively employed the imagery of 'medals' in his works.

JOSEPH ADDISON: 'HIS AUTOGRAPH FROM AN ORIGINAL IN THE POSSESSION OF JOHN THANE.' ADDISON WAS A COLLECTOR OF COINS AND MEDALS AND THE AUTHOR OF *DIALOGUES UPON THE USEFULNESS OF ANCIENT MEDALS.* AS WAS THE CASE FOR HIS CONTEMPORARIES, ADDISON USED THE TERMS 'COIN' AND 'MEDAL' INTERCHANGEABLY, BUT HAD MUCH WISDOM TO IMPART TO BOTH MEDAL AND COIN COLLECTORS. THUS, THE READER OF THE PRESENT VOLUME WILL ENCOUNTER QUOTATIONS FROM HIM IN THIS WORK. ALTHOUGH THE FIRST EDITION OF *DIALOGUES…*, A POSTHUMOUS EDITION, PUBLISHED BY THOMAS TICKELL, APPEARED IN 1721, ADDISON HAD COMPLETED IT IN 1715 AND HAD ORIGINALLY INTENDED TO PUBLISH IT AT THAT TIME WITH THE TITLE '*OF MEDALS.*'

Addison's *Dialogues upon the Usefulness of Ancient Medals* was not published until after his death in 1719. Guthrie, in his very worthwhile chapter on the uses of the medal in 18th-century Britain, comments that:

> Addison's *Dialogues* played a significant part in raising the profile of numismatics as a field of endeavour in Britain, where it had apparently received less attention than in continental Europe. The biographer Miles Davies observed that 'Of all the Sorts and Kinds of Writers and Writings Great Brittain [sic] has produc'd the fewest of *Medal-Tracts* and Numismatical Collectors. Tho' the Making or Striking of Medals be an old Practice, yet the Reading of History in and by them, is a new Study.[64]

[64] W. Guthrie, in J. C. D. Clark & H. Erskine-Hill, *The Politics of Samuel Johnson,* 2012, pp. 95, 107, cites as his sources for these comments: L. R. Gamez, 1988, pp. 257-258, and M. Davies, *Athenae Britannica*, 1716.

A BRONZE MEDAL OF JOSEPH ADDISON (41 MM., M.I.I 444/50, EIMER 483). BY EMILE ROGAT (1770-1852), FROM THE SERIES 'NUMISMATICA UNIVERSALIS VIRORUM ILLUSTRIUM,' ISSUED BETWEEN 1820 AND 1846 BY AMEDÉE DURAND. THE INSCRIPTION TRANSLATES AS: 'BORN 1672, AT MISTON IN WILTSHIRE, IN ENGLAND; DIED, 1719.' IMAGE © TRUSTEES OF THE BRITISH MUSEUM, EX AUGUSTUS W. FRANKS COLLECTION.

Guthrie notes that medals had 'important functions' in the 18th century, citing Addison's opinion that coins and medals could be useful as well as ornamental. He lists their use as 'vehicles of propaganda,' 'events in themselves,' '*casus belli,*' or,

> ...as a combination of visual symbolism and text impressed with meaning which were to be interpreted by the person who handled the object. [Thus] medals were not merely decorative, but at their best had 'verse and sculpture...'[65]

For Guthrie, 18th century numismatics:

> ...placed medals in their literary and historical context, and saw them as a vehicle for political and other statements conveyed by means of allegorical and apposite inscriptions.[66]

It is notable that while Addison concerned himself with writing about coins, using the then current custom of using the descriptor 'medals' as synonymous with 'coins,' his comments are also appropriate in their application to medals as we now know them.

> THERE is also a fine copy of verses upon the discourse on Medals, which is quite a new subject and very prettily treated by Mr. Pope...
>
> —Walter Molesworth writing to his brother John, Nov. 9, 1721, re Addison's *Dialogues* and Pope's comments on them. Cited by Guthrie, in Clark & Erskine-Hill, 2012.

[65] Guthrie, ibid, p. 103.

[66] Ibid.

Historical Commentary on Joseph Addison

I must confess, says Philander, the knowledge of medals has most of those disadvantages that can render a science ridiculous, to such as are not well versed in it. Nothing is more easy than to represent as impertinencies any parts of learning that have no immediate relation to the happiness or convenience of mankind... It is no wonder, therefore, that the science of medals, which is charged with so many unconcerning parts of knowledge, and built on such mean materials, should appear ridiculous to those that have not taken the pains to examine it.

—Ibid. p. 341.

§

...[Addison] is almost always spoken of as a man of fine intellect, lofty character, considerate and distinguished manners and great personal charm. He has been called the chief architect of public opinion in the 18th century. His posthumous fame, of course, rests almost exclusively on his contributions to the Toiler and the Spectator[67]... Addison brought English prose to a degree of finish and accessibility that had been wanting before.

—*Encyclopedia Americana*, 1918 ed., p.133.

§

The following excerpts are from Dialogues Upon the Usefulness of Ancient Medals, *1726 ed.:*

.....let us know the several uses of old coins...The first and most obvious one, says *Philander*,[68] is the shewing us the faces of all the great persons of antiquity. A cabinet of Medals is a collection of pictures in miniature (p. 13).

§

One may often find as much thought on the reverse of a medal as in a Canto of *Spenser* (p. 15).

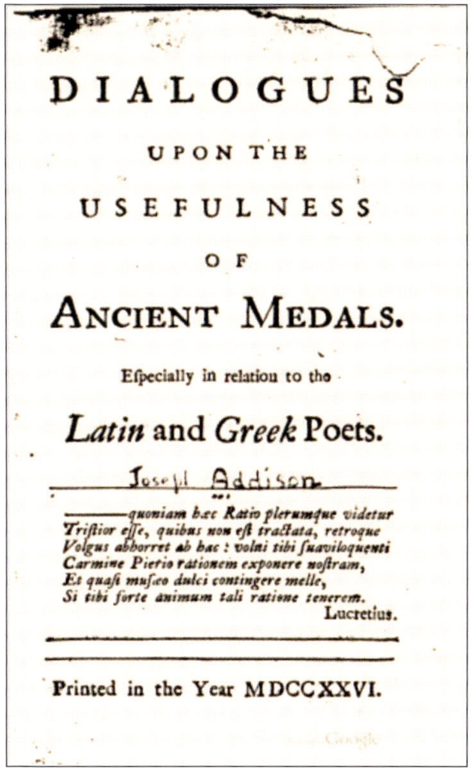
DIALOGUES
UPON THE
USEFULNESS
OF
ANCIENT MEDALS.
Especially in relation to the
Latin and *Greek* Poets.
Joseph Addison
——*quoniam hæc Ratio plerumque videtur*
Tristior esse, quibus non est tractata, retroque
Volgus abhorret ab hac: volui tibi suaviloquenti
Carmine Pierio rationem exponere nostram,
Et quasi musæo dulci contingere melle,
Si tibi forte animum tali ratione tenerem.
Lucretius.
Printed in the Year MDCCXXVI.

THE TITLE PAGE OF THE 1726 EDITION OF ADDISON'S *DIALOGUES...*, A WORK THAT GREATLY STIMULATED NUMISMATIC INTEREST IN 18TH CENTURY ENGLAND. A NUMBER OF SUBSEQUENT PRINTINGS EMPLOY THE SAME TITLE PAGE, DIFFERING ONLY WITH RESPECT TO THE DATE. *DIALOGUES ...* ALSO APPEARS IN VOLUMES OF ADDISON'S COLLECTED WORKS AS EARLY AS 1730 (E.G. JACOB TONSON, TWO VOLUME EDITION). IN THESE EARLY EDITIONS, THE AUTHOR'S NAME DOES NOT APPEAR ON THE TITLE PAGE; HERE IT HAS BEEN WRITTEN IN, EITHER IN CATALOGUING THE VOLUME OR BY A READER. IMAGE DIGITIZED BY GOOGLE.

---

[67] Daily 'news papers' widely read through their presence in coffee houses of the period.

[68] Philander was a character employed by Addison as a protagonist in his writing, e.g., in Dialogue ii of *Addison's Works*, the following narration appears:

> We will suppose the china dishes taken off [after tea], and a drawer of medals supplying their room. Philander, who is to be the hero of my dialogue, takes it in his hand, and, addressing himself to Cynthio and Eugenius, I will first of all, says he, show you an assembly of the most virtuous ladies that you have ever perhaps, conversed with. I do not know, says Cynthio, regarding them, what their virtue may be, but methinks they are a little fantastical in their dress. You will find, says Philander, there is good sense in it. They have not a single ornament that they cannot give a reason for. I was going to ask you, says Eugenius, in what country you find these ladies. But I see they are some of those imaginary persons you told us of last night, that inhabit old coins, and appear nowhere else but on the reverse of a medal (1811 ed., vol. iv, p. 33).

§

To come then to a more weighty use, says *Philander*, it is certain that medals give a very great light to history, in confirming such passages as are true in old authors, in settling such as are told after different manners, and in recording such as have been omitted. In this case a cabinet of medals is a body of history. It was, indeed, the best way in the world to perpetuate the memory of great actions, thus to coin out the life of an emperor, and to put every great exploit into the mint. It was a kind of printing, before the art was invented...For this too is an advantage medals have over books, that they tell their story much quicker, and sum up a whole volume in twenty or thirty reverses. They are, indeed, the best epitomes in the world, and let you see in one cast of an eye the substance of above a hundred pages. Another use of medals is, that they not only show you the actions of an emperor, but at the same time mark out the year in which they were performed. Every exploit has its date set to it. A series of an emperor's coins is his life digested into annals (p. 20).

§

What a majesty and force does one meet with in these short inscriptions: are not you amazed to see so much history gathered into so small a compass? (p. 155).

§

Medals are so many monuments consigned over to Eternity, that they may last when all other memorials of the same age are worn out or lost (p. 160).

—Above excerpts from: *Dialogues Upon the Usefulness of Ancient Medals,* 1726 ed.

EPISTLE TO MR. ADDISON, HIS *DIALOGUES ON MEDALS*

The Medal, faithful to its charge of fame,
Thro' climes and ages hears each form and name:
In one short view subjected to your eye,
Gods, Emperors, Heroes, Sages, Beauties, lie.
With sharpen'd sight pale Antiquaries pore,
The inscription value, hut the rust adore.
This the blue varnish, that the green endears.
The sacred rust of twice ten hundred years!
To gain Pescennius one employs his schemes,
One grasps a Cecrops in ecstatic dreams...

Oh, when shall Britain, conscious of her claim,
Stand emulous of Greek and Roman fame?
In living medals see her wars enroll'd,
And vanquish'd realms supply recording gold?
Here, rising hold, the patriot's honest face;
There, warriors frowning in historic brass:
Then future ages with delight shall see
How Plato's, Bacon's, Newton's looks agree;
Or in fair aeries laurell'd bards be shown,
A Virgil there, and here an Addison.
Then shall thy CRAGS (and let me call him mine)
On the cast ore, another Pollio, shine;
With aspect open shall erect his head,
And round the orb in lasting notes be read,
'Statesman, yet friend to Truth! of soul sincere,
In action faithful, and in honour clear;
Who broke no promise, serv'd no private end,
Who gain'd no title, and who lost no friend:
Ennobled by himself, by all approv'd,
And prais'd, unenvy'd by the Muse he lov'd.'

—Excerpted from Alexander Pope's Epistle v, To Mr. Addison. Occasioned by his *Dialogues on Medals...,* first published in 1721.

IF it were with Sciences as it is with Nobility, which draws its principal glory from its antiquity, The Science of Medals, without dispute, would be the most considerable and esteemed.

—Louis Jobert, *La Science des Médailles...*, 1697, p. 1.

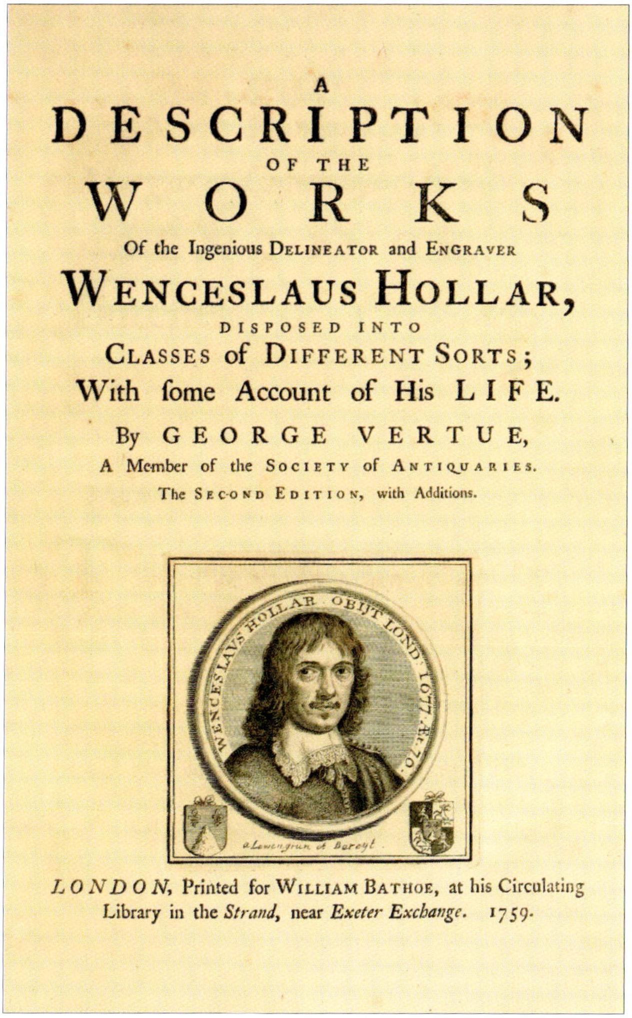

A
DESCRIPTION
OF THE
WORKS
Of the Ingenious DELINEATOR and ENGRAVER
WENCESLAUS HOLLAR,
DISPOSED INTO
CLASSES of DIFFERENT SORTS;
With ſome Account of His LIFE.
By GEORGE VERTUE,
A Member of the SOCIETY of ANTIQUARIES.
The SECOND EDITION, with Additions.

LONDON, Printed for WILLIAM BATHOE, at his Circulating Library in the *Strand*, near *Exeter Exchange*. 1759.

One can more fully visualize mid-17th century England, or at least London, by becoming familiar with the images left by the master etcher and portraitist Wenceslaus Hollar (1607-1677). Hollar has left us an *oeuvre* of over 2700 works which provides a contemporary view of life and place in England in the 17th century.* While visages of many illustrators of the period have never existed or have been lost, a self-portrait of Wenceslaus Hollar adorns the title page of George Vertue's catalogue of Hollar's work.** A Bohemian by birth, Hollar left Prague after his family's home was sacked during the Thirty Year's War, arriving in England in 1637 with his patron, Thomas Howard, 21st Earl of Arundel (1585-1646). Following the Earl's death, Hollar worked as a book illustrator. Leaving England during the Civil War, he worked in Antwerp. After his return in 1652, he briefly lived with William Faithorne, the engraver (1616–1691) while he reestablished himself as an artist. Hollar died in poverty in London in 1677. Image © Trustees of the British Museum.

* For examples, see pp. iii, xv, 7, 129, 157, 343 and 353.

**Although the above portrait is in the form of a medal, the authors are not aware of the existence of a medal which bears Hollar's image other than a modern one (ca. 2007).

'George Vertue, Engraver' (1684-1756). Oil on canvas painting by Jonathan Richardson the Elder (1665-1745), 1733. Image © National Portrait Gallery, London.

George Vertue

(1684-1756)

GEORGE VERTUE, English engraver and antiquary, was born in St Martin-in-the-Fields Parish, London, in November 1684. His parents, Mary Carter and James Vertue, had been domestic servants in the households of the exiled James II, his mother previously having been a household servant when James II was the duke of York. At the age of thirteen Vertue was apprenticed to a French heraldic engraver, likely Blaise Gentot (1658–1700), who, however, did not stay in business. Vertue was then apprenticed for seven years to the influential engraver Michael van der Gucht.[69] Both preceding and during this period, Vertue immersed himself in learning French, Dutch and Italian, as well as in studying music. With Sir Godfrey Kneller (1646-1723) as his patron, Vertue was a co-founder member of the Great Queen Street Academy of Painting (1711). His engravings of the portraits of George I and Archbishop Tillotson, after Kneller, which were commissioned by Lord Somers, established his reputation.

A ENGRAVED PORTRAIT OF GEORGE VERTUE BY JAMES BASIRE II AFTER AN ORIGINAL DRAWING BY JONATHAN RICHARDSON WHICH APPEARED IN NICHOLS' *LITERARY ANECDOTES...* (1812 ED.). IMAGE © TRUSTEES OF THE BRITISH MUSEUM.

Vertue was soon well set up in business, ultimately engraving over five hundred plates, mostly portraits for other artists, as well as illustrations for books. Vertue's engravings of Kneller's portraits brought him to the attention of the newly reconstituted Society of Antiquaries, and in 1717, he was appointed engraver to that body. This resulted in commissions for the execution of statuary, monuments, and other works of an antiquarian nature. He was eventually to be

[69] MICHAEL VAN DER GUCHT did the etchings for the 1715 edition of EDWARD HYDE CLARENDON's *History of the Rebellion...*, published by JOHN NICHOLS. Van der Gucht was born in Antwerp in about 1660, learned the skills necessary for success as an engraver there, and then moved to London, where he enjoyed much success, dying there in 1725. His sons GERARD (1695-1776) and JOHN (1697-1776) also became engravers, the former being a much sought after engraver for book sellers. Gerard also maintained his own printing and book-selling business and John achieved some success with his etchings. John's employment, like his father, included the engraving of anatomical illustrations. *For more information about the* van der Guchts, *see* Nichols, *Literary Anecdotes*, 1812, vol. ii, pp. 247 ff., *fn*.

"GEORGE VERTUE WHEN YOUNG BY HIMSELF." UNDATED, PEN AND INK ON PAPER. IMAGE © TRUSTEES OF THE BRITISH MUSEUM.

the first engraver to that society to become a fellow. During this time, Vertue developed many social contacts as his work was now increasingly recognized by his contemporaries, resulting in his becoming an active seller of his own productions as well as taking on commission work from the aristocracy. Vertue was also responsible for engraving a number of the plates appearing in *Heads of the Illustrious Persons of Great Britain*, published between 1734 and 1752, although the greater part was engraved by Jacobus Houbraken.[70] Houbraken came to replace Vertue in completing *Heads of the Illustrious Persons...*, the output of Vertue's work having become very slow and Houbraken's "more brilliant but less truthful"[71] portraits being preferred by the publisher. Yet, Vertue created fine line and mezzotint engravings of both persons and architecture and contributed to the history of British art through his accumulation of the details of the lives of British artists, which was to be later published by Horace Walpole.

Of course, Vertue's claim to a place in the history of British numismatics was his preparation of *Medals, Coins, Great Seals, Impressions from the Works of Thomas Simon...*, first published in 1753.[72] Here, his preparation of the work was likely, as was the case for Evelyn's *Numismata...*, in need of editing the numerous errors, which appeared in the first edition. Vertue's work received a critical review in the *Numismatic Chronicle* in 1842, when Nightingale, lamenting on the obscurity surrounding Thomas Simon, said:

> Vertue...has done something towards rendering Simon's name and merits known; but though his book displays both zeal and research, it appears to have been got up in haste; and while it is very defective (perhaps unavoidably so), as regards Simon's personal history, it is extremely incorrect in reference to many of the works ascribed to him, there being no authority beyond conjecture for many of the medals and coins published as his work.[73]

Vertue's output, in terms of literary work, was prodigious. From 1713, he had accumulated forty volumes of material on British art and artists, this material being intended for incorporation into a *History of the Arts in England.* Near completion in 1742, the project was abandoned when Vertue's patron, James West,[74] died in that year. Horace Walpole was to purchase the greater part of this material from Vertue's widow, some 40 volumes, using it (as well as Vertue's

---

[70] JACOBUS HOUBRAKEN (1698-1780) **the son of another artist and biographer, ARNOLD HOUBRAKEN (1660-1719), was perhaps the foremost portrait engraver in 18th c. Holland. His *oeuvre* included several hundred portraits of Dutch and English men of prominence, both contemporary and historically.**

[71] *DNB*, 1909 ed., vol. xx, p. 285.

[72] **A second revised and expanded edition, edited by Richard Gough, was later published in 1780.** *See this vol., pp. 396-397.*

[73] B. Nightingale, Notices of Thomas Simon, *Numismatic Circular*, 1842, p. 212.

[74] JAMES WEST, MP (1704?-1772) lawyer, antiquary and politician, treasurer and later president of the Royal Society and fellow of the Society of Antiquaries. West "...greatly assisted James Granger in his biographical work on portraits." (*DNB*, 1909, vol. xx, p. 1241-42). At his death, the sales of his prints and drawings and of his coin and medal collection, in January 1773, lasted thirteen days and seven days respectively.

'George Vertue and Margaret his Wife (née Evans) in the very Habits they were Married...,' an etching (ca. 1720) by Vertue, later published (1765-1810) by William Humphrey (1742/45?-1810/15?). Note the numerous portraits on the wall as well as the artist's palette and mahl stick that rest on the window sill. Image © National Portrait Gallery, London.

History...) in his preparation of *Anecdotes of Painting in England...*, published in five volumes between 1762 and 1771. This work incorporated a biography of Vertue as well as a catalogue of his engravings. In addition to the work most known to numismatists, *Medals, Coins, Great-Seals, Impressions, from the Elaborate Works of Thomas Simon...* (1753), Vertue prepared *On Holbein and Gerard's Pictures* (1740), and *Description of the Works of that Ingenious Delineator and Engraver, W. Hollar* (1745). At the time of his death, Vertue had been working on several catalogues of collections— Vanderdoort's of Charles I (1757), Chaffinch's of James II, as well as the collection of Queen Caroline (1758) and George Villiers, duke of Buckingham (1758). Vertue had substantially completed these surveys. After his death, all but the first (of Charles I's collection) were published from Vertue's manuscripts with annotations added by Walpole.[75]

[75] In 1786, Walpole purchased the inventory of Charles I's pictures at Whitehall which had been annotated by Abraham van der Doort, Charles I's keeper of the royal pictures, and later owned by Vertue. In this case, although Vertue had prepared an inventory, the one prepared by Walpole was not taken from Vertue's manuscript. In the case of the inventory of James II's collection, the existing copy of the inventory was transcribed by Vertue from the original inventory prepared by William Chaffinch, keeper of the king's closet. It appears that Vertue himself prepared the inventory of art in Queen Caroline's apartments at Kensington (*see* Smith, M. M., *Index of English Literary Manuscripts,* vol. 3, part 2, p. 243).

Vertue died on July 24, 1756, and was buried in Westminster Abbey. He was survived by his wife Margaret.

Vertue's collection of books, drawings and prints were sold at Ford's Auction in six sales beginning March 16, 1757 (*A Catalogue of the...collection of Prints, Drawings, and Books of Prints of G. Vertue, engraver; to be sold by auction, etc. London*). As noted above, in 1758 Horace Walpole purchased from Vertue's widow the approximately forty volumes of Vertue's 'notebooks' on the lives of English painters and their portraits as well as other prints and drawings. Additional antiquarian plates owned by Vertue were also purchased from his widow by the Society of Antiquaries or were sold at Langford's auction rooms on February 24 and 25, 1777. Horace Walpole ultimately came to possess 470 of George Vertue's prints and drawings which he kept in two folio volumes.

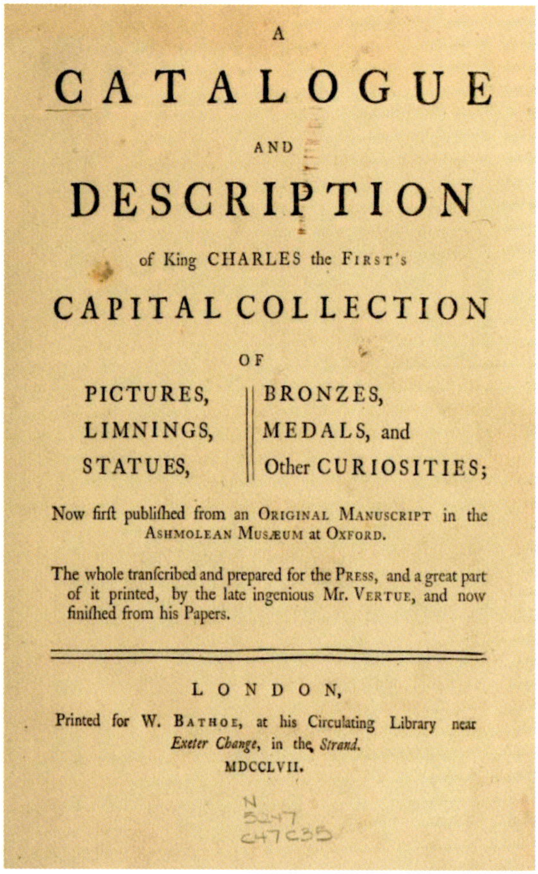

A

CATALOGUE

AND

DESCRIPTION

of King CHARLES the FIRST's

CAPITAL COLLECTION

OF

PICTURES,	BRONZES,
LIMNINGS,	MEDALS, and
STATUES,	Other CURIOSITIES;

Now firſt publiſhed from an ORIGINAL MANUSCRIPT in the ASHMOLEAN MUSÆUM at OXFORD.

The whole tranſcribed and prepared for the PRESS, and a great part of it printed, by the late ingenious Mr. VERTUE, and now finiſhed from his Papers.

LONDON,

Printed for W. BATHOE, at his Circulating Library near *Exeter Change*, in the *Strand.*

MDCCLVII.

THE TITLE PAGE OF THE CATALOGUE OF KING CHARLES I'S COLLECTION THAT WAS PREPARED BY ABRAHAM VAN DER DOORT AND TRANSCRIBED BY GEORGE VERTUE. IMAGE BY INTERNET ARCHIVE.

> WHEN one offers to the public the labours of another person, it is allowable and precedented to expatiate in praise of the work. Of this indulgence, however, I shall not [t]ake advantage. The industry of Mr. Vertue was sufficiently known; the antiquarian world had singular obligations to him. The many valuable monuments relating to our history, and to the persons of our monarchs and great men, which he saved from oblivion, are lasting evidences of his merit.
>
> —H. Walpole, *Anecdotes of Painting in England*, preface to the 1798 ed., vol. iii, p. 3.

THE TITLE PAGE TO VERTUE'S 1753 WORK ON THE MEDALS OF THOMAS SIMON, WHICH ALSO APPEARS IN THE 1780 EDITION. ENGRAVED BY GEORGE VERTUE.

GEORGE VERTUE'S RENDITION OF THOMAS SIMON'S 'GREAT SEALE' AS IT WAS ORDERED BY PARLIAMENT IN 1659. THIS SEAL, WHICH APPEARS AS PL. XXIV IN VERTUE'S *MEDALS, COINS, GREAT SEALS...OF THOMAS SIMON...*, WAS INTENDED TO REPLACE THE PREVIOUS SEAL, THAT OF RICHARD CROMWELL, WHICH WAS ORDERED TO BE BROUGHT IN AND BROKEN WHEN THE LONG PARLIAMENT WAS REASSEMBLED IN 1659. THIS SEAL WAS, HOWEVER, NEVER ACTUALLY USED AS THE GREAT SEAL OF ENGLAND.

George Vertue's
MEDALS, COINS, GREAT-SEALS... OF THOMAS SIMON...
(1753)

GEORGE VERTUE'S volume on the *Medals, Coins, Great Seals,...of Thomas Simon...*, first published in 1753 (with a second edition, revised by Richard Gouth, in 1780[76]) was the next work on British medals to appear after Evelyn's and stood alone for some time as a study of the work of an individual British medallist. The full title of this work is "**MEDALS, COINS, GREAT-SEALS, Impressions**. *From the Elaborate WORKS of* THOMAS SIMON, Chief *Engraver of the* MINT, *To K. Charles The 1st to the* COMMONWEALTH, *The* LORD PROTECTOR **Cromwell**, *and in the Reign of* K. CHARLES ye IID *To* MDCLXV, *by Geo. Vertue*."

Thomas Simon was the most prominent figure in the design and production of British coins and medals for a significant part of the early to mid-seventeenth century, having served in turn, Charles I, Oliver Cromwell, Richard Cromwell, and Charles II. The coverage of Vertue's work is thus necessarily broad, including those medals, coins, and seals (e.g., the 'Jamaica Island' Seal) which Simon either designed and/or produced under these four heads of state. The engravings in this volume are magnificent. The reader's attention is particularly called to plates VII and XXIV in Vertue's work—the 'Great Seal of England'—that represent the 'House of Commons sitting, with the Speaker in the Chair…' It the same view of Parliament that appears on the reverse of a number of Parliamentarian medals, including the one struck to celebrate the victory at Dunbar. While most of the plates in Vertue's volume deal with coinage and seals, there are several of medals that may well have been 'military rewards.'

AN ETCHED AND ENGRAVED SELF-PORTRAIT BY GEORGE VERTUE (1750), AFTER AN 1715 ENGRAVING BY THOMAS GIBSON (*CA.* 1680-1751). NOTE THE ENGRAVER'S TOOLS—COMPASSES, PAINTBRUSHES, PEN AND TUBE AND BURINS FOR ENGRAVING. THE INSCRIPTIONS READ 'BY MR. GEORGE VERTUE, WITHIN A FEW / YEARS OF HIS DEATH / PROOF / VERY RARE / OB. 1756.' IMAGE © TRUSTEES OF THE BRITISH MUSEUM.

[76] For which the antiquarian RICHARD GOUTH (1735-1809; *q.v. pp. 396-397*), has received little credit.

Title Pages for the Second Edition of Vertue's Classic Work

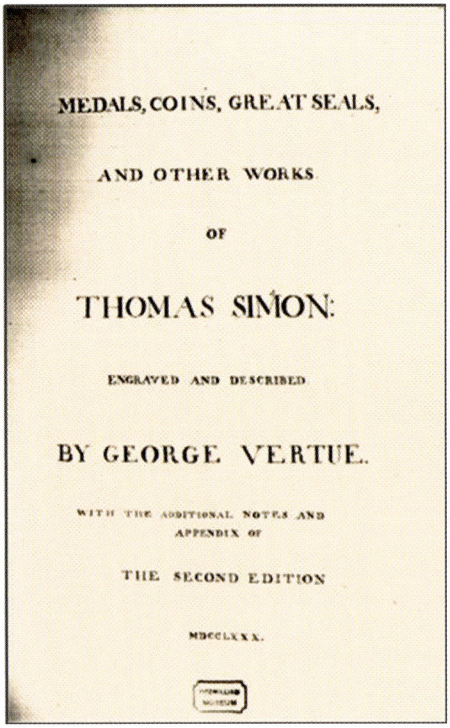
MEDALS, COINS, GREAT SEALS,

AND OTHER WORKS

OF

THOMAS SIMON:

ENGRAVED AND DESCRIBED

BY GEORGE VERTUE.

WITH THE ADDITIONAL NOTES AND APPENDIX OF

THE SECOND EDITION

MDCCLXXX.

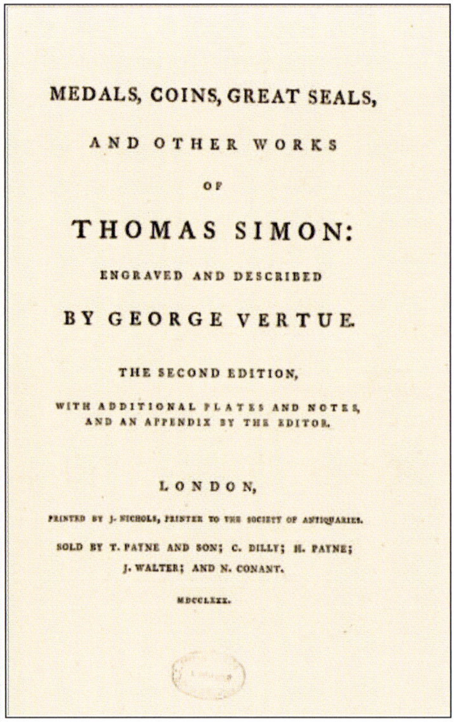
MEDALS, COINS, GREAT SEALS,

AND OTHER WORKS

OF

THOMAS SIMON:

ENGRAVED AND DESCRIBED

BY GEORGE VERTUE.

THE SECOND EDITION,

WITH ADDITIONAL PLATES AND NOTES, AND AN APPENDIX BY THE EDITOR.

LONDON,

PRINTED BY J. NICHOLS, PRINTER TO THE SOCIETY OF ANTIQUARIES.

SOLD BY T. PAYNE AND SON; C. DILLY; H. PAYNE; J. WALTER; AND N. CONANT.

MDCCLXXX.

Two versions of the title page of the second edition of Vertue's work on *The Medals...of Thomas Simon*, published in 1780. The one on the *left* would appear to be a draft of the published page which appears on the *right*. The size of the volume is crown quarto (10 x 7-1/2 in.). The image on the *left* is from the Fitzwilliam Museum's collection, and that on the *right*, from the British Museum's holdings. The images are copyrighted by and reproduced with the kind permission of (*left*) The Fitzwilliam Museum, University of Cambridge and (*right*) The Trustees of the British Museum, respectively. The following annotation, possibly in Richard Gouth's own hand (*q.v. pp. 396-397*), appears on an old slip of paper inserted into the Fitzwilliam Museum's copy:

Simons Medals to 1753
This is a very fine Copy of the first Edition, having (in M.S.) the additional Notes and Appendices of the Second Edition by George Vertue the editor Rd. Gough, 1780.

These include the medals with the likeness of the earl of Essex on the obverse, and on the reverse, his coat of arms or a representation of the sitting Houses of Lords and Commons. It is notable that, on many of these medals, in concordance with the original intent of some Parliamentarian leaders, the king is represented as sitting at the head of the House of Lords.[77] This design was not in error, for at the beginning of the Civil War, only a few Parliamentarian leaders intended that the king should be deposed.

As noted above, there are two editions of this work—1753 and 1780. While a number of copies of the 1753 edition were updated with the additions and corrections that then appear in the second

[77] See, e.g., M.I.I. 295/113, 296/114, etc.; also Platt, vol. i, pp. 79-81.

edition, the Fitzwilliam Museum, Cambridge, possesses a draft copy of the 1780 edition[78] with handwritten annotations, presumably by Richard Gouth. In comparison with the present authors' copy of Vertue, which ends with p. 66, the Fitzwilliam Museum's copy,[79] with substantial handwritten additions, contains 109 pages. This additional material provides further detail of Thomas Simon's life, his several appointments as 'Meddall-maker,' as well as copies of various warrants for the production of medals, seals and coins, including a detailed list of the latter. The copy in the possession of the Department of Coins and Medals at the British Museum is 68 pages in length, and contains the following comments on pages 66-68:

> The Works and Description of the Medals, Coins and curious Seals of the Commonwealth, by T. Simon, a book in Quarto, with 40 Plates.
>
> The Favours and free Access to the Cabinets of several of my honour'd Friends, I justly acknowledge with all due Thanks; and would, on this Occasion, more largely express: But having, in these Memorials of *Simon's* Work's, studied Clearness and Brevity; only here and there, where it was absolutely requisite, I have endeavour'd to deliver my self more fully, without being thought, I hope, either tedious to the present Readers, or offensive to Posterity, in this particular Attempt to embellish the History of those Times.
>
> George Vertue

John Nichols, in his *Literary Anecdotes of the Life of William Bowyer* (1812), comments that Richard Gough:

> Having also purchased the plates of the Medals, Coins, and Great Seals, executed by the celebrated Simon, and first published by Vertue in 1753, he gave a new and enlarged edition of them in 1780.[80]

Historical Commentary on George Vertue

...Vertue's MSS are not only a heap of immethodical confusion, but are written in so diminutive a hand, that many years ago, when I collected my *Anecdotes* from them, and had very strong eyes, I was often forced to use a magnifying glass.

—Horace Walpole, in a letter to John Pinkerton, dated Oct. 15, 1788, cited in W. S. Lewis & A. D. Wallace, *Horace Walpole's Correspondence...*, p. 299.

§

The Society of Antiquaries having republished some of Vertue's historical prints,...it has so happened that I have fortunately met with Van Voerst's original print of Charles I and his Queen, and upon comparing it with what has hitherto been supposed to be Vertue's copy, I find the impressions to be from the same plate, only retouched by Vertue, who has totally omitted Voerst's name, and although he has only added *excudit* to his own, yet this is a proceeding I knew [sic] not how to reconcile with the well known candour of that honest engraver...

—The Rev. Michael Lort,[81] letter to Horace Walpole, June 11, 1776, in Lewis & Wallace, ibid. p. 166.

---

[78] The present authors' copy has the handwritten note on a preliminary blank page: *"With the additions to the second Edition."* These have been added by hand in the appropriate locations, but it is still incomplete in comparison with the Fitzwilliam's copy.

[78A] For further details of Richard Gouth (1735-1809), *q.v. p. 397.*

[79] This copy bears LORD KENYON'S bookplate and was donated by him to the Fitzwilliam Museum in 1945.

[80] Nichols, *Literary Anecdotes...*, vol. vi, p. 284. JOHN NICHOLS (1745-1826) was an author, antiquarian and publisher (from 1778) of the popular publication *Gentleman's Magazine*. Edited by the Nichols and Gough families for almost two centuries (1731-1922), the accumulated contents of *Literary Anecdotes...* serve as an important anecdotal history of their times. RICHARD GOUGH (1735-1809) was an antiquarian and author of a number of works on Anglo-Saxon literature and archeology and British topography. He maintained a close friendship and collaboration with John Nichols who was also his neighbor (*q.v. pp. 391-392).*

[81] Antiquary and Regius professor of Trinity College, Cambridge.

PLATE XXXVIII FROM VERTUE'S WORK ON THOMAS SIMON. IN ADDITION TO THE PRIVY SEAL AND CHARLES II RESTORATION MEDALS:

> The other small Seals in this Plate, are the Portraits of private Persons, of which Kind, for Seals, *Simon* made great Variety (p. 65).

THE AUTHORS' COPY OF THIS WORK CONTAINS THE FOLLOWING HANDWRITTEN ENTRY:

> *Mr. Nicholas shewed the Society of Antiquaries 1723, an intaglio of his grandf. the Secretary, by Simon finely done. Dr. Cromwell Mortimer exhibited there 1735, a Steel Seal, about the size of the hatheread of a steel Pencil, formerly belonging to his father's first wife, a Daughter of Richard Cromwell, having the head of Oliver Cromwell by Symon* (p. 36).

PLATE XXII FROM VERTUE'S WORK ON THE MEDALS OF THOMAS SIMON. THE ILLUSTRATED MEDALS ARE OF (A) JOHN LILBURNE (M.I.I 385/3); (B) IBID. (385/4); (C) HENRY IRETON (387/6); (D) SIR JOHN HOTHAM (314/145); (E) DORCAS BRABAZON, LADY LANE (479/89); (F) BARON JOHN DE REEDE (320/156); (G) SIR ALBERT JOACHIM (324/162); AND (H) MONSIEUR "LA MARTINAY" (329/171). THE WIDE BORDER ON (A) SUGGESTS THAT IT MAY HAVE BEEN DRAWN FROM THE FORGERY BY 'STUART' (*see pp. 221 ff., this work*).

§

The Rev. Mr. *Gilpin*, in his "Essay upon Prints," says of *Vertue*, that "he was an excellent antiquarian, but no artist; he copied with painful exactness in a dry, disagreeable manner, without force or freedom: in his whole collection of heads we can scarce pick out half a dozen which are good." This character seems scarcely, or but little, overcharged, especially when it is considered that *Vertue* applied so much to portrait engraving; and as we have upwards of 500 portraits by him, it might therefore have been expected he should have made a greater progress in his art. His sketches and notes were purchased by the Hon. *Horace Walpole*, whom they furnished with the outlines of his Anecdotes of Painting and Engravings in England, and Memoirs of the Artist himself. A list of his works, much too long to be inserted here, may be seen in those Memoirs, which were abstracted in the Supplement to the "Biographia Britannica." His books, prints, and drawings, were sold by auction in *March* 1757; as were his pictures, models, plaster and wax impressions, limnings, coins, and medals, in May the fame year. His widow presented the Society of Antiquaries with a number of his plates of English antiquities; and they purchased of her his large historic plates, all which they have republished. On Mrs. *Vertue's* death, the remainder of his plates and prints were sold by Mr. *Langford* in 1776 and 1777. Mr. *Ford* in the *Haymarket* sold by auction, in 1766, the drawings of his brother James, who had followed the profession of a painter at *Rath,* where he then died.

—J. Nichols, *Anecdotes of Mr. Bowyer*, 1782, p. 238, *fn.*

§

Vertue's work as an engraver, although of no great artistic merit, forms a valuable historical record, and his antiquarian writings were of the highest importance.

—M. Bryan, *Dictionary of Painters and Engravers*..., 1889, vol. ii, p. 663.

§

...Mr. *Vertue was* buried, in the cloysters of Westminster-abbey, where there is a marble monument to his memory, with the following inscription, perfectly characteristic of its subject:

"Here lies the body of GEORGE VERTUE,
Late Engraver,
And Fellow of the Society of Antiquaries.
He was born in *London,* 1684;
And departed this life on the 24th of *July*, 1756.

With manners gentle, and a grateful heart,
And all the genius of the graphic art;
His fame will each succeeding artist own,
Longer by far than monuments of stone."

—ibid. p. 238.

Two other friends—not better poets indeed,—inserted the following lines in the papers, on viewing [Vertue's] monument:

Proud artist, cease those deeds to paint on stone:
Why should your skill so vainly thus be spent?
For Vertue ne'er can need a monument.

—H. Walpole, *Anecdotes of Painting*, 1786, pp. 269-270.

Rev. David Jennings

(1691-1762)

THE REV. JENNINGS was born at Kibworth, Leicestershire, the son of a minister to an Independent congregation. Educated for the ministry, David Jennings passed through a number of minor appointments until in 1718 he was ordained and called to be pastor to the Independent congregation at Wapping New Stairs where he remained for the rest of his life. Initially an advocate of religious liberty, he later became strictly Calvinistic in his views. In 1758, he opened a theological academy and began the tutoring of divinity students, an undertaking which eventually resulted in his training of a number of students for the Presbyterian ministry. Jennings' lectures on the Old Testament figures Moses and Aaron were eventually published posthumously as *Jewish Antiquities* (1837), his best-known work.[82] A number of his sermons were published, as was *An Introduction to the Use of the Globes &c.* (1747), a work reflecting his interest in science and in particular astronomy. In 1763, a single work on medals, entitled *An Introduction to the Knowledge of Medals, &c.* appeared.[83] In it, Rev. Jennings laid out the rationale and plan of this work in his introduction:

The Rev. David Jennings. A mezzotint by James McArdell (1729?–1765) after the portrait by (?) Jones, Henrietta St., Covent Garden, and published by Carington Bowles of No. 69, St. Paul's Churchyard.

> As the knowledge of medals is confessed to be not only entertaining, but in several respects of great use to the Chronologist, Historian, and Divine, as well as in particular to the Lovers and Professors of the fine Arts; it is presumed there is some ground to expect the following little Treatise on that subject, will meet with a favourable reception from the Publick; to whom it is offered; not as containing anything new, but as comprehending, in a small compass, a compleat Introduction to that Science: and as peculiarly calculated for those, who desiring a general acquaintance with the subject have neither time nor opportunity for studying larger Treaties, which enter into it more minutely. For the use of some young persons to circumstanced, it was originally drawn up; and it is now printed from the Author's Copy, corrected by his own hand.[84]

§

[82] *DNB*, 1908, vol. 10, p. 762; A. Rustin, *Oxford Dictionary of National Biography (ODNB)*, 2013.

[83] With respect to nomenclature, Jennings suggested that if, among other criteria, a piece weighed two ounces and a half or more and was found in copper rather than gold or silver, was not used as current coin but was "struck on such particular occasions…," it should be called a 'medallion' rather than a 'modern medal' (*Introduction to the Knowledge of Medals,* 1764 ed., p. 24).

[84] Jennings, ibid. p. A2.

The Rev. Jennings opines that medals were made for two reasons:

[For the] *Missilia*, which were scattered among the People on Days of Triumph, Jubilees, and Solemn Processions, as is usual among us at the Coronation: or for *Donativa*, of which Presents were made to Princes, or their Ambassadors, or to others in a way of honorary Reward, for some worthy Action; as our *Royal Society* presenteth every Year, a gold Medal to one of its Members, who hath distinguished himself by some valuable discovery in Natural Philosophy. [and the second reason for the medal] ...of which there is the greatest quantity, are taken to have been originaly, the Current Coin of their respective nations; but which through their scarcity, are now laid up in the cabinets of the curious.

—Rev. D. Jennings, *An Introduction to the Knowledge of Medals,* 1764, p. 2.

§

A Comment by John Pinkerton

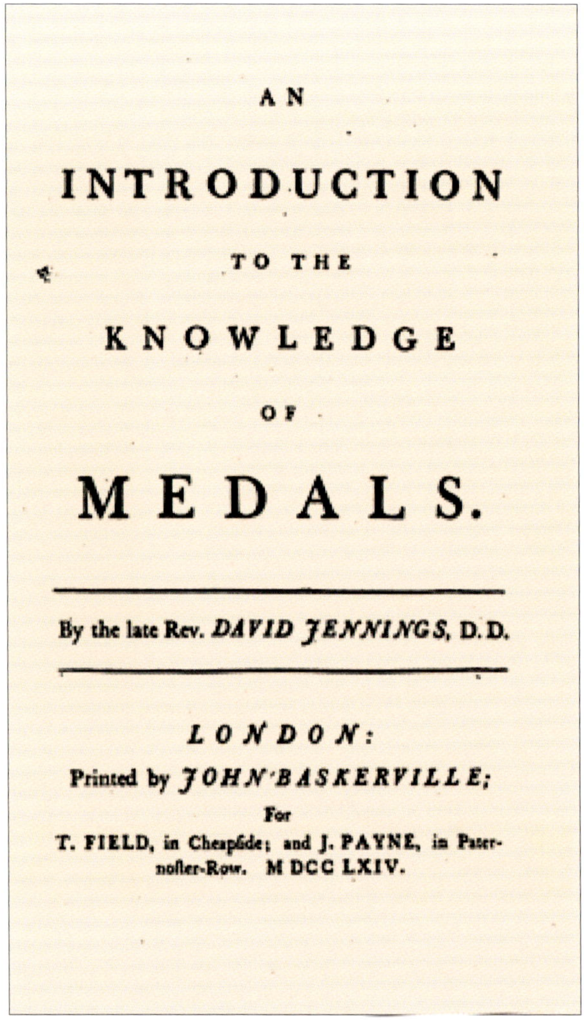
AN
INTRODUCTION
TO THE
KNOWLEDGE
OF
MEDALS.

By the late Rev. *DAVID JENNINGS*, D.D.

LONDON:
Printed by *JOHN BASKERVILLE;*
For
T. FIELD, in Cheapſide; and J. PAYNE, in Paternoſter-Row. M DCC LXIV.

THE TITLE PAGE OF REV. JENNINGS' BOOK ON THE SUBJECT OF MEDALS (1764 ED.). MANVILLE, IN HIS *NUMISMATIC GUIDE TO BRITISH AND IRISH PRINTED BOOKS* (2005) NOTES THAT THE CONTENT OF THIS WORK, IS ORIENTED TO THE BEGINNING COLLECTOR OF ANCIENT COINS AND "DERIVES STRONGLY FROM JOBERT" (P. 42).

An Introduction to the Knowledge of Medals by the late Reverend David Jennings, D. D. printed by Baskerville, 1764: 12mo. But this being the only other attempt in the language, it is necessary to mention it in a few words, It consists only of about 60 pages, most of which are occupied with Jewish shekels and divinity, as in duty bound to pray. The only apology which can be made for it is, that it was drawn up by the author, as would seem, without the most distant view of publication; but was sent into the breathing world, not half made up, by some officious friend. Its innumerable blunders, and holy verbosity, stamp it the most childish work which ever appeared in any science whatever.

—J. Pinkerton, *An Essay on Medals*, vol. i, 1808, pp. xi-xii.

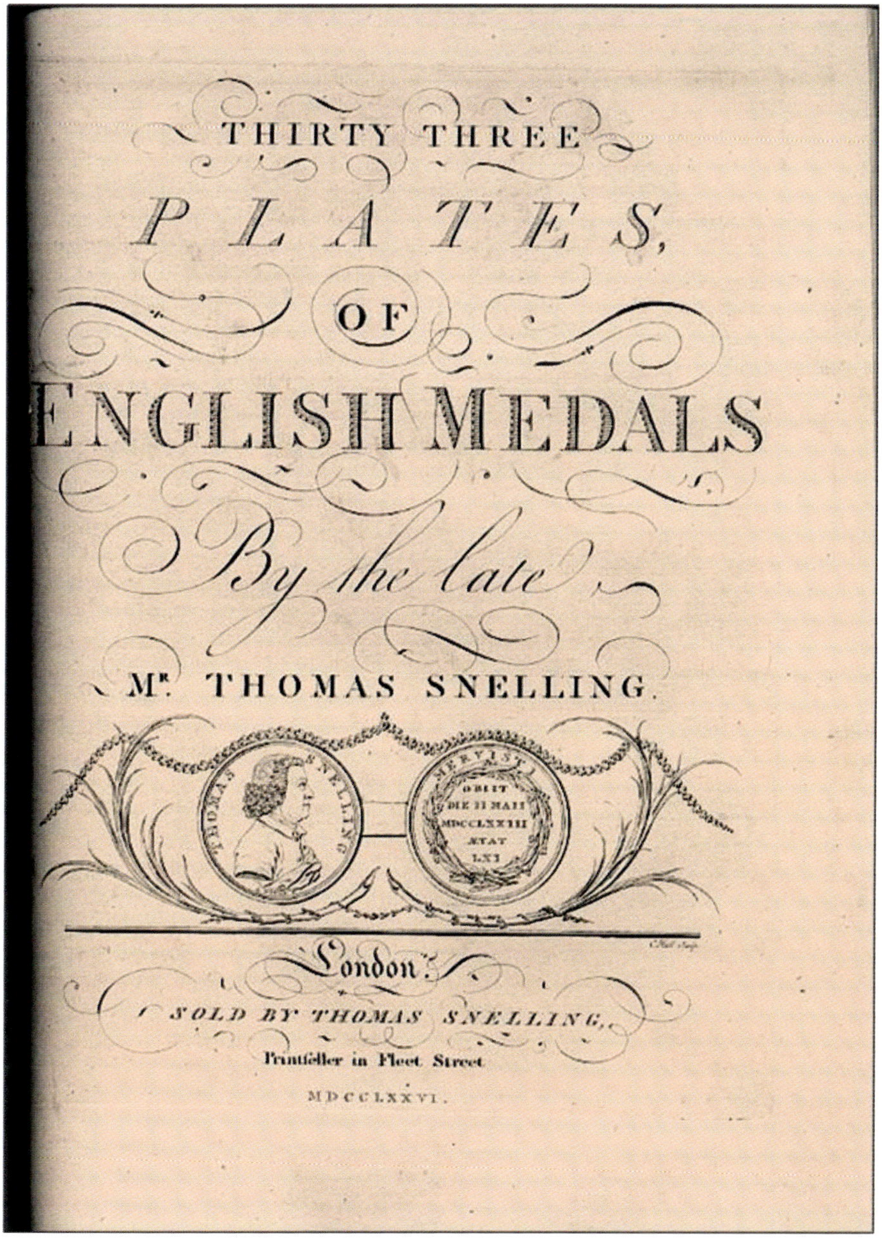

THIRTY THREE
PLATES,
OF
ENGLISH MEDALS
By the late
M^r. THOMAS SNELLING.

London:
SOLD BY THOMAS SNELLING,
Printfeller in Fleet Street
MDCCLXXVI.

THE TITLE PAGE FROM SNELLING'S *THIRTY-THREE PLATES OF ENGLISH MEDALS,* 1776. THE SIZE IS QUARTO (12-1/2 X 9-1/2 IN.). THIS WORK WAS TO REAPPEAR IN FOUR SUBSEQUENT EDITIONS, REFLECTING ITS CONTINUING POPULARITY AMONG COLLECTORS. FOR MANY DECADES, THIS WORK AND THE DERIVATIVE EDITIONS ATTRIBUTED TO JOHN PINKERTON WERE THE ONLY CATALOGUES OF ENGLISH MEDALS WHICH EXISTED. WITH THE EXCEPTION OF A CREDIT IN THE PREFACE TO THE 1790 EDITION, NONE OF THE FOUR SUBSEQUENT EDITIONS CARRIED SNELLING'S NAME (*Q.v. pp. 53-57, 69-78).*

Medals Commemorating Thomas Snelling

Three Medals commemorating Thomas Snelling in the year of his death. (*Top*) by Lewis Pingo* (1773, in copper, 40 mm., Eimer 749). Image courtesy of Dix Noonan Webb, Ltd. (*Center*) by J. Kirk** (1773, in bronze, 30 mm., British Museum acc./reg. no. SSB,228.17). (*Bottom*) by G. Rawle*** (1773, in silver, 40 mm., B. M. reg. no. M.4788) and also found in bronze (B.M. reg. no. SSB,228.16, 40 mm.). The second and third medals were donated to the British Museum by Dorothea, Lady Banks, ex Sarah Sophia Banks collection. Both images © Trustees of the British Museum. Eimer comments that Snelling:

> *...was the most celebrated London coin dealer of his day, with premises in Fleet Street patronized by members of the royal family (2010, p. 115).*

* Translated inscription: 'Merit / Died on May ii, 1773 aged 61.'

** Inscription: 'Let the art he loved and understood preserve his memory / born MDCCXII dyed MDCCLXXIII.'

*** *fl.* 1773, translated inscription: 'A student of coins, born MDCCII, died MDCCLXXIII.'

Thomas Snelling

(1712-1773)

THOMAS SNELLING, late 18th century numismatist, bookseller, and dealer in coins and medals, of no. 163 Fleet Street ('next the Horn Tavern.' at no. 145), is remembered as a prolific author of works on these subjects. His works included *Seventy-two Plates of Gold and Silver Coins*, published in 1757; *A View of the Gold and Silver Coinage of England* (1763); *A View of the Coins at this Time Current throughout Europe* (1766); *The Doctrine of Gold and Silver Computations* (1766); *Miscellaneous Views of the Coins Struck by English Princes in France* (1769); *A View of the Origin, Nature and Use of Jettons and Counters* (1769); and *Thirty-Three Plates of English Medals by the Late Mr. Thomas Snelling* (1776). It is this last work that is of primary interest to collectors and scholars of medals.

A PORTRAIT OF THOMAS SNELLING, BY JOHN THANE (HIS SON-IN-LAW), 1770. SNELLING WAS THE AUTHOR OF *THIRTY-THREE PLATES OF ENGLISH MEDALS*, WHICH AFTER HIS DEATH WAS TO BE PUBLISHED IN FOUR EDITIONS WHICH HAVE USUALLY, IF INCORRECTLY, BEEN ATTRIBUTED TO JOHN PINKERTON. SNELLING, A COIN-DEALER AND PRINTER, WAS THE AUTHOR OF TEN OTHER VOLUMES ON ENGLISH NUMISMATICS, BEGINNING IN 1757.

Snelling's *Thirty-Three Plates of English Medals…* was published posthumously in 1776. It was not seen through to completion by Snelling himself because of his death in 1773 at the age of 61. His son, also named Thomas, presumably brought the work to publication. The generally accurate and well drawn images on the plates were a boon to medal collectors, and the work appears to have sold well—certainly well enough that the plates were to reappear in four 'editions' of *The Medallic History of England.* The first of these four editions was published in 1790 and its authorship is usually, although incorrectly, credited to John Pinkerton. The titles of this and the next three editions vary somewhat and Pinkerton's name sometimes appears only on the volumes' spines, but not on the title page or within the text (*q.v. pp. 71-78).* It appears that Pinkerton was hired by the Edwards & Sons firm of printers to expand Snelling's original edition of 33 plates and to provide a commentary. All four editions since publication, however, have generally been attributed to Pinkerton despite the fact that the original 33 plates were in fact originally acquired and prepared for publication by Snelling. Pinkerton appears to have only been involved in the preparation of the first edition under a 'work made for hire' arrangement with Edwards & Sons (*q.v. p. 72*).

Three medals were struck commemorating the life of Thomas Snelling. One, executed in the classical style and by G. Rawle, presents Snelling's draped bust on the obverse, while those by

Kirk and Pingo have contemporary busts of Snelling on the obverse, the one by Kirk being partially draped.[85]

Little is known about Thomas Snelling's life, and probably the best biography is that prepared by R. H. Thompson for the *Oxford DNB*. Thompson's reading of the evidence, as available in contemporary records, indicates that Thomas Snelling was born to John and Phillis Snelling [sic], and was baptized at St. James's, Clerkenwell, London, in 1712. He had a business as a bookseller and coin dealer located at 163 Fleet Street:

> ...next the *Horn Tavern*, in *Fleet-Street*. Who buys and sells all Sorts of Coins and Medals.[86]

Thompson reports that the first numismatic-related mention of Snelling was in a letter to:

> ...the antiquary Joseph Ames (1689-1759) [about the latter's] Typographical Antiquities (1749) on the manner of distinguishing mints by letters of the alphabet.[87]

ANOTHER PORTRAIT ETCHING OF THOMAS SNELLING BY JOHN THANE (*SEE ENTRY FOR THANE, THIS VOL.*). POSSIBLY A STUDY FOR PINGO'S MEDAL. IMAGE © TRUSTEES OF THE BRITISH MUSEUM.

Snelling, whose name Thompson finds as a purchaser at London coin sales from circa 1766, appears to have been successful in his occupation as a coin and medal dealer. Among his clients was Dr. William Hunter, who retained Snelling to bid on his behalf for numismatic material at auction.[88] Thompson quotes the *Gentleman's Magazine* as referring to Snelling as being:

> Known among the Antiquarians for his skill in coins and medals.[89]

Thompson opines that:

> Snelling's works were highly valuable to collectors, and are still useful to students, [90]

an evaluation with which the present authors would concur. The only caveat would seem to be that Snelling may have been dishonest in the way he procured the plates he used in his *Thirty-three plates of English medals* (*q.v. p. 57, 'The Case Against Mr. Snelling'*).

Thomas Snelling was married to Elizabeth and they had seven children, a daughter, Mary Lord, having married the print seller and engraver John Thane (1747?-1818, *q.v. p. 375ff.*). At Snelling's death, "...the copyright, copies and copper-plates...," along with his stock and interest in his works were left to his wife, with instructions that upon her death, they should be divided among their children. Here, Thompson notes that there were twenty plates existent of the *Thirty Three Plates of English Medals*.[91] Additionally, Wroth notes that 'two'[92] of Thomas Snelling's

[85] L. Brown (1987), *Catalogue of British Historical Medals*, 1760-1960, vol. i, p. 41, nos. 178, 179, 180 (*q.v. p. 48 for illustrations of these medals).*

[86] *Thirty Three Plates*..., however, differs in the detail in that it reads: "London. Sold by Thomas Snelling, Print-seller in Fleet Street." This was to become the site, in 1898, of the new Anderton's Hotel.

[87] G. H. Thompson, 'Thomas Snelling.' *ODNB Online* (2004-2008).

[88] W. Wroth, *DNB* (1898 ed.), vol. 53, p. 207. *See the entry for Dr. Hunter, this vol., pp. 275ff.*.

[89] *Gentleman's Magazine,* 1st series, no. 43 (1773), p. 255; cited by Thompson.

[90] Thompson, ibid. p. 2.

[91] Ibid, p. 3.

works were published posthumously by his son, also named Thomas, who appears to have continued the family business. Neither Wroth nor Thompson further addresses the publication of the plates, it now appearing, as noted above, that the publisher, Edwards & Sons, employed John Pinkerton to provide text to accompany the plates for the 1780 edition.

After his death, Snelling's collections of coins, medals, and antiques were sold by auction in 1774 over four days at Langford's, 'at their house in the Great Piazza,' Covent Garden. The sale took place on Jan. 21 'and the three following days.' Among the purchasers of medal lots were Messrs. Thane, Young, Bell, Edwards, Griffiths and Powell. These purchasers did not confine their purchases to medals, as their names also appear next to coin lots, both classical and contemporary to that time. Snelling's books were sold separately. Obviously, they included many works of interest to numismatists. A 19th century description of this sale lists it as a:

> CATALOGUE of the curious Library of Thomas Snelling, (comprising an uncommon collection of books and MSS. on Coins and Medals) 8vo. with prices, half mor. extra, 5s 1774.
>
> —*Choice, Useful, and Curious Books, on sale by John Russell Smith, 4, Old Compton Street, Soho,* 1846, p. 32.

A copy of the sale catalogue, with prices realized, is held in the Department of Coins & Medals at the British Museum:

> Bibliotheca Snellingiana; a Catalogue of the Library of the late ingenious Mr. Thomas Snelling (Author of the Works on the Coins and Coinage of England, Scotland, &c.) Sold by Auction in London, March 1774, with prices, 8vo. London, 1774. Portrait inserted.
>
> > As might have been anticipated from the learning and research displayed in the works of Snelling, this Catalogue contains a very extensive and valuable collection of works on coins, medals, commerce, finance, and political economy. It also contains, what one would hardly have expected to find in it, a great number of books in different languages on tactics, the art of war, and military subjects generally! The library brought only 298*l*.; but were such a collection now to be disposed of, it would bring several thousand pounds.
>
> —J. E. McCullough, *A Catalogue of Books*, 1857, p.30.

> ALTHOUGH now superseded for most purposes, eighteenth-century numismatic works should not be neglected today, and not only for their own elegance and interest as early books with charming though often quaint engravings.
>
> —I. Stewart, in A. S. Bell, *The Scottish Antiquarian Tradition...*, 1981, p. 238.

[92] Wroth's biography of Snelling in the 1909 edition of *DNB* specifies "two," while Thomson's *O.D.N.B.* article states "...of Thirty Three Plates of English Medals twenty plates only."

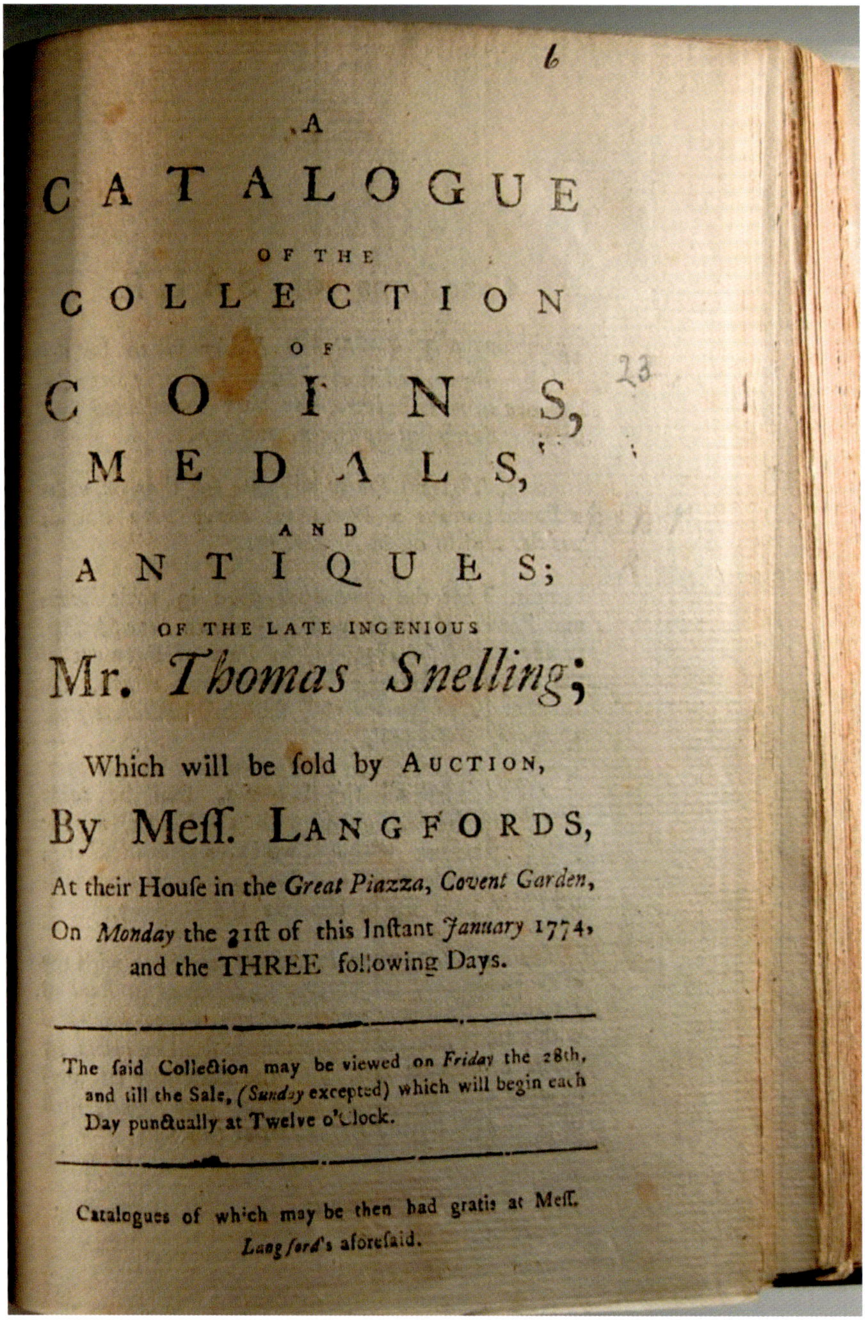

6

A
CATALOGUE
OF THE
COLLECTION
OF
COINS,
MEDALS,
AND
ANTIQUES;
OF THE LATE INGENIOUS
Mr. *Thomas Snelling*;

Which will be ſold by AUCTION,
By Meſſ. LANGFORDS,
At their Houſe in the *Great Piazza, Covent Garden*,
On *Monday* the 21ſt of this Inſtant *January* 1774,
and the THREE following Days.

The ſaid Collection may be viewed on *Friday* the 28th, and till the Sale, (*Sunday* excepted) which will begin each Day punctually at Twelve o'Clock.

Catalogues of which may be then had gratis at Meſſ. *Langford's* aforeſaid.

THE TITLE PAGE OF THE SALE CATALOGUE FOR THOMAS SNELLING'S STOCK OF COINS, MEDALS, ANTIQUES AND LIBRARY AT LANGFORD'S ON JANUARY 21-24, 1774. IMAGE COURTESY OF THE DEPARTMENT OF COINS AND MEDALS, BRITISH MUSEUM.

Thomas Snelling's
THIRTY THREE PLATES OF ENGLISH MEDALS
(1776)

THE title page of *Thirty Three Plates of English Medals* (1776) contains a portrait medal of the 'late Mr. Thomas Snelling,' who was:

> ...one of the principal London coin dealers of the day and needless, to say, a prolific author...[whose]...works...are of considerable significance. [93]

This work, which contains 33 engraved plates, is the last of a number of volumes on British numismatics that Snelling prepared before his death in 1773. To the authors' knowledge, Snelling's volume on medals appeared in only one edition. Certainly the next edition of the plates, published in 1790, and perhaps the 1802 edition as well, appear to have been prepared with the involvement of John Pinkerton. Pinkerton was not involved in the publication of the last two editions—1831 and an undated issue—as he died in 1826. Five previous works by Snelling, published between 1762 and 1769, dealt with English gold, silver, and copper coinage from the Norman Conquest, as well as lead, tin, and laton,[94] tradesmen's tokens, jetons, counters, and Abbey pieces. Also covered were: ...*Coins Struck By English Princes In France, Counterfeit Sterlings, Coins Struck By The East India Company, Those In The West India Colonies And In The Isle Of Man, Also Of Pattern Pieces For Gold And Silver Coins And Gold Nobles Struck Abroad In Imitation Of English.* Only the volume published in 1776 dealt primarily with medals.

DRAWINGS OF TWO OF THE THREE MEDALS OF THOMAS SNELLING, 1773. FROM ANTHONY DURAND'S* *MÉDAILLES ET JETONS DES NUMISMATES*, GENEVA, 1865, PLATE XIII, NOS. 7 AND 8.

*NOT TO BE CONFUSED WITH AMEDÉE DURAND, WHO MAY OR MAY NOT HAVE BEEN A RELATION (*Q.V. P. 306*).

The plates in Snelling, which are copperplate etchings, are generally excellently drawn and printed. Plate 12, reproduced on the following page, is an example of the typical style of illustration in this volume. Unfortunately, Snelling's volume on English medals does not contain any explanatory text, and we can only assume that this is a result of Snelling's having died before publication—his son Thomas then published the work posthumously. This was indeed a loss, for as George Frederick Kolbe, the numismatic book dealer, commented, these several volumes were:

(Continued on p. 55)

[93] G. F. Kolbe. Auction catalogue: *The John Frederick Bergman Numismatic Library, Part 1* (Oct. 6, 2001).
[94] A amalgam metal resembling brass.

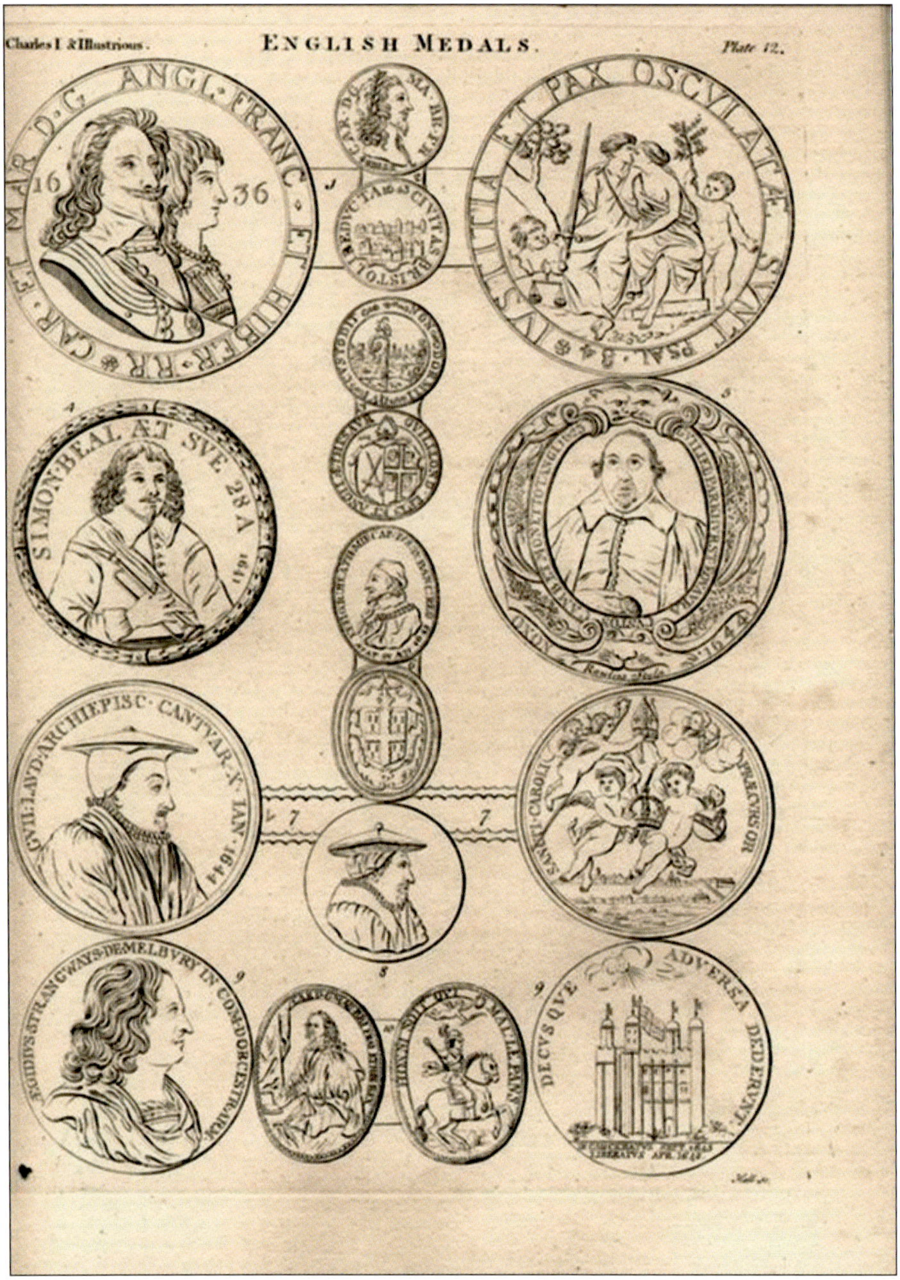

Plate 12 from Snelling's *Thirty Three Plates...* (1776) is typical of the style of his illustrations. This plate is numbered XVIII in all four of the editions of *The Medallic History of England*. The left margin is somewhat truncated due to the tight binding of the copy of the volume in which this plate appears. *See medal identifications on the facing page.*

LEGEND FOR THE ILLUSTRATIONS FROM SNELLING

THE PLATE ON THE PRECEDING PAGE FIRST APPEARED IN SNELLING' S *THIRTY THREE PLATES OF ENGLISH MEDALS BY THE LATE MR. THOMAS SNELLING,* POSTHUMOUSLY PUBLISHED IN 1776. THEY NEXT APPEARED IN THE FOUR EDITIONS OF *THE MEDALLIC HISTORY OF ENGLAND.* THE TITLES OF THE FOUR EDITIONS VARIED SOMEWHAT, AS DID THE NUMBERING OF THE PLATES. THE DETAILS OF THE MEDALS ILLUSTRATED ON PAGE 54 ARE NOT INCLUDED IN SNELLING'S VOLUME. THEY ARE AS FOLLOWS:

(1) *DUTCH FISHERY, 1636.* M.I.I 278/82; M.I.ILL XXIII/5. SEVERAL VERSIONS OF THIS CAST MEDAL, DIFFERING IN METAL (SILVER, BRONZE, AND LEAD), SIZE, DETAILS, AND DEGREE OF FINISHING (E.G., CHASING), WERE ISSUED IN TWO SIZES TO COMMEMORATE THE TREATY SIGNED BY ENGLAND AND HOLLAND TO ALLOW THE LATTER TO FISH IN ENGLISH WATERS IN EXCHANGE FOR A PAYMENT OF £30,000.

(2) *BRISTOL TAKEN, 1643.* M.I.I 307/131; M.I.ILL XXVI/16. THERE IS ANOTHER VARIETY OF THIS RARE MEDAL, PERHAPS UNIQUE, WHICH CONTAINS THE LETTERS O X, FOR OXFORD, THE SITE OF THE KING'S MINT (M.I.I 307/132; M.I.ILL XXVI/17).

(3) *WILLIAM JUXON, BISHOP OF LONDON AND LORD TREASURER, JETON, 1637.* M.I.I 279/85; M.I.ILL NOT ILLUSTRATED. PINKERTON (1802) COMMENTED THAT "...JUXON WAS A GREAT FRIEND OF LAUD, BUT OF A QUITE DIFFERENT CHARACTER, AS THE MILDNESS AND GENTLENESS OF HIS MANNERS GAINED HIM UNIVERSAL ESTEEM" (PP. 51-53).

(4) *SIMON BEAL, THE KING'S TRUMPETER, 1645.* M.I.I 323/160; M.I.ILL XXVIII/9.

(5) *SIR WILLIAM PARKHURST, WARDEN OF THE ROYAL MINT, 1644.* M.I.I 301/140; M.I.ILL XXVII/3.

(6) *SIR ROBERT HEATH, CHIEF JUSTICE OF THE COURT OF KING'S BENCH, 1645.* M.I.I 319/154; M.I.ILL XXVIII/2.

(7) *WILLIAM LAUD, ARCHBISHOP OF CANTERBURY, BEHEADED 10TH JANUARY 1644.* M.I.I 315/147; M.I.ILL XXVII/10.

(8) *WILLIAM LAUD. ANOTHER, SMALLER MEDAL, CA. 1645.* M.I.I 315/146; M.I.ILL XXVII/9.

(9) *COLONEL GILES STRANGWAYS, 1648.* M.I.I 333/177; M.I.ILL XXIX/9.

(10) *CHARLES I, BATTLE OF EDGEHILL, 1642.* M.I.I 298/118; M.I.ILL XXVI/5. PINKERTON LABELS THIS MEDAL, "A CURIOUS OVAL MEDAL."

(Continued from p. 53)

...written from an eighteenth century London coin dealer's point of view, and undoubtedly with the collector very much in mind.[95]

When one seeks to attribute the plates, it would appear to be Francis Perry[96] who engraved the plates, or at least ten—or possibly thirteen—of them, but these are all unsigned. Snelling's *Thirty-three Plates of English Medals* (1776) appear later in the four subsequent 'editions' of *The Medallic History of England.* These have been generally attributed to John Pinkerton under titles which vary somewhat: *The Medallic History of England to the Revolution, with Forty Plates* (1790), *The Medallic History of England, Illustrated by Forty Plates* (1802), *384 Medals of England, Engraved on Forty Plates* (1831) and *The Medals of England, Consisting of 384 Specimens Engraved on Forty Plates (*unknown publication date).

[95] Kolbe/Spink Joint Public Auction, December 10, 1989, lot 847.

[96] FRANCIS PERRY (D. 1765), *q.v. pp. 354-359, for further details.*

An illustration of Thomas Pingo's medal of Thomas Snelling from a catalogue for a coin and medal sale held in 1789 by Henry Young, No. 89, Fleet St.

Historical Commentary on Thomas Snelling

Dr. Ducarel[97] had some view to forming a series of English medals, which, by admitting such as have been struck abroad relative to the history of this kingdom, he thought could be carried beyond the conquest, provided the medals proved genuine. But when he engaged Francis Perry[98] to engrave a series, of which the late Mr. Hollis[99] gave the outline, he began no earlier than Henry VIII. and closed it with James I. in ten plates. Three supplemental ones were afterwards published of the same period. Mr. Hollis intended it should be more extensive, by taking in the Roman medals; he, however, assisted Perry in his own way. It was taken up by Mr. Snelling, who did not publish it in Mr. Hollis's life-time.—Mr. Snelling's being a posthumous publication, there is no letter-press to accompany his 33 plates, which reach from the conquest to 1742. It will be easily seen that the medals of the first five kings are by Dassier.

–A. Chalmers, *General Biographical Dictionary*. Revised ed., 1813, vol. xii, p. 377.

§

Mr. Snelling died May 2, 1773; and in the following year was published, "A View of the Silver Coins and Coinage of Scotland, from Alexander the First to the Union of the Two Kingdoms. By the late Mr. Thomas Snelling. To which are added Four Plates of the Gold, Billon, and Copper Coins of the same Kingdom, 1774." All these Tracts were collected into a volume by Mr. Thane, who prefixed to them the title of "Snelling on the Coins of Great Britain, France, and Ireland;" and an excellent Portrait, a small oval, under which is, "Mr. Thomas Snelling, Author of the Views of the Coins and Coinage of England, &c. &c. &c. *John Thane del. et sculp.*"

–J. Nichols, *Literary Anecdotes*, 1812, vol. iii, p. 620.

§

Dr. Hunter's comps. To Mr. Snelling and draws his attention to the following Lots of Mr. West's medals...Receipt given by Mr. Snelling to Dr. Hunter on payment of £302.18.6 12 Aug. 1872.

—Extracts showing transactions from: *Dr. William Hunter's papers*..., H.350 and H.361, pp. 41, 42.

[97] *See the textbox on the following page, as well as the entry for* ANDREW COLTÉE DUCAREL, *pp. 351-352.*
[98] *See the entry for* FRANCIS PERRY, *this volume, pp. 355-359.*
[99] THOMAS HOLLIS (1720-1774), bibliophile and medal collector (*q.v. pp. 361-365*).

'THE CASE *AGAINST* MR. SNELLING' —AS STATED BY MR. GOUGH*[100]

fn: "In order further to illustrate his design [*Table of English Gold Coins from the Eighteenth Year of King Edward the Third*, undertaken for the Society of Antiquaries], Mr. [Martin] Folkes* engraved 42 plates, containing near 480 coins, but not entirely filled up, and in 1745 exhibited it to the Society of Antiquaries. They then resolved to complete it, and Mr. Folkes furnished the plan of plates, and letter-press for 50, offering his assistance, and to make up his own plates, and give them to the Society. Upon his death, they purchased his 44 plates and copy for 120*l.* the mere cost of engraving; and Mr. William Folkes gave them some of his brother's MS papers. Thus was Mr. Folkes's valuable design carried into execution by this learned Body, by republishing, at their own expense, his Tables and Plates, with explanations, in 4to, 1763...As Mr. Folkes's book, published in 1745...related wholly to the History of the English Mint, the Society subjoined a particular description of the several coins, their weights, legends, &c. by Dr. John Ward, then Director, who drew up great part of the letter-press for Mr. Folkes, and on his demise by Dr. Andrew Gilford. This, new edition of both his pieces was completed from his corrected copy of his own edition. To which copy Professor Ward, Dr. Gilford, Dr. Ducarel,* and Mr. Colebrook, had in 1756 largely contributed their observations. Upon the decease of Professor Ward, the conduct of the new edition devolved on his coadjutor, Dr. Gilford. The Plates were begun to be completed by James Green, who had before been appointed engraver to the Society. Mr. Green died in 1758, and on his resignation of that office, on account of ill health, some of them were given to Wood the engraver. At length, at the desire of the Editor, the execution of the whole engraving was committed to Francis Perry*..., who finished his Work in 1758, and received for it 39*l.* 11*s.* The explanations subjoined, and the improved copy of Mr. Folkes's Work, were not put to press till 1761, in which year the first 15 sheets were printed in 14 weeks, as was exactly stated by Mr. Bowyer,* in his letter to the Council, in March 1782, in answer to a charge of unnecessary delay brought against him. But unexpected interruptions arising on the part of the Conductor, the next 14 sheets took up 39 weeks to print, and the new edition was not published till 1763...—The Advertisement, in two pages, was drawn up by Dr. Taylor, then Director. The Supplement, in 40 pages, with a Postscript of four more, and six Plates, were by Dr. Gifford. *During a long interval between the commencement and completion of this great Work, the publick was surprized, and the Society more so, by the appearance of 27 Plates of English Silver Coins, engraved by Francis Perry above mentioned, published by Mr. Thomas Snelling,* evidently copied from the Society's Plates, though not continued beyond the reign of King George the Second."* (*Italics added for emphasis—au.*)*R. G.*—I retain the foregoing note as written originally by Mr. Gough,* that I may correct it by the following remarks of Mr. Tutet: "It is too harsh to say in general terms 'evidently copied from the Society's plates,' as himself has given the names of several gentlemen who lent him rare and valuable Coins for the express purpose of being engraven in his Work, besides several in his own possession which he has specified, and many others which are well known to have been put into his hands, but the possessors names were not mentioned, on account of the Coins not being of any great rarity. There is also a proof of Snelling having published several Coins totally unknown to the Editor of the Society's Plates, the latter having frequently referred to the 'View of the English Silver Coin.' What Snelling was to blame for is in having availed himself somewhat unhandsomely of the Society's *unpublished* Plates; whence, however, he copied only a very small number of Coins, the originals of which were not then to be got at, and those few are wrong engraven by both Editors; therefore *fiat justitia!*"

—R. Gough,, *Literary Anecdotes*..., 1812, vol. ii, fn., pp. 586-587.

[100] *The asterisk indicates that a biographical entry may be found in the present volume.*

Pierre (Peter) Duby

(1721-1782)

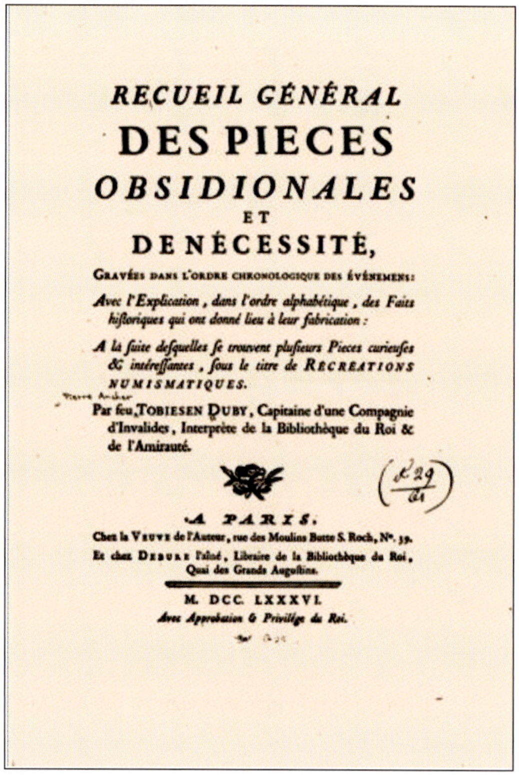

RECUEIL GÉNÉRAL
DES PIECES
OBSIDIONALES
ET
DE NÉCESSITÉ,
GRAVÉES DANS L'ORDRE CHRONOLOGIQUE DES ÉVÉNEMENS:
Avec l'Explication, dans l'ordre alphabétique, des Faits historiques qui ont donné lieu à leur fabrication:
A la suite desquelles se trouvent plusieurs Pieces curieuses & intéressantes, sous le titre de RECREATIONS NUMISMATIQUES.
Par feu TOBIESEN DUBY, Capitaine d'une Compagnie d'Invalides, Interprête de la Bibliothèque du Roi & de l'Amirauté.
A PARIS.
Chez la VEUVE de l'Auteur, rue des Moulins Butte S. Roch, Nº. 39.
Et chez DEBURE l'aîné, Libraire de la Bibliothèque du Roi, Quai des Grands Augustins.
M. DCC. LXXXVI.
Avec Approbation & Privilège du Roi.

DUBY'S RARE 1785 POSTHUMOUS WORK, PUBLISHED BY HIS WIDOW, WHICH DESCRIBES MEDALS, TOKENS, AND COINS ISSUED BY BESIEGED CITIES OR BY THEIR BESIEGERS.

DUBY (PETER AUCHER TORIESEN) a Swiss medalist of considerable antiquarian research, especially with respect to ancient numismatics. He was born at Housseau in 1721, and the earlier part of his life was passed in military service, till, having lost a limb at Fontenoy, he retired, turned his attention to literature, and became linguist to the king's library at Paris. He made a curious collection of French coins, especially of those struck by the earlier feudal seigneurs, and was the author of a work on medals in three quarto volumes, printed in 1790, eight years after his decease. —Dict. Hist.

— J. Gorton, *A General Biographical Dictionary,* 1851, vol. iv (unpaginated).

§

Possessing a mind equally unclouded by ambition and the love of pleasure, he employed all his leisure hours in the study of coins and medals, in which he acquired great proficiency. He began with considering and collecting such as had been struck during sieges, and in times of necessity; a pursuit analogous to his taste, and to the profession to which his early life had been devoted. Having completed this task, he undertook to form and to publish a more complete collection of the different, species of money struck by the barons of France, than any that had hitherto appeared. In this, which may be called a national work, not content with consulting all the authors who had treated on the subject, he also searched a number of different cabinets, on purpose to verify the original pieces, and to satisfy himself as to their existence and authenticity [but] he was snatched from his favourite avocations by the hand of death, Nov. 19, 1782, when his family were left to mourn the loss of a good husband and father, society to regret an estimable and a modest man, and the sciences to lament an able and an indefatigable investigator.

—A. Chalmers, *The General Biographical Dictionary*, 1813, vol. xii, pp. 373-374. Taken by Chalmers from *The Analytical Review, or History of Literature, Domestic and Foreign…,* 1791, vol. xi, p. 472.

§

Duby, Peter Ancher Tobiesen, a celebrated Swiss medallist and antiquary, was born in 1721 and died in 1782. He was an interpreter to the royal library at Paris and the author of an able and extensive work on medals.

—S. Maunder, *The Biographical Treasury, a Dictionary of Universal Biography*, 1838, pp. 38-39.

Mr. Pinkerton's Proposal for a 'Book on Medals'

Excerpted from: *The Numismatic Chronicle*, April 1841-January 1842, vol. iv, pp. 180-181.

Letter From John Pinkerton To Robert Dodsley —The following letter from Pinkerton to Dodsley, the publisher, contains the original proposals for the publication of his "Essay on Medals," which were accepted, the first edition being shortly afterwards published in the same year (1784) in one volume, octavo. Whatever were Pinkerton's faults it is certain that he was an ingenious and laborious writer; had he possessed less pedantry and self-conceit, he might have been a still more useful and correct one. The "Essay" here alluded to is a work of much merit, particularly the subsequent edition, which was enlarged into two volumes. Pinkerton had little practical knowledge of coins, but in these volumes he has brought together a mass of curious information digested into a popular form. He liberally abuses nearly every previous writer with a virulence and scurrility peculiar to the man, though his book shows that on every occasion he availed himself of their information.

B. Nightingale.

§

Knightsbridge, 12th January, 1784.

Dear Sir,

In a late conversation I started an idea of an Essay on Medals, in the way of Mr. Gilpin's Essay on Prints, and as you seemed not averse to that idea, I enclose a view of the proposed contents, in order that you may judge with more certainty than is possible from the evanescent nature of conversation. That this is the very land of connoisseurs, and that yet to this day no treatise of the kind has appeared, though every body wishes for it, is a very strong argument for a rapid sale. But of this you are the only judge, and I wish not to influence you either one way or the other.

My plan would make a neat little half-crown volume of about 200 pages, and should you like it upon farther thoughts I shall be glad to have your proposals. I have so many materials (this having always been a favourite amusement of mine) that I could engage to let you have it in a month, should you wish to publish this Parliament. As to knowledge of the subject and composition, should you not like them, I shall not murmur at your burning my M.S.

If you do not like the scheme, I shall drop it entirely, as I do not wish to offer my labour to every one, and, indeed, am too lazy to go to work with the humiliating view of afterwards hawking my little labours.

I am always, yours sincerely,

J. Pinkerton.

...A very little and very thin old man, with a very small, sharp, yellow face, thickly pitted by the smallpox, and decked with a pair of green spectacles.

—J. Nichols, *Literary History*, 1817, vol. v, p. 661.

John Pinkerton (1758-1826), is the author of *An Essay on Medals, or An Introduction to the Knowledge of Ancient Coins and Medals,* which appeared in three editions in the late 18th and early 19th century. Pinkerton's name is also associated with the four editions of Thomas Snelling's *Thirty-Three Plates of English Medals* which were published with various titles and with minimal or no attribution to Snelling—a credit appears only in the foreword to the 1790 edition. The portrait, *ca.* 1804, is a stipple engraving by William Hopwood (1784-1853), published in 1804 by H. D. Symonds, and is likely after Sylvester Harding's 1796 portrait, also a stipple engraving. Harding's portrait is absent the dark background and signature.

John Pinkerton

(1758-1826)

JOHN PINKERTON was born in Edinburgh on February 17, 1758. His parents were James Pinkerton, a prosperous dealer in hair,[101] and Mary, whose maiden name was Heron.[102] The youngest of three sons,[103] John attended the local village school and then grammar school at Lanark for six years, where he was an indifferent, often bored student. He showed an interest in the classics, and applied himself to this subject, as well as to French, Latin, and mathematics, translating some of Livy.[104] His father, "being of a severe and morose disposition,"[105] found a university education objectionable so his son John's formal education did not extend further. Afterwards, he was apprenticed as a law clerk for five years to William Aytoun, a well-known solicitor and writer. During this time, Pinkerton wrote and published *Ode to Craigmillar Castle* (1776), the castle being a romantic ruin, dedicated to a Dr. Beattie.[106] Beattie gave Pinkerton 'faint praise' with respect to his poetic abilities, commenting that the poem needed further development:

> There are many good lines in your poem; but when you have kept it by you a week or two, I fancy you will not think it correct enough as yet to appear in public.[107]

About this time, Pinkerton traveled to London in search of books he could not obtain in Scotland, and the volume and variety available led him to a decision to move there, and enter upon a career as an author. In 1780, his father died, leaving him £300 a year, allowing him to pursue his goals of a literary career. Moving to London in 1781, he settled in Knightsbridge. Several small works of poems he penned were not particularly successful, although his *Scottish Tragic Ballads*, published by John Nichols[108] in 1781, achieved some modest success. This work was expanded and republished in 1783 as *Select Scottish Ballads*. This last volume, however, contained a forged second stanza to the Scottish epic war ballad 'Hardyknute.'[109] If Pinkerton's goal was to gain notoriety, he had begun well in his new career. Discovery of his forgery by the literary critic Joseph Ritson[110] and the eminent scholar William Porden[111] resulted in much notoriety for the novice author. In April 1782, Porden wrote to Pinkerton:

---

[101] Wigs, of course, being very much in style at the time.

[102] ROBERT HERON and H. BENNET were names Pinkerton would later use as literary pseudonyms.

[103] The eldest son, James, died in military service, while the next son, Robert, succeeded to the father's estate in Lancashire.

[104] 59 B.C.-A.D. 17 TITUS LIVUS, the Roman historian, author of the *Annals of the Roman People,* covering the period from before the founding of Rome in 753 B.C. through 9 B.C.

[105] And quite hypochondriacal, a trait John also possessed. Obituary for James Pinkerton in *The Gentleman's Magazine*, May 1826, pp. 469-472.

[106] JAMES BEATTIE (1735-1803), a distinguished Scottish poet and author of *Minstrel.*

[107] D. Turner, *Literary Correspondence of John Pinkerton,* letter from Dr. Beattie dated Dec. 13th, 1775, vol. i, pp. 1-2.

[108] Nichols also published Pinkerton's later volumes on 'English Medals.'

[109] The origins of 'Hardyknute' itself are vague. It commemorates the Scottish victory over the forces of Haakon Haakonsson of Norway at the Battle of Largs on August 1, 1263, although it may be based on more than one ancient Scottish warrior. It is also possible that it was partly written in 1719 by the ballad writer ELIZABETH, LADY WARDLAW (1677–1727) who is alleged, without further evidence, to have discovered the *Hardyknute* manuscript in a vault at Dunfermline.

[110] JOSEPH RITSON (1752-1803) was a conveyancer, or real estate attorney, who spent his spare time writing particularly caustic literary criticism and managed to find fault with many eminent contemporary authors, including SAMUEL JOHNSON. A letter from ROBERT SOUTHEY to SAMUEL TAYLOR COLERIDGE contained the observation that:

> I am, however, going to be more impertinent still. When I read the tales, I read over again the second part of *Hardyknute*; and I must inform you that I have made up my mind with respect to the author of it. I know not whether you will value a compliment paid to your genius at the expense of your imitative art; but certainly that genius sheds a splendor upon some passages which betrays you. [112]

However, Ritson was much more direct and cynical, as Hustvedt relates:

> In the *Gentleman's Magazine* for November, 1784, Ritson denounced Pinkerton in the strongest terms as a forger... To give point to his acrimonious attack he made use of the pen-name "Anti-Scot" ...Ritson, branding the first part of "*Hardyknute*" as "certainly spurious," charges Pinkerton with the invention of the second part... Ritson's strictures, although perfectly justifiable, were so snarling in tone as to call forth a sort of apology from the editor for the "insertion of so singular a literary curiosity and complete specimen of modern criticism." [113]

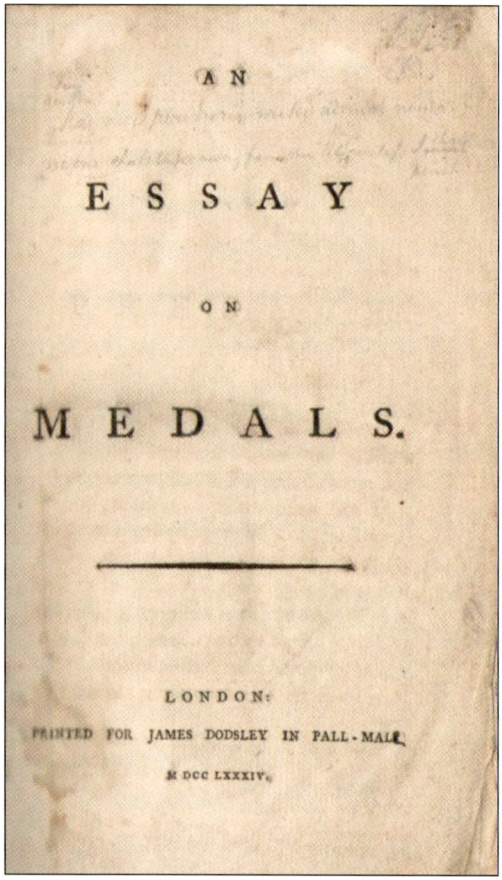

AN

ESSAY

ON

MEDALS.

LONDON:

PRINTED FOR JAMES DODSLEY IN PALL-MALL.

M DCC LXXXIV.

THE TITLE PAGE OF THE FIRST EDITION OF JOHN PINKERTON'S *AN ESSAY ON MEDALS*, WHICH WAS PUBLISHED IN 1784 AS A SINGLE VOLUME. SUBSEQUENT TWO-VOLUME EDITIONS THEN APPEARED IN 1789 AND 1808.

This attack by Ritson was not to be the only occasion on which he took Pinkerton to task for his improprieties, despite Pinkerton's admission of transgression. As Robert Triphook, the author of Pinkerton's obituary, observed:

> In 1784 [Ritson] demonstrated in a letter signed "Anti-Scot"...that 'Select Scottish Ballads (1783) was largely composed of modern forgeries by the alleged collector... Although Pinkerton frankly admitted the deceit, Ritson's wrath did not abate, and he resolved to teach Pinkerton how his work ought to be done. [114]

> Ritson is the oddest, but most honest of all our antiquarians, and he abuses Percy and Pinkerton with less mercy than justice (R. Southey, *Life...of Robert Southey*, 1855, p. 159).

[111] WILLIAM PORDEN (ca. 1755–1822) was an eminent and socially connected architect.

[112] Turner, *Literary Correspondence...*, letter from W. PORDEN to Pinkerton dated Apr. 5, 1782, vol. i, p. 25.

[113] Hustvedt, S. H., *Ballard Criticism in Scandinavia and Great Britain During the Eighteenth Century*, pp. 252-253.

[114] "Obituary of John Pinkerton," *The Gentleman's Magazine*, May 1826, vol. xcvi, p. 469-472. John Pinkerton was not the only author to be attacked by Ritson in his self-appointed role as guardian of literary honesty. In another letter, Joseph Ritson comments:

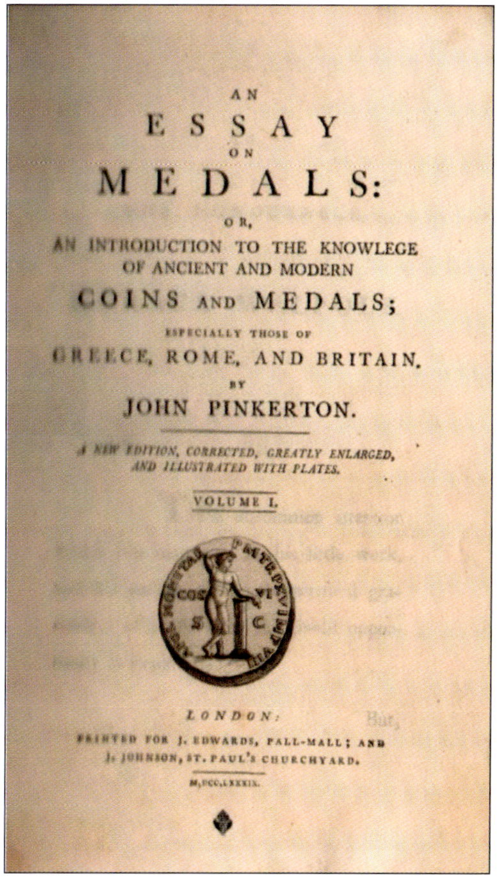

THE TITLE PAGE OF THE SECOND EDITION OF JOHN PINKERTON'S *AN ESSAY ON MEDALS*, 1789 (TWO VOLS.). NOTE THE MISSPELLING OF KNOWLEDGE.

Possibly, because of the notoriety now associated with his name, Pinkerton adopted a pseudonym, Robert Heron,[115] under which he published *Letters on Literature* (1785), a volume that contained an essay 'On Literary Forgery.' Never free of criticism of a personal sort when it came to other writers, Pinkerton continued to alienate many contemporary literary figures, as well as classical scholars, although he later was to express regret for this behavior. Yet, the publication of this work resulted in an introduction to the prominent politician, author, and architect Horace Walpole, and through him a further introduction to the eminent historian Edward Gibbon.

Ancient Scottish Poems, published in 1786, contained "previously unpublished Scottish poems," and is considered to be Pinkerton's finest work in terms of his contribution to Scottish literature.[116] It also contained a confession of his earlier plagiarism. Yet, his repudiation of the Old Testament in this work only served to alienate supporters such as Sir Walter Scott. *The Treasury of Wit*, a collection of aphorisms also appeared in 1786, although Pinkerton used the *nom de plume* H. Bennet for authorship. When a three-volume work entitled *Scottish Poems, Reprinted from Scarce Editions* appeared in 1792, so did criticism from Joseph Ritson, who was never far from pen and paper when a new work by Pinkerton appeared. Yet, it would not have been in Pinkerton's character to passively accept such criticism:

> In 1785, Pinkerton sent out his eccentric Letters of Literature under the penname of Heron... One of the letters deals with the question of literary forgery. In it, the author asserts that "those innocents who call such forgery criminal forget that they are blaspheming their savior and their religion; for Jesus represented his parables to contain the truth."[117]

But you know that Mr. Pinkerton is neither the first, nor likely to be the last fabricator of *Old Scottish Ballads* (J. Frank, *The Letters of Joseph Ritson...*, vol. ii, p. 180).

[115] S. Couper, 'John Pinkerton,' *ODNB*, (2004-2006). JOHN PINKERTON's choice of a pen-name was to create another problem for him, in that there existed in Scotland at that time a newly emerging, if minor author, who in actuality was named 'ROBERT HERON' (Obit., *Gentleman's Magazine,* op. cit., p. 471).

[116] Ibid.

[117] Hustvedt, *Ballard Criticism...*, pp. 252-253.

It is not clear whether the battering, which Pinkerton received from Ritson and other critics, led him to abandon his purely literary works for numismatics, but having had from boyhood an interest in:

> ...collecting medals, minerals, and other curiosities, [the acquisition by him of a rare coin] laid the foundation of a little collection, and [he] used to read Addison's *Dialogues on Medals* with infinite delight. These pursuits led him to see the defects of common books on the subject, and he drew up a manual and tables for his own use, which afterwards grew to the excellent and complete "Essay on Medals," the first edition of which was published by Dodsley in two 8vo volumes, 1784.[118] He was materially assisted in its completion by the late Mr. Southgate of the British Museum and Mr. Douce. The third and last edition was edited by Mr. Harwood.[119]

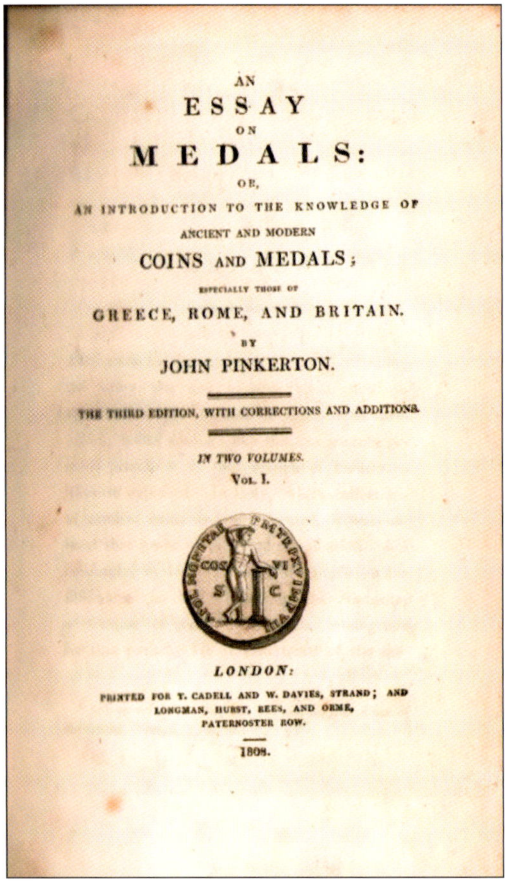
AN
ESSAY
ON
MEDALS:
OR,
AN INTRODUCTION TO THE KNOWLEDGE OF
ANCIENT AND MODERN
COINS AND MEDALS;
ESPECIALLY THOSE OF
GREECE, ROME, AND BRITAIN.
BY
JOHN PINKERTON.
THE THIRD EDITION, WITH CORRECTIONS AND ADDITIONS.
IN TWO VOLUMES.
VOL. I.
LONDON:
PRINTED FOR T. CADELL AND W. DAVIES, STRAND; AND
LONGMAN, HURST, REES, AND ORME,
PATERNOSTER ROW.
1808.

THE TITLE PAGE OF THE THIRD EDITION OF JOHN PINKERTON'S *AN ESSAY ON MEDALS*, 1808 (2 VOLS.).

An Essay on Medals appeared in 1784. This work was then very much respected and is still of interest to numismatists. It was first published in a one-volume format, which was later expanded into two volumes, which were published in 1789, with a third two-volume edition appearing in 1808. As described above, Pinkerton had had a genuine interest in numismatics from an early age. *Essay...* is a survey of ancient and modern coins, and contains notes on numismatic literature, counterfeiting and prices of old coins. The second edition contains six plates of coins while there are five in the first edition. *An Essay...* also contains comments on important contemporary 'cabinets' or collections in the chapter 'Directions for forming Cabinets:'[120]

> The King of France has the most opulent cabinet of this kind in existence,...which is calculated to have cost, since its institution till now, when arrived at a point of perfection which it can but little exceed, near 100,000*l.* sterling.[121]

---

[118] This is incorrect, as the first edition consisted of only one volume.

[119] Obituary, *The Gentleman's Magazine*, *op cit*., 1826 (May), vol. xcvi, p. 471.

[120] One of the copies of the 1808 edition of *An Essay on Medals*... held by the British Library contains HORACE WALPOLE's bookplate and manuscript notes.

[121] *Essay on Medals,* 1808 ed., vol. ii, p. 229.

Pinkerton noted that "The large and complete cabinet" should include every issue of the mint, in every age, and of every country:

> This, it may easily be seen requires a vast expense, and few but kings ought to attempt it. [122]

He estimated that the cost of such a collection could exceed that of Dr. Hunter's:

> ...perhaps one of the best private cabinets ever formed in this style, and cost about £21,000.[123]

Pinkerton further commented that he considered Dr. Hunter to be the foremost collector in Europe, with the exception of the French king:

> [Dr. Hunter's cabinet] was not only formed at vast expense, but with great care and ability; many medals of foreign cabinets, that flowed into it, having been rejected by the severity of English skill.[124]

Pinkerton noted that Dr. Hunter's will stipulated that upon his death his collection would ultimately pass to the University of Glasgow, which was indeed the case.[125] One also learns from Pinkerton, as he enumerates the collections of 17th century notables, that:

> Henry prince of Wales bought the collection of Goræus, amounting...to 30,000 coins and medals, and left it to his brother Charles I...the unhappy hero of his tale,...that impudent monarch, with an utter hatred for liberty, the parent of the fine arts...had a very fine cabinet of medals. [126]

Pinkerton also describes some other collectors of the period:

> Archbishop Laud, who bought 5,500 coins for 600*l.*, and gave them to the Bodleian library[;] Thomas earl of Arundel and Surrey, earl marshall of England...the dukes of Buckingham, and Hamilton...[and] the earl of Clarendon. Oliver Cromwell had also a small collection. [127]

As usual, Pinkerton had a good deal to say about other writers and their 'blunders.' For example, he stated that Jennings, in *An Introduction to the Science of Medals* (1764):

> ...seems to say that all the Roman emperors appear with diadems. He certainly had never seen a dozen coins; nor a single medallic writer of this century.[128]

Pinkerton did receive some positive critical review. His correspondence with eminent contemporaries yielded many strong endorsements of his work—more; it would seem than required by politeness. Cooper Walker, for example, wrote to Pinkerton with respect to a proposed work:

> The portraits of illustrious persons of Scotland, with biographical notices from your pen, will be a valuable accession to collections of taste, and serve to increase the stock of elegant literature.[129]

Further, Cooper Walker states that he was "rejoiced" that Pinkerton's:

---

[122] Ibid, *Essay...,* 1808 ed., vol. ii, p. 229.

[123] Ibid. A footnote notes that:
...23,000*l.* were expended [by Dr. Hunter in forming his collection]; 2000*l.* worth of duplicates were sold. (*q.v. pp. 275-277.*)

[124] Ibid. vol. i, p. 13.

[125] Ibid. vol. i, p. xxxix. *See pp. 274-277.*

[126] Ibid. vol. i, pp. 10-11. GORÆUS refers to the Flemish antiquary ABRAHAM GORLAEUS (1549-1608), *also known as* ABRAHAM VAN GOORLE (*q.v. p. 239*).

[127] *Essay...*, ibid. vol. i, pp. 10-11.

[128] Ibid, vol. i, 1808 ed., p. xii, fn.

[129] JOSEPH COOPER WALKER, (1761–1810) the eminent Irish antiquary and writer. Letter from Walker to Pinkerton, August 7, 1795. In Turner, *Literary Correspondence...*, vol. i, p. 389.

> *History of Scotland under the House of Stuart* is ready for the press. I shall await its appearance with impatience; and I shall expect with equal impatience the appearance of your *General History*. Deep and extensive erudition, assiduous research, and luminous arrangement render your productions inestimable to the lovers of historic truth.[130]

Horace Walpole was equally generous with praise of Pinkerton, declaring that the latter's understanding was:

> One of the strongest, most manly and clearest he ever knew. [131]

As was also Edward Gibbon, who wrote, in a letter to Pinkerton:

> ... that the best judges must have acknowledged his merit; and your rising fame will gradually extinguish the early prejudices and personal animosities which you have been too careless of provoking...[132]

A compliment to Pinkerton's ambition also appears in a letter from the eminent Sir Joseph Banks:

> Nothing can, in my opinion, be more honorable to a man who has any pretensions to literature, than being allowed to enrol himself as an early approver of the valuable undertaking you have in view: it is surely a disgrace to this country not to have a regular edition of its early historians: our literary progress as a nation is in that point materially behind hand. To you, Sir, and my friend Gibbon, who busy yourselves in an attempt to rescue us from the reproach of having neglected our early history, not thanks only, but all possible assistance and encouragement are surely due from those who cultivate letters in every shape.[133]

Having published on numismatics, Pinkerton now sought to use his literary accomplishments to secure a formal position in the numismatic world. Couper[134] notes that in 1788 Pinkerton had attempted to obtain Horace Walpole's support in obtaining a position at the British Museum, but Sir Joseph Banks, then a trustee of the British Museum, would not act on the appeal, or on a second one in 1795. About this time, Pinkerton was also seeking an improvement in his public and professional prestige through membership in literary organizations. In this regard, his letter to the earl of Buchan is both transparent and revealing of his own self-awareness with respect to his personality and his precarious position professionally:

---

[130] Ibid, p. 390.

[131] HORACE WALPOLE's tolerance of Pinkerton's requests did appear to wear thin, as evidenced by the former's response to Pinkerton in 1795, when Pinkerton was compiling a book of portraitures of important Scottish personages. Pinkerton wrote numerous letters to various prominent individuals to request either pictures of themselves or others with whom they were acquainted. His frequent requests of Horace Walpole to provide a means of introduction to prominent individuals resulted in this response:

> I have told you over and over, that knowing I have not a glimpse of interest with any one man in power, nor claim to asking favors of any one, I am extremely averse from attempting to make use of that no-interest.

Walpole tells Pinkerton that he sent his letter on to LADY DIANA BEAUCLERC, a lady connected to the House of Marlborough, for her review without endorsement due to his inability of moving both of his arms because of "the gout" (Letter, Walpole to Pinkerton, February 5, 1795, reprinted in W. S. Lewis & A. D. Wallace, *Horace Walpole's Correspondence*, 1967, p. 327).

[132] Letter from Gibbon to Pinkerton dated July 25, 1793. In Turner, *Literary Correspondence*..., vol. i, p. 332. EDWARD GIBBON (1737-1794) was the author of *History of the Decline and Fall of the Roman Empire*.

[133] Letter from Banks to Pinkerton dated December 8, 1793, in Turner, *Literary Correspondence*..., vol. i, p. 336. Eventually, Pinkerton was to wear out Banks' good will towards him. In a letter to GEORGE NICHOL (1740?-1828), a bookseller and publisher ('the king's bookseller'), dated June 26, 1799, Banks comments negatively on Pinkerton's character, referring to him as "a Little wasp." Nichol's reply comments on "the malicious Letter of that wicked wasp Pinkerton so full of all kinds of falsehoods."

[134] S. Couper, 'John Pinkerton,' *Oxford DNB*, 2004-2006.

> Being a *homo umbratilis*, of a hypochondriac, unsocial disposition, I have hitherto abstained from any intention or exertion to become a member of literary societies; but, having received a diploma of election as an honorary member of the Royal Society of Icelandic Literature at Copenhagen, under the patronage of the Prince of Denmark, and being about to be elected a member of the Royal Society of Sciences in Norway, under that [sic] of the Danish king's brother, I should wish to be a member of your Antiquarian Society at Edinburgh, as I am of that of Perth. I must confess that I should prefer such titles from my own country to those from any other; but I leave this matter entirely to your lordship's discretion...for I have, it seems, enemies at home, who prefer what is sweet in the mouth to those bitter draughts which invigorate the body. [135]

In 1802, Pinkerton moved to Paris, where he continued to promote a literary magazine with which he had become associated—*Critical Review*—but by 1805, the magazine had gone into bankruptcy. This, together with the difficult political situation between Britain and France at the time, led him to return home, where he published *Recollections of Paris*, on his experiences there.[136]

Pinkerton's private life seems to have been a shambles. In 1789 he lived at Mansfield Place, Kentish Town, with Ann whom he led others to believe was his wife, when in fact she was not. Pinkerton and Ann had two daughters, one of whom was named Sophia, and a son, Frederick. The other daughter's name is unknown. He left this family "on account of [Ann's] bad conduct and drunkenness."[137] According to Couper Walker, Pinkerton at this time was likely bargaining for the hand of Henrietta Maria Burgess. His efforts paid off; they were married on August 14, 1793, and took up housekeeping at Flask Walk, Hampstead. For a while, the marriage obviously contributed both to Pinkerton's personal and financial contentment, as he wrote to Lord Buchan:

> My health and spirits, thank Heaven, have never in my life been so good as within these two years, and my finances increase with what little reputation I can pretend to; nor has my marriage to a quiet, good wife, with some money, been without its share in contributing to my health and finances. [138]

To which, characteristically, he added:

> My literary temper, formerly very irritable, I also trust to have completely tamed; insomuch that I have just read over Buchanan's vast 8vo of abuse against me...to my wife, with no emotion but laughter. It is indeed a work of eminent absurdity; but, as no book is so bad but something may be learned from it, I find one typographical error pointed out...Yet on this he rings peals and changes, as if I were answerable for all the errors of John Nichols' incorrect press.[139]

The union with Henrietta lasted until 1802. Pinkerton and Henrietta had two daughters; another child died. In his will, he acknowledged only these two children, omitting those from his relation-

---

[135] Letter to the earl of Buchan, Dec. 19th, 1791. Quoted by Turner, vol. i, p. 277. DAVID STEUART (sic) ERSKINE, 11TH EARL OF BUCHAN (1742–1829), was a Scottish antiquarian very much involved in the literary affairs of his day.

[136] Couper, *ODNB*, entry for John Pinkerton, 9/4/2013, p.3.

[137] Ibid. citing E. H. Wood, *Letters to an Antiquary: The Literary Correspondence of G. J. Thorkelin (1752-1829)*, PhD thesis, University of Edinburgh, 1972, p. 195.

[138] From Turner, *Literary Correspondence*..., letter dated 21st April, 1794, vol. i, pp. 350-351. Partially quoted by Couper; p. 4.

[139] Turner, ibid. It should be noted that JOHN NICHOLS would later publish two editions of Pinkerton's *Medallic History of England.* The REV. JOHN LANNE BUCHANAN (1780-1816) was a literary critic who derided Pinkerton's views on the origins of the Celts (cf. J. L. Buchanan, *A Defence of the Scots Highlanders*, 1804).

ship with Ann. According to Couper, Pinkerton stated that his brother-in-law Thomas Burgess, the future bishop of Salisbury, had induced him to marry Henrietta:

> ...by splendid promises never performed. [140]

After ten years there was a divorce, but it was likely not legal. This did not stop Pinkerton, in 1812, from marrying Elizabeth Brown Becken, characterized by Wood as:

> ...another bitch of the modern hot-bed race quite unfit for the society of men of sense or spirit... [141]

However, perhaps not very surprising, considering Pinkerton's character, Elizabeth was "possessed of a rich uncle." Whether this marriage lasted is unknown; but what is clear is that after his marriage his financial situation became quite limited, as he had to sell a portion of his library. He now returned to Edinburgh, where he attempted to write a play, an endeavor he had relished even as a young man. The play, *The Heiress of Strathern or The Rash Marriage,* was a complete failure and closed after one performance. Unable to find employment, likely due to his reputation, he attempted other projects, none of which came to anything. Ultimately, Pinkerton returned to Paris where he lived at no. 10, 26 Rue de Ponthieu, Champs-Elysées, in an increasingly precarious financial and health situation. He died there in March 1825, at the age of 67 years.

It is somewhat difficult to reconcile the accolades heaped upon Pinkerton by some of his contemporaries with the many negative characteristics of his personality, his outright fraudulent literary practices, his generally offensive personality traits and, as will be seen, his aberrant racial beliefs (e.g., a belief in racial superiority). Even his friend Sir William Scott, wrote of Pinkerton, that in:

> ...*Recollections of Paris* in 1802 to 1805 we have abundant evidence of the low level of his moral standard. [142]

Pinkerton was an avowed racist, believing in Germanic racial superiority. In his opinion, the Celts—to him, the Irish, the Scottish Highlanders, the Welsh, the Bretons, and the Basques of Spain—were the surviving descendents of 'original Europeans.' He believed, to an obsessive degree, that members of these 'racial' groups could be identified by their physical characteristics. In particular, he held disdain for the Scottish Highlanders, as a 'degenerate imposter race with few achievements.' One doubts that he voiced such opinions when in the presence of members of these so-called 'inferior racial groups.' In any event, his contemporaries took up pen and paper to challenge his ideology.[143]

In sum, Pinkerton was many things to many people:

> His studious and laborious disposition deserves praise; and the defects we have had to notice with pain arose in youth from the arrogance of inexperience, and in his later years from mortification at the failure of a long series of literary attempts, some of which merited another fate...[144]

---

[140] Couper, p. 4.

[141] Couper, ibid. citing E. H. Wood, op cit.

[142] Constable, T. (ed.), *Archibald Constable and his Literary Correspondence*, 1873, vol. i, Edinburgh: Edmonston & Douglas, p 505.

[143] See, e.g., *The Gentleman's Magazine*, vol. lx, part 2, pp. 601-605.

[144] P. 327 in Sir Walter Scott, 'Ancient History of Scotland,' In *The Miscellaneous Prose Works of Sir Walter Scott, Bart.*, vol. xx, (Personal Criticism vol. iv, Miscellaneous Criticism), article xiii, pp. 301-376. This article is a reply to: J. Ritson's, 'Annals of the Caledonians, Picts, and Scots; and of Stratheclyde, Cumberland, Galloway and Murray,' *Quarterly Review*, 1829, vol. 41, p. 135.

In the present authors' view, Ferguson seems to have the right explanation for the dynamics underlying PINKERTON's repugnant ideas and frequently abhorrent behavior. The present authors would argue, however, that it would be too generous to Pinkerton's reputation to allow him to escape both full responsibility and condemnation for his behavior.

His obituary, "generally attributed to Sir Walter Scott," continues, for the most part, in the positive vein characteristic of the early reviews of his work by Walpole and Gibbon (*see above, p. 66*)—being perhaps more 'balanced' than would an obituary written by more modern writers. Yet, despite all the character flaws, professional and personal failings, a number of Pinkerton's works remain in print and he remains a subject of academic study to this day.[145]

In Re John Pinkerton's *Essay on Medals*

THE most valuable writer on this subject is, without doubt, Mr. Pinkerton, the second edition of whose *Essay on Medals* will, indeed, almost preclude the necessity of reference to any other work. This edition is enriched and illustrated with numerous engravings, forming specimens corresponding exactly in size and shape with the originals, of all the principal varieties of medals. It is in two small volumes, and was published in London in 1729.[146]

—J. A. Eames (1826). *General and Bibliographical Dictionary of the Fine Arts...*, no pagination.

§

[THEN] comes John Pinkerton, with his useful (although, in some instances, faulty) Essay on Medals, cutting right and left at the very authors preceding him, from whom he had *stolen* (from Jobert in particular). This was very unfair; but his book, indeed, was made to sell. He was paid a certain sum for his compilation; and although an old and highly respected friend of mine, Mr. Richard Miles, offered to correct the copy for him, and divest it of their errors, his reply was, "I have agreed to do it for a stipulated amount, and I shall take no further trouble with it."

So much for an author writing on a subject of which he knew little or nothing, merely for the sake of a trifling consideration. Such was the case with Pinkerton. It has been the fashion to censure this work, indeed much more than it deserves; at any rate it has been a serviceable *compilation,* and the standard by which our country collectors have been guided for the last forty years.

—William Till (1838), *An Essay on the Roman Denarius...*, 2nd ed., pp. 119-120.

In Re John Pinkerton's *Medallic History of England*

I am rather sorry to hear that you are going to be the *editor of another's* work, who art so infinitely better employed when composing yourself—however, as it will be on a branch of *vertù* that I love, I comfort myself from your taste and accuracy that it will be better executed than by anyone else.

—Horace Walpole, commenting on John Pinkerton's letter informing him that he was undertaking the publication of Snelling's *Thirty-three Plates of English Medals* (1776), in a letter to Pinkerton dated Oct. 15, 1788.[147] —Lewis & Wallace, *Horace Walpole's Correspondence...*,1976, p. 299.

The quotations from WALKER, WALPOLE, GIBBON, and SCOTT, *above,* are all cited by TURNER, *Literary Correspondence...*, 1830, vol. i, pp. vi-ix. Turner attributes the quotation from Scott (fn. 141, above) to *Quarterly Review*, vol. xli, p. 138. Turner, unfortunately, seems to not have had a great interest in numismatics and omits Pinkerton's correspondence on this subject from his work.

145 See, e.g., Ferguson, W. (1998). *The Identity of the Scottish Nation* and O'Flaherty, P. (2014) *Scotland's Pariah: The Life and Work of John Pinkerton, 1758-1826.*

146 The date is obviously in error. It should be 1784.

147 It is unfortunate that Pinkerton's letter of October 14, 1788, to which Walpole replied, appears to be lost. This letter might have provided further information concerning the details of John Pinkerton's involvement with Snelling's plates and the publication of *The Medallic History of England* by Edwards & Sons.

A SAMPLE PLATE (NO. XVI) FROM THE 1790 EDITION OF *MEDALLIC HISTORY OF ENGLAND TO THE REVOLUTION…* (WITHOUT THE MARGINS). IT IS EXACTLY THE SAME AS "PLATE 11" IN SNELLING'S *THIRTY-THREE PLATES OF ENGLISH MEDALS*, PUBLISHED IN 1776. THE SIZE IS QUARTO. THE ILLUSTRATED MEDALS ARE ALL MEMORIALS OF CHARLES I, CA. 1649.

John Pinkerton

The Medallic History of England…

SNELLING's thirty-three plates reappeared, in four later editions, all bearing some version of the title *Medallic History* or *Medals of England.*[148] The first three editions appeared in 1790, 1802, and 1831 while the date of the fourth edition is not known. All the editions except for the first were published without attribution, although it is generally assumed that John Pinkerton was very much involved in the publication of the first edition in 1790, and perhaps the 1802, but not the 1831 and undated editions as he died in 1826. Where original bindings remain legible, Pinkerton's name appears on at least some of them. It is only in the preface to the first edition that any reference to Snelling appears.

A YOUNGER JOHN PINKERTON. FRONTISPIECE FROM THE *LITERARY CORRESPONDENCE OF JOHN PINKERTON, ESQ. NOW FIRST PRINTED FROM THE ORIGINALS IN THE POSSESSION OF DAWSON TURNER, ESQ., M.A., F.R.S.*, 1830 ED., VOL I. THIS STIPPLE ENGRAVING OF A TASSIE PORTRAIT MEDALLION, DATED 1798, IS ATTRIBUTED TO W. C. EDWARDS, AFTER TASSIE.

Edwards & Sons published the first edition, entitled *The Medallic History of England to the Revolution, with Forty Plates*, with the date 1790 on the title page. The present authors' copy, with a badly worn but apparently original binding, has Pinkerton's name on the title strap of the spine: "*Pinkerton / Medallic / History of / England.*" This edition also contains commentary on each of the illustrated medals. The second edition, also with 40 plates and entitled *The Medallic History of England, Illustrated by Forty Plates*, appeared in 1802. This edition also contains the commentary that accompanied the plates in the 1790 editions, but does not contain the preface of the 1790 edition. The type of the 1802 edition has been reset. Another edition, dated 1831, exists, this containing only the plates, without the accompanying preface or text, and is entitled *384 Medals of England. Engraved on Forty Plates.* There is also an undated edition, entitled *the Medals of England, Consisting of 384 Specimens Engraved on Forty Plates.* It is without either the preface to the 1790 edition or the commentary of the 1790 or 1802

[148] *The Medallic History* volumes (*q.v. pp. 62-65, above*) should not be confused with another, more general in scope and perhaps more well-known, numismatic work by Pinkerton, *An Essay on Medals: Or an Introduction to the Knowledge of Modern Coins and Medals; especially those of Greece, Rome, and Britain.* The latter was first published in 1784 in two parts, but as a single volume which dealt primarily with coins, and later, in 1789, in a two volume revised second edition. The second edition, which is very scarce, has the original title to which is added: *A new edition, corrected, greatly enlarged, and illustrated with plates.* More frequently encountered is an expanded *Third Edition, With Corrections and Additions*, also in two volumes, published in 1808. Interestingly, one of the copies of the 1808 edition of *An Essay on Medals…* held by the British Library contains HORACE WALPOLE's bookplate and manuscript notes.

editions. The table, which appears in this volume on pp. 77 and 78, presents the physical characteristics of the four editions Snelling's original 33 plates are numbered in both Roman (I-IX) and Arabic (10-33) while those plates in the four later editions are all numbered in Roman (I-XL).

How Pinkerton's name came to be associated with Snelling's work is an interesting question. In the light of Horace Walpole's comment in his letter of October 15, 1788, in which Walpole admonished Pinkerton when he learned that the latter was "going to be the *editor of another's work*,"[149] Pinkerton was most likely hired by Edwards & Sons under a 'work made for hire' arrangement to prepare the additional plates and letterpress material in the 1790 edition.

A new biography of John Pinkerton addresses this question.[150] O'Flaherty, the author, indeed concludes that the publisher, Edward & Sons, hired Pinkerton to complete Snelling's *Thirty-three Plates of English Medals* (1776) by adding an additional seven plates and descriptions of the medals. Pinkerton, ever extremely sensitive about his reputation, likely understood very well the advice given him by Walpole. Financially insecure, however, Pinkerton probably felt that he could not turn down this piece of work.

O'Flaherty does not, however, provide any additional clarification concerning who initiated the idea of Pinkerton's working on the *Thirty-three Plates* volume, i.e., did the publisher approach Pinkerton or was it the other way around? In either case, Flaherty is probably right in concluding that the reason Pinkerton's name did not appear on the 1792 work was either that Pinkerton "...didn't wish to appear as an author in such a humble role..." or that the publisher, on his part, wished to avoid the notoriety which might arise and the resultant risk to his investment in the project by having Pinkerton's name appear on it.

O'Flaherty also concludes that Pinkerton used Charles Combe (*q.v. p. 85*) as his consultant in preparing the plates and descriptive commentary. He notes Pinkerton's acknowledgement of Combe in the first edition of *Thirty-three Plates of English Medals,* i.e., Combe had a "capitol Collection of Prints and Drawings of English Medals" (p. 63) upon which Pinkerton could draw in having the additional plates prepared, as well as Combe's previous assistance during the preparation of the second edition of *An Essay on Medals.*

Historical Commentary on John Pinkerton

The life of Mr. Pinkerton was...entirely and exclusively that of a literary man...

—Dawson Turner, *Literary Correspondence of John Pinkerton, Esq....*, Preface, 1830, vol. i, p. vii.

§

The Letters which form the greater part of the present Volumes were selected by Mr. Pinkerton himself for the purpose of publication. They include, among others from personages known to fame, epistles by Lord Buchan, Gibbon the historian, and Horace Walpole, besides a copious store of curious anecdotes, exhibiting the history of a literary man from the beginning to the end of his career; a man of a capacious mind, great acuteness, strong memory, restless activity, and extraordinary perseverance. These anecdotes afford a striking proof of the power of talents and industry to raise their possessor in the scale of society, as well as in the opinion of the world. Unfortunately, they are also calculated to read us another and not less instructive lesson, that somewhat more is required to turn such advantages to their full account; and that the endowments of the mind, unless accompanied by sound and consistent principles, can tend but little to the happiness of the individual, or

[149] HORACE WALPOLE'S letter to PINKERTON dated Oct. 15, 1788 (*q.v. p. 69 above*).

[150] O'Flaherty, P. (2014) *Scotland's Pariah: The Life and Work of John Pinkerton, 1758-1826.* Toronto: Univ. of Toronto Press. SNELLING'S son, also named THOMAS SNELLING, took over the business at 163 Fleet street after his father's death in 1776.

to the good of society. The close of Mr. Pinkerton's life was sadly dissimilar to what was promised at its outset.

—Ibid. preface, vol. i, pp. v-vi.

§

Pinkerton seems busy in his intended history of Scotland; whether it is to be the same with that advertised with the name of Robert Heron, I cannot learn. His treatment...is to be speedily [p]resented in print by the Reverend John Lane Buchanan...who seems in fact, to be as very a Celt as his antagonist could possibly wish for. I am sorry to find so good a cause in the hands of such an incompetent advocate...

—Ritson, J. (1833). *The letters of Joseph Ritson to Mr. George Paton*..., p. 46, letter dated Mar. 5 1794.

§

Our friend Pinkerton, I am told, to complete the infamy of his character, has turned critical reviewer, a situation, of course, which admits neither truth or honesty. He will therefore have the pleasure of thundering his own damnation upon the heads of others, among whom, I suppose, he will take care not to forget...J. Ritson.

—Ibid. pp. 67-68, letter dated Jan. 19, 1795.

§

The true Ishmael among archaeologists of that day was John Pinkerton, who seldom praises others, and of whom no one seems to have a good word to say. Neither shall I enter on his defense...Mr. Pinkerton was notorious as well for suppression as misquotation of authorities, for *suppressio veri* and *suggestio falsi*. In his collection of "Scotish Ballads," [sic] 1783, he inserted as ancient a Second Part of " Hardyknute," etc., which were proved to be modern; yet, in the Preface to his "Dissertation on the Scythians or Goths," he says: "In Germany or Scandinavia, if an author were to quote falsely, he would go near to incur the character of a scoundrel and a liar." He must have presumed too confidently on the greater lenity of his countrymen in estimating his own productions. Sir Walter Scott says of him that "he understood in an extensive sense Horace's maxim, *quidlibet audendi*."[151]

—A. Constable, et al. (1876) *Personal Reminiscences*, 1876, pp. 144-145.

§

I have heard the reviewer laughed at for the logic in his conclusion that because Pinkerton has been convicted of falsehood and interpolation, honest men should be suspected, and not Pinkerton disbelieved, even when he does write truth, according to the common maxim about liars. But there seems to be a Pinkerton mania in Scotland.

—A. Constable, et al., ibid. p. 123.

§

Perhaps the less that I say of John Pinkerton the better, inasmuch as my notice of him cannot be very favorable. He became afterwards my frequent guest, and in the autumn of that year spent three months with us in the country...I should have been willing to bear with or overlook his overweening egoism and numberless eccentricities, in consequence of which, when he left Edinburgh in 1814, there were but three individuals in the whole community with whom he remained on speaking terms, namely, Sir Walter Scott, Mr. Thomas Thomson, and my obscure self. He had ample worldly shrewdness (in pecuniary matters at least), great perseverance and power of research, was a fierce and uncompromising critic of all works, either in prose or verse, excepting his own; and for one who did not feel disposed to quarrel with his dictatorial manner and bizarre notions, his conversation, from its variety, afforded an inexhaustible stock of amusement.

—Ibid. p. 276-277.

§

Obituary: At Paris, aged 67, John Pinkerton, Esq, F. S. A. Perth, a voluminous and celebrated Author and Editor...Mr. Pinkerton claimed descent from an ancient family seated at Pinkerton [sic] near Dunbar... [In conclusion, it] will have been perceived that Mr. Pinkerton was an eccentric, but highly industrious literary workman, and that his talents, although in some instances ill-directed, were commensurate with undertakings of no ordinary rank in literature.

—*The Gentleman's Magazine*, May 1826, vol. xcvi, pp. 468, 472.

[151] *'Daring anything.'*

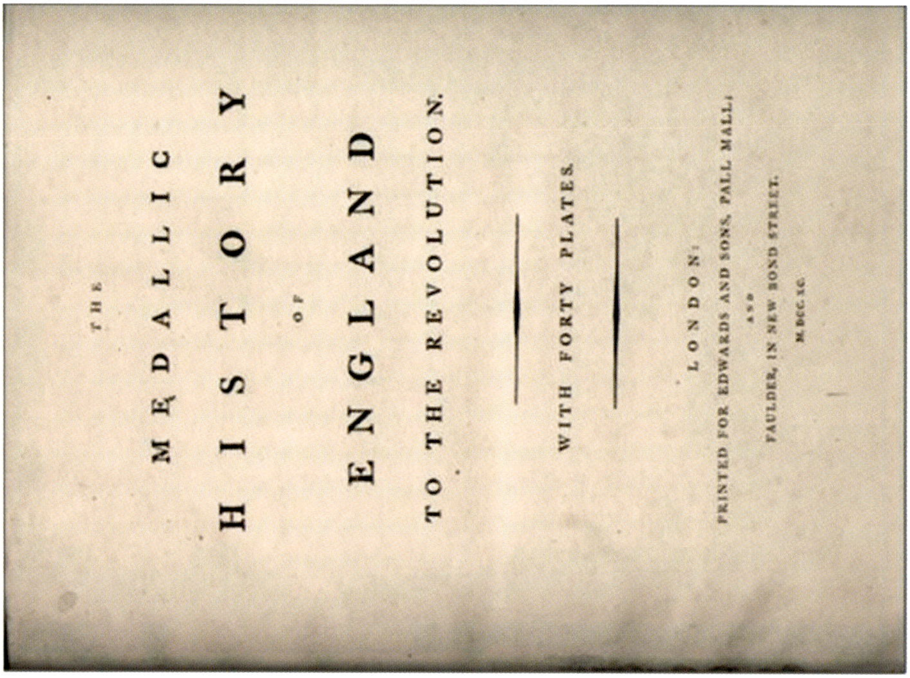

THE

MEDALLIC

HISTORY

OF

ENGLAND

TO THE REVOLUTION.

WITH FORTY PLATES.

LONDON:

PRINTED FOR EDWARDS AND SONS, PALL MALL;

AND

FAULDER, IN NEW BOND STREET.

M.DCC.XC.

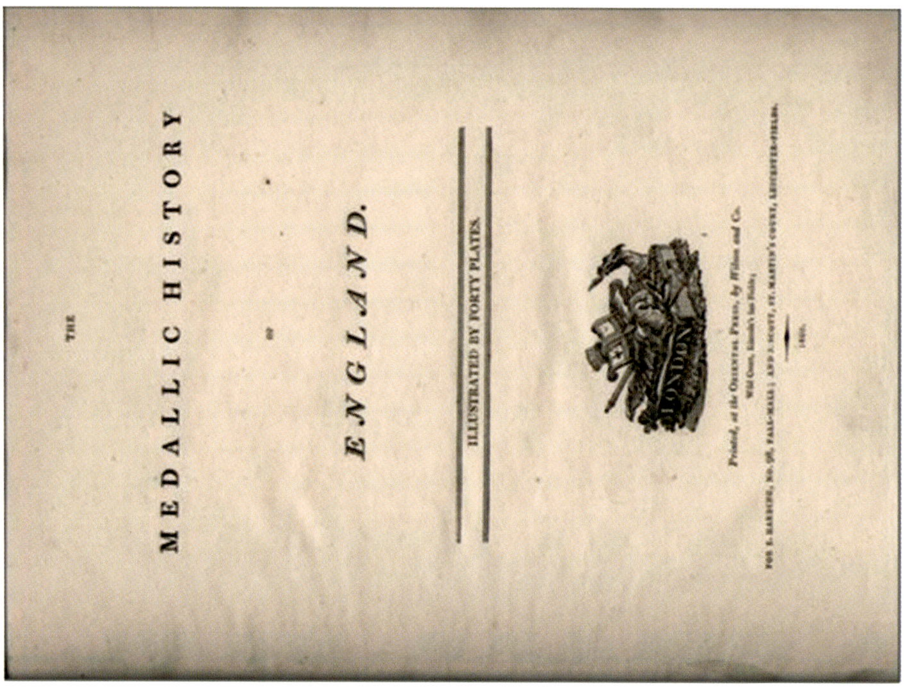

THE

MEDALLIC HISTORY

OF

ENGLAND.

ILLUSTRATED BY FORTY PLATES.

Printed, at the Oriental Press, *by Wilson and Co.*

Wild Court, Lincoln's Inn Fields;

FOR E. HARDING, NO. 98, PALL-MALL; AND J. SCOTT, ST. MARTIN'S COURT, LEICESTER-FIELDS.

1802.

THE TITLE PAGES OF THE 1790 (TOP) AND 1802 (BOTTOM) EDITIONS OF THE REISSUE (NOW WITH 40 PLATES) OF SNELLING'S *THIRTY-THREE PLATES OF ENGLISH MEDALS.* MANVILLE (2005) NOTES THAT SOME COPIES OF THE 1790 EDITION HAVE HAD THE REFERENCE TO FAULDER OBLITERATED (P. 51).

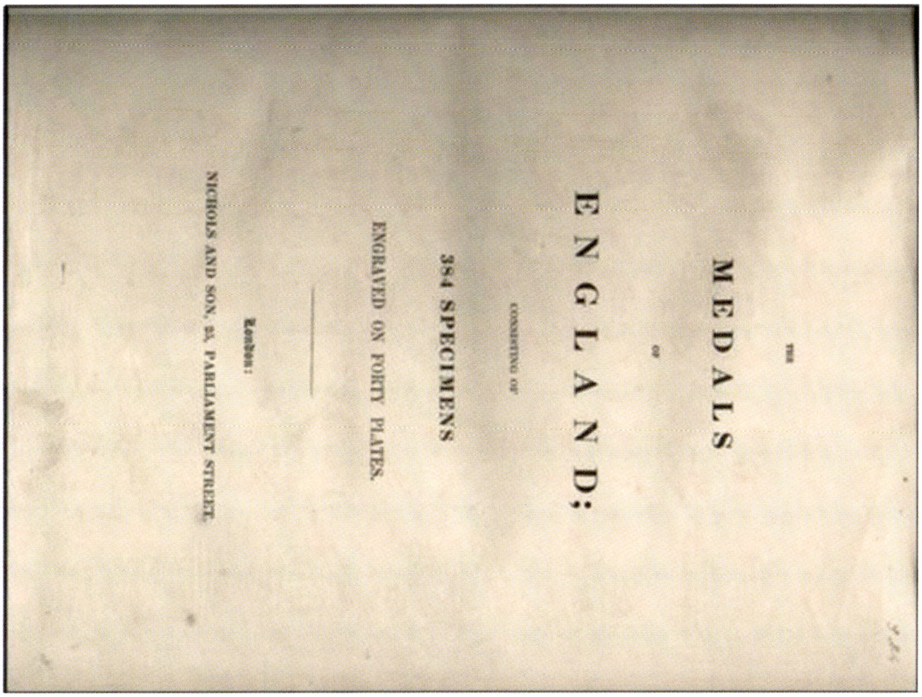

THE
MEDALS
OF
ENGLAND;
CONSISTING OF
384 SPECIMENS
ENGRAVED ON FORTY PLATES.

London:
NICHOLS AND SON, 25, PARLIAMENT STREET.

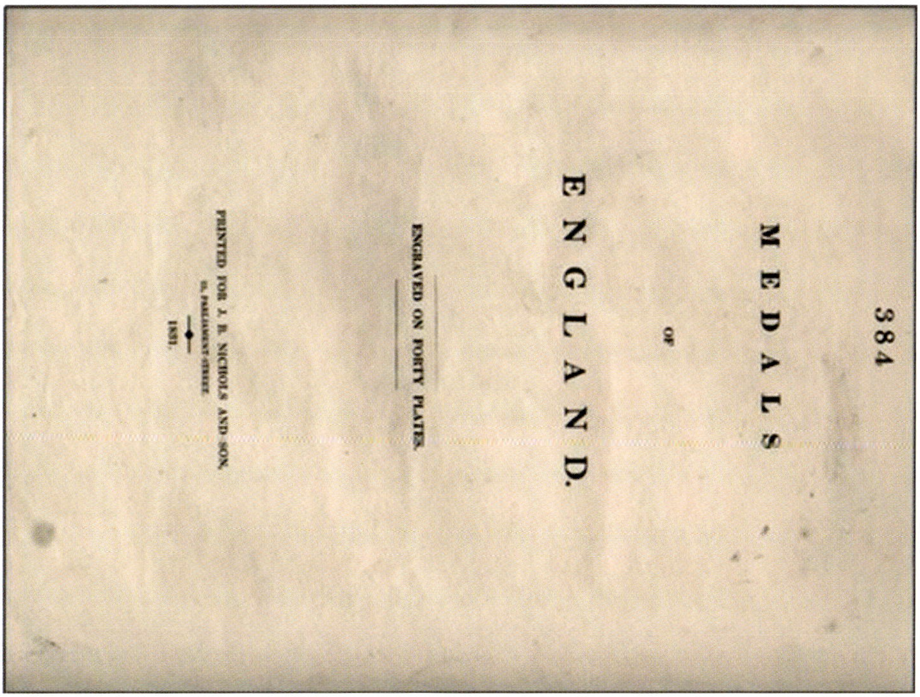

384
MEDALS
OF
ENGLAND.

ENGRAVED ON FORTY PLATES.

PRINTED FOR J. B. NICHOLS AND SON,
25, PARLIAMENT-STREET.
1831.

THE TITLE PAGES OF TWO OTHER REISSUES, BOTH WITH 40 PLATES, OF SNELLING'S ORIGINAL *THIRTY-THREE PLATES OF ENGLISH MEDALS*. THE PUBLICATION DATE OF THE EDITION SHOWN AT THE TOP IS UNKNOWN, WHILE THAT OF THE ONE SHOWN BELOW IS 1831.

THE PREFACE FROM PINKERTON'S FIRST EDITION OF *THE MEDALLIC HISTORY* (1790).

P R E F A C E.

THIS Work is the firſt which lays before the Reader a complete ſeries of Engliſh Medals down to the Revolution. Mr. Evelyn, in his NUMISMATA, publiſhed many Engliſh Medals, and about the middle of this century Mr. Perry engraved ſome plates of them; but Mr. Snelling's plates greatly exceeded all former attempts in this way.

The Publiſhers of the preſent Work have improved upon Mr. Snelling's plan, in ſupplying his deficiencies, and giving a deſcription with the plates. Their expence has been conſiderable, and the fruit of it is now ſubmitted to the Public.

Mr. Snelling's Collection, though meritorious, was ſo incomplete, that more than a third of the plates now appear for the firſt time, and in thoſe ſome of the moſt rare and curious Medals are contained.

If

[iv]

If we except the Medals of the Popes, this Collection may boaſt of being the firſt genuine and complete one of its kind. Notwithſtanding the eminence of France in books of ſcience muſt be acknowledged, yet that country has as yet only the fabulous and imaginary Works of De Bie and Typotius, and a few detached plates by Le Clerc. Germany, Spain, and the other countries of Europe*, have no Collection of this kind, though all muſt allow that its importance to the hiſtory and arts of a country ought to render it a national object every where.

The Publiſhers beg leave to acknowledge, with gratitude, the liberality of that eminent Medalliſt Dr. COMBE in favour of this Work. To his capital Collection of Prints and Drawings of Engliſh Medals they are entirely indebted for many of the curious articles here publiſhed. To him they alſo owe ſeveral explanations in the deſcription.

* The Medallic Hiſtory of the United Provinces begins at ſo late a period, that it hardly deſerves to form an exception.

NOTE: THE REFERENCE TO 'DR. COMBE' IS PRESUMABLY TO DR. CHARLES COMBE F.R.S. (1743-1817). HIS SON TAYLOR COMBE (1774–1826) WAS KEEPER OF ANTIQUITIES AT THE BRITISH MUSEUM (1807-1826). *See this vol., p. 85.*

CHARACTERISTICS OF THE FOUR EDITIONS
OF
'*THE MEDALLIC HISTORY OF ENGLAND.*'

As noted previously, there are four variously titled editions of THE MEDALLIC HISTORY OF ENGLAND *which have often been attributed to John Pinkerton. The information on the four volumes in the authors' library is summarized below. All four editions contain 384 illustrations on 40 plates. The details of a second copy of the 1790 edition are included to illustrate the fact that Pinkerton's name may or may not appear on a rebound work, depending on the bookseller's, bookbinder's or owner's knowledge of the volume's authorship. The present authors have, however, never seen a copy dated 1790 or later with Thomas Snelling's name on the binding.*

(A_1) *THE MEDALLIC HISTORY OF ENGLAND TO THE REVOLUTION, WITH FORTY PLATES.*

Dated M.DCC.XC.
Overall size: 13-1/2 x 11 in.; page size: 13-1/4 x 10-3/8 in.
No author's name on the title page, *but* Pinkerton's name appears on the original spine.
Pp: ii+112 + 40 pl.; plates numbered in Roman, pages in Arabic.
Title page states: "PRINTED FOR EDWARDS AND SONS, PALL MALL; /AND/ FAULDER, IN NEW BOND STREET/M.DCC.XC."
This volume contains a preface, 40 plates *and* descriptive commentary on the medals.
Original calf binding, with ornately decorated banded spine and title strap: "PINKERTON / MEDALLIC / HISTORY OF / ENGLAND." Binding severely worn, boards and flyleaves detached, thus rebound in 2013, red cloth, black title label stamped in gold, mounted on spine.

(A_2) *THE MEDALLIC HISTORY OF ENGLAND TO THE REVOLUTION, WITH FORTY PLATES.*

Another copy with the content identical to (A_1).
Dated M.DCC.XC.
Overall size: 14-3/8 x 11-3/4 in., page size: 13-3/4 x 11-1/4 in.
Bound in original 7/8 leather and cloth, with ornately decorated spine and embossed title on strap: MEDALLIC / HISTORY OF / ENGLAND.
Title page states: "PRINTED FOR EDWARDS AND SONS, PALL MALL; /AND/ FAULDER, IN NEW BOND STREET/M.DCC.XC."
Forty plates Roman numbering. descriptive commentary and preface present.
Binding: 7/8 green cloth, leather spine, appears to be original.

(B) *THE MEDALLIC HISTORY OF ENGLAND, ILLUSTRATED BY FORTY PLATES.*

Dated 1802.
Overall size: 12-11/16 x 11-1/4 in.; page size: 12-3/8 x 9-1/2 in.
Pinkerton's name did *not* appear on the original spine, which was in severely deteriorated condition due to wear. Rebound in 2013, red cloth, black title label stamped in gold, mounted on spine, as for copy (A_1).
"*Printed, at the* ORIENTAL PRESS, *by Wilson and Co.*, / Wild Court, Lincoln's Inn Fields; / FOR E. HARDING, NO. 98, PALL-MALL; AND J. SCOTT, ST. MARTIN'S COURT, LEICESTER-FIELDS / 1802."

(*continued on following page*)

(B) *(Continued from preceding page)*

112 pp. +40 plates numbered in Roman.

This edition contains 40 plates, no preface, but with the same descriptive commentary on the plates as contained in (A_1) and (A_2).

Bound in original 7/8 card boards, with ornately decorated spine and embossed title: "MEDALLIC / HISTORY OF / ENGLAND."

*The characteristics of two copies of this edition are presented here. It is interesting to note that of these two volumes, both of which retain the original bindings, Pinkerton's name only appears on one (A_2).

(C) *384 MEDALS OF ENGLAND, ENGRAVED ON FORTY PLATES.*

Dated 1831.

Overall size: 13-3/8 x 10-7/8 in.; page size: 13-1/8 x 10-1/2 in.

No author attribution.

"PRINTED FOR J. B. NICHOLS & SON, / 25, PARLIAMENT-STREET. / 1831."

Forty plates. All plates numbered in Roman numerals. No preface or commentary.

112 pp. +40 plates numbered in Roman. No preface or commentary on the plates as contained in (A_1) and (A_2).

Bound in red leather (sheepskin?) which appears to be a later replacement for the original. Title stamped on cover in gold: "MEDALS/ OF /ENGLAND/ LONDON/1831."

(D) *THE MEDALS OF ENGLAND, CONSISTING OF 384 SPECIMENS ENGRAVED ON FORTY PLATES.*

Undated, exact date of publication unknown.

Overall size: 11-7/8 x 9-3/4 in.; page size: 11-9/16 x 9-1/4 in.

No author attribution.

"London: / NICHOLS & SON, 25 PARLIAMENT STREET."

This edition contains 40 plates numbered in Roman, but no preface or commentary.

This copy has been rebound in 1/8 leather, together with Adam de Cardonnel's, *Numismata Scotiæ* (1786), review of the latter and handwritten comments bound with leaves.

Embossed title on the spine: "ENGLISH/ & /SCOTTISH/ COINS."

Note: While Snelling's original edition contained 33 plates, the editions associated with Pinkerton all contain 40 plates and the order of appearance was modified from that of Snelling, with plates by '— Barlow' having been inserted. Snelling's name appears only in the preface to the first (1790) edition.

> Pinkerton's constructive abilities left much to be desired.
>
> —Ferguson, *The Identity of the Scottish Nation*, 1998, p. 245.

PAMPHLETS upon single medals, and the like, are commonly written by the authors only to show that old women are not the only persons who can say a great deal upon nothing. These particularly swarm; and I will be bold to say that not one of them deserves perusal, even though the name of a first-rate medallic author stands at the head of it.

—J. Pinkerton, On the state of the literature on medals. In, *An Essay on Medals…*, 1808, vol. i, preface, p. xxiv.

§

THE less an author says at any time about his own productions the better; so it shall only be added, that, though this little Essay was begun as a mere amusement and relief from idleness, yet I soon found that infinite labour was required to answer my own expectations. As it is disagreeable to relinquish a design when entered upon, this toil has not been spared. Indeed the reader will hardly believe how much attention is required in a work of this kind, for every page almost contains a number of minute facts, for each of which considerable information is necessary: insomuch that perhaps in two or three lines the fruit of much research into a dozen or two of authors is presented...I will venture to say, that in no science whatever have so many bad books, and so few good ones, been given as in this.[152]

—J. Pinkerton, commenting on his own work, in *An Essay on Medals*, 1808, pp. xiii, xiv, xvi.

SOME, indeed, apprehend that none of the Ancient Pieces we now stile Medals, were ever Current Coin, but all struck on particular occasions; like those Modern Pieces which are called by that Name, to distinguish them from Common and Current Coin.

—Jennings, *An Introduction to the Knowledge of Medals*, 1764, p. 1

[152] This paragraph reveals much of JOHN PINKERTON's personality—in particular his narcissism, self-pity, contempt for other authors and even for those readers who, in his view, do not realize the investment he believes he has made in preparing the work. For a balanced evaluation of the man, the authors recommend O'Flaherty's biography of Pinkerton, *Scotland's Pariah: The Life and Work of John Pinkerton, 1758-1826* (op cit). O'Flaherty comments that:

> [Pinkerton's] life story is one of high ambition thwarted, great promise only partly fulfilled, and talent too often misdirected. It is full of struggle and pathos... (—O'Flaherty, preface)

It is surprising that it has taken this long for such a work to appear on a man who played such a large role, even if much of was notorious in nature, in late 18th century Scottish letters.

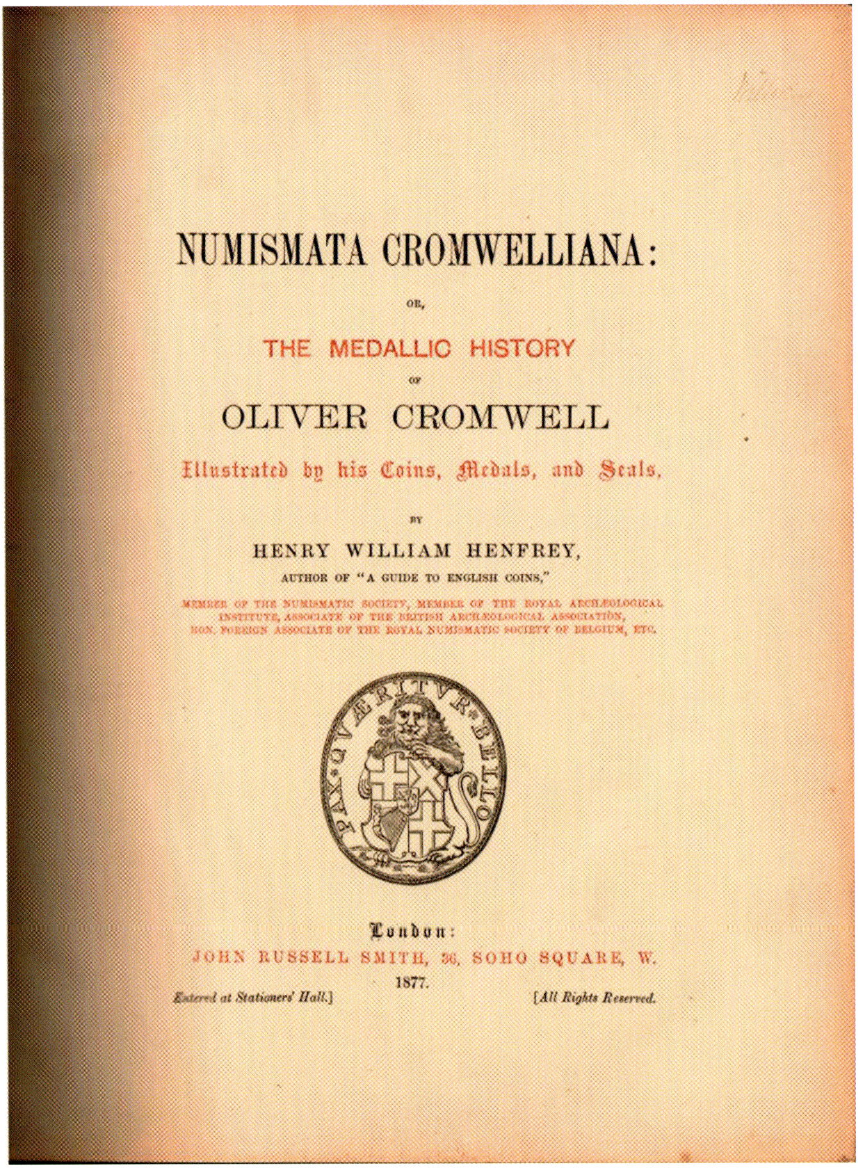

NUMISMATA CROMWELLIANA:

OR,

THE MEDALLIC HISTORY

OF

OLIVER CROMWELL

Illustrated by his Coins, Medals, and Seals,

BY

HENRY WILLIAM HENFREY,

AUTHOR OF "A GUIDE TO ENGLISH COINS,"

MEMBER OF THE NUMISMATIC SOCIETY, MEMBER OF THE ROYAL ARCHÆOLOGICAL INSTITUTE, ASSOCIATE OF THE BRITISH ARCHÆOLOGICAL ASSOCIATION, HON. FOREIGN ASSOCIATE OF THE ROYAL NUMISMATIC SOCIETY OF BELGIUM, ETC.

London:

JOHN RUSSELL SMITH, 36, SOHO SQUARE, W.

1877.

Entered at Stationers' Hall.] [*All Rights Reserved.*

THE TITLE PAGE FROM HENFREY'S *NUMISMATA CROMWELLIANA* (1877). THIS VOLUME IS SLIGHTLY SMALLER THAN QUARTO IN SIZE (11-7/8 X 8-1/2 IN.).

Henry W. Henfrey

(1852-1881)

HENRY WILLIAM HENFREY, the author of *Numismata Cromwelliana*, was the eldest son of Arthur Henfrey, the botanist, and his wife Elizabeth Anne, of London. His father, a fellow of the Royal Society, was a professor and fellow of King's College, University of London. The younger Henfrey was educated at Brighton College, where:

> ...he showed great talent for languages, and attained distinction in the school.[153]

He was, however, unable to attend Oxford University due to injuries he sustained as the result of an accident. At Brighton, with the support of a number of family friends (in particular, Mr. Peter Cunningham, Mr. Joseph Bonomi the Younger, and Admiral Henry Smyth[154]), Henfrey pursued his interest in archeology and numismatics and published a number of articles in the *Numismatic Chronicle*. Gaining some reputation for his publications on English coins and medals, he advanced from initial membership in 1868, at age sixteen, in the Numismatic Society of London to membership on its council, contributing twelve papers, primarily on English coins and medals, to its *Proceedings*. The first edition of his *Guide to English Coins* was published in 1870. He was elected to membership in the British Archeological Association and he contributed papers on Cromwellian medals, among other topics, to its *Proceedings*.

In addition to *Numismata Cromwelliana* and journal articles, Henfrey also wrote and published *A Guide to the Study and Arrangement of English Coins: Giving a description of every denomination of every issue in gold, silver, and copper, from the conquest to the present time, with all the latest discoveries* (1870, 1885). Another numismatic work, a history of English country mints, was in progress when he suddenly died in July 1881, after returning from a trip to Italy. This work was never completed. Both the obituaries in the *Numismatic Chronicle* and the 1891 *DNB* considered *Numismata Cromwelliana* to have been his principal work.

Henry Henfrey's *NUMISMATA CROMWELLIANA...*

Henfrey's *Numismata Cromwelliana: or, The Medallic History of Oliver Cromwell, Illustrated by his Coins, Medals, and Seals*,[155] was published in 1877. As the title implies, the work dealt exclusively with the coins, medals and seals of the Cromwellian period. Printed in a small private subscription edition, and now very scarce, the work focused on coinage and mint affairs for the period 1650-1658, and covers the Dunbar, Lord General, and Inauguration medals, as well as the very rare medal of Cromwell and Fairfax (M.I.i 411/48). It also covers Dassier's medal, the 'octagonal medal,' Kirk's medal, Smith's medal, copper and lead tokens containing portraits of Cromwell, as well as the Dutch satirical medals of Cromwell and the funeral medals. Henfrey of course focused exclusively upon coins, medals and seals pertaining to Oliver Cromwell. It is indeed unfortunate that Henfrey died so young, as it is likely that this young medallic scholar would likely have made many more contributions to numismatic literature.

[153] *Numismatic Chronicle*, 1882, ser. iii, vol. ii, pp. 21-22.

[154] Ibid.

[155] This volume should not be confused with *Cromwelliana: A Chronological Detail of Events in which Oliver Cromwell was Engaged...*, by JAMES CAULFIELD, published in 1810 by MACHELL STACE, *Bookseller*, Princes street, Leicester Square.

"OMNIA ANTIQUITATIS MONUMENTA COLLIGO."

15, Eaton Place, Brighton________ , 187__

Sir,

Being at present engaged in collecting materials for a complete account of the Coins and Medals of Oliver Cromwell, I beg to solicit your kind assistance towards the accomplishment of my object.

If you are possessed of any unpublished information relative either to the Medallic History of the Protectorate, or to the Life and Works of Thomas Simon, I should feel obliged for any communication from you.

The following brief catalogue of all the Coins, Pattern Pieces, Medals and Dutch imitations, is intended for comparison with any specimens that may be preserved in your own cabinet. If, on examination, you are able to furnish any new variety, it is requested that you should state in your reply:—

The *number* which your piece resembles in the following printed catalogue,

Also whether it differs in respect of:

Metal, *Type* or *Design*, *Legend* or *Inscription*, *Edge*, plain or milled, *Weight*, *Size*, *Shape*, oval or circular.

If your coins and medals all exactly resemble those in my list, will you please to note the numbers, and state the weights of the coins in Troy grains, and the sizes of the medals in inches and tenths of an inch?

I remain, Sir,

Yours very faithfully,

HENRY W HENFREY.

F.H.S. M.N.S., M.R.A.I., ETC.

THE TEXT OF THE LETTER CIRCULATED BY HENRY HENFREY IN SOLICITING INFORMATION FOR HIS VOLUME ON THE COINS AND MEDALS OF OLIVER CROMWELL. SOME 250 COPIES OF THE COMPLETED WORK WERE PREPARED AND DISTRIBUTED, MAINLY TO SUBSCRIBERS, WHO RECEIVED IT IN SIX PARTS.

§

Historical Commentary on Henry Henfrey

This work, the publication of which in part has been somewhat irregular, in consequence of the illness of the author, is now complete, and we may fairly congratulate Mr. Henfrey upon a very honourable achievement. For the first time it is here attempted to give a complete historical description of all the Coins, Medals, and Pattern Pieces of Cromwell, and the exploration necessary to make such an undertaking of permanent use, among State Papers and other manuscript sources of information, has brought to light many matters of value not only to the history of art, but also to the general history of the period. To many, possibly, the result of such labour as embodied in this book may appear dry and uninteresting, but we trust (to borrow the words of an eminent reviewer) that the reading public of this country has not yet sunk so low as to be incapable of appreciating "works of original research," illustrative of the national history, because they are unavoidably wanting in dramatic elements....The number and variety of medals and coins connected with Cromwell which Mr. Henfrey has succeeded in discovering are very astonishing; some of these, indeed, exist only in one or two specimens. Ample descriptions of all, accompanied by collotype illustrations, are given, together with historical notes adequate enough to show their connexion with public events...The numerous autotype illustrations add much to the value of the work, being executed with unusual care and delicacy.

— J. J. Cartwright. Review of *Numismata Cromwelliana*. In *The Academy*. (August 11, 1877) London: J. Murray, 1877, pp. 150-151.

§

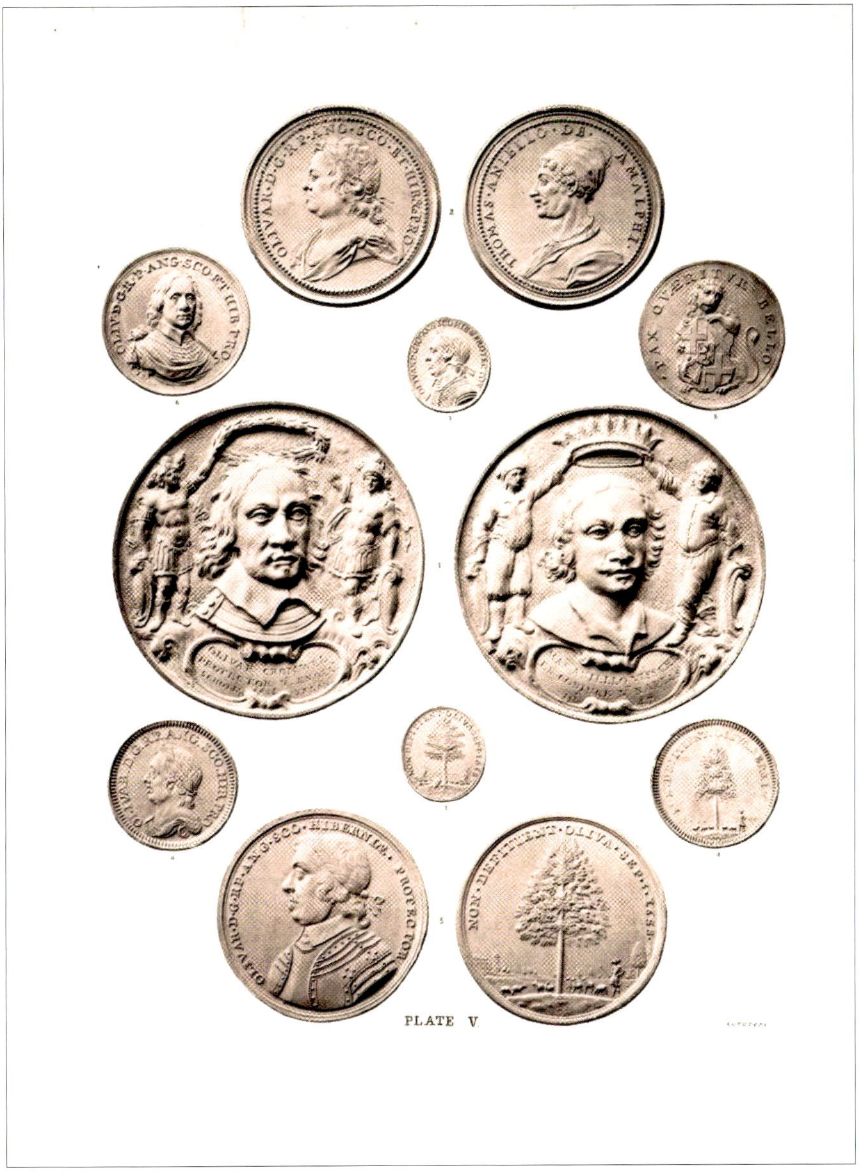

PLATE VI FROM *NUMISMATA CROMWELLIANA*. HENFREY'S ACHIEVEMENT IN COMPLETING THIS REMARKABLE WORK AT THE AGE OF TWENTY-FIVE IS HIGHLY DESERVING OF CREDIT. HENFREY'S DESCRIPTIONS OF THE MEDALS SHOWN ARE: (1) A 'DUTCH SATIRICAL MEDAL' (THE 'CROMWELL & MASANIELLO' MEDAL, M.I.I. 432/78, M.I.ILL XL/1, PLATT I/345/TYPE A) AND (2) ANOTHER (M.I.I.432/79, M.I.ILL XXXIX/11, PLATT I/346/TYPE C); (3) THE 'FUNERAL MEDAL' BY SIMON (M.I.I. 433/82, M.I.ILL XL/3, PLATT II/26/A); (4) 'FALSE FUNERAL MEDAL' (M.I.I. 434/84, M.I.ILL XL/5, PLATT II/26/B) AND (5), ANOTHER (435/85, M.I.ILL XL/4, PLATT II/26/C); (6) A 'FALSE INAUGURATION MEDAL' (M.I.I. 410/46, M.I.ILL XXXIII/9, PLATT I/340/C). HENFREY'S 'FALSE' DESIGNATIONS COULD ALSO HAVE BEEN APPROPRIATELY LABELED 'DUTCH COPIES,' THE PRIMARY INTENTION OF THEIR MAKERS MORE LIKELY HAVING BEEN TO SUPPLY A PERCEIVED MARKET IN ENGLAND FOR MEMENTOES AND REPRODUCTIONS RATHER THAN TO DECEPTIVELY SELL AS 'ORIGINAL' MEDALS.

§

Mr. Henry W. Henfrey exhibited three scarce contemporary pamphlets relating to King Charles I. This famous tract was reprinted in the Harleian Miscellany, London, 1810:

> "The King's Cabinet opened; or certain Packets of Secret Letters and Papers, written with the King's own hand, and taken in his Cabinet at Naseby-Field, June 14, 1645, by Victorious Sr Thomas Fairfax; wherein many mysteries of State, tending to the Justification of that Cause for which Sir Thomas Fairfax joyned battell that memorable day, are clearly laid open; Together with some Annotations thereupon. Published by speciall Order of the Parliament." London, 1645. Small 4to. 56 pages, and two portraits.
>
> This famous tract was reprinted in the Harleian Miscellany, London, 1810, vol. v, p. 514. Thomas Carlyle says: "The King's carriage was also taken, with a cabinet and many royal autographs in it, which, when printed, made a sad impression against His Majesty; gave, in fact, a most melancholy view of the veracity of His Majesty,—on the word of a king! All was lost."* It has been remarked that these letters equally prove "Charles' systematic insincerity, timeserving, double- dealing, arrogance, and thirst for revenge; and the reading of these letters is generally considered to have been as fatal to his cause as the field of Naseby where they were taken."
>
> *Vol. I, p. 191, 1871 ed. of *Oliver Cromwell's Letters and Speeches.*

—*Journal of the British Archaeological Association*, 1873, v. 29, p. 311.

§

To all those who pursue numismatic or historical studies we cordially recommend the *Numismata Cromwelliana*, or the *Medallic History of Oliver Cromwell*; illustrated by his coins, medals, and seals, by our able associate and auditor, Henry W. Henfrey, F. Roy. Hist. Soc., etc., author of a Guide to English Coins. In this work a complete historical description of all the coins, medals and pattern pieces of Oliver Cromwell is attempted for the first time. The general reader will also derive much information from the new light thrown upon the history of the Protectorate by these reliable witnesses, and may gain some idea of the beauty of those splendid specimens of seventeenth century art, hitherto unrivalled in any country, the works of Thomas Simon. The collector and student of English coins will find amongst the numismatic information, numerous facts, details, and elucidations which are absolutely unpublished; and the numerous autotype plates will furnish the first correct, and in some instances, the only illustrations yet published of many pieces. As only two hundred and fifty copies of the work will be printed, application should be made by those wishing to possess it to the author, 14, Park Street, Westminster.

—Review of *Numismata Cromwelliana...* In *The Journal of the British Archaeological Association*, 1873, v. 29, p. 443.

Discussing the development and spread of 'antiquarianism' Woolf notes that from the:

. . . LATE Elizabethan period, antiquaries and interested noblemen...and scholars... assembled cabinets of marvels and curiosities to adjoin and adorn their libraries...The size of such collections became an index of honour and intellectual sophistication...The genuine virtuoso had much in common with the antiquary; frequently including an appetite for objects such as coins and medals.

—Woolf, D. R. (2003). *The Social Circulation of the Past: English Historical Culture, 1500-1730,* p. 173.

MR. TAYLOR COMBE AND DR. CHARLES COMBE

THE MEDAL OF TAYLOR COMBE OF THE BRITISH MUSEUM BY BENEDETTO PISTRUCCI AND W. J. TAYLOR (46 MM., *B.H.M.* I/1258).

TAYLOR COMBE (1774-1826)

TAYLOR COMBE GRADUATED M.A. FROM ORIEL COLLEGE, OXFORD IN 1798. IN 1803, HE WAS APPOINTED TO THE BRITISH MUSEUM STAFF WITH RESPONSIBILITY FOR COINS AND MEDALS. IN 1807, HE WAS ADVANCED TO KEEPER OF ANTIQUITIES, WHILE STILL MAINTAINING RESPONSIBILITY FOR COINS AND MEDALS. COMBE WAS ELECTED TO MEMBERSHIP IN THE SOCIETY OF ANTIQUARIES (1796) AND THE F. R. S. (1806). HE MAINTAINED HIS APPOINTMENT AS KEEPER AT THE BRITISH MUSEUM UNTIL HIS DEATH IN 1826. HIS COLLECTION OF CLASSICAL AND NUMISMATIC LITERATURE AND PRINTS, ALONG WITH A FEW MEDALS, WAS SOLD AT SOTHEBY'S ON DECEMBER 7, 1826. TAYLOR COMBE WAS THE SON OF THE PHYSICIAN, NUMISMATIST AND RARE BOOK COLLECTOR DR. CHARLES COMBE.

CHARLES COMBE, M.D., F.S.A., F.R.S. (1743-1817)

DR. COMBE WAS A FRIEND OF WILLIAM HUNTER, THE ANATOMIST AND COLLECTOR, FROM ABOUT 1773. COMBE ASSISTED HUNTER IN ORGANIZING HIS COIN COLLECTION AND PROPOSED A CATALOGUE OF THE HUNTER COLLECTION, BUT ULTIMATELY COMPLETED ONLY ONE INSTALLMENT (*NUMMORUM VETERUM POPULORUM ET URBIUM QUI IN MUSEO GULIELMI HUNTER ASSERVANTUR DESCRIPTIO, FIGURIS ILLUSTRATA)*, WHICH WAS PUBLISHED IN 1782. THE PREFACE TO HIS WORK INCLUDES A HISTORY OF THE HUNTER COLLECTION. COMBE ALSO SOLD MANY COINS TO HUNTER AND HE WAS ONE OF THREE INDIVIDUALS APPOINTED BY HUNTER AS A TRUSTEE OF THE COLLECTION FOR A PERIOD OF 30 YEARS FOLLOWING HIS DEATH, AFTER WHICH THE COLLECTION WAS TO GO TO GLASGOW UNIVERSITY. DR. COMBE ALSO WROTE THE MEMOIR FOR THE REV. RICHARD SOUTHGATE THAT WAS APPENDED TO THE SALE CATALOGUE OF SOUTHGATE'S COLLECTION, AS WELL AS THE APPENDIX TO THE SECOND EDITION OF GEORGE VERTUE'S *MEDALS OF THOMAS SIMON*.

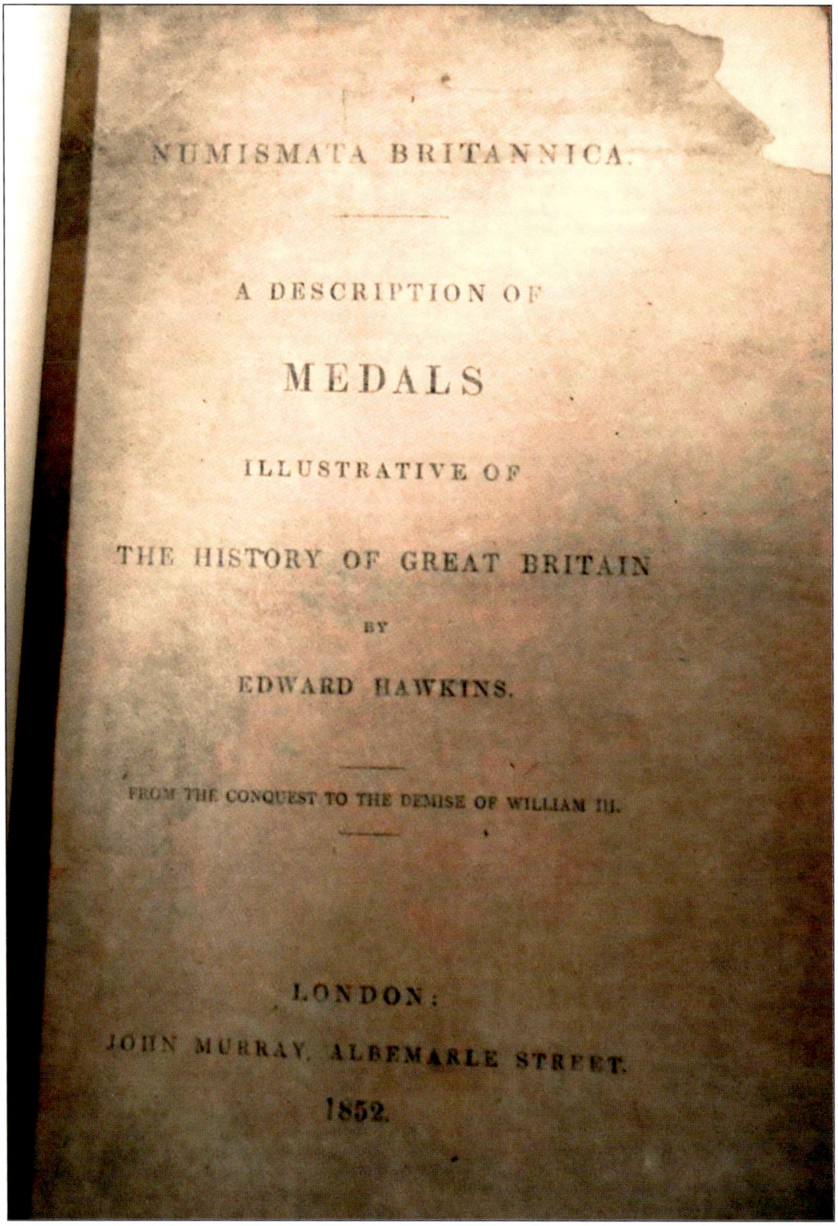

NUMISMATA BRITANNICA.

A DESCRIPTION OF

MEDALS

ILLUSTRATIVE OF

THE HISTORY OF GREAT BRITAIN

BY

EDWARD HAWKINS.

FROM THE CONQUEST TO THE DEMISE OF WILLIAM III.

LONDON:
JOHN MURRAY, ALBEMARLE STREET.
1852.

The title page of one of the very few surviving copies of *Numismata Britannica*, Hawkins' original work, which in 1852 was denied publication and ordered to be destroyed by the Trustees of the British Museum. Totaling 718 pages, this work included an index of die engravers in addition to a general index. The last medal for which there is an entry is for the death of William III in 1702. The final notation of the work is "End of vol. I," indicating that a second volume had been planned. Image courtesy Dept. of Coins & Medals, British Museum.

Edward Hawkins

(1780-1867)

EDWARD HAWKINS, whose name appears first on the classic work *Medallic Illustrations of Great Britain and Ireland to the Death of George II*, was appointed assistant keeper in the Department of Antiquities at the British Museum in May 1825. One year later, upon the death of the keeper, Taylor Combe,[156] to whom he had been deputy, Hawkins was advanced to that position, in which he remained for thirty-five years, retiring in 1860.

EDWARD HAWKINS, AUTHOR OF *NUMISMATA BRITANNICA*, THE PREDECESSOR TO *MEDALLIC ILLUSTRATIONS...*, WHICH IN **1852** WAS DENIED PUBLICATION BY THE TRUSTEES OF THE BRITISH MUSEUM. THIS WORK WAS LATER REVISED AND EXPANDED BY A. W. FRANKS AND H. GRUEBER AND PUBLISHED IN **1885**. IMAGE © TRUSTEES OF THE BRITISH MUSEUM.

Hawkins was the first-born son of Edward, a banker, and Ellen Hawkins. He received his education at the local grammar school and by private tutoring provided by George Ormerod, the vicar of Kensington. Upon completion of his education and following his commission in the local volunteer corps, Hawkins entered the work world through employment in his father's bank. Although he remained employed in a similar position and as a superintendent of a copper works until the age of forty-five, he displayed strong scholarly inclinations, first in botany, for which he was elected a fellow of the Linnaean Society, and as a collector of historical works on Chester. Elected a fellow of the Royal Society in 1821 and of the Society of Antiquaries in 1826, he was a founding member and president of the Numismatic Society of London.[157] In 1826, at age forty-six, Hawkins undertook the position of keeper of antiquities at the British Museum.

As keeper of antiquities, Hawkins successfully oversaw the expansion of what was then a department incorporating a broad spectrum of specialist areas, including coins, medals, prints and drawings. In a key position during the period of rapid expansion of the museum, Hawkins was a dynamic and exacting department head, often following his own lead rather than those of the museum trustees, a not totally unknown situation for the British Museum at that time.

---

[156] TAYLOR COMBE (1774-1826), keeper of coins and medals, and later of antiquities, at the British Museum. His father CHARLES COMBE, M.D., F.R.S. (1743-1817) is also mentioned in the preface to the first (1790) edition of John Pinkerton's *Medallic History of England (q.v. pp. 72, 76 and 85).*

[157] Blackburn, M. A. S. 'Edward Hawkins, (1780–1867),' *ODNB*, online ed., Oct. 2009.

Maintaining a scholarly output in numismatics, Hawkins produced two works of signal importance—*Silver Coins of England,* published in 1841, and *Numismata Britannica...*, both of which reflected the interest he had developed in the subject from the time of his appointment. He was, however, unable to obtain funding to publish *Numismata Britannica...*, a descriptive catalogue of British historical medals. The work was based on both his own and the Museum's collections. Hawkins had intended publishing it himself, but the British Museum decided to publish it. The work, the full title of which was *Numismata Britannica—A Description of Medals Illustrative of the History of Great Britain—from the Conquest to the Demise of William III,* was completed in 1852.[158] Hawkins then had it typeset, bound and printed, but the work was refused publication by the museum trustees due to Hawkins having expressed within it gratuitous controversial comments about historical figures, as well as "strong anti-Catholic sentiments."[159] The trustees found these comments unacceptable and ruled that they could not appear in a Government-sanctioned publication.[160] Further, when the printing was destroyed, in 1852, Hawkins was denied a copy for his own use. [161] Syson notes that this refusal led to questions being raised in the House of Commons by a member, John Ball:

> [Mr. Ball] would mention another instance of the gross mismanagement of the Trustees. A distinguished officer of the Museum, Mr. Hawkins, had for years been engaged in the preparation of an important work, illustrative of British history, at the request of the Trustees. The work was nearly completed, and had, in fact, gone through the press, when the Trustees decided that it was unfit for publication. The reasons assigned for this decision were various. Some said it was offensive to the adherents to the Stuarts, and others said it was offensive to the Roman Catholics, and a third party said it was offensive to the memory of William III., of whom the right hon. Member for Edinburgh (Mr. Macaulay) was so warm an admirer. But the most remarkable fact was, that Mr. Hawkins had literally been denied a copy of his own book, though he requested one, that he might correct or defend what was considered offensive. He might also state, that the scientific department of the Museum was in such a condition, that students could derive no instruction from the collections.[162]

It is not clear that raising this question accomplished anything at the time. In 1864, with the approval of Hawkins, now retired,[163] the then keeper of coins and medals, W. S. W. Vaux, and Augustus W. Franks, then in charge of Oriental Antiquities, again raised the matter of publication:

---

[158] Hawkins explicitly stated the purpose of the work in his foreword:

> The object of this work is to describe all the Medals, wherever executed, which illustrate the History of British Affairs or Persons.
>
> The subject of the Medal is pointed out, and the allusion of the device explained.
>
> Reference is made to Cabinets where the Medals described are to be found, or to Plates where they are represented.
>
> The sizes of the Medals are stated, and authorities given for the Medals in which they exist.
>
> The continuation of the Work is in progress.
>
> EDW. Hawkins, May 1852.

[159] Ibid. p. 2. Syson cites as examples:

> ...Mary Tudor's 'drivelling attachment to her cold-hearted husband' and said of General Fleetwood that 'as he was a great prayer monger, Cromwell thought that he would make a good tool for his hypocrisy' (*The Legacy of Edward Hawkins: Franks as Numismatist...,* In Caygill & Cherry, *A. W. Franks...*, 1997, p. 296).

[160] M.I.I, preface, vol. i, p. vi.

[161] Both L. Syson, in M. Caygill & J. Cherry (1997, p. 296) and *DNB* (1909, vol. 22, pp. 665-668) state that six bound copies of *Numismata Britannica* have survived, of which one copy is in the possession of the British Museum's Department of Coins and Medals (M. Jones, The Medal Collection of the British Museum. *The Medal*, 1985, no. 6, pp. 8-11).

[162] *Hansard's Debates,* July 3,1854.

[163] Hawkins submitted his resignation in October 1860, with an effective date of year's end. Upon his retirement, three new departments were formed from his previous purview.

> ...the Trustees will remember that when they decided on reprinting the volume in question, they obtained the consent of Mr Hawkins that his old friends Mr Vaux and Mr Franks should make such alterations in the suppressed edition as would remove the objections which the Trustees had entertained to the publication.[164]

The trustees granted permission to publish a revised and expunged version, and provided two copies of the original book for Vaux and Franks to work from, while Hawkins provided his original manuscript. A revised work was presented to the Trustees in 1861, but while Vaux was satisfied with it, this was not the case for Franks. Now, the delay reflected Franks' expressed need to examine original specimens in private collections in Britain and museums on the Continent of medals that Hawkins only knew through published descriptions.[165] Further, Franks obtained many of the electrotypes of rare medals in the present collection on his European trips. A second revised work, incorporating the new material, was presented to the trustees in 1870, which now approved it. However, this version, too, was not to reach the publication stage, and Syson suggests that:

ANOTHER PORTRAIT OF EDWARD HAWKINS, THE PRINCIPAL AUTHOR OF *MEDALLIC ILLUSTRATIONS....* A 1833 LITHOGRAPH BY MAXIM GAUCI AFTER THE ORIGINAL BY EDEN UPTON EDDIS. PUBLISHED BY THE BRITISH MUSEUM AND COLNAGHI, SON & CO. IMAGE © TRUSTEES OF THE BRITISH MUSEUM.

> ...One suspects that Franks himself recognized a lack of completeness and, with his now very personal commitment to the project, preferred to continue his researches.[166]

Franks was now over his head with professional commitments, and recognizing this, in 1881, he invited Herbert A. Grueber to help him complete the work. As Syson notes, Franks had indeed become very invested in the project, as may be gathered from the following excerpt from a letter written by him:

> The work in question is not merely a catalogue of the English medals in the Museum, but a general work on the subject, including all known specimens [...] with explanations of a general kind. It is not therefore a work on numismatics only, but one that will be of use to the student of English history.[167]

The final version of the revised work, now expanded to cover the period through the reign of George II, was not, however, to see publication until it was published in two volumes in 1885 as Hawkins et al.'s *Medallic Illustrations....* To Hawkins' authorship, the names of Franks and Grueber were added. Franks enriched the work in many ways, including information on medals in Continental collections. Incorporation of this material not only expanded the range of medals covered but also allowed for estimates to be made as to the relative scarcity of each medal.

[164] Ibid, p. 298, citing British Museum (Central Archive) *Officers' Reports*, 5 July 1881. W.S.W. VAUX (1818-1885) resigned from his post as keeper of coins and medals in October 1870 due to ill health.
[165] In fact, Hawkins had only been to the Bibliothèque Nationale in Paris.
[166] Syson, p. 299.
[167] Ibid. p. 299.

Grueber contributed his own additional research to the volumes, wrote the introduction, and prepared the indices.

The work was followed by a companion set of plates, with the same title, published between 1904 and 1911 and reissued by Seaby in 1979. Both remain the standard works on the subject to this day.

Hawkins and his wife Eliza had three sons and a daughter. He died in 1867, some six years after his retirement from the British Museum. His large collection of historical medals was purchased in 1860 by the British Museum. Although the Trustees were still hesitant to purchase it, its acquisition (upon its *third* offer by Hawkins) was quite a coup for the museum, given that it contained 4,347 medals while the Museum at that time owned only 1,581. The price of £2,288 8*s* 0*d* had been set some time before, in 1855, when Hawkins had first offered the collection to the British Museum, and had been refused.[168]

LINKS WITH THE PAST

To the Editor of THE TIMES:

Sir,—The late Mr. Edward Hawkins, of the British Museum, whom I knew well in my boyhood, used to tell his friends that when he was a child he was once touched—i.e., patted on the head—by Dr. Samuel Johnson. Dr. Johnson had himself been touched, for King's evil, by Queen Anne.

Your obedient servant,
R. A. Eden, M.A.
Vicar of Old Sr., Pancras,
Wilton Rectory, Salisbury,
Aug. 13.

—*The London Times*,
August 16, 1910

Historical Commentary on Edward Hawkins

We proceed to give a brief notice of some of the friends whom we have lost. First among these stands the name of Mr. EDWARD HAWKINS, F.S.A., who for many years took a warm interest in the affairs of this Society. From his early years he devoted much time and attention to the study of coins generally, and to the collection of a remarkably complete series of English medals (now in the National Collection). Hence, on the death of Mr. Taylor Combe, in 1826, he was deservedly appointed Keeper of the Antiquities in the British Museum—an office he held, greatly to the advantage of the students of Art as well as of Antiquities, till the end of the year, 1860. During the period of his Keepership, Mr. Hawkins published several valuable works on Numismatic subjects, all of which contain numerous plates, drawn with scrupulous accuracy under his own eye, chiefly by the late Messrs. Corbould and Fairholt. *As* such may be mentioned "An Account of the Anglo-Gallic Coins in the British Museum," and "The Silver Coins of England," which is still, and has been ever since it was published, the text-book on the subject. Mr. Hawkins also prepared and put in type fifteen years since a considerable portion of a complete history of all known English medals, under the title of "Numismata Britannica." This work, it is understood, is now in progress towards completion, and will shortly be made public. Mr. Hawkins was for many years Fellow and Vice-President of the Royal Society, Fellow and President of the Numismatic Society, and Vice-President of the Society of Antiquaries. To the *Transaction!* of each of the two last Societies he gave many valuable papers; and as keeper of his own department of the Museum, he contributed much to the efficiency and accuracy of the eighth, ninth, and tenth Parts of the "Account of the Ancient Marbles in the British Museum," printed between the years 1839 and 1845, at the expense of the Trustees.* He died at his house in Lower Berkeley Street, on the 22nd of May 1867, in the 88th year of his age.

* For this notice, we are indebted to the *Athenaeum* of June 15, 1867.

—*The Numismatic Chronicle and Journal of the Royal Numismatic Society*, 1867, vol. 7 (New Series), pp. 11-12.

[168] Ibid. p. 297.

Augustus W. Franks

(1826-1897)

SIR AUGUSTUS WOLLASTON FRANKS, K.C.B., joined the British Museum in 1851 as an assistant, with responsibility for overseeing the building of the Museum's collection of British and medieval antiquities, the establishment of which had been recommended that year by a royal commission. In this position, Franks reported directly to Edward Hawkins, then keeper of antiquities. In 1866, Franks was appointed keeper in the department of British and medieval antiquities. Upon Hawkins' retirement in 1860, his department was divided into oriental (i.e., Egyptian and Assyrian) antiquities, Greek and Roman antiquities, and coins and medals. A fourth department, British and medieval antiquities and ethnography, was amalgamated into oriental antiquities. Franks was initially in charge of this last entity, reporting to Samuel Birch, the keeper of oriental antiquities. Franks was subsequently keeper, and then senior keeper of his department, which included coins and medals, from 1866 until 1897. The success of the endeavors of Hawkins and Franks can be judged by the fact that their purview is now reflected in five current museum departments—medieval and later antiquities, prehistoric and Romano-British antiquities, ethnography, oriental antiquities and coins and medals.[169]

ONE OF TWO KNOWN BOOK PLATES ASSOCIATED WITH AUGUSTUS WOLLASTON FRANKS. THE ABOVE PLATE WAS CREATED BY THE SOCIETY OF ANTIQUARIES OF LONDON FOR INSERTION IN BOOKS INCLUDED IN HIS BEQUEST TO THE SOCIETY. THIS LIKENESS IS FROM THE ONLY KNOWN PHOTOGRAPH OF FRANKS. FRANKS AND HERBERT A. GRUEBER PREPARED THE FINAL VERSION OF EDWARD HAWKINS' *MEDALLIC ILLUSTRATIONS OF THE HISTORY OF GREAT BRITAIN AND IRELAND*, PUBLISHED IN 1885. THE LEGEND "BEQUEATHED TO THE SOCIETY OF ANTIQUARIES OF LONDON. BY SIR AUGUSTUS WOLLASTON FRANKS. PRESIDENT, MDCCCXCII-XCVII." IMAGE COURTESY OF ANTHONY PINCOTT AND THE BOOKPLATE SOCIETY.

Franks was born in Geneva to Captain Frederick Franks, a naval officer, and his wife, Frederika Anne. The family moved to Rome in 1828 and then to London in 1843. Born into a wealthy family, both his mother and father were collectors, the former of pictures, and the latter, trained as a chemist, of minerals. Further, as Franks himself noted in one of the few letters of his which have sur-

[169] M. Caygill & J. Cherry (1997). *A. W. Franks, Nineteenth Century Collecting and the British Museum.* London: Trustees of the British Museum.

vived, that a family history of collecting could be traced back through a number of generations.[170] Franks received his education at Trinity College, Cambridge, from which he was awarded his B.A. (1849) and M.A. (1862) degrees, and developed an interest in antiquarian studies, publishing his first paper while still at the university.

FRANKS' PERSONAL BOOKPLATE, DISPLAYING HIS FAMILY ARMS. FRANKS' MOTTO APPEARS *ABOVE:* NUNC MIHI MOX ALIIS ('NOW TO ME, SOON TO OTHERS'). DESIGNED BY C[HARLES] W[ILLIAM] SHERBORN (1831-1912), WHO UTILIZED THE SAME BASIC DESIGN FOR BOOKPLATES OF OTHER INDIVIDUALS AS WELL. SHERBORN ALSO EXECUTED THE PORTRAIT OF FRANKS WHICH APPEARS ON THE BOOKPLATE ON THE PRECEDING PAGE. IMAGE © TRUSTEES OF THE BRITISH MUSEUM.

In 1849, Franks established himself in London, where he quickly became active in antiquarian pursuits, including serving as honorary secretary of the Medieval Exhibition of 1850. He apparently did this job well. The Exhibition's sponsor, the Society of Arts, in whose rooms it was held, awarded him a life membership. From his early days at Cambridge, Franks was intensely involvement in professional societies, having been one of the founders of the Cambridge Architectural Society and an early member of the Cambridge Antiquarian Society and the Royal Archeological Institute. Additionally, he was active in the Society of Antiquaries. A polymath and eminent scholar, and widely recognized as such, his interests spanned the gamut from oriental glass and sculpture to Hans Holbein and Anglo-Saxon rings. Being independently wealthy, Franks purchased items for the museum utilizing his own funds, in addition to using the funds allotted for this purpose by the trustees. Additionally, he frequently donated items from his own collections to the museum. He also traveled throughout Europe to visit other museums, and although he did not like to speak in public, he did what was required of a leading scholar of his time.[171]

Although Franks was not primarily a numismatist, he recognized the value of coins, medals, tokens, jetons, and counters as possessing valuable information for historical researchers, particularly with respect to social history. This area was one of those in which he donated a number of important items from his own collection to the Museum. Soon after his arrival at the British Museum, he spent time in the medal room, serving in the place of absent members of staff. Here he found a productive use for his time, initially arranging the token collection and editing the exist-

---

[170] A. W. Franks. "The Apology of my Life," in M. Caygill & J. Cherry (1997), ibid. appendix 1, pp. 318-324. This letter, reprinted in its entirety, serves as an brief autobiography, in the absence of a more formal one, which given Franks' private nature, would have been an unlikely undertaking.

[171] D. M. Wilson, *The Forgotten Collector...*; *DNB*, 1909, vol. 22, pp. 665-668. L. Syson, 'The Legacy of Edward Hawkins: Franks as Numismatist.' In M. Caygilll & J. Cherry (eds.) (1997) *A. W. Franks: Nineteenth-century collecting and the British Museum...*, pp. 296-307.

ing catalogue of British medals.[172] Despite his handing over responsibility for coins and medals to William Vaux in 1861, Franks never lost interest in numismatics. In fact, he worked to convince the trustees that gaps in both the medal and coin collections, now incorporating those items purchased from Edward Hawkins, be filled upon availability at sales. Here again, he likely purchased as many medals (and other acquisitions) out of his own pocket as did the museum; one of those he secured being the John Kendal medal, the earliest known portrait medal of an Englishman (ca. 1480, *see Platt & Platt,*[173] *vol. i, p. xvi*).

Later in life, he served as president of the Society of Antiquaries. He declined appointment as principal librarian, and he twice declined appointment as director of the South Kensington Museum (now the Victoria and Albert Museum). He was also offered the directorship of the British Museum but declined this office as well. His honors included creation as K.C.B., honorary doctorates from both Cambridge and Oxford, fellowship in the Royal Society, antiquary to the Royal Academy, and following his retirement in 1896, he was appointed a trustee of the British Museum.

A WOOD ENGRAVING OF AUGUSTUS W. FRANKS FROM *THE ART JOURNAL ILLUSTRATED*, 1891, P. 167. IMAGE COURTESY VICTORIA & ALBERT MUSEUM.

Franks never married, living in a house on museum property, and finding friendship through his club, the Athenaeum, and a circle of influential individuals, both within and outside of the government. Unlike his museum and professional activities, and public honors, almost nothing is known about his private life. He died in 1897, renowned for his contributions to the British Museum and the antiquarian sciences. A dedicated collector-scholar to the end, his obituary notes that:

> He had in hand at the time of his death a catalogue of the enamels in the British Museum—one of his favorouite subjects.[174]

In his will, he bequeathed almost his entire personal collection, comprising some 3,300 pieces, to the Museum, as well as a smaller number of items to other museums. His contributions to the Museum overall were highly significant, and even his modesty did not prevent his summarizing them as follows in his *Apology*:

> So much for the British Museum and its collections. I think I may fairly say that I have created the department of which I am now Keeper, and at a very moderate cost to the country. When I was appointed to the Museum in 1851 the scanty collections out of which the department has grown occupied a length of 154 feet of wall cases, and 3 or 4 table cases. The collections now occupy 2250 feet in length of wall cases, 90 table cases and 31 upright cases, to say nothing of the numerous objects placed over the cases or on walls.[175]

---

[172] Syson, in Caygill & Cherry (eds.), *A. W. Franks…*, 1997, p. 297.
[173] J. J. Platt & A. K. Platt (2013). *The English Civil War: Medals, Historical Commentary & Personalities*, London: Spink (2 vols.). Subsequent citations of this work will be referred to simply as 'Platt.'
[174] Obituary of Sir A. W. Franks. *London Times*, May 24, 1897.
[175] Franks, *Apology*, in Caygill and J. Cherry, Appendix 1, p. 324.

Historical Commentary on Augustus W. Franks

If Franks's first interests were not numismatic, he nevertheless contributed substantially to the study of British medals, tokens and counters. His scholarship in the area has remained underrated because, to a great extent, it lies hidden in a book which bears the name of Edward Hawkins. His first Keeper was his dominant influence but, in a quiet way, Franks added an extra dimension to Hawkins's work by his investigation of technique and artistry...

— L. Syson, "The Legacy of Edward Hawkins: Franks as Numismatist," in Caygill & Cherry (eds.), *A. W. Franks*..., 1997, p. 301.

§

In the Notes of the Month in the Antiquary for June we announced the re-election, on St. George's Day, of Sir A. W. Franks as president of the Society of Antiquaries. This announcement in our pages would only reach our readers after they had already learnt from the daily newspapers of Sir Augustus Franks's death. In him the Society of Antiquaries has lost one of the most distinguished antiquaries who have filled the presidential chair. It is not too much to say that the death of the president of the Society of Antiquaries is an irreparable loss. Sir A. W. Franks's profound knowledge was always at the service of others, and his decision on any point was at once accepted as final. It had only to be reported that Sir A. W. Franks assigned a particular character or date to an object for the matter to be accepted as settled. The writer remembers a remarkable instance of the kind which occurred a few years ago. An exhibition of maces and civic insignia was being held at the rooms of the Society of Antiquaries, and among the objects in the room was the crystal mace or sceptre belonging to the city of London. Mr. Franks (as he then was), holding the sceptre in his hands and carefully examining it, startled the meeting of the Society by stating that the greater portion of the mace was of Saxon date. Suppressed murmurs of astonishment greeted the announcement, and it was thought by many that the word "Saxon" was a *lapsus lingua* on the part of the speaker, who, however, repeated the statement with measured emphasis of enunciation. No one ventured to dispute his verdict, and the more leisurely examination by other experts has subsequently confirmed the judgment which was then passed at the time, at sight, by Mr. Franks as to the date of the very beautiful and remarkable object in question.

—Obituary in *The Antiquary*, July 1897, pp. 193-195.

§

Among our home Members, there is no one whose loss is more deeply and universally deplored than my life-long friend and in several capacities colleague Sir Augustus Wollaston Franks, the President of the Society of Antiquaries. Although a rare attendant at our meetings, and the author of but one communication to the Chronicle, he was an active and warm supporter of the study of numismatics. The paper I have mentioned added nearly 250 new varieties to the London Tradesmen's Tokens of the sixteenth century; but the important share that he took in preparing the Medallic Illustrations of British History for the press has a far higher claim upon our gratitude. In this exhaustive work he was assisted by our Secretary, Mr. Grueber. The Society will remember the account of a remarkable hoard of about 240 Anglo-Saxon coins from the time of Offa to that of Æthelwulf, communicated to us in 1894. The whole of this hoard was, with his accustomed liberality, added to the National Collection by Sir Wollaston Franks, but this is a mere trifle when compared with the marvelous treasures which he from time to time presented to the Museum and those which he has bequeathed to it. This is not the place to dilate upon his wonderful stores of knowledge, ever at the disposal of students, of his critical acumen and his powers of organization. Far less can I speak of his devoted friendship and the kindliness of his disposition. To many besides me his loss is incalculable and irreparable. For forty- five years he devoted the whole of his time and the bulk of his income to forwarding the interests of the British Museum and improving its archaeological collections, and his services to the Society of Antiquaries have also been unbounded. I may mention that in 1884 he had a medalet struck, with his crest and motto on the obverse and his name and family arms on the reverse, which he gave to his more intimate friends as a kind of numismatic memorial, which will now be doubly treasured. On it his university degree is recorded as M.A., but Cambridge, his alma mater, subsequently conferred upon him the degree of Litt.D., and Oxford that of D.C.L. He was born on March 20th, 1826, and died on May 21st, 1897, having been for thirty-six years a member of this Society, and for forty-four years a fellow of the Society of Antiquaries.

— Obituary in the *Numismatic Chronicle and Journal of the Numismatic Society*, Third Series. vol. xvii, pp. 23-24.

Historical Commentary on *Medallic Illustrations*

The review of *Medallic Illustrations* by Robert Vaughan
(The British Quarterly Review, 1886, vol. 82, pp. 162-163)

In these two portly volumes we have almost a consecutive history of England as told by our medals, from the time when these commemorative works of art were first introduced into this country in the reign of Henry VIII., to the death of George II., when medallic art ceases to possess much artistic value, and the medals become so numerous that several more volumes would be required to complete the catalogue. Although this is essentially a technical work, full of minute descriptions of devices and inscriptions, we have found it singularly interesting. In the first place there is an interest about medals which does not belong to mere coins. They are issued to place on record the great events and the great persons, the golden deeds and worthies, of our history; and these are things which possess a perennial charm for us all. The medal which was engraved at the very time the Spanish Armada was dispersed, with the laconic comment, 'The Spanish fleet came, went, was '—*Classis Hispanica venit, ivit, fuit*—is as interesting as that record of the rector of Carisbrook in the Isle of Wight who was so excited by the sight he witnessed one morning from the hill that he inserted a note in his parish register that the Armada had just sailed by. It may be said that hardly an event of importance after the accession of Elizabeth is left unrecorded in our medallic series; battles, treaties, statesmen, court ladies, soldiers, divines, martyrs, authors, all have their appropriate medallic record, generally with curious allegorical allusions, if events, and if persons, with speaking portraits. The quaint devices of many of the medals, notably those that have relation to the various attempts of Papists upon England— such as the Armada, the murder of Godfrey, the supposed trick about the birth of the elder Pretender, &c.—are often exceedingly humorous; while the legends or inscriptions that accompany these ingenious representations are instructive as showing the feeling of the time, and are not seldom in themselves amusing. But perhaps the chief charm of English medals lies in their portraits. Inferior to the engravers of Italy, the English medallists, or rather the foreign artists who as a rule made the English medals, were frequently men of remarkable genius, and bore a high reputation for fidelity to their originals. The extensive series of portraits of the leaders on both sides in the Civil War by such masters as the two Simons, Rawlins, and Briot, the medals of the beauties of the court of Charles II by Roettier and others, possess a high artistic value and cannot fail to interest the reader. The student of English history will find these volumes indispensable, and those who can take them with them to the British Museum and compare them with the splendid exhibition of medals now to be seen in the north gallery will learn much that is new and fascinating. It is needless to say that a work executed by such authorities as Messrs. Franks and Grueber is well done. The descriptions are clear and accurate, the historical notes appended to each medal, principally due to Mr. Grueber, are particularly able and careful, and the illustrations, though hardly numerous enough, are well engraved. The work forms a valuable addition to the publications of the Department of Coins and Medals, which already number nearly thirty volumes.

Herbert A. Grueber

(1846-1927)

HERBERT APPOLD GRUEBER, as a member of the Department of Coins and Medals at the British Museum, became involved in preparing *Medallic Illustrations...* in 1881 at the invitation of Augustus W. Franks who, by that point in his career, was fully occupied by his professional commitments. Grueber's assistance, including preparation of the introduction and indices, ensured that the volumes finally reached publication. Subsequently, Grueber undertook the preparation of the 'Plates' for publication.

HERBERT A. GRUEBER, WHO PREPARED THE SET OF PLATES (M.I.ILL) TO ACCOMPANY M.I. PUBLISHED BETWEEN 1904 AND 1911 AS A 19-PART SERIES OF ELEPHANT SIZE PORTFOLIOS OF UNBOUND PLATES. THE PLATES WERE REPRINTED, BOUND IN A SINGLE VOLUME, IN 1979. IMAGE © TRUSTEES OF THE BRITISH MUSEUM.

Grueber was the son of the Rev. and Mrs. Charles Stephen Grueber. Ordained in 1840, the Rev. Grueber was the vicar of Hambridge, Winchester, and a prolific author. Like his father, Herbert Grueber was also a prolific author. In addition to the preparation of *Medallic Illustrations...*, he was the author of *Roman Medallions in the British Museum* (1874); *A Guide to the Exhibition of British Medals* (1881; 2nd ed., 1891); *A Catalogue of English Coins in the British Museum. Anglo-Saxon Series. vol. ii., Wessex and England to the Norman Conquest* (1893); *Handbook of the Coins of Great Britain and Ireland in the British Museum* (with C. F. Keary, 1899);[176] *A Guide to the Department of Coins and Medals in the British Museum* (with B. V. Head, W. Wroth, and E. J. Rapson, 1901); and *Coins of the Roman Republic in the British Museum* (1910).

Grueber became keeper of Coins and Medals in 1906 and continued in this position until 1912. In 1909, he was awarded the medal of the Royal Numismatic Society. His correspondence and papers relevant to his interest in Egyptian archeology are at the National Archives at Kew.

> MEDALS serve for two purposes, for the illustration of history and as records of the contemporary state of the art. Some series, like that of Italy have more interests for their artistic merit than their historical import [...] but in the English and Dutch series the interest lies rather in their historical value than in the artistic qualities, the medallic art of neither country attaining at any time any high degree of excellence... [The medals] must therefore be considered interesting chiefly as records and illustrations of the History of England.
>
> —H. A. Grueber, *A Guide to the Exhibition of English Medals* (2nd ed.), 1891, Introduction, p. vii.

[176] GRUEBER and [CHARLES F.] KEARY'S methodology in compiling this work has relatively recently come under some criticism. Stewart (in Bell, 1981), in reviewing the history of Scottish numismatics, suggests that Grueber's classification of English coinage did not take heed of the then recent advances by Scottish numismatists (pp. 244-245).

Edward Hawkins, Augustus W. Franks, & Herbert A. Gruber's

Medallic Illustrations of the History of Great Britain and Ireland to the Death of George II

(1885; 1969)

THE most important works on the subject of British historical medals in general are Hawkins, Franks and Grueber's revised version of Hawkins' comprehensive *Medallic Illustrations of the History of Great Britain and Ireland, to the Death of George II* ('M.I.,' 1885; reprinted by Spink & Son in 1969), and Gruber's accompanying set of plates or 'illustrated companion,' of similar title ('M.I.ILL,' 1904-1911, 1979).[177] The latter consists of 183 large folio-sized plates with brief descriptions, published in 19 parts by the British Museum between 1904 and 1911, and in a single folio-sized volume, by Seaby, in 1979. Both works, M.I.ILL and M.I.I, are true classics in the field, and the 'gold standard' against which all subsequent works must be measured. Further, in their scope and comprehensiveness the *Medallic Illustrations* volumes are likely to remain preeminent for many years to come.

The importance of *Medallic Illustrations* compels that the story of its conception and publication be retold. Hawkins (1780-1867), assistant-keeper from 1826 and then keeper of antiquities and coins in the British Museum, a position that he held until his retirement in 1860, completed a substantial part of the work for the first two volumes some three decades before their actual publication. The final work was to include:

> ...descriptions of all medals at present known that illustrate the history of Great Britain and Ireland to the end of the reign of George II., whether struck in this country or abroad, whether relating to public works or private persons, and whether contemporary or executed at a later date[178]

This statement gives some idea of the wide breadth of the work's intended scope. Indeed, the fact that this goal was well met in terms of the available knowledge of the time reflects great credit upon the authors. A good part of this work, to the end of the reign of William III, was completed by Hawkins and printed in 1852. However, in that the work was to be a publication of the British Museum, and thus indirectly of the Government, the trustees' feelings were that it contained "some strictures upon public characters"[179] and thus should not be published. In 1864, upon again coming before the trustees, and its value being recognized, it received a more sympathetic reception.

The judgment was made, however, that some revision was necessary. Sometime later Hawkins consented to this to be undertaken by Augustus W. Franks, keeper of British and medieval antiquities, and W. S. W. Vaux, the then keeper of coins and medals. In his revision of the work,

---

[177] With the exception that the volume of plates omits "*to the Death of George II*" from the title.

[178] Franks, A. W., preface, p. v. In E. Hawkins, A. W. Franks, and H. GRUEBER (1885; 1969). *Medallic Illustrations of the History of Great Britain and Ireland to the Death of George II* (vols. I and II). The full title of Hawkins' original work was *Numismata Britannica: A Description of Medals Illustrative of the History of Great Britain.*

[179] *See the biography of Hawkins, pp. 87-90.*

MEDALLIC ILLUSTRATIONS

OF THE HISTORY OF

GREAT BRITAIN AND IRELAND

TO THE

DEATH OF GEORGE II.

COMPILED BY THE LATE

EDWARD HAWKINS, F.R.S., F.S.A.,

AND EDITED BY

AUGUSTUS W. FRANKS, F.R.S., F.S.A.,

AND

HERBERT A. GRUEBER.

VOL. I.

ORIGINALLY PUBLISHED BY

THE TRUSTEES OF THE BRITISH MUSEUM

1885

AND REPRINTED BY

SPINK & SON LTD.

1969

THE TITLE PAGE OF VOL. I *OF MEDALLIC ILLUSTRATIONS*, AS REPRINTED IN 1969. THIS WORK, WHEN ORIGINALLY PUBLISHED IN 1885, WAS A REWRITTEN AND EXPANDED VERSION OF HAWKINS' ORIGINAL WORK, *NUMISMATA BRITANNICA...*, WHICH WAS REFUSED PUBLICATION BY THE BRITISH MUSEUM TRUSTEES BECAUSE OF THE "POLITICAL AND PARTISAN REMARKS" WHICH IT CONTAINED. THE TITLE PAGE OF THE 1885 EDITION IS IDENTICAL TO THAT OF THE REPRINT WITH THE EXCEPTION THAT THE PUBLICATION INFORMATION READS: "PRINTED BY ORDER OF THE TRUSTEES OF THE BRITISH MUSEUM." IT ALSO LISTS THE VENUES WHERE THE WORK COULD BE PURCHASED: THE BRITISH MUSEUM, LONGMAN'S & CO., B. QUARITCH, A. ASHER & CO., TRŰBNER & CO., AND C. ROLLIN & FEUARDENT.

Franks expanded the scope of the work both in terms of the number of medals included, with some 446 medals being added, including some examples from cabinets on the Continent, as well as extending coverage through the end of the reign of George II in 1760.[180] Finally, in 1885, with the assistance of H. A. Grueber, assistant keeper of coins, who participated in the completion of the work particularly that part involving medals subsequent to the reign of William III, the work saw publication.[181]

Grueber began work on the accompanying "illustrated companion" volume of the same title in 1904 and this work was published by the British Museum between 1904 and 1911. As noted above, it was a series of 19 folders of individual plates, typically in sets of three parts of ten plates each, the plates having been prepared and the letterpress upon which they were printed having been set up by the Oxford University Press. The two-volume set of *Medallic Illustrations…* (hence referred to respectively as 'M.I.I' and 'M.I.II') was reprinted by Spink & Son, Ltd. in 1969, while, as noted above, the companion volume of plates (hence referred to as 'M.I.Ill') was reprinted in 1979 as a single volume of folio size by Seaby Publications in association with the British Museum.

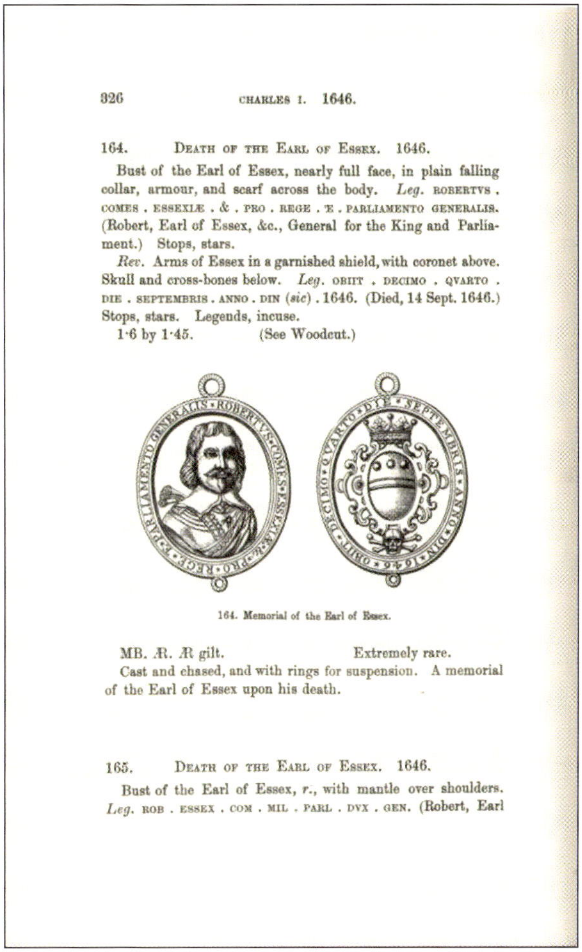

326 CHARLES I. 1646.

164. DEATH OF THE EARL OF ESSEX. 1646.

Bust of the Earl of Essex, nearly full face, in plain falling collar, armour, and scarf across the body. *Leg.* ROBERTVS . COMES . ESSEXIÆ . & . PRO . REGE . E . PARLIAMENTO GENERALIS. (Robert, Earl of Essex, &c., General for the King and Parliament.) Stops, stars.

Rev. Arms of Essex in a garnished shield, with coronet above. Skull and cross-bones below. *Leg.* OBIIT . DECIMO . QVARTO . DIE . SEPTEMBRIS . ANNO . DIN (*sic*) . 1646. (Died, 14 Sept. 1646.) Stops, stars. Legends, incuse.

1·6 by 1·45. (See Woodcut.)

164. Memorial of the Earl of Essex.

MB. Æ. Æ gilt. Extremely rare.

Cast and chased, and with rings for suspension. A memorial of the Earl of Essex upon his death.

165. DEATH OF THE EARL OF ESSEX. 1646.

Bust of the Earl of Essex, *r.*, with mantle over shoulders. *Leg.* ROB . ESSEX . COM . MIL . PARL . DVX . GEN. (Robert, Earl

A PAGE FROM VOL. I OF THE 1969 REPRINT OF THE 1885 EDITION OF M.I. THE REPRINT IS IDENTICAL TO THE ORIGINAL EDITION. THERE ARE A MODEST NUMBER OF ILLUSTRATIONS APPEARING THROUGHOUT THE TEXT. OF PARTICULAR INTEREST IS THE NOTATION IDENTIFYING COLLECTIONS WHERE EXAMPLES HAD BEEN FOUND TO RESIDE—IN THE CASE OF THIS 'EXTREMELY RARE' MEDAL, EXAMPLES WERE ONLY TO BE FOUND IN THE BRITISH MUSEUM ('MB') COLLECTION—ALTHOUGH IN BOTH SILVER AND SILVER-GILT.

[180] It is interesting to note that FRANKS observed that one of the reasons for only including medals through the reign of GEORGE II was that "…the medals of the reign of GEORGE III are almost as numerous as all the preceding series." This comment is well illustrated by COLONEL M. H. GRANT's listing of British medals since 1760, published in the *Numismatic Circular* between 1936 and 1941, which contains some 9,900 medals, three times the number listed in *Medallic Illustrations.*

[181] op cit.

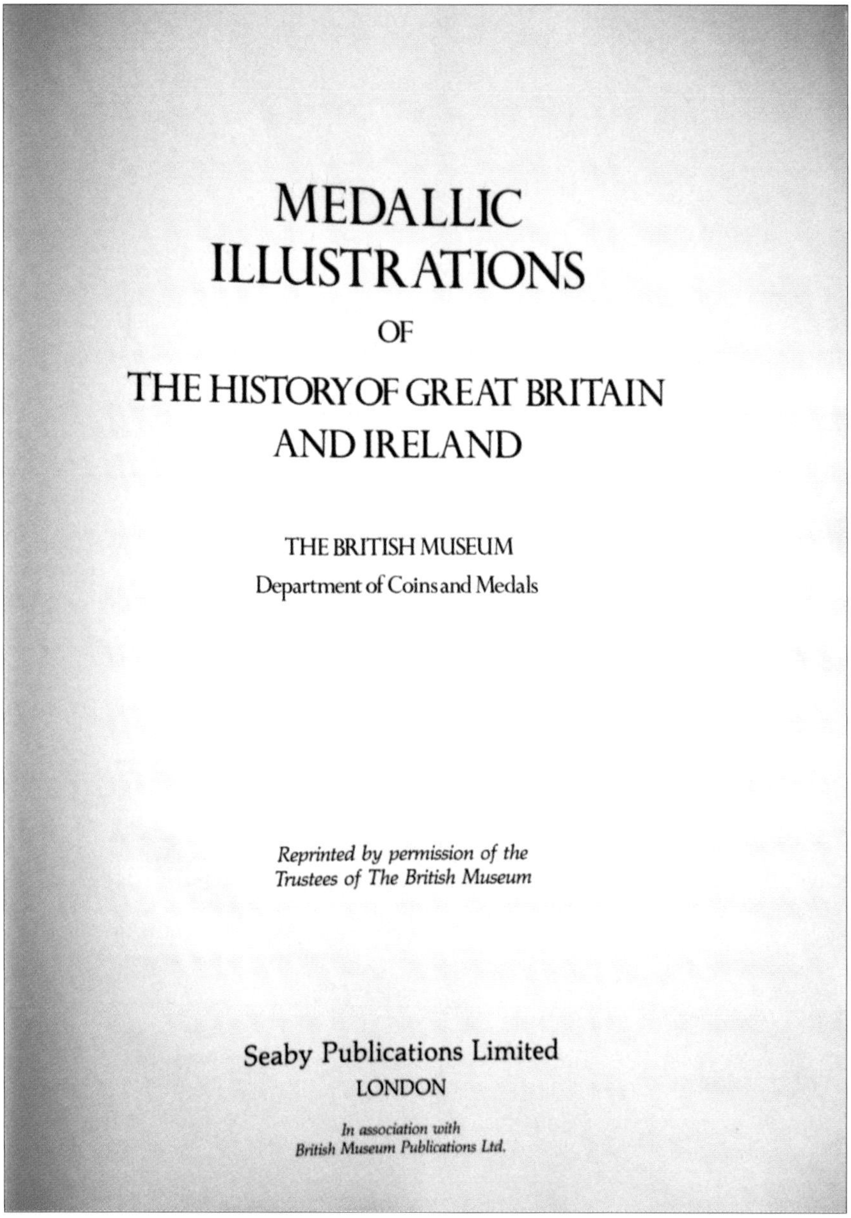

MEDALLIC ILLUSTRATIONS OF THE HISTORY OF GREAT BRITAIN AND IRELAND

THE BRITISH MUSEUM
Department of Coins and Medals

Reprinted by permission of the Trustees of The British Museum

Seaby Publications Limited
LONDON

In association with British Museum Publications Ltd.

The original set of 183 folio size plates to accompany Hawkins et al's *Medallic Illustrations* was published by the British Museum between 1904 and 1911. It consisted of 18 fascicules of ten plates each plus the indices. Illustrated above is the title page of the set of plates bound into one volume as reprinted by B. A. Seaby in 1979. Another identical volume of the bound plates, also dated 1979, was issued in the USA by Quarterman Publications Inc. The two bound volumes are folio size and identical with the exception of the publisher's name on the title page.

Herbert Gruber's
MEDALLIC ILLUSTRATIONS
OF THE
HISTORY OF GREAT BRITAIN AND IRELAND
—'THE PLATES'

(1904-1911; 1979)

Historical Commentary on '*M.I.—The Plates*'

Unsigned review from the *Saturday Review of Politics, Literature, Science and Art* of June 10, 1905, Vol. 99, pp.776-777.

BRITISH HISTORICAL MEDALS.

"Medallic Illustrations of the History of Great Britain and Ireland: Plates I.-XXX. Edward III. to Charles I." With a preface by H. A. Grueber. Published by the Trustees of the British Museum. 1904-5. 22s. 6d.

IT is now just twenty years since the authorities of the Coin Department of the British Museum published their " Medallic Illustrations of the History of Great Britain and Ireland" in four solid volumes. In 1885 the art of reproducing the aspect of coins and medals by means of the collotype process had not been invented, and the only illustrations that were to be found in the book were woodcuts, which gave in many cases a very poor idea of the originals. They were moreover few in number, and only reproduced unique or unpublished medals. To-day the improved methods of photography enable the British Museum to supplement the original "Medallic Illustrations" with a full set of plates, figuring every piece of importance; the first thirty of them, which cover the period down to the death of Charles I., are now before us. They are admirably executed, as indeed are all the illustrations of the later publications issued by the Museum. They cannot fail to be useful to every student of history, as well as to the medal collectors—a class that can never be very numerous, on account of the expensiveness of their pursuit, for medals, unlike coins, are seldom issued in large numbers, and the individual specimen is hard to find and costly to purchase.

It seems, at the first glance, a pity that this splendid series of plates could not be published in book-form, so as to enable it to be placed on the shelf alongside of the volumes of text which it illustrates. But a moment's reflection shows that the system adopted—that of large portfolios containing ten plates apiece—was necessary. For many early medals are so large that they could not have been reproduced on an ordinary octavo page— No. 3 of Plate I. for example is five inches broad. There was no possibility therefore of printing the illustrations in volumes uniform with the "Medallic Illustrations". It is an unfortunate but inevitable result that there will always be a certain difficulty in using the text and the plates together. It is comparatively simple to refer from the photographs to the printed description in the volumes of 1885, but the reverse process is not so easy. The text, published twenty years before the complementary plates, contains (of course) no cross-reference to them, and the student loses a certain amount of time in ascertaining the precise plate in which the medal that he is investigating is to be found. Sometimes, indeed, he will not find it at all; for there are many items in the catalogue which are not illustrated. But in such cases the student may console himself by reflecting that if the particular medal is not to be found in the plates, it must be either unimportant, badly preserved, or not contemporary with the person or event that it commemorates. For the editors have, very wisely, resolved not to illustrate any medals that were not struck at the time to which they purport to belong. We search in vain for reproductions of Passe's or Dassier's memorials of early Plantagenet monarchs, or for representations of King Alfred, Chaucer, William of Wykeham, Wycliffe, or other worthies whom eighteenth-century medallists delighted to honour with apocryphal portraits.

This exclusion from the plates of all pieces which are not contemporary forces on our attention, in an almost startling way, the lateness of the date at which the custom of striking commemorative medals was introduced into England. All the best of the Italian series had appeared, and decay in

PLATE LVI OF THE SET PREPARED BY HERBART A. GRUEBER TO ACCOMPANY *MEDALLIC ILLUSTRATIONS*. AS THE IMAGES OF MEDALS WERE MADE USING THE COLLOTYPE METHOD, THEY ARE OFTEN LESS THAN PERFECT REPRODUCTIONS, PARTICULARLY WHERE A MEDAL EXHIBITED WEAR. THE MEDALS ILLUSTRATED IN THIS PLATE ARE, HOWEVER, FOR THE MOST PART, IN HIGH RELIEF, THUS ALLOWING GOOD QUALITY REPRODUCTIONS. UNFORTUNATELY, THE 1904-1911 ISSUE OF PLATES WAS PRINTED ON WOOD-PULP PAPER WITH A HIGH ACID CONTENT AND/OR TREATED WITH BLEACH; THUS THEY ARE FOUND BROWNED AND OFTEN BEGINNING TO FLAKE AND CRUMBLE AT THE EDGES.

the medallic art was already setting in beyond the Alps, before a single real native medal had been issued on this side of the Channel. To all intents and purposes we may say that it was only in the reign of Henry VIII. that they began to be struck. Of the seven items that form the first plate of the first portfolio, all attributed to dates before 1509, not one can be called, in any true use of the word, a genuine English medal. Two of the pieces are mere "jetons" or reckoning-counters, employed in the treasury of Edward III.: there is nothing medallic or commemorative about them. Two are medals with portraits of British worthies—Sir John Kendal (a knight of Malta) and Archbishop Scheves of S. Andrews, but both were struck abroad, the one in Italy and the other in Flanders. Another, that of Federigo, Duke of Urbino, represents a foreign prince and was struck in his dominions, having no connexion with England save that it commemorates his nomination by Edward IV. to the honourable place of a Knight of the Garter. One, the supposed marriage-medal of Henry VII., is (as the editor confesses) wrongly attributed, and belongs in reality to a series of pieces struck at Prague about 1500: it contains no reference whatever to the union of the Two Roses. There remains only the interesting and peculiar medalet which is commonly known as "Perktn Warbeck's Groat". This is a small silver piece with the arms of England, the royal badges, the date 1494, and the inscription "Mene, mene, Tekel, Phares". It was usually said that Henry VII. was the person who is declared to be "tried in the balance and found wanting", and that the medalet was issued by the partisans of Warbeck, and circulated as a badge when he was preparing for his final invasion of England. But it must be confessed that there is no certain proof that this was the case, and the piece may be merely a jeton with a scriptural motto, like many others that have no political meaning. Even if we think that the juxtaposition of the inscription and the date suggests a connexion with Warbeck, we must still concede that the token would certainly have been struck not on this side of the Channel, but by Margaret of Burgundy somewhere in the Netherlands. For it was the Duchess who organised and financed all the impostor's plots, and, if such badges were ever issued, they would certainly have been made in one of her mints and then sent across to England.

The true series of British medals therefore commences with Henry VIII. in England and with James IV. in Scotland, and the fine silver piece with a portrait of the latter sovereign, which forms the first item in Plate II., must be regarded as the forerunner of all the innumerable tribe. There are some fine issues under Henry VIII. and Edward VI., but they are comparatively few in number, and it was only under Elizabeth that the custom of commemorating any important event by a medal became well rooted in this country. Excluding specimens struck in Holland, or elsewhere, in compliment to Elizabeth, there remains a large and interesting series of undoubtedly English work, which grows more and more numerous as the reign draws to a close. But the golden age of English medallic art was undoubtedly the time of Charles I., when not only did the engraver of the royal mint strike many scores of pieces, but private persons were in the habit of issuing and distributing similar memorials of themselves. When the Civil War broke out in 1642 we have another series added- the long list of military badges and rewards issued both by the King and by the Parliament. Despite the troublous times these nearly always display most beautiful and artistic work. The Simons, who worked for the Parliament, and Rawlings who dwelt at Oxford and struck the king's issues, were artists of the highest merit. Their medals are nearly always in high relief, and the subjects, whether portraits or allegorical scenes, are treated in a bold and realistic style, which contrasts most favourably with the pretty but shallow and commonplace pseudoclassical art of the succeeding generation. For with the accession of Charles II. the English medals fell into line with those of the continent, and both the portrait busts and the reverses begin to show that servile copying of the ancient Roman coinage which was the distinguishing mark of the succeeding age. The student will find the very best of the English issues in Plates XXV.-XXX., though there are good pieces still to come in the as yet unpublished Part IV., which will contain Cromwell's medals, and other excellent productions of that admirable artist the younger Simon.

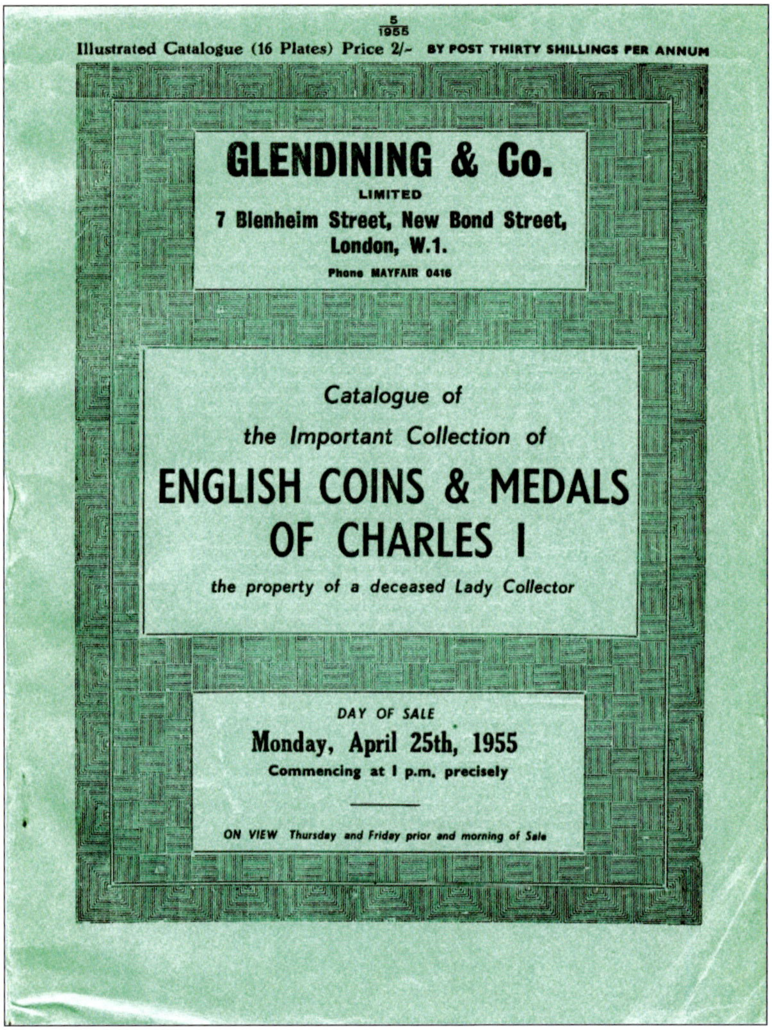

THE CATALOGUE FOR THE APRIL 25, 1955, SALE AT GLENDINING'S OF MS. HELEN FARQUHAR'S MEDAL COLLECTION. THE GREATER PART OF THE COLLECTION WAS SOLD AT THIS AUCTION UNDER THE ATTRIBUTION "THE PROPERTY OF A DECEASED LADY COLLECTOR." OTHER ITEMS FROM HER COLLECTION WERE DONATED TO THE BRITISH MUSEUM.

Helen Farquhar[182]

(1869-1953)

•On Tudor and Stuart Coins and Medals•

A most useful body of work more broadly focusing on the medallists of the 17th and 18th centuries and the medals and coins they designed and produced is Helen Farquhar's series of articles entitled *Portraiture of our Stuart Monarchs on their Coins and Medals,* which appeared in seven parts in the *Numismatic Chronicle* between 1909 and 1915. Farquhar also authored several articles on Nicholas Briot (1914), the 'Forlorn Hope' medal (1930), and the Shrewsbury medal (1929), as well as a series of articles that dealt with Thomas Simon's life and work (1929-1936), all of which appeared in the *Numismatic Chronicle*. The authors have encountered references to collections of Ms. Farquhar's articles bound into a single volume, published by Harrison & Sons in 1917.

Farquhar, a true scholar-collector of medals, was primarily concerned with the medals of the Tudor and Stuart periods, in particular the portraiture of the Stuart monarchs on coins and medals, and only secondarily focused on other medals of the Civil War period. Miss Farquhar was a founding member of the British Numismatic Society and a life member of the Royal Numismatic Society. For her contributions in numismatics, she received the John Sanford Saltus Medal of the B. N. S. in 1911, and in 1931, the gold medal of the R. N. S. During this period, Helen Farquhar's address was 11 Belgrave Square, a letter having been addressed to her there on December 8, 1913. Later, her address is indicated at 6 Lowndes Street, SW1 (letter dated January 23, 1933). Ms. Farquhar was a very private person, and attempts at learning further details about Ms. Farquhar's life, or to obtain a photograph of her, have met with failure.

The British Museum holds Ms. Farquhar's notebooks, which contain a list of the medals in her collection and the prices paid for them as well as casts in plaster of her collection of medals, which the authors have had the privilege of viewing. Fifty choice pieces from her collection were donated to the British Museum, where they now reside in the museum's collection. The greater part of her medal collection, comprising over 200 pieces was, however, sold at auction at Glendenning's' on April 25, 1955, under the attribution, "The Property of a Deceased Lady Collector."

Historical Commentary on Helen Farquhar

BRITISH NUMISMATIC SOCIETY.—*March* 25.—Mr. Carlyon-Britton, President, in the chair—Miss Helen Farquhar contributed a comprehensive and interesting treatise, from both the historical and the numismatic points of view, on "Artistic Portraiture of our Tudor Monarchs on their Coins and Medals." By means of contemporary descriptions of the personal appearance of the several monarchs, and photographic reproductions of portraits, and medals, preserved in the national and some well-known private collections, Miss Farquhar demonstrated how close is the relationship between certain portraits of the Tudors painted by the artists of the period and the representation of them on their coins and medals. Miss Farquhar's method was applied with particular success in the case of the coins issued by Henry VIII. in 1526. On these coins the King's head is presented in profile, and he is represented as clean shaven, which was not his custom. Miss Farquhar gave reasons for thinking that he really had discarded his beard for a short time at about that date; similarly she was able to adduce evidence for the belief that the beautiful medal of Elizabeth—"Medallic Illustrations," No. 129 —was the work of Nicholas Hilliard, the miniaturist, goldsmith, and carver to the Queen.—

[182] HELEN FARQUHAR qualifies as *both* an author *and* as an 'eminent collector in the present work.'

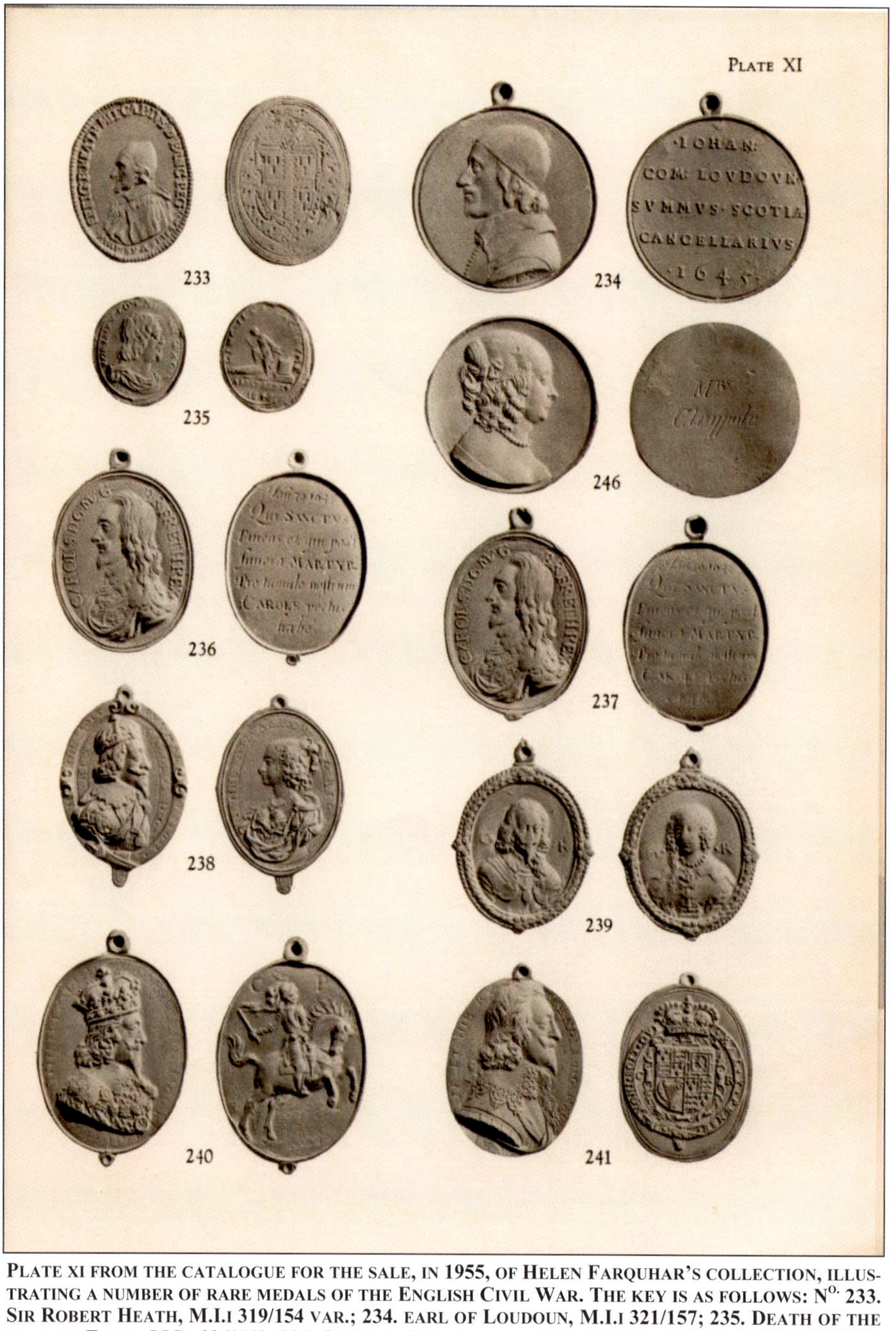

PLATE XI FROM THE CATALOGUE FOR THE SALE, IN 1955, OF HELEN FARQUHAR'S COLLECTION, ILLUSTRATING A NUMBER OF RARE MEDALS OF THE ENGLISH CIVIL WAR. THE KEY IS AS FOLLOWS: N^O. 233. SIR ROBERT HEATH, M.I.I 319/154 VAR.; 234. EARL OF LOUDOUN, M.I.I 321/157; 235. DEATH OF THE EARL OF ESSEX, M.I.I 326/165; 236. CHARLES I MEMORIAL, M.I.I 344/194; 237. *IBID.*, M.I.I 355/217; 238. CHARLES I AND HENRIETTA MARIA, M.I.I 355/217; 239. *IBID.*, M.I.I 257/222; 240. EDGEHILL, M.I.I 299/119; 241. CHARLES I, M.I.I 360/231; 246. ELIZABETH CLEYPOLE, M.I.I 430/74.

Exhibits: By Lieutenant-Colonel Morrieson, a series of shillings, groats, and half-groats of Henry VII., Henry VIII., and Mary, and silver coins of Elizabeth. By Mr. Max Rosenhein, a bronze gilt medal of Queen Mary, by Jacopo Nizolo da Trezzo, having FIDEI DEFENSATRIX added to the regal style; a leaden medal of Mary and Philip, by the same; a bronze gilt medal by Giovanni Cavino, of Padua, struck by command of Pope Julius III. to commemorate the marriage of Philip and Mary, and bearing the words ANGLIA RESURGENS on the reverse; a bronze medal of Henry VIII. of uniface, by a Dutch or German artist; a bronze medal, likewise unifacial, of Sir John Cheke (IOANNES CHECVS), the tutor of Prince Edward, designed by a medallist of Padua, where Cheke lectured in 1555; a miniature on vellum, and a cameo in onyx of Flizabeth; and a case of mathematical instruments made by Bartholomew Newsum, the Queen's clockmaker, perhaps for the Queen's own use. By Mr. S. M. Spink, six testoons of Henry VIII. and Edward VI., two of which were severally countermarked in Queen Elizabeth's reign with a greyhound and a portcullis, in order that they might serve for 2-1/4*d.* and -1/2*d.* respectively; shillings of Edward VI., Philip and Mary, and Elizabeth, one of the latter Queen's being milled and of small type; a pattern shilling and a pattern sixpence of Elizabeth, with a key and a mullet as mint-marks respectively.

—*The Antiquary*, 1908, vol. xliv, p. 193.

§

BRITISH NUMISMATIC SOCIETY.—*May* 20.—...The deterioration of the bronze coinage of the realm in the early part of the seventeenth century was commented upon, and the recent discovery, among abstracts of the State Papers of 1630, of a petition to King Charles I., made by the engraver Briot, was announced by Miss Helen Farquhar. In this petition Briot begged for leave to set up engines in the Tower in order to improve the coinage of bronze and prevent counterfeiting by hand. The acts of encroachment upon the minting rights of the Crown were so numerous that Mr. A. H. Baldwin estimated that not fewer than 15,000 different tokens were in currency during the seventeenth and eighteenth centuries. The practice was widely spread, and Mr. A. W. Barnes exhibited a collection of eighty-eight tokens of the seventeenth century current in Bedfordshire alone. Mr. L. Clements exhibited specimens of all the tokens issued in the Isle of Wight—forty-seven in number. In addition to these, he exhibited 228 specimens of Hampshire tokens, dating from 1652 onward, out of the 241 published, together with 50 others, of the same county, regarded as unique...

—*Ibid. p.* 271.

§

D.F.A. writes:—

With the recent death of Miss Helen L[aura] Farquhar, London, at the age of 93, this country has lost a distinguished figure in the study of seventeenth-century art and portraiture. Miss Farquhar started to take a keen interest in numismatics in 1903. She soon established a reputation at home and abroad as an authority on medals and *objects d'art* of the Stuart period. Her magnificent collection of medals, badges, touchpieces, and coins of the period is now bequeathed to the British Museum, where, by her wish, it is to remain intact for a period before incorporation into the general series. Her books and articles, especially on Tudor and Stuart portraiture and on touchpieces, will long remain standard works of scholarship.

Miss Farquhar was easily the *doyenne* of British numismatists. She was awarded the medals of both the Royal and British Numismatic Societies, and is the only woman ever to have had this honour. On her ninetieth birthday she was presented with a special testimonial from the Royal Numismatic Society. She was the last survivor of the generation of British numismatists which flourished before and after the first world war. Her many younger friends will always remember her with affection as a very great lady.

—*The London Times*, January 12, 1953.

§

BY the death of Miss Helen Farquhar, F.R.Hist.S., on 3 January1953, in her 94th year, the Council have lost [sic] one of their own body and the Society one of its most popular and valuable members. As possibly I may now be one of Miss Farquhar's oldest numismatic friends, yet I fear that no pen of mine can adequately do justice to her character, her vast knowledge, and her kindly disposition that endeared her to the Society...

Miss Farquhar was one of the Founder Members of the British Numismatic Society in 1903 and became one of the Life Fellows of the Royal Numismatic Society (or the Numismatic Society as it then was) in 1904. In being awarded the John Sanford Saltus Medal of the British Numismatic Society in 1911, and the Royal Numismatic Society Medal in 1931, Miss Farquhar became one of the three noted numismatists to receive the much-coveted awards of the two societies...Miss Farquhar had the proud distinction of being the first lady to receive the Royal Numismatic Society Medal. In 1950 she was elected to Honorary Membership of the British Numismatic Society. From the beginning Miss Farquhar was an enthusiastic supporter of the movement which inaugurated the Society and she retained that enthusiasm until the last. She was ever a generous supporter of the funds, but what can we say of her contributions in the matter of papers? Truly her works were a remarkable achievement! ... her total output during the heyday of her production was well over 1,100 pages. All this was the result of valuable and original research over ground that to the best of my knowledge and belief had never been broken before. Yet, if my memory be not at fault, all this was probably the result of a casual conversation between herself and the late W. J. Andrew—who was her sponsor into the Society. She was dilating on her interest in Stuart relics, &c., and the outcome of this conversation was that Mr. Andrew persuaded her to write a paper for the *Journal.* What an example of the proverb "From small beginnings come great things"!

From the...titles [of her papers], it will be readily seen how ardent a Stuart Royalist was Miss Farquhar. She had sound judgment and a knowledge of the Carolian and late Stuart coins, medals, and relics which was both deep and scholarly, and perhaps second to none. For many years she was a very regular attendant at the meetings, and as most of the years she was either on the Council or a Vice-President. [Her] counsel at the meetings was frequently sought and generously given, especially in regard to her knowledge of Stuart art and relics, &c. In later years her frail constitution, coupled with her very advanced years, claimed their limitations. Her genial disposition and popular personality will long be remembered by members of the Society, especially the older members who knew her for so many years. The Society, therefore, will mourn the loss of an accomplished and gracious lady and one that it was a privilege to have known.

—H. W. T[affs]. Obituary. *British Numismatic Journal*..., 1952-1954, vol. 27, pp. 101-102.

Two Rare Medals from Ms. Helen Farquhar's Collection

Helen Farquhar's splendid collection of coins and medals was dispersed after her death, with the greater part (over 225 items) being sold at Glendining's auction on April 25, 1955. Previously, in 1939, fifty choice items had been bequeathed to the British Museum. The two items shown above represent one medal from each disposition—the uniface openwork silver Royalist badge, ca. 1649, by Thomas Rawlins having gone to auction and the medal of Henry Cromwell by Abraham Simon having gone to the British Museum. Images © Trustees of the British Museum.

The details of the two medals are as follows: *(Left)* in silver, 46.5 x 32.5 mm., ca. 1649 (M.I.i and M.I.Ill: no entry). This medal possesses elements similar to three other medals: M.I.i 368/253; xxxiii/4 and M.I.i 301/122; pl. xxvi/8; Platt i/298/type B; and Farquhar, *Numismatic Chronicle*, 5th ser., v. 10, pl. XXIII/ I. This medal also possesses two small lugs or rivets for attachment on the reverse, possibly for adornment to a book or snuff box. *(Right)* Medal of Henry Cromwell, in silver, 28 x 22 mm., ca. 1654, M.I.i 412/49, M.I.Ill xxxvii/12, British Museum acc./reg. no. 1939,0703.1. This is a very rare medal of which only two original examples are known:

> ...one was Mr. Tyssen's, the other was in the possession of the late J. Delafield Phelps, Esq., Chavenage House, Gloucestershire (M.I.i, pp. 412-413).

Other Works on 17th-century British Medals

· A Brief Review of the Literature ·

ASIDE from Evelyn, Vertue, Snelling and Pinkerton's respective works in book form and *Medallic Illustrations ...*, there are few other works on seventeenth century British medals which could be considered 'classics,' if such status is reflected by their early dates, and continued recognition and usage over a period of centuries, even where some of their usefulness has become antiquated. Perhaps the major exception to this group is Helen Farquhar's series of articles on medals of the Stuart monarchs, as well as on the medallists Thomas Simon and Nicholas Briot, published in the early 20th century. In the case of Farquhar's works, these have been in use in excess of one century since their appearance, and in the case of Evelyn, Vertue, Snelling and Pinkerton, two to three centuries. There are, however, a number of other works that should be known to the collector or scholar of seventeenth century medals. These include volumes which more generally deal with British military medals but touch upon medals of the seventeenth century, even if only briefly. First, there are the late-nineteenth century works. Among these are John Horsley Mayo's *Medals and Decorations of the British Army and Navy* (1897), George Tancred's *Historical Record of Medals and Honorary Distinctions Conferred Upon the British Navy, Army, & Auxiliary Forces, from the Earliest Period* (1891) and Carter & Long's *War Medals of the British Army, 1650-1891* (1893). There is also the earl of Sandwich's later *British and Foreign Medals Relating to Naval and Maritime Affairs* (1939). The primary focus of these volumes is on British military and naval medals from the East India series through the Victorian period. The volume by Mayo, who died in 1895, with the work having been seen through publication by a nephew, does provide very useful detail on perhaps some one hundred medals and badges authorized or awarded during the reigns of James I through James II, including some not seen very often. These include, for example, Lord Lambert's jewel (1659), and the jewel awarded to the Swedish ambassador (1656). Tancred's volume only briefly touches upon seventeenth century medals. It is useful with respect to the naval and military medals, often unique, awarded to officers other than those with which we are usually familiar. These include awards during the reigns of James I through James II, the Parliamentarian medals and gold chains, and other rewards (usually monetary) awarded or authorized for award for land or sea service.[183] Carter & Long's volume is focused on 19th century awards.

Leonard Forrer's (1869-1953) work, *Biographical Dictionary of Medallists,* published in eight volumes beginning in 1904, the last of which appeared in 1930. This work provides a basic biographical reference source for information on those medallists who worked during the seventeenth century, as well as a chronological listing of their medallic productions. However, given the breadth of the work—500 B.C. through 1900 A.D.—it is not surprising that 17th century medallists occupy only a relatively small niche.

There are also other, more recent works, which are directly relevant to the subject of seventeenth century medals, but these generally focus on the Civil War through Commonwealth periods. Alan J. Nathanson's *Thomas Simon, his Life and Work, 1618-1665* (1975) is a brief but interesting work describing the life and career of this medallist, including both his work on coins and the great seals of the Commonwealth as well as those of Charles II. It also covers the impact upon the mint of Peter Blondeau's mechanization techniques from 1649 when he arrived in England. For a

[183] This distinction is made because in a number of cases, it is doubtful that the awards, although authorized, were actually received by the intended recipients.

number of reasons, however, his innovative mechanization techniques[184] for improving the production of coinage were not implemented in a meaningful way until 1656 when Oliver Cromwell contemplated a new coinage. Simon and Blondeau then collaborated in this work—Simon responsible for the design, and Blondeau, the production. Nathanson draws heavily upon the works by Vertue, Henfrey, and Farquhar, as well as the *Calendar of State Papers* in the Public Record Office, which is the primary (sometimes the sole) source of information for some of the medals and badges of the mid-17th century period. Unfortunately, relatively little information has survived regarding the life of Thomas Simon (and even less concerning his brother, Abraham), Nathanson brings together what is known in a highly readable and informative volume.

Edward Besly's *Coins and Medals of the English Civil War* (1990) focuses on the mints and coinages of the Civil War period, placing them "within the context of the time."[185] During this period there were two mints—the Royalist and Parliamentarian respectively—the former primarily being at Oxford. It was here that the Forlorn Hope 'badge' and a number of commemorative badges or medals were struck. These included those for the reunion of Charles I and Henrietta Maria at Kineton, the capture of Bristol, the medal of Sir William Parkhurst (the mint master at Oxford), and the unique award to Sir Robert Welch for rescuing the king's standard at Edgehill. The Parliamentarians, having taken possession of the Tower Mint in 1642, gained the main prize, and with it, many of the mint's highly skilled pre-war employees, including Thomas Simon. Simon had been apprenticed to Edward Greene, chief engraver, and jointly with Edward Wade had been advanced to Greene's position at his death in 1645. It was at the Tower Mint that the military rewards of the earls of Essex and Manchester, Ferdinando Fairfax and his son Sir Thomas Fairfax, and Sir William Waller were designed and produced. This well-illustrated and informative volume focuses primarily on the coins and secondarily on the medals of the Civil War period. This is quite understandable as the design and manufacture of medals occupied only a very small part of the activities of the several mints during this period, at least during their official working hours.

In addition to the works described above, there are also a number of journal articles that should be of interest to the collector of the 17th century period and numismatic scholar alike. By their very nature, articles can only effectively communicate in-depth information about more circumscribed issues—and usually these are specific medals or series of medals. Among these must be mentioned Besly's article on the 'Forlorn Hope' award which appeared in *The Medal* in 1991, and Marvin Lessen's series of superb articles on the Cromwell Dunbar, lord general, and funeral medals by Simon, as well as the Commonwealth naval medals of 1653, all of which appeared in the *British Numismatic Journal*. Lessen was the first to apply rigorous modern scientific methodology to the study of English Civil War medals.

Finally, there are a number of modern 'catalogues' or 'compendiums' (as opposed to *auction catalogues*, another very useful source of descriptive information) dealing with either historical or military medals or a combination of the two. Some of these are particularly useful for details and illustrations of medals of the Civil War period, as well as for information about the relative scarcity of medals and their provenance. These include Christopher Eimer's *British Commemorative*

---

184 At the time BLONDEAU arrived in England, coins were still being hammer-struck. Among the techniques which he introduced were milling and an improved method for the engraving of edge inscriptions on coinage. Upon OLIVER CROMWELL's death, Blondeau returned to France in 1658, only to have THOMAS SIMON sent there by CHARLES II in November 1661 to induce him to return to England. Blondeau did return with Simon in January 1662, when he was appointed engineer of the mint. Simon at this time was by now embroiled with the ROETTIERS brothers, who had come to England in Simon's absence to assist in the preparation of dies for the new coinage (*See also the entries for* PIERRE (PETER) BLONDEAU *and* THOMAS SIMON *under 'Medallists,'*).

185 E. Besly (1990). *Coins and Medals of the English Civil War*. London: Seaby/National Museum of Wales, 1990 p. v.

Medals and their Values (1987), an excellent survey of the entire series of British historical medals, a superbly illustrated second edition of which appeared in 2010. Eimer's work is a modern illustrated catalogue of the series of British medals in its full breath, and while valuable for its detail for the medals it presents, it is not inclusive with regard to all issues, which is not surprising, given the astounding 13,000 British medals that have appeared up to 1941.

Other helpful works are Daniel Fearon's *Spink's Catalogue of British Commemorative Medals, 1558 to the Present Day* (1984) and Michael Mitchiner's *Jetons, Medalets, and Tokens: British isles, 1558 to 1830* (vol. 3) which is useful in regard to jetons and counters in addition to medals of this period. Jetons, of course, are the primary focus of this volume, but some medals are also covered, as is the evolution of the medalet from the jeton. [186] Finally, and certainly not least of these works, is the important three-volume work on British commemorative medals by Laurence Brown—*British Historical Medals 1760-1960*—the writing of which Brown undertook to remediate the lack of reference works on the subject. More specifically focused on military medals, particularly those issued since the late 18th century, is Major L. L. Gordon's *British Battles and Medals,*[187] which has been the standard work on British military medals since its initial publication in 1947, and a sampling of seventeenth century medals is included.

Also very valuable are the sales catalogues for the 'Great Sales' of collections of 17th c. medals which have taken place at London auction houses—Sotheby's, Christie's, Glendining's, Bonham's, Seaby's and Baldwin's, among others. Most recently, two other auction houses—Morton & Eden and Woolley & Wallis—have held sales of large 17th c. medal collections. The major sales will be reviewed later in this volume.

Unfortunately, neither in these volumes or elsewhere is there much in the way of information relating to the commissions, instructions, and orders for *manufacture, bestowal* and *actual award* of medals during the 17th century. There are, happily, a few exceptions to this general state of affairs. There is clear documentation, for example, relating to the authorizations for both the Civil War period Forlorn Hope and Dunbar medals,[188] as well as for the 'jewels' presented to prominent high ranking individuals. There are also the awards for those officers and men whose gallant behavior came to the attention of sufficiently high levels of authority where awards could be authorized. Examples of both exist as well. The Forlorn Hope and Dunbar medals[189] are analogous to gallantry and campaign medals respectively under the present British system, while the 'jew-

---

[186] According to the *Oxford English Dictionary (OED)*, 'jeton' is a term of 13th or 14th c. origin applied to:

> ...a piece of metal, ivory, or other material, bearing an inscription or device, formerly used as a counter in casting up accounts or in card-playing.

Although in general use in England before the 15th century, jetons began to be struck in England about this time, and were more widely produced during Elizabethan times. The majority of those still in use during the latter part of this period were imported from the Continent, especially Nuremberg. By the early seventeenth century, cast and chased silver jetons were in wide use in England, although by the Civil War, this use declined significantly with the increased use of Arabic numerals in general accounting. Mitchiner notes that from the time of Charles I, the jeton evolved into a means of disseminating information or served as a presentation piece, thus evolving into the medalet. For the reader wishing more information on the topic of jetons, Mitchiner (1998) should be consulted.

[187] Most recently revised and published in 1988 under the editorship of E. C. Joslin, A. R. Litherland, and B. T. Simpkin. A seventh edition, edited by John Hayward, Diana Birch and Richard Bishop has since been published in 2006.

[188] There exists a royal warrant describing the intent of the Forlorn Hope medal, and a Parliamentary order authorizing the Dunbar medal.

[189] The only *known* surviving examples of the Forlorn Hope medal are in the collection of the National Museum of Wales (E. Besly, personal communication) and the British Museum, respectively. With respect to the Dunbar medal, Lessen, who has intensively studied these medals, is of the opinion that there are likely three original large medals (one gold, two silver) and six small medals in existence (two gold, one silver, one copper, one pewter, and one "silverish;" although he is not certain as to the authenticity of the last two). The British Museum collection contains the small gold, copper and pewter medals.

els' were unique awards somewhat analogous to present day orders. However, while documentation exists for the authorization of the Forlorn Hope and Dunbar medals, further information relating to the *actual awards* of both is generally lacking,[190] and it is of course just this information that is craved by the student of medals.[191] On the other hand, because of their very uniqueness and award to prominent commanders, information is available regarding authorization for the jewels in the form of royal warrants. Additionally, the British Museum recently acquired a small Fairfax medal in gold, with the accompanying citation, signed by Sir Thomas Fairfax.

•The History of Book Auctions•

"ADVICE TO THE BIDDER"

ALTHOUGH THE EARLIEST KNOWN BOOK AUCTION IN EUROPE APPEARS TO HAVE TAKEN PLACE IN HOLLAND IN 1599, THE PRACTICE DID NOT REACH ENGLAND UNTIL OCTOBER 31, 1676. THE FIRST SALE IN ENGLAND WAS OF THE LIBRARY BELONGING TO THE LATE 'REVEREND AND LEARNED DIVINE, DR. LAZARUS SEAMAN, SOMETIME VICE-CHANCELLOR OF CAMBRIDGE, MASTER OF PETER-HOUSE, AND LATE MINISTER OF THE GOSPEL IN ALL HALLOWS, BROAD STREET.' 'MR. MILLINGTON, THE NOTED AUCTIONEER, CONDUCTED THE SALE...' THE READER MAY FIND THE INTRODUCTION TO 'THE TERMS' OF THE SALE TO BE OF INTEREST.

READER,

It hath not been usual here in *England* to make Sales of BOOKS by way of *Auction, or who will give most for them*: But it having been practiced in other Countreys to the Advantage of Buyers and Sellers; It was therefore conceived (for the Encouragement of Learning) to publish the Sale of these Books this manner of way; and it is hoped that this will not be unacceptable to Schollars; and therefore we thought it convenient to give an Advertisement concerning the manner of proceeding therein.

—British Museum Trustees (A. W. Pollard, ed.). *List of Catalogues of English Book Sales, 1676*-1900. (1915), pp. ix-x.

[190] This should perhaps not be surprising since these medals would have been awarded to the nameless 'other ranks,' comprised of 'ordinary' individuals for whom, in most cases, little or no documentation of their existence is available. The Civil War period is the time at which individuality first began to be evidenced for members of the 'underclass,' from which most private soldiers were recruited. To some extent, this change is a result of Renaissance humanism appearing in works by fifteenth century writers such as THOMAS MORE (1478-1535) and THOMAS CROMWELL (earl of Essex, ca. 1485-1540), who as principal adviser to HENRY VIII (1532-1540) drafted most of the Reformation acts of the 1530's and implemented suppression of the monasteries. Thomas Cromwell was eventually accused of treason and beheaded. OLIVER CROMWELL was descended from Thomas' sister KATHERINE, and during the Civil War, Thomas' descendants fought on the Royalist side. The emphasis here is on 'first began,' as it is likely that the overwhelming majority of the upper and middle classes likely did not yet subscribe to this point of view.

The absence of records concerning the Forlorn Hope other than the original warrant (as well as for other Royalist medals), may be due to the destruction of all records of the Oxford Mint in a fire in 1644. In general, however, record-keeping of the period was rather haphazard at best, and as much of the actual work on medals was done by mint employees privately in other than normal work hours, official records may never have existed.

[191] Of course, one never knows what medal or badge-related document may emerge from obscurity, and this is just one more reason that the subject is so fascinating.

Medallists associated with 17th Century British Historical Medals

The *Oeuvre* of Nicholas Hilliard

The iconic 'Dangers Averted,' medal (1589) by Nicholas Hilliard, specifically commemorating the defeat of the Spanish Armada in 1598, and more broadly, both Queen Elizabeth I's ascendency in the domestic sphere and England's ascendency in Europe. While this particular medal was crafted in the late 16th century, it deserves inclusion as an example of Hilliard's mastery of medallic art. ***Obv. legend translation***: 'No other circle in the whole world so rich.' ***Rev. legend***: 'Not even dangers affect it' (in gold, 58 x 52 mm., M.I.i 154/130, M.I.Ill xi/9, Eimer 61A, British Museum acc./reg. no. 1866,1218.1). Only two examples in gold are known to exist—one in the British Museum and another in the Fitzwilliam Museum, Cambridge. Examples in other metals are believed to be later copies.

The 'Lyte Jewel,' a diamond-set gold and enamel pendant jewel containing a portrait miniature of James I by Nicholas Hilliard, ca. 1610 (64 x 28 mm., acc./reg. no. wb.167). The portrait is on card-backed vellum with a bareheaded King James I wearing a ribbon for the Lesser George of the Order of the Garter. All images © Trustees of the British Museum.

Nicholas Hilliard

(1542 *or* 1547-1619)

•Portrait Painter, Miniaturist & Medallist•

BORN into a family of goldsmiths,[192] Hilliard continued in the family tradition and prospered. He is closely associated with the reigns of two English sovereigns—Elizabeth I and James I. Nicholas Hilliard began his career as an apprentice to Robert Brandon,[193] Queen Elizabeth I's jeweler and chamberlain of the City of London. Hilliard's first commission for the Queen was painted between 1572-76 after which he departed England for France, possibly for further artistic training. Returning in 1578/79, he made a number of jeweled lockets for smaller miniatures, on which he concentrated for the rest of his life.[194]

"NICHOLAS HILLIARD, AGED 30," A MINIATURE SELF-PORTRAIT WATERCOLOR ON VELLUM PUT DOWN ON CARD (CA. 1577). HIS SKILL WAS SUCH THAT THE FRENCH POET PIERRE DE RONSARD IS REPUTED TO HAVE SAID OF HIM:

*THE ISLANDS INDEED SELDOM BRING FORTH ANY CUNNING MAN, BUT WHEN THEY DO IT IS IN HIGH PERFECTION.**

IMAGE © VICTORIA AND ALBERT MUSEUM, LONDON.

* STRONG, 1975, P. 6.

During Elizabeth I's reign (1558–1603), Hilliard produced a number of iconic images of both Elizabeth and members of her court. Elizabeth, however, maintained close control over images of herself and never granted an exclusive appointment as portraitist to a single artist. Hilliard was appointed her 'limner,' as well as miniaturist and goldsmith, although perhaps the favor with which he was viewed at court is reflected in the 40*l.* annual allowance granted him by Elizabeth in 1599. In 1591, he had been paid 400*l.* for a Great Seal, a large sum at the time. Despite his earnings, Hilliard was frequently in debt.

Early in his career Hilliard had invested heavily in a gold-mining venture in Scotland, and had lost a considerable sum, from which he seemed never to have fully recovered. The extent of his

[192] RICHARD HILLIARD, Nicholas' father, was a goldsmith and sheriff of Exeter while his mother, LAURENCE, was the daughter of a London goldsmith.

[193] ROBERT BRANDON (d. 1591) was also chamberlain of the City of London, in which role he had oversight for finances and apprentices as well as oversight of estates held in trust for orphans, and the management and maintenance of the City of London's properties.

[194] Although some of his productions were 'cabinet miniatures,' i.e., up to 10 inches in height.

Three Examples of the 'Peace with Holland' Medal

King James I, 'Peace between England and Holland,' 1604, by Nicholas Hilliard. The imagery on the reverse is consistent with the purpose of the medal, thus the legend 'Hence peace, plenty, and true religion.' (*Top)* a finely struck original gold example (37 mm., M.I.i 193/14, M.I.Ill xiv/15, Eimer 84a, ex 1st Marquess of Lansdowne); (*center)* a cast and chased example in bronze (34.5 mm.). Examples in silver also exist. A variant, M.I.i 193/15 (41.5 mm., M.I.Ill xiv/15) can be found in silver and lead with an openwork frame, ornamented hat brim and dress and stippled background to date in exergue. The variant shown at the bottom also has a stippled background in the *rev.* field and is absent the loop seen in M.I.Ill. Images, *top* and *center*, © Trustees of the British Museum (acc./reg. nos. 1844,0425.24 and M.7009); *below*, from a private collection.

penuriousness was reflected in his imprisonment at one point after he had failed to produce the monies he had pledged as surety for a friend's debt. Hilliard's artistic productions were not limited to miniatures and medals for he also painted illuminated manuscripts and documents and created designs for the ornate title pages of books.

Hilliard's involvement with the court continued into the reign of James I, when in 1617 the king granted:

> ...a patent to this effect: "Whereas our well-beloved servant, Nicholas Hilliard, gentleman, our principal drawer of small portraits, and embosser of our medals in gold, in respect of his extraordinary skill in drawing, graving, and imprinting, &c., we have granted unto him our special licence for twelve years, to invent, make, grave and imprint any pictures of our image, of our Royal Family, with power to take a constable and search for any pictures, plates, or works, printed, sold, or set up."[195]

Referring to the self-portrait shown on page 115, the curatorial comment of the Victoria and Albert Museum states that:

> Dating from Hilliard's visit to France in 1576-1578, its mood is very much that of the portraiture of the art-loving French court, where artists enjoyed a far higher status than their English counterparts. Its boldness and brilliance demand recognition of Hilliard's genius, and express his aspirations to the status of a gentleman, not a tradesman. The reality on Hilliard's return to England was less ideal. A permanent position at court with all its attendant privileges eluded him, and he was compelled to set up as an artist in the City of London like any other craftsman.[196]

Hilliard died in January 1619, and was buried in St. Martin-in-the-Fields, Westminster.

Attempted Union of England and Scotland

An attractive medal in silver, cast in 1604 and possibly by Hilliard, it was issued when James I was attempting to forge a complete union between England and Scotland. The reverse shows two scepters passing through a single crown under a radiant sun. The surrounding inscription: 'FURMANTVR BINA SVB VNO' ('The two are established under one') (54.5 x 44.5 mm., M.I.i 194/17). This example is from the Foley Collection (*q.v. p. 337*). Daniel Fearon, the cataloguer, noted that two other examples differing in some details are known, a silver example in the Hunter Collection, and a bronze one in the British Museum. Image courtesy Woolley & Wallis, Auctioneers.

[195] J. J. Foster (1908). *Chats on Old Miniatures*. London: T. Fisher Unwin, p. 123.

[196] http://collections.vam.ac.uk/item/O72550/self-portrait-aged-30-portrait-miniature-nicholas-hilliard/.

The James I Coronation Medal
by Charles Anthony

A James I coronation medal attributed to Charles Anthony, July 25, 1603. (*Above*) a cast medal in silver-gilt* (28 mm., M.I.i 191/11, M.I.Ill xiv/11, Eimer 80b), and (*below*) a struck silver example (ibid. 29 mm.). This was the first medal to be distrubuted at a coronation in England. The crowned lion rampant is holding a beacon and wheat sheaf, symbols for hope and abundance. The translation of the *obv.* legend is 'James I., Cæsar Augustus of Britain, Cæsar the heir of the Cæsars, presents this medal.' The silver-gilt example has obviously been damaged, and it also shows weakness on the reverse between 7:00 and 10:00. The silver example is in much better condition except for the scratch on the *obv.* at 10:00. Images courtesy of A. H. Baldwin & Sons Ltd, London, www.baldwin.co.uk (auction sale 74, lot 1705); and Noble Numismatics Australia (auction sale 99, lot 2996, ex Tom May Collection).

*Very rare in this metal.

Charles Anthony

(fl. 1599-1615)

•Medallist•

CHARLES ANTHONY, an engraver at the London mint during the reign of James I, although primarily responsible for the production of gold coinage, created several attractive medals, including the first coronation medal, that for James I. A member of a family of skillful engravers, Anthony had followed his father Derick[e] Anthony, as 'Graver at the Mint' in 1599, a position the latter had held since 1551.[197] Nicholas Hilliard displaced Charles Anthony for several years, although Hilliard finally withdrew from the post in favor of Anthony.[198]

MEMORIAL MEDAL IN GOLD AND SILVER FOR THE DEATH OF HENRY, PRINCE OF WALES, 1611/12. ATTRIBUTED TO CHARLES ANTHONY, IT WAS STRUCK FROM SEVERAL DIES IN BOTH GOLD AND SILVER (BOTH 28 MM., M.I.I 200/29, M.I.ILL XV/7, EIMER 90). HENRY'S DEATH RESULTED IN THE CROWN BEING PASSED TO HIS BROTHER CHARLES IN 1625. IMAGES © TRUSTEES OF THE BRITISH MUSEUM (ACC./REG. NO. M.7022) AND COURTESY OF A. H. BALDWIN & SONS LTD, LONDON, WWW.BALDWIN.CO.UK (AUCTION SALE 49, LOT 1245).

Anthony had again to face a threat to his situation when James I attempted to place John Acheson, then his goldsmith in Scotland, in Anthony's position, but Anthony was able to maintain his life tenure. When, in 1615, Anthony died, he was succeeded by his son, Thomas Anthony, who in 1618 was displaced by William Holles. Thus Anthony, as well as his father and son, all served as engravers and had to defend their positions during the reigns of four sovereigns—Edward VI, Elizabeth I, James I and Charles I.[199] Horace Walpole, in his *Anecdotes of Painting* (1762) comments that:

> The first graver I meet in the reign of James is CHARLES ANTONY, to whom Sir Thomas Knyvet, master of the mint in the second of that king, paid by warrant 40*l*. for gold and workmanship, for graving an offering piece of gold, Antony having then the title of the king's graver(fn.). Vertue supposes this person made the medal in 1604 on the peace with Spain, a medal not mentioned by Evelyn, and that he continued in office till 1620.

---

[197] The notice of the grant of this position is found in Walpole's...*Anecdotes of Painting in England:*

> I shall take notice that, among the patent rolls, is a grant in the sixth [year] of Edward, to Antony Deric of the office of capital sculptor of the monies in the Tower of London (1879, vol. i, p. 78).

[198] Perhaps because of the relationship he had had with DERICK[E] ANTHONY when Hilliard and Derick[e] had worked together to design ELIZABETH I's second Great Seal.

[199] Craig, J. (1953, 2010). *The Mint: A History of the London Mint from A.D. 287 to 1948.* Cambridge: Cambridge University Press, pp. 131, 146.

Medallic Portraits by Charles Anthony (?): Two Early 17th c. Queens

(Top) Queen Elizabeth I (1533-1603), 'Distress Relieved,' a struck medalet, or possibly a pattern for a groat, with the queen's monogram on the reverse. M.I. translates the inscriptions as 'With the help of God I sustain one with two' and 'preserver of the afflicted' (in silver, 1601, M.I.i 177/177 25 mm.). Although M.I. suggests the latter may relate to Elizabeth's provision for sick and wounded seamen and sailors, and reform of charities, the reference on the former remains enigmatic.

(Below) a medal of Queen Anne of Denmark (1574-1619), wife of James VI of Scotland, later James I of England (in silver, 1602 or 1604, M.I.i 192/12, 28.5 mm., Eimer 81). The obverse inscription reads: 'Anne, by the grace of God, Queen of Great Britain, France, and Ireland, Daughter and Sister of Kings of Denmark.' And, on the reverse: 'Cunning is fallacious, innocence is safer.' This piece is probably a coronation medal as it was struck in 1604, when James I assumed the title of 'king' (at least on coinage), having previously been crowned as 'emperor' in 1602. Anne therefore also obtained her title of 'queen' in 1604; thus the 'queen' reference dates the medal as 1604. The attribution of this medal to Charles Anthony is also less than perfectly clear. Both medals are rare and from the Christopher Foley Collection, lot 117 (bought at Baldwin's, March 1998), and lot 137 (bought, T. Millett, 2001). Images courtesy Woolley & Wallis, Auctioneers.

Mr. Anstis informed him of a warrant to a brother of Charles Antony, called THOMAS ANTONY, curatori monetae et sigillorum regis ad cudendum magnum sigillum pro episcopatu et comitatu palatino Dunelm. 1617.[200] But of neither of these brothers do I find any other traces.[201]

fn. I have a thin plate of silver larger than a crown piece, representing King James on his throne. It is very neat workmanship, probably by this Anthony [sic].

§

The following comment on the spelling of the name of Derrick[e] Anthony by an astute reader, Mr. Corney, appeared in *The Gentleman's Magazine* after his having read the first volume of the *New General Biographical Dictionary*.

Greenwich, May 18, 1840.

Mr. Urban,

Anthony (Derick).—The name of this seal engraver appears to have been introduced in order to serve as a vehicle for announcing a discovery. The Antony Doric of Horace Walpole should be Deric Antony! The new biographer deserves praise for his discovery. I cannot, however, convince myself that Derick Anthony has a better claim to be commemorated than Charles Anthony—who was engraver of seals, &c. to James I. for more than ten years; and on whom some interesting facts have recently become more accessible.

—Yours, &c. Bolton Corney.[202]

MEDALLIONS are medals of a larger size, and supposed to have been struck by the different emperors for their friends, or for foreign princes and ambassadors. That the smallness of the number of these, however, might not put to hazard the loss of the devices they bore, the Romans generally took care to stamp the subjects of them upon their ordinary coins. Medallions, in respect of other coins, resembled what modern medals, properly so speaking, are in respect to money, having had no current value, but merely an arbitrary one. Medallions are so scarce that no set can be made of them even with mixing the different metals.

—J. Elmes. (1826). *A General and Bibliographical Dictionary of the Fine Arts…*, pages unnumbered; found under 'Medals.' Cf. *Encyclopedia Britannica,* 1771 ed.vol. iii, p. 57, from which this quote was in large part taken by Elmes.

[200] This appears to be a reference to payment to the 'guardian' (master?) of the seals for the preparation of the great seal of County Palatine of Chester, ruled over by the earls of Chester.

[201] Walpole, *Anecdotes of Painting…*, 1762 ed., vol. ii, p. 39.

[202] 1840, vol. 167, p. 587.

The Restoration of Charles II

by Peter van Abeele

Two strikingly different Charles II Restoration medals by Peter van Abeele. (*Above*) 'Charles I and Charles II' (in silver, 1660, 70 mm., M.I.i 449/33, M.I.Ill xli/15, Ex Michael Hall Collection). (*Below*) 'The Embarkation at Scheveningen' (in silver, 1660, 70 mm., M.I.i 455/44, M.I.Ill xli/10, Eimer 210). The second medal celebrates the embarkation of Charles II and his court at Scheveningen, Holland, on his return to England from exile. Note that on both medals Charles I and Charles II are portrayed wearing the Garter George suspended from a chain or ribbon. On the reverse of the second medal, Fame flies over the fleet with a trumpet and scroll or pennant bearing the words 'soli deo gloria' (M.I.i: 'To God alone the glory'). Both medals were made in Holland, are hollow and made of two embossed plates joined by a broad rim with a suspension loop added to the second one. The first medal, when found in silvered copper, may be a copy. Original examples of the second may be found gilded. Both images courtesy of A. H. Baldwin & Sons Ltd., London, www.baldwin.co.uk (auction no. 64, lot 648; and no. 56, lot 3002).

Pieter (Peter) van Abeele

(1608-ca. 1677 or 1684?; fl. 1622-1677)

•Medallist•

FORRER had a high opinion of van Abeele, commenting that he was "...a medallist of great merit" and that he "was one of the best engravers of the Dutch school of the seventeenth century."[203] With respect to technique, Forrer compares van Abeele's work to that of his contemporary, O. Müller, another Dutch medallist,[204] noting that both used the *repoussé* method, which produced medals which were embossed, chased and in high relief. This method employs two separate hollow embossed and chased plates that are then joined at the rim with a band or ring of metal. The greatest advantage of the repoussé method is that it allows the use of higher relief in medallic portraits and design.[205] Abeele is credited with having first perfected this method. Van Abeele's most important medallic work may have been the Dutch issue, ca. 1655, commemorating the granting of arms to the city of Amsterdam in 1342 and the addition of the imperial crown to the arms in 1488. With respect to medals with British themes, van Abeele is best known for his medal of the embarkation of Charles II and his court at Scheveningen on his return to England to be restored to the throne (1660).

Mary, Princess of Orange, and her son William III

THIS MEDAL, LIKE OTHERS BY VAN ABEELE, CONSISTS OF TWO EMBOSSED PLATES, FASTENED TOGETHER BY A BAND WHICH FORMS THE EDGE. M.I.I NOTES THAT THIS MEDAL (SILVER, 1654, 64 MM., M.I.I 417/55, M.I.ILL XXXVIII/5, EIMER 192) WAS INTENDED TO MAINTAIN THE PRESENCE BEFORE THE PUBLIC OF THE HOUSE OF ORANGE AFTER CROMWELL HAD BY TREATY WITH THE PROVINCE OF HOLLAND EXCLUDED THAT FAMILY FROM POWER. PRINCE WILLIAM WAS TO LATER RULE ENGLAND AS KING WILLIAM III (1689-1702). NOTE VAN ABEELE'S INITIALS IN THE FIELD TO THE *LEFT* OF THE PRINCE. IMAGE © TRUSTEES OF THE BRITISH MUSEUM (ACC./REG. NO. M.7375).

[203] L. Forrer, *Biographical Dictionary of Medallists,* vol. i, p. 10.

[204] O. Müller (*also known as* Wouter Müller; fl. 1653-1688) is perhaps best known for his medal of Cromwell and Masaniello (M.I.I 432/78; M.I.ILL XL/1; Platt, I/345/A).

[205] L. Forrer, vol. iv, p. 195.

Two Medals by Christoph[er] Adolfszoon

Two Dutch medals commemorating the Peace of Breda which concluded the Second Anglo-Dutch War and established peaceful relations between the two countries. *Above*, a highly allegorical and very rare medal in gold, the obverse depicting *Hollandia* holding a scepter and spear while trampling *Discord* as a lion and lamb sit beside her. In the field a naval action appears to her right and a peaceful scene (of Breda) to her left. On the reverse, her sword is sheathed and decorated with an olive wreath. She holds a cornucopia and caduceus in her other hand (in silver, 1667, 71 mm., M.I.i 528/176, M.I.Ill lii/5; Eimer 240). Unfortunately, *Discord*, whom *Hollandia* treds upon, and whose name 'Mala Bestia' (pernicious beast), appears in the exergue, was seen by the English as an insult to Charles II, to whom the epithet had been applied during the war. M.I. comments that this medal, by depicting the burning of English ships in Chatham before the end of the war, also gave great offense to the English government. The English demanded and received an apology, recall of the medal and destruction of the dies, but the damage had been done, and the insult contributed to a renewal of hostilities in 1672. The real reason for resuming war, however, was more likely an agreement to assist France in her war against the Dutch under the Treaty of Dover.

(Below) another medal commemorating the Peace of Breda in 1667. The obverse of this medal depicts Dutch and English ships sailing together peacefully while the reverse contains the arms of the two countries on shields surmounted by a wreath of olive leaves and decorated with flowers and crossed and tied palm and laurel branches (1667, in silver-gilt, 71 mm., M.I.i 534/184, M.I.Ill liv/2, Eimer 242). M.I. notes the error in the placement of the Scottish lion on the British shield. Images courtesy of A. H. Baldwin & Sons Ltd, London, www. baldwin.co.uk (auction no. 62-63, lot 1213) and © Trustees of the British Museum (acc./reg. no. G3,FD.369).

Christoph[er] Adolfszoon

(fl. 1666-1676)

•Medallist•

CHRISTOPH[ER] ADOLFSZOON was a Dutch medallist of whom few details of his life have been left to posterity; indeed, there are also few medals which he has left behind as well. The three medals shown here, together with his medal commemorating the 'Naval Action with the Dutch, 1666' (M.I.i 518/164, M.I.Ill li/3) appear to be the sum total of his signed *oeuvre* of medals concerned with British themes. Other than his having produced medals in Holland over a period of ten years (1666-1676) and reputedly having received one thousand ducats for his medal of Michael De Ruyter, the Dutch admiral, nothing else is known of him.[206] Forrer repeats Grueber's comment to the effect that "His work is coarse, but characteristic of Dutch medallic art of that period,"[207] an opinion which is not shared by the present authors, particularly when the total, albeit small in size, of Adolfszoon's medallic output is examined.

Peace with Holland Concluded in London, 1674

Probably by an unknown contemporary of Chistropher Adolphszoon

Sometimes attributed to Christoph[er] Adolfszoon, but not likely his work, this very rare hollow cast medal in silver celebrates the signing of the 'Peace with Holland, 1674' treaty which ended the Third Anglo-Dutch War. The obverse depicts a mounted William III of Holland presiding over an assault on the seaside town of Naarden in Holland, above which is an orange branch intertwined with a ribbon on which there is an inscription which translates as: 'Beyond the power and condition of youth.' The reverse depicts a dove with palm and olive branches over a calm sea with the surrounding inscription that translates from the Latin as: 'From God comes Peace and happy Victory' (61.8 mm., M.I.i 561/225, M.I.Ill lvii/6, Eimer 253). Note that the date 1674 appears in the form of a chronogram. It was by this treaty that the Dutch lost the colony of New Amsterdam to the English. Image courtesy of Nomos AG, auction 5, lot 71.

---

[206] M.I.i, biographical notice, p. 719.

[207] L. Forrer, *Biographical Dictionary...*, v. i, p. 25, citing Grueber, *English Medals in the King's Library...*, p. 44.

Marriage of Charles I to Henrietta Maria
Medals by Pierre Regnier[208]

'Marriage of Charles I to Henrietta Maria' (1625, M.I.i 238/1, M.I.Ill xix/7, Eimer 105a), in gold and silver, respectively. Images courtesy Spink Auctions (sale no. 11023, lot 565) and A. H. Baldwin & Sons Ltd, London, www.baldwin.co.uk (auction no. 65, lot 1005).

'Marriage of Charles I to Henrietta Maria' (1625, M.I.i 238/2, M.I.Ill xix/8, in silver). Images courtesy of A. H. Baldwin & Sons Ltd, London, www.baldwin.co.uk (auction no. 68, lot 3001).

---

[208] *Images continue on p. 128.* Further details concerning these medals may be found in M.I.i and M.I.Ill, as well as in Platt, vol. i, pp. 115-116.

Pierre Regnier

(ca. 1577-after 1640)

•Medallist•

PIERRE REGNIER rose from humble origins, having begun his career as an apprentice engraver to Alexandre Oliver, conductor of the Monnaie du Moulin, the Paris mint. Having married Oliver's daughter Michelle in 1607, he succeeded to the position that his father-in-law Alexandre Oliver had held there until his death. During his early tenure at the mint, Pierre Regnier had disputes with Nicholas Briot over the extent of his purview, these ending in 1623 with Briot's flight to England. Upon Briot's departure, Regnier was appointed engraver-general, but he was never confirmed in this post. From 1625, he held this position on an alternating basis shared with his brother-in-law René Oliver, who had successfully claimed his late father's concession. In 1629, with the murder of René Oliver, Jean Warin (Varin) was appointed engraver-general in his place, but despite Regnier's protests, he was required to share the position of assistant-engraver with Warin until 1639 when Warin assumed the position full time. It is not known whether Regnier sold his position to Varin or was forced out.

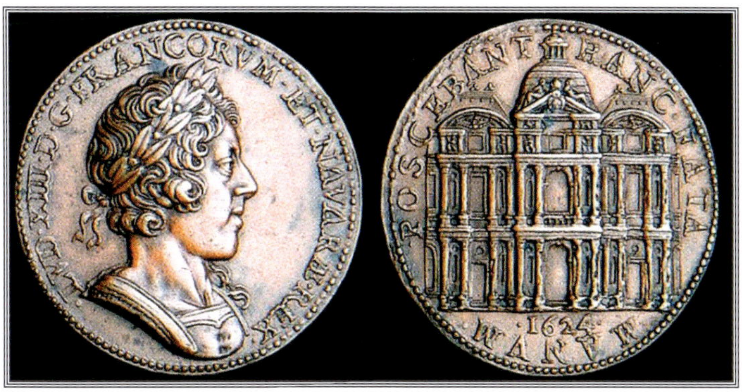

A French example, unsigned, of Pierre Regnier's work, in bronze (32 mm.). This medal commemorates the building of an extension to the Louvre in 1624 during the reign of Louis XIII (1610-1643). Image courtesy Morton & Eden Ltd.; ex Stack collection, May 2009; Jones 96.

A prolific medallist and engraver, Regnier had introduced new methods of mechanization for the manufacture of coins and medals at the mint. The main products were coins and jetons, but Regnier continued his involvement in both the design and manufacture of medals. The only English medals Regnier is known to have been involved with are those celebrating the marriage of Charles I and Henrietta Maria (*see previous and following pages*). This involvement would seem to have arisen from the fact that Henrietta Maria was the sister of King Louis XIII of France. [209] The difference in execution of the marriage medals when compared with Regnier's work as illustrated by the Louvre medal above is remarkable.

[209] L. Forrer, *Biographical Dictionary of Medallists*, vol. 5, pp. 62-65.

Marriage of Charles I to Henrietta Maria Medals by Pierre Regnier (*con't.*)

'Marriage of Charles I to Henrietta Maria 1625' (M.I.i 238/3, M.I.Ill xix/9, Eimer 105b, in silver, British Museum acc./reg. no. M.7079). Images © Trustees of the British Museum.

'Marriage of Charles I to Henrietta Maria 1625' (M.I.i 238/4, M.I.Ill xix/10, in silver, British Museum acc./reg. no. M.7080). Images © Trustees of the British Museum.

'Marriage of Charles I to Henrietta Maria 1625' (M.I.i 238/5, M.I.Ill xix/11, in silver. B. M. acc./reg. no. M.7081). Images © Trustees of the British Museum.

A view of London with London Bridge in the foreground, ca. 1647. This is the fifth panel of seven of Wenceslaus Hollar's 'Long View of London' showing the bridge and the east of the city from St. Magnus to Barking. The 'Angel of Fame' flies above, blowing a trumpet. A particularly interesting visual point in the etching is the structure in the middle of London Bridge, 'Old Nonsuch House.' Completed in 1579, it was possibly the first prefabricated building, having been built in the Netherlands and then reassembled on the Bridge. No nails, mortar or iron were used in its construction, only wooden pegs. During the 17th century, among the shops on or adjoining the bridge and in Nonsuch House proper were a number of booksellers, including those at the signs of 'The Three Bibles,' 'The Seven Stars,' 'The Sun and the Bible,' and the 'Hand and Bible.' Torn down ca. 1757, rebuilt and then damaged by fire the following year, London Bridge was finally demolished with the opening of a new structure in 1831. Image © Trustees of the British Museum, acc./reg. no. 1864, 0611.437.

Charles I's return to London following his Coronation in Scotland in 1633 By Nicholas Briot

The medal executed by Nicholas Briot to commemorate Charles I's return to London following his coronation in Scotland in 1633 (42 mm., M.I.i 266/62 (B_1), M.I.Ill xxii/4, Eimer 124b). Found as both struck and cast, the example here being cast. This medal depicts an event which never took place, for his state procession from the Tower of London to Westminster was cancelled because of the presence of plague in London. Illustration courtesy Morton & Eden, Ltd.

John Evelyn's depiction of the above medal in *Numismata* (1697, pl. xxxi). Note that the king is depicted wearing a crown, while this is not the case on the actual medal.

Nicholas Briot

(1579?-1646?)

•Medallist •

NICHOLAS BRIOT was born in Damblain, Lorraine, France, into a Huguenot family of patternmakers, die cutters, and craftsmen in pewter who had long been established in their profession.[210] Later, Briot was to become a celebrated medallist and coin-engraver in his own right in both France and England. As a young man, he worked as an engraver of coins of Lorraine from 1611-1624, then, following Philippe Danfrie, as 'engraver-general of the coins' at the Paris mint from 1606, for almost a decade. During this time, Briot produced a number of coronation medals for Louis XIII as well as medals of other prominent persons. Some of these medals were ascribed to Guillaume Dupré for whom Briot had worked for several years, although Forrer states that this work was certainly that of Briot and not of any other engraver. Forrer, for example, comments that the 1618 coinage issue of francs bearing Louis XIII's portrait, was:

> ...struck from dies engraved by N. Briot, after wax models by Dupré.[211]

Briot experimented with copper-plate engraving, producing portraits of Louis Potier de Gesvre and the botanist Johann (*or* Jean) Bauhin. Having learned of newly introduced methods in Germany of mechanically producing coins and medals with milled edges using a machine, Briot sought to employ these methods in France. Using the milling machinery, he was able to produce a perfectly round coin by striking a coin or medal through a process which incorporated a mechanical balance.[212] He approached the Paris mint with his invention, but the authorities of his native country refused to accept this process, and insisted that he continue to use the hammer to produce coins by striking.

Finding himself in financial straits, and pursued by creditors, in 1623 Briot left for England, bringing the milling process with him. There he was warmly greeted by Charles I who allowed him all the rights of a resident of England. Soon, Briot was engraving the king's image on coins with milled edges:

> On 16 Dec. 1628, the King granted him the privilege to be a free denizen, and also full power and authority to frame and engrave the first designs and effigies of the king's image in such size and forms as are to serve in all sorts of coins of gold and silver.[213]

By 1633, Briot had been appointed chief engraver to the Royal Mint, and was engaged in producing the crown and half-crown pieces. Two years later, Briot was appointed mint-master in Scotland as well, retaining this post until 1639.[214] Briot made a number of dies and moulds for medals of Charles I, at least during the early part of the latter's reign. These included the Dominion of the Sea and Scottish Coronation medals. During this period, he also made a medal of John Stuart, earl of Tracquair, when he was appointed Lord Treasurer. This medal is now exceedingly rare.[215]

---

[210] BRIOT's father DIDIER and his brother ISAAC were distinguished medallists, as was his uncle FRANÇOIS.

[211] Spink & Son, *Numismatic Circular,* Feb. 1899, vol. ix, p. 3213.

[212] The mill had been invented by ANTOINE BRUCHER (?-?, mid- to late-16th c.) in France during Henry II's reign (1547-1559) to replace the hammer. It was discontinued, however, in 1585 because of its great expense. It was also used in England during ELIZABETH I's time, but again discontinued after only about ten years of use. According to Pinkerton,

> ...the mill was not in constant and authorized use, in the English mint, till 1662 (pp. 133-134).

[213] L. Forrer, vol. i, p. 288; *DNB*, 1886 ed., vol. xi, p. 351, citing Thomas Rymer, *Fœdera*, xix, p. 40.

[214] Forrer noted that when BRIOT was nominated as mint-master in Scotland there were objections to his being appointed to the position because:

> ... the sinking of Irnes (*i.e., iron tools used in the minting process*) was incompatibill with the maister of Mynt, and that never in Scotland a Mr of Mynt was sinkar, or one that could sink (*sic*, Cochran-Patrick, *Records of the Coinage of Scotland*, vol. ii, p. 108; also cited by Forrer, vol. i, p. 288).

[215] L. Forrer, ibid. vol. i, pp. 287-289.

Nicholas Briot's Charles I Coronation Medals

Nicholas Briot's medal, in gold, commemorating the coronation of Charles I in 1626 (30 mm., M.I.i 243/10, M.I.Ill xx/1, Eimer 106, Platt I/117/A_1). There are two varieties—Type A, shown here with the sword piercing the word *Reddita** after the second d, and Type B, with *Reddita* pierced after the first d (30 mm., M.I.i 243/10, M.I.Ill xx/2, Platt I/117/b).

* 'donec·pax·reddita·terris' ('Until peace is restored to the Earth').

Another example of Nicholas Briot's work—the thistle reverse medal commemorating the coronation of Charles I in Scotland in 1633 (28 mm., M.I.i 266/60, M.I.Ill xxxii/2, Eimer 123, Platt I/134/c). This type is absent the edge inscription seen on the Type B medal. Images © Trustees of the British Museum.

During the English Civil War Briot spent two years in France, before returning to England:

> ...follow[ing] the English King in his capacity of Engraver to York and to Oxford.[216]

Mayo notes that while there, Briot improved coining machinery which included cylinder-presses:

> In the reign of Charles I, Nicholas Briot set up at the Mint his improved balance, which, although it could not be used for striking medals of large size, or in high relief, led to further improvements in the striking machinery which have enabled large medals to be made from dies.[217]

216 C. E. Challis, *A New History of the Royal Mint*, p. 283.
217 Mayo, p. lxxiv.

Nicholas Briot's 'Peace or War' Medals

CHARLES I, PEACE OR WAR, 1643, IN SILVER (28 MM., M.I.I 309/136, M.I.ILL XXVI/18, EIMER 142 VAR., PLATT I/206/'TYPE C'). BY NICHOLAS BRIOT, WHOSE INITIAL APPEARS BELOW THE BUST. FOUR VARIETIES OF THIS MEDAL, VARYING IN A NUMBER OF DETAILS AND METALS, EXIST. IMAGE COURTESY SPINK AUCTIONS, NO. 1011, LOT 317.

ONE VARIETY OF THE PEACE OR WAR MEDAL EXISTS WITH THE REV. DATE 1660, SHOWN HERE IN COPPER/BRONZE (28 MM., M.I.I 309/136, M.I.ILL XXVI/20, EIMER 142 VARIANT, PLATT I/206/'TYPE D'). RUST MARKS ARE PRESENT CONFIRMING THAT THE ORIGINAL DIES, WITH THE REVERSE DATE ALTERED, WERE USED IN ITS MANUFACTURE AT THE LATER DATE. IMAGE © TRUSTEES OF THE BRITISH MUSEUM.

Briot, having been engaged "quite specifically to engrave the royal effigy," was never allowed to engrave the reverse of Charles I's coins or to:

> ...intermeddle with the graving of anything that carried our arms. [218]

Briot was paid the going rate for producing the coins but he had to pay for his:

> ...own coinage ingots and cutting out the blanks and striking. [219]

Further, according to Challis, by 1638/9:

> Briot's coins differed from the normal run produced by the moneyers in being struck by machine. For his larger denominations oval blanks were punched out of metal strip and then fed sideways between convex dies which, being rocked from side to side, at one

[218] Challis, p. 301.
[219] Ibid, p. 301.

and the same time printed the coin and rendered it round. For the smaller denominations Briot appears to have punched out circular blanks which were then struck in a screw-press.[220]

During the Civil War, Briot remained in England and continued to serve Charles I as an engraver in York and Oxford from 1642 until his death in 1646. Challis states that Briot left his second wife Esther impoverished when he died, although he had been paid 50*l.* per annum.[221] At the Restoration, Charles II acknowledged the 3000*l.* debt owed to Briot as one of those individuals who had served his father Charles I.

Summarizing Briot's contributions, Forrer opines that many believe that his coins and medals were works of art. His implementation of producing a medal or coin using the laminating machine and a coining press or *monnoyoir*, a German invention which he improved, and the use of a cutter rather than a hammer to strike a coin, was an advance which resulted in the coining of a more perfect product. His students, Thomas Simon and Nicholas Blondeau, enhanced his machinery even further.[222] The French never took to his improvements of coin and medal production, and these were also resisted by mint employees in England. These objections were eventually overcome, bringing about, in Forrer's opinion:

...that revival in medallic art, which Simon and his school rendered so conspicuous.[223,224]

Historical Commentary on Nicholas Briot

...[Briot's] various productions all show a wonderful talent. Beyond introducing machinery...he reformed the method and style of engraving, which his pupils like Blondeau, and especially Thomas Simon, brought to a rare state of perfection. Mr H. A. Grueber of the British Museum says of Briot that "his dies for coins and medals are gems of medallic art...," an opinion which other writers fully endorse...Briot trained two great artists: Blondeau, and Thomas Simon, who mark the apogee of medallic art in this country.

H. A. Grueber, in Hawkins, et al., *Medallic Illustrations of British History...*, 1889, vol. i, pp. 292-293.

§

Of 'Nicholas Briot' and 'Mr. Symonds,' since they have the honour of a passing relation to the Lord General, and still enjoy, or suffer, a kind of ghost-existence in the Dilettante memory, we may subjoin, rather than cancel, the following authentic particulars. In the Commons Journals of 20th August 1642, it is: ' *Ordered*, That the Earl of Warwick,' now Admiral of our Fleet, be desired that Monsieur Bryatt may have delivery of his wearing apparel; and all his other goods stayed at Scarborough, not belonging to Minting and Coining of Moneys.' —This Nicholas Bryatt, or Briot, then, must have been Chief Engraver for the Mint at the beginning of the Civil Wars. We perceive, he has gone to the King northward; but is here stopt at Scarborough, with all his baggage, by Warwick the Lord High Admiral: and is to get away. What became of him afterwards, or what was his history before, no man and hardly any Dilettante knows

—T. Carlyle, *Cromwell's Letters...*, commentary on 'Nicholas Briot' and 'Mr. Symonds,' and their medals, 1904 ed., vol. ii, p. 176.

§

NICHOLAS BRIOT was a native of Lorraine, and graver of the mint to the King of France, in which kingdom he was the inventor, or at least one of the first proposers of coining money by a press, instead of the former manner of hammering. As I am ignorant myself in the mechanic part of this art, and have not even the pieces quoted by Vertue, I shall tread very cautiously, and only transcribe the titles of some memorials which he had seen, and from whence I conclude a literary controversy art,

---

220 Ibid.

221 *DNB*, ed., 1886, vol. vi, p. 351; Challis, p. 333.

222 L. Forrer, vol. i, p. 288.

223 Ibid. p. 294.

224 Briot signed his work 'Briot,' 'N. Briot,' 'N. Briot F.[ecit],' or with his initial(s): 'B' or 'N. B.,' the last particularly on counters and jetons, sometimes with a small flower or an anchor.

The Dominion of the Sea Medals: 1630 & 1639

The 'Dominion of the Sea medals' by Nicholas Briot, issued in 1630 (cast, in bronze, 59 mm., M.I.i 256/40, M.I.Ill xxiv/4, Platt i/123-126, British Museum acc./reg. no. M.7107) and 1639 (cast, in silver, 60 mm., M.I.i 285/97, M.I.Ill xxiv/10, Eimer 136, Platt I/147-148). The earlier medal (*above*) was issued to stress England's claim to 'dominion of the sea,' Charles I's assertion of England's control over the seas surrounding the British Isles. The later medal was issued at the time talks with Spain were underway concerning the presence of the Spanish fleet in the Downs off Dover and was a reassertion of England's dominion. Both medals are similar in overall design, bearing a portrait of Charles I on the obverse and on the reverse a ship under sail and a fort on land which can be seen in the distance. The earlier medal, executed in 1630, portrayed the king wearing a ruff collar and an ornately decorated cloak and armor. On the 1639 medal the image of Charles has been changed to more accurately reflect his age and then current style—he is wearing a soft falling collar over less ornate dress and armor. On the 1639 medal, Charles is also depicted with longer hair. The 1630 medal is found in gold, silver-gilt, silver and bronze. The 1639 medal is found in gold (very rare) and silver. There are at least two full size variants. Also, note that the reverse inscriptions differ, QVI having been grammatically incorrect, it was replaced with QVÆ. The medal images are respectively © Trustees of the British Museum (*top*) and a medal in a private collection (*bottom*).

and have not even the pieces quoted by Vertue, I shall tread very cautiously, and only transcribe the titles of some memorials which he had seen, and from whence I conclude a literary controversy was carried on in France on the subject of this new invention, to which, according to custom, the old practitioners seem to have objected, as probably interfering with the abuses of which they were in prescriptive possession...Nicolas Briot...This Coquerel, I find by another note, was generalis onetarius, or pope of the mint into which the reformation was to be introduced. The Luther, Briot, I suppose miscarried, as we soon afterwards find him in the service of the crown of England, where projectors were more favourably received. From these circumstances I conclude he arrived in the reign of King James, though he did not make his way to court before the accession of King Charles, the patron of genius. Briot's first public work was a medal of that prince exhibited in Evelyn, with the artist's name and the date 1628. To all or to almost all his coins and medals he put at least the initial letter of his name. He was employed both in England and Scotland. In 1631, as appears by Rymer's Foed., tom, xix., p. 287, a special commission was appointed for making trial of the experience, skill, and industry of Nicholas Briot, in the coinage of money at the mint, dated June 13, 1631, at Westminster. This was the project he had attempted in France, by instruments, mills, and presses, to make better money and with less expense to the crown than by the way of hammering. The scheme was probably approved, for in the very next year we find him coining money upon the regular establishment..Briot returned to France about 1642, having formed that excellent scholar Thomas Simon...

In a private family (the name of which he does not mention) Vertue saw a peach-stone, on which was carved the head of King Charles full-faced, with a laurel, and on the reverse, St. George on horseback, with the garter round it, and on one side above the king's head, these letters NB. The tradition in that family was, that the carver having been removed from the service of the crown, and at last obtaining the place of poor knight at Windsor, cut that curiosity to show he was not superannuated nor incapable of his office, as he had been represented. If the mark NB signified Nicholas Briot, as is probable, either the story is fictitious, or Briot did not return to France on the breaking out of the civil war. The latter is most likely, as in the Treasury, where the plate of St. George's Chapel is deposited, there is such another piece, though inferior in workmanship to that above mentioned. In the museum at Oxford are two small carvings in wood, Christ on the cross, and the nativity, with the same cypher NB on each. I have a bronze dish ornamented in a good grotesque taste in relief, with the elements and the seven liberal sciences. On the bottom of the outside is a good deal of Francis Briot, who was probably the brother of Nicholas.

—H. Walpole, *Anecdotes of Painting in England,* 1879 ed., pp. 134-136.

§

Briot continued in the service of the king; his relations with the parliament have been made the subject of special study by Miss Farquhar, who claims to have vindicated his loyalty to Charles...His influence on the technique of the English coinage was undoubtedly great and beneficial.

— G. F. Hill (1920), *Medals of the Renaissance*, p. 164.

Saliger deriveth the word Medal from the Arabic *Methalia*; a sort of Coin with a human head upon it.

But the opinion of *Vossius*, is generally received; *viz.* that it come from *Metallum*, Metal; of which substance Medals are commonly made.[225]

—D. Jennings, *An Introduction to the Knowledge of Medals,* 1764, p. 1.

[225] JULIUS CAESAR SCALIGER (*also* GIULIO CESARE DELLA SCALA), was an Italian classical scholar and physician of the late 16th-early 17th century (*q.v. pp. 238, 239*). GERHARD JOHANN ERNIE VOSSIUS (VOSS) was a Dutch classical scholar and theologian of roughly the same period.

A Rare and less well known Jeton by Nicholas Briot

William Juxon (ca. 1582-1663) accompanied Charles I when he ascended the scaffold and offered him last rites before his execution in January 1649. The late king's high regard for Juxon was clearly reflected in the latter's having been chosen for such a role. Juxon later attended Charles II as Archbishop of Canterbury (1660-1663) and officiated at his coronation in 1660. Juxon had been bishop of London from 1633, succeeding the previous occupant of that position, Archbishop William Laud. In 1649 Juxon was himself removed. Over a decade before, in 1636, Charles I had appointed Juxon Lord High Treasurer of England and First Lord of the Admiralty—he was the last member of the clergy to hold such high secular offices.

This rare silver jeton, or counter (28 mm., M.I.i 279/85, M.I.Ill xxiii/8) bears the arms both of Juxon and the See of London—the obverse shows the See's arms impaling Juxon's, with a mitre above. Juxon's arms appear on the reverse—a hand issuing from a cloud holding a crozier, on which stands a stork with a pebble in one claw, with a view of London in the distance. The surrounding legend on the obverse: GVIL' · LOND' · EPVS · ET · ANGLIÆ · THESAVR' · is interpreted by M.I. as 'William, Bishop of London, and Treasurer of England.' The reverse bears the surrounding legend: NON · DORMIT · QVI · CVSTODIT (M.I.: 'The sentinel does not sleep'). This example of the medal was sold at Spink in 1984 and at Baldwin's in 2007 (auction 51, lot 1286), where it brought over three times the estimate. Image courtesy of A. H. Baldwin & Sons Ltd, London, www.baldwin.co.uk.

The Medals of James I and his Family by Simon de Passe

A MAGNIFICENT SET OF SILVER PORTRAIT MEDALS—BOTH FROM THE VIEWPOINT OF ART AND OF TECHNIQUE—BY SIMON DE PASSE CA. 1616. *CLOCKWISE FROM 12:00:* (A) QUEEN ELIZABETH I, (B) FREDERICK, COUNT PALATINE, PRINCESS ELIZABETH AND THEIR SON PRINCE FREDERICK, (C) QUEEN ANNE, (D) JAMES I, QUEEN ANNE, AND PRINCE CHARLES, (E) MARIA, INFANTA OF SPAIN, (F) JAMES I, AND IN THE CENTER, (G) CHARLES, PRINCE OF WALES. IMAGES COURTESY OF MORTON & EDEN, LTD. FROM THEIR MAY 21, 2003, AUCTION. FOR FURTHER DETAILS CONCERNING THESE MEDALS AND THE METHODS OF MANUFACTURE SEE PP. 140-141.

Simon van de Passe

(ca. 1595/96-1647)

• Portrait Painter and Medallist •

As was the case for Nicholas Hilliard and Charles Anthony, Simon van de Passe came from a family of engravers and initially at least, he worked engraving plates for publication. De Passe's father Crispijn (1565?-1637) was a line-engraver as were his brothers Crispin (1597?-1667?) and Willem (1598?-1637?) and his sister Magdalena (1600–1638), the three of the eight van de Passe children selected to be brought up as engravers.[223] Born in Cologne, he first lived in Utrecht where the family had settled, and then in London (1615-1622).

Simon van de Passe's first work, a portrait of Henry, Prince of Wales, appeared in 1612, the year of Henry's death. In London he worked for Nicholas Hilliard, obtaining a license from Hilliard to engrave counters of the royal family. As Forrer points out, Simon van de Passe was responsible for producing most of the counters during the reign of James I, with the new appearance of these counters coinciding with van de Passe's taking up their design in 1616. Such counters were sold in sets of thirty-six, either mixed or of the same design. The sets consisted of pieces containing portraits of the English sovereigns. These counters were

THREE EXAMPLES OF EARLY 17TH C. SILVER COUNTERS* WHICH APPEAR TO HAVE BEEN STRUCK IN IMITATION OF ENGRAVING BY SIMON VAN DE PASSE OR HIS FOLLOWERS, CA. 1616-1630. (*TOP*) EDWARD II (CA. 1632, 27 MM., M.I.I 379/281, M.I.ILL XXXIV/9); (*CENTER*) JAMES I AND PRINCE CHARLES (CA. 1625, 27 MM., M.I.I 376/272, M.I.ILL XXXIV/1, EIMER 174, PLATT I/141); (*BOTTOM*) CHARLES I AND HENRIETTA MARIA (27 MM., CA. 1630, M.I.I 378/279, M.I.ILL XXXIV/7). IMAGES COURTESY (*TOP*) NOBLE NUMISMATICS (AUSTRALIA), INFO@NOBLE.COM.AU (AUCTION SALE 102, LOT 2019); (*BOTTOM*) STACK'S COIN GALLERIES, 2008, LOT 1396.

*SEE COMMENTS, PLATT, VOL. I, P. 141. COLOR ADDED TO IMPROVE CONTRAST.

[223] *DNB*, 1909 ed., vol. xv, p. 443.

widely used at the time for both arithmetic calculations and gaming, and that business was at the very least steady, and possibly very good.[224] The method of manufacture of these counters appears to have been stamping in imitation of engraving. Their issue continued past van de Passe's departure from England in 1622, his pupils having continued to engrave them until about 1638.

Another example, this one in gold, of Simon van de Passe's medal, medallion or plaquette of James I (ca. 1616, 60 x 49 mm., M.I.i 215/62, M.I.Ill xvi/2, British Museum acc./reg. nos. M.7045 and BNK,EngM.34, ex Bank of England Coll.). The prevailing expert opinion is that the gold medallions of James I and Elizabeth I in this series have been engraved while the silver ones have been cast (*see textbox on following page*).

George Villiers, marquess and 1st duke of Buckingham, and favorite of James I. An oval silver medallion by Simon van de Passe. The obverse inscription translates as: 'The most noble Lord George Villiers, Marquess of Buckingham, Viscount Villiers, Baron of Waddon, Admiral of England, &c.' The reverse displays his arms with the Latin inscription for 'The cross the test of Faith' (ca. 1618, 59 x 49 mm., M.I.i 220/74, M.I.Ill xvii/5, British Museum acc./reg. no. M.7058, signed S P. *fe*). Images © Trustees of the British Museum.

Simon van de Passe is, however, better known for his medallic portraits than for his counters. These finely worked and very attractive pieces, some engraved by hand, others cast, exist for many members of the royal family and aristocracy. Typically, they are of silver, although occasionally found in gold, have a portrait on the obverse, the sitter's coat of arms on the reverse and measure approximately 2.2-2.5 x 1.8-2.0 inches. Forrer suggested that these plaques were intended to be used as plates for printing the portraits they contained. More recent interpretations have rejected this view.[225]

In 1622, Simon may have already decided to leave London. His brother Willem moved to London at this time, possibly to take up Simon's work. Another brother, Crispijn II, moved from Utrecht to France at about the same time and Simon himself moved to Utrecht in that year where he continued to engrave plates. Then, in about 1624/25, Simon moved to Copenhagen where he became principal engraver to King Christian IV of Denmark. Simon died in Copenhagen in 1647, having completed his final plate the previous year.

---

[224] L. Forrer, vol. iv, p. 396-400.

[225] Ibid. p. 400; L. Brown, *B. N. J.*, 2003, vol. 73, pp. 175-185; M. Jones, *N. C.*, 1983, 143, pp. 227-230, *q.v. text box on facing page*.

Medallions Portraying the Royal Family · by Simon de Passe ·

Three silver plaques or medallions* of the royal family by Simon de Passe, ca. 1615-1620. (*Left*) King James I (signed S P. *fe*, 54 x 42 mm., M.I.i 214/61, M.I.Ill xvi/1, Eimer 94 var.), *rev.* legend: 'Blessed are the Peace-Makers'; (*Center*) the King with Anne of Denmark and Prince Charles, later King Charles I (62 x 50 mm., unsigned, M.I.i 217/68, M.I.Ill xvi/6) *rev.* legend: 'The most potent James, by the grace of God, King of Great Britain and Ireland, and the most serene Anne, by the grace of God, Queen of Great Britain, together with the most illustrious Prince Charles, Prince of Great Britain' and (*Right*) Charles, Prince of Wales (56 x 43 mm., M.I.i 216/66, M.I.Ill xvi/4), *rev.* legend: 'The most illustrious and potent Prince Charles, Prince of Great Britain and Ireland, Duke of York and Albany,' signed S P. *sc*. The first medallion is known in gold as well as silver. Images © Victoria and Albert Museum, London.

*M.I. states that these plaques are stamped in imitation of engraving, and there has been some disagreement on this point for many years (*see, e.g.*, L. Brown, A discourse of medals, *British Numismatic Journal*, 2003, vol. 73, pp. 175-185, in particular pp. 178-179, where Brown summarizes the conflicting views and the evidence). Brown concludes by stating his agreement with Mark Jones' conclusion that the silver pieces of de Passe in the British Museum had simply been cast although the gold medals of Elizabeth I and James I had been engraved ('The technique of Simon van De Passe reconsidered,' *Numismatic Chronicle*, 1983, 143, pp. 227-230). Jones concluded that "De Passe engraved models for his medals" and:

> *...on occasion, directly engraved medals not intended for reproduction: the reproductive technique used in his workshop was neither stamping in imitation of engraving nor engraving, whether or not assisted by transfers, but simple casting* (p. 228).

Several Medals by Claude Warin

Medals of Thomas Carey,* Gentleman of the Bedchamber to King Charles I (ca. 1633, 73 mm., acc./reg. nos. 1926,0811.1) and Margaret Carey, his wife (71.5 x 67.5 mm., acc./reg. no. 1926,0811.2). Both medals are uniface, in silver, cast and chased, with an incuse reverse and are not listed in M.I. or M.I.Ill. The medal of Thomas Cary is signed 'va' below the truncation while the medal of Margaret Carey is unsigned. Both are attributed to Claude Warin (Varin). The inscriptions are translated as 'Thomas Carey, Gentleman of the Bedchamber to King Charles, aged 35, 1633' and 'Margaret, wife of Thomas Carey, aged 26,' respectively. The British Museum description notes that these medals "appear to be reproductions by Warin of the round portrait medals of the Careys [and] were not known to the compilers *of Medallic Illustrations* and do not appear to have been published since." Both medals were donated to the British Museum by Ms. Helen Farquhar following their purchase at Sotheby's sale of July 14, 1926 (lot 454), for £41. Similar portraits appear on three other medals: M.I.i 268/66, M.I.Ill xxii/8 and M.I.i 269/67, M.I.Ill xxii/9 (Thomas Carey) and M.I.i 269/68, M.I.Ill xxii/10 (Margaret Carey). At right is the obverse of a uniface medal, also by Claude Warin, of Anne Blake, wife of William Blake, Chirographer[226] (1603-1677) and the younger brother of Admiral Robert Blake (ca. 1634, in silver, cast, 72 mm., British Museum acc./reg. no. 1882,0706.2, M.I.i 272/71). The treatment of the portraits on the two medals is almost identical and obviously by the same artist.** This medal was donated to the British Museum by A. W. Franks.

*Also spelled 'Cary.' **The medal of Anne Blake is signed 'varin.'

[226] A court official who oversees the preparation of legal opinions and other documents for printing and dissemination.

Claude Warin (Varin)

(1606/7?-1654; fl. 1630–1654)

• (French) Medallist •

THE family of Claude and Jean Warin (*or* Varin) is thought to have been engravers and possibly coin forgers who were employed by the minor French aristocracy near Sedan and Liège. Claude and Jean learned their trade in the family business—one that appears to have been somewhat less than totally honest, for as Jones notes, the princely employers of the Warins:

> ...made a profit from producing coinage of inferior alloys which was intended to pass at par with the coins of neighboring countries.[227]

A WELL-KNOWN FRENCH MEDAL OF THE CONSTANT DE SILVECANE, PRESIDENT OF THE COUR DES MONNAIES IN LYON, AND PRESIDENT OF PARLEMENT. BY CLAUDE WARIN, 1647, 75.5 MM., STRUCK IN SILVER WITH STIPPLED BACKGROUND AND INCUSE REVERSE. NOTE THE SIGNATURE BELOW THE TRUNCATION: 'C. WARIN 1647.' IMAGE © VICTORIA & ALBERT MUSEUM, LONDON.

The details of Claude Warin's life are somewhat elusive. More is known about his work, for he was an engraver working at the Lyons mint (1647–1654; *see following entry for Jean Warin*). A prolific medallist, some 70 medals have been attributed to him by Jones.[228] It has been assumed that he was a brother of Jean Warin, engraver-general of coins in France.[229] In his 1894 paper on foreign artists working in England, reflecting the state of knowledge about the Warins at that time, Parkes Weber commented that:

> Claude Warin was probably a relation of Jean Warin, and seems to have worked for some period in England before he finally settled at Lyons. His medals are cast and of a somewhat sculpturesque style, imitating that of Guillaume Dupré[230] rather than that of Jean Warin (p. 2).[231]

Most of Claude Warin's work was carried out in France and most of his subjects were French. He did, however, spend the years 1630/31-1636 in England where he produced a number of attractive portrait medals, including those of Thomas Carey and his wife Margaret Carey (1633, signed 'VA'). After his return to France, Claude Warin completed work on a medal of John Prideaux (signed 'C WA' and dated 1638).[232] Hill notes the similarity of this medal to the one of Sir Thomas Bodley *(see overleaf)* and attributes the latter to Claude Warin as well. The issue of signatures continues, however, to be problematic for two reasons—first, many medals are simply signed 'WARIN,' 'WA' or 'VA,' the latter attributed by Hill to Jean Warin before his association with the French mint.[233] Secondly, the possibility exists, as suggested by Rondot and Parkes Weber, that:

---

[227] M. Jones (1979). *The Art of the Medal,* p. 78.

[228] Ibid.

[229] L. Forrer, *Biographical Dictionary of Medallists*, vol. vi, p. 352.

[230] GUILLAUME DUPRÉ (1574-1643), French sculptor and medallist to Kings Henry IV, Louis XIII and until Dupré's death in 1643, Louis XIV.

[231] F. Parkes Weber (1894). 'Medals and Medallions of the Nineteenth Century, Relating to England, by Foreign Artists,' *Numismatic Chronicle*, Ser. 3, vols. xiii–xiv.

[232] JOHN PRIDEAUX (1578-1850), Regius Professor of Divinity, Oxford (1615-1641) and vice-chancellor of the University and bishop of Worcester (1641-1650).

[233] G. F. Hill (1920). *Medals of the Renaissance;* Hill & Pollard (1978), op. cit., p. 157. Forrer stated that: [Claude Warin's] "works are signed: C. WARIN; — C. VARIN; — C.V.; — WARIN; — VARIN, AND VA" (vol. vi, p. 352).

An Interesting Pair of Medals of Thomas Bodley Associated with Claude Warin (Varin)

Two examples of a medal, in the classical style, of Sir Thomas Bodley (1545-1612). Both are cast, the one at the top in lead and the one below in silver. Both are signed with the usual 'Warin' and each has the *obv.* and *rev.* inscriptions: 'TH · BODLY · EQ · AVR · PVBL · BIBLIOTH · OXON · FVNDATOR · RP · LITERARIAE ·' ('Thomas Bodley, Knight, founder of the Public Library, Oxford') and '· AETERNITAS ·' ('Eternity of the Republic of Letters'). Each bears a profile portrait of Bodley on the obverse and on the reverse a female in classical dress holding the heads of Apollo in her right hand and of Diana in her left. These medals were cast in 1646, possibly to coincide with the publication of Bodley's autobiography. The details are: *(above)* 51 mm. overall, 44.5 mm. without the rim, British Museum acc./reg. no. M.7020, M.I.i 200/28, M.I.Ill xv/6. ex Edw. Hawkins collection; (*below, a slightly enlarged image*) 43 mm., British Museum acc./reg. no. M.8908. M.I.i notes that :

> An entry in the Bodleian Library accounts for 1646 which reads 'Item to ye painter yt drew Sr. Thomas Bodley's picture & to Mr Warren that made his medale to each of them 2s. In toto 4s',...appears to date the medal.

The present authors have found no further information. They are in agreement with *The Burlington Magazine for Connoisseurs* which comments that:

> The Bodley medals [are] a puzzle (vol. xii, Oct. 1907-Mar. 1908, p. 355, fn. 6).

> ...many of the Medals hitherto attributed to Jean Varin, as he signed in later times, were executed by Claude Warin, an engraver who worked at Lyons from 1630 to 1654[234]...Mon. Natalis Rondot has shown that the medals of Englishmen signed WARIN or VARIN are all probably the work of Claude Warin. Although this is contrary to the view which has been most frequently expressed, I feel confident that those who carefully examine the medals will confirm me (p. 287).[235]

---

[234] F. Parkes Weber (1894, op. cit.) citing M. Natalie Rondot, *Les Sculpteurs de Lyon...,* 1884 , pp. 46-47.

[235] R. Natalis, 'English Medals by Foreign Artists,' *Numismatic Chronicle*..., 1888, vol. xiii, p. 287, fn.

Jean Warin (Varin)

(1604/6?-1672; fl. 1629-1672)
• (French) Medallist •

LITTLE is known of Jean Warin's (*also* Varin) early life, despite his later prominence as an engraver of mid-seventeenth century French coins and medals. What is known is that he was born in Liège, that his father was an engraver for Ferdinand of Bavaria (the prince-bishop of Liege, 1577-1650), that Varin moved to Paris in 1626/27 and that he became a naturalized French citizen in 1650.

JEAN WARIN, A LINE ENGRAVING BY GÉRARD EDELINCK (1640-1707), LATE 17TH C. IMAGE © NATIONAL PORTRAIT GALLERY, LONDON.

Having settled in Paris, Warin worked as an engraver at the Louvre mint and by 1629 he was designated the "garde et conducteur des engines de la monnoye du Moulin de Paris." In 1636, Warin had persuaded King Louis XIII to grant him a one-quarter interest in the mint, the other shareholders being Pierre Regnier (*q.v. pp. 127ff.*), Pierre Olivier and Aubin Olivier. Between 1639 and 1648, he had bought out the remaining partners and was the sole proprietor. By 1646, having obtained the patronage of Cardinal Richelieu, he was appointed the conductor of the mint and engraver-general of coinage, likely equivalent to today's comptroller-general of currency. In these positions he oversaw the issue of numerous coins and medals by the mint and thus exerted a very significant influence over the design of French coinage of this period. Part of his contribution was the reintroduction, against the opposition of established interests at the mint, of milling machinery.[236] Unlike his brother Claude, Jean Warin did not work in England and his 'death medal' of Charles I (M.I.i 292/107), which was obviously intended as a tribute to the martyred king, is the only medal of his which has a clearly English theme.

Historical Commentary on Jean Varin

JOHN VARIN or WARIN was an eminent medallist in France, but appears by some works to have been in England, at least to have been employed by the English. There are four such pieces in the collection of Mr. West.[237] The first, a large medallion cast, 'Guil. fil. Rob. Ducy mil. et baronet, astat. suas '21, 1626.' Another, a cast medal of Philip Howard S. R. E. Card. Norfolk. Endymion Porter,

---

[236] L. Forrer, *Biographical Dictionary of Medallists*, vol. vi, pp. 361-372.

[237] JAMES WEST MP (1703-1772), a politician and antiquary, was secretary of the treasury, vice-president and later president (1768-1772) of the Royal Society and a vice-president of the Society of Antiquaries. West was also an enthusiastic 'Grangerizer' (*see p. 369*).

The 'late Mr. West' is mentioned twice as a collector in Vertue's *Medals of Thomas Simon*..., i.e., (i) "Bought at his sale by Mr. Morrison for *Mr. Browne*" (p. 77) and (ii) "Mr. *West* shewed one of these at the Antiquary Society, 1734" (fn., p. 12). p. 56.

Two Medals by Jean Varin

A so-called 'death medal' of Charles I (silver, 69 mm., uniface, M.I.i 292/107, M.I.Ill xxv/4, Platt 1/241/A). This particular example was sold at Morton & Eden's auction of December 9, 2009 (lot 307). It is unsigned but dated 1649. Ex Montagu, Murdoch, Sloane Stanley and Farquhar collections (*see* Platt, 2013, vol. i, pp. 241-243 for further details, including a variant with a reverse design by Jacopo Nizolla da Trezzo). Image courtesy of Morton & Eden, Ltd.

Bust of Armand Jean du Plessis, Cardinal Richelieu of France (1585-1642) (in silver, 1630, 76 mm., British Museum acc/reg. no. G3,IP.1101). The allegorical reverse portrays France as a passenger in a chariot driven by Fame with Fortune chained to it while a flying Victory prepares to place a laurel crown upon France's brow. The arms of Richelieu appear on a banner attached to Fame's trumpet. Image courtesy of A. H. Baldwin & Sons Ltd, London, www.baldwin.co.uk (no. 67, lot 2030).

Medals Bearing Portraits of Jean Warin (Varin)

Two medals bearing the image of Jean Warin. *(Above)* by Jean-Baptiste Dufour (1656-1683) (bronze, 1684, 51 mm., Jones, British Museum acc./reg. no. 1931,0507.43). The three figures on the *rev.* represent *Painting, Medallic Art* and *Sculpture* respectively, with Medallic Art holding in her hand a portrait of Warin. The inscription: 'A single one would have sufficed to render him imortal.' (*Below*) The medal by Jacques-Édouard Gatteaux (1788-1881) from the series 'La Galerie Métallique des Grands Hommes Français' (in bronze, struck examples dated either 1817 or 1823, 40 mm.). Images *(above)* © Trustees of the British Museum and (*below*) of a medal in a private collection.

aetat. 48, 1635. And Margareta, uxor, st. 26, 1633. I have a good medal of Cardinal Richelieu by Warin, who died in 1675, as I learn from a jetton of him by Dacier. Warin was exceedingly fond of money; and having forced his daughter, who was beautiful, to marry a rich and deformed officer of the revenue, she poisoned herself a few days after the wedding, saying, 'I must perish, since my father's avarice would have it so.' Lettres de Guy Patin; and Recreations Histor., vol. i., p. 75, 1768

— H. Walpole, *Anecdotes of Painting in England*, 1871 ed., p. 206

The 'Oxford Crown' Coin by Thomas Rawlins

The 'Oxford Crown' coin was produced by Thomas Rawlins in 1644, and is included here to further illustrate Rawlins' skill. It depicts Charles I on horseback brandishing a sword, with the walled city of Oxford in the lower background of the obverse. The obverse has a Latin inscription translatable as: 'Let God arise and let his enemies be scattered.' This coin bears Thomas Rawlins' monogram engraved into the city wall (at 7:00) in the background.* The reverse inscription reflects Charles I's ambitions for the Civil War—upholding the Protestant religion, the laws of England and a free parliament. Because of its scarcity and the clever way in which Rawlins engraved his monogram, this coin is highly desirable to collectors. It illustrates the evident masterful work of Rawlins.

The first specimen here (top) is an original issue** with a line of provenance which extends back to its sale at Gerard's on January 18, 1786. It was sold at Christie's auction of November 15, 2001 (sale 1286, lot 68, £34,500). The bottom one is an 18th c. copy, one of two which were sold by Dix Noonan Webb at their auctions of December 17, 2007 (lot 277, £230) and June 16, 2010 (lot 1009, £370). Images courtesy of Christie's and Dix Noonan Webb, Ltd.

* The walls were later torn down by the Parliamentarians.

**The original coin, rated 'extremely fine' (as is also the case for the forgery) shows the typical weakness at the sides of a coin produced on a 'rocker press.' It is one of a small number of known specimens, possibly no more than 15, none of which have a fully struck legend.

Thomas Rawlins

(1620?-1670)
•Medallist•

THOMAS RAWLINS was one of the great medallists of the Civil War period, and in addition, was a playwright, goldsmith and gem engraver. Rawlins apprenticed at the London mint under the tutelage of Nicholas Briot and was appointed chief engraver of the king's mints during the Civil War. While Thomas Simon, an acknowledged Puritan, remained faithful to the Parliamentarian cause, Rawlins was a firm Royalist. The first medal on which Rawlins' signature appeared was that of William Wade, in 1641.[238]

Given his loyalty to the king, in 1643 Rawlins moved to Charles' headquarters at Oxford where he produced coins and medals for him. In 1644 he created the 'Oxford crown,' (*see preceding page*) which Nathanson, in his volume on Thomas Simon,[239] judged to have been Rawlins' best work. The following year Rawlins produced the 'Forlorn Hope' medal and the unique medal which was conferred upon Sir Robert Welch, as well as the medal struck to commemorate Prince Rupert's taking of Bristol. He also produced the medal commemorating the meeting of Charles I and Henrietta Maria at Kineton in 1643. Rawlins was appointed chief engraver of the mint in March 1647, likely following Briot's death.

A VERY NICE EXAMPLE OF A PORTRAIT MEDAL OF KING CHARLES LAUREATE AND QUEEN HENRIETTA MARIA BY THOMAS RAWLINS (CA **1649**, IN SILVER, **26** X **20** MM., **M.I.I 355/218, M.I.ILL XXXI/10, PLATT I/193/B**). IMAGE COURTESY SPINK AUCTIONS, NO. **9026**, LOT **158**.

Rawlins' 'Oxford Crown,' issued in 1644, is a silver piece, with the image of the mounted and armed king on the obverse. The reverse shows plumes with the inscription stating Charles' war aims, i.e., the promotion of the Protestant religion, the laws of England and a free Parliament. Rawlins also made the pattern for the medal given to Bishop Juxon immediately before the king was beheaded.[240]

Rawlins continued his work in this role in Oxford for the king and his supporters until March 1648, when he fled to France, not returning to England until 1652. When he did return, his status was greatly reduced and until the Restoration he could only find work as a die maker of tradesmen's tokens. Forrer notes, however, that:

> There is no doubt that, during the Commonwealth the Engraver earned his livelihood by cutting private seals and badges, or "suspension medalets, which the disheartened cavaliers wore in remembrance of their beloved sovereign."[241]

[238] *See text box on following page.*

[239] A. J. Nathanson (1975). *Thomas Simon: His Life and work, 1618-1665.* London: Seaby.

[240] L. Forrer, *Biographical Dictionary of Medallists*, vol. v, p. 38.

[241] Ibid, vol. v., p. 51, citing B. Nightingale, *Numismatic Chronicle*, xiii, p. 129 ff. *For examples of these medalets, see this vol., p. 336, and Platt, vol. i, pp. 286-295.*

Medal of William Wade by Thomas Rawlins

This medal (M.I.i 289/103, M.I.Ill xxiv/13) was made before the Civil War, although during the war a William Wade was a major in the Parliamentarian Army. M.I.i notes that there was no officer by this name in the Royalist Army. Thus, if this medal was made by Rawlins, who was at the Royalist mint, it was probably unrelated to the events of the war. A recent image of the electrotype specimen (in base medal) in the British Museum is illustrated on the left, while the collotype image of this medal from M.I.Ill appears to the right. Note the differing visual effects. The details are: 1.5 x 1.1 in. (38.0 x 28.3 mm.), 15.9 gms. acc./reg. no. PI.1221. The electrotype specimen of the medal is soldered to a thicker metal plate. Both images © Trustees of the British Museum.

This work apparently did not provide Rawlins with a sufficient living for in 1657 he was placed in debtor's prison at the 'Hole in St. Martin's.' He sought help from John Evelyn, an acquaintance, who wrote that Rawlins was:

> ...an excellent artist, but debash'd fellow. [242]

Rawlins' fortune and position changed for the better when Charles II came to the throne. He was reinstated as chief engraver at the mint while Thomas Simon was named 'chief engraver of arms and seals' and was given a residence in the mint. During this time some of Rawlins' work consisted of engraving the king's effigies for coins, likely designing copper farthings of Charles II as well as producing the privy seal for Ireland and five judicial seals for the counties in Wales. Rawlins continued to hold the position of chief engraver to the mint until his death in 1670.[243]

---

[242] *DNB*, vol. xvi, p. 770. debash'd=A sudden awareness of, or being overcome by shame or other fault.

[243] D. Allen (pp. 50-51) attributed the following medals to Thomas Rawlins: *Signed and dated:* William Wade (??,1641, M.I.i 289/103); Sir William Parkhurst (1644, M.I.i 311/140); Sir Robert Heath (1645, M.I.i 319/154); Thomas Harper (1647, M.I.i 330/172); Sir Robert and Lady Bolles (1655, M.I.i 420/59); Edward Wray (unpublished, 1657). *Unsigned, dated, and "doubtfully attributed to Thomas Rawlins:"* Simon Beal[e] (?,1646, M.I.i 323/160); Sir Henry Slingsby (1658, M.I.i 427/71). *Signed and dated, or bearing the portraits of signed and dated medals:* Forlorn Hope (1643, M.I.i 302/123); Sir Robert Welch (1643, M.I.i 302/124); Charles meets Henrietta Maria at Kineton (1643, M.I.i 306/130); Bristol Taken (1643, M.I.i 307/131-2); Peace or War (1643, M.I.i 308/134); Death of Charles (1649 or after, M.I.i 341/190, 344/195); Charles & Henrietta Maria (M.I.i 354/215-18; 356/221, 359/229, 369/256); Charles I and Charles II (?, M.I.i 371/261, 301/122); Charles II, (M.I.i 371/262); Coronation of Charles II (1661, M.I.i 474/80, 474/81, 474/82); Charles II, Dominion of the Sea (1665, M.I.i 506/144). Key: ?=doubtfully attributed, ??=very doubtfully attributed.

'The Meeting at Kineton' by Thomas Rawlins

'Charles I and Henrietta Maria meet at Kineton on July 13, 1643' (1643, 36 mm., M.I.i 306/130, M.I.Ill xxvi/15, Platt i/209/a). A medal by Thomas Rawlins created to celebrate the reunion of the royal couple at Roundway Down near where the Parliamentarian Army had that same day been defeated. Queen Henrietta Maria had just returned to England from the Continent where she had sought to procure arms for the Royalist cause. The quality of this production is remarkably inferior when compared with Rawlins' other work, likely reflecting haste in producing it. Image © Trustees of the British Museum.

According to Forrer:

> Rawlins, although a very talented artist, was an uneven worker, and some of his productions betray no doubt the great haste with which he had to execute the King's commands.[244]

Mayo seems to have shared this opinion, for he commented that:

> Rawlins executed almost all the Royalist medals and badges, but his work does not equal Simon's.[245]

Rawlins signed his coins and tokens with an R, a bold **R** rotated 90 degrees to the right, or ℛ. His medals, which are usually cast and chased, are signed R;—T. R: or with his full name. The 'Oxford Crown' bears his initials combined into a monogram. Forrer notes that:

> In technical finish and sureness of touch, Rawlins is inferior to Thomas Simon, the great Medallist of the Commons, yet much of his work is decidedly pleasing and elegant. Evelyn says that he excelled in medals and in intaglios, and in Flecknoe's 'Miscellanies' there is a poem on that excellent cymelist [sic] or sculptor in gold and precious stones, Thomas Rawlins.[246]

Hill & Pollard observed that of the coins, medals and badges prepared during the latter part of Charles' reign:

> A great many of these are of very indifferent quality; but the portraits of Charles I and the young Prince Charles on the 'Forlorn Hope' badge are beautiful.[247]

---

[244] L. Forrer (1912), *Biographical Dictionary*..., vol. v, pp. 51-52.

[245] J. H. Mayo (1897) *Medals and Decorations*, vol. i, p. lxxv.

[246] L. Forrer, ibid. vol. v, p. 40, quoting Wroth, *DNB*, 1909, vol. xlvii, p. 326-327.

[247] G. F. Hill & G. Pollard, *Medals of the Renaissance*, p. 158. *Also see Platt, vol. i, pp. 303-306.* The present authors would go further and question whether the very great differences in portraiture seen on Rawlins' pieces are not a question of 'indifference,' but perhaps of production by a 'different hand,' that of an assis-

As noted above, Rawlins was also an author and playwright, publishing in 1640 the tragedy '*The Rebellion*,' a play set in Seville and casting tailors as its main characters, as well as a collection of poems and two posthumously published comedies.[248]

A SILVER-GILT ROYALIST BADGE OF CHARLES I AND QUEEN HENRIETTA MARIA BY T. RAWLINS, (CA. 1649, 37 X 29 MM., M.I.I, 354/215, M.I.ILL XXXI/5, EIMER 169, PLATT I/195/A). THE STYLES OF THE OBVERSE AND REVERSE DESIGNS HERE APPEAR MISMATCHED. ALSO, THE PORTRAIT OF CHARLES BEARS A GREAT DEAL OF SIMILARITY TO THE ONE ON THE DEATH MEDAL ATTRIBUTED TO JEAN WARIN WHICH APPEARS ON P. 146. IMAGE COURTESY DIX NOONAN WEBB, LTD.

Historical Commentary on Thomas Rawlins

An ardent Royalist, he served both Charles I. and Charles II, undergoing great hardships during the Commonwealth.

—L. Forrer, *Biographical Dictionary of Medallists*, 1912, vol. v, p. 38.

§

Little is known of this artist except during the Civil War, when he made the majority of the Royalist badges.

—D. Allen, Thomas Simon's Sketch-book, *Walpole Society*, 1937-38, vol. 27, p. 45.

§

THOMAS RAWLINS, author of The Rebellion, was principal Engraver of the Mint in the reign of Charles I. and Charles II., a vocation which, in his preface, he prefers to the threadbare occupation of a poet. It is an argument, as well of his personal respectability, as of his easy circumstances, that no fewer than eleven copies of prefatory verses, by the wits of the time, are prefixed to the old edition. Notwithstanding the popularity of the piece, and several passages of real merit. It was never republished; perhaps because Rebellion soon assumed the whole kingdom for its stage.

—R. Dodsley, et al., *The Ancient British Drama...*, 1810, vol. iii, p. 544.

§

---

tant or apprentice, the sculpted medal thus perhaps being more accurately described as being 'in the style of' Thomas Rawlins.'

[248] Brydges notes that Rawlins:

> ...was author of a Tragedy, called "Rebellion," 4to, 1640...He also published a book of Poems, under the title of "Calanthe," 8vo. 1648; and likewise, if not the same "Good Friday; or, divine Meditations on the Passion of Christ;" and with it some other small pieces of poetry, 4to, 1663 (*Censura Literaria...*, 1805, vol. i, p. 37).

A VERY ATTRACTIVE MEDAL BY THOMAS RAWLINS (1643, 42 X 33.1 MM., BRITISH MUSEUM ACC./REG. NO. M.9082, M.I.I 301/122, M.I.ILL XXVI/8, PLATT I/298/A), THIS EXAMPLE IN SILVER-GILT BEARS A PORTRAIT OF CHARLES I ON THE *OBV.* AND OF PRINCE CHARLES ON THE *REV.*; OTHER EXAMPLES HAVE NO REVERSE. A UNIFACE EXAMPLE WITH ONLY THIS OBVERSE WAS UNTIL RELATIVELY RECENTLY BELIEVED TO BE THE SO-CALLED 'FORLORN HOPE' MEDAL UNTIL THE ACTUAL MEDAL OF THAT NAME WAS IDENTIFIED. THE BRITISH MUSEUM SUGGESTS THAT THE UNIFACE OBVERSE-ONLY EXAMPLES MAY HAVE SERVED AS MEMORIAL MEDALS FOR SUPPORTERS OF THE LATE KING. THIS MEDAL COULD POSSIBLY HAVE SERVED AS A MILITARY REWARD FOR HIGHER RANKING OFFICERS, ALTHOUGH CONFIRMATION AWAITS THE DISCOVERY OF CORROBORATING EVIDENCE. IMAGE © TRUSTEES OF THE BRITISH MUSEUM.

§

I shall now set down what little I have to say of the medallists of King Charles. Briot has been mentioned under the preceding reign: he and T. Simon, his disciple, possessed the royal favour till the beginning of the troubles; when Simon falling off to the parliament, a new medallist was employed on the few works executed for the king during the remainder of his life: his name was THOMAS RAWLINS.

The first work by which he was known to the public was of a nature very foreign from his profession; in 1640 he wrote a play called 'The Rebellion,' and afterwards a comedy, called 'Tom Essence.' He was appointed engraver to the Mint, now become ambulatory, by patent in 1648; having in the preceding year, while the king was at Oxford, struck a medal on the action of Kineton-field. Under the date on the reverse is the letter R, sideways (Evelyn, p. iii., No. 32).[249] The next year he struck another, after many offers of peace had been made by the king and rejected; on the reverse are a sword and a branch of laurel; the legend 'In utrumque paratus.' The letter R. under the bust of the king.[250] In 1644 he made a large oval medal, stamped in silver, with the effigies of a man holding a coin in his hand, and this inscription, 'Guliel. Parkhurst, eq. aurat. custos camb. et monet. totius

[249] 'Charles meets Henrietta Maria at Kineton' (1643, M.I.I 306/130, M.I.ILL xxvi/15, Platt I/209/A).

[250] The 'Peace or War' medal (1643, M.I.I 308/134, Platt I/205/A).

'CORONATION OF CHARLES II, 1661,' IN COPPER/BRONZE, BY THOMAS RAWLINS (33 MM., M.I.I 475/81, M.I.ILL XLV/12, EIMER 220). THERE ARE AT LEAST FOUR VARIETIES OF THIS MEDAL, ALL RARE TO VERY RARE AND DIFFERING IN DETAILS, INCLUDING THE SIGNATURE, PRESENCE OF AN EDGE INSCRIPTION, *REV.* DESIGN, METAL (SILVER, Æ GILT, COPPER/BRONZE), AND PRESENCE (OR ABSENCE) OF A DIE CRACK. IMAGE COURTESY SPINK AUCTIONS, NO. 1011, LOT 319.

Anglias' 1623. Oxon. 1644.' T. R.[251] ...I take for granted this Mr. Parkhurst had been either a patron or relation of Rawlins, or one cannot conceive why he should have gone back twenty-one years to commemorate an obscure person, so little connected with the singular events of the period when it was struck. This medal was in the collection of Sir Hans Sloane, and is now in the museum, as was, and is, an oval piece of gold of Charles II., the reverse a ship; better workmanship than the preceding.[252] There is but one piece more, certainly known for his, a cast in lead, thus inscribed, 'Rob. Bolles de Scampton in com. Lincol., bart.;' under the shoulder, 'T. Rawlins, F. 1665.'[253] There might be, and probably were, other works of his hand, to which in prudence he did not set his name. Such is the bold medallion of Archbishop Laud, struck in 1644.[254]

—H. Walpole, *Anecdotes of Painting in England*, 1879 ed., pp. 205-206.

§

...Thomas Rawlins, an engraver of considerable excellence, and, before the civil wars, an officer in the Tower Mint. When Parkhurst and Bushell were appointed masters of the mint established at New Inn, Oxford, in February 1642-3, Rawlins at the same time was constituted chief engraver; but on the

ANOTHER VERY RARE MEDAL ATTRIBUTED TO THOMAS RAWLINS WHILE HE WAS RESIDENT IN ENGLAND. THIS MEDAL CELEBRATES THE BETROTHAL OF CHARLES I LOUIS, ELECTOR PALATINE, AND CHARLOTTE OF HESSE CASSEL. THE OBVERSE INSCRIPTION '❀ VNIENDO ❀ MVLTIPLICAMINI.' ('YE MULTIPLY BY UNION') AND *REV.* 'PERFECI 1648' ('I HAVE SUCCEEDED'). IN SILVER, (21 MM., M.I.I 339/185, XXIX/17, BRITISH MUSEUM ACC./REG. NO. M.7229, EIMER 156). THE REVERSE DESIGN OF THIS MEDAL WAS ALSO USED AS THE REVERSE OF M.I.I 384/1 (M.I.ILL XXXIV/19, ACC./REG. NO. M.7317) SIGNIFYING THE INTENTION OF CHARLES II TO ASSUME THE ROYAL PREROGATIVE. THE USE OF THIS REVERSE DESIGN MAY HAVE BEEN BASED SIMPLY UPON THE DESIGN'S AVAILABILITY AS IT APPEARS TO HAVE NO OBVIOUS SYMBOLIC OR OTHER CONNECTION WITH THE SUCCESSION. IMAGE ©TRUSTEES OF THE BRITISH MUSEUM.

[251] SIR WILLIAM PARKHURST, master of the mint under Charles I (M.I.I 311/140, Platt II/249).

[252] CHARLES II, 'Dominion of the Sea' (1665, M.I.I 506/144).

[253] SIR ROBERT AND LADY BOLLES (1655, M.I.I 420/59, Platt I/57).

[254] Presumably the larger medal of ARCHBISHOP WILLIAM LAUD, (1644, M.I.I 315/147, Platt II/190/B).

king's affairs becoming hopeless, Rawlins fled to Paris. On his returning to England, his mark is found on the town-pieces of 1652, struck for the cities of Bristol and Oxford; and there are doubtless others to which he did not affix his initial. In 1658 his mark is again distinguished on the Houndsditch and one or two other tokens. He was then in extreme distress, as evidenced by a letter addressed by him, from "the Hole in St. Martin's, Febru. 27, 1657-8," to John Evelyn, pathetically imploring his aid:

> Sir: It is my misfortune since my coming into England, to rancounter [sic] many misfortunes. I am now a prisoner*, and am resolved to make use of the Act for Relief of Poore Prisoners, and only want money to sue out my Habeas Corpeas. Sir, it is for God's sake I begg your charitye, and I shall returne it ether in worke, in which, I thank God, I have much bettered myselfe since I had the honor to see you at Parris, or in what quantity of money you shall be pleased to furnish me with. Sir, I once more for Heaven's sake implore your assistance, to him that writs him selfe, however distressed at this tyme,
>
> "Yo[r] faithfull and ever gratefull servant,
>
> THO: RAWLINS."

Two examples of a very rare medal of Cecil Calvert, 2nd Lord Baltimore (1605-1675). It is attributed to Thomas Rawlins. It was likely executed by Rawlins during his residence in Oxford, the Royalist court, after Calvert gave up his plans to reside in America. The *rev.* bears a map of Maryland, the sun above. The *rev.* inscriptions 'TERRAMARIÆ' (Maryland) and 'VT : SOL : LVOEBIS : AMERICÆ' ('As the sun thou shalt enlighten America'). The suspension loop of the example in the British Museum (*top*) appears to have been removed (1632, cast and chased in silver, 35 x 32 mm., M.I.i 261/53, B.M. acc./reg. no. M.7113, Eimer 121). A specimen of this medal, in extremely fine condition (*bottom*), sold for $176,250 at the Heritage Auctions sale of January 2013 (lot 3587). The research reported in the sale catalogue indicates that this was:

> The First Indian Peace Medal created specifically for use with the Indians...Only three examples of this medal are known: the present example, one in the British Museum without loop and one in the Maryland Historical Society (this last a different variety and size, without the rosette mint mark). The medal offered here is the only specimen retaining its attached hanger or loop and is almost certainly the piece that spent more than 30 years in the hands of the powerful Susquehannocks, who could have easily overrun the new and under populated colony of Maryland but for the pledge of peace represented by this historic piece of silver.

* *fn.* The "Hole in St. Martin's," where Rawlins intimated he was then a prisoner, was one of the many cells called public prisons, which disgraced the metropolis in the seventeenth century. Cromwell, in his war with

the Dutch, crammed it with prisoners; and in October, 1663, the Dutch captains there confined addressed petition to General Monk, praying his good offices towards their liberation; it was dated "from the Prison in the Mewes," and from that appellation was possibly a place of confinement created under the Stuarts; subsequently it became the parish watch-house, of which there is an excessively rare print. It stood on the east side of the Mews, the site being the now roadway in front of the east end of the Royal Academy.

—H. B. H. Beaufoy, *Descriptive Catalogue of the…Tokens Current in the Seventeenth Century*, 1855, pp. 137.

§

Evelyn, in his endorsement of the letter, described him as "an excellent artist, but debash'd [debauch'd] fellow;" nor is there the slightest inference to be drawn that this urgent appeal was otherwise than unfavourably received. The engraving of traders' irons was at best but precarious and unremunerative, and although he is known to have competed for the proposed state farthings, to displace those issued by traders and ale-house keepers, yet he was thoroughly unsuccessful. The piece with Oliver's profile on the obverse, and having on the reverse the attributes of the three kingdoms entwined on columns, inscribed THVS VNITED INVINCEABLE, and again issued in four or five varieties known as patterns, were the productions of Thomas Rawlins. After the restoration of Charles the Second, Rawlins's patent as chief engraver was but slightly recognized; he however worked in the mint on the official seals; the money-dies being supervised by younger, more energetic, and more skilfully practised hands.

—Ibid. H. B. H. Beaufoy, *Descriptive Catalogue of the…Tokens Current in the 17th Century*, 1855, pp. 137-138.

In addition to being a medallist, Thomas Rawlins was a playwright and also did related artwork. The title page of the above play by James Yorke, whose image is incorporated into the design, is an example, having been engraved by Rawlins in 1641. Note the monogram, a combined T and R, at the lower center left. Image © Trustees of the British Museum.

§

THOMAS RAWLINS (who was Engraver of the Mint under both Charles I and Charles II), the author of a tragedy called The Rebellion, which while containing one situation of surprising novelty, is otherwise unmarked by originality.

—A. W. Ward, *A History of English Dramatic Literature…*, 1875, v. 2, p. 358.

• Two states of an Etching of Westminster Hall •

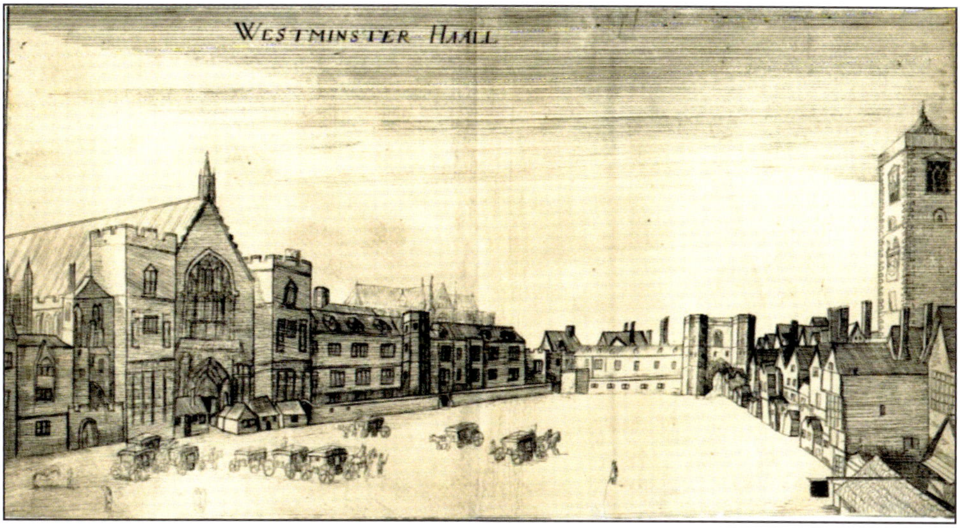

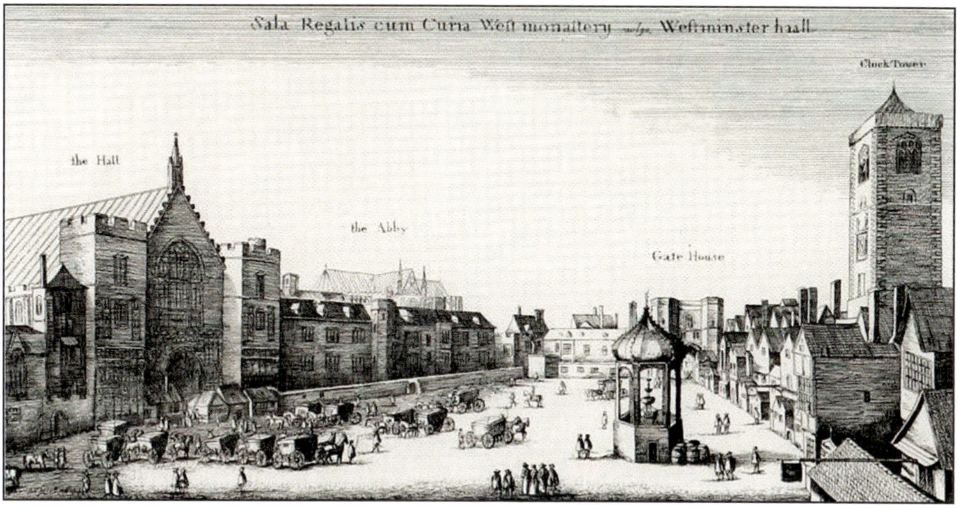

Wenceslaus Hollar's *Sala Regalis cum Curia West-monasterÿ, vulgo Westminster haall (Westminster Hall)*, ca. 1647. The first and second (of four) states of this etching. Note how the scene has become populated between the first two states—people, additional coaches, and even a fountain* have appeared. Westminster Abbey is visible in the background at center-left, its definition increasing in subsequent states. The difference in color between the two images likely reflects in part printing considerations, the first state of the etching having been printed on laid ivory paper. Images © Trustees of the British Museum.

*The fountain, the octagonal canopied structure shown to the right, was built in 1443 by Henry VI. It was connected to a 12th century conduit and remained in place until the late 17th century. In 1977 a fountain commemorating Queen Elizabeth II's Silver Jubilee was built in the yard which now has been made into a formal garden.

Blondeau's Commonwealth Milled Coinage

Two rare and attractive milled coins of the Commonwealth period. (*Above*) A half-crown coin in silver, 1658, the dies for which were produced by Thomas Simon. Minted in 1658 at the order of Oliver Cromwell, using Peter Blondeau's milling machine. Produced until 1662, the coin was worth 30 pennies, two and a half shillings, or one-eighth of a pound. (*Below*) A gold broad dated 1656. Worth 20 shillings, the broad anteceded the early guinea, which was in use between 1663 and 1814, although the latter's worth was fixed at 21 shillings from 1717. The broad was often retained as a memento by (the more prosperous) former supporters of Oliver Cromwell. Today it is the rarer of the two coins. Images courtesy of Heritage Auctions, September 13, 2009, lot 21003 and January 6-7, 2013, lot 20788.

Peter (Pierre) Blondeau

(*d.* 1664)

• Medallist •

PETER BLONDEAU was a coin engraver and medallist whose most important contribution was the invention of a machine that struck coins and medals with a milled edge, thus much improving their manufacture and appearance over previous methods. A contemporary of Abraham and Thomas Simon, Blondeau collaborated with the latter in the production of coins under both Oliver Cromwell and Charles II.

Through the mid-sixteenth century, coins had been manufactured by hammering. This practice was superseded by the introduction of milling which used a horse-powered screw press, a process which produced improved coins with much more uniformity and a distinct appearance, but at a slower rate. According to Henfrey,

> ...the coining-press or mill was known to Benvenuto Cellini...in the sixteenth century, and it was introduced into France by Aubry Olivier about 1553. It was not, however, until March, 1645, that coinage by the hammer was entirely suppressed in that country.[255]

Although Eloy[e] Mestrelle, a French moneyer, had first introduced the milling process in England during the reign of Elizabeth I, he was very much resented by the workers at the mint, who saw his machinery as a threat to their livelihoods. Milled coins, likely attributable to Mestrelle, appeared between 1561 and 1575. Mestrelle was, however, eventually dismissed after a decade of employment. Turning to counterfeiting, he was apprehended and hanged in 1578. Milling was not reintroduced in England until 1628, when Nicholas Briot, also a Frenchman, became chief engraver. In the early 1630s, Briot had produced a high quality series of coins for the Crown, but once again the introduction of a milling machine encountered the hostility of mint employees who feared loss of their jobs. Briot was, in effect, banished to the mint in Scotland, where he was appointed master (1635-1639).

With Oliver Cromwell now in power, the Council of State and Parliament desired to improve the quality, appearance and soundness of the coinage. To this end, in 1649 Peter Blondeau, who had improved upon the milling process, but had returned to France in 1656 and was then residing in Paris, was invited to bring his milling machinery to England. Blondeau had:

> ...invented and brought to perfection certain improved machinery for striking money of equal sizes and shapes, having a beautiful polish, and with graining or inscriptions on the edges; thus preventing the clipping of the current coins, and the counterfeiting of them to any extent.[256]

Blondeau's own version of the invitation is as follows:

> The Honourable Councell of State had prudently resolved to have the money well Coyned, if they could but meet with an excellent Workman to have the conduct of that Work: A year since (*i.e.* about June 1649) I had notice of it, whereupon I sent hither (to London) some Paterns of Coyn, which were esteemed and approved of by the said Honourable Councell of State, which occasioned my coming into England.[257]

Following his having sent examples of his work to London, Blondeau arrived there on September 3, 1649, and was paid £40, but told that if the Council could not come to some kind of agreement as to his pay he would be reimbursed for the expenses of his journey. The £40 appears to have been compensation for the clothes and personal items Blondeau lost to pirates when he made the crossing by sea from France. In fact, he was never paid for the expense of his journey.

---

[255] H. W. Henfrey (1877), *Numismata Cromwelliana: or, the Medallic History of Oliver Cromwell...*, p. 65.

[256] Ibid. p. 61.

[257] *Proposals to the Parliament*, June 1650, folio sheet in the British Museum, cited by Henfrey, p. 62.

A SCREW PRESS FOR MINTING COINS, *CA.* 1750. RATHER THAN BEING STRUCK, IMAGES WERE PRESSED ONTO BLANK METAL DISKS OR PLANCHETS WHICH HAD BEEN SOFTENED PRIOR TO BEING INSERTED INTO THE PRESS BY A BOY AS SHOWN HERE. THE WEIGHTED ARMS PROVIDED FORCE WHICH WAS THEN CONVERTED INTO VERTICAL PRESSURE AT THE POINT AT WHICH THE COIN DIE CAME INTO CONTACT WITH THE BLANK METAL DISK. THIS OFT-REPRODUCED IMAGE ORIGINALLY APPEARED IN *L'ENCYCLOPÉDIE DIDEROT ET D'ALEMBERT*, CA. 1751-1757.

Blondeau's appearance in London did not please everyone—Dr. Aaron Guerdain, the master of the mint, who claimed that there were already too many workers at the mint, stated that if he:

> ...was come to be an Officer of the Mint, they were already too many, and that the Workmen were more than they had need for the Coyning of their Money, which they would doe so well, that the State would be satisfied.[258]

Blondeau remained idle in London for nine months, at his own expense, when he finally wrote a paper on:

> ...the evils occasioned by the counterfeiting, clipping, and transporting of the current coin.[259]

Stating that the prevention of these evils was the reason that the committee wanted him to remain in England, Blondeau also reiterated the Council of State's proposition that:

> ...by a new Invention of mine, to make a more handsomer Coyne, than it can be found in all the world besides, *viz.* That shall not only be Stamped on both Flatsides, but shall even be marked with Letters upon the thicknesse of the Brim, whereby the Counterfeiting, Casting, and Clipping of the Coyne shall be prevented.

[258] H. W. Henfrey (1877), ibid. p. 62.

[259] Ibid. p. 63. In fact, it was not until 1656 that milled coins designed by THOMAS SIMON and bearing the Protector's portrait were produced; the use of hammered coins only ceased in 1662, after the Restoration. From that point on, coins were milled.

An 'improved' screw press for coinage illustrated on a French copper token of 1797. The inscription refers to it as having an improved beam or arm designed to avoid the accidents associated with earlier models. This token was issued privately by the Monneron brothers, French bankers, with the approval of the French government, in response to a shortage of small change in circulation and a loss of confidence in the paper 'Assignats' issued by the new government. The tokens themselves were minted by Matthew Bolton at the Soho Mint in Birmingham. Image © Trustees of the British Museum (acc./reg. no. 1870,0507.6250).

> [Blondeau went on to say that the Master of the Mint]:...hath told me himself in plaine terms, That he would doe his utmost to hinder my Proposition; and for that end he hath brought in an Irish Lock Smith, one *David Rammage*, a man ill-affected to the present Government, who hath been Servant formerly [to] the late deceased Master *Briot*, for whom he forged his Tools, and marked his Brasse Counters.[260]

He then alluded to the low prices set by the minters:

> ...to discourage him and make him go home, when they would return to their old ways. He says that the moneyers have tried to imitate his patterns, and to discover his secrets, but without the slightest success. [261]

In another letter, Blondeau answered his critics who stated that his coins could easily be counterfeited. He responded that his machines were too large and expensive, thus requiring many men to operate them, concluding that:

> ...his money cannot be successfully moulded and cast, nor can it be clipped without taking away the letters or graining on the edge, thereby causing immediate detection [and that his] pieces with inscribed edges cannot be successfully or expeditiously made in the Tower Mint by the old methods. [262]

Despite his protestations, the mint officers continued to oppose Blondeau. Their opposition was vitriolic, and played heavily upon English xenophobia toward Blondeau's being French. The lieutenant of the Tower was engaged to protect him and his assistants from mischief by giving them rooms at Worcester House both for their safety and where Blondeau could continue his work in peace.[263]

[260] Ibid. p. 62.
[261] Ibid. p. 64.
[262] Ibid. p. 64.
[263] Nathanson, p. 26.

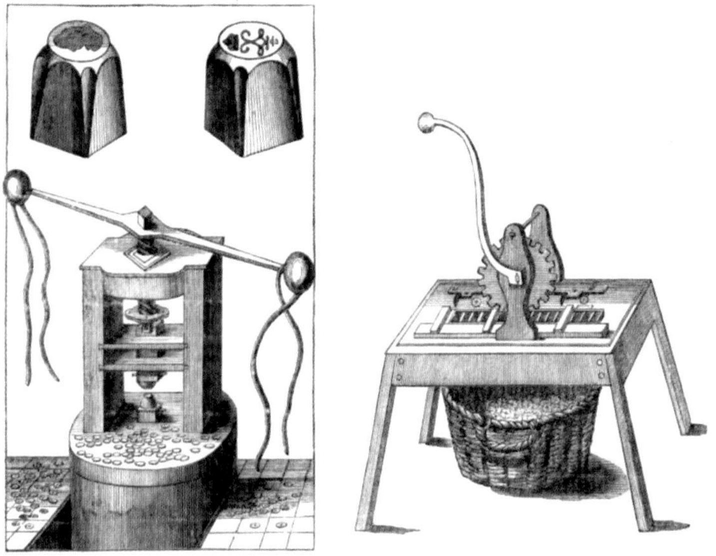

LATE 17TH C. ENGRAVINGS OF (*LEFT*) A MILL AND [SCREW] PRESS FOR IMPRESSING DESIGNS ON TO PLANCHETS FROM DIES. (*RIGHT*) A MACHINE FOR 'MILLING' OR INSCRIBING THE EDGES OF COINS. IMAGES ORIGINALLY IN BOIZARD'S* *TRAITÉ DES MONNAIES, DE LEURS CIRCONSTANCES ET DÉPENDENCES* (CA. 1692) AND REPRINTED IN COCHRAN-PATRICK, *RECORDS OF THE COINAGE OF SCOTLAND* (1876), PP. LII, LV.

*ALSO BOISARD. BOIZARD (D. 1725) WAS COUNSELOR AT THE FRENCH ROYAL 'COUR DES MONNAIES,' IN PARIS, THE LEGAL BODY WHICH REGULATED COIN-MAKING AND THOSE OCCUPATIONS WHICH USED OR DEALT IN THE USE OF GOLD AND SILVER (E.G., MONEYERS, MONEY-CHANGERS, JEWELERS, GOLDSMITHS, ETC.). HE IS CONSIDERED BY SOME TO HAVE BEEN A 'FOUNDER' OF THE SCIENCE OF NUMISMATICS.

Thereupon, the Committee suggested holding a competition to see who could make the most impressive and attractive coin. The winner would gain the employment. Thomas Simon helped Blondeau, supplying the dies during this contest.[264] Blondeau was an engineer and thus needed Simon to engrave the dies. One of the mint's objections to Blondeau was that two hundred families would lose their jobs at the mint if Blondeau won. Whether this consideration affected the outcome is not known. Although Blondeau's coinage was much improved over the mint's work, a decision was not made, only deferred.[265] Blondeau continued to work on the fringes of the mint, having been granted working space at Drury House.

Blondeau was finally allowed to employ his coining machines in May 1651. Conditions changed, however, when Oliver Cromwell, upon assuming power as Protector, promised Blondeau funds for equipment. An inquiry conducted by a committee including Major-general Lambert and Sir Charles Wolseley into the use of Blondeau's machine for coining resulted in a positive report to the Council:[266]

---

[264] According to Nathanson, Blondeau and Simon:

> ...were close collaborators in the execution of the famous Cromwell portrait series...Simon engraved the dies, and thus he was responsible for the high quality of medallic art...while Blondeau, concerned with the mechanics of striking, was responsible for the excellence with which they were struck (pp. 18, 28).

[265] For details of the entire matter, see Henfrey, 1879, pp. 77-80 and Forrer, vol. i, p. 199.

[266] The Committee for the Mint, report dated March 7, 1653/54.

A CHARLES II LOYALTY BADGE BY BLONDEAU

'LOYALTY BADGES' OF A SIZE TO ALLOW CONCEALMENT WERE WORN BY CHARLES I'S FOLLOWERS AFTER HIS DEATH IN 1649. THIS PRACTICE CONTINUED TO BE POPULAR WITH BADGES BEARING THE IMAGE OF CHARLES II BEING WORN BY THE LATTER'S SUPPORTERS DURING HIS ABSENCE FROM THE THRONE OF ENGLAND. THE SMALL SIZE OF THE BADGES ALLOWED THEM TO BE WORN SURREPTITIOUSLY. THEY MAY ALSO HAVE BEEN WORN OPENLY FOR A FEW YEARS AFTER THE RESTORATION. THIS RARE CAST AND CHASED SILVER BADGE (18 X 15 MM., M.I.I 438/7, M.I.ILL XL/12, BRITISH MUSEUM ACC./REG. NO. M.7407) WAS MADE BY PIERRE BLONDEAU, CA. 1649-1664. THE REVERSE DESIGN OF TWO ANGELS SUPPORTING A CROWN IS RELATIVELY UNCOMMON AMONG THESE BADGES, APPEARING ON ONLY TWO OTHER EXAMPLES (I.E., M.I.I 5, M.I.ILL XL/10 AND M.I.I 444/18, M.I.ILL XL/22). EX EDWARD HAWKINS COLLECTION. IMAGE © TRUSTEES OF THE BRITISH MUSEUM.

> According to yor Lordships Order of reference, We have considered of the petition and proposealls tendred by Mr Blondeau concerning the Mint, wherein he proposeth severall wayes of advantage to the State in reference to Coyning, vizt, ...That the money coyned in this way shall not be subject to Clippinge,...That all pieces of the same Species shall be of the same weight,...That it shall be very Chargeable and difficult to be counterfett, and not at all to be done by ordinarie privat persons as now, nor by any but good Artists, and at a great Charge,...And lastly, That this coyne shall be very handsome to ye eye.[267]

The report concluded that Blondeau should be allowed to set up a mint in Ireland as:

> Money being there so generally corrupted, to the great prejudice of the inhabitants.[268]

The Council now compensated Blondeau with 100*l.* for his past expenses and ordered that he be paid an annual pension of 100*l.* and be given the Tower of London house which Briot had used as a workplace. However, despite this turn of affairs for the better, Blondeau, having been generally shabbily treated, and with Oliver Cromwell's death, looked askance at his future in England. He returned to France, discouraged and tired of conflict after four years in England, never having received appropriate compensation for his efforts.

In 1662, Simon urged Charles II to recall Blondeau to England to develop and employ techniques and machinery for the production of coinage with milled and engrained edges, and it was agreed:

> ...to furnish all the mills, rollers, presses, and other instruments, to cut, flatten, make round and size the pieces; the engine to mark the edges of the money with letters and grainings, the great presses for the coinage of monies, and all other tools and engines for the new way of coining,[269] [and] on May 17, 1662, Blondeau was officially appointed Engineer of the Mint with the handsome salary of £100 per year with living accommodations at the mint. He also received a coinage licence for twenty-one years with the provision that his invention would be kept secret.[270]

---

[267] *Interregnum Letters and Papers*, London: P.R.O., bundle No. 820; cited by Henfrey, p. 81.

[268] Henfrey, p. 83.

[269] L. Forrer, p. 199.

[270] Nathanson, p. 37.

But, Blondeau did not live to complete his contract. He left England for Poland in April 1664 to obtain screw presses for coining, and died there later that same year, but not before he had sworn mint employees to secrecy about the details of his coining machinery. The work of producing coins was then undertaken by the Roettier brothers.

Peter (Pierre) Blondeau: Historical Commentary

THE Council of State, and Commons in Parliament, having had it represented to them, that the Coins of this Government might be more perfectly and beautifully done, and made equal to any Coins in *Europe*, proposed to send to *France* for an Artist there, who had invented and improved a Machine and Method to make all Coins, by a *Screw Press*, and Mill, with the most beautiful Polish, and Equality, on the Edge, or any proper Inscription, or Graining, which might denote the Time of coining, or prevent the falsifying of Coins, or from being clipt (as usually) and counterfeited; for this Purpose they resolved to send for the Person proposed to be employed in this Service for the State.

By the Council of State, ordered 8th of *August* 1649 to send for *Peter Blondeau*, from *Paris*, to come to *London*, to treat with him, upon the Price and Expence of coining Money after his new Invention. He arrived at *London* the 3d of *Sep.* 1649, being allowed for his Journey and Expence.

...And [the Committee of the Mint] having heard all Objections that could be alleged by the Masters, Officers, and Workmen of the Mint, the said Committee concluded, and voted that, the Manner of Coining by *Blondeau*...was better, more advantageous, and honorable for the State, than that which was already used by the Common-wealth.

—G. Vertue, *Medals, Coins, Great-Seal, Impressions, From the Elaborate Works of Thomas Simon ...*, 1753 ed., p. 17.

§

By coach to Whitehall with Colonel Slingsby[271] (carrying Mrs. Turner with us) and there he and I up into the house, where we met with Sir G. Carteret: who afterwards, with the Duke of York, my Lord Sandwich, and others, went into a private room to consult: and we were a little troubled that we were not called in with the rest. But I do believe it was upon something very private. We staid walking in the gallery; where we met with Mr. Slingsby, that was formerly a great friend of Mons. Blondeau, who showed me the stamps of the King's new coyne; which is strange to see, how good they are in the stamp and bad in the money, for lack of skill to make them. But he says Blondeau will shortly come over, and then we shall have it better, and the best in the world.

—S. Pepys, *Diary*, February 19,1660/1666, 1942 ed., vol. ii, p. 36.

§

Wednesday, the 24th of December, 1656.

A BILL for Naturalizing of Lewis De Moulyn, Gyles Dury, **Peter Blondeau**, Adam de Cardonell, Stephen Hammon,...Gustavus Myles Fleetwood, George William Fleetwood, Adolphus Jacobus Fleetwood, Prudence Van Acker, now the Wife of James Butler, Nicholas Van Acker, John Archer, was this Day read the Third time.

—*House of Commons Journal* (24 December 1656), vol. 7, 1651-1660 (1802), pp. 474-75.

§

The researches of Mr. Henfrey into the history of the artist Peter Blondeau will lead to a better recognition of his merits. Thomas Simon, it seems, only engraved the dies, while Blondeau performed all the other processes of making the coins of Cromwell; and these coins are usually admitted to be the most beautiful and best executed in the whole of the English series. Leake, in his Historical Account of English Money, 1793, remarks that they exceed anything of the kind done since the time of the ancient Romans. The Rev. Rogers Ruding calls them "eminently beautiful," and "coined with the greatest care and exactness." The testimonies of Folkes, Snelling, Wyon, and others are to the same effect. As Blondeau feared that the jealous workmen of the Mint would discover his secret processes, "the kitchen, larder, cellars, coach houses," &c., of Drury House (on the site of the present Drury Lane Theatre) were assigned him as workshops.

—J. J. Cartwright, *The Academy*. (August 11, 1877) London: J. Murray, pp. 150-151.

§

---

[271] HENRY SLINGSBY (1602-1658), mint-master at Kippax, near Leeds. *For biographical information, see Platt, vol. ii, p. 284-288.*

Chelsea, September 25, 1838

MY DEAR SIR,

Having had occasion lately to look into the library of the British Museum for notices respecting Thomas Simon, the celebrated engraver of Coins and Medals about the middle of the seventeenth century, I was surprised to find a printed paper on a loose sheet, without date, but bearing that of 1650 *written* at the bottom of the page, to which the name of Simon is attached also in MS., although the paper itself is evidently the production of a foreigner; whereas I had always understood that Evelyn's assertion was correct, that Simon was born in Yorkshire.

On a perusal of the document, which is an address from the writer to the Parliament of the Commonwealth of England, there can be no doubt that it must be ascribed to Peter Blondeau, a French engineer, who came over to England about that time, for the purpose of prevailing upon the council of state to accept of some new improvements, which he had introduced into the practice of coining money, for the use of the British Mint. The paper recites the countenance he received at first from the committee of the mint, and the difficulties he afterwards experienced from the master and officers of that establishment.

The supposition that this paper [A], a copy of which I beg leave to enclose to you for the Numismatic Society, was really written, or at least addressed, by Peter Blondeau to the Parliament, is fully established by another paper [B], also in the British Museum, in which his name occurs evidently relating to the same subject, and which seems to have been addressed to the Parliament a few years after. In this, Blondeau enlarges upon the difficulties placed in his way, the motive of those obstacles, and upon the advantages which would accrue, both to the mint and to the public, if the Parliament would enforce the adoption of his new process: this process being simply the substitution of the mill and screw, for the hammer to strike the coin. This machinery was not, however, finally provided for the mint, as stated by Folkes in the introduction to his "Table of English Coins," till the year 1662.

These two documents together present several curious circumstances respecting the state of the British Mint, and the coinage issued from it at this period: and as they seem to have escaped the notice of the learned writers on the subject—at least, I do not find them attended to by Folkes, although he mentions generally the fact to which they relate,—I have thought that perhaps you would not consider them undeserving of being brought under the notice of the society, as illustrative of the history of our coinage.

Ever, my dear Sir,

Yours very truly, W. R. HAMILTON

—*The Numismatic Chronicle and Journal of the Royal Numismatic Society*, 1839, vol. 1-2, pp. 165-167.

MEDALLIST, *n. s. medallist,* [Fr.] A man skilled or curious in medals.—As a *medallist,* you are not to look upon a cabinet of medals as a treasure of money, but of knowledge. —*Addison.*

—Entry in *The Encyclopaedia Perthensis or, Universal Dictionary of the Arts, Science, Literature, &c., Intended to supercede the use of other books of reference*, 1816, vol. xiv, p. 179.

Two Medals by Heinrich Reitz the Younger

The 'Dutch Fisheries' medal (1636, 78 mm., M.I.i 279/84, M.I.Ill xxxiii/5, British Museum acc./reg. nos. 1865,0724.2 [M.7135], Eimer 128), cast and chased in silver. The allegorical design on the reverse depicts Justice and Peace kissing with infant genii holding an olive branch and scales respectively. The legend translates as 'Justice and Peace have kissed each other. Psalm 84.' Both this and the medal shown below are rare.

A later memorial medal of Charles I and Queen Henrietta Maria (in silver, 1649, 75 mm., M.I.i 350/209, M.I.Ill xxxi/1, British Museum acc./reg. no. bnk,engm.52 [P.I. 1380], Eimer 159, Platt i/259/b). Both examples are cast and chased. This medal uses the same *obv.* portrait by Heinrich Reitz as shown above, but it is perhaps somewhat more finely worked. Certainly the surrounding legend is more carefully worked. The reverse legend: 'Alas, what a madness this is of the rabble.' M.I.i interprets the many-headed monster as symbolizing "the variety of evil passions which agitated the people of England at this time." Both images © Trustees of the British Museum.

Heinrich Reitz the Younger

(1622?-1692?; fl. 1636-1649)

• Medallist •

LITTLE is known about this medallist other than he was German and worked during the first half of the seventeenth century. Grueber writes that Reitz "…worked principally for Christian I of Saxony and the princes of the houses of Brandenburg and Brunswick."[272] Reitz's productions include the Dutch Fisheries medal (1636; M.I.i 279/84), issued to commemorate the agreement between the two countries under which the Dutch agreed to pay for the right to fish in English waters as well as the production of a Charles I memorial medal (1649; M.I.i 350/209). M.I.i interprets the many-headed monster on the reverse of this medal as symbolizing "the variety of evil passions which agitated the people of England at this time" (*see illustration on preceding page*). The 'cut-out' of the image of the king on the obverse which appears to the right was likely used to adorn snuff boxes and book covers, but the presence of a means of suspension suggests that they were also worn. Another, possibly unique, Charles II reward (M.I.i 452/36) attributed to Reitz appears on the following page.

THE 'CUT-OUT' HEAD OF CHARLES I, IN SILVER (51.5 X 29.7 MM., M.I.I 370/259, M.I.ILL XXXIII/10, PLATT I/221/A_2) MADE FROM THE MEMORIAL MEDAL BY HEINRICH REITZ (M.I.I 350/209; M.I.ILL XXIII/5, PLATT I/259/B; *ILLUSTRATED ON PREVIOUS PAGE*). THESE PIECES ARE OFTEN FOUND AS DECORATIVE ATTACHMENTS TO BOOKS OR BOXES, BUT MOST SEEN BY THE AUTHORS HAVE LOOPS AND RINGS ON THE REVERSE SUGGESTING THAT THEY WERE PROBABLY WORN SUSPENDED FROM A CHAIN.

AN ILLUSTRATION FROM A. T. MALKIN, *A GALLERY OF PORTRAITS*, 1835, VOL. V, P. 34 OF MEDALS OF EDWARD HYDE, EARL OF CLARENDON AND CHARLES II. *SEE FOLLOWING PAGE.*

[272] H. A. Grueber (1881). *Guide to the English Medals Exhibited in the King's Library*, p. 16.

A Unique Medal in Gold of Charles II
by Heinrich Reitz the Younger (?)

One of the two medals in the illustration from Malkin's book on the preceding page. The British Museum tentatively attributes it to Heinrich Reitz the Younger. It apparently is a unique medal, cast and chased in gold. The obverse inscription translates as: 'Charles II, by the Grace of God, King of Britain, France and Ireland,' and the reverse as: 'For zeal and fidelity in adversity.' M.I.i comments that:

> *This fine medal was evidently given by Charles to some faithful and valued adherent, whom, unfortunately, it has not been possible to trace (p. 452).*

M.I.Ill provides the following history:

> *This medal was presented by K. Charles 2 to a Scotch gentleman, whose descendents sold it about 1820 to Mr. Whiteaves, from whom it was purchased by Lord Ashbrook. His Lordship's house having been robbed with a view of his collection of gold coins and medals, he resolved to remove their temptation and sold them to Mr. Young, from whom this medal was purchased for the National Collection. The artist who made it is uncertain (pl. xlii).*

It should be noted that the illustration from Malkin on the previous page distorts the sizes of the two medals—the Clarendon medal is 44 mm. and the Charles II medal, 75 mm. The details of the two medals are as follows: (i) Edward, Earl of Clarendon: M.I.i 478/87, M.I.Ill xlv/17, Platt II/162/a and (ii) Charles II: M.I.i 451/36, M.I.Ill xlii/1. Above image © Trustees of the British Museum.

During the reign of Emperor Charles VI, 1711-1740, who was an enthusiastic student of coins and medals, the curator C[arl]. G[ustav]. Heraeus (1671-1730) had Renaissance bronze and lead medals replaced with copies cast in precious metal. This was done in order that the imperial persons could handle the medals—base metals not being worthy of them.

—J. G. Pollard (2007). *Renaissance Medals*, vol. II, p. xv, citing O. Kurz, *Fakes: A Handbook*… pp. 190-191.

Wenceslaus Hollar's View of Whitehall, 1647

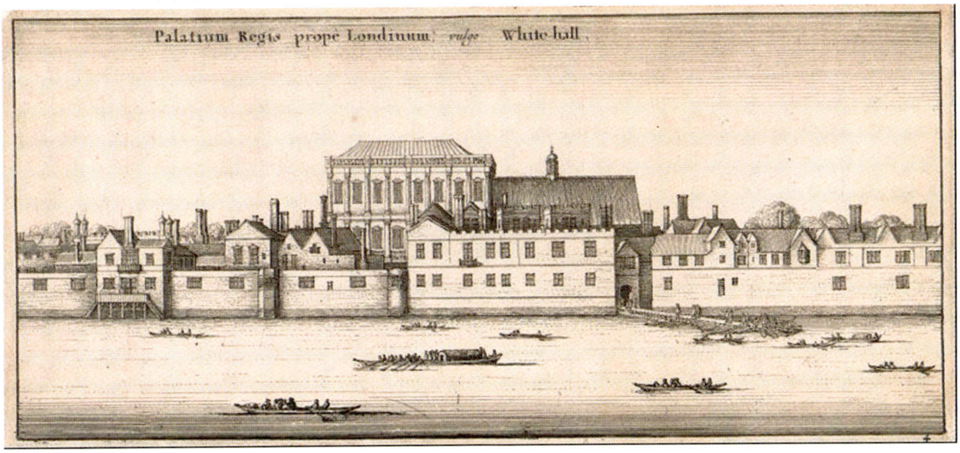

Palatium Regis Prope Londinum, Vulgo Whitehall **(*The King's Palace, or Near Whitehall*), a line engraving by Wenceslaus Hollar, ca. 1647, part of his series of four views of London etched while he was in Antwerp, most likely from drawings made earlier in London. The Banqueting Hall at Whitehall occupies the center of the image and dominates it in this highly formalized representation of a part of 'Royal London.' Image courtesy of the Yale Center for British Art.**

GEORGE VERTUE'S DRAWING OF ABRAHAM SIMON, IN GREY WASH OVER RED CHALK WITH PEN AND BROWN INK, AFTER THE PORTRAIT BY SIR GODFREY KNELLER (1646-1723). NOTE THE SMALL OBJECT CONTAINING A PORTRAIT IN SIMON'S RIGHT HAND, PERHAPS AN INITIAL MODEL FOR A MEDAL. IMAGE © TRUSTEES OF THE BRITISH MUSEUM.

Abraham Simon

(Baptized 1617 or 1622-ca. 1692)

•Artist & Medallist•

THE elder brother of Thomas Simon and an artist and medallist of great skill, Abraham Simon (*also* Simons) was the son of Peter (Pierre) and Anne Simon and was baptized at the French Protestant church in Threadneedle Street, London. He was educated with a view that he would enter the Church.[273]

Abraham acquired the skill of modeling in wax, and as a result of his execution of a number of portraits during a stay in Sweden, he was appointed to a position in Queen Christiana's court as a purchaser of works of art. He later accompanied her during a state visit to France. Abraham was awarded a gold medal and chain by the queen for his services, which, as is pointed out by *DNB,* he is to be seen wearing in the 'wax model' portrait of himself [*q.v. p. 174*]; close examination reveals that he is indeed wearing a medal suspended by a chain. It is also seen on the 'portrait medal' which appears below on page 173.

AN OIL ON CANVAS PORTRAIT OF ABRAHAM SIMON ATTRIBUTED TO HIM. (CA. 1670). IMAGE © THE NATIONAL PORTRAIT GALLERY, LONDON.

All surviving portraits illustrate the long hair and full beard which were characteristic of Abraham Simon's appearance. He is described as small in stature and:

> ...'of a primitive philosophical aspect'...[whose] eccentric dress excited derision in the street, but he was an excellent artist, and a man of the same independent character as Benedetto Pistrucci... Evelyn calls him 'fantastical Simons [sic], who had the talent for embossing so to the life.'[274]

According to Horace Walpole, Abraham Simon was rumored to have been in love with Queen Christiana, but this has not been confirmed by other sources. During his attendance on the queen on her visit to the court of Louis XIII he was allegedly arrested as a "suspicious person while trying to model the king from the gallery of the Royal Chapel."[275]

Arriving in England from France in or after 1642 or 1643, Abraham Simon was kept busy modeling the effigies of leading Parliamentarians. Evelyn commented that he was:

[273] *DNB*, 1897, vol. vii, p. 264.
[274] Ibid. pp. 264-265.
[275] Ibid. p. 264.

> ...a virtuoso fantastical Symons, who had the talent of embossing so to ye life... Abraham Simons, a strange character, but most excellent modeller after life, and engraver of medals[276]

It would appear that while Abraham Simon worked from life, his brother Thomas worked from drawings. Included among Abraham's works are a number of wax models which he prepared for medals Thomas completed through the casting and chasing processes. It would also appear that Abraham was at times involved in the final stages of the chasing process. Abraham also created a number of medals himself, using the same process, signing them 'A. S.' *DNB* describes these as:

> ...graceful and simple in treatment, but being usually in low relief and of small module, seem[ing to be] occasionally deficient in vigour.[277]

During the earlier part of his career, Abraham seems to have been the better known of the Simon brothers. Allen attributes 10 portrait medals to Abraham Simon, all of which are round in shape, cast, and signed and dated.[278] Additionally, he attributes to Abraham Simon the round portrait medal of Baron de Reede (M.I.I 320/156; Platt II/44/A). This last medal is dated but unsigned. Two misattributions, i.e., Civil War medals incorrectly attributed to Abraham Simon, are: Henry Cromwell (M.I.I 412/49) and Colonel Desborough (M.I.I 423/63; Platt II/75/A). No medals by Abraham Simon appear after Thomas Simon's death in 1665.[279]

Following the Restoration, Abraham Simon was employed modeling a portrait of Charles II, for which he was paid 100*l*. When similarly employed by the duke of York who only proposed to pay him half the amount paid by the king, Abraham allegedly defaced the duke's portrait in his presence.[280] This and other similar 'acts of impatience' when his works were criticized eventually cost him further commissions. He appears to have died in obscurity about 1692. He was married and had two daughters.

> READERS of the best authentick Writers; only having drawn out in some Sort of Succession the Works done to commemorate Acts of those Times, wherein *T. Simon*, or his Brother *Abraham Simon*, were concerned, to illustrate I hope thereby some Parts in History, and to hand to Posterity the Fame of those excellent and much admired Artists.
>
> —Vertue, *Medals, Coins, Great Seals...of Thomas Simon,* 1780 ed., p. iv.

---

276 Bray, ibid. *Memoirs of John Evelyn...*, 1871 ed., vol. ii, p. 226.

277 *DNB*, 1897, vol. lii, p. 264.

278 Allen, ibid. p. 49. These are the medals: the EARL OF LOUDOUN (1645, M.I.I 321/157); WILLIAM POPE (1645, M.I.I 322/158); LORD INCHIQUIN (1646, M.I.I 324/161); ALBERT JOACHIM (1646, M.I.I 324/162); SIR SIDENHAM POYNTZ (1646, M.I.I 325/163); the EARL OF DUNFERMLINE (1646, M.I.I 328/168); THE EARL OF LAUDERDALE (1646, M.I.I 328/169); MARTINAY[?] (1647, M.I.I 329/171); MANTEAU VAN DALEM (1647, not in M.I.I, but appears in the Murdoch sale, 1904, lot 116; *see below*); and SIR CHARLES ERSKINE (1647, M.I.I 330/173).

279 Allen, ibid. pp. 46-50. *See Historical Commentary, below*.

280 Vertue, ibid. p. 60. Farquhar, reporting this event, observed that:

> A curious commentary on the way in which the "persons of honour and distinction" of those days were swayed by the royal displeasure is the opinion expressed by Evelyn, who, as a connoisseur, should have risen above such sordid considerations, but who, instead of commiserating the unfortunate disgrace of the artist, spoke of him after his death as "the late squalid Embosser" (*Portraiture of our Stuart Monarchs on their Coins and Medals*, Part ii, *B.N.J.*, 1910, vol. vi, p. 248). This, despite his earlier description of Abraham as 'Fantastical Simon.'

A Portrait Medal of Abraham Simon

(*Left*) (A_1) Portrait medal of Abraham Simon (ca. mid-18th c., in silver, 45 x 37 mm., M.I.i 512/154, M.I.Ill l/2, British Museum acc./reg. no. M.7554). (*Right*) Illustration of this medal as it appears in Vertue's *Medals, Coins, Seals...of Thomas Simon...* 1753; 1780, pl. xxxv. The medal is nearly identical in design to the one of his brother Thomas Simon (M.I.i 512/155) which appears on pp. 180 and 187 of this volume. There is, however, no evidence that these two medals are older than the early to mid-18th century—M.I.i attributes them to '— Stuart.' Further, given that the medals and Vertue's portraits are not contemporary to the lifetimes of the Simons, the only known likenesses of either of the Simons done during their lifetimes are the self-portrait of Abraham on page 171 and (probably) the small plaque (c), also of Abraham, on p. 174. Medal image © Trustees of the British Museum.

Identification, Examined Specimens, and Measurements:

M.I.i 512/154; M.I.Ill l/2. *Ca.* 1750 (?)

(A_1) British Museum. Oval cast and chased uniface medal in silver from a wax model. Solid, acc./reg. nos. M.7554, H132; PI.1833. The measurements are 1.8 x 1.5 in. (45 x 37 mm.), 36.4 gms. The ticket states: "Ab. Simon, Trattle 2.2." Edward Hawkins Collection. This medal is similar to the one illustrated and described for Thomas Simon below (i.e., M.I.i 512/155), except that the subject is Abraham Simon, not Thomas, and it is on a thicker flan.

(A_2) British Museum. Oval cast and chased solid uniface medal in silver from a wax model. Acc./reg. nos. BNK,EngM.96; PI.—. The measurements are 1.85 x 1.3 in. (47 x 33.5 mm.), otherwise it is identical to (A_1).

Not in M.I. or M.I.Ill. *Ca.* 1666 (?) *Not illustrated*

(B) British Museum. Oval embossed plate in silver filled with red wax. acc./reg. no. BNK,EngM.96, PI.1832. The measurements are 1.86 x 1.5 in. (47.2 x 38.7 mm.), 8.1 gms. Similar to the medal of Thomas Simon, with paper backing, now detached. The obverse of the ticket reads: "Bank [of England] Coll. Eng. Med 96," and on the reverse, "AR 1.85 Abraham Simon 1666."

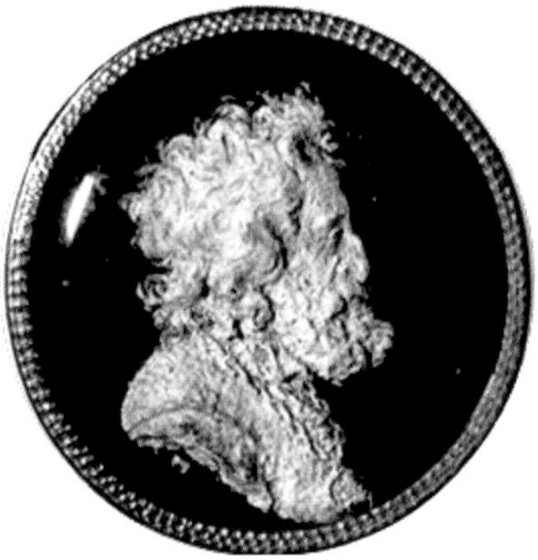
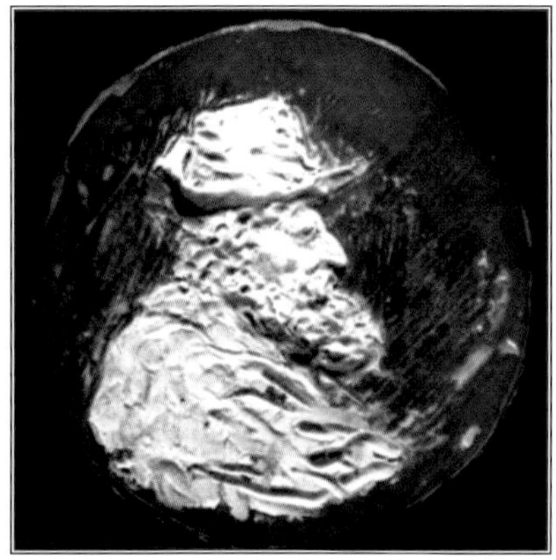

TWO SELF-PORTRAITS (?) BY ABRAHAM SIMON. *L.* (C) A SMALL PLAQUE IN WAX AND GLASS (44 MM., BRITISH MUSEUM ACC./REG. NO. SLPICTURES.290); *R.* (D) ANOTHER PLAQUE IN WAX ON SLATE (CA. 1650-1700, 65 MM., B.M. SLPICTURES.289). ILLUSTRATIONS © TRUSTEES OF THE BRITISH MUSEUM.

NOT IN M.I. OR M.I.ILL.

(C) British Museum. The acc./reg. no. is SLPictures.290. The measurements are: 1.7 in. (44 mm.). This is the medal illustrated above, *l.*, which is more of a brooch. It consists of a bust of an elderly man (Abraham Simon?), facing right, wearing a medal on a ribbon and done in wax and glass, with a decorative surround in gold. Acquired by the British Museum from Hans Sloane in 1753.

NOT IN M.I. OR M.I.ILL.

(D) British Museum. A self-portrait of Abraham Simon, facing right, wearing a hat. A medallion in pink wax on slate, with a mount. acc./reg. no. SLPictures.289. The measurements are: 2.55 in. (65 mm.). Also acquired by the British Museum from Hans Sloane in 1753.

Description, Details, and Comment:

Medal (A) has a bust of Abraham Simon on the obverse, facing right, with medium length hair and beard. He is wearing a plain falling collar, doublet and medal (perhaps of Queen Christiana?) around his neck suspended from a double chain. This medal is illustrated on the preceding page as reproduced from Vertue, and is similar in design to the medal of Thomas Simon illustrated both on the same plate (*q.v. pp. 180 and 187*), and also in a cast copy in base metal (M.I.I 512/155), which is in a private collection. The reverse is blank. Example (C), *above*, may perhaps be a small plaque or possibly a brooch intended for wearing. It may be a self portrait, produced by Abraham Simon himself, perhaps as a memento to be given as a gift. In this regard, Derek Allen comments that:

> It was remarked of Abraham...[that he] used to carry round with him a box containing glass and wax prepared for making models from the life. [281]

This is the only specimen of this medal or plaque that the authors know to exist; it appears to be the example that Derek Allen reproduced in his 1938/39 article (pl. ix, no. 29). The other plaque, (D) for which no further information is available, does not appear to be a self-portrait.

[281] D. Allen, 'Thomas Simon's Sketch-book,' *Walpole Society*, 1937-38, vol. 27, p. 32.

Historical Commentary on Abraham Simon

Only having drawn out in some Sort of Succession the Works done to commemorate Acts of those Times, Wherein *T. Simon*, or his Brother *Abraham Simon*, were concerned,—to illustrate I hope thereby some Parts in History, and to hand to Posterity the Fame of those excellent and much admir'd Artists.

—G. Vertue, *Medals, Coins, Great-Seals*..., 1753, p. lv.

§

And as these Times of Action, for, and against the Republic, or Change of Monarchical Government, frequently employed and encouraged many Men of Learning, Parts, and Capacity, as the Public was affected more or less: So, the Use of Medals was multiplied, and they were then more handed about to denote their respective Leaders, in Favour of the Parties they espoused. Upon such Occasions, many having been performed by *Thomas Simon* the engraver of Medals, and some others from Models in Wax, after the Life, by *Abraham Simon*, and cast in Gold and Silver; whose Fame was in high Repute, at the same time with his Brother, who often highly repaired his Works.

—G. Vertue, *Medals, Coins, Great-Seals*..., 1753, p. 25.

§

It is difficult to say exactly how much Thomas Simon was indebted to the eccentric and clever Abraham for the designs of some of his medals and coins; although the signature T. S. appears on pieces which may have been the joint work of the two brothers, this might be because of Thomas's official position; that either was capable of working alone is abundantly proved, but it is said that Abraham often made the original wax sketch, Thomas the finished portrait from it, Abraham excelling in portraiture, Thomas above all men in die-sinking, engraving, and chasing.

—Helen Farquhar, Portraiture of the Stuarts on the Royalist Badges, *British Numismatic Journal*, vol. ii, p. 285-286 (cited by Forrer, vol. v, p. 514).

"An Unpublished Medal by Abraham Simon"
Sold at Auction in 1904

"Manteau van Dalem, 1647, by Abraham Simon. Bust, *right*, hair long, in plain collar and armour, with baldric; on truncation, 'A. S.' On reverse: 'PR MANTEAV VAN DALEM ESS INGEN GEN 1647' in fine lines across field, very fine, unpublished and possibly unique; from the Montagu collection."

—*The John G. Murdoch Sale of the Series of English Historical Medals in Gold, Silver and Bronze, from Henry VI (1422- 1471) to George II (1727-1760)*, Sotheby, Wilkinson & Hodge, 1904, lot 116, sale price: 45*s*.

Note: The present authors have recently learned that the Victoria & Albert Museum possesses an example of this medal, cast in silver (acc/.reg. no. 814-1904). Not having examined it they cannot opine as to whether it is an original or a copy.

§

In this Plate,[282] I have taken the Opportunity to represent the Pictures of the ingenious Brothers and coeval Artists, *Abr.* and *Tho. Simon*. As to their first setting out in Art, or from whom they had their Rudiments, like many other Genius's in their early Bud; is usually unobserved, till Time gradually expands them, and ripens them to a Degree of Perfection, worth the Notice of the Curious. The elder Brother, *Abraham*, was trained to Scholarship, with Intention to recommend himself to some ecclesiastical Preferment; but by what Means his Studies were diverted, does not appear. Upon some Account, or the Offer of some Opportunity, he went to *Sweeden*, and there by his Art and Ingenuity, in modelling in Wax the Portraits of several noted and eminent Persons, he obtained the favour of Queen *Christiana*, and attended in her Court, as a Gentleman of her Retinue. There he so ingratiat-

[282] *q.v. p. 180, this vol.*

Two medals by Abraham Simon (?)

Two medals attributed to Abraham Simon. (*top*) Murrough O'Brien, Lord Inchiquin (silver, 1646, 35 mm., M.I.i 324/161, M.I.Ill xxviii/10, British Museum acc./reg. no. M.7201, Eimer 150, Platt ii/242/a) and (*bottom*) John Maitland, 2nd Earl of Lauderdale (silver, 1646, 36 mm., M.I.i 328/169, M.I.Ill xxviii/18, B. M. acc./reg. no. M.7212, Platt ii/212/a1). Both are 1.4 in. in diameter and in silver, although examples of the former also exist in silver-gilt and gold. The present authors are divided in their opinion as to whether the Lord Inchiquin medal is by Abraham Simon; certainly the two medals appear to differ greatly in style of execution. Images © Trustees of the British Museum.

ed himself, that in Consideration of his Services and Merit, she presented him with a golden Chain, and Medal; which he commonly wore. When that Queen, who was a curious Collector of the Works of Art, in Paintings, Sculpture, &c. from Italy, and other Parts of *Europe*; he was one of her principal Agents; for, when, that Queen went to visit the Court of *France*, Simon was in her Train. As he was a Man of small Stature; of a primitive philosophic Aspect, always wearing his Hair and Beard, according to the Mode of his Ancestors, this was the Occasion of an odd Adventure to him.

—G. Vertue, *Medals, Coins, Great-Seals…of Thomas Simon…*, ibid. pp. 57-58.

§

Lewis the XIII King of *France*, then living; it so happened, that Queen *Christiana* went to the Royal Chapel, and *Simon*, being of her Retinue, he placed himself in a Gallery, within View of the King; so that he might, as he intended, draw the King's Picture in Wax, modell'd, according to his Manner of Working. During this Operation, the King, remarking how busy he was, and the Oddness of the

A Medal and Two Portraits of John Campbell, Earl of Loudoun
• An interesting Comparison •

Portraits apparently drawn from a medal of John Campbell, Earl of Loudoun (1598-1662). The earlier of the portraits (*R*) is ca. 1768-1780 and by John Record (fl. 1768-d. 1784). It appears to have been based upon the medal by Abraham Simon designed over a century earlier (*center*, in silver, ca. 1645, 36 mm., M.I. 321/157, M.I.Ill xxviii/5, Eimer 148, Platt ii/63/A$_1$). An example of this very rare medal in gold is in the Fitzwilliam Museum collection; an enlarged illustration of it may be found in Platt/ii/63. The portrait (*L*), is by an anonymous copyist, ca. 1819. It is from John Thane's *British Autography* and appears to have been taken from Record's portrait (British Museum acc./reg. no. gg.1.497). The earlier work (*R*) was done in grey wash over black and red chalk and graphite. The images are respectively (*L*) from a private collection and (*center* and *right*) © Trustees of the British Museum.

§

Man, did not know what he was about; therefore ordered one of the Captains of the Guard, to take that Man into Custody, till he had leisure to understand, who he was, and what he was doing. The next Morning, the King was told, that he was an Artist and Attendant on the Queen of *Sweeden*. He being ordered to appear before the King, was asked several Questions, as if he was taken for a suspicious Person. Being therefore strictly examined, he boldly said to the King; *Sire, What are you afraid of, to see a Man, with his own Hair, and a Beard, which the King your Father, would have been ashamed to have been seen publicky without, for Fear of being thought to be a Boy, or no wise Man?* Finding himself, little employed, after the Queen left *Sweeden*, he went to *Holland*, and resided there some Time. But his Countenance and Habit, constantly wearing Boots, and Spurs, with his long Sword *en Cavaliere*, made him everywhere remarkable, and to some People ridiculous.

About this Time, he became acquainted with several *Sweedish* Gentlemen, sent to *England*; from that Court, whose Portraits he model'd; as he did also, those of some *Hollanders*, Embassadors from the States; as that of old *De Joachim*, &c. so much approved of, before mentioned. When the Restoration of King *Charles*, and the Royal Family came about, He, with many others, returned to *England*; where he soon got recommended to the Court, and to the King; to whom he was well known, for his Skill and Merit, no less for the Singularity of his Figure, and his cynical Humour.

—G. Vertue, ibid. pp. 58-59.

A VERY RARE MEDAL OF HENRY CROMWELL

A CAST AND CHASED MEDAL OF HENRY CROMWELL IN SILVER (27.2 X 22.7 MM., M.I.I 412/49; M.I.ILL XXXVII/12; PLATT, II/44/A1). IMAGE © TRUSTEES OF THE BRITISH MUSEUM (ACC./REG. NO. 1939,0703.1; ENLARGED 1.75 X ACTUAL SIZE). ***ALSO SEE PAGE 108, THIS VOLUME.***

As the authors have noted elsewhere (Platt, 2013, vol. 2, p. 44), this is the only medal with a contemporary image of Henry Cromwell known to the authors and it does not appear to be the work of the Simons. Thus, the following reference to the Simons having taken an 'effigy' of Henry would seem to be of interest to the reader as it was to the authors.

IT appears that his effigy was taken by Abraham and John[283] Simon,* but it is singular, that we should have neither any engraved portrait or medal of so good and great a man. I have heard that miss Cromwells [sic] are in possession of an original portrait of him, perhaps it is the same as was mr. William Cromwell's, the grandson of Henry; mr. Panton possesses also an original one of the lord lieutenant, when a child. Vertue has engraved his seal as lord deputy of Ireland; it has his arms, with the same quarters as his Father's privy seal, impaling those of his ladies; with his own crest, viz. a lion with a double tail, holding a spear or javelin, the whole emblazoned and inscribed, SIGILL. HENRICI. CROMWELL. HIBERNIÆ DEPVTATI; the original was in the possession of the late mr. William Cromwell.

—M. Noble, *Memoirs of the Protectorate-House of Cromwell*, 1784 ed., vol. i, pp. 284-285.

* *fn.*: List of effigies executed by Abraham and John Simon, made out by mr. Pennington, cheese-factor, of London; and given to mr. George Copland, engraver, who gave it to Thomas Hollis, esq. october 2, 1759, and is printed in the life of the last gentleman; there are mentioned in that publication, the names of the following persons, whose lives are given in these volumes; earl of Warwick, lord Kimbolton, Oliver and Richard, protectors, mr. and mrs. Cleypole, mr. and mrs. Ireton, Fleetwood, St. John, Waller, Hampden, Hammond, Lockhart, Desborough, Jones, Scroop, Hazilrig, Lenthall, Hewson, Harrison, Ireton, Lambert, and Monk.

[283] It is not clear as to why REV. NOBLE refers to THOMAS SIMON as 'John.'

Albert Joachim, Ambassador of the United Provinces Medals by Abraham Simon (*and others*)

Type A_1. An original medal, 1636, cast and chased in silver, ex George III collection, donated by George IV. Image © Trustees of the British Museum.

Type A_2. An original medal, 1636, also cast and chased in silver. Image © Trustees of the British Museum.

Type B_2. A late 18th c. forgery signed 'A. S.' on the bust truncation, in silver, and likely by '— Stuart.' Image courtesy of Spink & Son Ltd.

Type C. Another forgery, also of the late 18th c., this in silver and unsigned. Image courtesy of A. H. Baldwin & Sons Ltd, London, www.baldwin.co.uk.

The medals of Albert Joachim (1646, M.I.i 324/162, M.I.Ill xviii/11) provide interesting examples of the several varieties of a single 17th century medal that can be found. Here, in addition to the original castings, there are at least two varieties of a forgery by '— Stuart' and/or another medallist, both of which have been made to a higher standard than the original medal.

The illustration of this medal from Pinkerton, 1802. ed., pl. xxiv, no. 5. The prominent border suggests that it was drawn from a restitution/forgery.

Example (A_1), cast in silver (1646, British Museum acc./reg. no. G3,IP.523), is about as good an example of an original of this medal as can be found. Example (A_2) is another original medal (35 mm., British Museum acc./reg. no. M.7202), also cast and chased in silver, but of somewhat poorer definition. The British Museum also possesses another example (acc./reg. no. BNK,E.M.67) in silver similar to (A_2), as well as one in base metal, likely copper (36.6 mm., acc./reg. no. M.7203). Example B_2[284] is a late 18th c. copy in silver (38 mm., *Spink Numismatic Circular*, August 2004, lot CM0802) incorrectly attributed to James 'Athenian' Stuart. It has the characteristics of a forgery by '— Stuart' after Abraham Simon's work. The final example, Type C, is 37.5 mm., cast and chased in silver, and from the Michael Hall Collection (Part 3) sold at Baldwin's Auction no. 67 on September 28, 2010 (lot 2526). Original examples of this medal are quite rare.

[284] Note that the numbering (e.g., A_1, A_2, etc.) follows the system used in Platt, 2013.

A PAGE FROM VERTUE'S CLASSIC WORK, *MEDALS, COINS, GREAT SEALS…, FROM THE ELABORATE WORKS OF THOMAS SIMON…*, INITIALLY PUBLISHED IN 1753, WITH A SECOND REVISED EDITION PREPARED BY RICHARD GOUTH IN 1780 (*Q.V. PP. 396-397*). THIS VOLUME IS, IN EFFECT, A HOMAGE TO THE TWO MEDALLISTS, ILLUSTRATING EXAMPLES OF THEIR BEST WORK.[285]

[285] Note the famous 'Petition Crown' coin illustrated here. This work was created by THOMAS SIMON for CHARLES II as his entry in a competition for a new design for the crown. The competition grew from the

Thomas Simon

(1618 or 1623?-1665)[286]

• Medallist to Parliament, & later, to King Charles II •

THOMAS SIMON (*also* Simons, Simmons, Simmonds) was born in Yorkshire to Peter (Pierre) and Anne Simon, Walloonians and formerly inhabitants of London or as is equally likely, Guernsey, where there was a Simon family. Simon appears to have initially been apprenticed to a London goldsmith, George Crompton. At an early age, Simon is said by George Vertue to have come to the attention of Nicholas Briot, the engraver at the London mint.[287] He was apprenticed for the usual seven year period to Edward Greene, 'the chief graver at the Tower,' in or about 1635.[288] There, he was also likely instructed by Briot, Greene's supervisor. Simon's first work was the 'Scottish Rebellion' medal (1639), issued to commemorate the Treaty of Berwick which was concluded in that same year. Simon's apprenticeship ended in 1642, and in 1645 he was appointed—(along with Edward Wade) 'joint chief graver of the stamps for coins,' which carried with it the authorization for engraving the royal arms and seals. This joint appointment likely represented the split in loyalty of the mint's 'management,' in that William Parkhurst, the warden of the mint at Oxford, supported the king, while in London, Greene supported

THERE IS NO KNOWN PORTRAIT OF THOMAS SIMON OTHER THAN THIS SUPPOSED LIKENESS, WHICH APPEARS ON A MID TO LATE-18TH C. MEDAL AND IS ILLUSTRATED IN VERTUE, *MEDALS, COINS, SEALS... OF THOMAS SIMON...* (1780, PL. XXXV; *SEE PREVIOUS PAGE*). A MEDAL, IDENTICAL IN DESIGN, OF HIS BROTHER ABRAHAM ALSO EXISTS (*SEE ABOVE, P. 173*). BOTH APPEAR TO BE OF THE SAME DATE OF MANUFACTURE.

---

inability of Simon and JOHN ROETTIER to work together on the project. Simon, however, did not submit his design for some time, and Roettier won by default (*q.v. p. 186*). The portrait medal of ABRAHAM SIMON (M.I.I 512/154; M.I.ILL pl. L/2) is executed from a wax model of the subject and was also the subject for a mid-18th c. chasing by '— STUART,' and an earlier repoussé work. The medal worn by Abraham Simon was believed to have been given to him by QUEEN CHRISTIANA OF SWEDEN and to contain her portrait. Abraham served in her retinue, apparently as both an artist and agent in the acquisition of artistic works. The portrait badge of THOMAS SIMON (M.I.I 512/155; M.I.ILL pl. L/3; *illustrated on p. 187*) also exists as a chasing by '— STUART' (*ibid.*), but the original artist is unknown.

286 The later of the two dates for Simon's birth is questioned by Nathanson, who notes that Simon's first work, the seal for ALGERNON PERSON, Lord High Admiral, was produced in 1637. He cites Farquhar's evidence (i.e., 'New Light on Thomas Simon,' *Numismatic Chronicle*, 5th Series, xvi (1936), pp. 211-234) for acceptance of the 1618 date as correct. The later date would have made Simon 16 years of age at the beginning of his apprenticeship, when he executed the Scottish Rebellion medal. DEREK ALLEN, in his important article 'Thomas Simon's Sketchbook' (1938-1939), stated that THOMAS SIMON was born in London in 1618. A 19th century offering of a biography on Thomas Simon may be found in Nightingale's "Notices of Thomas Simon," which appeared in the *Numismatic Chronicle* in 1842.

287 Although Nathanson suggests that BRIOT may have been repeating Vertue's conjecture.

288 EDWARD GREENE had been at the Tower mint since 1624, first as 'joint chief graver,' and then as sole 'chief graver' (1628-1644).

AN EXAMPLE OF THOMAS SIMON'S EARLY WORK EXECUTED AT THE TIME OF THE SCOTTISH REBELLION IN 1639. THIS MEDAL (31 MM., M.I. 282/91 M.I.ILL XXIV/4, EIMER 134B, PLATT I/150/B), ILLUSTRATED ABOVE IN SILVER-GILT, WAS MANUFACTURED USING A NUMBER OF DIES WHICH DIFFER SLIGHTLY IN DETAIL (*SEE PLATT, VOL. I, PP. 149-153*). IT IS FOUND IN BOTH SILVER AND GOLD. ILLUSTRATION COURTESY OF DIX NOONAN WEBB LTD.

Parliament. Briot, meanwhile, vacillated between the two sides. Simon appears to have never wavered in his support for Parliament. The annual salary for this position was 30*l*., to be shared by Simon and Edward Wade.

Simon was subsequently confirmed in his loyalty to the Parliamentarian cause when he received authorization to engrave the great seal of the Commonwealth, an act which was viewed as 'high treason' by the Royalists.[289] He subsequently engraved a number of medals for Parliament.[290] Following the death of Wade in 1648, in 1649 Simon was appointed "sole chief graver to the mint and seals." In September 1650, he was sent by Parliament to Edinburgh to take Cromwell's portrait for the 'Dunbar medal.' Cromwell, despite his protestations about a portrait of him appearing on a medal, must have liked it, for he recommended Simon for promotion, commenting:

> ...indeed the man is ingenious and worthie of incouragement.[291]

During 1649-1651, Simon, now focusing exclusively on medals rather than coinage, engraved the great seal of the Commonwealth. By 1655 Simon was engraving and producing seals and medals for Cromwell. His annual salary of 30*l*. as chief graver of the mint and seals was now supplemented by 13*l*. 6*s*. 8*d*. in payments for making medals for Oliver Cromwell and for the 'public

---

[289] Nathanson, p. 11, also notes that the King, ignoring this appointment, made his own, that of THOMAS RAWLINS, as chief engraver.

[290] Illustrations of most of Simon's medals may be found in the present work, in M.I.ILL and in Platt (2013). With respect to Simon's work, Allen noted that while:

> There are various signed medals of Thomas Simon from 1639 onwards, but no portrait medal of his, other than military rewards or official pieces, is signed T.S. or dated before 1653. In this year there are two dated medals [i.e., those of Bulstrode Whitelock and Sir James Harrington]. From 1658 to 1664 there are a number more [i.e., those of Edward Montague, 1658; George Monke, 1660; Dorcas Brabazon, 1662, the Earl of Clarendon, 1662; and the Earl of Southampton, 1664]. In addition to the medals signed and dated, there are one or two signed and undated which link themselves in boldness of relief with the later rather than the earlier group [i.e., those of John Thurloe, Henry Scobell, Elizabeth Claypole]. Besides this group, there are some seven or eight unsigned and undated medals in low relief which do not even bear the names of the sitters on the reverse [i.e., those of Sir John Hotham, Peter Carey, Archbishop Laud, &c.] (p. 23).

[291] *DNB*, vol. xviii, p. 266.

service.' That same year Simon received orders to engrave the great seal, privy seal, and seal manual.[292] During the following two years, Simon also engraved the great seals of Ireland and Scotland, as well as seals for the English, Scottish and Irish councils and the English law courts and admiralty. During 1656-1658, he was engaged in engraving the dies for the Commonwealth coinage, the specimens for which were struck by Blondeau.[293]

AN ORIGINAL AND VERY RARE SMALL DUNBAR MEDAL IN GOLD. THE DUNBAR MEDAL IS PERHAPS THE BEST KNOWN OF THOMAS SIMON'S MANY MEDALLIC WORKS (1650, 25.6 X 21.8 MM., M.I.I 392/13, M.I.ILL XXXV/4, EIMER 181B.1, PLATT I/325/I1). IMAGE © TRUSTEES OF THE BRITISH MUSEUM.

As the "sole chiefe Engraver…for life" at the mint, Simon was now receiving, in addition to his salary, a fee for each die he produced, often amounting to over 100*l*. per medal.[294] Problematically for him, however, the expenses and fees incurred for executing the commissions awarded him substantially exceeded the 700*l*. that had been advanced for this purpose in 1655. Thus, in January 1658, he submitted his bill to the council for 1,728*l*., 5*s*. 8*d*. (less of course the 700*l*.). In the face of no reply in August 1658, Simon again submitted his bill, noting:

> I beg you to consider that I and my servants have wrought five years without recompense, and that the interest I have to pay for gold and silver eats up my profit. [295]

In 1659, he received a further 278*l*. towards the arrears owed to him.

In 1660, at the Restoration, Simon lost his position as chief engraver to Thomas Rawlins, who had been originally appointed to this position by Charles I and was now reinstated as 'sole chief graver' by Charles II. Thomas Simon petitioned King Charles II to become the chief engraver as well as for a pardon for having worked for the Commonwealth. Charles denied the former most likely because of his father's promise of the position to Rawlins, while still granting Simon a pardon, no doubt because of his great skill. Simon was reemployed making coinage dies, and in

---

292 An engraved stamp, used for making an impression in wax to seal documents.

293 Given his great skills as medallist and the quality of the sketches present in his *Sketchbook*, it is surprising that Allen came to the conclusion that:

> …[Thomas] Simon was not regarded as capable of making his own drawings from the life (p. 38).

If so, ABRAHAM SIMON'S skill in drawing likenesses from life may have been essential to Thomas' work.

294 Nathanson, p. 24.

295 *DNB*, vol. xxvii, 266.

AN ATTRACTIVE EXAMPLE IN GOLD OF THOMAS SIMON'S SMALL MEDAL OF THOMAS FAIRFAX (1645; 25 x 20 MM.; M.I.I 318/151; M.I.ILL XXVII/14; EIMER 146B; PLATT II/98/B). IT IS RARE IN THIS METAL. IMAGE COURTESY SPINK AUCTIONS (NO. 11009, LOT 782).

May 1661, he received a grant as 'one of the engravers of the king's arms, shields and stamps.[296] Nathanson, comparing Rawlins' reinstated salary of 30*l.* with that of Simon's 50*l.* concludes that Rawlins' position was honorific, with the latter's work being confined solely to badges and medals for the period 1660-1662. Simon, on the other hand, was involved in the broad array of work performed by the mint, including the production of new dies for coinage, and as Nathanson notes, the great seal of Charles II and the coronation medal were both Simon's work.[297]

Simon, now back to working with inferior hammer-struck coinage rather than the new milled coinage which he had produced together with Blondeau, was slow in meeting production goals, and was rebuked by the Lords Commissioners of the Treasury for this, being ordered to:

> ...forbeare all other services, until he hath perfected all things which belonge to him. [298]

When this admonishment did not have the desired effect, Charles II had to personally intervene, ordering Simon to prepare the coinage. Despite the Crown's frustration with the pace of his work, in June 1661 Simon was made by patent one of the king's 'chief gravers of the mints and seals,' at an annual salary of 50*l.*[299]

At this point in time, Charles, acknowledging the need to mint coinage in such a manner as to prevent clipping and counterfeiting, ordered that all coins were henceforth to be made by machinery. Pierre Blondeau was recalled from France by Simon, as engineer of the mint, to produce coinage by machine. With Blondeau still in France in November 1661, Simon was sent there in order to convince him to return to England, a task at which he was successful. In his absence, however, the Roettier brothers, John and Joseph, whose family had contributed to Charles II's upkeep during the latter's exile in France, had been invited to come to England from the Netherlands to help prepare the new coinage dies.[300]

---

[296] M.A.E. Green (ed.). *Calendar of State Papers, Domestic Series, of the Reign of Charles II: 1660-1661...*, vol. xxxvi, p. 599.

[297] Nathanson, p. 31.

[298] Vertue, 1793, p. 83, cited by Nathanson.

[299] *DNB*, vol. xviii, pp. 266.

[300] Nathanson, p. 35.

TWO VERSIONS OF THOMAS SIMON'S LARGE SILVER MEDAL OF SIR THOMAS FAIRFAX. (*ABOVE*) AN ORIGINAL EXAMPLE (34 X 28 MM.; M.I.I 318/151; M.I.ILL XXVII/14; EIMER 146A; PLATT II/97/A). (*BELOW*) ANOTHER VERSION, BY ANOTHER HAND, OF THIS MEDAL, UNIFACE, ALSO 34 X 28 MM. AND PREVIOUSLY UNPUBLISHED. SECOND IMAGE COURTESY OF NOBLE NUMISMATICS, PTY. LTD. (AUSTRALIA), INFO@NOBLE.COM.AU (AUCTION SALE 99, LOT 3004).

In 1662, Charles II ordered Thomas Simon and John Roettier to engrave dies for the new 'milled' coinage. Unable to reach agreement, Simon and the Roettiers prepared competing designs. With the Roettiers' design being selected by default when Simon failed to submit a timely entry, Simon lost his position at the mint, and the Roettiers were appointed engravers in his place. In this same year, Blondeau returned to the mint, having been appointed engineer, with a salary of 100*l*. and living accommodations, as well as a license with the guarantee that his striking machinery would be kept secret for 21 years.

The following year, in 1663, seeking to demonstrate his skill as an engraver, and thus his value to the king, Simon created a pattern crown piece, the so called 'Petition Crown,' which had engraved upon its edge the following inscription:

> THOMAS SIMON MOST HUMBLY PRAYS YOUR MAJESTY TO COMPARE THIS HIS TRYALL PIECE WITH THE DUTCH,[301] AND IF MORE / TRVLY DRAWN & EMBOSSED, MORE GRACEFULLY: ORDER'D, AND MORE ACCURATELY ENGRAVEN TO RELIEVE HIM.

---

[301] I.e., the crown produced by John Roettier.

THE FAMED 'PETITION CROWN' (1663) COIN, IN SILVER, BY THOMAS SIMON. THIS COIN, WHICH BEARS AN INSCRIPTION OF SOME 200 CHARACTERS ON TWO LINES ON ITS EDGE, IS THE 'PROTOTYPE' PRODUCED BY SIMON IN HIS COMPETITION WITH THE ROETTIER BROTHERS FOR DESIGN OF THE NEW COINAGE FOR CHARLES II. SIMON SUBMITTED HIS DESIGN LATE AND HAD DIFFICULTY MAKING A DIE STRONG ENOUGH TO USE WITH THE NEW MECHANICAL PRESS. ONLY 12 ORIGINAL EXAMPLES OF THIS COIN ARE BELIEVED TO STILL BE IN EXISTENCE TODAY. THE EXCELLENCE OF SIMON'S ENGRAVING IS EVIDENT IN THE ENLARGED REVERSE DETAIL *BELOW*. IMAGES © TRUSTEES OF THE BRITISH MUSEUM.

The 'Petition Crown,'[302] was unsuccessful in getting Charles II to change his mind and select Simon's design over the one by the Roettiers which he had already chosen. It did, however, seem to have been instrumental in obtaining more work for Simon, for in 1664 he was engaged in engraving seals, medals and coins. Sometime after completing the 'Dominion of the Seas' medal commemorating the defeat of the Dutch fleet in June 1665, Thomas Simon was stricken with the plague and died at the age of 47, although there is some doubt as to whether this was the actual cause of his death.[303] Simon was buried on July 26, 1665[304] at the parish church of All Saints, Maidstone, Kent, and was later reinterred in the churchyard of St. Clements Dane, London. Simon left several surviving children by his wife

---

[302] An example of the 'Petition Crown' coin sold for a record £207,100 at the Spink auction of September 27, 2007. A prior sale of this piece in May 2003, also by Spink, realized £138,000 (including premium). In 1775, this coin had realized £12. *Also see fn. 398, p. 294.*

[303] Nathanson, p. 44, suggests that deaths from the plague had receded by the time of Simon's death and thus plague was a possible, but not certain, cause of his death.

[304] There is some dispute about the date—*see, e.g.,* Whetmore, *B.N.J.*, vol. 30, (1960-61), pp. 159-173.

Elizabeth including his daughters Elizabeth and Ann and a son, Samuel. Another daughter, Hibberd, inherited Simon's sketchbook. In his will he left his son Samuel his farm in Shorne, near Gravesend, Kent, as well as his paintings, drawings, and medals. His punches and graving tools were left to his nephew William. In 1669 Simon's wife petitioned the king for 2,164*l.* as the amount of arrears owed him and the following year was paid a settlement of 1,564*l.*, 10*s.*[305]

A PORTRAIT MEDAL OF THOMAS SIMON

(LEFT) (A1) OVAL PORTRAIT MEDAL APPARENTLY OF THOMAS SIMON IN SILVER **(45.8 X 38.1 MM., M.I.I 512/155, M.I.ILL L/3, BRITISH MUSEUM ACC./REG. NO M.7555). THE EXECUTION AND STYLE OF THE MEDAL ARE DEFINITELY NOT THOSE OF HIS BROTHER ABRAHAM, WHOSE WORKS REFLECTED GREAT ARTISTIC SKILL. IMAGE © TRUSTEES OF THE BRITISH MUSEUM.** *(RIGHT)* (A3) **A LATER CAST COPY OF THIS MEDAL. IT IS OF BASE METAL, LIKELY A MID-18TH C. PRODUCTION, POSSIBLY BY 'STUART.'**

Identification, Examined Specimens, and Measurements:

M.I.I 512/155; M.I.ILL PL. L, NO. 3. *CA.* 1750 (?).

(A1) British Museum. Oval cast and chased uniface medal in silver. Solid. acc./reg. no. M.7555, H133; PI.1835. The measurements are 1.8 x 1.5 in. (45.8 x 38.1 mm.), 43.3 gms. On a thicker flan than the similar medal of Abraham Simon, otherwise, identical (*q.v. p.173*). Waxed paper backing detached. Ex Edward Hawkins Collection. It is identified by the British Museum as: "A chasing by Stuart, but from what original it is not known."

(A2) British Museum. Another oval cast and chased uniface medal in silver. acc./reg. no. BNK,EngM.95, PI.1834. The measurements are: 1.8 x 1.5 in. (46.5 x 39.0 mm.), 7.9 gms. There is a card backing, now detached, which bears the inscription: "T. Simon. The four — Bank of England Collection. Acquired in 1877."

[305] A brief 19th c. biography on THOMAS SIMON may be found in B. Nightingale's 'Notices of Thomas Simon,' which appeared in the *Numismatic Chronicle* in 1842 (vol. iv, pp. 211-232). Additional useful biographical information may be found in A. H. Whetmore's 'Some further notes on Thomas Simon,' (*B.N.J.*, vol. 30, 1960-1, pp. 159-73) and Derek Allen's 'Thomas Simon's Sketch-book' (*Walpole Society*, 1938-39, xxvii, pp. 13-53). The Sketchbook itself was sold at Christie's on July 14, 1987. It contains illustrations which would be of great interest to anyone interested in Thomas Simon and his *oeuvre*.

(A₃) Private collection. Cast in base metal. The measurements are: 1.9 x 1.6 in. (47.3 x 40.2 mm.), 60.0 gms. The reverse bears an inscription in ink, in running script, which reads "Tho's Simon."

Description and Details:

A uniface plaque, with the half-length image of Thomas Simon, turned slightly left, long hair over collar, wearing a plain falling collar and buttoned doublet. Blank reverse. M.I.ILL. suggests that:

> [Like the similar one of Abraham Simon, M.I.I. 512/155], this medallic portrait was executed about the middle of the eighteenth century; probably from a model by Abraham Simon, which does not appear to be extant.[306]

Other Variation(s): None known.

Metals and Rarity:

In silver, this medal (A₁) is noted by M.I.I to be rare. Given the absence of other examples of these medals, all must be considered very rare to excessively rare. In fact, other than the examples above, and the silver example in the Farquhar collection sale (Glendining's, April 1955, lot 299) which was resold at Glendining's at their March 16, 1989, sale (lot 152), no others are known by the authors to have come onto the market. The Glendining's sale catalogue description of Helen Farquhar's collection states:

> ...AR portrait plaque, *obv.* only (M.I. 554/214), and a pair of chasings by Stuart of Abraham and Thomas Simon, *both extremely fine.*

One of the medals (in base metal) was resold at the Glendining's auction of 25 March 1998, and the catalogue notes:

> Although of uncertain date and origin the medal is, especially by nature of the subject, very rare. The Farquhar example [lot 299, part], was re-sold by "An English Collector", Glendining's, 16 March, 1989 [lot 152, part]. An inscription in ink on the rev. reads "Tho's Simon." The image is possibly taken from Vertue.

Comment:

M.I.I has little to say about this set of medals. Nathanson contains an illustration, in silver, which he identifies as "a uniface chased silver plaque," by Stuart, and of mid-18th century origin. He notes that this medal is likely based on an original wax model, now no longer in existence. There is an illustration of this medal in Forrer,[307] but it is not clear as of which metal it was made or if it was solid or hollow. This medal is likely among the copies of Abraham Simon's work produced by '— Stuart' during the mid-18th century and sold at auction in the early 20th century "for a high price."[308]

ʃʃʃʃ

> Thomas Simon, the great medallist of the Commons...
>
> —*DNB*, vol. 1900 ed., vol. xlvii, p. 770.

[306] M.I.ILL, plate L/2.

[307] Vol. v, p. 519.

[308] L. Forrer, vol. v, p. 704.

A MOST INTERESTING LATER (CA. MID-18TH C.), AND IN ALL PROBABILITY, DUTCH, RESTRIKE IN SILVER OF THE 'LORD GENERAL' MEDAL BY THOMAS SIMON (27 X 29 MM., M.I.I 388/7, M.I.ILL XXXIV/25, EIMER 180B, SIMILAR TO PLATT I/336/A). THE WORDS '*ECCE HOMO*' (TRANSLATED IN THE KING JAMES VERSION OF THE BIBLE AS 'BEHOLD THE MAN') WERE ORIGINALLY ATTRIBUTED TO PONTIUS PILATE WHEN HE PRESENTED THE SCOURGED JESUS CHRIST TO THE CROWD PRECEDING HIS CRUCIFIXION (JOHN 19:5). NOTE THAT THERE HAS BEEN AN ATTEMPTED REMEDIATION TO THE DIE FAULT AT 11:30 AND THAT A LOOP HAS BEEN ADDED. IMAGE COURTESY OF CLASSICAL NUMISMATIC GROUP, INC. (HTTP://WWW.CNGCOINS.COM).

Historical Commentary on Thomas Simon

...and to what degree of perfection [medallic art] is since ascended by our *Symons*...appears not only in our common and current moneys, but in sundry noble *Medals* and *Medalions* for Work and Elegancy, emulous of the most celebrated Antients.

—J. Evelyn, *Numismata*..., 1697, p. 22.

§

Here it may be observed, that *Thomas Simon* having displeased the late King *Charles* I, by accepting the Employment under the Commonwealth, of making other Great Seals for the Parliament, by their Order, in Imitation of his; it was yet thought necessary at the present, to employ him on the Acount of his superior Skill, and even to grant him a fresh Patent, as one of his Majesty's chief Gravers of the Mint, and Seals, with the Fee of Fifty Pounds, *per Annum*; which Patent was dated *June* 2. 1661.

—G. Vertue, *Medals, Coins, Great-Seals*..., 1753, p. 48.

§

Thomas Simon, who was formed in England by Briot, a celebrated French medalist, rivalled the classic artists of antiquity. He and his master were retained in the service of Charles I but almost all the capital works of the former were executed during the protectorate of Cromwell, the dies for whose crown, half-crown, shilling, and sixpence, were exquisitely cut by him, as were also his great seal, and that of the Commonwealth. His trial-piece of the crown of Charles II shews to equal advantage the excellence of his hand. He was sometimes assisted by his brother Abraham, the ingenious modeller in wax...

—J. Granger, *Biographical History*, 1824 ed., vol. Iv, p. 73.

§

The celebrated Thomas Simon was employed by Parliament to design the Medals of this period. As an artist he takes the first rank, and the beautiful Medals he produced have left him a name imperishable in the records of time.

—G. Tancred, *Historical Record*..., 1891, p. 28.

§

In the preparation of many of his portrait medals Simon had the advantage of working from the admirable wax models of his brother Abraham, but his own work on coins and seals proves that he was an accomplished designer, endowed with a keen sense of what was appropriate for the circular 'flan' of the coin and the seal. His technical skill is triumphantly evinced by his Petition Crown, and, taken altogether, he must be pronounced the finest medallist who ever worked in England. His usual signature is **T. S.**

—*DNB*, 1897 ed., vol. xxviii, p. 267.

§

His fame as an Engraver of coin- and metal-dies stands unrivalled in the British series.

—L. Forrer, *Biographical Dictionary of Medallists*, 1912, vol. xxviii, p. 519.

§

The two brothers Simon produced medals singly or together; in the case of a joint work, it seems that Abraham made the model, while Thomas, a more skilful engraver, did the after-chasing. The Simons appear to have first made their models in wax, and then to have cast the medals from models in sand.

—Ibid. 1912, vol. v, p. 531.

§

Symonds, Symons or as the moderns call him, Simon, is still known as an approved Medal-maker. In the Commons Journals of 17th December 1651, we find: *Ordered,* That it be referred to the Council of State to take order that the sum of 300*l.*; be paid unto Thomas Symonds, which was agreed by the Committee appointed for that purpose to be paid unto him, for the Two Great Seals made by him, and the materials thereof: And that the said Council do take consideration of what farther recompense is fit 'to be given unto him for his extraordinary pains therein; and give order for the payment of such sum of money as they shall think fit in respect thereof.'

An earlier entry, which still more concerns us here, is an Order, in favour of one whose name has not reached the Clerk, and is now indicated only by stars, That the Council of State shall pay him for 'making the Statue of the General,'—doubtless this Medal or Effigies of the General; the name indicated by stars being again that of Symonds. The Order, we observe, has the same date as the present Letter.[309] (The Medal of Cromwell, executed on this occasion, still exists, and is said to be a good likeness)[310]...Vertue published Engravings of all these Medals of Simon (as he spells him) in the year 1753.

The 'Two Great Seals,' mentioned in the Excerpt above, are also worth a word from us. There had been a good few Great Seals to be made in the course of this War; all by Symonds: of whom, with reference thereto, we find, in authentic quarters, various notices, of years long prior and posterior to this. The *first* of all the 'new Great Seals' was the one made, after infinite debates and hesitations, in 1643, when Lord Keeper Lyttleton ran away with the original:[311] Symonds was the maker of this, as other entries of the same Rhadamanthine Commons Journals instruct us: On the 11th July 1648, Henry Marten[312] is to bring 'the man' that will make the new Great Seal, and let us see him 'tomor-

---

[309] *fn.: Commons Journals*, 4th February 1650-1.

[310] *fn.*: W. Harris, *Life of Cromwell,* p. 518, of which THOMAS CARLYLE states in a footnote:

> *Life of Cromwell*: a blind farrago, published in 1761, 'after the manner of Mr. Bayle,'—a very bad 'manner,' more especially when a Harris presides over it! Yet poor Harris's Book, his three Books (on Cromwell, Charles and James I.) have worth: cartloads of Excerpts, carefully transcribed,—and edited, in the way known to us, 'by shoving- up the shafts.' The increasing interest of the subject brought even these to a second edition in 1814 (*Letters*..., p. 70, *fn.*).

The medal referred to presumably being that commemorating the victory over the Scots at Dunbar.

[311] This reference would appear to be to Lyttleton's removal of the Great Seal from the mint and conveyance to Charles I who was then at York. A Parliamentarian moderate, LYTTLETON (EDWARD, 1ST BARON LYTTLETON, 1589-1645), as Lord Keeper of the Great Seal, had previously incurred the king's displeasure when he had refused to put the Great Seal on the order to arrest the 'five members' of Parliament and had voted for the Militia Ordinance.

[312] HENRY MARTEN (1602-1680), a confirmed leader of the Leveller faction, sat in both the Short and Long Parliaments, where he actively opposed both the Scottish alliance of 1643 and Presbyterianism. Surprisingly, he was a supporter of the Catholics, which likely contributed to his not being executed at the Restoration. Marten was usually at odds with OLIVER CROMWELL for his Leveller sympathies. At one point, the rumor abounded (spread mostly by JOHN LILBURNE) that Marten intended to assassinate Cromwell in the same manner as JOHN FELTON had assassinated BUCKINGHAM (Fraser, *Cromwell*, p. 224), although Gardiner directly quotes Wildman as suggesting his having said that "...he himself would be another Felton" (*Civil War*, vol. iii, p. 372). Marten was later the chairperson of the committee to decide on Lilburne's

row;' which man it turns out, at sight of him, not 'tomorrow,' but a week after, on the 19th July, is 'Mr. Simonds'[313]—who, we find farther, is to have 100*l.* for his work; 40*l.* in hand, 30*l.* so soon as his work is done, and the other 30*l.* one knows not when. Symonds made the Seal duly but as for his payment, we fear it was not very duly made. Of course when the Commonwealth and Council of State began, a couple of new Great Seals were needed; and these too, as we see above, Symonds made; and is *to be* paid for them, and for the General's Statue;—which we hope he was, but are not sure!

Other new Seals, Great and Not-so-great, in the subsequent mutations, were needed; and assiduous Symonds made them all. Nevertheless, in 1659, when the Protectorate under Richard was staggering towards ruin, we find 'Mr. Thomas Symonds Chief Graver of the Mint and Seals,' repeatedly turning up with new Seals, new *order* for payment, and new indication that the order was but incompletely complied with.[314] May 14th, 1659, he has made a new and newest Great Seal; he is to be paid for that, and 'for the former, for which he yet remains unsatisfied.' Also on the 24th May 1659[315], the Council of State got a new Seal from him. Then on the 22d August; on the Rump Parliament's re-assembling, he makes a 'new Parliament Seal;' and presents a modest Petition to have his money paid him: *order* is granted very promptly to that end, 'his debt to be paid for this Seal, and for all former work done by him;'—we *hope*, with complete effect.[316]

The Restoration soon followed, and Symonds continued still in the Mint under Charles II.; when it is not very likely his claims were much better attended to; the brave Hollar, and other brave Artists, having their own difficulties to get life kept-in, during those rare times, Mr. Rigmarole!—Symonds, we see, did get the place of Nicholas Briot; and found it, like other brave men's places full of hard work and short rations- Enough now of Symonds and of Seals and Effigies.

—T. Carlyle, *Cromwell's Letters…*, commentary on 'Nicholas Briot' and 'Mr. Symonds,' and their medals, 1857, vol. ii, pp. 254-255.

§

Under the commonwealth the celebrated Simon produced medals which are deservedly reckoned the most admirable pieces of modern workmanship.

— J. Elmes, *A General and Bibliographical Dictionary of the Fine Arts…*, pages unnumbered, 1826, under entry for "Medals."

§

Sir George Hill has frankly confessed that he can perceive no difference in style between the work of the two brothers. Certainly the medals of Abraham bear a very close resemblance to the early unsigned and undated pieces, but they may be easily distinguished from Thomas's signed medals. They are lower in relief and less statuesque in conception. They have besides a certain humorous or satirical quality which is quite lacking in the puritan work of Thomas. There are also technical details which distinguish them. The form of truncation used by Abraham differs appreciably, and it is often cross-hatched, a treatment which never occurs on Thomas's medals or on the unsigned group. His are the only medals with a raised rim. They are, so far as I can tell, the only medals regularly cast in lead.

—D. Allen, *Thomas Simon's Sketchbook,* 1938-1939, vol. 27, p. 31, citing G. F. Hill, *Medals of the Renaissance*, 1920.

---

continued imprisonment (Gardiner, *ibid*, vol. iii, pp. 361-362). Jailed in 1643 by JOHN PYM for calling for the deposing of the King, he went on to reconcile with Cromwell who appointed him to sit on the High Court of Justice where he was one of those to sign the death warrant in 1649. Fraser relates the story attributed to COLONEL EWER that:

> …he and Henry Marten inked each other's faces with pens after signing, as the warrant lay in the Painted Chamber [a chamber of Westminster Palace], like grotesque schoolboys (ibid. p. 287).

Although Marten avoided execution at the Restoration because of his kindness towards Royalists, he died in imprisonment in 1680, allegedly having choked on his dinner.

[313] *fn: Commons Journals*, iii, 162, 174.

[314] *fn:* ibid. vii. 664.

[315] *fn:* ibid. vii. 663.

[316] *fn:* ibid. vii. 654, 663, 765.

The 'Fairfax Jewel' or 'Naseby Enamels' (1)

In November 1645, Parliament ordered the creation of a 'jewel' of 700 (*or* 800, depending upon the account) pounds value to be given to Sir Thomas Fairfax as a reward for his victory over Royalist forces at the battle of Naseby on June 14, 1645. The Jewel, the commission for which was given to the Huguenot artist Pierre Bordier, was to be in the form of a gold locket or watch-case, surrounded by diamonds. The 'jewel' has three paintings on enamel—of Parliament in session, a mounted Sir Thomas Fairfax, and a battle scene showing the Royalist forces being routed—two of these scenes are shown above and the third on page 195, *below*. In subsequent years the jewel passed from the executors of Thomas Fairfax's estate through the hands of Ralph Thoresby, Horace Walpole and Lord Hastings. At some point, the three paintings were mounted in the case seen here. Recently purchased by the National Trust, since late 2009 the jewel has been kept at Seaton Delaval Hall, a Grade I listed country house in Northumberland just north of Newcastle upon Tyne. *Cf.* Markham (1870, pp. 435-436), Mayo (vol. i, pp. 14-17), and Platt (ii/pp. 109-111). Images © The National Trust.

Note: The legend in the first roundel reads:

"These Enamels, painted by P. Bordier, were given by the Parliament to General Fairfax on his Victory at Naseby. [They] were purchased of his Executors by M. Ralph Thoresby, and at his sale by M. Horace Walpole. 1764."

Jean Petitot & Pierre Bordier

(1607/8-1691) (1676-1763)

· Artists and Miniaturists ·

JEAN (JOHN) PETITOT the elder was French-Swiss in origin, the fourth son of a Burgundian wood-carver who, with his family, had fled France because of religious persecution. A goldsmith, then portrait painter, and later, enameller and miniaturist, it was Petitot who introduced painted miniatures to the court of Charles I during the late 1630s. The actual process of painting on enamel is credited to Jean Toutin (1578–1644), a French goldsmith who developed a method of painting colors on white enamel, then firing the enamels in a furnace without any resultant change in color. Petitot then adapted this technique to the painting of miniatures.

Pierre (Peter) Bordier was a painter of miniatures to whom Petitot had been apprenticed and later worked with closely. While apprenticed to Pierre Bordier, Petitot's brilliance was quickly noticed by the latter:

> [Bordier, having] frequent occasion to make use of enamel, Petitot attained such a tone of colour, that Bordier, who afterwards became his brother-in-law, conceived that if Petitot would apply himself to portrait, he might carry the art to great perfection (—Walpole, *Anecdotes*..., 1879 ed., p. 197).

JEAN PETITOT, A PORTRAIT EXECUTED BY WILLIAM BOND (FL. 1772-1827), CA. 1826, USING ETCHING AND STIPPLE ENGRAVING AFTER A SELF-PORTRAIT BY PETITOT. IT APPEARED IN THE 1826 EDITION OF WALPOLE'S *ANECDOTES OF PAINTING IN ENGLAND* (VOL. II, P. 301). *ANECDOTES...* WAS BASED ON GEORGE VERTUE'S NOTES WHICH HAD BEEN PURCHASED BY WALPOLE AFTER VERTUE'S DEATH. IMAGE © TRUSTEES OF THE BRITISH MUSEUM.

Seeking to advance themselves, Petitot and Bordier traveled to France, Italy and finally England, arriving in England in about 1643. King Charles I's physician, Sir Theodore Turquet de Mayern[e], aware of the fine portraits being produced by the pair, introduced them to the king and soon they were working at court where they painted a number of portraits of Charles and the royal family. With advice in painting technique from Van Dyck, the leading court painter at the time, they completed a number of works, with Petitot copying his own works in miniature. When painting miniatures, Petitot painted the heads and hands while Bordier did the hair, draperies and backgrounds. Charles, impressed by the resulting work, commissioned Petitot to paint a George of the Order of the Garter, although this was one of only a small number of medallic portraits completed by Petitot.[317]

Following Charles I's execution in 1649, Petitot, fearing the violence then taking place, joined the royal family in exile in Paris where he was introduced to Louis XIV by Prince Charles. Wornum comments on Petitot's leaving England and his production of the 'Fairfax Jewel:

[317] CHARLES I appears to have been so taken by PETITOT'S work that he provided him with an apartment at Whitehall and occasionally went to observe Petitot at work (G. C. Williamson, vol. iv, p. 424).

PIERRE BORDIER, A SCARCE PRINT PORTRAIT, CA. 1657, BY PIERRE VAN SCHUPPEN (1627-1702) AFTER A PAINTING BY JEAN DE DIEU (CA. 1625-1709). PETITOT DEVELOPED HIS SKILLS WHILE APPRENTICED TO BORDIER AND SOON WAS COLLABORATING WITH HIM, PETITOT DOING THE DRAWING AND PAINTING, AND BORDIER THE ENAMELING. IMAGE © TRUSTEES OF THE BRITISH MUSEUM.

> The tragic death of his royal protector was a dreadful stroke to Petitot, says his biographer, who attended the exiled family to Paris. I question, as so few English portraits appear by his hand, and none, that I know, later than 1642, whether the Civil War did not early drive him back to France; but Bordier undoubtedly remained here some time longer, having been employed by the Parliament to paint a memorial of the battle of Naseby, which they presented to Fairfax, their victorious general. This singular curiosity is now in my possession, purchased from the museum of Thoresby, who bought it, I with other rarities, from the executors of Fairfax. It consists of two round plates, each but an inch and half diameter, and originally served, I suppose, for the top and bottom of a watch, such enamelled plates being frequent to old watches instead of crystals. On the outside of that which I take for the bottom, is a representation of the House of Commons, as exhibited on their seals by Simon. Nothing can be more perfect than these diminutive figures; of many, even the countenances are distinguishable. On the other piece, within, is delineated the battle of Naseby; on the outside is Fairfax himself, on his chestnut horse, men engaging at a distance. The figure and horse are copied from Vandyck, but with a freedom and richness of colouring, perhaps surpassing that great master. Under the horse one reads P. B. fecit.[318]

Meanwhile, Pierre Bordier remained in England working for Cromwell and Parliament, later being commissioned by the latter to paint the 'Fairfax Jewel.'[319]

---

[318] From R. N. WORNUM'S annotation of Walpole's *Anecdotes of Painting...* (1888 ed.). Wornum notes his dependence upon JAMES BURGESS' *Lives of Eminent Painters* (1754) for this information.

[319] In this regard, Wornum comments:

> I have the receipt of the executors of Fairfax to Thoresby, who paid 185*l.* for his purchases. He has, at the end of his *Ducatus Leodiensis*, in the account of his own museum, given a more minute description of these enamels.
>
> A jewel, enamelled upon gold—General Fairfax, on a chestnut horse—army in the distance. Motto, "Sic radiant fideles." On the reverse, the battle of Naseby. An inch and half diameter; 700*l.* value. Three members deputed to carry the present to him -*Ludlow's Memoirs*, fol. p. 62.—D.

The 'Fairfax Jewel' or 'Naseby Enamels' (11)

THE REVERSE OF THE FITTED CASE CONTAINING THE THREE PAINTINGS COMPRISING THE 'FAIRFAX JEWEL.' THE FAIRFAX JEWEL WAS PRESENTED TO SIR THOMAS FAIRFAX BY PARLIAMENT AS A REWARD FOR HIS VICTORY AT NASEBY. THE EMPTY PLACES APPEAR TO HAVE ALWAYS BEEN THAT WAY. IMAGE © THE NATIONAL TRUST.

In Paris, Petitot met Jacques Bordier, a cousin of Pierre, who, like Petitot, was a goldsmith and enameller. From this point on, Petitot and Jacques Bordier worked as partners in painting miniatures—the faces and hands being painted by Petitot while Bordier did the hair, dress, jewels, and backgrounds. The painting was usually done on gold and silver plates, only rarely on copper. This partnership, which collaborated in commissions received from Louis XIV, was to last for 35 years. Petitot and Jacques Bordier were given apartments in the Louvre and produced over 300 miniatures of French and other prominent Continental figures, including those of Louis XIV's mother Anne of Austria and Queen Maria Theresa. So enamored of Petitot's work was Louis XIV that even after Petitot's three decades of residence in France, he initially refused to grant his request to be allowed to retire to Switzerland.[320] From 1685 until about 1687, Petitot and his Calvinist Protestant (Huguenot) brethren faced persecution in France, and with his niece, he was imprisoned for refusing to renounce his religion. In failing health, he eventually complied and was allowed to leave France for Geneva. Arriving there, he was the subject of a church investigation. Ultimately cleared of wrongdoing, he was allowed to rejoin the Huguenot community in Geneva, where he resumed his work, in which he was engaged when he died in 1691.

---

[320] R. E. Graves (ed.) (1886). *Bryan's Dictionary of Painters and Engravers*..., vol. ii, p. 280; *Encyclopedia Britannica*, 1911 ed., vol. xxi, p. 308.

Historical Comment on Jean Petitot and Pierre Bordier

[Petitot] was patronised by the two monarchs who of late years have given the noblest encouragement to artists—Charles I. and Louis XIV. He deserved their protection as a genius, and has never been equalled in enamel...his talent was not only copying a portrait with exact resemblance, but also designing a head most perfectly after nature. To this he added a softness and liveliness of colouring which will never change—a circumstance which greatly increases their value.

—Walpole, H. (1888, R. N. Wornum, ed.). *Anecdotes of Painting*..., vol. ii, pp 31-37.

§

Richelet, in his "Remarques Preliminaires," Paris, 1680, says that MM. Bordier and Petitot are the most famous painters in enamel in Paris, and the first who have made portraits in enamel; before then there were only flowers and prettiness; "the enamel is done on plates of gold or copper covered with white enamel." Sometimes the enamels were after original sketches, and sometimes after portraits by contemporary artists, Lebrun, Mignard, Rigaud, Nanteuil, Philippe de Champagne, Largilliere, &c.

An example of the fine portraiture work of Jean Petitot & Pierre Bordier is seen in this miniature of Queen Henrietta Maria likely done before the death of Charles I. Image © Victoria & Albert Museum.

Petitot's enamel portraits are, as a rule, on gold, covered with a pure white enamel ground, and on this the colours are laid with a marvellous delicacy and minuteness of execution. They fire as painted, touch for touch, with very slight changes of colour, but their surfaces are different from those of the true vitreous enamels. The school of enamelling projected by Petitot had an immense vogue abroad in the latter part of the seventeenth century, and the earlier part of the eighteenth. Both Dutch and French jewellers gladly made use of the new and beautiful art for the decoration of watch cases, among the most successful of them may be mentioned Jan Berninck, of Amsterdam; Jean Hebrat, of Brussels; Gribelin, of Paris; and Huard le Puisne. The work of the English enameller, J. Tompion, of London, is also found on watch cases. His flesh tints are pleasing.

—C. Davenport, 'Portrait Enamels.' *Journal of the Royal Society of Arts*, April 17, 1908, pp. 573-578.

§§§§

ALTHOUGH now superseded for most purposes, eighteenth-century numismatic works should not be neglected today, and not only for their own elegance and interest as early books with charming though often quaint engravings.

—I. Stewart, in A. S. Bell, *The Scottish Antiquarian Tradition*..., 1981, p. 238.

THE FRONTISPIECE TO *LIBRA SEX DE LITERIS INVENTIS* (1711), BY SAMUEL GRIBELIN. THE LEGEND IS FROM CLAUDIUS—'...THY MIND [INTELLECT] IN TURN EITHER BESTOWS ITS EFFORTS ON THE STATE OR ITS LEISURE ON THE MUSES' (CLAUDIAN, *PANEGYRIC ON THE CONSULSHIP OF FL. MANLIUS THEODORUS*, A.D. 399). THE BRITISH MUSEUM SUGGESTS THAT THE FIGURE MAY HAVE BEEN INTENDED TO REPRESENT THOMAS HERBERT, 8TH EARL OF PEMBROKE (1664-1732; *Q.V. P. 282*), WHO WAS AN AVID COLLECTOR OF CLASSICAL ANTIQUITIES—GEMS, COINS, MEDALS, INTAGLIOS, AND BUSTS. NOTE THE FRAME, POSSIBLY CONTAINING COINS OR MEDALS, AT THE LOWER RIGHT. THE INSCRIPTION IN GREEK OVER THE DOOR 'IATREION PSYCHES' TRANSLATES AS 'HEALING PLACE OF THE SOUL.' IT IS TO BE FOUND OVER THE ENTRANCES TO LIBRARIES.

Two Medals of Charles II by John Roettier

A magnificent gold medal, designed by John Roettier(s), depicting on the obverse Charles II as a Roman general viewing a naval engagement (ca. 1665, 62 mm., M.I.i 503/139, M.I.Ill xlviii/11, British Museum acc./reg. no. M.7545, Eimer 230). This medal was struck after the defeat of the Dutch fleet on June 3, 1665, by an English fleet under the duke of York, Prince Rupert, and the earl of Sandwich. It was given as a reward to those captains and admirals who had distinguished themselves in the action. The reverse inscription is from Virgil's *Aeneid*: 'For such enterprises.' Image reduced in size by approximately 20 per cent; © Trustees of the British Museum.

Another very attractive medal designed by John Roettier, this in silver, the obverse portraying the conjoined busts of Charles II and his queen, Catherine (ca. 1670, 41 mm., M.I.i 546/203, M.I.Ill lv/9, British Museum acc./reg. no. G3,EM.209, Eimer 245). The reverse design refers to the dissemination of British influence and colonization throughout the world, thus one possible translation for the legend: 'The Briton spread over the world.' Image approximately actual size; © Trustees of the British Museum.

John Roettier[s] & Family

(1631-1703)

·Medallists·

APPOINTED an engraver at the royal mint in 1661, John Roettier (*also* Jan Roettier[s] *or* Rotier; 1631-1703) was born in Antwerp or Brussels where he learned the trade of medal-engraving from his father, Philip Roettiers (1596-1669), a goldsmith and medallist. An assistant engraver at the Antwerp mint, he and his brothers Joseph (1635-1703) and subsequently, Philip (b. 1640), accepted the invitation of Charles II and came to England in 1661. Forrer cites Horace Walpole[321] as stating that this invitation resulted from the Roettier brothers' father having loaned money to Charles II during his exile, in return for which he obtained a promise of employment for his sons following Charles' restoration to the throne. Thus, Norbert and James Roettier were appointed 'joint assistant engravers' at the royal mint, and John became chief engraver upon the death of Thomas Rawlins in 1662. Challis comments that:

> To some, then as now, this was a most puzzling appointment, for it was made at the expense of Thomas Simon, one of the greatest engravers the mint has ever had.[322]

THE REVERSE OF JOHN ROETTIER[S]'S MEDAL OF GILES STRANGWAYS, IN SILVER (1648, 60.5 MM., M.I. 333/177, M.I.ILL XXIX/9, EIMER 153, PLATT II/292/B). THE SURROUNDING INSCRIPTION: 'AND ADVERSITY CONFERRED HONOR [GLORY?].' IN THE EXERGUE: 'GILES STRANGWAYS OF MELBURY, IN THE COUNTY OF DORSET, ENGLAND.' IMAGE © TRUSTEES OF THE BRITISH MUSEUM.

Work was divided at the mint, with John producing the puncheons, and Joseph and Philip sinking the dies. This arrangement continued until 1679 when Joseph left his position as assistant engraver at the royal mint sometime before 1680 and went to France where in 1682 he was appointed engraver-general of coins, a post he held until his death in 1703.[323] In 1684, Philip, who had been away from the mint some time, lost his salary there and was appointed 'engraver-general of coins to the king of Spain in the Low Countries' and then engraver at the mint in Antwerp.

John Roettier remained at the mint in London, being named 'engraver in the mint' in 1690, now in the absence of Joseph, being assisted by Norbert. John was removed from his position in 1697 or 1698, when a committee of the House of Commons reported that he was a 'violent papist' and

---

321 Walpole, *Anecdotes of Painting*, v. ii, p. 184.

322 C. E. Challis, 'Roettier [Roettiers] family.' *Oxford DNB (online)*. Challis suggests the reasons for this having been done included CHARLES II's dislike of his portrait as executed by Simon when compared with that produced by the Roettier brothers, SIMON's history of appointment as chief engraver at the mint during the Protectorate, and Simon's delay in the production of the dies.

323 JOSEPH CHARLES ROETTIERS (1693-1779), the son of JOSEPH ROETTIERS, was also an engraver, having been appointed 'Graveur des Medailles du Roi' in 1715 and in 1727, 'Engraver General at the Paris mint.'

therefore unfit to have custody of the dies for coins.[324] In actuality, the reason was his failure to prevent the misuse of dies for which he had held responsibility.[325] John (Jan) Roettier retired to a house in Red Lion Square, London, where he died in 1703 and was buried in the Tower.

A design frequently employed by Jan (John) Roettier in his medals of Charles I (ca. 1641-1648, ? mm., M.I.i 360/231, M.I.Ill xxxii/8, similar to Eimer 173, Platt i/168/A_2). Here, a silver-gilt example, ca. 1649, in a possibly unique ornamental brooch setting. Image courtesy of Noble Numismatics Pty. (Australia), info@noble.com.au, auction sale 99, lot 3008.

Norbert Roettier and his brother James, having been in all but title, joint engravers-general to the mint, continued in this position until about 1695 when Norbert left for France. James remained in his position until 1697, when he was summarily dismissed. Norbert, a fervent Jacobite, had left to join the court of James Stuart to which he was styled 'engraver of the mint.' While with the Stuarts, he produced several medals for them. He then was appointed 'engraver-general of the Monnies of France,' succeeding his uncle Joseph Roettiers in the position. Fashioning himself 'Graveur général des monies de France et d'Angleterre,' he died in France in 1727. Norbert's eldest son, James Roettier (1707-1784), was appointed 'goldsmith to the king of France' and upon his father's death succeeded him as 'engraver of the mint' to the Stuart pretender. Returning to London in 1731, he produced a number of medals for the English nobility and other prominent individuals, signing his name IAC. ROETTIERS.[326]

[324] L. Forrer, vol. v, p. 163.

[325] S. Handley, op cit., p. iii. It appears that workers at the mint had copied the dies for James II gold guineas and provided them to coiners in the Fleet Prison who used them to strike counterfeit guineas on gilded copper, an act for which John Roettier was held responsible.

[326] *DNB*, 1897, vol. xlix, pp. 98-101. *DNB* states that John Roettier usually signed his medals "J. R." in monogram…, [but] also sign[ed] ROTI.; ROETTI; IAN. R.; JOAN. ROTI.

Waller's Epigram Upon the Golden Medal

The so called 'Golden Medal' issued in gold (rare), silver-gilt and silver to commemorate the marriage of Charles II and Catherine of Braganza. Designed by John Roettier, the original dies are in the British Museum. (*Top*) in silver-gilt (43 mm., M.I.i 489/111, M.I.Ill xlvii/1, Eimer 224), sold at Dix Noonan Webb Auction of March 15, 2011, lot 1033; (*bottom*) in silver, same details, British Museum acc./reg. no. M.7525).* The medal, issued in 1662, is believed to derive its name from Edmund Waller's *Epigram Upon the Golden Medal*.

Our guard upon the royal side!
On the reverse our beauty's pride!
Here we discern the frown and smile,
The force and glory of our isle.
In the rich medal, both so like
Immortals stand, it seems antique;
Carved by some master, when the bold
Greeks made their Jove descend in gold,
And Danae wondering at their shower,
Which falling, stormed her brazen tower.
Britannia there, the fort in vain
Had battered been with golden rain;
Thunder itself had failed to pass;
Virtue's a stronger guard than brass.

*Images courtesy of Dix Noonan Webb (*above*) and © the Trustees of the British Museum (*below*).

The Duchess of Richmond as Britannia

FRANCES TERESA STEWART (1647-1702) CAME TO ENGLAND FROM PARIS IN 1663. HER FATHER, A PHYSICIAN IN QUEEN HENRIETTA MARIA'S COURT, HAD BEEN IN EXILE THERE. SHE RETURNED AT THE INVITATION OF HENRIETTA MARIA TO SERVE AS MAID OF HONOR TO CATHERINE OF BRAGANZA AT HER MARRIAGE TO CHARLES II. AS A RESULT OF HER WIT, BEAUTY AND CHARM, STEWART QUICKLY GAINED A HIGH DEGREE OF POPULARITY. SHE ALSO ATTRACTED THE AMOROUS ATTENTION OF KING CHARLES II WHO IS SAID TO HAVE PURSUED HER FERVENTLY, EVEN CLIMBING OVER A GARDEN WALL TO VISIT HER, LEADING TO RUMORS THAT CHARLES INTENDED TO DIVORCE CATHERINE IN ORDER TO MARRY HER. STEWART IS BELIEVED TO HAVE RESISTED HIM, CHOOSING INSTEAD TO ELOPE WITH AND MARRY THE 3RD DUKE OF RICHMOND IN 1667. THE UNFINISHED MEDAL SHOWN HERE DEPICTS THE DUCHESS OF RICHMOND AS BRITANNIA, AND APPEARS TO HAVE BEEN INTENDED FOR USE AS THE REVERSE OF A MEDAL THAT WAS NOT ISSUED (IN PEWTER, 1667, 68 MM., M.I.I 537/188, M.I.ILL LIV/6, B.M. ACC./REG. NO. M.7574, IMAGE © TRUSTEES OF THE BRITISH MUSEUM, EX HANS SLOANE AND MATTHEW YOUNG COLLECTIONS). IN 1829, THE DIES FOR THIS MEDAL AND OTHERS BY THE ROETTIERS WERE GIVEN TO THE BRITISH MUSEUM BY MR. MATTHEW YOUNG (*Q.V. P. 301, BELOW*).

ʃʃʃʃ

Another Candidate for the 'Golden Medal'?
A Comment by Robert Bell on Edmund Waller's
·Epigram Upon the Golden Medal·

While Catherine of Braganza's visage on the 'Golden Medal' may have been the inspiration for Waller's 'Epigram,' as M.I.I suggests, another candidate surely also exists in the person of Frances Teresa Stewart, Duchess of Richmond and Lennox, known because of her beauty and charm as 'La Belle Stewart.'

THIS epigram alludes to the well-known original of the figure of Britannia. Philippe Rotier, the medallist, being employed to cut the die for the new coinage, transferred the portrait of the reigning favourite, La Belle Stewart, to the reverse of the coin, where it may still be seen,* the likeness being transmitted with tolerable accuracy through the hands of subsequent artists. He afterwards engraved her profile for a medal, which Horace Walpole pronounces the most perfect face he had ever seen. It is said of Rotier, that while Miss Stewart sat to him, he conceived so violent a passion for her, that he nearly lost his senses. That exquisite loveliness was afterwards fearfully impaired by the ravages of the small-pox, which deprived her of the use of one of her eyes. Waller repeats in his verses the compliment to Miss Stewart's virtue, which, whether well or ill founded, appears to have been generally credited at court.

—R. Bell (ed.) (1854), *Poetical Works of Edmund Waller*, London: Charles Griffin, *fn.* p. 226.

*This statement remained true into the 21st century, with Ms. Stewart's image as Britannia being depicted on the 2006 fifty pence piece.

Frances Teresa Stewart, Duchess of Richmond & Lennox

Left, a mezzotint engraving of the original painting by Sir Peter Lely of Frances Teresa Stewart, Duchess of Richmond & Lennox, published in 1779 by Thomas Watson. Right, the obverse of a uniface medal of Frances Stewart by John Roettier, ca. 1667 (70 mm., M.I.i 541/195, M.I.Ill lv/i, B. M. acc./reg. no. M.7585). Ex Edw. Hawkins collection. The die for this medal was later purchased by Mr. Matthew Young, who struck several examples in bronze. Images © Trustees of the British Museum.

Historical Commentary on John Roettier[s]

...that excellent engraver... who emulates even the ancients in both metal and stone.

—J. Evelyn, *Diary*, July 20, 1678.

§

There dined with us to-day Mr. Slingsby, of the Mint, who showed us all the new pieces both gold and silver (examples of them all), that are made for the King, by Blondeau's way; and compared them with those made for Oliver. The pictures of the latter made by Symons [Thomas Simon], and of the King by one Rotyr [Roettier], a German, I think, that dined with us also. He extols those of Rotyr's above the others; and, indeed, I think they are the better, because the sweeter of the two; but, upon my word, those of the Protector are more like in my mind, than the King's, but both very well worth seeing. The crowns of Cromwell are now sold, it seems, for 25s. and 30s. apiece.

—S. Pepys, *Diary*, March 9, 1662/1663, 1942 ed., vol. iv, pp. 63-64.

§

My Lord Brouncker and I to the Tower, to see the famous Engraver, to get him to grave a seal for the office. And did see some of the finest pieces of work, in embossed work, that ever I did see in my life, for fineness and smallness of the images thereon.

—ibid. March 26, 1666.

§

In [the reign of Charles II], the family of Roettier, a goldsmith and banker of Paris, were the principal artists in this line. This person had supplied Charles II. with money during his exile; and when he was restored, the king, according to a previous agreement, sent for the sons of Roettier, two of whom came over, John and Joseph. Simon, that admirable artist, who had worked for Cromwell, and the commonwealth, was superseded by them. They were established in the Mint, with a good salary

THIS DESIGN FOR A MEDAL BY JOHN ROETTIER, AS WAS THE CASE FOR THE ONE SHOWN ON PAGE 203, WAS NEVER USED. IT IS THE OBVERSE OF A MEDAL OF BARBARA VILLIERS (1640-1709), ANOTHER FAVORITE OF CHARLES II, INTENDED TO COMMEMORATE HER HAVING BEEN RAISED TO THE PEERAGE AS THE DUCHESS OF CLEVELAND (1670, IN LEAD, 62 MM., BRITISH MUSEUM ACC./REG. NO. 1887, M.I.I 547/204, M.I.ILL LV/10, EX HANS SLOANE COLLECTION). IMAGE © TRUSTEES OF THE BRITISH MUSEUM.

and a house; they were allowed 200*l.* for each broad seal, and they gained 300*l.* per annum by the sale of their medals to foreign countries; they became rich, and then the third brother, Philip, came over, and was employed by the government. John Roettier was reckoned the best artist of the three, but Philip was the only one of them that put his name or initials upon our medals. Simon, displeased at the preference given to persons so inferior to himself, struck the famous "pattern crown" piece, which, although it did not displace his rivals, caused the restoration of his salary, with a portion of the Mint work. John Roettier employed two of his three sons (James and Norbert) very much, which disgusted their uncles. Joseph went to France, and Philip to Belgium, and each of them was employed by the respective governments of those countries. The youngest son of John died, and he, with his remaining son, Norbert, continued in employment until the revolution; and, singular enough, although John, the head of this family, was offered to be continued in his employment, nothing could prevail upon him to work for king William. He thus made himself an object of suspicion; guards were placed round his house in the Tower, and lord Lucas, the governor, made him so uncomfortable that he soon left the place. Roettier, sen. was, however, wealthy, but infirm in health. He retired to a house in Red-lion square. His son Norbert still worked for the government. It is said he did the coronation medal of king William and queen Mary; also some dies for the copper coinage. In 1694, it was decided that both these sovereigns' heads should be placed on the same side, Britannia on the reverse: but some "circumspective eyes" pretended that they discovered a satyr's head couched in that of the king. This caused a good deal of noise. A report was spread, that James II. was in England, concealed in Roettier's house in the Tower. Norbert Roettier left the Tower, and went to France, where Louis XIV. gave him employment; and he there struck several medals for the pretender. Harris, a player, who succeeded Roettier, was quite incapable of filling the situation. This intruder was obliged to employ workmen to strike the medal for the new sovereign, queen Anne. One of these workmen was Mr. Croker,[327] who afterwards got the appointment. A detailed account of the principal work in medals and coins struck by this family will be found in Evelyn, Pinkerton, &c. Du Four was another medallist, of whose work not many specimens are extant. George Bower produced several large medals of Charles II. with the queen's head on the reverse, of the duke of York's shipwreck, of king James II., another of his queen, of the dukes of Albemarle, Ormond, and Lauderdale, and of the earl of Shaftesbury.

— W. B. S. Taylor (1841). *The Origin, Progress, and Present Condition of the Fine Arts in Great Britain and Ireland*, v. i, pp. 392-395.

[327] *See entry for John Croker, pp. 211-212.*

Two Later Medals By John Roettier(s)

Another example of an attractive medal made by John (Jan) Roettier in 1667, this one in silver celebrating the Peace of Breda (56 mm., M.I.i 535/186, M.I.Ill liv/4, Eimer 241). The *rev.* imagery is of Britannia reviewing her fleet, the sitter for the depiction of Britannia having been Frances Teresa Stewart, Duchess of Richmond and Lennox, 'La Belle Stewart.' Image courtesy Dix Noonan Webb, Ltd., auction of March 15, 2011, lot 1037.

Medal of John Maitland, duke of Lauderdale, 1672, also by John Roettier (in silver, 62 mm., M.I.i 550/208, M.I.Ill live/1, Eimer 248, Platt II/212/b). The reverse depicts the goddess *Minerva* holding the duke's crested helmet in her left hand and a spear in her right hand. She rests her right arm on a shield emblazoned with the Lauderdale arms which includes the motto of the earls of Lauderdale, *Consilio et Animis* ('by counsel and courage'). Image courtesy of Ben Weiss. Another medal of Maitland by Abraham Simon (M.I.i 328/16.9, Platt II/326/a) appears on page 176.

Charles II Marriage Medals by George Bower[s]

Celebratory medal of Charles II & Catherine of Braganza (in silver, 1662, 62 mm., M.I.i 491/115, M.I.Ill xlvii/1, British Museum acc./reg. no. M.7528, Eimer 222). Artistically, perhaps Bower's best medallic work. Compare with, e.g., the marriage or 'golden medal' by John Roettier (M.I.i. 489/111), which appears on page 201.

Another celebratory medal of the marriage of Charles II and Catherine of Braganza, also by George Bowers (in silver, 1662, 52.5 mm., M.I.i 480/90, M.I.Ill xlvi/3, British Museum acc./reg. no. M.7496, Eimer 223). It possesses an interesting reverse design; a finely sculpted image of Fame depicted blowing her trumpet while holding an olive branch in her left hand. The bust portraits are, however, of lesser artistic quality than for example, those of John Roettier. Readers will undoubtedly note that the portraits on two medals depicted here, although of the same persons, differ significantly in execution. Ex Edward Hawkins collection. Both Images © Trustees of the British Museum.

George Bower[s]

(fl. 1664–1689; d. 1690?)

·Medallist·

A CONTEMPORARY of the Roettiers, Bower[s] is often compared unfavorably with them as a medallist. Little is known of George Bower's life aside from his professional activities for the period 1664–1689/90 and the fact that he probably died in the latter year. During this time he was employed as an 'embosser in ordinary,' or engraver, at the royal mint and served as a medallist to three kings—Charles II, James II and William III. He also executed private commissions.

Although Bower's medals lack the finer portraiture and finishing of the Roettiers' medals, many of them are well known to collectors. In particular, the Charles II Restoration (1660; M.I.i 458/50; *q.v. p. 208*) and marriage medals (1662; M.I.i 491/115; M.I.i 480/90; *q.v. p. 206*). Bower's work under James II included a medal commemorating the defeat and trial of the seven bishops (1688, M.I.i 622/37, M.I.Ill lxv/9, Eimer 288) and the coronation of William and Mary (1689). *DNB* notes that Bower's execution of a medal (M.I.i 583/259, *see illustration below*) commemorating the acquittal of the earl of Shaftesbury on charges of treason led John Dryden to write his satire, 'The Medal:'

> Five days he sate for every cast and look,
> Four more than God to finish Adam took;
> But who can tell what essence angels are,
> Or how long Heaven was making Lucifer?

BOWER'S MEDAL COMMEMORATING THE DISCHARGE OF ANTHONY ASHLEY COOPER, 1ST EARL OF SHAFTESBURY, ON CHARGES OF TREASON (1681, IN SILVER, 40 MM., M.I.I 583/259, M.I.ILL LX/8, BRITISH MUSEUM ACC./REG. NO. M.7632, EIMER 261). THE INSCRIPTION 'LÆTAMVR' ('[LET US] REJOICE'). SHAFTESBURY HAD BEEN A FERVENT SUPPORTER OF THE RESTORATION, BUT IN 1673 HE WAS DISMISSED FROM HIS POSITION AS LORD CHANCELLOR AND CHARGED WITH TREASON FOR HAVING SUPPORTED THE CLAIMS TO THE CROWN OF JAMES SCOTT, 1ST DUKE OF MONMOUTH. WHEN ACQUITTED OF THESE CHARGES IN 1681, THE POPULAR PARTY HAD THIS MEDAL, WHICH WAS THEN WORN BY HIS SUPPORTERS, STRUCK BY BOWER. HERE AGAIN, BOWERS' STYLE DIFFERS FROM THAT EMPLOYED ON THE TWO MEDALS ILLUSTRATED ON THE FACING PAGE. IMAGE © TRUSTEES OF THE BRITISH MUSEUM.

The 'Gigantomachia' Medal by George Bower and ?

The stylized allegoric reverse of this struck silver medal, celebrating the victory of Charles II over his enemies, depicts an angry Jupiter ending the war with his enemies, the Titans ('Giants'), who wished to reconquer the kingdom. Jupiter does so by hurling thunder and lightning down from the heights of heaven until the Titans (i.e., the Regicides), depicted here as vague and emaciated forms, are defeated and cast into the depths of the earth. (1660, 64 mm., M.I.i 458/50, M.I.Ill xlii/5, Eimer 213).

An interesting variant of this medal resides in the Victoria and Albert Museum, London. This medal, also struck in silver and acquired by the Museum in 1992, possesses much of the same design, but was clearly executed by a different medallist. The edge bears the inscription: 'Matthew Raper* born November the 19th 1705. Given him by his uncle Mos(e)s Raper Iunr. 19th Novr. 1706.' The V&A attributes the medal to Bower but comments that the design is based on a work by the Italian sculptor Guglielmo della Porta (ca. 1500–1577). Image © Victoria and Albert Museum, London (acc./reg. no. A.6-1992).

*Matthew Raper (1705-1778) was a British polymath whose areas of erudition included astronomy, mathematics, modern languages and classical Greek and Roman numismatics. He was elected to the Royal Society in 1754.

Jan Smeltzing

(1656-1693; (fl. 1669-1693)
•Medallist•

JAMES SCOTT, 1ST DUKE OF MONMOUTH (1649-1685), ON HIS DEFEAT AT THE BATTLE OF SEDGEMOOR, JULY 6, 1685. THIS MEDAL BY JAN SMELTZING (IN SILVER, M.I.I 613/22; M.I.ILL LXIV/7; EIMER 277; 48 MM. B. M. ACC./REG. NO. G3,FD.244) COMMEMORATES THE ATTEMPT BY SCOTT, THE OLDEST ILLEGITIMATE SON OF CHARLES II, TO DEPOSE HIS CATHOLIC UNCLE, JAMES II, AN ATTEMPT FOR WHICH SCOTT WAS BEHEADED. THE REVERSE LEGEND: 'IT HAS SUCCEEDED LITTLE, BUT I ACTED DILIGENTLY.' EX GEORGE III COLLECTION; IMAGE © THE TRUSTEES OF THE BRITISH MUSEUM.

THE son and brother of medallists, Jan (*or* Johannes) Smeltzing was a technically proficient and productive medallist during the latter half of the 17th century, working in France and the Netherlands. While active for a long period (1669-1693), most of his work was completed during the years 1684-1693. Having begun his career in his native Holland, he was forced to leave that country for France in 1690 as a result of the satirical medals which he had designed. He then worked at the Paris mint, but soon left France to return to the Netherlands. Back in his home country, he returned to the design of satirical medals of the French king, Louis XIV. England did not escape his critical gaze—several of his medals of James II are very much satirical in nature. Among his best known productions are the medals for the 'Birth of Prince James' (1688, M.I.I 630/51, 630/52), 'Seven Bishops Imprisoned' (1688, M.I.I 621/36), and the 'Flight of James II' (1689, M.I.I 649/3).[328] Attwood notes that after Smeltzing's death, his brother Martin, among others, reused a number of his dies in combination with new ones.[329] *See overleaf.*

IN every age and nation, distinguished for arts and learning, the inclination of transmitting the memory, and even the features of illustrious persons to posterity, has uniformly prevailed. The greatest poets, orators, and historians, were contemporaries with the most celebrated painters, statuaries, and engravers of gems and medals; and the desire to be acquainted with a man's aspect has ever risen, in proportion to the known-excellence of his character, and the admiration of his writings.

—Granger, *A Biographical History of England*, 1779 (3rd ed.), vol. i, p. i.

[328] L. Forrer, *Biographical Dictionary…*, vol. v, pp. 544-550.

[329] P. Attwood (1998), *Grove Art Online* (now *Oxford Art Online*).

The Flight of James II

Two Dutch Medals By Jan Smeltzing

Jan (Johannes?) Smeltzing, working in the Netherlands in the late 17th c., not only was a prolific maker of medals commemorating Dutch events, but also produced a number of medals with English themes. The two medals illustrated here commemorate James II's departure from England after he was deposed in the 'Glorious Revolution' of 1688. As the last Roman Catholic monarch, he raised both the fear of absolutism and the reestablishment of Catholicism in England following the baptism of his first son into the Catholic faith. The first medal bears the image of a column broken by a bolt of lightning with Jehovah's name in Hebrew. In the distance is a view of London. M.I.i makes the comment that:

> The circumstances of James's "desertion or abdication" of the throne were so very extraordinary, that the Revolutionists might have well considered it the effect of Divine interference, and might also wish to have it generally understood that he voluntarily quitted the throne, and was not driven from it (p. 649).

The reverse of the second medal bears an allegorical representation of the offer by the House of Lords of the crown to William of Orange. It bears an image of two trees on the reverse—a broken oak and a flourishing orange tree, representing the end of the house of Stuart and the rise of the house of Orange. Behind is a sun rising over the sea.

Both medals are in silver and were struck in Holland in 1688. The details of the two medals are as follows: (*Above*) M.I.i 649/3, M.I.Ill lxix/3, 49 mm., British Museum acc./reg. no.: G3,EM.136. The obverse and reverse inscriptions are translated by M.I.i as: 'James II, King of England, voluntarily fled from London 20 Dec., taken 23 Dec. 1688, again fled 2 Jan. 1689.' and 'Not by the blow of man, but by the blast of Heaven.' This medal, from the collection of George III, was donated to the British Museum by George IV in 1825. (*Below*) in silver, 48 mm., M.I.i 651/6, M.I.Ill lxix/5, British Museum acc./reg. no.: M.7723. The obverse and reverse inscriptions are translated by M.I.i as 'For acorns, oranges.' After the flight of James II, the crown was offered to the Prince of Orange on January 3, 1689. The obverse portraits of James II on both medals shows his hair in a bag, a reference to his readiness for hurried flight. The initials S. N. in the reverse exergues of both medals signify '[Jan] Smeltzing of Nijmegen.' Both medals ex Edward Hawkins' collection, images © Trustees of the British Museum.

John Croker

(1670–1741).

·Medallist·

QUEEN ANNE, 'UNION OF ENGLAND AND SCOTLAND' (SILVER, 1707, 70 MM., M.I.II 298/115, M.I.ILL CXXIV/16, EIMER 423). ALTHOUGH UNSIGNED, IT IS BELIEVED TO BE BY JOHN CROKER. IMAGE COURTESY OF BEN WEISS.

JOHN CROKER was born in Dresden, Germany as Johann Crocker. His father was a woodcarver and cabinet-maker to the electoral court of Saxony. Johann was taken in as an apprentice by his godfather, a goldsmith and jeweler, when his father died at an early age.

Medal design and engraving were self-taught skills acquired in John Croker's off-time. Arriving in England from Holland in 1691, Croker anglicized his name and obtained an appointment as assistant engraver to Captain Henry Harris, the chief-engraver at the London mint,[330] where he was immediately set to designing medals, the first of which he completed that same year. Seen by the mint officers as 'a very able artist,' Croker gained advancement to chief engraver in 1705, following Harris' death, a position he held until his own death. In this role, he engraved the majority of coins during the reigns of Anne and George I.[331]

---

330 'CAPTAIN' HENRY HARRIS (ca. 1634-1704) deserves some further mention as a colorful and rather disreputable minor character who achieved some notoriety in his time. Apparently Harris was an 'actor, singer, dancer, theatre owner/manager and painter of scenery' who had numerous appearances in court for matters relating to his theatrical career, as well as for unpaid debts, contracts, matrimonial and other matters. Harris eventually secured paid posts as chief engraver at the mint as well as 'Yeoman of the Revels,' among others. Harris was a frequent dinner companion and friend of SAMUEL PEPYS, who admired him for his acting and mentions Harris positively in his *Diary* on a number of occasions. Harris seems to have also introduced Pepys to some of the racier aspects of London life. In 1665, upon the death of THOMAS SIMON, Harris unsuccessfully applied for the position of chief engraver of seals. He was, however, successful upon his re-application five years later. It is not clear that Harris carried out many duties connected with his official positions aside from collecting his salaries. He was, however, proficient at obtaining sinecures—losing his chief engraver of seals position about 1680, he was soon appointed an assistant engraver! He regained the chief engraver position with the accession of William and Mary, agreeing to employ JAMES and NORBERT ROETTIER[S] as assistants. In 1694, at the age of 63, he appears to have been appointed to a 'military' position and in 1697, as commissioner of stamps (at a salary of £300 per annum). At his death, he was described as "Captain Harris, her majesties engraver of money and medalls" (Highfill, et al. *Biographical Dictionary of Actors…in London, 1660-1800*, 1982, vol. 7, pp. 123-132).

331 *DNB*,vol. xiii, pp. 122. For a detailed biography see Pfister, *Numismatic Circular*, 1852/53.

It would appear that Croker had by 1713 begun to introduce "distinctly historical" designs into the reverses of coinage.[332] Commenting specifically on Croker's work as a medallist, *DNB* observed that:

> From 1702 till 1732 Croker was constantly engaged in medal engraving. His medals, which are nearly all commemorative of events and not of persons, are always struck, not cast, and are, like his coins, very neatly turned out. The work of his reverses recalls that of his predecessors, the Roettiers, but is in lower relief; his designs are very pictorial and full of minute detail. A manuscript volume purchased by the British Museum at the sale of the library of Mr. Stanesby Alchorne, once an officer of the mint, contains many of Croker's original designs for medals as well as autographs of Sir Isaac Newton as master of the mint. Croker's earliest medals are—like all his coins and patterns for coins—unsigned. His 'Queen Anne's Bounty' medal of 1704 is signed I. C., and from that date this is his almost invariable signature. A few specimens (of 1704 and 1706) are signed CROKER. In official documents he is called both 'Croker' and 'Crocker.' Croker was the public medallist of his time; but he had a private pecuniary interest in the sale of his works, as appears from a report of the officers of the mint to the lord high treasurer, stating that the officers were of 'opinion that good graving was the best security of the coin, and was best acquired by graving medals;' the gravers of the mint should therefore 'have leave to make and sell such medals of fine gold and silver as did not relate to state affairs, and such medals as were made to reward persons by her majesty for good services, also such as had historical designs and inscriptions for great actions'[333]

'GEORGE II, QUEEN CAROLINE AND THEIR CHILDREN.' OBVERSE BY JOHN CROKER, REVERSE BY J. S. TANNER (IN SILVER, 1732, 69 MM., M.I.II 500/47, M.I.ILL CLI/5, BRITISH MUSEUM ACC./REG. NO. G3,EM.100, EIMER 528). JOHN SIGISMUND TANNER (*D.* 1775), LIKE CROKER, A GERMAN, SUCCEEDED CROKER AS CHIEF ENGRAVER AT THE MINT.[334]

---

[332] Ibid. vol. xiii, pp. 122. *DNB* suggests that:

> ...it would appear that Croker was thus attempting to carry out the novel recommendation of Dean Swift, that the English farthings (and half-pence) 'should bear devices and inscriptions alluding to the most remarkable parts of her majesty's reign'—a suggestion ...the lord treasurer had at last fallen in with...

[333] Ibid. Source cited as: *Cal. Treasury Papers*, report 'dated 20 June 1706. Read 18 Aug. 1706.'

[334] TANNER served in his position at the mint for almost 40 years, occupied primarily with the engraving of dies for use in producing coinage. *DNB* notes that:

> He also engraved...dies in imitation of Thomas Simon's pattern-coins made for Oliver Cromwell, partly utilising the old punches...Tanner's puncheons and dies for medals, as well as those made by John Croker [q. v.], the medallist, were sold at auction by Gerard in Soho, London, on 18 June 1783 (*DNB*, vol. 55, p. 358)...

Later Medallists Associated with 17th c. British Medals

Dassier's 'Kings and Queens of England'

A restruck set (ca. 1825) of 35 gilded Æ medals comprising a complete set of Jean Dassier's 'Kings and Queens of England' series, in an original presentation case. A selection is shown above enlarged. *The legend continues on page 216.*

Jean Dassier[s][335]

(1676-1763)

· Medallist ·

DESCRIBED by Forrer as "one of the greatest of the eighteenth century Medallists," Jean Dassier[s] was born in Geneva in 1676 and learned his trade from his father, Domaine Dassier (1640/1?-1719), chief-engraver at the Geneva mint,[336] and from Norbert and John Roettier[s] in Paris. Jean Dassier was assistant-engraver at the Geneva mint from 1711-1720, and then in 1720, upon his father's death, succeeded him as chief-engraver to the Republic of Geneva, maintaining this position until 1763 when he died[337]

***Portrait of Monsieur Jean Dassier* by Jean-Étienne Liotard (1702-89). Image from the collection of the Cabinet d'Arts Graphiques des Musées d'Art et d'Histoire, Genève, N° d'inventaire D 1998-0502.**

Although his life as a medallist lies mostly outside the period addressed by this work, Jean Dassier's major association with English medals was his series of medals of the kings and queens of England from William I through George II, the dies for which were executed in 1731. An early visit to England, in 1728, was motivated by his unfulfilled hopes of obtaining a position at the royal mint. A second visit, in 1731, during which he was introduced to Queen Caroline, was much more successful, and with the Queen's blessing, he prepared and executed a series of illustrations for Paul Rapin de Thoyras' *History of England*, basing the portraits upon George Vertue's engravings. Following his return to Geneva, he resumed his duties as chief engraver at the Swiss mint until his death in 1763, when he was succeeded by his son Antoine (1718-1780), who remained in this position from 1764 until 1780. Jean's other son, Jacques-Antoine (1715-1759), had worked as 3rd assistant-engraver at the royal mint (1741-1745) but died at an early age.

Hawkins, et al. note that Dassier's medals, which were issued "in silver, bronze, and soft metal" may also be found "*damasked*, that is, the device and legend have been gilded, and the field bronzed," and that one set:

---

335 Forrer, L., *Spink's Monthly Numismatic Circular*, 1899, Vol. 8, p. 3743. For a listing of his medallic works, *see* Forrer, vol. 1, pp. 512-517. Eisler's *Medals of the Dassiers of Geneva* (2010) contains illustrations of all of DASSIER'S *oeuvre*.

336 Baker, M., 'John [Jean] Dassier.' *Oxford DNB (online)*, p. i.

337 Lewis & Wallace comment that JOHN PINKERTON, in *An Essay on Medals* (*1784*), confuses DOMAINE AND JEAN DASSIER, and that this confusion is repeated in the second edition (*Horace Walpole's Correspondence*…, 1951, fn. 13, p. 300).

...from the cabinet of George III, is in the British Museum; another set, wanting the medal of George II., was sold at Mr. Thane's sale in 1819... The dies of these medals came into the possession of Mr. Thomason, of Birmingham, by whom several sets have been issued; but they want the sharpness and freshness of the original impressions...[338]

It should be noted that Dassier also produced a set of seventy-two medals of 'celebrated persons of the age of Louis XIV (1723-24) as well as a set of 24 medals of men of the Reformation period (1725).

A DAMASCENED BRONZE MEDAL OF OLIVER CROMWELL, LAUREATE, AS LORD PROTECTOR OF ENGLAND (1658; 37 MM.; M.I.I 435/87; M.I.ILL CLI/2 (PART); EIMER 203; PLATT II/30/C) FROM THE SERIES OF ENGLISH SOVEREIGNS BY JEAN DASSIER (1731). THE MEDAL, AT 37 MM., IS SLIGHTLY SMALLER THAN OTHERS IN THIS SERIES, WHICH ARE 40 MM. THIS WOULD SEEM TO HAVE BEEN INTENDED TO REFLECT CROMWELL'S STATUS AS AN UNCROWNED RULER. THE PORTRAIT IS BASED ON THE BUST DESIGNED BY THOMAS SIMON FOR THE PATTERN COINAGE OF 1656. NOTE THAT CROMWELL WAS BORN ON APRIL 25, 1599, AND NOT ON APRIL 3, 1603, AS STATED ON THE MEDAL. ILLUSTRATION COURTESY OF A. H. BALDWIN & SONS LTD, LONDON, WWW.BALDWIN.CO.UK (AUCTION 65, LOT 1010).

LEGEND FOR DASSIER'S '*KINGS AND QUEENS OF ENGLAND*'

(See illustrations on page 214)

THIS SET INCLUDES THE ADDITIONAL MEDALS OF GEORGE III AND GEORGE IV BY J. MARRIAN WHICH WERE ADDED LATER. THE ORIGINAL SET, ISSUED IN 1731, CONSISTED OF 33 MEDALS, WITH AN ADDITIONAL ONE OF CAROLINE, QUEEN TO GEORGE II. THE ORIGINAL 1731 ISSUE WAS AVAILABLE IN SILVER, DAMASKED BRONZE OR BRONZE. FURTHER SETS WERE STRUCK BY DASSIER, LIKELY TOGETHER WITH HIS SON, JACQUES-ANTOINE, AROUND 1755. ADDITIONAL ISSUES OF THE SETS TOOK PLACE ABOUT 1773 (BY LEWIS PINGO*), AND 1825-1830 (BY SIR EDWARD THOMASON), AND SOMEWHAT LATER, AGAIN BY THOMASON. THIS LAST ISSUE WAS OF MEDALS STRUCK FROM REWORKED DIES, SOME OF WHICH CLEARLY SHOW THE WEAR ON THE DIES. THE SETS BY THOMASON ARE READILY DISTINGUISHABLE BY THE BIOGRAPHICAL COMMENTS ON THE REVERSE (EIMER 1236). IT SHOULD BE NOTED THAT SOME OF THE DATES ON THE MEDALS ARE INCORRECT. IMAGES COURTESY CLASSICAL NUMISMATIC GROUP, HTTP://CNG@CNGCOINS.COM (AUCTION NO. 88, LOT 2128).

*A MEMBER OF THE IMPORTANT FAMILY OF 18TH C. ENGLISH ENGRAVERS AND MEDALLISTS.

[338] M.I.I, pp. 1-2. Medals from the 'Kings and Queens of England' set were later restruck and reissued by SIR EDWARD THOMASON. Thomason (1769-1849) was an inventor and prodigious manufacturer of "...medals, tokens, works in bronze, and silver and gold plate" who had learned his trade as an apprentice under MATTHEW BOULTON and assumed his father's buckle factory upon the latter's retirement in 1793. Thomason later opened his own medal manufacturing business. For a biography and listing of his works, including a bibliography, see Forrer, vol. vi, pp. 73-81.

Dassier's medal of Charles I in silver and bronze (1731, 40 mm., M.I.i 353/212, M.I.Ill *no entry*, Eimer 164, Platt I/272/a). It is from the same set as the medal of Oliver Cromwell, *above and previous page*. *Top:* Stack's Bower Galleries Auction, April 4, 2010, lot 3630. *Bottom:* In a private collection.

Historical Commentary on Jean Dassier

JOHN DASSIER, though never in England,[339] is certainly entitled to a place in this catalogue. He was medallist to the republic of Geneva,* and aspiring to be employed in the mint here, struck a series of the Kings of England, in a better style than our medals had been of late years. Some of the heads indeed were not taken from true originals, but the temples and monuments on the reverses were well designed and executed. He published them by subscription in 1731, at six guineas for 33 medals in copper, and fifteen in silver. His brother James had been here three or four years before to endeavour to procure a place in our mint for John, but none being vacant, Sir Andrew Fountaine, the celebrated virtuoso and patron of artists, and Mr. Conduit, who had married Sir Isaac Newton's niece, and who were the persons then directing the mint, offered a pension of 50*l* a year to Dassier till Mr Croker should die; but he was not content with the offer. James Antony Dassier, nephew of John, came over, and on Croker's death in 1740, was next year appointed second engraver to the mint,

[339] Walpole has substituted the English names John for Jean, Anthony for Antoine and James Anthony for Jacques-Antoine. He was incorrect in stating that Jean had never been in England.

and returned to Geneva in 1745. The uncle had executed a set of the reformers in smaller brass, and begun large medals of some of our great men then living; the nephew did several more, which were sold in copper at seven shillings and sixpence** each, and are very good performances, though inferior to the medals of the popes by Hamerani, and more inferior to those of St. Urbain, medallist to the last Dukes of Lorrain. There is a beautiful and numerous suite of Roman history in small medals of bronze by the younger Dassier.

*About 1740, and for some years, before and after, Dassier, a native of Geneva, settling in London, engraved a series of medals of all the English kings, with great taste and spirit. They are struck upon fine copper, and amount to thirty-six in number. He likewise gave [sic] medals of many illustrious men of this and other nations; all of which deserve considerable praise. Pinkerton on Coins, v. ii. p. 115.
** At Dr. Mead's sale in 1755, ten medals in copper of eminent persons were sold for two guineas, and the set of kings, thirty-six in number, produced only 4*l.* 4*s.* The resemblance was imaginary.

H. Walpole, *Anecdotes of Painting*..., 1782 ed., vol. iv, pp 217-218.

§

Of Dassier I know no more than I have said in the *Anecdotes of Painting*.

—H. Walpole, in a letter to John Pinkerton, dated Oct. 15, 1788, cited in W.S. Lewis & A.D. Wallace, p. 300.

§

About 1740, a series of medals was engraved in London by Dassier, a native of Geneva, containing all the kings of England, being thirty-six in number. They are executed upon fine copper, in high taste. There are besides numerous medals of eminent private persons in England; and those who are desirous of further information concerning them are referred to Pinkerton's Essay, already cited, and Mr. Snelling's plates of them.

—J. Elmes (1826). *A General and Bibliographical Dictionary of the Fine Arts...*,
Pages unnumbered; entry found under 'Medals.'

§§§§

A Curator's Comments
on
Commemorative Medals

WITH the revived interest in fifteenth-century Italy in the history of ancient Greece and Rome, came a new passion for collecting antique coins. Rulers and scholars realised that coins, struck in durable metals, had outlasted all the other achievements of the ancients, preserving the names and appearances of the emperors for posterity. Seizing on the possibility similarly to commemorate themselves, men and women commissioned medals, which retained the profile portrait but were often bigger and more elaborate than their prototypes.

—T. Richard Blurton (ed.). *The Enduring Image: Treasures from the British Museum* (exhibition catalogue, 1997).

On the Study of Coins and Medals

THERE are few countries, Italy excepted, in which a greater number of coins have been discovered than in Britain, though we are by no means well acquainted with the time when the study of them commenced amongst us. Mr. Pinkerton suspects that Camden[340] was one of the first, if not the very first British author who produced medals in his works, and who must have had a small collection. Speed's Chronicle, published in the seventeenth century, was illustrated with coins from Sir Robert Cotton's cabinet. Gordæus's collection was purchased for Henry Prince of Wales, brother of Charles I., to whom he left it at his death. According to Joseph Scaliger, this fine assortment comprised thirty thousand coins and medals, but they were dissipated and lost among the civil commotions which ensued. A collection of upwards of five thousand was presented by Archbishop Laud to the Bodleian library. The Dukes of Buckingham and Hamilton, Sir Thomas Fanshaw, Sir Thomas Hanmer, Mr. Selden, and many others, are enumerated as having collections. Vaillant speaks of that of Charles II., and we believe our present august sovereign is in possession of a considerable assortment; indeed, several noble cabinets have been recently formed, which we have not space to particularize. That of the late Dr. Hunter, however, claims notice, as having been one of the very- greatest in Europe...

—*Encyclopedia Britannica*. 1839 (6th ed.), vol. 13, p. 142.

[340] Presumably WILLIAM CAMDEN, in his *Britannia*... (1722).

Medals of James 'Ash' or 'Pasch'? One a 'Stuart' copy?

(*Top*) A uniface piece in an 18th c. velvet lined snakeskin case (British Museum acc./reg. no. M.7383), probably by 'Stuart,' misidentified in both Vertue (1753, pl. xx) and Pinkerton (*Medallic History…*, 1790, pl. xxiv) as a 17th c. medal of James Ash, MP in 1640 and 1656, and later recorder for Bath. The British Museum points out that it is in reality a medal, not of James Ash, but of James Pasch, who is also represented on another 17th c. medal, *below*, the 'original' likely produced in Holland and having no association with England.

The details are: *(top,* the 'Stuart copy'*)* 34 x 29.5 mm., M.I.i 422/1, British Museum acc./reg. no. M.7383. (*bottom,* the Dutch 'original'*)* 35 x 30 mm., also M.I.i 422/1, the same M.I. number as for the previous medal, British Museum acc./reg. no. M.7382. The medallist for the original medal is unknown. Both medals are ex the Edward Hawkins collection. The reverse inscription: ❀ 'in te domine speravi. ps. 70.' ❀ ('In Thee, O Lord, have I put my trust. Psal. 70'). Both medals are cast and chased in silver, the workmanship being described as "coarse" and "fine," respectively. An example of the Dutch medal was sold at Baldwin's auction sale no. 49, on September 25, 2006, lot 1256. The catalogue states:

> Many of these Stuart copies, whilst a flight of fantasy, are extremely rare 18th century medals. ex Papillon Collection (lot 37), and Spink Auction 24 (lot 157). It should be noted, however, that this medal shares little, design-wise, in common with other medals attributed to 'Stuart.'

Images courtesy (*top)* Woolley & Wallis, Ltd. (The Christopher Foley, F.S.A., Collection of Early English Medals, lot 381, October 16, 2014) and (*bottom)* © Trustees of the British Museum.

'— Stuart'

(fl. 1740-1780)

· Medallist and Forger ·

STUART,' whose Christian name and dates of birth appear to be lost to history, worked during the mid- to late-18th century as a medal chaser and die-engraver. According to Forrer, among his employers were Thomas Hollis and Thomas Pingo.[341] Forrer comments:

> Stuart made some very clever copies of some of the medals by Abraham and Thomas Simon, and many others, which vary in degree of excellence. But it is quite possible that many of the retrospective medals usually ascribed to Stuart are not by him.[342]

Many late 18th and early 19th c. copies and/or forgeries of seventeenth century medals have been misattributed to James 'Athenian' Stuart, the celebrated designer, artist, architect and designer (*q.v. pp. 224-228*). Among the copies of original medals attributed to '— Stuart' are Abraham Simon's medals of Admiral Blake, Bulstrode Whitelocke and Thomas Fairfax, including the 'Cromwell & Fairfax' medal, the portrait medals of Abraham and Thomas Simon as well as the medals of Lord Inchiquin and Sir John Hotham.

Examination of medals attributed to '— Stuart' reveals several distinct styles. None of these, in the opinion of the present authors, appear to be attributable to James 'Athenian' Stuart. Stylistic characteristics which define works by '— Stuart' include a broad border and often poorly detailed portraits which appear to be poor likenesses of the subjects. Examples of several of these medals appear on the following pages and on the reproduced full page of illustrations from the catalogue of Glendining's' March 16, 1989, sale of British historical medals on p. 331, *below*. These examples may be compared with the medals by James 'Athenian' Stuart. The medals by '— Stuart' may have been used to satisfy the desire by contemporary collectors to fill gaps in their collections. Alternatively, they may have been offered for sale as 'original' medals. Given the absence of detailed works which could be consulted, there simply was a dearth of knowledge which could be used to identify forgeries. What would be ideal in resolving the question of the purpose for which the '— Stuart' medals were made would be the surfacing of a circular or advertisement for them. An order or sale confirmation from a potential seller with details would be even better.

ʃʃʃʃ

---

[341] THOMAS HOLLIS (1720-1774) was a member, with JAMES 'ATHENIAN' STUART, of the medal committee of the Royal Society of Arts. Otherwise, little attention was paid to him until recently, when his diary was found. Laurence Brown, in *British Historical Medals*, notes that Hollis was a:

> ...noted Republican. Being opposed to Tory principles he chose to propagate his feelings by the purchase and production of books and medals which he gave to various libraries (*B.H.M.* vol. i, p. 39 fn.).

At Hollis' death, his collections of "Ancient & Modern Coins and Medals" were sold by Mr. Sotheby at the latter's home and sales rooms, no. 145 Strand, opposite Catherine Street. The sale covered six days beginning on May 14, 1817. A total of 727 lots yielded £3223 15 *sh (q.v. pp. 360-365)*.

THOMAS PINGO JR. (1714–1776) was a member of the illustrious family of medallists and die engravers that flourished in England during the 18th century. THOMAS worked for the royal mint, having first been appointed assistant engraver in 1771. Of his sons, LEWIS PINGO (1743–1830) succeeded him at the mint in 1776 while JOHN PINGO succeeded him as the 'engraver of punches to the assay office at Goldsmith's Hall.' BENJAMIN PINGO was Rouge Dragon Pursuivant (1780-1786) and York Herald (1786-1794) at the College of Arms.

[342] L. Forrer, *Biographical Dictionary of Medallists*, 1907, vol. v, p. 702.

Some Original Medals and Forged Copies by 'Stuart'

'MARTINAY (?).' M.I.I 329/171. (*LEFT*) ORIGINAL MEDAL BY ABRAHAM SIMON, ASHMOLEAN MUSEUM, OXFORD; 35.6 MM. (*RIGHT*) FORGERY, BRITISH MUSEUM, 32.6 MM.

JOHN THURLOE. M.I.I 406/40. (*LEFT*) ORIGINAL BY THOMAS SIMON IN GOLD. (*CENTER AND RIGHT*) FORGERIES, 34.3 MM., 33.1 MM., AND 44.5 MM., RESPECTIVELY. IMAGES © TRUSTEES OF THE BRITISH MUSEUM.

Some Original Medals with 'Forged' copies by 'Stuart' (continued)

Sydenham Poyntz. M.I.i 325/163. (*Top left)* original medal by Abraham Simon, Victoria & Albert Museum, 35 mm. (*Top right)* A forgery, Fitzwilliam Museum, Cambridge, 35.7 mm., by '—Stuart'(?). (*Below)* a forgery by Stuart (Glendining's auction, March 16, 1989, lot 143, 41 mm., *obv.* only shown here. The images are only to approximate scale.

§

Legend for the Illustrations

On this and the preceding page are shown original medals, *c*1. Civil War period, as well as later restitutions or forgeries which have been attributed to '— Stuart.' The original medals have all been attributed by M.I. and other authorities to the Simons—Martinay and Poyntz to Abraham, and Thurloe to Thomas—and indeed the styles match other known medals by both Abraham and Thomas Simon, particularly the former. There are a number of similarities in design among the 'forgeries,' most notably the broad border. Larger images of each of the medals and their details may be found in Platt, *op cit*. Images © and courtesy of the indicated museums. Note that the images are not to scale.

James 'Athenian' Stuart and Classical Design

One of the medals designed by James 'Athenian' Stuart and executed by Thomas Pingo. It was prepared for the Society for the Promotion of Arts, Manufactures and Commerce in 1759 and commemorates the taking of Guadeloupe from the French in that year (bronze, 39 mm., M.I.ii 697/427, M.I.Ill cxxix/8). This medal should be compared with the 'forgeries' attributed to Stuart which appear on pages 222 and 223. Note in particular the use of a beaded border both here and on the restituted medal of Sydenham Poyntz. Both James 'Athenian' Stuart and Thomas Pingo employed this decorative element on several of their medals, most notably on the medals they produced for the Society of Arts. Claude Warin also used this design element on his medal of Thomas Bodley (*see p. 144*). Image © Trustees of the British Museum.

Steeped in the classical art and architecture of Italy and Greece, James 'Athenian' Stuart brought back many sketches and concepts from his long excursion there. His book, *The Antiquities of Athens and Other Monuments of Greece* (1762), written with Nicholas Revett upon their return to England, stimulated a revival of classical design. The above pen, ink and gray wash study of five Athenian medals appeared as the headpiece to chapter I of vol. II of this work, published in 1787. Of particular interest is the image of *Minerva* which appears on the medal to the right and which Stuart likened to *Phidias'* description of the gold and ivory statue of *Athena* which stood in the Parthenon. The similarity to the figure on Thomas Pingo's medal (British Museum acc./reg. no. 1853,1210.502) perhaps suggests the genesis of this particular medallic design.* Image © Trustees of the British Museum.

*Minerva was the Roman goddess of wisdom and the arts, as well as of medicine, wisdom and commerce, equivalent to the Greek goddess Athena. Phidias, the great Greek sculptor, designed the statues of Athena which stood in the Parthenon.

James 'Athenian' Stuart

(1713-1788)

•Classicist, Architect, Designer and Medallist•

JAMES 'Athenian' Stuart was an important architect, designer and medallist of the mid-18th century. His *oeuvre* in the neoclassical manner led to his achieving popularity and influence in architectural and decorative style in England and he went on to design a series of medals for the Royal Society of Arts. Many other 'false' medals—forgeries and reconstitutions—including those on pp. 222 and 223—have been attributed to him. The present authors do not believe that 'Athenian' Stuart either designed or was involved in the later manufacture of false 17th c. medals.[343] Yet, his name is frequently cited in auction catalogues as the medallist responsible for the late 18th c. reproductions of medals by Abraham and Thomas Simon. Judging by catalogue descriptions, it would seem this presumed relationship is widely accepted by modern auction house specialists and collectors. But there is simply no evidence to suggest that James 'Athenian' Stuart was involved in producing these medals.

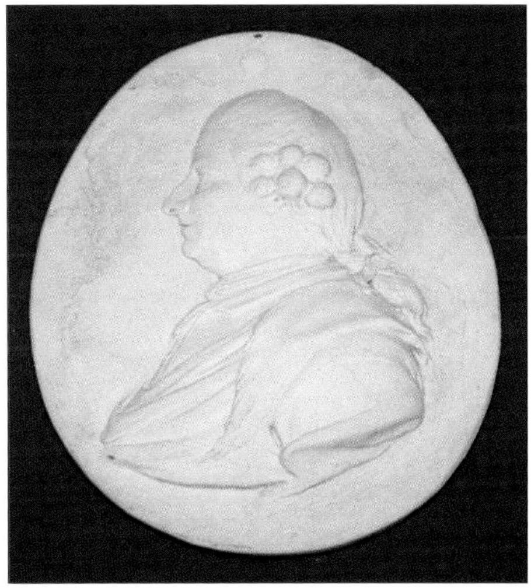

A BUST MEDALLION (3.5 IN. IN HEIGHT) IN FIRED CLAY, OF JAMES 'ATHENIAN' STUART, THE CLASSICIST PAINTER, ARCHITECT AND DESIGNER TO WHOM A WIDE RANGE OF COPIES AND/OR FORGERIES OF 17TH C. MEDALS HAVE BEEN, AND CONTINUE TO BE, INCORRECTLY ATTRIBUTED (*SEE PLATT, VOL. II, PP. 39 AND 218, FOR A DISCUSSION OF THIS POINT*). THE BUST IS LIKELY BY JOHN FLAXMAN (1755-1826). IMAGE © TRUSTEES OF THE BRITISH MUSEUM (ACC./REG. NO. 1909,1201.180).

Aside from the complete absence of factual evidence as well as stylistic considerations, there simply would have been no rational motivation for 'Athenian' Stuart to have engaged in such activity. Having been financially secure in both middle and later life, the modest possible financial gain would presumably not have been an incentive. Also, he was arguably a better artist than whoever produced the restitutions of the Simons' medals. Given the association of his name with that of another Stuart, most likely the one employed as a medal chaser by Thomas Hollis and Thomas Pingo, students and collectors of this period's medals should be aware of the details of 'Athenian' Stuart's involvement in medal design.

James 'Athenian' Stuart was truly a 'self-made' man in an age when such an accomplishment was no mean feat. Born into poverty, the son of a seaman and the main financial supporter of his family after the death of his father, Stuart, a youngster with artistic talent, somehow managed to escape the world of his origins. In 1742, he travelled (on foot!) to Italy where he worked as a *cicerone* (guide) for foreign visitors. This journey to Rome clearly identifies the young Stuart as having been, from a relatively young age, an intellectually curious and adventurous person. In 1750, along with Nicholas Revett, a young English nobleman, Stuart undertook the arduous and

[343] This opinion is also stated by Christopher Eimer in his chapter on 'Stuart and the Design and Making of Medals,' in S. W. Soros (2007), *James "Athenian" Stuart, 1713-1788, The Rediscovery of Antiquity*, pp. 494-512.

hazardous journey to Athens in order to 'study antiquities.' Returning to London in late 1762, the publication of *The Antiquities of Athens and other Monuments of Greece*, immediately gave him and Revett standing in the early years of the Greek revival period in England.

Elected to membership in the Society of Antiquaries and to fellowship in the Royal Society, Stuart became a highly sought after architect and interior designer who became involved in medal design through his association with Thomas Hollis. Arbuthnott, in her chapter *The Life of James 'Athenian' Stuart,* comments that:

> It seems that Stuart's opinions as much as his designs were the commodity that his patrons sought from him.

Yet, Arbuthnott notes that many contemporaries thought his work products sometimes shoddy, one commenting: "He is certainly no painter."[344]

ANOTHER, EARLIER, ILLUSTRATION OF JAMES 'ATHENIAN' STUART. LIKELY BY JAMES BASIRE THE ELDER (1730–1802). POSSIBLY A PROOF FOR A BOOK ILLUSTRATION. IMAGE © TRUSTEES OF THE BRITISH MUSEUM; ACC./REG. NO. 1848,1125.381.

Earlier, in 1757, Stuart's designs for medals to be issued by the Royal Society of Arts were adopted after problems had arisen in their production[345] by the jewelry manufacturer Nicholas Crisp. Stuart and the wealthy antiquary Thomas Hollis were both members of the medal committee of the Society when the need for new designs for the medals had arisen. Stuart's designs were accepted and Thomas Pingo, a member of the celebrated family of engravers,[346] was selected for the execution of the medals. The successful completion of the commission led to further collaboration in medal design and manufacture between Stuart, Hollis, and Pingo, who were later joined in this endeavor by John Kirk (*q.v. pp. 228-233*). The classical design of the medals which emerged from this collaboration is evident in the example on page 224 and it would appear that Hollis was involved closely with Stuart in the design of many, if not all, of them. Eimer notes that Stuart also designed medals for other clients, including the royal family. Most of these medals were manufactured by either Pingo or Kirk, the former accounting for the great majority of them.

Acquiring appointments as serjeant-painter to the Office of Works and surveyor to the Greenwich Naval Hospital, as well as private commissions as an architectural design consultant, gave Stuart a good living. Later in life, however, his working habits, as well as his health, deteriorated. Projects he had contracted for progressed slowly if at all. Seemingly more often than not, he absented himself from his responsibilities. He began to receive criticism and not surprisingly, his

344 C. Arbuthnott (2007). "The life of James 'Athenian' Stuart, 1713-1788," in Soros, S. W., *James "Athenian' Stuart...,"* pp. 73, 74.

345 The then new name of the Society for the Promotion of Arts, Manufactures and Commerce.

346 C. Eimer (1998). *The Pingo Family & Medal Making in 18th Century Britain.* London: British Art Medal Trust.

'In James 'Athenian' Stuart's hand'

Two examples, in James 'Athenian' Stuart's hand, of the architectural and decorative design which he so carefully studied in Italy and Greece and brought to England. *Above*, a pen and ink and grey wash drawing of the Temple of Theseus (Temple of Hephaestus) in Stuart and Revett's *The Antiquities of Athens* (1794, vol. iii, Chap. 1, Pl. iii). The annotations at the top are in Stuart's hand:

> *The architectural lines are drawn from a Plate in my [A]thenian work by a friend of yours whose name I do not / recollect / he lives next door to Mr Smith / the engraver"* [in faded ink at top] *'Mr Walker,'* [and on the metopes and on the right] *'Mars & a giant / Perseus slays Medusa / Oedypus & Sphinx / Cadmus & serpent.'*
>
> --British Museum description.

This etching appeared in Stuart and Revett's work presenting classical design based on observations and measurements obtained during their tour of Greece during the early 1750's. This volume, the first accurate work on classical Greek architecture, contributed to the Greek revival in architecture and the decorative arts in Britain. This particular design portrays a couple and two fauns in a Bacchanalian dance (British Museum acc./reg. nos. 1853,1210.503 and 1892,0714.646). Both Images © Trustees of the British Museum.

reputation faltered. He developed severe gout and subsequent joint problems—the disease of the prosperous at that time—as well as an increasingly problematic drinking problem, which, while it negatively affected his work, does not seem to have led to a significant reduction in his financial situation. He did not live to see publication of the second volume of his *Antiquities of Athens*, which he had worked on during this period of illness. It, as well as the two subsequent volumes and a supplement, were completed and published by others after his death in 1788. At his death, he left a moderately large estate which was unfortunately squandered by the executor, Stuart never having gotten around to writing a will.

Three Medallions by John Kirk

A group of three signed portrait tokens or medallions by John Kirk which recently sold at auction. They are, from left: Oliver Cromwell (bronze, 25.5 mm., B.H.M. 171), Queen Charlotte (bronze, B.H.M. 168, 25.5 mm.), and Lord Chatham (silvered bronze, 26 mm., B.H.M. 175). The medal of Cromwell is one of the scarcer of the series, and the silvered example of the Chatham medal is rare. Images courtesy of Spink auctions (no. 12026, lot 838). These three medals are from a series issued by the *Sentimental Magazine* during the period 1773-1774. According to Brown,* examples in "silver were issued to those correspondents who had submitted the best contributions to the previous month's issue." The other personalities to appear in this series, which consisted of thirteen medals, were: King George II, King George III, the Duke and Duchess of Gloucester, William Beckford (mayor of the City of London), David Garrick (the actor and stage manager), the duchess of Cumberland, Lord Camden, John Wilkes, MP, and the marquis of Granby. ***See below, pp. 232-233, for further details on this series.***

***Brown, L. (1980). *British Historical Medals*, 1760-1960. London: Seaby, vol. i, p. 39.**

John Kirk

(1724?-1776/8??)

· Medallist ·

WORKING during the latter part of the 18th century, John Kirk had been a student of another medallist, Jacques-Antoine Dassier (the son of Jean Dassier, *q.v. pp. 214-218*), likely around 1740. Although many of the medals attributed to him were concerned with contemporary events (fl. 1745-1778) and commemorative in nature, such as those memorializing the 'Repulse of the Rebels by the Duke of Cumberland' (1745) and the 'Battle of Culloden' (1776), he also reproduced a number of 17th century medals—including those of Elizabeth Claypole (M.I.I 430/75) and Oliver Cromwell (M.I.I 435/86). He signed his work KIRK or I. KIRK.

A UNIFACE CAST SILVER MEDAL OF ELIZABETH CLEYPOLE (NÉE CROMWELL; CA. MID-18TH C.), BELIEVED TO BE BY JOHN KIRK AND POSSIBLY CHASED BY '— STUART' (45 X 41 MM., M.I.I 431/76, PLATT II/40/D1). IMAGE © TRUSTEES OF THE BRITISH MUSEUM (ACC./ REG. NO. M.7391).

Few details of Kirk's life can be confirmed, but his residence and/or place of business in the early 1760s appears to have been St. Paul's Churchyard. There is, however, uncertainty over the date of his death as more than one John Kirk may have lived and/or worked in St. Paul's churchyard. A John Kirk of St. Paul's Church Yard died in either November or December 1776. A John Kirk, 'engraver', of St. James's died in 1778, but there is also a report in the *Gentleman's Magazine* of March 31, 1791, of the demise of "Mr Kirk, seal-engraver, in St Paul's Churchyard." Handley, in the entry for John Kirk in the *Oxford D.N.B*, appears to doubt that either of the John Kirks (who died respectively in 1776 and 1791) was the medallist, but that he was the previously mentioned John Kirk of St James's who died in 1778. This may be the John Kirk who made his will on November 13, 1778, it having been proved by his wife Catherine on December 5, 1778. Also, previously, the *Gentleman's Magazine* of November 19, 1761, had reported the death of a "Mr. Kirk, senior of the same address," which Handley suggests may have been John Kirk's father or brother. This Kirk's will was proved on the same date. Finally, "A John Kirk, engraver, [likely John Kirk, senior], was a member of the Freemason Lodge at 'Fountain' in the Strand in 1725 & after at the 'One Tun,' 1 Noble Street in 1731."[347]

As Hadley notes that as a medallist John Kirk had achieved a degree of professional success, having received premiums from the Society of Arts (1762/63) and had at least twice, in 1773 and 1775/76, "exhibited medals of the royal family and others." This would be consistent with an upwardly mobile move from St. Paul's Church-yard to St. James's.

347 S. Handley, 'John Kirk,' *Oxford DNB (online)*; British Museum, 'biographical details for John Kirk;' L. Forrer, *Biographical Dictionary*...,1907, vol. 3, pp. 162-165. Handley notes that in 1745-1746 several medals were struck by 'John Kirk and A. Kirk' but does not comment further.

Two brass 'advertising tickets' or trade tokens (ca. 1750) for I. Kirk's shop in St. Paul's Church Yard, 'where may be had a Variety of Dutch and English toys.' (*Top*) brass, 30 mm., British Museum acc./reg. no. SSB,192.2, Mitchiner 1998, vol. 3, 1738/5095). (*Bottom)* brass, 30 mm., Mitchiner, ibid. 1738/5096. It is not clear if this I. Kirk is one of the two Kirks—John and James, both of whom maintained businesses in St. Paul's church yard, or yet another Kirk. Images actual size and © Trustees of the British Museum.

John Kirk's trade card, now in the British Museum collection, and illustrated here, sheds some light on his business. The card, from the collection of Sir Ambrose Heal,[348] is mounted on a cardboard sheet on which the details of research on the two Kirks—John and James—who maintained businesses in St. Paul's Church Yard during the 18th c. are noted. The card contains handwritten notes of Heal's research. Note also the existence in St. Paul's church Yard of I. [*for* J.] Kirk's shop selling Dutch and English toys—These most likely were for one or the other of the John Kirks of St. Paul's Churchyard (*See text box, following page*).

[348] Sir Ambrose Heal (1872-1959), the chairman of Heal's furnishings store in Tottenham Court Road, was a wealthy collector and "authority on London shops and trades on which he published many articles and books." He bequeathed to the British Museum his own collection of some 9,000 trade-cards as well as a separate group of trade cards, primarily from the Banks, Franks, Fielden and other collections (British Museum Merlin database, acc./reg. no: Heal,59.95).

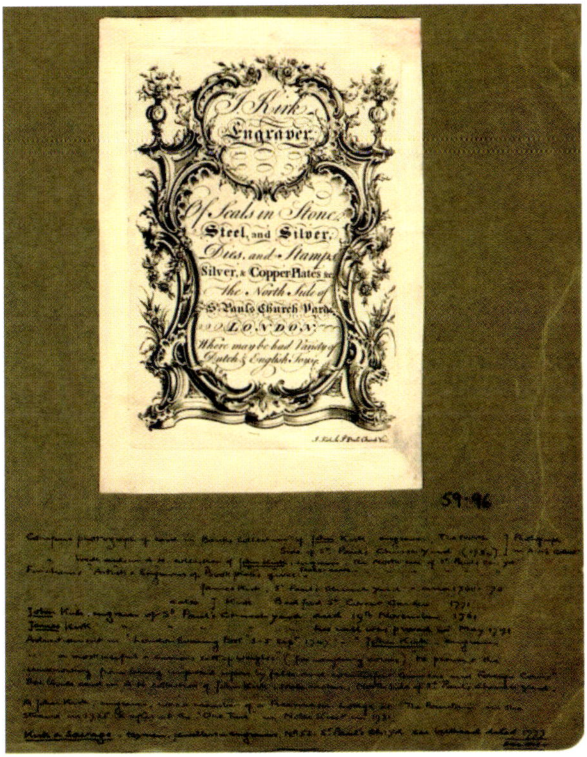

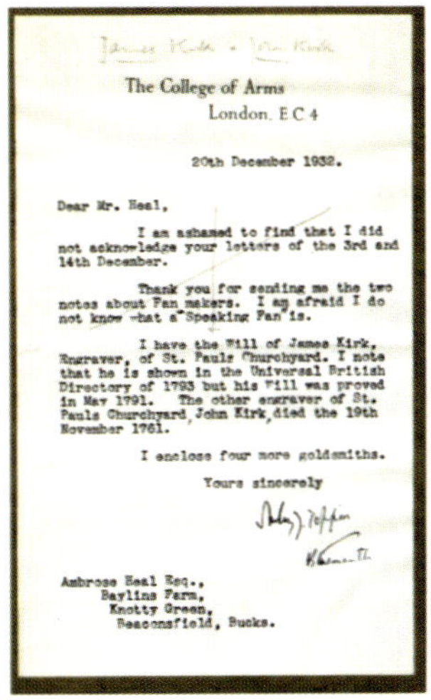

James Kirk & John Kirk

The College of Arms
London, E C 4

20th December 1932.

Dear Mr. Heal,

I am ashamed to find that I did not acknowledge your letters of the 3rd and 14th December.

Thank you for sending me the two notes about Fan makers. I am afraid I do not know what a "Speaking Fan" is.

I have the Will of James Kirk, Engraver, of St. Pauls Churchyard. I note that he is shown in the Universal British Directory of 1793 but his Will was proved in May 1791. The other engraver of St. Pauls Churchyard, John Kirk, died the 19th November 1761.

I enclose four more goldsmiths.

Yours sincerely

Ambrose Heal Esq.,
Baylins Farm,
Knotty Green,
Beaconsfield, Bucks.

John Kirk's trade card, from Sir Ambrose Heal's collection, together with biographical notes and a letter to Heal from the College of Arms regarding the two Kirks, John and James, both engravers of St. Paul's Churchyard. Images © Trustees of the British Museum.

Compare photograph of card in Banks Collection of <u>John</u> Kirk, engraver, The North Side of St Paul's Churchyard (1789.) [Photograph in A. H.'s Collect.]
" trade card[s?] in A. H.'s collection of <u>John Kirk</u>, engraver, The North side of St Paul's Ch'yd.
scale-maker " " " "
Fincham's "Artists & Engravers of Bookplates" gives:—
James Kirk, St Paul's Church Yard – circa 1760-'70
& also J. Kirk Bedford's St. Covent Garden 1771
<u>John</u> Kirk, engraver of St Paul's Church Yard died 19th November 1761
<u>James</u> Kirk " " " "his will was proved in May 1791
Advertisement in "London Evening Post" 3-5 Sept. 1747: — = <u>John Kirk</u>, engraver
"...a most useful and curious sett (sic) of weights" (for weighing coins) "to prevent the unknowing from being imposed upon by false and counterfeit Guineas and Foreign Coins."
See trade card in A. H. collection of John Kirk, scale maker, North Side of St Paul's Church Yard.
A John Kirk, engraver, was a member of a Freemason Lodge at "The Fountain" in the Strand in 1725 & after at the "One Tun" in Noble Street in 1731.
<u>Kirk & Salvage</u>, toymen, jewelers & engravers, No. 52, St. Paul's Ch'yd. See [billhead?] <u>dated 1777</u>.

Transcription of Sir Ambrose Heal's notes on the card on which is mounted John Kirk's trade card (*above, left*). Heal (1872-1959) was a furniture designer and manufacturer of the Arts and Crafts movement and a collector of 17th and 18th century historical ephemera, including records of tradesmen, goldsmiths and furniture makers. Heal bequeathed his collection of trade cards to the British Museum.

Kirk's Cromwell & other Medalets

'*Olivar* Cromwell,' laureate. Another example of the bronze medalet struck in 1775-1778? (25.6 mm., M.I.i 435/86; Platt II/10/A1). Image courtesy Woolley & Wallis Auctioneers, 'The Foley sale,' 2014, lot 394.

The following article appeared on p. 69 of the September 1853, issue of Willis's Current Notes: A Series of Articles on Antiquities, Biography…:

Cromwell Medallet.—The piece described by your Correspondent, Current Notes, p. 3, as "a small copper coin; the reverse, Oliver Cromwell, 1658," is one of the Medallets presented by Kearsly the publisher, to the purchasers of the *Sentimental Magazine,* in 1773, and 1774. The Dies were very creditably engraved by James Kirk, who died in Nov. 1776. The Cromwell Medallet was presented with the Magazine for October 1773; but the practice began in April of that year; the first being a Medallet of King George the Third.

The advertisements announced "with every Number of the *Sentimental Magazine,* will be given a curious medal, struck on fine metal, about the size and weight of a guinea, executed by Mr. Kirk, who is universally esteemed the first artist in London, in his profession. The medal is, of itself, exclusive of the Magazine, superior to many sold for half-a-guinea; it will represent some reigning toast, some great personage, some hero celebrated in the annals of our own kingdom, or in those of the Continent; some patriot, or some uncommon Literary Genius.

"To expatiate on the utility of perpetuating the names and traits of Beauties, Kings, Heroes, and Philosophers, would appear absurd; but we must insist on it, so far as it is a proof of our originality; nor let it be suspected that the cheapness of the purchase, shall result from the want of delicacy in the execution, as the celebrated Mr. Kirk is well known in this walk of science; his name is sufficient to gain us the patronage of every one who has taste and judgment.

"The medal to be given with each number, will be sealed up in a kind of silky paper, provided for that purpose, to prevent any injury to the fine impression of the Die; and it will be so affixed to the Magazine, as to render it portable without any inconvenience.

"Those correspondents who furnish us with the best poem, or the best article in prose, in the course of every month, shall be entitled to a silver prize medal, with their names or signatures engraved there on."

"Persons who are desirous of having any of the medals given in the course of the work, struck on gold or silver, may, by applying to the publisher, be supplied with them, on reasonable terms."

The scheme appears to have become highly popular, as on April 13th another advertisement stated: "The very extraordinary demand for the *Sentimental Magazine,* with which a curious medal of his Majesty is given, engraved by Kirk, has occasioned its being out of print these two days; a new edition was published at noon, price only sixpence, when those persons who have been disappointed, may be supplied by G. Kearsly, removed from Ludgate-hill, to No. 46, opposite Fetter-lane, in Fleetstreet, and by all other Booksellers and Pamphlet shops in London and Westminster."

(Continued on following page)

Kirk's Cromwell & other Medalets (Con't)

Two additional bronze medalets from the series issued by *The Sentimental Magazine* in 1773-1774—of David Garrick, the actor (25 mm., Brown, *British Historical Medals,* M.I.i 40/173, British Museum acc./reg. no. M.4790) and the Duke of Gloucester (25 mm., B.M. acc./reg. no. 2010,4008.3). Images © Trustees of the British Museum.

(Continued from previous page)

"N.B. Several curious impressions struck on silver and gold may be had tomorrow, the 14th." In January 1774, the proprietors announced—

"It may appear extraordinary to some, that a medal worth half a crown, can be afforded in a magazine sold only for sixpence; the public therefore are desired to observe, that all valuable medals are cut merely for the curious, and have hitherto been purchased only by Connoisseurs; consequently the demand for them is inconsiderable. To have a die well executed is very expensive; it will cost as much for two hundred, as for twenty thousand; and were it not for an extensive sale of the Magazine, we could not sell a medal for less than half-a-crown; but as we flatter ourselves we shall merit the encouragement of the public, we are sensible, we can afford a medal worth half-a-crown for sixpence."

The sale was very great, and there are medallets for every month; that of the Duchess of Gloucester, finished the series in April 1774.

—A Collector.

"COINS AND MEDALS WERE HIS AMUSEMENT..."

From: *The Life of John Sharp, D.D. ...**

AMIDST the variety of business that he went through, and frequent avocations from home while he lived upon his cure, he took no kind of diversion, unless the study of coins and medals may be called so...Coins and medals were his amusement and delight for several years after he was Archbishop. When he so improved and enlarged his collection, that at length it was inferior to few in England, especially in regard of the Saxon and English coins... He likewise wrote and left a large MS. For of these he was fond, and begun a collection very early, which, in progress of time, came to be large and curious.

Sharp, T. (1825). *The Life of John Sharp, D.D...*, vol. i, pp. 47-48. Image © Trustees of the British Museum.

*(1664/65-1714)

Some Eminent Collectors and Collections of 17th c. British Medals

EMINENT COLLECTORS AND COLLECTIONS

Today's collectors of both early and modern medals have a natural interest in the collectors who preceded them, particularly those that have previously owned 'their' medals. Thus, in the present authors' opinion, it would be remiss to discuss the medals of the 17th century without also noting several early personages who built great collections of these 'pieces of history.' The collecting of 'medals' (a term which at least through the early 19th century encompassed both coins and medals) may have existed from antiquity—certainly it is traceable to the middle ages. Prince Henry, the eldest son of James I, appears to have been the first English royal collector that can be identified, with Charles I succeeding to the ownership of his collection as well as the throne after Henry's death. We may deduce from the publications of Evelyn, Vertue, and Pinkerton that the collecting of medals or 'memorials' of the principal figures associated with the English Civil War likely began soon after the end of the period of hostilities. It has continued unabated since then, with such items becoming ever more sought after. In the 18th century, collecting in all its forms became a frequent pursuit for gentlemen and, although less so, for ladies as well. Possession of a 'cabinet of medals' provided both personal diversion as well as a basis for social conversation. The accoutrements of numismatic collecting—cabinets, magnifying lenses and published reference works are visible in a number of contemporary prints (see, e.g., this volume, pp. ii, 2, 239, 259.).

By the early 1770s, Thomas Snelling was conducting public auctions of both coins and medals, a practice also engaged in by both Leigh & Sotheby's (and its predecessor firm—Baker & Leigh—which had opened in 1744) and Christie's, founded in 1766 by James Christie. By 1800, entire sales were devoted to numismatic material, as for example, evidenced by the catalogue for the dispersal of Samuel Tyssen's collection in 1802 at Leigh, Sotheby, & Son. Today, a medal (or coin) which possesses the 'pedigree' of having resided in Samuel Tyssen's or another of the great early collections usually commands a premium at auction.

Significant portions of these collections have also found their way into modern museum collections. These include the royal collection originally formed by Prince Henry which was presented to the nation by George IV in 1823 and which since 1825 has resided at the British Museum. Unfortunately, this collection had been decimated by fire and mysterious disappearance, the latter most likely the result of pilfering during and following the Civil War period. Edward Hawkins sold his extensive personal collection of over 4,300 pieces to the British Museum in 1860 following his retirement as keeper of antiquities. Dr. William Hunter's cabinet became the core of the Hunterian Museum's collection of coins and medals. The Tangye collection now resides at the Museum of London. Sir Joseph Banks' modest collection, as well as that of his sister, Ms. Sarah Sophia Banks, went to the British Museum. Surgeon-major J. W. Fleming's collection was donated by him to the Victoria and Albert Museum, while a number of very rare pieces in Ms. Helen Farquhar's collection were given to the British Museum.[349]

Finally, the collectors and sales described here, which the authors believe are representative of the 'higher end' of medal collecting of their times, do not provide a complete compendium of sales or collections. Other sales include, for example, the George Hamilton Smith (Glendining's, November 1927) and James O'Byrne (Christie, Manson & Woods, May 1962). Additionally, many more modest collections have been formed and dispersed over the years.

[349] The greater part of Ms. Farquhar's collection was sold at Glendining's in 1955, some nineteen years after her death in 1936.

The Royal Collections

of Prince Henry & King Charles I[350]

In 1874, Henry Henfrey published the following article in the Numismatic Chronicle. *After some consideration, the authors of the present volume have decided not to abstract it, but rather to reprint it in its entirety, given the wealth of information it provides concerning the 'Royal Collection.' With much taken directly from the original sources, and the further research conducted by Henfrey which appears in the 'Postscript,' it provides a useful introduction to this collection. It appears that while most of this collection was composed of coins, it also obviously contained at least a modest number of what we now consider as proper 'medals.'*

KING CHARLES THE FIRST'S COLLECTION OF COINS & MEDALS[351]

WHILE looking through a volume of original letters and warrants at the British Museum, I happened by chance to notice the following curious warrant of Charles I., and as it does not seem to have ever been printed, or noticed by any numismatic writer, I considered that a copy, together with the partial explanation that I can render of it, would not be unacceptable to this society.

Whereas wee have remayning in our Library at St. James divers Medalls and ancient Coines, Greeke, Romane, and others. Wee doe hereby authorize, constitute, and appoint, our trusty and welbeloved Sir Simonds D'Ewes of Stowhall in the County of Suffolck [sic] Knight & Baronet, and Patricke Young Gentl. keeper of our Libraries, to sort and put ye said Coines and Medalls into their Series and order, and to lay aside to bee disposed by us all duplicates among them wch are genuine and true, and to separate, and divide the novitious, adulterate & spurious peeces from ye said genuine. All which said peeces so separated and divided, are to remaine in our said Library at St. James, in the custody of the said Patricke Young, untill our further pleasure bee knowne. And that ye said Sir Simonds D'Ewes have free liberty from time to time to take into his owne custodie and keeping, such and soe many of them as hee shall have occasion to make use of, hee giving under his hand a note for the true & faithfull restoring of the number received. Given under our Royall hand at Newport in the Isle of Wight this 19th day of October, in the foure and twentieth yeare of our Raigne. [1648].—(Additional MSS., No. 6,988, fo. 216.).

CHARLES K.

CHARLES' OLDER BROTHER, PRINCE HENRY. AS MIGHT BE EXPECTED OF A ROYAL COLLECTION, IN THIS CASE, HENRY'S, IT WAS SUBSTANTIAL IN SIZE, REPORTEDLY, DEPENDING ON THE SOURCE, CONTAINING AS MANY AS 12,000 OR MORE ITEMS. IMAGE © TRUSTEES OF THE BRITISH MUSEUM.

Sir Simonds d'Ewes, Knight and Baronet, was an eminent historian and antiquary, who lived 1602–1650. He was a burgess for Sudbury in the celebrated Long Parliament; but his sympathies inclining to the Court, he was one of the members "purged" on the 6th December, 1648. He then retired to his antiquarian studies and pursuits, and we are told that

[350] Given the dates associated with it, the collection owned by PRINCE HENRY and CHARLES I obviously did not include items related to the Civil War. Yet, both were collectors of coins and medals, although a relatively small number of these found their way into the British Museum's holdings through KING GEORGE III's collection, which was acquired in 1824.

[351] From the *Numismatic Chronicle*, 1874, vol. 14, pp. 100-104.

he formed a noble collection of Roman coins. Patrick Young, a Scotchman by birth (born 1584, died 1652), was appointed the first librarian of the English Royal Library after its complete settlement. He was also a prebendary and treasurer of St. Paul's Cathedral.

Having premised these facts, which will be found in the "Biographia Britannica," I will now give, from the same source, a short account of the proceedings taken by the Commonwealth with regard to the Royal Library at St. James's. It was first seized by the Parliament in August, 1648, and committed to the trust of Hugh Peters, who preserved the library and coins for three or four months, when he delivered up the keys and custody of them to Major-General Ireton: The well-known and enlightened Sir Bulstrode Whitelocke, fearing that these national treasures might be sold to foreigners, and so lost to the country, and at the instance of the learned John Seiden, undertook the care of them in July, 1649. He appointed, in the same year, John Dury, a German, to be his deputy librarian, and instructed him "to go for an inventory of the books and medals to Mr. Young." Mr. Dury continued in charge of the Royal Library and Medals probably until the Restoration, and from an account taken by him, on the 27th April, 1652, we learn that 12,000 coins were then in the library. *

Returning to the warrant, one is led to inquire why such orders should be given by the King to Sir Symonds d'Ewes and Patrick Young on the 19th October, 1648, when the coins were actually under the control of the Parliament, and in the custody of their agent, Hugh Peters? Charles I. was then at Newport, released on parole from his prison at Carisbrook Castle, in the Isle of Wight. During the negotiations which took place from the 18th September to the 27th November between the King and the Parliamentary Commissioners, and which resulted in the Treaty of Newport, Charles was allowed to occupy the house of a private citizen in that town. From this house the warrant in question must have been dated, on the 19th October, and it is not improbable that the King then expected to be very shortly reconciled with the Parliament, and again installed in his former power and possessions. In fact, until the famous " Pride's Purge," the Parliament was very well disposed towards a reconciliation with him, and by a vote of the 5th December, 1648, accepted the King's concessions as a ground for proceeding to the settlement of the peace of the kingdom. But after Colonel Pride's exclusion of the forty-one members on the following day, all such hope was at an end. Charles had been seized by the army, and removed from Newport on the 29th November, and on the 30th January, 1649, he was executed, within three months and a half from the date of his signing this "Warrant.

HENRY "W. HENFREY.

POSTSCRIPT

Since writing the above I have, at the request of the Editor, collected all the notices that I can find relative to Charles I.'s collection of coins and medals.

Lilly says that Charles "was well skilled in things of antiquity," and "could judge of medals whether they had the number of years they pretended unto." He acquired, on his brother's death, the cabinet which was founded by Prince Henry.

John Pinkerton, in the third edition (1808) of his "Essay on Medals," remarks, that " Henry Prince of Wales bought the collection of Gorlæus, amounting, as Joseph Scaliger says, to 30,000 coins and medals, and left it to his brother, Charles I." —(p. 10, vol. i.)

It is believed that Charles I. added considerably to this collection, and Horace Walpole, in his "Anecdotes of Painting", states that, upon his accession, he appointed Abraham Vanderdort a Dutchman, keeper of his cabinet of pictures, medals, &c., at a salary of £40 a year.

There are several copies extant in manuscript of the catalogue which Vanderdort drew up at the King's command, entitled "An inventory of pictures, medals, agates, and other rarities in the privy-garden at Whitehall." The original inventory is said to be in the Ashmolean Museum at Oxford, but a copy of it, in Vanderdort's handwriting, may be seen in the British Museum, Harleian MSS., No. 4718. A rough list of the King's medals is given on fos. 23-28. A fair copy of this catalogue was lately bought by her Majesty the Queen for the library at Windsor, from the sale of Sir William Tite's collection.

"Soon after this, about August, 1660, he was appointed by the King to make a Description of his Medals, and had them delivered into his Hands, and King Henry the VIIIth's Closet assigned for that purpose."

The subsequent history of Charles I.'s cabinet until the Restoration has been noticed in the preceding article; but upon the return of Charles II., he ordered Elias Ashmole to draw up an account of the

ABRAHAM GORLÆUS (1549-1609)*

...AN EMINENT ANTIQUARIAN WAS BORN AT ANTWERP, AND GAINED A REPUTATION BY HIS CARE IN COLLECTING A GREAT NUMBER OF MEDALS AND OTHER ANTIQUES... IN 1608, HE PUBLISHED A COLLECTION OF MEDALS: WHICH, HOWEVER, IF WE MAY BELIEVE THE SCALIGERANA,** IT IS NOT SAFE ALWAYS TO TRUST. WE MEET THERE WITH THE FOLLOWING WORDS: "GORLÆUS CASTS MEDALS; HE SHEWED ME SOME, BUT I FOUND THEY WERE NOT ANCIENT; SINCE THAT TIME HE SHEWED ME NONE BUT GENUINE ONES: HE IS A GOOD MAN"...HIS COLLECTIONS OF ANTIQUES WERE SOLD BY HIS HEIRS TO THE PRINCE OF WALES.

—*A NEW AND GENERAL BIOGRAPHICAL DICTIONARY*; **1761, VOL. V, P. 492.**

*SEE TEXT, PREVIOUS PAGE. IMAGE © TRUSTEES OF THE BRITISH MUSEUM.

**LITERALLY 'SCALINGER'S TABLE TALK,' THE SOURCE BEING JULIUS CAESAR SCALIGER (*ALSO* GIULIO CESARE DELLA SCALA; 1484–1558), AN ITALIAN PHYSICIAN AND PHILOSOPHER OF SCIENCE.

royal cabinet, as we learn from the following passage in the Memoirs prefixed to Ashmole's "Antiquities of Berkshire," 8vo., 1719, vol. i. p. x.:—

John Evelyn, in his "Numismata," supplies the next notice:

"I conclude this Recension where indeed I ought to have begun, when I mention'd the Great and most ulustrious [sic] Persons of *England* (emulating the most celebrated Cabinets of the Greatest *Princes* of other *Countries),* namely, that *Royal Collection* of *Medals* at St. *James's,* begun by that Magnanimous and Hopeful Prince *Henry,* and exceedingly augmented and improved by his Brother King *Charles* the *Martyr,* from the Testimony of his own Learned Library keeper *Patrick Junius* (in his *Notes* on St. *Clement's* Epistle to the *Corinthians), Quem locum* (speaking of St. *James's) si vicinam Pinacothecam, Bibliothecæ celeberrima conjunctam; Si* NUMISMATA *Antiqua Græca, ac Romana; Si statuas & Signa ex ære & Marmore consideres; non immérito Thesaurum Antiquitatis &* Ταμιεῖον *Instructissimum nominare potes, &c.* To which add, that of another Learned *Medalist Carolas Primus ille Magnæ Britanniæ Rex, cæteris Europa: Principes omnes hoc possessionum Genere, vincebat;* which how at this Day impair'd, and miserably imbezel'd, not only by the *Rebels* during the late *Civil Wars,* but even since, thro' the Negligence of others, is of deplorable Consideration; if any hopes yet remain of its revival again to some tolerable degree of Lustre and Repair, we must be oblig'd to the indefatigable Industry of the late Supervisor, the obliging and universally Learned (whilst he lived, my excellent Friend) and lately deceas'd... Monsieur *Justel;* and from hence forward to the no less accomplish'd (in all solid Learning and severer Studies) Dr. *Bentley,* his worthy successor.

"This for the *Books* and Manuscripts, among which there are still many Choice and Inestimable Volumes, besides the Famous and Venerable *Alexandrian Greek Bible* of St. *Tecla;* but the *Medals* have been taken away and purloin'd by *Thousands,* and irrecoverable. Their late Majesties (Charles II. and James II.) had yet a very rich and ample *Collection,* which I well remember were put in Order, and Methodiz'd by Mr. *Ashmole,* soon after the Restauration of King *Charles* the Second, which I hope, and presume may be still in being and to be recovered" (Pp. 246, 7, of J. Evelyn's "Numismata," fol., London, 1697).

However, very soon after the publication of Evelyn's book, the royal collection was irrecoverably lost in the great fire which consumed all that remained of the palace of Whitehall (except the Banqueting House) on Tuesday, 4th January, 1697-8.

The reader may thus trace the history of the ill-fated royal collection from its foundation by Prince Henry, its augmentation by Charles I., and its partial dispersion during the Commonwealth, to its final destruction in 1698.

30th June, 1874. HENRY W. HENFREY.

The Royal Collections: Commentary

[Charles I's] Love and Protection of the Arts...He was well skilled in things of antiquity, could judge of medals whether they had the number of years they pretended unto; his libraries and cabinets were full of those things on which length of time put the value of rarities. In painting he had so excellent a fancy, that he would supply the defect of art in the workman, and suddenly draw those lines, give those airs and lights, which experience and practice had not taught the painter...After the restoration endeavours were used to reassemble the spoils—A commission was issued out to examine Hugh Peters concerning the disposal of the pictures, jewels,' etc., that had belonged to the royal family—but without effect, by the obstinacy or ignorance of Peters, who would not or could not give the desired satisfaction...it is plain from the catalogue of the collection of James II. that the crown still possessed a great number of valuable pictures; but the fire of Whitehall destroyed almost all that the rage of civil war had spared...The royal library escaped better; this was founded by James I. It contained the collection belonging to the crown, among which were several fine editions on vellum, sent as presents from abroad, on the restoration of learning, to Hen. VII., Hen. VIII., and Queen Elizabeth; the library of the Lord Lumley, purchased by James for Prince Henry; the collection of Casaubon, bought of his widow, and some curious MSS. brought from Constantinople by Sir Thomas Roe. These books have been given to the British Museum by his late majesty. To this library Prince Henry had added a large number of coins, medals, cameos, and intaglias, the Dactyliotheca of Gorlaeus. Mr. Young, librarian to Charles I. was removed by the council of state in 1649, at which time an account of the books and coins was taken; of the latter there were 1200, of which 400 only remained at the restoration. Among the Duke of Ormond's letters is one dated April 2, 1649, where he says, 'All the rarities in the king's library at St. James's are 'vanished.' Yet it is evident many remained; for in June 1659 a vote passed that the Lord Whitlocke be desired and authorised to take 'upon him the care and custody of the library at James House, and of all the books, manuscripts and medals, that are in or belonging to the said library, that the same be safely kept and preserved, and to recover all such as have been embezzled or taken out of the same.' Charles II. after his return ordered Ashmole to draw up an account of the medals that were left, and placed them in the closet of Henry VIII. at Whitehall, where they were lost at the fire.

—H. Walpole, *Anecdotes of Painting in England*, 1879 ed., pp. 137, 155-156.

§

HENRY PRINCE OF WALES, SON OF JAMES I., A COIN COLLECTOR.— Extract from the "Accounts of the Revels at Court in the Reigns of Queen Elizabeth and James I.," edited by Mr. Peter Cunningham, and published by the Shakespeare Society.

In the "Accompte of the Money expended by Sir David Murray, K[t]., as Keeper of the Privie Purse to the late noble Prynce Henry Prynce of Wales, from the 1 October 1610 to 6 November 1612, (the daye of the decease of the said Prynce) &c[a.], &c[a.], the following entry occurs: —

Antiquities of Medall and Coynes .... £2200.

No further mention is made in these "Accounts," nor was any record found in the Audit Office, as to the nature of this collection, or whence obtained. Nor in any English work to which we have had access, could we find anything to satisfy our curiosity; until chancing to look into "Chalmers' Biographical Dictionary," in the notice of Abraham Gorlaeus, it is said that he "gained a great reputation by collecting Medals and Antiquities, and that after his death at Delph in April 1609, his collections were sold to the Prince of Wales."

This is all the information we have been able to glean relative to this interesting transaction. It shews the tastes and inclinations of this young Prince, who was willing to devote so large a sum (large for those days) in furtherance of Numismatic pursuits; and the presumption is that the collection must have been valuable and extensive.

After the death of Prince Henry the collection became the property of his brother Prince Charles, subsequently King Charles I., celebrated for his love of modern as well as ancient art; and it remained carefully preserved until that unfortunate sovereign fell under the power of the Parliament, when the "Rulers of Fanaticism" as D'Israeli calls them, caused the whole of the King's furniture, pictures, and collections of every kind, to be appraised, preparatory to sale, and the library, and medals, and coins only escaped the dispersion that befell the pictures through the antiquarian zeal of Selden, who apprehensive of their loss, induced his friend Bulstrode Whitelocke, then Lord Keeper of the Commonwealth, to apply for the office of Librarian. "This contrivance," adds D'Israeli, "saved the valuable collection." Whitelocke continued in this office until 1660; but at the Restoration nearly two-thirds of the medals were missing, said to have been abstracted by Hugh Peters the Puritan, and others, between 1649 and 1652, before they came under the guardianship of Whitelocke. Ultimately, the library, and remaining medals and coins, were deposited in the British Museum, soon after the foundation of that institution.

— B. N., *Numismatic Chronicle*, 1849, pp. 187-188.

§

The first distinct intimation, however, of a cabinet of medallic character, that is to say, of medals and coins selected on account of their illustrative and artistic value, is associated with a relatively modern epoch and with an English prince. Books, manuscripts, painting, statuary, ceramics, bronzes, even gems, had found admirers long before Prince Henry, eldest son of James I., directed his attention to numismatics in conjunction with his pursuits as a book-lover. At his death in 1612 his medals and coins were valued at something like £3000; it must have been a large and important body of examples, if we take into account the difference in the monetary standard. The most remarkable point seems to be, that the taste developed itself thus strongly and abruptly in the Stuarts, a Scottish house influenced by French culture, if not by Spanish magnificence and fondness for display.

—H. Carew, *The Coin Collector*, 1896, pp. 21.

§

FOR thus has a cabinet of ten thousand medals, not inferior to most abroad, & far superior to any at home, which were collected by that hopefull cherisher of greate and noble things Prince Henry, been imbezil'd and carried away during our late barbarous rebellion, by whom & whither none can or is like to discouer. What that collection was, not onely of bookes and medals, but of statues & other elegant furniture...

—W. Bray (1906). *Diary and Correspondence of John Evelyn*, vol. iii, p. 449.

§

Charles I himself collected coins and medals, and had a collection which was kept in the cabinet room at Whitehall. The collection consisted of both antique and modern specimens. His interest in the Royal image as represented on numismatic items only increased upon his accession to the throne, as he appears to have realized the importance of representation of the Royal image as good 'public relations.' The collection had been begun by his older brother, Prince Henry, and was continued by Charles. The curator was Abraham Van der Doort, who compiled a catalogue in the late 1630s. Under Charles I, the collection not only consisted of items inherited from his brother, but also specimens, and additionally books on the subject which appear to have been purchased during Charles' reign.

—J. Peacock (1999). 'The visual image of Charles I,' in C. Corns (ed.), *The Royal Image*.....p. 180.

§§§§

Samuel Pepys' Visit to the London Mint

May 19,1663

UP pretty betimes, but yet I observe how my dancing and lying a morning or two longer than ordinary for my cold do make me hard to rise as I used to do, or look after my business as I am wont... [and] to the Tower; and by Mr. Slingsby, and Mr. Howard, Controller of the Mint, we were shown the method of making this new money, from the beginning to the end, which is so pretty that I did take a note of every part of it and set them down by themselves for my remembrance hereafter. That being done it was dinner time, and so the Controller would have us dine with him and his company, the King giving them a dinner every day. And very merry and good discourse about the business we have been upon, and after dinner went to the Assay Office and there saw the manner of assaying of gold and silver, and how silver melted down with gold do part, just being put into aquafortis, the silver turning into water, and the gold lying whole in the very form it was put in, mixed of gold and silver, which is a miracle; and to see no silver at all but turned into water, which they can bring again into itself out of the water. And here I was made thoroughly to understand the business of the fineness and coarseness of metals, and have put down my lessons with my other observations therein. At table among other discourse they told us of two cheats, the best I ever heard. One, of a labourer discovered to convey away the bits of silver cut out pence by swallowing them down into his belly, and so they could not find him out, though, of course, they searched all the labourers; but, having reason to doubt him, they did, by threats and promises, get him to confess, and did find 7*l.* of it in his house at one time. The other of one that got a way of coyning money as good and passable and large as the true money is, and yet saved fifty per cent. to himself, which was by getting moulds made to stamp groats like old groats, which is done so well, and I did beg two of them which I keep for rarities, that there is not better in the world, and is as good, nay, better than those that commonly go, which was the only thing that they could find out to doubt them by, besides the number that the party do go to put off, and then coming to the Comptroller of the Mint, he could not, I say, find out any other thing to raise any doubt upon, but only their being so truly round or near it, though I should never have doubted the thing neither. He was neither hanged nor burned, the cheat was thought so ingenious, and being the first time they could ever trap him in it, and so little hurt to any man in it, the money being as good as commonly goes.

—S. Pepys, *Diary*, May 19, 1663, 1942 ed., vol. iv, pp. 126-128.

NOTE: The portrait of Pepys (ca. 1689/90) is an engraving by Robert White (1645-1704) after the portrait by Sir Godfrey Kneller (1646-1723). It appeared as the frontispiece to Pepys' *Naval Memoirs* (1690).The motto is that of Pepys, taken from Cicero, which translates as: 'The mind's the man.' This portrait also appears on one of Pepy's personal bookplates. Each volume owned by Pepys contained two bookplates—one at each end. Image © Trustees of the British Museum.

Samuel Pepys

(1633-1703)

IN addition to having been an Admiralty official, and now known as a diarist, Samuel Pepys was an avid book collector and also had an interest in medals of which he maintained a small collection. Pepys' interest in medals was likely no different from those of other gentlemen of his day, to whom a cabinet of coins and medals provided an agreeable and to a great extent, an unremarkable pastime. Pepys' *Diary* provides us with several examples of his own and his peers' interest in medals, e.g.:

SAMUEL PEPYS AT AGE 33, AN OIL ON CANVAS PORTRAIT (1666) BY JOHN HAYLS (1600?-1679). THE NPG NOTES THAT 'PEPYS PAID HAYLS £14 FOR THE PICTURE AND 25*s* FOR THE FRAME.' IMAGE © NATIONAL PORTRAIT GALLERY, LONDON.

> I went this morning with Sir W. Pen by coach to Westminster, and having done my business at Mr. Montagu's, I went back to him at Whitehall, and from thence with him to the 3 Tun Tavern, at Charing Cross, and there sent up for the maister's of the house's dinner, and afterwards had him and his fayre sister (who is very great with Sir W. Batten and Sir W. Pen in mirth) up to us, and looked over some medals that they shewed us of theirs; and so went away to the theatre...[352]

The following entry gives us an interesting comment about John Roettier's 1667 medal celebrating the Peace of Breda (M.I.I 535/186, M.I.ILL LIV/4; *see this vol., p. 205, for an illustration of this medal*).

> ...at my goldsmith's did observe the King's new medall, where, in little, there is Mrs. Steward's face as well done as ever I saw anything in my whole life, I think: and a pretty thing it is, that he should choose her face to represent Britannia by.[353]

[352] S. Pepys, (Wheatley, H. B., et al., eds.) (1893). *The Diary of Samuel Pepys...*, November 1, 1661.

[353] Ibid. *Diary...*, February 25, 1667. *Also see pp. 202-204.*

A Letter To S. Pepys from H. Slingsby[354]

A PORTRAIT MEDALLION OF SAMUEL PEPYS, CA. 1700-1705, IN IVORY (13.3 CM.) BY DAVID LE MARCHANT (1674-1726). IMAGE © THE TRUSTEES OF THE BRITISH MUSEUM; ACC./REG. NO. 1884,0105.1.

The following letter accompanies a list of "modern English medals" offered for sale by Mr. Slingesby.

11 October, 1687

Sir—

You being my ancient friend and good acquaintance, I cannot doe lesse than offer to putt into your hands a generall collection of all the medalls made by Roettiers, of which I had an opportunity to chuse the best struck off; and I am sure soe full a collection noe man in England has beside myself, which you shall have at the same rate I paid for. When Roettier happens to die, they may be worth five or ten pounds more, and yett are not to be had, many of the stampes being broke and spoiled. I have sent you the list to peruse, which, if you approve of, I shall much rejoyce at; if not, pray returne the list againe, for I have severall friends will be glad to have them of,

Sr, yours, &c.,
H. Slingesby,

If you desire any of the King and Queen's coronation medalls, I have 6 of them that I can spare at 6s. each.

A List Of Monsieur's Roettier's Medalls, With Cases [sic].

1. The great Brittania, with Felicitas Brittania..., 1 10 0 (£. s. d.)
2. The Duke of Yorke's, with Nec Minor in Terns..., 3 14 0
3. The late King's for the Hospitall, with Institutor Augustus..., 3 2 0
4. The Comte de Monterey, with Belgii et Burgundice Gubernator..., 3 2 0
5. The new Brittannia, with Nullum numen abest..., 2 3 0
6. The Duke of Yorke, with Genus antiquum..., 2 3 0
7. The Duke of Lauderdale, with Concilia et Animis..., 2 0 0

[354] Text of the letter from *The Diary and Correspondence of Samuel Pepys, F.R.S...*, 1854, Vol. 4, 5th ed., pp. 238. The original is in the British Library. This HENRY SLINGESBY, a friend of Pepys, appears to be the son of SIR HENRY SLINGSBY a Royalist who commanded the trained bands of York against SIR JOHN HOTHAM and later served at the capture of Leicester, Naseby and Newark. After the war, having refused to take the oaths and to compound, Sir Henry went into hiding and his estates were sequestered. Arrested by JOHN LILBURNE after his involvement in the planned 'Northern Rising,' OLIVER CROMWELL decided to make an example of him. He was subsequently beheaded in 1658.

8. The King, for the Pyre Ships, with Pro talibus amis..., 1 19 0
9. The King, with Religionis Reformats Proiectori..., 1 17 0
10. Collo" Strangways, with Decusque adversa dederunt..., 1 17 0
11. The Bpp of Canterbury, with Sancti Caroli Precursor..., 1 15 0
12. Another of the same..., 1 15 0
13. The King, for Bruges, with Redeant Commercia Flandris...,1 9 0
14. The First Brittania, with Favente Deo 1 9 0
15. The King, for the Pyre Shipps, with Pro talibus ausis..., 1 8 0
16. The King's New Invention for Fortifications...,1 7 0
17. The King, with his Armes..., 1 4 0
18. The King on one side and the Queen on the other..., 0 18 0
19. The King of Spaine, with Flandria. Ostendae..., 0 18 0
20. The Queen Dowager and S' Katherine, with Pietate insignis..., 0 18 0
21. Another of the same..., 0 18 0
22. The King of Sweeden's Inauguration, 29 May, 1671..., 0 18 0
23. The King and Queen together, with Diffuses in Orbe Britannus..., 0 16 0
24. The little one, the King on one side and the Queen on the other..., 0 10 0
25. Sr Samuel Morland's..., 0 10 0

Total . . . . 43 0 0 (£. s. d.)

Samuel Pepys' Bookstamp and Bookplates

Not surprisingly for a book collector of means at the time he lived, Pepys' owned a large number—some 3,000 volumes. Thus, the inscription *Mens cujusque is est Quisque* ('mind makes the man'[355]) is reflective of Pepys' view of the intellectual life. Describing his library, Fletcher noted:

***"With the exception of a few in morocco or vellum, Pepys's books were bound in calf. Almost all of them bear Pepys's arms on the lower cover; while on the upper is found a shield with [an] inscription…* 'Sam. Pepys Car. et Iac. Angl. Regib. a Secretis Admiraliae' (Samuel Pepys: Private Affairs of the Admiralty for Charles and James, Kings of England). *This shield (L.) is surmounted with his helmet and crest, and is surrounded by mantling, in which are introduced two anchors, indicating his office. He also used three bookplates—one with his arms, quartering Talbot of Cottenham (center); a second with his portrait by Robert White (q.v. p. 242); and a third (R.) bearing his initial, with two anchors crossed, together with his motto* Mens cujusque is est Quisque…."**

— W. Y. Fletcher, *English Book Collectors*, 1902, pp. 118-121).

355 'The mind's the man,' *or* 'Mind makes the man,' the original Latin phrase' from Cicero's *De re publica.*

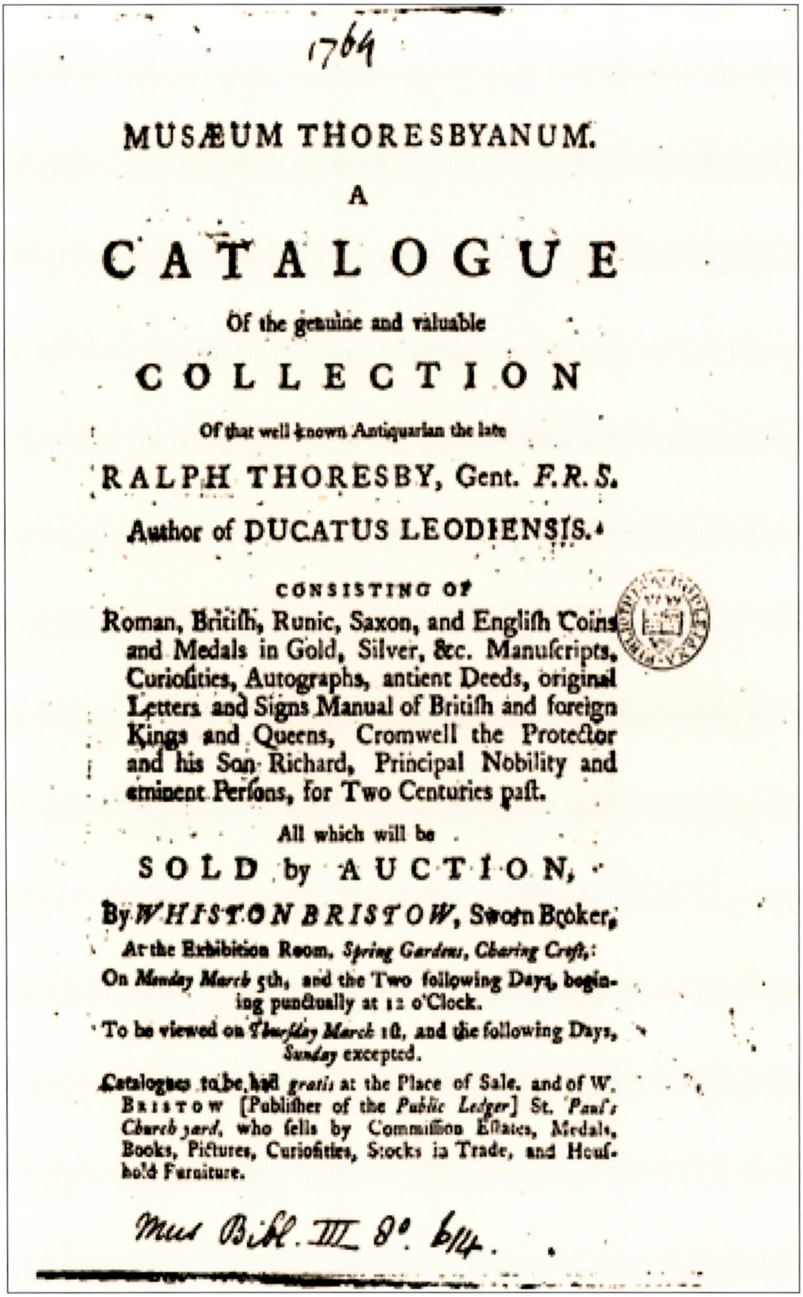

1764

MUSÆUM THORESBYANUM.

A

CATALOGUE

Of the genuine and valuable

COLLECTION

Of that well known Antiquarian the late

RALPH THORESBY, Gent. *F.R.S.*

Author of DUCATUS LEODIENSIS.

CONSISTING OF

Roman, British, Runic, Saxon, and English Coins and Medals in Gold, Silver, &c. Manuscripts, Curiosities, Autographs, antient Deeds, original Letters and Signs Manual of British and foreign Kings and Queens, Cromwell the Protector and his Son Richard, Principal Nobility and eminent Persons, for Two Centuries past.

All which will be

SOLD by AUCTION,

By *WHISTON BRISTOW*, Sworn Broker,

At the Exhibition Room, *Spring Gardens, Charing Cross*;

On *Monday March* 5th, and the Two following Days, beginning punctually at 12 o'Clock.

To be viewed on *Thursday March* 1st, and the following Days, *Sunday* excepted.

Catalogues to be had *gratis* at the Place of Sale, and of W. BRISTOW [Publisher of the *Public Ledger*] St. *Paul's Church yard*, who sells by Commission Estates, Medals, Books, Pictures, Curiosities, Stocks in Trade, and Houshold Furniture.

Mus Bibl. III 8° 6/4.

THE TITLE PAGE OF THE CATALOGUE FOR THE SALE, ON MARCH 5-7, 1764, OF THE REMAINING CONTENTS OF RALPH THORESBY'S 'MUSEUM THORESBYANUM.' THE SALE, BY THE BROKER WHISTON BRISTOW, TOOK PLACE AT SPRING GARDENS, CHARING CROSS. IMAGE DIGITIZED BY GOOGLE.

•Eminent Collectors and Collections•[356]

Ralph Thoresby

(1658-1725)

RALPH THORESBY was an antiquarian and collector whose father John, a devout Presbyterian, had served as an officer under Thomas Fairfax in the Parliamentarian Army. In 1679, Thoresby inherited his father's 'Museum of Oddities,' and also Thomas Fairfax's collection of coins and medals for which his father had paid 30*l*. Together with two friends, Ralph purchased a significant portion of Fairfax's library for 182*l*.[357]

Thoresby is a biographer's delight—the figure who kept a detailed diary of his life.[358] Intended for a life as a merchant, and having inherited his father's wool and cotton business, he was, however, an indifferent businessman, spending a good deal of his time in antiquarian pursuits. With literary and antiquarian interests, he produced a history of Leeds and, as he aged, turned increasingly to his museum, which gained some notoriety. It did not, however, survive after his death in 1725, the last items remaining in it, including books, coins and medals, finally going to auction in March 1764. Some items were acquired by the British Museum. Horace Walpole and Dr. Ducarel also acquired some of Thoresby's manuscripts, Walpole's being later sold at the 1830 Strawberry Hill sale.[359] Today, the Bodleian Library possesses a collection of antiquarian documents relating to Thoresby while the Yorkshire Archeological Society has many of Thoresby's manuscripts and letters.

'Radulphus Thoresby,' the proof of an engraving after the original portrait by George Vertue, dated 1712, and later used as the frontispiece for Thoresby's *Ducatus Leodiensis, or, the Topography of the Ancient and Populous Town and Parish of Leedes...* (1725), to which is appended a catalogue describing his collection and museum. Image © Trustees of the British Museum (acc./reg. no. 1868,0509.619).

---

[356] It should be noted that the 'Eminent Collectors' were not necessarily collectors exclusively of medals but most often collected both coins and medals, as well as other categories of items. Among those who collected only numismatic material, coins were usually the predominant interest.

[357] The £ symbol as we know it today had originally been an *l*., representing *libra*, the unit of weight in the Roman Empire.

[358] Rev. J. Hunter (ed.). *The Diary of Ralph Thoresby, F.R.S.; Author of the Topology of Leeds.* London: Colburn & Bentley, 1830 (2 vols.).

[359] *See entry for Dr. Ducarel, this vol., p. 351.*

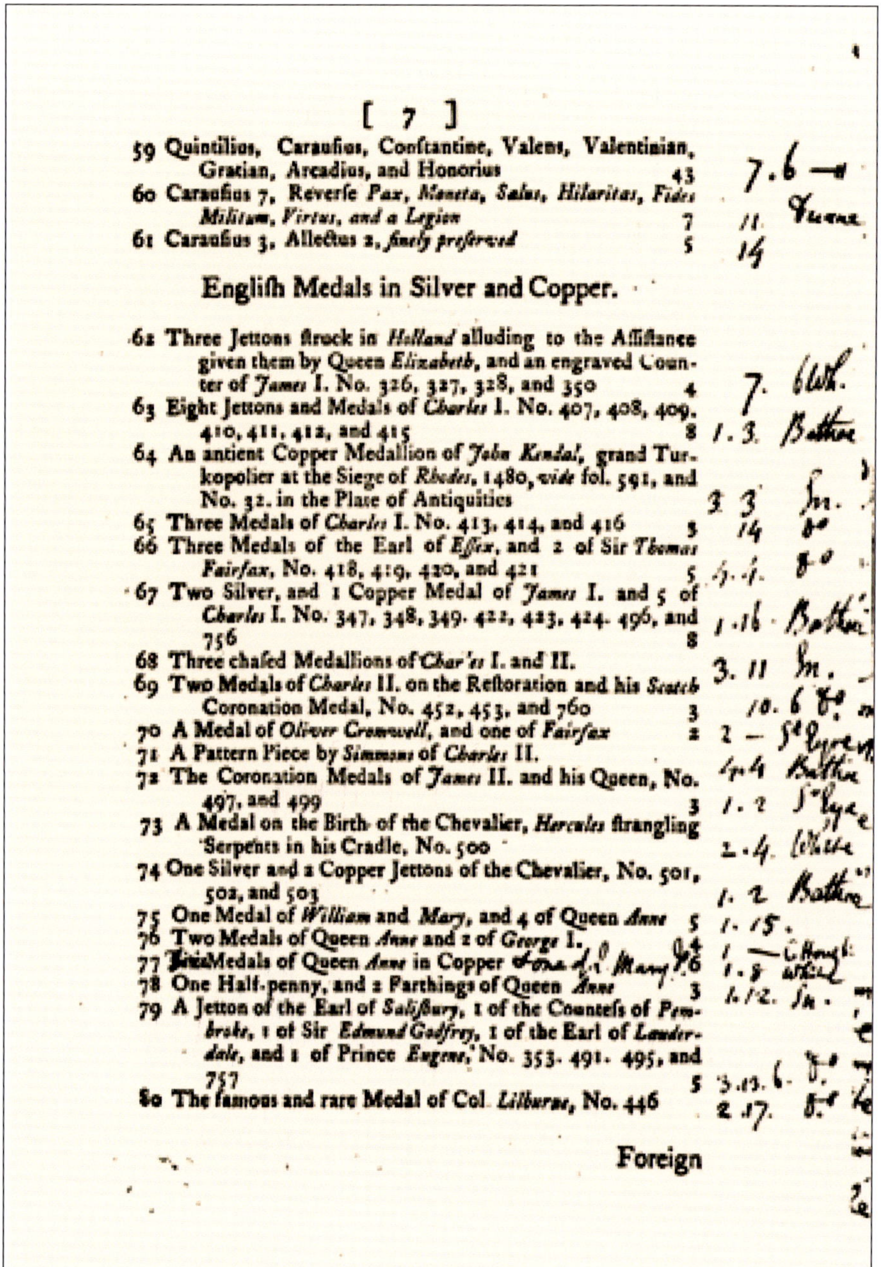

[7]

59 Quintilius, Carausius, Constantine, Valens, Valentinian, Gratian, Arcadius, and Honorius 43

60 Carausius 7, Reverse *Pax*, *Moneta*, *Salus*, *Hilaritas*, *Fides Militum*, *Virtus*, *and a Legion* 7

61 Carausius 3, Allectus 2, *finely preserved* 5

English Medals in Silver and Copper.

62 Three Jettons struck in *Holland* alluding to the Assistance given them by Queen *Elizabeth*, and an engraved Counter of *James* I. No. 326, 327, 328, and 350 4

63 Eight Jettons and Medals of *Charles* I. No. 407, 408, 409, 410, 411, 412, and 415 8

64 An antient Copper Medallion of *John Kendal*, grand Turkopolier at the Siege of *Rhodes*, 1480, *vide* fol. 591, and No. 32. in the Plate of Antiquities

65 Three Medals of *Charles* I. No. 413, 414, and 416 3

66 Three Medals of the Earl of *Essex*, and 2 of Sir *Thomas Fairfax*, No. 418, 419, 420, and 421 5

67 Two Silver, and 1 Copper Medal of *James* I. and 5 of *Charles* I. No. 347, 348, 349. 422, 423, 424. 496, and 756 8

68 Three chased Medallions of *Charles* I. and II.

69 Two Medals of *Charles* II. on the Restoration and his *Scotch* Coronation Medal, No. 452, 453, and 760 3

70 A Medal of *Oliver Cromwell*, and one of *Fairfax* 2

71 A Pattern Piece by *Simmons* of *Charles* II.

72 The Coronation Medals of *James* II. and his Queen, No. 497, and 499 3

73 A Medal on the Birth of the Chevalier, *Hercules* strangling Serpents in his Cradle, No. 500

74 One Silver and a Copper Jettons of the Chevalier, No. 501, 502, and 503

75 One Medal of *William* and *Mary*, and 4 of Queen *Anne* 5

76 Two Medals of Queen *Anne* and 2 of *George* I. 4

77 Medals of Queen *Anne* in Copper 6

78 One Half-penny, and 2 Farthings of Queen *Anne* 3

79 A Jetton of the Earl of *Salisbury*, 1 of the Countess of *Pembroke*, 1 of Sir *Edmund Godfrey*, 1 of the Earl of *Lauderdale*, and 1 of Prince *Eugene*, No. 353. 491. 495, and 757 5

80 The famous and rare Medal of Col. *Lilburne*, No. 446

Foreign

A PAGE FROM THE CATALOGUE FOR THE SALE OF RALPH THORESBY' COLLECTION CONTAINING A SELECTION OF ENGLISH MEDALS. NOTE THE SALES PRICES AND PURCHASERS' NAMES TO THE RIGHT, AS WELL AS 'AN ANCIENT COPPER MEDALLION OF *JOHN KENDAL*.'* DIGITIZED BY GOOGLE.

*THE FIRST KNOWN MEDAL TO BEAR THE PORTRAIT OF AN ENGLISHMAN (*SEE* M.I.i 17/3, PLATT i/xvi).

Commentary on Ralph Thoresby

A Mr. RALPH THORESBY informs us, in the account of, his own "Museum," that Lord Fairfax made a collection of engraved portraits of warriors. He also made a collection of coins and medals, which were purchased by Mr. Thoresby's father... It should be remembered, to his honour, that he allowed a considerable pension to that able and industrious antiquary, Roger Dodsworth,[360] who had the greatest hand in the "*Monasticom.*"

—J. Granger, *Biographical Dictionary,* 1824, vol. iii, p. 64, *fn*

§

[Thoresby is] now most frequently mentioned, as the possessor of a very extensive and curious Museum, in which were deposited rarities both of nature and art; fossils and shells, books, manuscripts, prints, coins, and autographs. A descriptive catalogue is annexed to the Ducatus. We see in this Diary how a private person, in a country town, and with a small fortune, was able to amass a treasure which may excite the envy of the more opulent but less fortunate collector of these times. Thoresby was pre-eminently a collector. He was one of the fathers of that still increasing and flourishing family. Like some of his successors, he had stored up some things as valuable rarities, which better judgment and superior knowledge would have led him to reject. But compare his Catalogue with that of the Tradescants,[361] and how superior was his Museum to theirs! There was in it very little to be despised, and a great deal to be coveted.

—Review of *The Diary of Ralph Thoresby.* In *Gentleman's Magazine,* vol. C, no. 23 (Jan-Jun, 1830), pp. 153-156.

§

Thoresby often complains of the loss of time occasioned by showing his collection of coins and other rarities to strangers, who were often persons unable to appreciate them, or to benefit by the sight of them. The publication of Camden[362] had made him known, and his curious museum talked of, so that scarcely a week passed in which he was not visited by persons for the express purpose of inspecting it. This was a means, however, of increasing his collection, for many returned the favour by making additions to the museum... Who shall presume to say what his coins, medals, prints, manuscripts, books, and autographs would bring on a sale by auction at the present day? Would 5000*l.* be too large a sum?

—Rev. J. Hunter (ed.) (1830). *The Diary of Ralph Thoresby... (1677-1724)*, vol. i, p. 201, fn.

360 ROGER DODSWORTH (1585-1654), was an English antiquary. He is most remembered for his history of Yorkshire, *Monasticon Anglicanum*. Upon Dodsworth's death, the manuscript for this work and others were bequeathed to THOMAS FAIRFAX, 3RD LORD FAIRFAX OF CAMERON, who in turn left them to the Bodleian Library, where they still reside.

361 JOHN TRADESCANT THE ELDER (ca. 1570-1638) and his son, JOHN TRADESCANT THE YOUNGER (1608-1662), established the *Musæum Tradescantianum*, the first public museum in England, ca. 1634. Objects in the collection were classified as natural (*naturalia*) or man-made (*artificialia*). In 1656 ELIAS ASHMOLE published the younger Tradescant's encyclopedic catalogue of its contents as *Musæum Tradescantianum, or a Collection of Rarities Preserved at South-Lambeth neer London*. In 1659, by deed of gift, the collection came into the possession of Ashmole who incorporated it into his 'cabinet of curiosities.' In 1677 Ashmole donated the cabinet to the University of Oxford which in 1679 erected a purpose-built building to house it.

362 WILLIAM CAMDEN'S (1551-1623), *Britannia*, a topographical and historical survey of the British Isles. First published in 1586, in Latin, with the aim of "restor[ing] antiquity to Britaine, and Britaine to its antiquity," the work went through six editions, with a seventh English edition appearing in 1607.

Four Items from Sir Hans Sloane's Collection

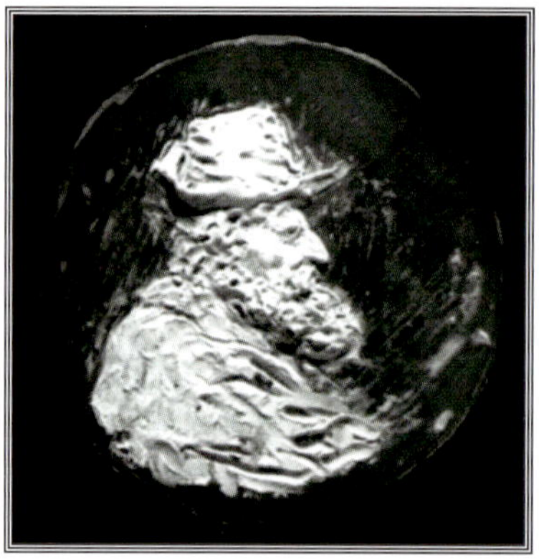

These medals and medallions from Sir Hans Sloane's collection are among those which came to the British Museum by a bequest/purchase in 1753. (*Top*) the uniface medal in lead of Barbara Villiers, Dutchess of Cleveland, by John Roettier(s), ca. 1670 (62 mm., M.I.i 547/2904, British Museum acc./reg. no. M.7590). (*Center*) uniface medallion busts by Abraham Simon, the one on the left a possible self-portrait (65 mm., acc./reg. no. SLPictures.289), and to the *right*, an unknown man (64 mm., acc./reg. no. SLPictures.292). (*Below*) the small Dunbar medal in gold by Thomas Simon (25 x 21 mm., M.I.i 391/13, M.I.Ill xxxv/4, Platt I/325/I_1, Eimer 181B_1). Image sizes not to scale. Images © Trustees of the British Museum.

Sir Hans Sloane

(1660-1753)

MEDAL OF SIR HANS SLOANE, IN BRONZE (1744; 54 MM., M.I.II 558/185, M.I.ILL CLIX/13, EIMER 588), DESIGNED BY JACQUES ANTOINE (JAMES ANTHONY) DASSIER AND THE FIRST IN HIS SERIES OF MEDALS OF ILLUSTRIOUS MEN THEN LIVING IN ENGLAND (CA. 1740). [363] **EX EDWARD HAWKINS COLLECTION. IMAGE © TRUSTEES OF THE BRITISH MUSEUM.**

A physician and naturalist, Hans Sloane collected a variety of items, including antiquities, books, paintings and prints, manuscripts, medals and coins and 'natural curiosities,' particularly botanical specimens and minerals.[364] Sloane was the son of Alexander Sloane, the agent for James Hamilton, 2nd viscount Claneboye. A collector from an early age, he was educated as a physician with a particular interest in the medicinal qualities of plants. Trained on the Continent, he collected botanical specimens, gaining him sufficient attention and election first to the Royal Society and soon after, fellowship in the College of Physicians. Sloane traveled to the West Indies as physician to Christopher Monck, the duke of Albemarle (and son of General George Monck), returning with a large collection of previously unknown tropical plants which he catalogued. He also returned with cocoa, which he mixed with milk to make it palatable, thus inventing 'milk chocolate,' introducing the concoction to England and making a considerable profit in the process.

ILLUSTRATION OF THE ABOVE MEDAL FROM ANTHONY DURAND'S *MEDAILLES ET JETONS DES NUMISMATES*. (1865, PL. XIII, NO. 4).

[363] The son (*or* nephew?) of JEAN DASSIER (1717-1779), he worked at the royal (1740/41-1745), and the St. Petersburg (1756-1759) mints. Other subjects of medals in the series, which was sold by subscription—four guineas for 13 medals—were ALEXANDER POPE, JOHN CAMPBELL, 2ND DUKE OF ARGYLL, WILLIAM PULTENEY, 1ST EARL OF BATH AND EDMOND HALLEY. Dassier died while returning to Geneva from St. Petersburg.

[364] As well as insects (5,500), and human and animal skeletons.

Sloane soon developed a fashionable and highly lucrative society practice, serving as physician to Queen Anne and George I and later George II. Created a baronet in 1716, he soon advanced to the presidency of the Royal College of Physicians and, in 1727, the presidency of the Royal Society, succeeding Sir Isaac Newton. It was in the same year that he was appointed physician to George II.

A MEZZOTINT PORTRAIT OF HANS SLOANE AT AGE 69, CA. 1729 AFTER THE PAINTING BY SIR GODFREY KNELLER (1646-1723) AND PRINTED BY JOHN FABER THE YOUNGER AFTER THOMAS MURRAY (1663-1735). SLOANE'S COLLECTION, GIVEN TO THE BRITISH NATION FOR A FRACTION OF ITS VALUE, FORMED A PART OF THE FOUNDATION OF THE BRITISH MUSEUM COLLECTION. IMAGE © TRUSTEES OF THE BRITISH MUSEUM; ACC./REG. NO. 1863,0725.213.

Upon his death in 1753, Sloane's library and collections (i.e., his 'cabinet of curiosities') expanded by the purchase of other extensive collections, were bequeathed to the nation by his daughters, Sarah Stanley and Elizabeth Cadogan, in return for the sum of £20,000—a large figure, yet one believed to be far below their true value—a transfer referred to as the 'Sloane Bequest.' Sloane's collections, together with the Royal library and the Cottonian and Harleian collections of books and other items were, in the period 1753-1757, combined to form the British Museum Sloane collection. The Museum's collection alone included 23,000 coins and medals; 50,000 books, prints and manuscripts; a herbarium (a collection of dried plants); 1,125 'things relating to the customs of ancient times.' In 1881, the natural history collection became the foundation of the collection for the Natural History Museum which until 1963 remained a part of the British Museum.[365] Sloane's house in Bloomsbury Place (no. 3), London, is now open to the public. Sloane also purchased the house next door, no. 4, for storage for his collection.

[365] Anon. SIR HANS SLOANE (1660-1753) the founder of the British Museum. *Journal of the American Medical Association,* 1969, vol. 207, no. 5, pp. 943–910.

Dr. Richard Mead

(1673-1754)

ANOTHER physician of note as a collector is Dr. Richard Mead. Preeminent as a scientist remembered primarily for his contributions to an understanding of the transmission of infectious diseases, Dr. Mead also developed a magnificent collection of medals, including a large number from the 17th century.

Dr Richard Mead, a mezzotint portrait, ca. 1734-1775, by Richard Houston (c.1721-1775), printed by Allan Ramsey (1713-1784). Image © Trustees of the British Museum.

As one of eleven children born to Matthew Mead, an Independent clergyman, of Stepney, London and his wife Elizabeth, Mead obtained his education at the University of Utrecht followed by three years of further studies in Padua, Rome and Naples. Mead returned to London in 1696 and opened a medical practice in which he gained sufficient prominence to become, in time, physician to Queen Anne, King George II and Sir Isaac Newton. This was quite an achievement as Mead had started his practice without a license from the College of Physicians. It took until 1708 for him to be admitted to membership in that body. Among Mead's greatest contributions to medicine were his avoidance of the more questionable treatments offered by physicians of his time, as well as his promotion of inoculation for small pox and measles and the implementation of public health measures in controlling bubonic plague.

Mead was elected to the Royal Society in 1703 following the publication of his work on poisons, and his dissemination of knowledge about the existence of the 'itch' mite—previously it had been believed that the itching caused by such infestations resulted from constitutional dysfunction. Mead was a founder of the Foundling Hospital in London, a home for abandoned children, and pressed for the inclusion of a sick room, pharmacy and exercise yard, rare facilities for a children's shelter in the late 18th century.

A serious collector of rare books, portraits, drawings, natural history, coins, gems and medals, Mead's library contained over 10,000 volumes, a massive number for that time. At Mead's death in February 1754, his various collections were catalogued and sold at auction. The auction of numismatic items took place over eight days (February 11-19, 1755) and was conducted at Mr. Langford's rooms in Covent Garden and at Mr. Baker's room in York Street. The catalogue for the sale was 210 pages in length. Forty-nine lots of 'gold and silver medals' were sold at the seventh day's sale while 'Miscellaneous Medals, English and Foreign' (lots 9-42) and 'Large Brass Medallions cast' (lots 43-46) were sold on the eighth day.

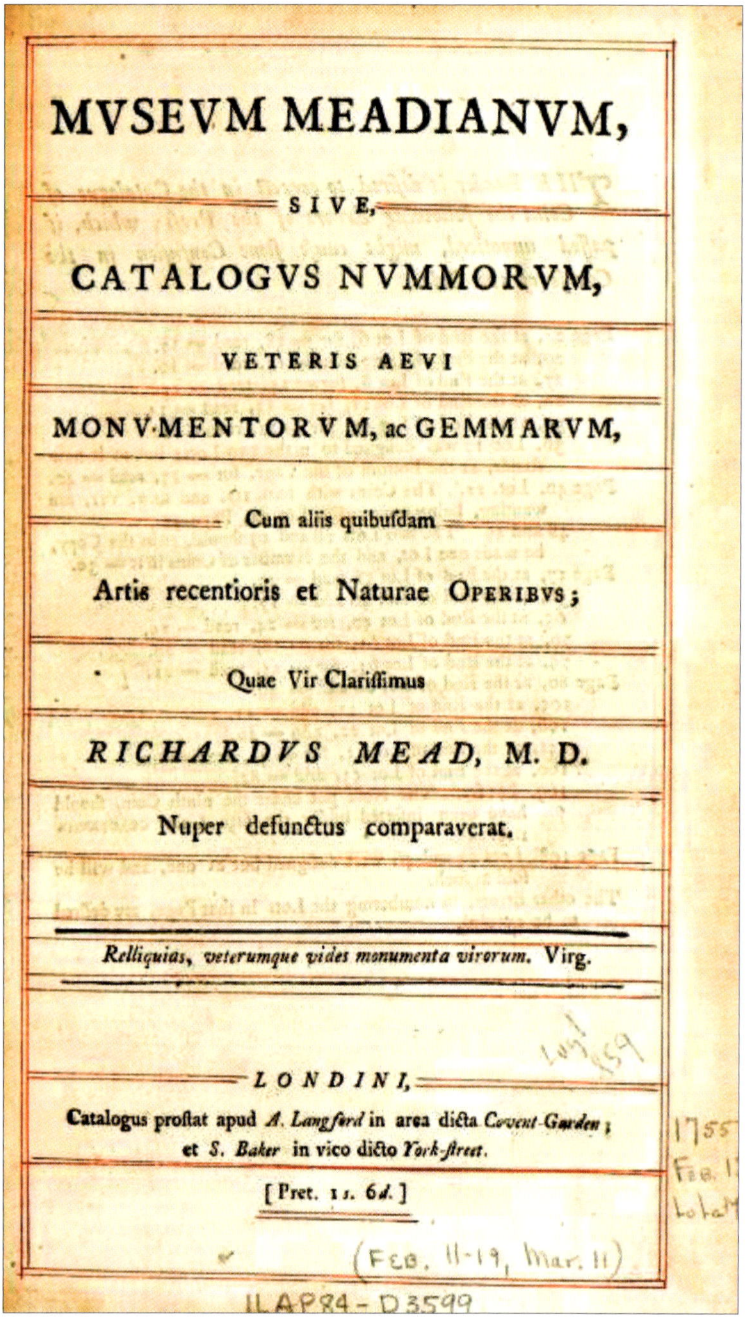

MVSEVM MEADIANVM,

SIVE,

CATALOGVS NVMMORVM,

VETERIS AEVI

MONVMENTORVM, ac GEMMARVM,

Cum aliis quibusdam

Artis recentioris et Naturae OPERIBVS;

Quae Vir Clarissimus

RICHARDVS MEAD, M. D.

Nuper defunctus comparaverat.

Relliquias, veterumque vides monumenta virorum. Virg.

LONDINI,

Catalogus prostat apud *A. Langford* in area dicta *Covent-Garden*; et *S. Baker* in vico dicto *York-street*.

[Pret. 1*s.* 6*d.*]

(Feb. 11-19, Mar. 11)

ILAP84-D3599

THE TITLE PAGE OF THE SALE CATALOGUE FOR THE NUMISMATIC MATERIAL IN THE RICHARD MEAD AUCTION. THIS PARTICULAR COPY IS ONE OF TWO HELD BY THE GETTY RESEARCH INSTITUTE. WHAT MAKES THIS COPY SO INTERESTING AND VALUABLE ARE THE NOTATIONS OF THE PRICES REALIZED.

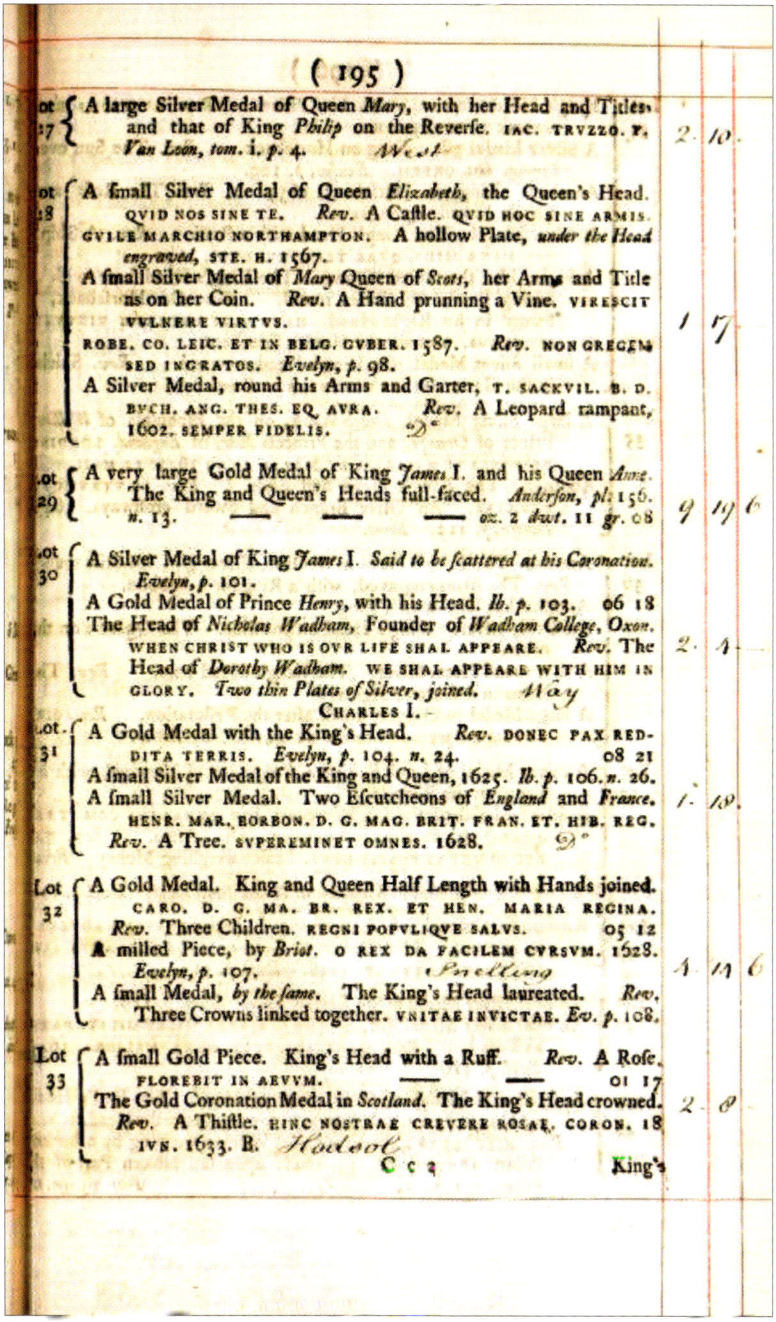

(195)

Lot 27 — A large Silver Medal of Queen *Mary*, with her Head and Titles, and that of King *Philip* on the Reverse. IAC. TRVZZO. F. *Van Loon, tom.* i. *p.* 4. *West* — 2. 10.

Lot 28 — A small Silver Medal of Queen *Elizabeth*, the Queen's Head. QVID NOS SINE TE. *Rev.* A Castle. QVID HOC SINE ARMIS. GVILE MARCHIO NORTHAMPTON. A hollow Plate, *under the Head engraved*, STE. H. 1567.
A small Silver Medal of *Mary* Queen of *Scots*, her Arms and Title as on her Coin. *Rev.* A Hand prunning a Vine. VIRESCIT VVLNERE VIRTVS.
ROBE. CO. LEIC. ET IN BELG. GVBER. 1587. *Rev.* NON GREGEM SED INGRATOS. *Evelyn, p.* 98.
A Silver Medal, round his Arms and Garter, T. SACKVIL. B. D. BVCH. ANG. THES. EQ. AVRA. *Rev.* A Leopard rampant, 1602. SEMPER FIDELIS. *D°* — 1. 7

Lot 29 — A very large Gold Medal of King *James* I. and his Queen *Anne*. The King and Queen's Heads full-faced. *Anderson, pl.* 156. *n.* 13. — — — *oz.* 2 *dwt.* 11 *gr.* 08 — 9. 19. 6

Lot 30 — A Silver Medal of King *James* I. *Said to be scattered at his Coronation. Evelyn, p.* 101.
A Gold Medal of Prince *Henry*, with his Head. *Ib. p.* 103. 06 18
The Head of *Nicholas Wadham*, Founder of *Wadham College*, *Oxon.* WHEN CHRIST WHO IS OVR LIFE SHAL APPEARE. *Rev.* The Head of *Dorothy Wadham.* WE SHAL APPEARE WITH HIM IN GLORY. *Two thin Plates of Silver, joined.* *Way* — 2. 4.

CHARLES I.

Lot 31 — A Gold Medal with the King's Head. *Rev.* DONEC PAX REDDITA TERRIS. *Evelyn, p.* 104. *n.* 24. 08 21
A small Silver Medal of the King and Queen, 1625. *Ib. p.* 106. *n.* 26.
A small Silver Medal. Two Escutcheons of *England* and *France.* HENR. MAR. BORBON. D. G. MAG. BRIT. FRAN. ET. HIB. REG. *Rev.* A Tree. SVPEREMINET OMNES. 1628. *D°* — 1. 18.

Lot 32 — A Gold Medal. King and Queen Half Length with Hands joined. CARO. D. G. MA. BR. REX. ET HEN. MARIA REGINA. *Rev.* Three Children. REGNI POPVLIQVE SALVS. 05 12
A milled Piece, by *Briot.* O REX DA FACILEM CVRSVM. 1628. *Evelyn, p.* 107. *Snelling*
A small Medal, *by the same.* The King's Head laureated. *Rev.* Three Crowns linked together. VNITAE INVICTAE. *Ev. p.* 108. — 4. 14. 6

Lot 33 — A small Gold Piece. King's Head with a Ruff. *Rev.* A Rose. FLOREBIT IN AEVVM. — — 01 17
The Gold Coronation Medal in *Scotland.* The King's Head crowned. *Rev.* A Thistle. HINC NOSTRAE CREVERE ROSAE. CORON. 18 IVN. 1633. B. *Hodsol* — 2. 8

C c 3 King's

A PAGE FROM THE PRICED CATALOGUE FOR THE SALE OF NUMISMATIC MATERIAL FROM DR. MEAD'S COLLECTION. THE MEDALS LISTED HERE WILL BE READILY RECOGNIZED BY THE MODERN COLLECTOR OF 17TH C. ENGLISH MEDALS.

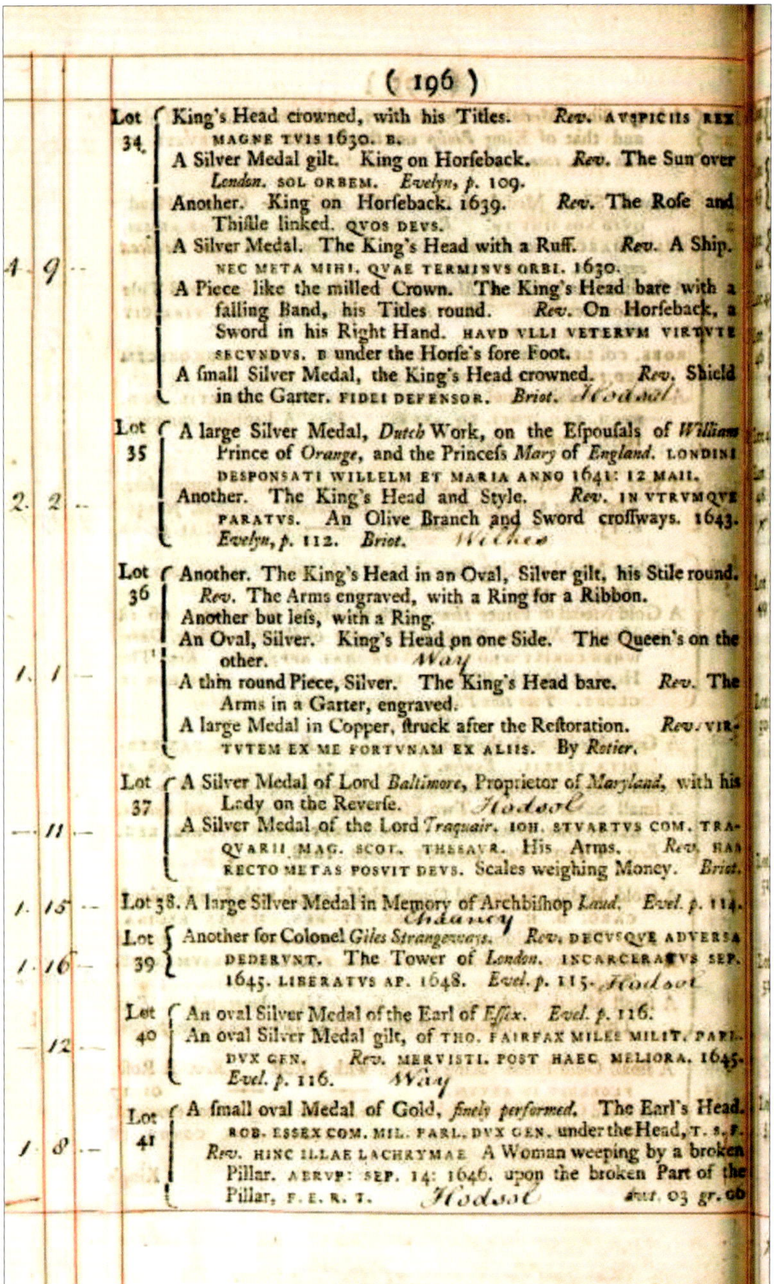

(196)

4. 9 .. Lot 34 { King's Head crowned, with his Titles. *Rev.* AVSPICIIS REX MAGNE TVIS 1630. B.
A Silver Medal gilt. King on Horfeback. *Rev.* The Sun over *London.* SOL ORBEM. *Evelyn, p.* 109.
Another. King on Horfeback. 1639. *Rev.* The Rofe and Thiftle linked. QVOS DEVS.
A Silver Medal. The King's Head with a Ruff. *Rev.* A Ship. NEC META MIHI, QVAE TERMINVS ORBI. 1630.
A Piece like the milled Crown. The King's Head bare with a falling Band, his Titles round. *Rev.* On Horfeback, a Sword in his Right Hand. HAVD VLLI VETERVM VIRTVTE SECVNDVS. B under the Horfe's fore Foot.
A fmall Silver Medal, the King's Head crowned. *Rev.* Shield in the Garter. FIDEI DEFENSOR. *Briot.* Hodsol

2. 2 .. Lot 35 { A large Silver Medal, *Dutch* Work, on the Efpoufals of *William* Prince of *Orange*, and the Princefs *Mary* of *England*. LONDINI DESPONSATI WILLELM ET MARIA ANNO 1641: 12 MAII.
Another. The King's Head and Style. *Rev.* IN VTRVMQVE PARATVS. An Olive Branch and Sword croffways. 1643. *Evelyn, p.* 112. *Briot.* Wilkes

1. 1 — Lot 36 { Another. The King's Head in an Oval, Silver gilt, his Stile round. *Rev.* The Arms engraved, with a Ring for a Ribbon.
Another but lefs, with a Ring.
An Oval, Silver. King's Head on one Side. The Queen's on the other. Way
A thin round Piece, Silver. The King's Head bare. *Rev.* The Arms in a Garter, engraved.
A large Medal in Copper, ftruck after the Reftoration. *Rev.* VIRTVTEM EX ME FORTVNAM EX ALIIS. By *Rotier.*

— 11 — Lot 37 { A Silver Medal of Lord *Baltimore*, Proprietor of *Maryland*, with his Lady on the Reverfe. Hodsol
A Silver Medal of the Lord *Traquair*. IOH. STVARTVS COM. TRAQVARII MAG. SCOT. THESAVR. His Arms. *Rev.* HAS RECTO METAS POSVIT DEVS. Scales weighing Money. *Briot.*

1. 15 -- Lot 38. A large Silver Medal in Memory of Archbifhop *Laud.* *Evel. p.* 114. Chauncy

1. 16 — Lot 39 { Another for Colonel *Giles Strangeways*. *Rev.* DECVSQVE ADVERSA DEDERVNT. The Tower of *London*. INCARCERATVS SEP. 1645. LIBERATVS AP. 1648. *Evel. p.* 115. Hodsol

— 12 — Lot 40 { An oval Silver Medal of the Earl of *Effex*. *Evel. p.* 116.
An oval Silver Medal gilt, of THO. FAIRFAX MILES MILIT. PARL. DVX GEN. *Rev.* MERVISTI. POST HAEC MELIORA. 1645. *Evel. p.* 116. Way

1. 8 — Lot 41 { A fmall oval Medal of Gold, *finely performed*. The Earl's Head. ROB. ESSEX COM. MIL. PARL. DVX GEN. under the Head, T. S. F. *Rev.* HINC ILLAE LACHRYMAE. A Woman weeping by a broken Pillar. ABRVP: SEP. 14: 1646. upon the broken Part of the Pillar, F. E. R. T. Hodsol *Aur.* 03 *gr.* 06

PAGE 196 FROM THE PRICED CATALOGUE FOR THE SALE OF NUMISMATIC MATERIAL FROM DR. MEAD'S COLLECTION. OF PARTICULAR INTEREST ARE THE PRICES REALIZED ON THIS, AS WELL AS ON THE LAST PAGE, WHICH DEMONSTRATE A HIGH LEVEL OF INTEREST IN MEDALS ON THE PART OF BIDDERS.

Edward Harley, 2nd Earl of Oxford

(1689–1741)

A major collector and patron of the arts, Harley was a:

> ...close friend and constant patron of the antiquary and engraver George Vertue, who made frequent use of Harley's library.[366]

The son of Robert Harley, 1st earl of Oxford and Mortimer (1661-1724), politician, and his first wife Elizabeth, Edward Harley was a very wealthy man, having both inherited wealth and married into a sizable fortune of which he made ample use in expanding his interests in the arts and the collecting of manuscripts, books, coins, medals and miniatures. A patron of poets, writers, antiquaries and artists, his proclivity for collecting appears to have been inherited from his father to whose personal collection of 3,000 printed and manuscript books and 13,000 charters were added those inherited from his mother-in-law, Lady Margaret Cavendish, duchess of Newcastle and Tyne, and those he himself purchased through agents and from booksellers. At the time of his death, Harley had amassed some 50,000 printed books, 350,000 printed pamphlets and 41,000 prints. After his death, Harley's collections of antiquities, coins, medals, and pictures were sold at Mr. Cock's[367] auction rooms in March 1742 while his book collection was sold outright to the bookseller Thomas Osborne for £13,000, also in 1742. The manuscripts and rolls were willed to his widow, Henrietta, née Cavendish Holles (d. 1755), for her lifetime, and then to their daughter, Margaret Cavendish Bentinck, Duchess of Portland (d. 1785). In 1753, the manuscripts were sold by them to the nation for £10,000.[368] This sum was far below their market value.

Edward Harley, 2nd Earl of Oxford, wearing the robes of a peer. Oil painting on canvas, after 1728, by Michael Dahl (1659-1743). Image © Trustees of the British Museum.

---

[366] D. Stoker, 'Edward Harley,' *ODNB on line*, 2004.

[367] Christopher Cock (d. 1748), 'auctioneer of St Paul Covent Garden.' Cock was a major London auction house proprietor for almost three decades from 1717. The name 'Cock' also appears in sales catalogues as a successful buyer from ca. 1711-1740. Cock conducted business:

> Next the Vine Tavern, Broad St, St James's, London 1722, upper end of Broad St, next Golden Square 1722-1724, Broad St 1725-1726, The Two Blue Spires, Broad St 1725, Poland St, corner of Broad St 1726-1731, Great Piazza, Covent Garden 1731-1748.

Abraham Langford is listed by Cock as the latter's business agent to whom responsibility was given to make an accounting of Cock's estate upon his death. Cock's collection of pictures was sold at Langford's in May 1749 (www.npg.org.uk/research/programmes/directory-of-british-picture-restorers/british-picture-restorers-1600-1950-c.php).

[368] Ibid. The acquisition by the nation of Harley's manuscript collection (the 'Harleian Collection'), together with the libraries of Hans Sloane, Robert Bruce Cotton, and King George II formed the basis of the British Museum Library collection, now the British Library.

AN ENGRAVED PORTRAIT OF EDWARD, EARL OF OXFORD, CA. 1728, IN A CLASSIC POSE VERY MUCH REMINISCENT OF GEORGE VERTUE'S SELF-PORTRAIT *(CF., P. 39)*. IT WAS DRAWN BY GEORGE VERTUE AFTER A PAINTING BY MICHAEL DAHL (1659-1743), AND PORTRAYS THE EARL HOLDING A PORTRAIT MEDAL OF QUEEN ANNE IN HIS LEFT HAND WHILE OTHER MEDALS LIE ON THE TABLE BEFORE HIM. THE BRITISH MUSEUM COMMENTS THAT "VERTUE SEEMS TO HAVE INTENDED THIS PRINT AS THE FRONTISPIECE TO HIS HISTORY OF ART IN ENGLAND." IMAGE © TRUSTEES OF THE BRITISH MUSEUM.

THE FRONTISPIECE BY GEORGE VERTUE FOR THE AUCTION SALE OF THE COLLECTION(S) OF THE LATE EDWARD HARLEY, 2ND EARL OF OXFORD, IN 1741/42. NOTE THE COIN AND MEDAL CABINET AND THE SMALL PORTRAIT LABELED "HOLLAR" IN THE RIGHT CENTER. OTHER IMAGES OF THE SALE CATALOGUE PAGES, INCLUDING MEDALS OFFERED FOR SALE, APPEAR ON THE FOLLOWING PAGES. IMAGE © TRUSTEES OF THE BRITISH MUSEUM.

The First Major Collection of Coins and Medals to be Sold at Auction in England

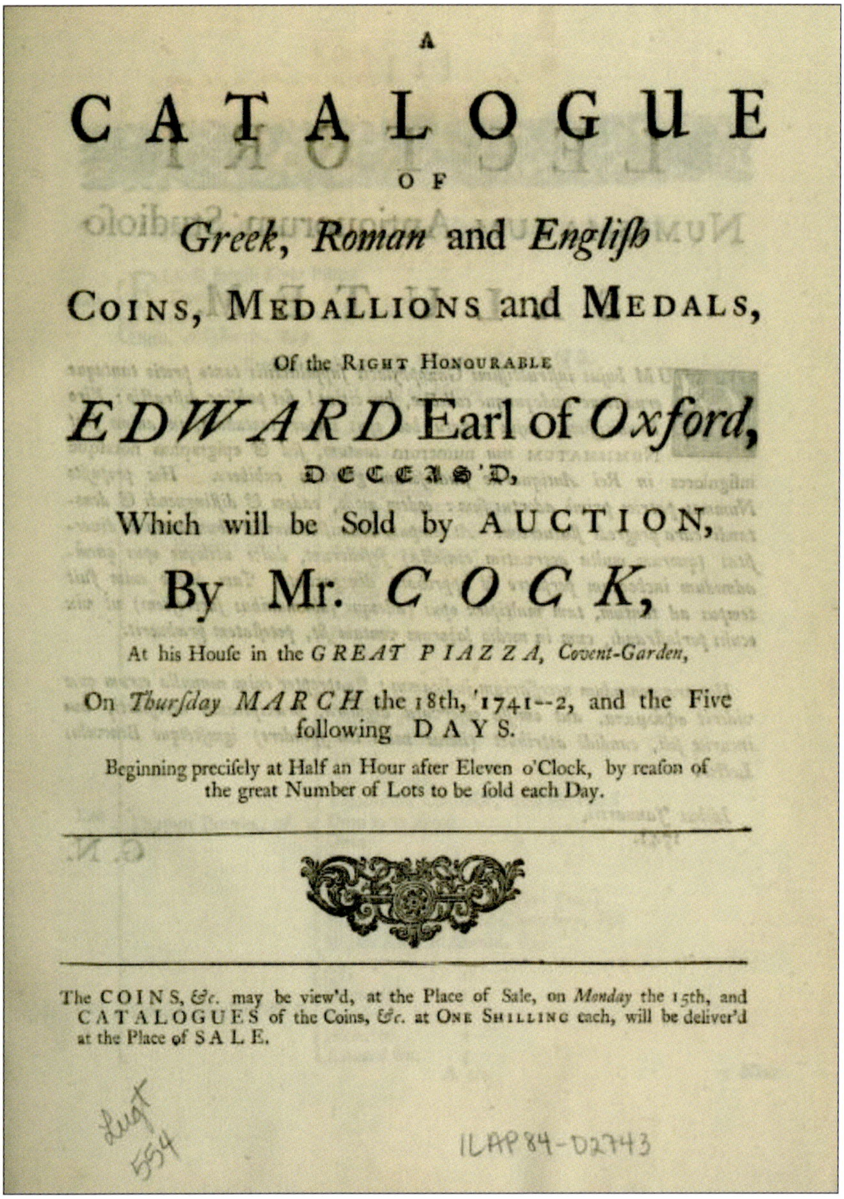

A

CATALOGUE

OF

Greek, *Roman* and *English*

COINS, MEDALLIONS and MEDALS,

Of the RIGHT HONOURABLE

EDWARD Earl of *Oxford*,

DECEAS'D,

Which will be Sold by AUCTION,

By Mr. *COCK*,

At his House in the *GREAT PIAZZA*, *Covent-Garden*,

On *Thursday MARCH* the 18th, 1741--2, and the Five following DAYS.

Beginning precisely at Half an Hour after Eleven o'Clock, by reason of the great Number of Lots to be sold each Day.

The COINS, &c. may be view'd, at the Place of Sale, on *Monday* the 15th, and CATALOGUES of the Coins, &c. at ONE SHILLING each, will be deliver'd at the Place of SALE.

Lugt 554

ILAP84-D2743

A copy of this very rare catalogue was offered for sale in Baldwin's numismatic literature sale (Winter 2013-14). The catalogue notes:

> *Only 1 copy cited in Manville and only 4 copies coming onto the market in the past 40 years, none of these with both the prices and buyers names. Of the utmost rarity…*

This page image and the following two digitized by Internet Archive.

A Page from the Catalogue of the earl of Oxford Sale listing Medals in Gold and Prices Realized

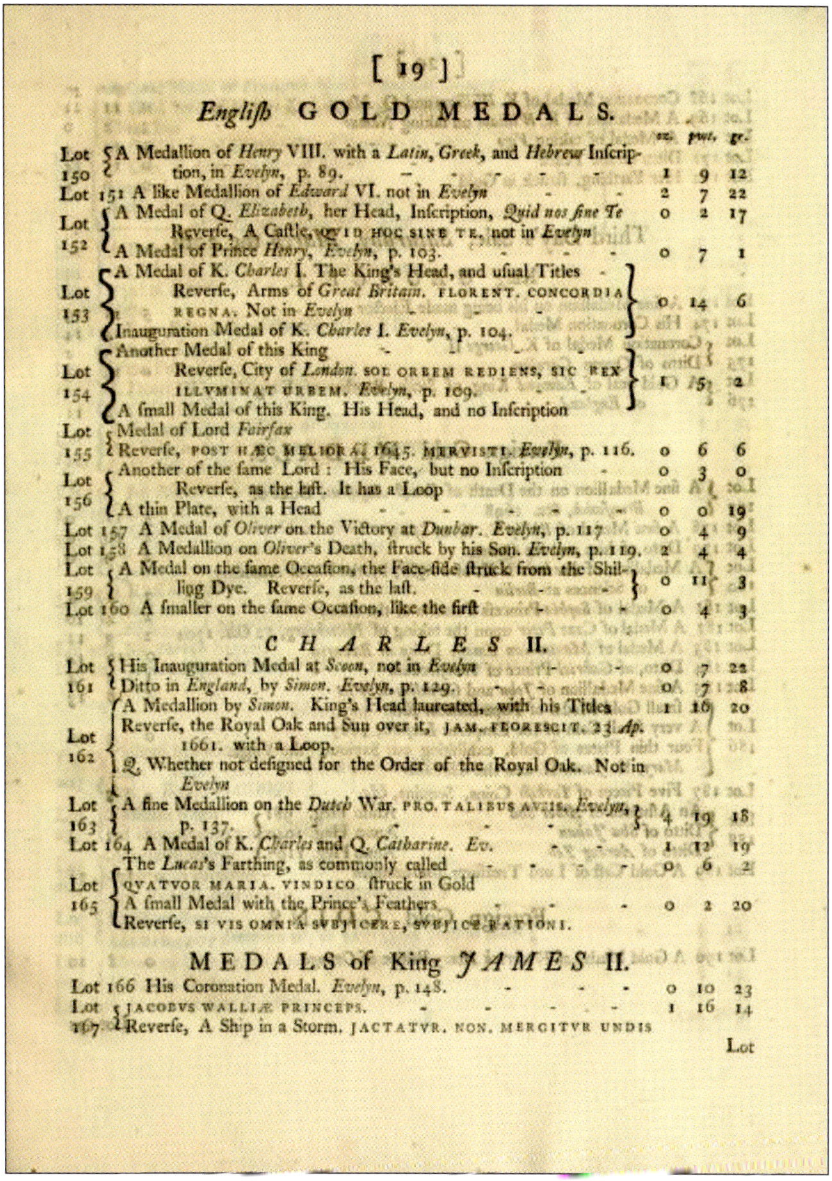

[19]

English GOLD MEDALS.

Lot		oz.	pwt.	gr.
Lot 150	A Medallion of *Henry* VIII. with a *Latin*, *Greek*, and *Hebrew* Inscription, in *Evelyn*, p. 89.	1	9	12
Lot 151	A like Medallion of *Edward* VI. not in *Evelyn*	2	7	22
Lot 152	A Medal of Q. *Elizabeth*, her Head, Inscription, *Quid nos sine Te* Reverse, A Castle, QVID HOC SINE TE. not in *Evelyn*	0	2	17
	A Medal of Prince *Henry*, *Evelyn*, p. 103.	0	7	1
Lot 153	A Medal of K. *Charles* I. The King's Head, and usual Titles Reverse, Arms of *Great Britain*. FLORENT. CONCORDIA REGNA. Not in *Evelyn* Inauguration Medal of K. *Charles* I. *Evelyn*, p. 104.	0	14	6
Lot 154	Another Medal of this King Reverse, City of *London*. SOL ORBEM REDIENS, SIC REX ILLVMINAT URBEM. *Evelyn*, p. 109. A small Medal of this King. His Head, and no Inscription	1	5	2
Lot 155	Medal of Lord *Fairfax* Reverse, POST HÆC MELIORA. 1645. MERVISTI. *Evelyn*, p. 116.	0	6	6
Lot 156	Another of the same Lord: His Face, but no Inscription Reverse, as the last. It has a Loop	0	3	0
	A thin Plate, with a Head	0	0	19
Lot 157	A Medal of *Oliver* on the Victory at *Dunbar*. *Evelyn*, p. 117	0	4	9
Lot 158	A Medallion on *Oliver*'s Death, struck by his Son. *Evelyn*, p. 119.	2	4	4
Lot 159	A Medal on the same Occasion, the Face-side struck from the Shilling Dye. Reverse, as the last.	0	11	3
Lot 160	A smaller on the same Occasion, like the first	0	4	3

CHARLES II.

Lot		oz.	pwt.	gr.
Lot 161	His Inauguration Medal at *Scoon*, not in *Evelyn*	0	7	22
	Ditto in *England*, by *Simon*. *Evelyn*, p. 129.	0	7	8
Lot 162	A Medallion by *Simon*. King's Head laureated, with his Titles Reverse, the Royal Oak and Sun over it, JAM. FLORESCIT. 23 *Ap.* 1661. with a Loop. Q. Whether not designed for the Order of the Royal Oak. Not in *Evelyn*	1	16	20
Lot 163	A fine Medallion on the *Dutch* War. PRO. TALIBUS AUSIS. *Evelyn*, p. 137.	4	19	18
Lot 164	A Medal of K. *Charles* and Q. *Catharine*. *Ev.*	1	12	19
Lot 165	The *Lucas*'s Farthing, as commonly called QVATVOR MARIA. VINDICO struck in Gold	0	6	2
	A small Medal with the Prince's Feathers Reverse, SI VIS OMNIA SVBJICERE, SVBJICE RATIONI.	0	2	20

MEDALS of King *JAMES* II.

Lot		oz.	pwt.	gr.
Lot 166	His Coronation Medal. *Evelyn*, p. 148.	0	10	23
Lot 167	JACOBVS WALLIÆ PRINCEPS. Reverse, A Ship in a Storm. JACTATVR. NON. MERGITVR UNDIS	1	16	14

Lot

The listing of lots of gold medals in the Harley sale. Note the references to John Evelyn's *Numismata...* (1697), the only work on English medals then in existence. It is not difficult to identify the pieces, although lot 158, 'A Medallion on *Oliver's* Death, struck by his Son' would appear to refer to M.I.i 435/85 (*see text box on following page*). One can but wonder whether the idea for George Vertue's *Medals of...Thomas Simon* (1753) was in any way stimulated by the association with a patron who possessed such a strong interest in medals as well as a sizeable collection.

The March 1741/42, sale at Cock's consisted of 520 lots, of which there were some 14 gold and 36 silver medals of Charles I, 7 gold and 44 silver medals of Charles II, and 25 "Silver Medals of the Nobility," i.e., Oliver Cromwell, Essex, Brown, Monk, Fairfax, etc., as well as a number of foreign medals. The description of the catalogue in the 2014 sale in which it was sold states that it is the only known priced catalogue among the four copies believed to still be in existence. It further notes that it could be argued that:

> The Oxford sale was the first auction to really promote numismatics to a wider audience in London...it was this sale that gave credence to the idea that there was indeed a burgeoning market for coins... and... they warrant[ed] auctions in their own right.[369]

In the Earl of Oxford's Sale (1741/42) Lot 158)

It is not clear as to which medal is referenced as lot 158 in the sales catalogue on the previous page. The illustration on page 119 of Evelyn's *Numismata*... is unmistakably that of the large Cromwell death medal (1658, M.I.i 435/85, M.I.Ill xl/3, Eimer 202a, Platt ii/25/c). Yet, this medal is described by M.I.i as having been 'executed in Holland' and does not suggest that it was struck by an order of Richard Cromwell. It seems unlikely that Richard would have had a medal struck in his father's honor in Holland. Perhaps the medal in question is the smaller one attributed to Thomas Simon (1658, M.I.i 433/82, M.I.Ill xl/3, Eimer 200, Platt ii/25/a).

(*Top*) illustration from Evelyn, 1697, p. 119. (*Center*) The large Oliver Cromwell death medal, produced in Holland (M.I.i 435/85), in silver. (*Below*) the Oliver Cromwell death medal, produced in England by Thomas Simon (M.I.i 433/82), in silver. Images from a private collection and © Trustees of the British Museum, respectively.

369 *Baldwin's Fixed Price List Winter 2013-14 Catalogue*. Numismatic Literature section.

A Page from the Sale Catalogue of the Earl of Oxford
Sale Catalogue listing Medals in Silver

[26]

Q. ELIZABETH.

Lot 276
- A Medallion on the triple League againſt Spain. *Ev.* N° 16.
- A Medal. Q. Head. *Quid nos ſine te?*
  Reverſe, a Caſtle. *Quid hoc ſine te?* Not in *Ev.*
- A Medal on this Queen, by the States of Holland. *Ev.* N° 14.
- The Silver Pledge of a Penny.

JAMES. I.

Lot 277
- His Coronation Medal. *Ev.* N° 18.
- A large Oval Medal
  Reverſe, *Noah's* Ark, STET. SALVVS IN VNDIS. Not in *Ev.*
- A Medal of Q. *Anne* his Conſort. *Ev.* N° 23.

CHARLES I.

Lot 278
- A thin Plate, while he was Duke of *York*
- His Coronation Medal. *Ev.* N° 24
- His Marriage Medal. *Ev.* N° 26
- Ditto on the Expedition to *Rochelle*. *Ev.* N° 27
- A Medal of this King not in *Evelyn*, round the Arms and Garter FIDEI. DEFENSOR
- Another not in *Evelyn*; round the Arms, FLORENT. CONCORDIA REGNA

Lot 279
- A Medal engrav'd in *Evelyn*, N° 29
- N° 30 in *Ev.*
- N° 31
- N° 33 in *Ev.*
- Ditto a little different
- N° 34

The following Medals of K. *Charles* I. are not in *Evelyn*

Lot 280
- An oval Medal, one Side K. Head, on the Rev. his Queen's, by *Rawlins*
- Ditto, but no Inſcription
- Another with the K. and Q. Head
- A Medal with a Trident and Sceptre 1628. REGIT. VNVS. VTROQVE
- Medal with the K's Head. Reverſe, PRISCI. DECVS. ORDINIS AVCTVM.

Lot 281
- A large Caſt. Reverſe, A Ship at Sea. NEC. META. MIHI. QVÆ TERMINVS ORBI.
- A Medal of the ſame Deſign, but ſomewhat different
- A ſmall Medal of the ſame Device and Inſcrip. by *Briot*

Lot 282
- A ſmall Medal of Princeſs *Mary's* Birth. STAT. PROLE. HAC ALTERA. DELOS.
- A Medal with the King on Horſeback
  Reverſe, Hand holding a Roſe and Thiſtle. QVOS DEVS
- Ditto leſs
- Ditto

Lot

Page 26 from the Edward Harley auction sale catalogue. A priced copy of the catalogue recently sold at auction contains many names of buyers whose names are familiar among the antiquaries and dealers of the period—Martin Folkes, Horace Walpole, Henry Young, Roger Gale, Bishop [Richard] Rawlinson, Lord Pembroke, Robert Bootle and Mrs. Katherine Bridgeman. The last, a book collector described by Vertue as being 'one of the principal collectors of English coins.'

Hugh Percy, 1st Duke of Northumberland & Elizabeth, his Duchess

(1715-1786; 1716-1776)

HUGH PERCY AND ELIZABETH, THE 1ST DUKE AND DUCHESS OF NORTHUMBERLAND. THESE ARE MEZZOTINTS BY EDWARD FISHER (1722-1781/82) AFTER THE PORTRAITS BY JOSHUA REYNOLDS, CA. 1759-1782. IMAGES © TRUSTEES OF THE BRITISH MUSEUM.

THE collection of medals and other items assembled by Elizabeth, the 1st duchess of Northumberland,[370] is remarkable in several ways. First, it was one of very few assembled by a woman of the Georgian period. Secondly, it was very broad in its scope, including both naturalistic specimens and medals. Further, a nine-volume *Musæum* catalogue of it exists.[371] Having started collecting at an early age, she is quoted as having described her habit as a "rage of medals." She amassed a collection of which her most recent chronicler says:

> The next category, medals and coins, was the real point of excellence of the entire collection. Building on her father's collection, either autonomously or through the services of Louis Dutens,[372] a French diplomat and numismatist, Elizabeth managed over time to amass one of the largest numismatic collections of Georgian Britain, particularly strong in north European medals. As the inventory reports, they were kept in medal cases distributed between the "Museum Room" and the "second room in the gallery."[373]

This collection is remarkable in that it appears to have survived intact from the death of the duchess in 1776 until the time of its partial dispersal by auction in 1980-1981. The auction catalogue states:

> Virtually all of the medals in the collection (the main exception being the Napoleonic series) were struck before 1786, the year of the death of the first Duke of Northumber-

[370] ELIZABETH SEYMOUR PERCY, 2nd Countess, later 1st Duchess of Northumberland.

[371] Aymonino, A. "The Musæum of the 1st Duchess of Northumberland…," 2012, pp. 101-120.

[372] LOUIS DUTENS (1730–1812), French author and later member of the Royal Academy, was business manager and travel companion to the Duke of Northumberland as well as tutor to the Duke's children.

[373] Aymonino, ibid. p. 109.

land, and it is probable that such medals were collected by him or his wife Elizabeth, the first Duchess (1716-1776).[374]

The collection of coins and medals, after remaining intact for two centuries, was partially dispersed at the Sotheby's sales of December 3, 1980, and June 17, 1981. Examination of the catalogues for these sales reveals, however, that the lots in these sales consisted almost entirely of European medals, with only a small number of English medals, beginning with those of the reign of Charles I, being represented. There were a total of 964 lots, of which only 26 were of English medals, these having been duplicates of the English collection being retained at Alnwick Castle. The inventory of English gold and silver medals in the retained collection totals some 70 pages and it is expected that the full listing will at some point be available on the Getty Provenance Index.[375] Given the comprehensiveness of the partial collection sold in 1980, it is highly likely that the retained collection will be found to contain a significant number of 17th century British medals.

A Scarce Medal of Charles II by Philip Roettier

Rarely seen outside of museum collections, this 'State of Britain' medal is found in silver (ca. 1667, 28 mm., M.I.i 541/193; M.I.Ill liv/11, British Museum acc./reg. M.7579, Eimer 244) and bronze (M.7580). The reverse inscription, 'qviescit britan' (Britain at rest), likely refers to the peace following the Treaty of Breda. Signed P. R. (Philip Roettier) on the obverse. Image © Trustees of the British Museum.

[374] Sotheby Parke Bernet (December 3, 1980). *European Historical Medals from the Collection of his Grace the Duke of Northumberland...Removed from Alnwick Castle.* Introduction to the sale catalogue.

[375] Christopher Hunwick, personal communication, February 7, 2014.

THE TITLE PAGE, ILLUSTRATED WITH A WOOD-ENGRAVING, FOR THE SALE CATALOGUE OF STRAWBERRY HILL AND ITS CONTENTS IN APRIL AND MAY 1842. THE AUCTION TOOK PLACE OVER 24 DAYS. IMAGE BY INTERNET ARCHIVE, FROM THE UNIVERSITY OF TORONTO LIBRARY.

Horace (Horatio) Walpole

(1717-1797)

AS the youngest son of the Chancellor of the Exchequer and first Prime Minister, Sir Robert Walpole, the leader of the Whig party, and his wife Catherine, Horace Walpole, as 4th earl of Orford, was able to lead a privileged life. Educated at Eton College and King's College, Cambridge, his father's influence brought him sinecures in the way of well paid appointments requiring little or no effort. Able to lead a leisurely life, Walpole stood for election as a Whig MP from Callington, Cornwall. He held this seat for 13 years despite never having visited his constituency.

'HORACE WALPOLE' BY JOHN GILES ECCARDT (FL. CA. 1740, D. 1779), AN OIL PAINTING ON CANVAS, DONE IN 1754 FOR THE 'BLUE BEDROOM' AT STRAWBERRY HILL, A GLIMPSE OF WHICH APPEARS HERE IN THE BACKGROUND. IMAGE © NATIONAL PORTRAIT GALLERY, LONDON.

After his father's death in 1745, Walpole built a home, 'Strawberry Hill,' at Twickenham, London, where he lived from 1753 until his death. Regularly expanding the house over the next 30 years, its design was a major influence on English architecture and has been credited with initiating the Gothic revival style in England. An enthusiastic collector of antiquarian books, articles of *vertu* and other curiosities, Walpole's collection achieved great celebrity. Visitors and sightseers of all social standings came to see Strawberry Hill, and although Walpole was happy to receive them, and enjoyed the celebrity, he eventually found them to be a mixed blessing—a burden intruding on his personal privacy, although at the same time, a validation of his personal tastes.[376]

In 1757, Walpole established his own printing press at Strawberry Hill, and published a number of his own works. Not surprisingly, one of the works he published was *A Description of the Villa of Mr. Horace Walpole* (1784). His *Catalogue of the Royal and Noble Authors of England* was his first work of substance to be published by the press in 1758, although it is now considered of relatively minor importance. Foremost among Walpole's works in historical importance is his reworking of George Vertue's manuscript notebooks as *Anecdotes of Painting in England*, which first appeared in 1762 and which he edited twice and reprinted several times at Strawberry

[376] It is clear that HORACE WALPOLE possessed a striking appearance as well as some very idiosyncratic personal tastes (*q.v.* '*Historical Commentary*,' *below*)

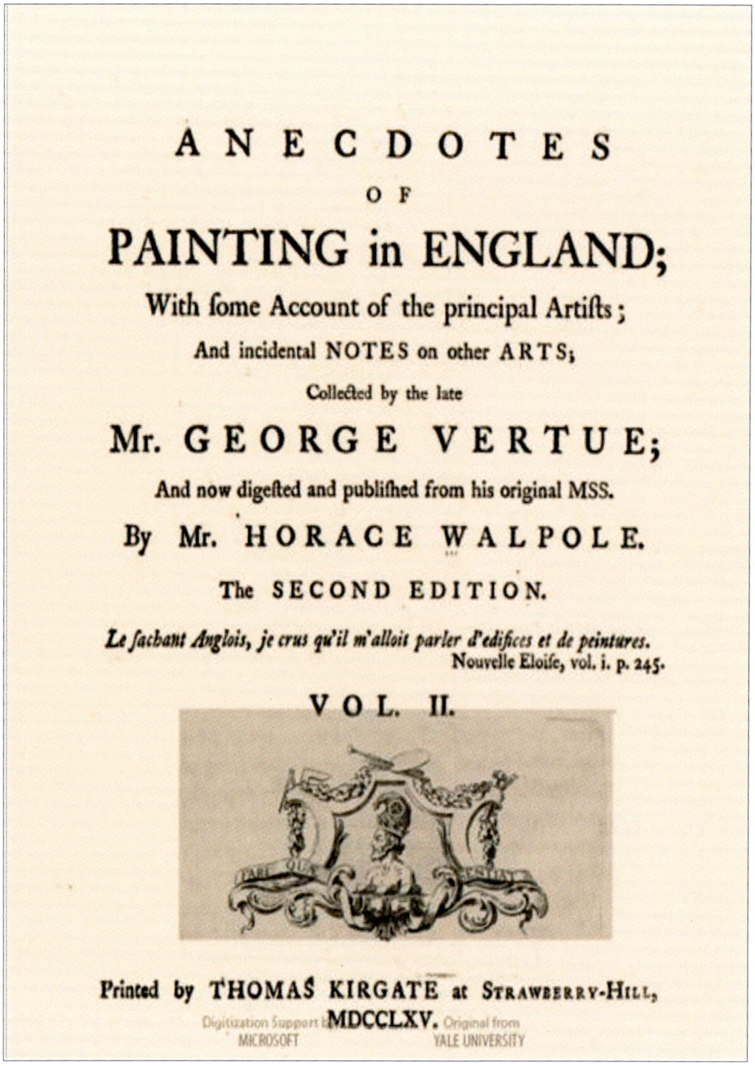

ANECDOTES
OF
PAINTING in ENGLAND;
With ſome Account of the principal Artiſts;
And incidental NOTES on other ARTS;
Collected by the late
Mr. GEORGE VERTUE;
And now digeſted and publiſhed from his original MSS.
By Mr. HORACE WALPOLE.
The SECOND EDITION.
Le ſachant Anglois, je crus qu'il m'alloit parler d'edifices et de peintures.
Nouvelle Eloiſe, vol. i. p. 245.
VOL. II.

Printed by THOMAS KIRGATE at STRAWBERRY-HILL,
MDCCLXV.

THE TITLE PAGE OF VOL. II OF THE VERY RARE SECOND EDITION OF *ANECDOTES OF PAINTING…*, PUBLISHED IN 1765. EVEN RARER IS THE FIRST VOLUME, PUBLISHED IN 1762. IMAGE FROM THE YALE UNIVERSITY COLLECTION, DIGITIZED BY MICROSOFT.

Hill. From 1762 on, Walpole addressed himself to revising and publishing *Anecdotes of Painting…*, the fifth volume of which appeared in 1771.[377] Since its publication, this work has been of great importance to historians of the artistic, political and social life of the 17TH century and earlier.[378]

---

[377] *Anecdotes of Painting…* in its original format, as prepared by GEORGE VERTUE, only appeared in print relatively recently. It was published in six volumes, between 1930 and 1955, by the Walpole Society.

[378] Horace Walpole's correspondence exists as searchable page images of W. S. Lewis' *Yale Edition of Horace Walpole's Correspondence* (1937-83), 48 volumes (Lewis Walpole Library, launched 2010).

A REPRESENTATION OF HORACE WALPOLE'S LIBRARY AS IT APPEARED IN *ANECDOTES OF PAINTING....* ILLUSTRATION FROM THE 1849 ED., VOL. II, P. 643.

Earlier, on August 22, 1758, Walpole had purchased from Vertue's widow more than 40 of the latter's manuscript notebooks which contained his observations on British art and artists to the mid-18th century. There had been rumors about the existence of the notebooks for some years, and Walpole had unsuccessfully searched for them a decade earlier.[379]

Horace Walpole was a dedicated collector of medals as well as of many other kinds of objects. This was evident at the sale of Strawberry Hill and its contents in May 1842. The sale catalogue contained the following preamble by the auctioneer:

> The individual who has received instructions from the Right Honorable the Earl of Waldegrave, to distribute to the world the unrivalled and wondrous Collection at Strawberry Hill, formed by his Lordship's great ancestor, Horace Walpole...approaches his present herculean undertaking with feelings such as he has never experienced on any former occasion, fully sensible that the distribution of this precious museum, crowded with the tangible records of past ages—treasures consecrated by the hand of time and of genius—far exceeding in interest and importance all that has preceded it in the chronicles of auctions, and that no future sale can by possibility enter into rivalry.[380]

The overall auction covered 32 days and realized in excess of £33,000.[381] The coins and medals were sold on the tenth day, May 5, 1842, and consisted of the following: "English patterns and proofs in gold, silver and copper" (32 items in 16 lots) from Edward VI pattern shilling to patterns for Commonwealth farthing and a George III pattern for a Guinea; "Scotch gold and silver coins" (39 items in 6 lots); "English medals in gold" (seven medals in four lots), including.

> The Celebrated Medal of Henry VIII, on his Head side a Latin inscription of his titles, as head of the church, &c., reverse same inscription in Hebrew and Greek. This is of ex

[379] M. Myron (2004). 'Vertue, George (1684–1756),' *Oxford DNB*, online edition., accessed Jan. 2008.

[380] Sale catalogue, 'Prefatory Remarks.'

[381] P. Langford. 'Walpole, Horatio (Horace),' *O.D.N.B*, 2004-2006

> treme rarity, being a struck medal in a high state of preservation. Vide Plate 4, No. 1, Edwards' Medallic History.[382]

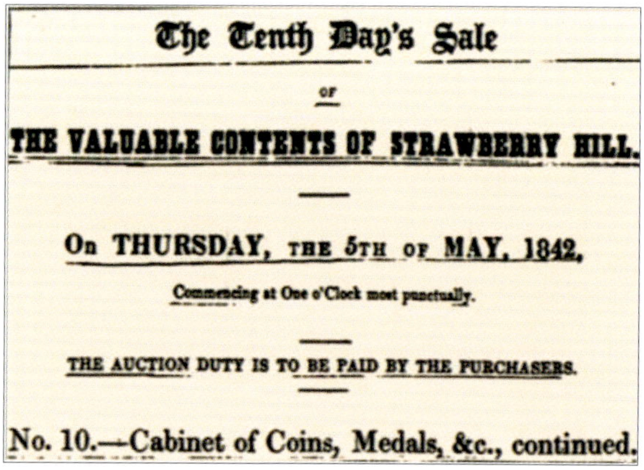
The Tenth Day's Sale
OF
THE VALUABLE CONTENTS OF STRAWBERRY HILL.
On THURSDAY, THE 5TH OF MAY, 1842,
Commencing at One o'Clock most punctually.
THE AUCTION DUTY IS TO BE PAID BY THE PURCHASERS.
No. 10.—Cabinet of Coins, Medals, &c., continued.

THE SALE CATALOGUE HEADING FOR THE SECTION LISTING THE CONTENTS OF HORACE WALPOLE'S CABINET OF COINS AND MEDALS.

More medals continued to be auctioned—"English medals in bronze," (190 medals in 13 lots), "English medals in silver," (155 medals in 44 lots), including the medals of Thomas Wriothesley, Lord Inchiquin, "Abraham and Thomas Simon, most beautifully chased by Stewart"[sic], Lord Kimbolton, reverse his Arms in a Shield …,"[383] These are followed by "Foreign medals in silver, copper, &c." (972 medals in 22 lots), "Foreign silver medals" (52 medals in 11 lots). In addition, there were "foreign coins in silver" (280 coins in 15 lots) and "Foreign gold coins" (145 coins in 25 lots). Overall, the sale of numismatic material consisted of 1,872 items, of which 352 were English medals, and 1,076 foreign medals.

Horace Walpole knew John Pinkerton well and the two met frequently in Walpole's home. They carried on a correspondence on the subject of medals and Pinkerton's publications. In response to Pinkerton's expressed interest in a position at the British Museum, Walpole solicited Sir Joseph Banks on Pinkerton's behalf:

> I wrote a letter to Sir Joseph Banks, soliciting his interest for you, should there be a vacancy at the Museum. He answered (and I will show you his answer when I see you) that he is positively engaged to Mr. Thorkelin, should Mr. Planta resign; but that, the Chancellor having refused to sign the permission for the latter, who will not go abroad without that indulgence, no vacancy is likely to happen from that event. Sir Joseph has since called on me, to make excuses for not complying with my request; and he then told me he thought Mr. Planta might go abroad, with the consent of the Archbishop and Speaker, without the signature of the Chancellor. I do not care about that, which would not promote your interest. I am very sorry, for your sake, that I have none; but I knew as much before.[384]

After this episode, however, Walpole's enthusiasm for Pinkerton appears to have diminished as measured both by the frequency of his letters and their tone.[385]

---

[382] Sale catalogue, 10th day, lot 23. This reference is to JOHN PINKERTON'S *Medallic History…*, 'Edwards' being the name of the publisher. The medal referred to is M.I.I 47/44, dated 1545, which commemorates Henry VIII as the 'Supreme Head of the Church' on what is believed to be the first medal to have been made in Britain (*q.v. p. 25*).

[383] This page from the sale catalogue, with marginal notes of the buyers and the successful bids, is illustrated below on p. 271.

[384] Letter dated Feb. 11, 1788. *See* Turner, *Literary Correspondence*, vol. I, p. 180; also Lewis, *Walpole Correspondence*, vol. 16, pp 294-295 (*q.v. p. 66*).

[385] See, e.g., Walpole's letters to Pinkerton of July 31 and Aug. 19, 1789, and his comment on Pinkerton's undertaking publication of Snelling's work on medals, letter of Oct. 15, 1788. *See this vol., p. 69.*

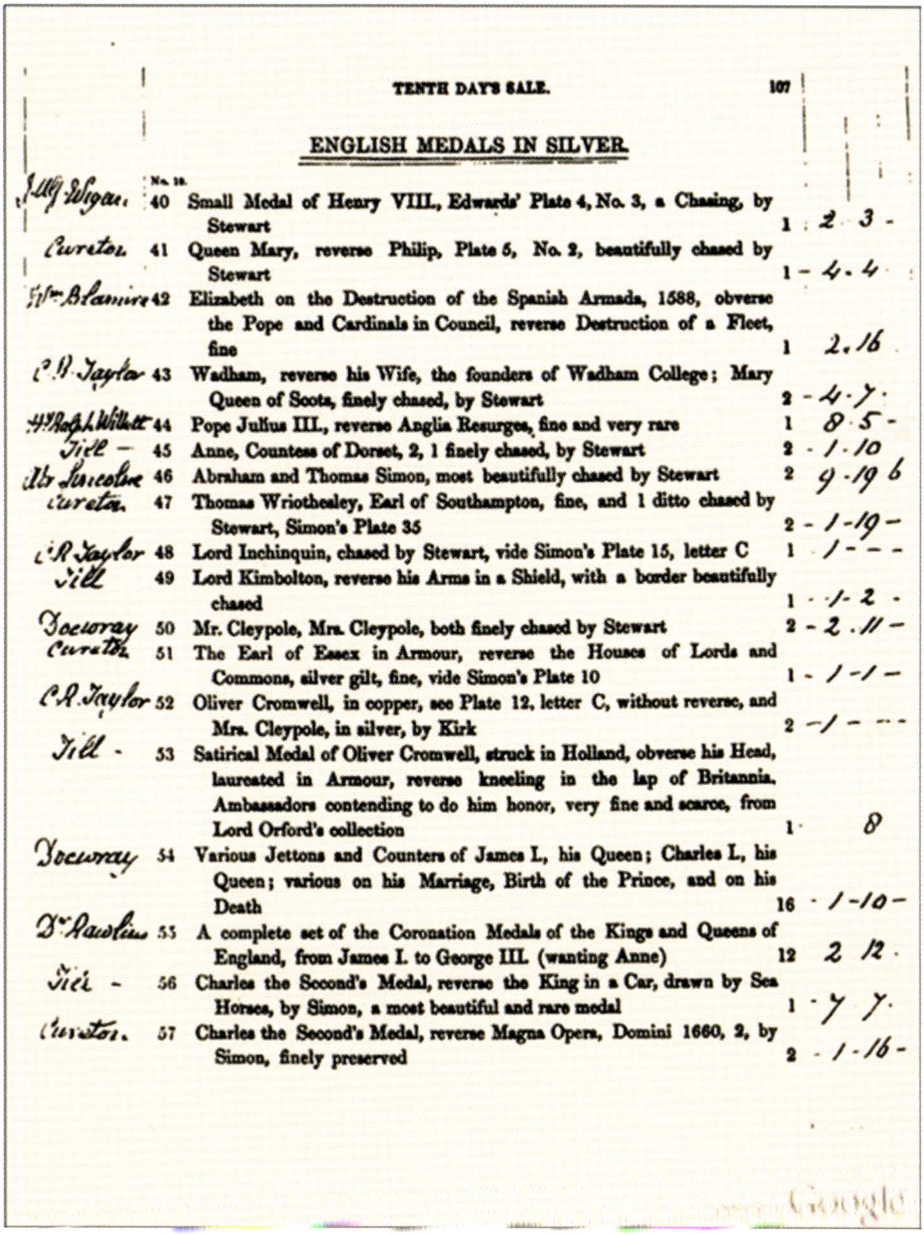

TENTH DAY'S SALE. 107

ENGLISH MEDALS IN SILVER.

Buyer	No.	Lot	Qty.	Price
Jelly Wigan	40	Small Medal of Henry VIII., Edwards' Plate 4, No. 3, a Chasing, by Stewart	1	2 3 -
Cureton	41	Queen Mary, reverse Philip, Plate 5, No. 2, beautifully chased by Stewart	1	4. 4
Wm. Blamire	42	Elizabeth on the Destruction of the Spanish Armada, 1588, obverse the Pope and Cardinals in Council, reverse Destruction of a Fleet, fine	1	2. 16
C. R. Taylor	43	Wadham, reverse his Wife, the founders of Wadham College; Mary Queen of Scots, finely chased, by Stewart	2	4. 7
Mr. Ralph Willett	44	Pope Julius III., reverse Anglia Resurges, fine and very rare	1	8 5 -
Till	45	Anne, Countess of Dorset, 2, 1 finely chased, by Stewart	2	1. 10
Mr. Lincoln	46	Abraham and Thomas Simon, most beautifully chased by Stewart	2	9. 19 6
Cureton	47	Thomas Wriothesley, Earl of Southampton, fine, and 1 ditto chased by Stewart, Simon's Plate 35	2	1. 19 -
C. R. Taylor	48	Lord Inchinquin, chased by Stewart, vide Simon's Plate 15, letter C	1	1 - - -
Till	49	Lord Kimbolton, reverse his Arms in a Shield, with a border beautifully chased	1	1. 2 -
Jocwray	50	Mr. Cleypole, Mrs. Cleypole, both finely chased by Stewart	2	2. 11 -
Cureton	51	The Earl of Essex in Armour, reverse the Houses of Lords and Commons, silver gilt, fine, vide Simon's Plate 10	1	1 - 1 -
C. R. Taylor	52	Oliver Cromwell, in copper, see Plate 12, letter C, without reverse, and Mrs. Cleypole, in silver, by Kirk	2	1 - -
Till	53	Satirical Medal of Oliver Cromwell, struck in Holland, obverse his Head, laureated in Armour, reverse kneeling in the lap of Britannia, Ambassadors contending to do him honor, very fine and scarce, from Lord Orford's collection	1	8
Jocwray	54	Various Jettons and Counters of James I., his Queen; Charles I., his Queen; various on his Marriage, Birth of the Prince, and on his Death	16	1 - 10 -
Dr. Rawlins	55	A complete set of the Coronation Medals of the Kings and Queens of England, from James I. to George III. (wanting Anne)	12	2 12
Till	56	Charles the Second's Medal, reverse the King in a Car, drawn by Sea Horses, by Simon, a most beautiful and rare medal	1	7 7
Cureton	57	Charles the Second's Medal, reverse Magna Opera, Domini 1660, 2, by Simon, finely preserved	2	1. 16 -

A page from the May 5, 1842, Strawberry Hill sale catalogue, with descriptions of several of the medals which were to be sold that day, along with the realized prices and names of the buyers — Till, Taylor and [Richard] Rawlins are names that appear often in priced catalogues for sales of the period which contain medals. Image by Google.

At Walpole's death in 1797 from a cold after a cold spell at Strawberry Hill, the estate, in the absence of male heirs, passed out of the Walpole family to the Cholmondeley family into which his sister Mary had married, and eventually to the Waldegraves, who sold it in 1842.

Walpole's legacy has had its ups and downs. Samuel Egerton Brydges (1762-1837), writing in 1825, commented that:

> In his life, [Walpole's] literary reputation stood, as it surely deserved, very high; but since the lion died, from some strange causes, not yet entirely developed, the tide turned against him, and he has been in many quarters most severely and uncandidly animadverted on.[386]

Very popular and stylish during his lifetime, Walpole's reputation in this regard did not endure for long past his death, and as Langford has pointed out, Boswell, for example, labeled him "genteel, fastidious, priggish." This particular view, however, was likely influenced by Walpole's dislike of Samuel Johnson.[387]

'PORTRAIT OF HORACE WALPOLE.' A PRINT BY T. EVANS (FL. 1797-1812) AFTER A STIPPLE ENGRAVING CA. 1795/96 BY SIR THOMAS LAWRENCE (1769-1830). IMAGE © NATIONAL PORTRAIT GALLERY, LONDON.

Historical Commentary on Horace Walpole

His figure was...not merely tall, but more properly *long* and slender to excess; his complexion and particularly of his hands, of a most pale unhealthiness...His eyes were remarkably bright and penetrating, very dark and lively:—his voice was not strong, but his tones were extremely pleasant, and if I may say, highly gentlemanly...he always entered a room in that style of affected delicacy, which fashion had then made almost natural;—*chapeau bras* between his hands as if he wished to compress it, or under his arm—knees bent, and feet on tip-toe, as if afraid of a wet floor...His dress in visiting was most usually, in summer when I most saw him, a lavender suit, the waistcoat embroidered with a little silver or of white silk worked in the tambour, partridge silk stockings, and gold buckles, ruffles and frill generally lace. I remember... thinking him very much under-dressed, if at any time except in mourning, he wore hemmed fabric. In summer, no powder, but his wig combed straight, and showing his very smooth pale forehead, and queued behind:—in winter powder.

—L. M. Watkins (1822). *Anecdotes, Biographical Sketches and Memoirs*, vol. i, p. 105-106.

§

---

386 E. Lodge (1835). *Portraits of Illustrious Personages of Britain*, vol. xii, pp. 5.

387 I. S. Lustig & F. A. Pottle (eds.). 1986, p. 217; cited by P. Langford, op cit.

Among the MSS in Walpole's library were notebooks and loose papers of the engraver George Vertue, bought from the latter's widow, 22 August 1758. Walpole digested Vertue's rough notes on English painters, engravers, and works of art into his *own Anecdotes of Painting in England*, which is still a principal source for the history of the visual arts in England. Comparison with the notebooks has shown that Walpole's continuous prose is only infrequently close to Vertue's fragmented notes, even in the *Catalogue of Engravers* where Walpole was effectively writing a history which Vertue had seriously contemplated and assembled especially full materials.

— A. Lindsay (1997). *Index of English Literary Manuscripts: Vol. 3: 1700-1800*, London/ Mansell Pubs. for Cassell. Part 2, p. 242.

§

At Rome he had a favourable opportunity of making acquisitions of the objects he so much desired —for three of the principal collections, the Barberini, the Sacchetti, and the Ottoboni, were disposed of during his stay in the Eternal City. He mentions having obtained some curious medals and coins. He bought also some bronzes and medals, a few busts, and two or three pictures. One of the busts was the famous Vespasian, in touchstone, reckoned the best in Rome, except the Caracalla of the Farnese: he gave but twenty-one pounds for it, at Cardinal Ottoboni's sale. One of his medals he thought as great a curiosity: it was of Alexander Severus, with the amphitheatre in brass; this reverse is extant on his medals, but Walpole's purchase was a medagliuncino, or small medallion, and the only one with this reverse then known. It was found by a peasant while he was in Rome, and sold for sixpence to an antiquarian, to whom Walpole paid for it seven guineas and a half.

— E. Warburton (ed.) (1852). *Memoirs of Horace Walpole and His Contemporaries*. vol. 1 p. 291.

The Rev. Clayton Mordaunt Cracherode (1730-1799), a collector of books, prints, coins, medals and natural history whose name appears among collectors of the mid- to late-18th c. period and who was a competitor of Horace Walpole at auctions. A cleric and trustee of the British Museum, he bequeathed his collection to that institution. Fletcher commented that Rev. Cracherode:

> ***...devoted his life to his favourite pursuit, the formation of his collections......[he] lived entirely among his collections, and it is said that he never mounted a horse, nor travelled a greater distance than from London to Oxford*** **(1902, pp. 222-223).**

Cracherode is considered to be second only to Sir Hans Sloane in the importance of his contribution to the building of the British Museum's collections. At his death, Rev. Cratcherode left all but two books of his library of 4,500 volumes to the nation. Among the items donated were 4,500 'remarkable' books, 107 portfolios of drawings and prints, including some by Rembrandt and Dürer, coins and medals (valued at a substantial £6,000), engraved gems, shells and minerals. The remaining items were sold at Sotheby's on the 1st of June, 1805.

The Hunter Prize Medals

The existence of multiple medal types of the two Hunter brothers—William and John, both prominent physicians—can create some confusion; thus information is provided on both men's medals.

·1. The William Hunter Medals·

The [William] Hunter Prize medals have been awarded by the medical faculty of the University of Glasgow since ca. 1774. Their purpose was (and remains) to reward excellence in the medical program of study. The authors have seen a number of variants—the only constant among them being a portrait of Dr. Hunter, *left*, in surgical cap and gown, on the obverse. The obverse and/or reverse inscriptions vary somewhat. There are two basic types of the [William] Hunter Prize medals.

(a) The Hunter Prize medal, Type A, by Edward Burch, R.A., 1774, cast in iron. Other examples have been found in bronzed lead. Eimer lists this medal in silver, copper/bronze, iron and tin. The silver vase or urn depicted on the reverse was presented to Dr. Hunter in 1761. Image © Trustees of the British Museum .

Type A by Edward Burch, R.A. (ca. 1730-1814), cast in iron and bronze,* ca. 1774 (in iron, 70 mm., Cochran-Patrick 109/29, British Museum reg./acc. no. M.4799, M.4800, Eimer 754) and corresponding in description to Cochran-Patrick. For Type A, *top*, the *obv.* bears a portrait of Dr. Hunter with the inscription: 'gvl · hvnter · anatomicvs' (William Hunter, Anatomist), in surgical cap and gown. The *rev.* bears an urn decorated with a scene depicting a dissection, with the date 1774 divided by the vase stem; the motto *olim·meminisse ivvabit* ('time heals all things' *or* 'hereafter, it will be pleasant to remember'). Such a cup was presented to William Hunter in 1761. Signed burch · fec · on the obverse. Some examples of this medal are unnamed and/or undated.

*Cochran-Patrick lists 'bronze and tin.' A silver example sold at auction in 2002 bears on the edge the inscription: 'Anatomical Prize awarded to Mr. Tho. Forder, St. Georges school of Medicine, Session 1851 & 1852.'

(b) The Hunter Prize medal, Type B, by Neil MacPhail, ca. 1870, struck in copper. Eimer lists this medal in silver and copper/bronze.

The *Type B* medal, by Neil MacPhail (1861-1907), struck in silver and copper** (70 mm., Cochran-Patrick 153/11-13, Eimer 806). The Type B medal bears the same *obv.* portrait as the Type A medal, but

(Continued on page 276)

Dr. William Hunter

(1718-1783)

WILLIAM HUNTER was from South Lanarkshire, Scotland. Having studied divinity at the University of Glasgow from ages 13 through 18, he then turned to medicine, and following further training at the University of Edinburgh, he went to London in 1740 to study anatomy. There he made significant contributions as an anatomist and achieved financial and social success as an obstetrician. The physician extraordinary to Queen Charlotte, he was elected to fellowship in the Royal Society and then to a professorship of anatomy at the Royal Academy. From 1746 on, numerous anatomists and obstetricians were trained under him, attending lectures at his private 'anatomy theatre,' and from 1768, at his 'museum' in Great Windmill Street, London. Hunter was among those physicians who created the discipline of obstetrics, which previously had been the provenance of the midwife. Returning to Glasgow, he built a house there in 1770 which evolved into the Hunterian Museum and Art Gallery of the University of Glasgow (1807). The Hunterian Museum celebrated its bicentenary in 2007.[388]

WILLIAM HUNTER, M.D., A STIPPLE ENGRAVING, CA. 1764, MOST LIKELY AFTER THE (1758) PORTRAIT BY ALLAN RAMSAY (1713-1784). DR. HUNTER FORMED A COLLECTION WHICH STILL EXISTS INTACT AT THE HUNTERIAN MUSEUM, UNIVERSITY OF GLASGOW. HE INSISTED ON REPLACING LESS THAN PERFECT PIECES WITH ONES OF BETTER QUALITY WHEN HE COULD, THUS RESULTING IN A COLLECTION OF MAGNIFICENT SPECIMENS. IMAGE © NATIONAL PORTRAIT GALLERY, LONDON.

Hunter was a fervent and eclectic collector of many things, including natural history specimens, especially fossil elephants, and anatomical and pathological specimens. In addition to books and art, including paintings, prints and drawings, his collection of coins and medals was to become the famed 'Hunter Coin Cabinet.' King George III and Horace Walpole both donated choice items to Hunter's cabinet from their own collections. Hunter's collection is considered by some as possibly the finest ever assembled by an individual.

Building the extensive collection that was to form the 'Hunter Coin Cabinet' required not only a deep pocketbook but also agents who could be employed to find and obtain material, as well as experts to advise on and order the collections. Hunter, preferring to buy established collections through private treaty rather than at auction, purchased numerous cabinets belonging to other collectors as well as individual items in this manner. He also made purchases from Thomas Snelling

[388] WILLIAM HUNTER's brother JOHN HUNTER (1728-1793) was also a famed physician in his own right.

THE HUNTER PRIZE MEDALS

(*Continued from p. 274*)

WITH THE INSCRIPTION 'GVILIELMUS·HVNTER·ANATOMICVS. MDCCXVIII•MDCCLXXXIII,' AND SIGNED: 'BURCH FEC.' ON THE REVERSE IS THE INSCRIPTION: 'IN ACADEM. GLASGUENS. FACUTATE MEDICA DISCIPULUS INGENIO AC LABORE INSIGNIS PRŒMIUM HOCCE MERITO CONSECUTUS EST' ('A STUDENT IN THE FACULTY OF MEDICINE OF THE UNIVERSITY OF GLASGOW [WHO IS] DISTINGUISHED BY ABILITY AND EFFORT RECEIVED THIS AWARD FOR MERIT'). THE EXAMPLE ABOVE IS NAMED, HAVING THE DETAILS ENGRAVED IN SMALL CAPITOL LETTERS ON THE EDGE: 'ANDREAS M^CMILLAN, A.M., IN CLASSE GEOLOGICAE, 1904-5.' UNNAMED, UNDATED AND/OR UNSIGNED EXAMPLES OF THE TYPE B MEDAL ALSO EXIST.

·2. The John Hunter Medal·

(C) THE JOHN HUNTER PRIZE MEDAL FOR ACHIEVEMENT IN MEDICINE AND THE BIOLOGICAL SCIENCES, IN COPPER/BRONZE, BY NEIL MACPHAIL.

THERE IS ANOTHER 'HUNTER MEDAL,' TYPE C, SOMEWHAT SIMILAR IN DESIGN, WITH AN IDENTICAL REVERSE TO TYPE B AND ALSO BY NEIL MACPHAIL. THIS MEDAL, BEARING THE PORTRAIT OF JOHN HUNTER (1728-1793; WILLIAM HUNTER'S YOUNGER BROTHER), ON THE OBVERSE, IS ALSO AWARDED BY GLASGOW UNIVERSITY, AND HAS A REVERSE IDENTICAL TO THAT OF THE TYPE B MEDAL. DATED FROM 1793, IT IS 70 MM. AND IS FOUND IN SILVER AND COPPER/BRONZE (EIMER NO. 852).

JOHN HUNTER WAS A RENOWNED ANATOMIST, INNOVATIVE SURGEON AND COLLABORATOR WITH EDWARD JENNER IN THE DISCOVERY OF SMALLPOX INOCULATION. HE ADVOCATED THE SCIENTIFIC METHOD IN INVESTIGATIONS. THERE ARE OTHER 'HUNTER PRIZE MEDALS' AS WELL, INCLUDING ONE AWARDED BY ST. GEORGE'S HOSPITAL, LONDON, AND ANOTHER BY THE UNIVERSITY OF LEEDS (*SEE* EIMER, NO. 806, AND TIMOTHY MILLETT LTD. HISTORICAL MEDALS AND WORKS OF ART, 2003 CATALOGUE, ITEM 520).

** SEE COCHRAN-PATRICK (PL. XXI, NO. 1) FOR AN ILLUSTRATION OF THE MEDAL WITHOUT THE DATE ON THE REVERSE. AN EXAMPLE IN SILVER SOLD AT DIX NOONAN WEBB (DECEMBER 11, 2002, LOT 885) WAS BOTH UNSIGNED AND UNDATED.

and John Kirk, among others. Ultimately, in the purchase of the cabinet built by Matthew Duane, a London lawyer, he is known to have incorporated items from the collections of the earl of Oxford, Richard Mead, and Martin Folkes.[389]

A number of the medals examined in the preparation of the companion volume to the present work[390] are part of the Hunterian collection at Glasgow University. The collection was built by Dr. Hunter between about 1770 and 1783, a relatively short period of time. Yet, it was perhaps unsurpassed up to that point, except possibly by the French and British royal collections. While actively collecting, Hunter spent some £22,000 of his own funds, an enormous amount for the time, equivalent to well over £2,000,000 today, on the acquisition of coins and medals. At his death, Dr. Hunter bequeathed his collection to Glasgow University. In 1807, the major part of his

[389] D. Bateson. 'Great Collectors. William Hunter (1718-1783).' http://inc-cin.org/assets/pdf/articles/ collectors-hunter.pdf. Accessed May 26, 2015.

[390] J. J. Platt & A. K. Platt (2013). *The English Civil Wars*…, op cit.

collection was sent to Glasgow by ship, accompanied by a Royal Navy frigate. A second group of coins and medals deemed to be too valuable to be sent by sea was shipped overland accompanied by an armed escort. The collection contains items in superb condition. The fact that there is absolute certainty that no items have been added to it since its arrival at Glasgow University in 1807 allows the narrowing of estimates of age for specific items in the collection to the years before that date. Dr. Hunter died in 1783, age 64, and was buried in St. James-in-the-Fields Church, Piccadilly.

Historical Commentary on Dr. William Hunter

Dr. Hunter died July 30, 1783; and bequeathed his invaluable Museum to the University of Glasgow. His memory was embalmed, in "An Account of the Life and Writings of the late William Hunter, M. D. F. R. S. and S. A...; read on the 6th of August 1783, at a General Meeting of the Society of Physicians, of which he was President, and published at their Request. By Samuel Foart Simmons, M. D. F. R. S. &c. &c...1783; an elegant little publication, which, at the time, was thus characterized: "The commemoration of a person who deserved highly of a profession in which he attained so eminent a rank, will, we doubt not, be received with pleasure by the Publick. The ingenious Writer seems to have taken due pains to procure correct information relative to his subject; and he has shewn much judgment in proportioning the strictly biographical, to the critical and scientific part of his narration, according to the degree of consequence of each. The piece is (what the memoirs of a professional man should be) no less a sketch of what the recorded person did for the advancement of his peculiar Art or Science, than of what he was as a private character. It is written in an elegant, unaffected style; and incidental matters are occasionally interspersed, which convey curious or instructive information."

—*Monthly Review*, vol. lxx, 155...

A WILLIAM HUNTER PRIZE MEDAL BY EDWARD BURCH ('TYPE A'; EIMER NO. 754). FROM A. DURAND, *MÉDAILLES ET JETONS DES NUMISMATES*, 1865, PL. VI.

§

"*Nummorum Veterum Populorum et Urbium qui in Musæo Gulielmi Hunter asservanteur Descriptio, Figuris illustrata. Operâ et Studio Caroli Combe, S. R. et S. A. Londini Socio.*" This Work contains accurate descriptions, and good engravings, of a vast number of medals, collected with much industry, and at a great expence, by the late Dr. Hunter. The Medals are arranged in alphabetical order, according to the names of the Nations and Cities to which they belong.—The descriptive part, short as it is, 'takes up 354 pages; and is followed by the engravings, which are very well executed by Mr. Charles Taylor, and exact copies of the originals.—Mr. Combe, in his Preface to this Work, gives an account of the nature of it, of the rise and progress of Dr. Hunter's Museum, together with the names of those gentlemen whose contributions enriched it—*Monthly Review*, vol. LXVIII, p. 436.

—J. Nichols & S. Bentley, *Literary Anecdotes of the Eighteenth Century*..., 1812, vol. viii, pp. 121-122.

§

The Hunter brothers were like squirrels amassing large quantities of various medical and non-medical curiosities. William Hunter's collection of anatomical and pathological specimens range from the mundane to the exotica. His book collection consisted of some 10,000 volumes, including 534 incunabula.

—W. W. Buchanan, "William Hunter (1718–1783)," *Rheumatology*, 2003, vol. 42, pp. 1260-1261.

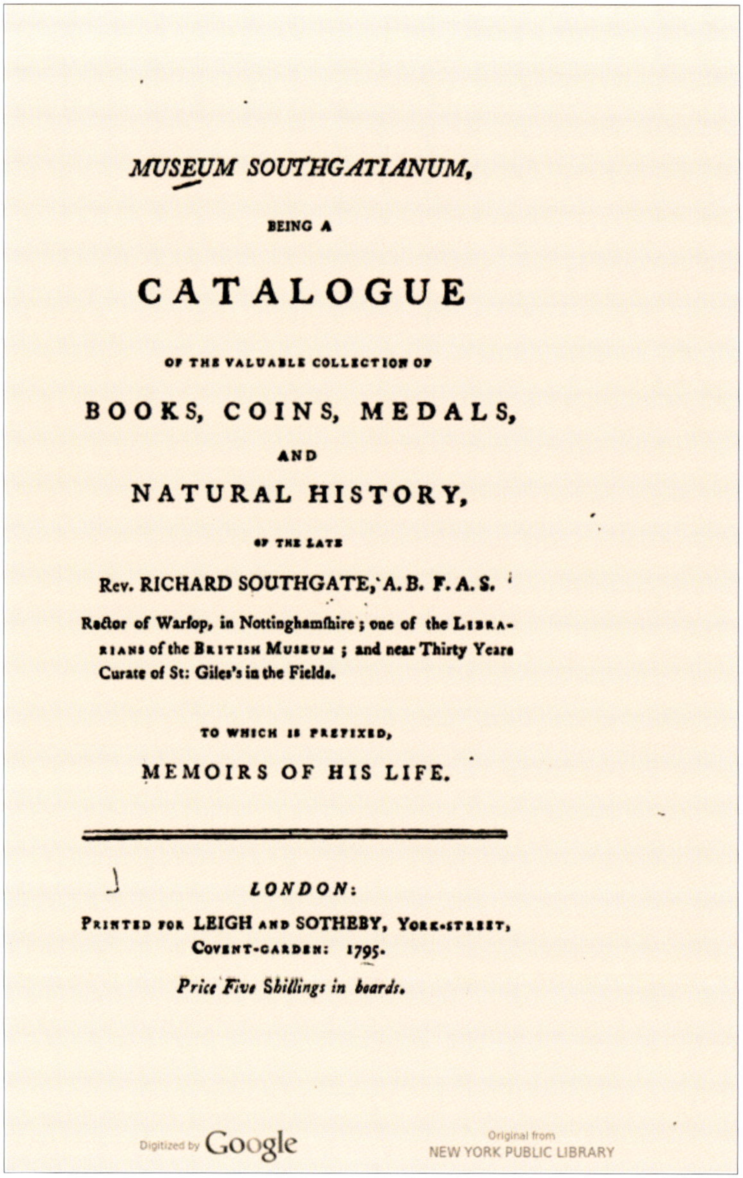

MUSEUM SOUTHGATIANUM,

BEING A

CATALOGUE

OF THE VALUABLE COLLECTION OF

BOOKS, COINS, MEDALS,

AND

NATURAL HISTORY,

OF THE LATE

Rev. RICHARD SOUTHGATE, A. B. F. A. S.

Rector of Warsop, in Nottinghamshire; one of the LIBRARIANS of the BRITISH MUSEUM; and near Thirty Years Curate of St: Giles's in the Fields.

TO WHICH IS PREFIXED,

MEMOIRS OF HIS LIFE.

LONDON:

PRINTED FOR LEIGH AND SOTHEBY, YORK-STREET, COVENT-GARDEN: 1795.

Price Five Shillings in boards.

THE TITLE PAGE FROM LEIGH AND SOTHEBY'S SALE CATALOGUE FOR *MUSEUM SOUTHGATIANUM,* WHICH CONTAINS REV. SOUTHGATE'S COLLECTION OF COINS & MEDALS, DIVIDED INTO EIGHT DAY SALES. EXAMINATION OF THE CATALOGUE REVEALS VERY FEW ENGLISH MEDALS; HOWEVER, THE REV. SOUTHGATE'S COLLECTING ACTIVITIES WERE VERY TYPICAL OF GENTLEMEN-COLLECTORS OF THE PERIOD AND A GOOD DEAL OF DOCUMENTATION EXISTS CONCERNING THEM. FROM 1784 TO 1795 SOUTHGATE WAS RESPONSIBLE FOR THE COIN AND MEDAL COLLECTIONS AT THE BRITISH MUSEUM. IMAGE DIGITIZED BY GOOGLE.

The Rev. Mr. Richard Southgate

(1729-1795)

BORN at Alwalton, Huntingdonshire, Southgate's father was a 'farmer,' but he must have been a prosperous one, for young Richard received a private education followed by matriculation at St John's College, Cambridge. Never having married, he served first as a curate in a number of parishes primarily in Lincolnshire and in 1763 took the position of curate of St James's, Westminster, soon moving to St. Giles-in-the-Fields, London. A collector of books, coins, medals and natural history, Southgate received an acknowledgement from John Pinkerton for his assistance in the latter's preparation of *An Essay on Medals* (1784).

THE REV. RICHARD SOUTHGATE AT AGE 55. THE ILLUSTRATION, CA. 1784, WHICH WAS ENGRAVED BY THOMAS TROTTER (CA. 1750–1803). IT IS A PROOF OF THE FRONTISPIECE FOR *MUSEUM SOUTHGATIANUM* (1795), THE SALE CATALOGUE FOR SOUTHGATE'S COLLECTION(S). IMAGE © TRUSTEES OF THE BRITISH MUSEUM.

Offered the position, in 1784, of assistant librarian in the Department of Manuscripts at the British Museum, with responsibility for its coin collection, Southgate accepted it and literally spent the remainder of his life there, living at the Museum and in 1795, dying there. After his death, his collections, excluding coins and medals, totaling some 2,599 lots, were sold by Leigh & Sotheby in a sale which covered some twelve days. The scheduled eight-day follow-on sale of his coins and medals was cancelled when the better part of the collection was purchased *en bloc* by Samuel Tyssen.[391] That the collection was of interest to Mr. Tyssen, a very serious collector, confirms the opinion given by Southgate's biographer to the effect that:

> [The] ENGLISH AND FOREIGN MEDALS [in Southgate's collection are] of the finest preservation and among them some of the greatest rarity ('Memoirs...,' in the *Museum Southgatianum* catalogue, Leigh & Sotheby, 1795, p. xx).

[391] The year before, in 1794, SAMUEL TYSSEN had also purchased THOMAS SNELLING'S collection. In 1802, the Trustees of the British Museum acquired a substantial part of Tyssen's collection through purchase

Historical Commentary on the Rev. Mr. Southgate

The reverend Mr. Southgate, who to much learning adds the inferior praise of an eminent skill in medals, possesses, in his chosen cabinet, as neat and complete a series of this kind as is perhaps to be found.

— John Pinkerton, *An Essay on Medals*, 1784, pp. 84-85.

§

His finances were small; but, having no pride, very little ambition, and great prudence, he was able, even at that time, to begin his collections of Books and Coins; and though what he bought of the latter were of little value, yet so nice was his taste, that he never purchased any which were not in the highest preservation and perfection (p. 362).

Mr. Southgate now began to find himself in tolerably easy circumstances; and by the death of a near relation, in 1786, he became heir to an estate of 100*l.* a-year in Whitechapel. This addition to his income allowed him to indulge his inclination for buying books and coins in a manner more suitable to his taste; for though he never bought any books but of the best edition, and in good condition, yet they were confined to the more useful and least expensive. Now, being long accustomed to habits of œconomy, which he ever retained, he was able to purchase such as were more ornamental and of a higher price (p. 367).

—J. Nichols & S. Bentley (1812). *Literary Anecdotes, of the Eighteenth Century...,* vol. 6, pt. i.

§

Both Samuel Tyssen and John Pinkerton were associated with the Rev. Richard Southgate. Comments regarding these associations with Dr. Southgate appear in DNB, Nichols & Bentley's Literary Anecdotes *and Southgate's obituary:*

On Christmas-day 1765 [Rev. Southgate] accepted the same position at St. Giles-in-the-Fields, London, and held it for the rest of his days. On settling in London Southgate took pupils in classics, and with his augmented income collected books, coins, and medals...

In medallic science few could be compared with [Southgate], and he owned 'the most neat and complete series' of English pennies to be found in this country. He materially assisted Pinkerton in his 'Essay on Medals' (1784). Considerable collections were made by him for a 'History of the Saxons and Danes in England,' illustrated by their coins, but the work was not completed.

Southgate's books and prints were sold by Leigh & Sotheby in 2,599 lots on 27 April 1795 and eleven following days, and fetched 1,332*l.* 12*s.* His coins and medals were announced for sale in eight days, but, according to Nichols, they passed by private contract to Samuel Tyssen. The shells and natural curiosities were sold on 12 and 13 May 1795. Each catalogue was printed separately, and the whole was bound up with life prefixed by Dr. Charles Combe, as 'Museum Southgatianum.'[392] The frontispiece was a medallion portrait of him at the age of fifty-five.

—*Dictionary of National Biography,* 1898, vol.53, p. 291.

§

As to his medallic knowledge, very few were to be compared with him; and it was from this source that his historical knowledge was so considerable, and from his mode of collecting that it was so well retained. He was well acquainted both with the early and modern English Poets, as well as the prose writers, and was extremely well informed about the ecclesiastical history of this country, the various religious disputes, and the characters of the persons who were principally concerned in them; and had rather more than a superficial knowledge of natural history and the Linnæan system. He left behind him a choice and very valuable collection of books, coins, medals, shells, and other natural curiosities, which, in April and May 1795 were sold by auction, by Messrs. Leigh and Sotheby, the sale continuing 21 days. The books consisted of the best editions, fine copies mostly, in excellent condition, and many in superb bindings. The coins and medals, the knowledge of which he was singularly eminent and accurate so as to be equaled by very few persons, if any.

---

[392] *Museum Southgatianum, Being a Catalogue of the Valuable Collection of Books, Coins, Medals, and Natural History, by Rev. Richard Southgate, A.B., F.A.S., Rector of Warsop, in Nottinghamshire, one of the librarians of the British Museum; and near thirty years Curate of St: Giles's in the Field to Which Is prefixed Memoirs of his Life.* London: Printed for Leigh and Sotheby, Covent-Garden, 1795 (Price Five Shillings in boards).

fn.: Of these the most valuable part was purchased by Samuel Tyssen, esq. F. R. S. and F. S. A. well known among the lovers of literary virtu...(*q.v. Samuel Tyssen, pp. 289 ff.*).

—Ibid. pp 377-378.

§

[The Rev. Southgate] left -five brothers; and, dying intestate, his valuable Library was sold by Messrs. Leigh and Sotheby in the month of April following. His Cabinet of Coins and Medals was purchased, by private contract, by Samuel Tyssen, esq. of Yarborough Hall in Norfolk; at whose decease they were dispersed by public auction, together with his own magnificent Collection, in York-street, Covent Garden, April and May 1802.

—*Literary Anecdotes..*, 1812, v. 6, pt. i, p. 113.

§§§§

THERE is a disposition in the human mind, which leads us to inquire, with some avidity, into the Lives and Characters of those who have raised, in an eminent degree, either the esteem or admiration of their Friends or Country.

—Anon., 'Memoirs of the Life of the Rev. Richard Southgate.' A biographical sketch of his life which introduces the sales catalogue for the auction of his collection of books, coins, medals and natural history. Leigh & Sotheby, 1795.

§

[REV. Southgate] was an excellent medallist, and was engaged in drawing up an account of Dr. Hunter's Saxon coins. In numismatic knowledge he stood almost unrivalled... His knowledge of books was considerable; and he was employed by the Trustees of the British Museum in making purchases of many curious articles.

—*Literary Anecdotes..*, 1812, v. 6, pt. i, p. 112-113 fn.

Edward Burch, R.A. (1730-1814)

Burch, the medallist responsible for William Hunter's 1774 medal, is an interesting personality. He was a self-taught miniaturist and seal-engraver who started life as a waterman on the Thames, later advancing in life to election as a member of the Royal Academy. During his career, Burch worked for both James Tassie and Josiah Wedgewood and also made seals for Sir Joshua Reynolds. This gilded cameo bearing a likeness of Burch (British Museum acc./reg. no. 1887,0307,I.6) was made at the Wedgewood factory, ca. 1785-1795, and donated to the British Museum by Sir A. W. Franks in 1887. Image ©Trustees of the British Museum.

Before …*Medallic Illustrations*…

THE MODERN COLLECTOR MAY WONDER WHAT 'STANDARD SOURCES' THE SERIOUS COLLECTOR OF BRITISH MEDALS CONSULTED BEFORE THE PUBLICATION *OF MEDALLIC ILLUSTRATIONS* IN 1885. A PARTIAL ANSWER IS PROVIDED IN THE SALE CATALOGUE FOR THE PEMBROKE COLLECTION FORMED BY THOMAS HERBERT (1656-1733), THE 8TH EARL OF PEMBROKE AND 5TH EARL OF MONTGOMERY. PRECEDING THE SMALL GROUPING OF ENGLISH MEDALS IN THE SALE, HELD IN JULY AND AUGUST, 1848, IS THE FOLLOWING 'NOTE' (*RIGHT*):

CATALOGUE

OF

THE ENTIRE

PEMBROKE COLLECTION

OF

GREEK, ROMAN, ENGLISH, SCOTCH, IRISH,

AND FOREIGN MEDIÆVAL

COINS AND MEDALS,

As published in 1746, 4to, under the following Title:—

" Numismata Antiqua, in tres partes divisa. Collegit olim et æri incidi vivens curavit THOMAS PEMBROCHIÆ ET MONTIS GOMERICI COMES. Prelo demum mandabantur, A. D. MDCCXLVI."

WHICH WILL BE SOLD BY AUCTION,

BY MESSRS.

S. LEIGH SOTHEBY & CO.

AUCTIONEERS OF LITERARY PROPERTY AND WORKS ILLUSTRATIVE OF THE FINE ARTS

AT THEIR HOUSE, 3, WELLINGTON STREET, STRAND,

On MONDAY, 31st of JULY, 1848, and Eleven following Days, (Sunday excepted) at One o'Clock precisely each day.

To be Viewed on the Thursday, Friday, and Saturday previous to the Sale, from Ten o'clock in the Morning until Four in the Afternoon, and also on the Mornings of the Sale until Twelve o'clock.

J. DAVY & SONS, Printers, 137, Long Acre.

ENGLISH MEDALS,

IN GOLD, SILVER, AND COPPER.

NOTE.—The reference *Snel.* is to the 33 plates of English Medals prepared for publication by Snelling, and published in 1776, after his decease, without letter-press. The reference *Pink.* is to the plates of the anonymous work by John Pinkerton, entitled "*The Medallic History of England to the Revolution, with 40 plates,*" London, 4to. 1790; most of the plates in this work are the same which were prepared for publication by Snelling, but are numbered differently.

252 SILVER. Henry VIII. *obv. m. m.* rose, or cinquefoil, HENRIC'. 8. DI'. GRA'. ANGL'. FRANC'. Z. HIB'., the King's Bust, to the waist, in armour, and crowned; seen nearly full face, but to *r.*; sword in *r.* hand; orb and cross in *l.* *rev.* PARCERE. SVBIECTIS. ET. DEBELLA'. SVPBOS., an heraldic Lion passant, to *l.*, his fore paw resting on the orb and cross; in the *exergue*, two small scrolls with foliage. *Pink.* iv. 3. *Snel. Medals, pl.* iii. *Pemb. p.* 4, *t.* 43. *well preserved, and presumed to be unique.* - *size* 9. *wt.* $78\frac{6}{10}$ *grs.* 1

∴ In the Pembroke Plates this very early medal is called, "*the first English Medal.*" The inscription, from Virgil, on the reverse, recurs on the very rare Scottish Gold Coin of James VI, forming lot 189, page 38.

THE AUCTION CATALOGUE NOTE READS:

"THE REFERENCE SNEL. *IS TO THE 33 PLATES OF* ENGLISH MEDALS *PREPARED FOR PUBLICATION BY* SNELLING, *AND PUBLISHED IN 1776, AFTER HIS DECEASE, WITHOUT LETTER-PRESS. THE REFERENCE* PINK. *IS TO THE PLATES OF THE ANONYMOUS WORK BY* JOHN PINKERTON, *ENTITLED* "THE MEDALLIC HISTORY OF ENGLAND TO THE REVOLUTION, WITH 40 PLATES," *LONDON 4TO. 1790; MOST OF THE PLATES IN THIS WORK ARE THE SAME WHICH WERE PREPARED FOR PUBLICATION BY SNELLING, BUT WERE NUMBERED DIFFERENTLY."*

AND BELOW, IN THE DESCRIPTION FOR ITEM 252:

IN THE PEMBROKE PLATES THIS VERY EARLY MEDAL IS CALLED, "THE FIRST ENGLISH MEDAL." *THE INSCRIPTION, FROM VERGIL, ON THE REVERSE, RECURS ON THE VERY RARE SCOTTISH GOLD COIN OF JAMES VI, FORMING LOT 189, PAGE 38.**

§

THE PEMBROKE COLLECTION HAD PREVIOUSLY BEEN EXTENSIVELY CATALOGUED BY ITS OWNER, HENRY HERBERT, THE 9TH EARL, IN 1746. IT WAS ONLY ONE OF A NUMBER OF SUCH CATALOGUES WHICH HE HAD COMMISSIONED TO INVENTORY THE HUGE COLLECTION, THE FORMATION OF WHICH DATED BACK TO PHILIP HERBERT, THE 4TH EARL. THAT EARL HAD BEEN A PATRON OF ARTISTS AND WRITERS, INCLUDING SUCH LUMINARIES AS ANTHONY VAN DYCK, INIGO JONES AND WILLIAM GIBSON, THE MINIATURIST. WILLIAM SHAKESPEARE'S FIRST FOLIO OF COLLECTED WORKS IS DEDICATED TO PHILIP HERBERT AND HIS BROTHER WILLIAM.

*AN ILLUSTRATION OF THIS MEDAL APPEARS ON P. 25 OF THE PRESENT VOLUME.

Thomas Dimsdale

(1758-1823)

THOMAS DIMSDALE, the youngest son of Dr. Thomas Dimsdale (1712-1800), the physician who had vaccinated Queen Catherine II of Russia against smallpox, was an avid collector of coins, medals, books, drawings and paintings. His collection, for example, included drawings by Michelangelo and Raphael. Like many other eminent collectors, Dimsdale competed vigorously with his collecting peers for items that came onto the market, and purchased entire collections or at the very least the most important works in them. Even while seriously ill, Dimsdale purchased many important works through the dealer Samuel Woodburn.[393] Following his death, Dimsdale's rival collector, Sir Thomas Lawrence,[394] acquired many important pieces from Dimsdale's collection through Woodburn. In 1824, following his death the previous year, his wide-ranging collections came up for sale at Sotheby's. His collection of books, coins and medals was dispersed at auction—the library in June, and the coins and medals in July. An important collection, the latter sold "at most extraordinary and unheard-of prices."[395]

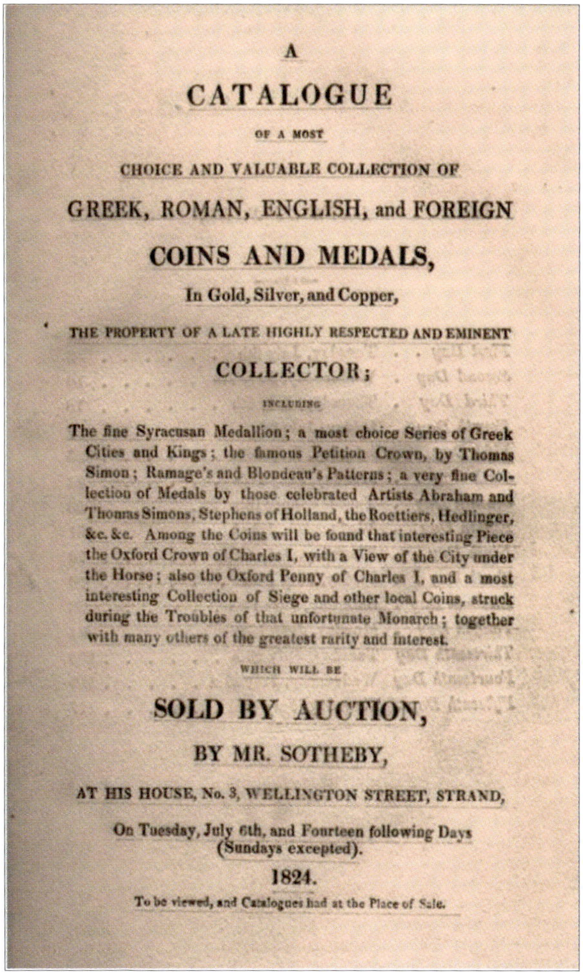

A
CATALOGUE
OF A MOST
CHOICE AND VALUABLE COLLECTION OF
GREEK, ROMAN, ENGLISH, and FOREIGN
COINS AND MEDALS,
In Gold, Silver, and Copper,
THE PROPERTY OF A LATE HIGHLY RESPECTED AND EMINENT
COLLECTOR;
INCLUDING
The fine Syracusan Medallion; a most choice Series of Greek Cities and Kings; the famous Petition Crown, by Thomas Simon; Ramage's and Blondeau's Patterns; a very fine Collection of Medals by those celebrated Artists Abraham and Thomas Simons, Stephens of Holland, the Roettiers, Hedlinger, &c. &c. Among the Coins will be found that interesting Piece the Oxford Crown of Charles I, with a View of the City under the Horse; also the Oxford Penny of Charles I, and a most interesting Collection of Siege and other local Coins, struck during the Troubles of that unfortunate Monarch; together with many others of the greatest rarity and interest.
WHICH WILL BE
SOLD BY AUCTION,
BY MR. SOTHEBY,
AT HIS HOUSE, No. 3, WELLINGTON STREET, STRAND,
On Tuesday, July 6th, and Fourteen following Days (Sundays excepted).
1824.
To be viewed, and Catalogues had at the Place of Sale.

THE TITLE PAGE OF THE CATALOGUE FOR THE SALE BY AUCTION, BEGINNING ON JULY 6, 1824, AT SOTHEBY'S, OF THOMAS DIMSDALE'S COLLECTION OF COINS AND MEDALS. UNDOUBTEDLY, THE BRIEF SYNOPSIS ON THE COVER WOULD DRAW MANY ATTENDEES TODAY.

393 SAMUEL WOODBURN (1783-1853) a well-known and perhaps 'principal' dealer of portraits and prints at the time, did business at 112 St Martin's Lane and then Park Lane. He lived at 184 Piccadilly.

394 SIR THOMAS LAWRENCE (1769-1830), self-taught portraitist to 'polite society' and the royal family.

395 Stewartby, (Lord) (1996). 'Scottish Coin Collectors,' *BNJ*, vol. 287, p. 95.

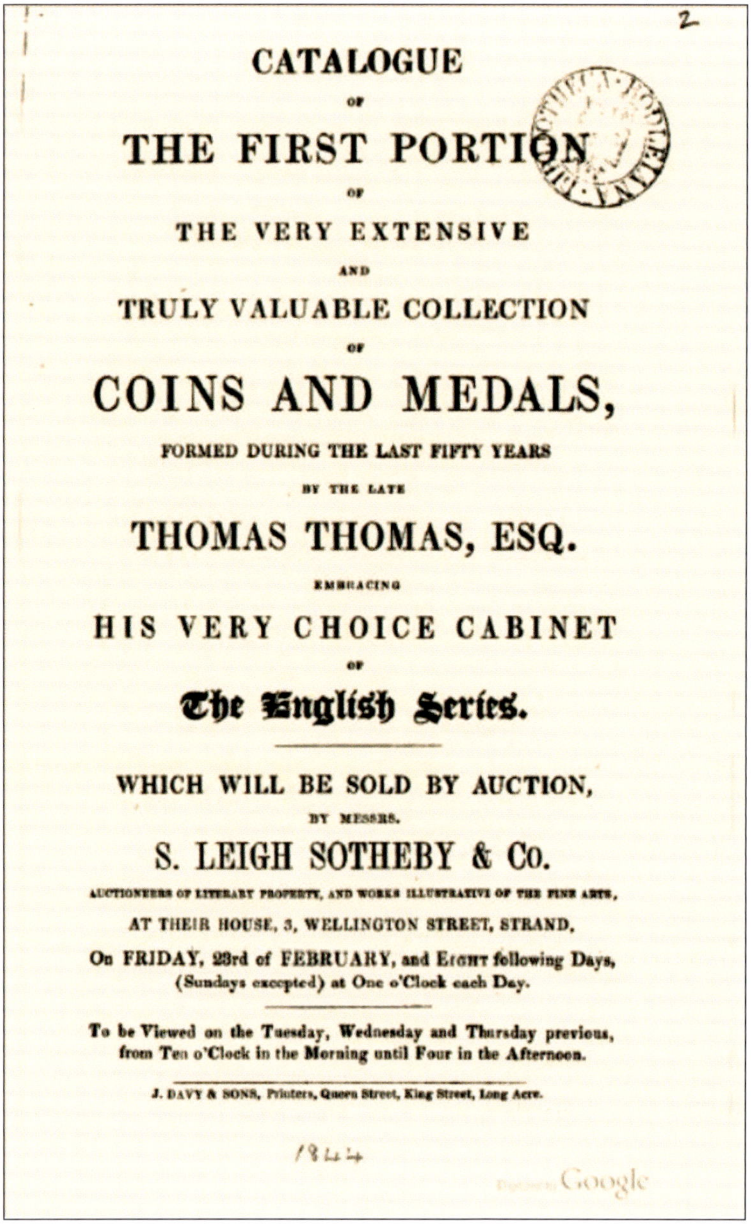

CATALOGUE

OF

THE FIRST PORTION

OF

THE VERY EXTENSIVE

AND

TRULY VALUABLE COLLECTION

OF

COINS AND MEDALS,

FORMED DURING THE LAST FIFTY YEARS

BY THE LATE

THOMAS THOMAS, ESQ.

EMBRACING

HIS VERY CHOICE CABINET

OF

The English Series.

WHICH WILL BE SOLD BY AUCTION,

BY MESSRS.

S. LEIGH SOTHEBY & Co.

AUCTIONEERS OF LITERARY PROPERTY, AND WORKS ILLUSTRATIVE OF THE FINE ARTS,

AT THEIR HOUSE, 3, WELLINGTON STREET, STRAND,

On FRIDAY, 23rd of FEBRUARY, and EIGHT following Days,
(Sundays excepted) at One o'Clock each Day.

To be Viewed on the Tuesday, Wednesday and Thursday previous,
from Ten o'Clock in the Morning until Four in the Afternoon.

J. DAVY & SONS, Printers, Queen Street, King Street, Long Acre.

1844

THE TITLE PAGE OF THE SALE CATALOGUE FOR THE FIRST PART OF THOMAS THOMAS' COLLECTION. THE COLLECTION HAD BEEN FORMED OVER HALF A CENTURY AND CONTAINED MANY SEVENTEENTH CENTURY MEDALS IN GOLD. IMAGE BY GOOGLE.

Thomas Thomas

(?-d. 1843)

THOMAS THOMAS, Esq., was a green grocer and tea dealer in Oxford Street, London. His collection of coins and medals, noted by the cataloguer to have been formed over 50 years, was dispersed in 1844 by Leigh & Sotheby's in three auctions which covered a total of 34 days. Three separate catalogues were issued—the first sale began on February 23, 1844, and took nine days. The catalogue described the sale as including a:

> ...very extensive and truly valuable collection of coins and medals.

The second sale began on July 8, 1844, lasted 12 days and consisted of the first portion of Greek, Roman, and foreign medieval coins and medals. The third sale commenced on July 29, 1844, was 13 days in length, and covered the same categories.

When one examines the entries for 17th century items in the sales catalogues, it is immediately apparent that in addition to Mr. Thomas' collection having been large, it was also comprised of items of extraordinary rarity and apparent quality. It is surprising that this collection (and auction) remains relatively unknown. One reason may be that few copies of the auction catalogue have survived and thus they themselves are rare.

A PROOF OF A STIPPLE AND ETCHED ENGRAVING OF THOMAS THOMAS, ESQ., BY H. A. OGG, HOLDING A COIN OR MEDAL IN HIS RIGHT HAND, PRINTED BY A. ARCHER. IMAGE COURTESY DIX NOONAN WEBB, LTD.

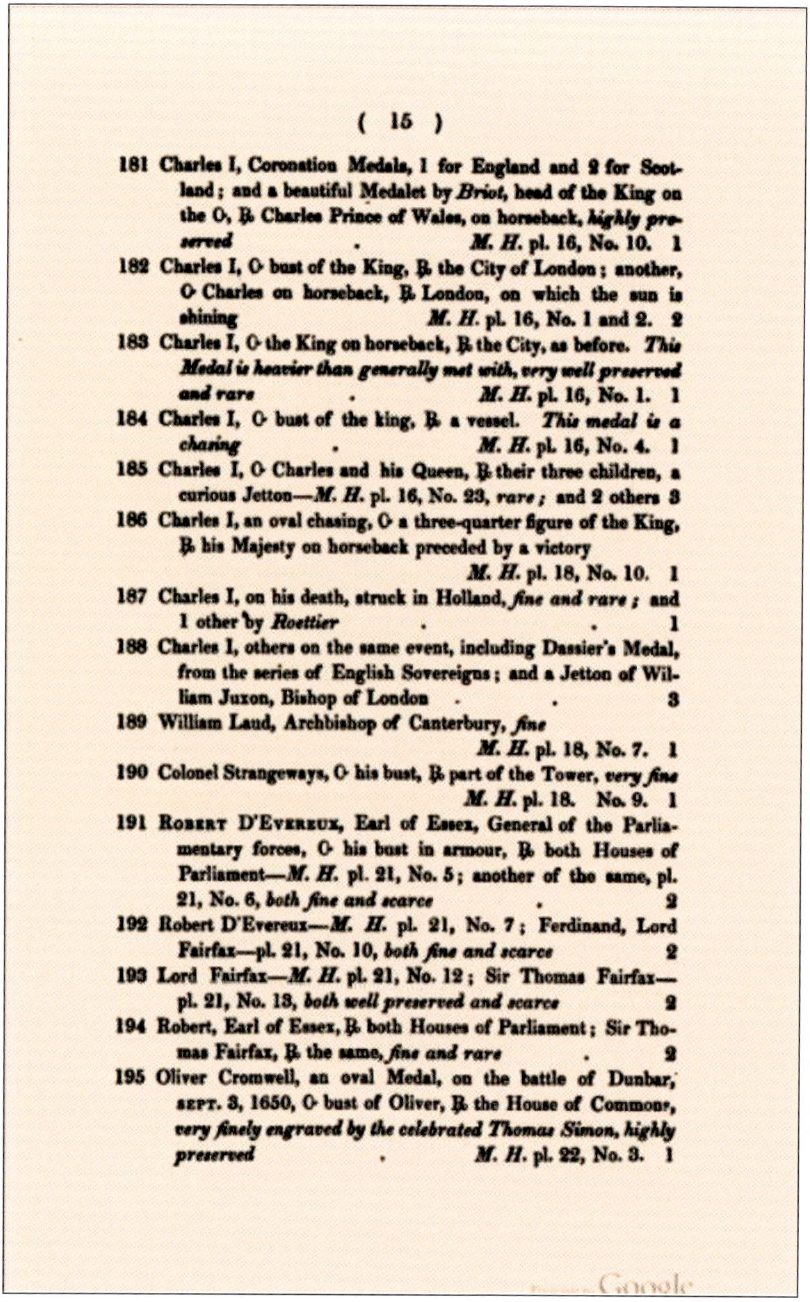
(15)

181 Charles I, Coronation Medals, 1 for England and 2 for Scotland; and a beautiful Medalet by *Briot*, head of the King on the O, ℞ Charles Prince of Wales, on horseback, *highly preserved* . *M. H.* pl. 16, No. 10. 1

182 Charles I, O bust of the King, ℞ the City of London; another, O Charles on horseback, ℞ London, on which the sun is shining *M. H.* pl. 16, No. 1 and 2. 2

183 Charles I, O the King on horseback, ℞ the City, as before. *This Medal is heavier than generally met with, very well preserved and rare* . *M. H.* pl. 16, No. 1. 1

184 Charles I, O bust of the king, ℞ a vessel. *This medal is a chasing* . *M. H.* pl. 16, No. 4. 1

185 Charles I, O Charles and his Queen, ℞ their three children, a curious Jetton—*M. H.* pl. 16, No. 23, *rare;* and 2 others 3

186 Charles I, an oval chasing, O a three-quarter figure of the King, ℞ his Majesty on horseback preceded by a victory *M. H.* pl. 18, No. 10. 1

187 Charles I, on his death, struck in Holland, *fine and rare;* and 1 other by *Roettier* . . 1

188 Charles I, others on the same event, including Dassier's Medal, from the series of English Sovereigns; and a Jetton of William Juxon, Bishop of London . . 3

189 William Laud, Archbishop of Canterbury, *fine* *M. H.* pl. 18, No. 7. 1

190 Colonel Strangeways, O his bust, ℞ part of the Tower, *very fine* *M. H.* pl. 18. No. 9. 1

191 Robert D'Evereux, Earl of Essex, General of the Parliamentary forces, O his bust in armour, ℞ both Houses of Parliament—*M. H.* pl. 21, No. 5; another of the same, pl. 21, No. 6, *both fine and scarce* . 2

192 Robert D'Evereux—*M. H.* pl. 21, No. 7; Ferdinand, Lord Fairfax—pl. 21, No. 10, *both fine and scarce* 2

193 Lord Fairfax—*M. H.* pl. 21, No. 12; Sir Thomas Fairfax—pl. 21, No. 13, *both well preserved and scarce* 2

194 Robert, Earl of Essex, ℞ both Houses of Parliament; Sir Thomas Fairfax, ℞ the same, *fine and rare* . 2

195 Oliver Cromwell, an oval Medal, on the battle of Dunbar, sept. 3, 1650, O bust of Oliver, ℞ the House of Commons, *very finely engraved by the celebrated Thomas Simon, highly preserved* . *M. H.* pl. 22, No. 3. 1

A page from the sale of the Thomas Thomas collection showing Charles I and Civil War period medals in silver which were sold in July 1844. 'M. H.' refers to Pinkerton's *Medallic History*... Image by Google.

(33)

ENGLISH MEDALS. GOLD.

See Medallic History of England.

446 Henry VIII, O profile portrait of the king, head decorated with a bonnet, and his bust with a collar of rubies, surrounded with name and title, as defender of the faith and head of the church, under Christ, ℞ two inscriptions, one in Hebrew and the other in Greek, bearing the same meaning, *very well preserved, and of great rarity—weight,* 1 *oz.* 9 *dwts.* 12 *grs.* *M. H.* pl. 4, No. 1. 1

*** From the Strawberry Hill Collection.

447 Mary I, O head of the queen, ℞ her consort, Philip of Spain. *The likenesses of both are faithfully portrayed, and finely engraved by Trezo, very similar to M. H.* No. 2, pl. 5, *only differing in having their names and titles; very well preserved, and extremely scarce weight,* 1 *oz.* 21 *grs.* 1

448 Elizabeth, on the dispersion of the Spanish Armada, O an assembly of Catholics, ℞ vessels in a storm, *fine and very rare—weighing* 1 *oz.* 19 *dwts.* 12 *grs.* *M. H.* pl. 8, No. 7. 1

449 Elizabeth, a Jetton, O head of the queen, with portcullis and rose, ℞ a castle and globe, *rare and very fine—weight,* 2 *dwts.* 14 *grs.* *M. H.* pl. 8, No. 3. 1

450 Robert Dudley, Earl of Leicester, a fine oval engraving, with his bust, &c. *elegantly adorned;* plain ℞; *highly preserved and very rare size,* 2½ *in. by* 2¼*—weight,* 15 *dwts.* 19 *grs.* 1

451 Mary Queen of Scots, *an exquisite engraving,* on an oval plate, 3 in. by 2½, having the portrait of the queen in the elegant costume of her day, *in fine preservation weight,* 18 *dwts.* 23 *grs.* 1

452 James I, O a fine bust of the sovereign, his person elegantly attired, ℞ two figures, representing Peace and Religion, one bearing a cornucopia, the other a beacon, *very fine and rare —weighing* 1 *oz.* 3 *dwts.* 5 *grs.* *M. H.* pl. 12, No. 6. 1

453 James I, another, similar, *very well preserved weight,* 16 *dwts.* 5 *grs.* 1

454 James I, O bust of the king, clothed in armour, head laureated, surrounded with name and title, ℞ the royal arms, with an ornamented cross, *fine and very rare—not in the Med. Hist. of England* . *weight,* 8 *dwts.* 10 *grs.* 1

GOLD MEDALS FROM THE REIGNS OF HENRY VIII THROUGH JAMES I WHICH WERE DISPERSED IN THE THOMAS THOMAS SALE. IMAGE BY GOOGLE.

A portrait of Samuel Tyssen (1756-1800), whose collection was sold by Leigh, Sotheby & Son on thirteen days beginning on December 7, 1801. This page appeared as the frontispiece to the auction catalogue. The original of this stipple engraving is by William Evans (fl. 1797-1812), after the portrait by Henry Jacob Burch (1763-1840). the British Museum's copy of this print was given to the Museum by Dorothea, Lady Banks. Previously it had been in Ms. Sarah Sophia Banks' collection.

Samuel Tyssen

(1756-1800)

ALTHOUGH known as a great collector, Samuel Tyssen seems to have led an otherwise unremarkable life of which only the barest details are known. There is a good deal known, however, about his collecting activities. In 1794, he purchased from Hodsoll's[396] John Thane's collection of coins and medals which had been built by Thomas Snelling. The following year Tyssen purchased a significant block of Rev. Richard Southgate's collection. In 1802, Tyssen's own collection of Anglo-Saxon coins (but apparently not the medals) was purchased in its entirety by the trustees of the British Museum. The medals appear to have been dispersed at the Leigh, Sotheby & Son sale of Tyssen's remaining numismatic collections which began on April 12, 1802, and lasted for 25 days, ending on May 31, 1802. The sales of Tyssen's entire 'museum' had begun in December 1801. The May 30, 1802, sale was the last to be held. The announcement of the first sale was as follows:

> A catalogue of the entire and valuable library of the late SAMUEL TYSSEN, ESQ. of Narborough Hall in the county of Norfold (sic); comprehending a very extensive collection of books on coins, English history, voyages and travels, arts and sciences, and belles-lettres: together with missals, manuscripts, &c. Which will be sold by auction by Leigh, Sotheby and son ... on Monday, December 7, 1801, and twelve following days.

AN ILLUSTRATION OF THE TYSSEN MEDAL (M.I.I AND M.I.ILL: NO ENTRY, EIMER 920) FROM *DURAND'S MÉDAILLES ET JETONS DES NUMISMATES,* 1865, PL. XIV, NO. 8.

It is of interest to note that the December 6, 1802; session was devoted exclusively to duplicates of coins and medals! A catalogue of this sale was sold at Spink's auction of February 2006. The catalogue's description is enlightening:

> *A Catalogue of an Entire Collection of Antiquities and Curiosities of the Late Samuel Tyssen 18 May 1802* (Octavo, pp. 12; 109 lots). Hand-priced with buyers' names throughout the coin section. Buyers included the great dealers and collectors of the day including Young, Trattle, Miles, Banks, Rashleigh, Bird, Coombe, Thane, Dimsdale. Lord Northwick being amongst the most eminent of the names. A remarkable collection

---

396 Hodsoll & Stirling, located at 345 Strand, was originally the business of WILLIAM HODSOLL (CA. 1712-1752), a "goldsmith & banker at the sign of the Sun, opposite Katherine Street in the Strand," who also sold coins and medals. In 1770, EDWARD HODSOLL's name appeared in the London Directory as a banker, located "near Katherine Street in the Strand." In 1776 the name of the firm changed to Hodsoll and Mitchell and in 1795, SIR WALTER STIRLING entered the firm as a junior partner. From 1799 until 1824, the firm's name was Hodsoll and Stirling, and in 1824, it became "Sir W. Stirling, Bart., Stirling, and Hodsoll." After 1825 the firm disappeared from the list of London bankers and "in 1828, it ceased doing business and its accounts were transferred to Snows." (F. G. Hilton Price, *London Bankers*..., 1890-91 ed., p. 158). Nichols comments that Mr. Hodsoll was a:

> Banker in the Strand, and possessed of a most curious Collection of Coins and Medals, which, after the death of his son, were bought entire by the late Samuel Tyssen, Esq. and have been since dispersed by auction. (*Literary Anecdotes*..., 1812, vol. iv, p. 704, fn.).

The Medal Commemorating Samuel Tyssen's Death

The medal, shown here in silver and bronze, commemorating the death of Samuel Tyssen of Narborough Hall, Norfolk (41 mm.; Eimer 920), by J. Milton, 1800. The obverse bears the following inscription: 'samuel · tyssen · arm · a. s. s.' ('Samuel Tyssen, Fellow of the Society of Antiquaries') while the reverse bears an inscription in eight lines, within a wreath crown: 'de narborough hall / in / agro norfolciensi / effigiavit /amica manus / ioan . milton / mdccc' ('of Narborough Hall in the county of Norfolk. The friendly hand of John Milton made this likeness, 1800') (41 mm., Eimer 920, B.H.M. 491). This medal is very rare in silver and somewhat rare in bronze. Eimer lists it in white metal as well. Tyssen's collection was sold in 1802. Top image courtesy of Timothy Millett Historical Medals, Ltd.

and one of the most famous of the early English sales: Samuel Tyssen, like so many of the early eminent collectors, purchased collections en bloc, such as those of Edward Solly,[397] Rev. Richard Southgate and Edward Hodsoll.

SSSS

[397] Edward Solly (1776-1844) was an English merchant with a connoisseur's eye for fine art, whether it be in paintings, coins or medals (*See textbox on p. 295, below*).

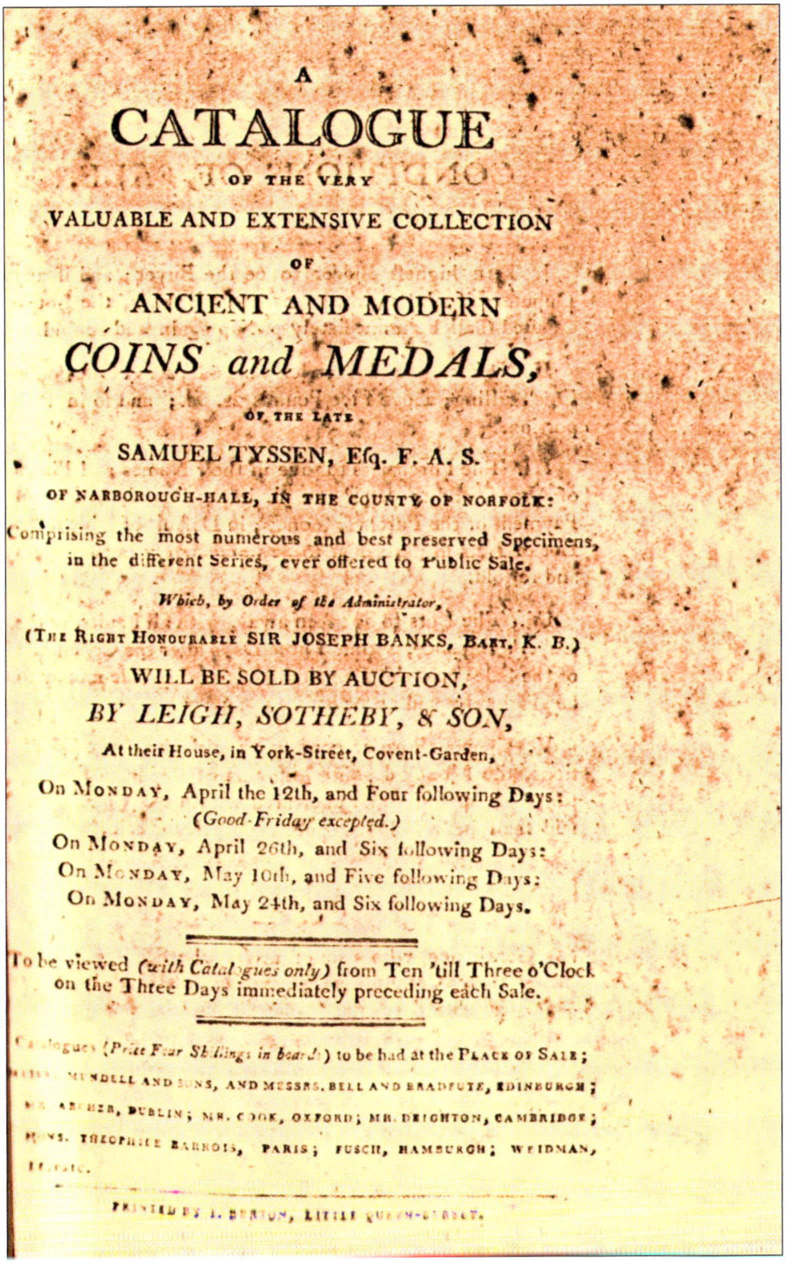

A

CATALOGUE

OF THE VERY

VALUABLE AND EXTENSIVE COLLECTION

OF

ANCIENT AND MODERN

COINS and MEDALS,

OF THE LATE

SAMUEL TYSSEN, Efq. F. A. S.

OF NARBOROUGH-HALL, IN THE COUNTY OF NORFOLK:

Comprising the most numerous and best preserved Specimens, in the different Series, ever offered to Public Sale.

Which, by Order of the Administrator,

(THE RIGHT HONOURABLE SIR JOSEPH BANKS, BART. K. B.)

WILL BE SOLD BY AUCTION,

BY LEIGH, SOTHEBY, & SON,

At their House, in York-Street, Covent-Garden,

On MONDAY, April the 12th, and Four following Days:

(Good-Friday excepted.)

On MONDAY, April 26th, and Six following Days:

On MONDAY, May 10th, and Five following Days:

On MONDAY, May 24th, and Six following Days.

To be viewed *(with Catalogues only)* from Ten 'till Three o'Clock on the Three Days immediately preceding each Sale.

Catalogues *(Price Four Shillings in boards)* to be had at the PLACE OF SALE; MUNDELL AND SONS, AND MESSRS. BELL AND BRADFUTE, EDINBURGH; MR. ARCHER, DUBLIN; MR. COOK, OXFORD; MR. DEIGHTON, CAMBRIDGE; MONS. THEOPHILE BARROIS, PARIS; FUSCH, HAMBURGH; WEIDMAN, LEIPSIC.

PRINTED BY J. BURTON, LITTLE QUEEN-STREET.

THE TITLE PAGE OF THE CATALOGUE FOR THE SALE OF SAMUEL TYSSEN'S COLLECTION OF COINS AND MEDALS SOLD AT SOTHEBY, LEIGH, & SON, APRIL 12–MAY 31, 1802. *COLOR ADJUSTED.*

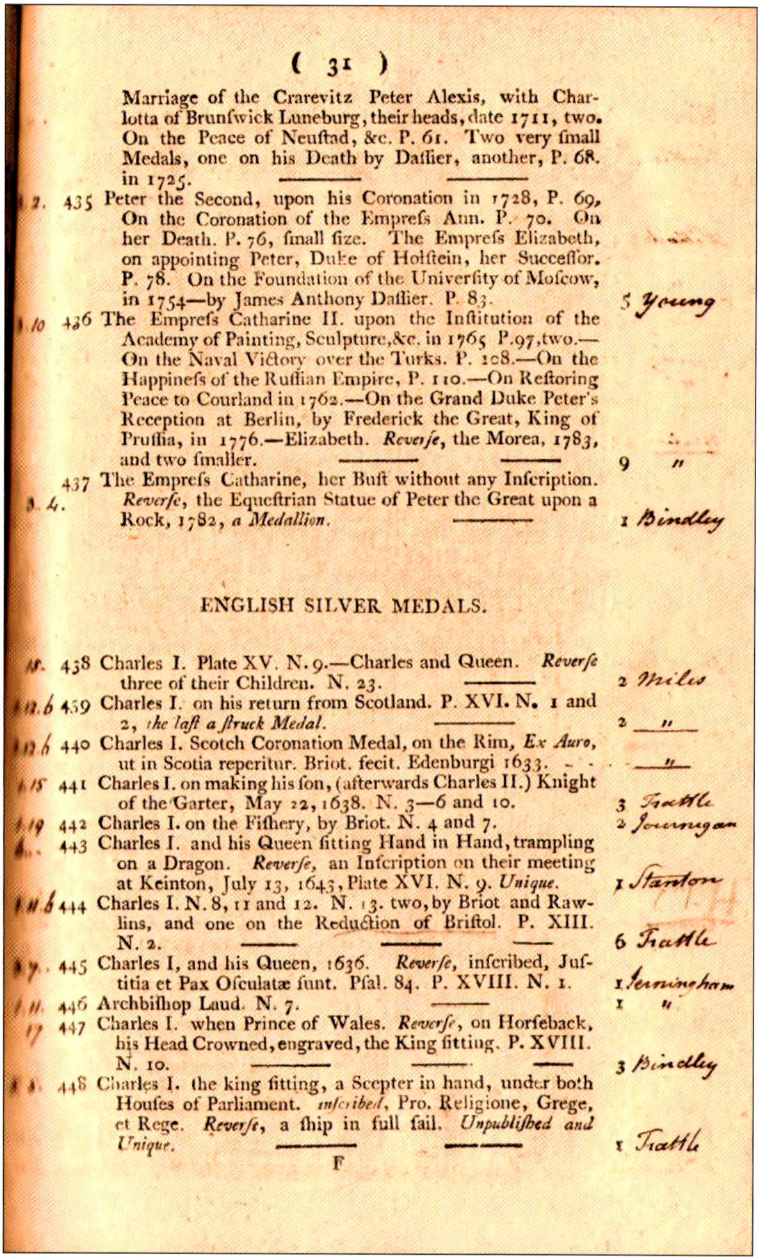
(31)

Marriage of the Czarevitz Peter Alexis, with Charlotta of Brunswick Luneburg, their heads, date 1711, two. On the Peace of Neustad, &c. P. 61. Two very small Medals, one on his Death by Dassier, another, P. 68. in 1725.

435 Peter the Second, upon his Coronation in 1728, P. 69, On the Coronation of the Empress Ann. P. 70. On her Death. P. 76, small size. The Empress Elizabeth, on appointing Peter, Duke of Holstein, her Successor. P. 78. On the Foundation of the University of Moscow, in 1754—by James Anthony Dassier. P. 83. — 5 Young

436 The Empress Catharine II. upon the Institution of the Academy of Painting, Sculpture, &c. in 1765 P. 97, two.—On the Naval Victory over the Turks. P. 108.—On the Happiness of the Russian Empire, P. 110.—On Restoring Peace to Courland in 1762.—On the Grand Duke Peter's Reception at Berlin, by Frederick the Great, King of Prussia, in 1776.—Elizabeth. *Reverse*, the Morea, 1783, and two smaller. — 9 "

437 The Empress Catharine, her Bust without any Inscription. *Reverse*, the Equestrian Statue of Peter the Great upon a Rock, 1782, *a Medallion.* — 1 Bindley

ENGLISH SILVER MEDALS.

438 Charles I. Plate XV. N. 9.—Charles and Queen. *Reverse* three of their Children. N. 23. — 2 Miles

439 Charles I. on his return from Scotland. P. XVI. N. 1 and 2, *the last a struck Medal.* — 2 "

440 Charles I. Scotch Coronation Medal, on the Rim, *Ex Auro*, ut in Scotia reperitur. Briot. fecit. Edenburgi 1633. - - — "

441 Charles I. on making his son, (afterwards Charles II.) Knight of the Garter, May 22, 1638. N. 3—6 and 10. — 3 Trattle

442 Charles I. on the Fishery, by Briot. N. 4 and 7. — 2 Jernigan

443 Charles I. and his Queen sitting Hand in Hand, trampling on a Dragon. *Reverse*, an Inscription on their meeting at Keinton, July 13, 1643, Plate XVI. N. 9. *Unique.* — 1 Stanton

444 Charles I. N. 8, 11 and 12. N. 13. two, by Briot and Rawlins, and one on the Reduction of Bristol. P. XIII. N. 2. — 6 Trattle

445 Charles I, and his Queen, 1636. *Reverse*, inscribed, Justitia et Pax Osculatæ sunt. Psal. 84. P. XVIII. N. 1. — 1 Jerningham

446 Archbishop Laud. N. 7. — 1 "

447 Charles I. when Prince of Wales. *Reverse*, on Horseback, his Head Crowned, engraved, the King sitting. P. XVIII. N. 10. — 3 Bindley

448 Charles I. the king sitting, a Scepter in hand, under both Houses of Parliament. *inscribed*, Pro. Religione, Grege, et Rege. *Reverse*, a ship in full sail. *Unpublished and Unique.* — 1 Trattle

F

One page from a priced 1802 sale catalogue for the sale of Samuel Tyssen's coins and medals. Of particular interest is not only the notation of the hammer price for each lot but also the name of the successful bidder. Some of the names are known to today's collectors, not least of which is Marmaduke Trattle, the successful bidder for lots 441, 444, 448, 450 and 460, who was then well on his way to building a large and remarkable collection.

(32)

Bird 449 Charles I. all *Reverse*, the Queen with Rings to wear round the neck. 4

Trattle 450 A thin plate of Sir William Packhurst, Warden of the Mint, done at Oxford, by Rawlins, in 1644. P. XVIII. N. 5. *and an engraved Plate of* Rycraft.
And the head of a young Man, ÆT. 20. unknown. 5

Willock 451 Colonel Strangeways. *Reverse*, the White Tower. P. XVIII. N. 9. 1

" 452 Charles I. and his Queen, *without* the date. P. 18. N. 1. *Reverse*, a Monster with 7 heads, the King's head under it, with the Crown and Scepter, *inscribed*, Heu Quænam. Hec Insania Vulgi, probably on his Death. 1

Young 453 Charles I. on his Death, Plate XVII. N. 1—3—4 and 5. 4

" 454 Charles I. on his Death. P. XVII. N. 7—8—9, by Rotier. 3

" 455 Charles I. on his Death. P. XVII. N. 10—11, and one *inscribed on the Reverse*, but not legible. 3

Miles 456 Robert Devereux, Earl of Essex, General of the Parliament Forces. *Obverse*, riding full speed, Sword in Hand. Inscription *engraved*, Robertus Comes Essex. *Reverse*, his Arms, *unpublished*. 40

Young 457 Lord Essex, Plate XXI. N. 4—5—6. two and 7. 5

" 458 Sir Thomas Fairfax, General of the Parliament's Forces, Plate XXI. N. 10—11—13. and *one struck, not published. Same Obverse and Reverse, but round.* 4

" 459 Jetton's Bishop Juxon. P. XVIII. N. 3. John Gidley. P. XX. N. 5. and Lord Traquair. *Obverse*, his Arms. *R.* Scales and Weights. 3

Trattle 460 Oliver Cromwell, Lord Protector, on his Victory at Dunbar. Plate XII. N. 3 and 4, *this without a Reverse*. N. 5, and one *an imitation* of it. *Reverse*, like N. 6, supposed to have been done in Holland —2. 2

Jerningham 461 Olivar. *Reverse*, Massaniello. P. XXII. N. 10. -2. 1

ROMAN IMPERIAL COINS in SILVER.

Miles 462 Caligula, 1. Claudius, 2. Claudius and Nero, 1. Nero, 3. Galba, 3. 10

Coombe 463 Nero and Agrippina, 2. Nero, 1. *(all finely preserved.)* 3 2.

" 464 Nero, 2. Galba, 2. Otho, 2. Vitellius, 2. *(all well preserved.)* 8 2.

465 Nero, 3. Galba, 2. Otho, 2. Vitellius, 2. Vespasianus, 3. 12

Stanton 466 Vitellius, 2. Vespasianus, 3. Titus, 3. *(all finely preserved.)* 8

467 Otho, 2. Vitellius, 2. Vespasianus, 4. Titus, 2. Domitianus, 4. 14

Young 468 Vitellius, 2. Vespasianus, 4. Titus, 4. Julia Titi, 1. 11

Coombe 469 Vespasianus, 2. Titus, 2. Julia Titi, 1. Domitianus, 1. *(all well preserved.)* 6

Willock 470 Vespasianus, 4. Titus, 3. Julia Titi, 1. Domitianus, 4. 12

These medals are of course known to today's collector. With *Medallic Illustrations* yet to be written, the plate numbers refer to 'Pinkerton's' *Medallic History*.... then a current and well-known reference.

Historical Commentary on Samuel Tyssen

SAMUEL TYSSEN, Esq., F.S.A...of Narborough Hall, Norfolk... The principal owner of the soil and lord of the manor is Samuel Tyssen, Esq., owner of Narborough Hall, an ancient mansion of brick and stone, formerly encompassed by a moat, and built in the reign of Henry VIII by Judge Spelman. The late Mr. Tyssen collected here in extensive and valuable collection of coins, medals, and other antiquities, said to have cost him about £20,000, but sold after his death, by auction, for less than a tenth part of that sum.

—W. White, *History, Gazetteer, and Directory of Norfolk*, 1845, p. 378.

§

Of [those medals of Rev Southgate], the most valuable part was purchased by Samuel Tyssen, esq. F.R.S. and F.S.A. well known among the lovers of literary virtù. [Tyssen] married the heiress of Edward Bodicoat, esq. and obtained by it the manor of the rectory of Hackney, as well as that of *Lord'shold* and *King'shold*. By this lady, who died before him, he had several children; and afterwards married a second wife, who survived him. He died Oct. 31, 1800 and his valuable and extensive Collection of antient and modern Coins and Medals came afterwards, by order of his Administrator, the Right Hon. Sir Joseph Banks, bart. K. B. (in April and May 1802) under the hammer of Messrs. Leigh and Sotheby, in a sale which lasted 25 days;[398] and to the Catalogue of which was prefixed a portrait, engraved by W. Evans, from a painting by H. Burch;[399] and the following Advertisement:[400]

> The great reputation acquired by the late Samuel Tyssen, esq. as a collector of coins and medals, both antient and modern, is so universally acknowledged, and so firmly established, that it seems almost unnecessary to dwell, a single moment, upon the extent and value of the cabinet now offered to the publick, which, it may be truly said, is rich beyond all example. To a fortune extremely ample Mr. Tyssen added the most indefatigable perseverance, by which scarcely a day was suffered to elapse without some addition being made to his Collection; nor, in the zeal which he shewed for attainments of this kind, was any expence spared, for, if his wealth and industry were alike notorious, so was his liberality equally conspicuous. In addition to the immense number of single articles, which his own judgment enabled him to purchase at sales and of private hands, throughout a long and unremitted attention to numismatic pursuits, his cabinet became gradually enriched by three of the most elegant and important collections which have ever been formed, by individual exertion at least, in this country.
>
> After what has been said, it may be almost superfluous to mention the collections of **Edward Solly, esq. the Rev. Richard Southgate, and Edward Hodsoll, esq**. collections sufficient, of themselves, to confer the highest celebrity upon any cabinet, in which they were united.[401] But these were not the only aids, of which Mr. Tyssen availed himself;

---

[398] Included in the sale of Tyssen's collection in 1802, as lot 3016, was the famous 'Petition Crown' coin, which sold for £105. As noted earlier *(q.v. fn. 302, p. 186)*, when it was sold at Spink on May 21, 2003, the Petition Crown realized a hammer price of £120,000 (£138,000 including premium), against a pre-sale estimate of £40,000-60,000, a record for sale of a single coin. When it was next sold, once again by Spink, on September 27, 2007, it also realized a record price for English silver coins—£207,100—against an estimate of £120,000-150,000. There are no more than four 'Petition Crown' coins in private collections. Most recently, the so-called 'Reddite crown,' named for its differing edge inscription: REDDITE QVÆ CÆSARIS CÆSARI &CT ('Render unto Caesar things that are Caesar's...') sold in March 2007, at Spink for £396,000 ($657,818 US), against a pre-sale estimate of £100,000-£120,000. The price included the 20 percent buyer's premium.

[399] This is the portrait which appears in the present work on page 288.

[400] From the preface to the sale of Mr. Tyssen's collection at Sotheby, Leigh & Son in 1802.

[401] The following passage, from the *Diary of Sir William Staunton*..., allows us to trace the provenance of the so-called 'Edgehill medal,' i.e., the medal referred to by Mr. Staunton (i.e., "The Queene removed...from Stratford to Wroxton, meeting ye King at ye foote of Edgehill"), and which was purchased by him at Tyssen's auction after first having passed through Mr. Hodsoll's collection. As WILLIAM HAMPER, the editor of Staunton's *Diary*..., relates it:

the consolidated labours of many lives, and now affords an infinitely larger and richer assemblage of medallic treasures than was ever yet sold by public sale in any part of Europe. In the following Catalogue care has been taken, that the best only of every specimen should be inserted; the others having been invariably consigned to the furnace. Having stated this, it only remains to be added, that, whatever was the extent and the value of Mr. Tyssen's Collection, the whole of it is now submitted, without any reserve, to the publick, with the exception only of what has been converted into bullion, and of the series of antient British and Saxon coins, which later have been purchased by the British Museum, a repository of all others the most fit for so noble, and, in this country, so interesting a suite; and the publick are highly indebted to the Trustees for the zeal and vigilance, which, upon this occasion, they have manifested...

—J. Nichols & S. Bentley, *Literary Anecdotes of the Eighteenth Century...*, 1812, v. 6, pt. i, pp. 376-377. This passage first having seen publication in the auction catalogue for the Tyssen sale at Sotheby, Leigh & Son.

Edward Solly, A Dedicated Collector

Edward Solly (1776-1844) was an English merchant living in Berlin, later Stockholm, and finally in London, who was involved in the Baltic timber trade and then the supply of provisions to the Allied nations during the Napoleonic Wars. Later in life he sold art works in London from his house at 7, Curzon Street, London. A connoisseur and serious collector of 13th through 15th century Italian and Dutch art, including works by Vermeer, the van Eycks, Raphael and Fra Filippo Lippi, he amassed an unprecedented collection, concerning himself with provenance and documentation at a time when this was not customary. In the end, several thousand paintings sold by Solly in his lifetime and later by his heirs, formed the core of numerous major 19th through 21st century collections, including those of the Alte National-Galerie, Munich, the Gemälde-Galerie, Berlin, the National Gallery, London, the Kress and Mellon collections, and the National Gallery, Washington. Solly was also a collector of English coins, medals and tokens. There does not appear to have been an auction sale of Solly's numismatic collection. The *Anthenæum* newspaper of December 18, 1886, however, announced the auction of "The Collections of Coins, Medals, and Tokens, the Properties of the late Prof. Edward Solly, F.R.S., F.S.A. and others," among which is: "...an interesting Series of English Silver Medals..." This Edward Solly (1819-1886) would appear to have been a son and the items sold in 1886 by Sotheby, Wilkinson & Hodge may well have included medals from the elder Solly's collection which had passed to him.

On this occasion the unique commemorative Silver Medal, represented at the end of the Diary, from the original in the Cabinet of William Staunton, Esq. of Longbridge House, near Warwick, was struck at Oxford. It is of very rude execution, the metal seeming to have been cut out of a piece of Plate, and weighs [illegible] The present engraving [illegible] of the original, but it had been previously copied in Evelyn's Discourse on Medals 1697 (being casually found in a field of his), in Snelling's thirty-three Plates of English Medals 1776, and in The Medallic History of England to the Revolution, 1790, evidently from the same Plate as Snelling's. —It was purchased at Mr. Bartlett's sale in 1787, by Mr. Hodsoll at the price of £25. 10. 0. The Cabinet of the latter Gentleman passed entire in that of Mr. Tyssen [sic], at whose auction Mr. Staunton became the enviable possessor of this distinguished Warwickshire Rarity (p. 53).

Two medals portraying Sir Joseph Banks

The medal created in 1816 by William Wyon to commemorate Sir Joseph Banks (in silver, 40 mm., B.H.M. 911, Eimer 1088). Eimer suggests that the Royal Society was responsible for this medal as a tribute to Banks, who had served as president from 1778 to 1819. It is also found in copper/brass and white metal. The *rev.* portrays an open book decorated with a garland and wheatsheaf, with a forget-me-not below. Image © Trustees of the British Museum (British Museum acc./reg. no. SSB,227.5, ex Sarah Sophia Banks Collection).

An unnamed example of the Banksian medal of the Horticultural Society of London, also by Wyon (1820, copper alloy, 38 mm., Eimer 1138). An example of this medal in gold was presented by the Society to Lady Banks. Other medals were awarded in silver and later in bronze (38 mm., B.H.M. 1041, Eimer 1138). Image © Trustees of the British Museum (British Museum acc./reg. no. M.3871).

Sir Joseph Banks, Bart.

(1743-1820)

BORN in 1743, the son of a wealthy Lincolnshire land owner, Joseph Banks was the beneficiary of an inheritance that allowed him a life in which he could pursue his intellectual interests. After attending Harrow and Eton, he entered Christ Church College, Oxford, in 1761, but found a lack of intellectual stimulation in the study of botany. As a result, he undertook tutoring in the subject at Cambridge. Beginning in 1764, Banks travelled widely as an explorer and naturalist, collecting specimens of botanical and animal life in Newfoundland, Labrador, and western England while studying natural and human history. In many ways, this was a predictable extension of his childhood interest in plants and animals. Providing some £10,000 of his own money, Banks outfitted and accompanied Lieutenant James Cook on H.M.S. *Endeavour* during 1768–71 on the latter's initial voyage circumnavigating the globe. This was just one of many trips he undertook to gather specimens and knowledge about the natural world. Banks was intending to accompany Cook on his second voyage, but Banks' many demands during the outfitting of the ship resulted in conflict with Cook, and he did not accompany the expedition, although he still remained friends with Cook. Among Bank's achievements were his identification of wheat rust and the fungus associated with the barberry family of shrubs, and the earlier emergence of marsupial mammals when compared to placental mammals. Returning home to London, Banks established what many considered to be the premier scientific botanical collection in the country. He also helped establish the Royal Botanical Gardens at Kew as a major botanical institution, and served as president of the Royal Society for four decades, from 1778 until 1819, a year before his death in 1820. His generosity and willingness to share his knowledge and specimens gained him many friends in the intellectual communities. Most of his library of works on natural history now resides in the British Library and his botanical collection and a portion of his library are in the Museum of Natural History. Ever an advocate of science and scientists, he used his personal influence to promote and protect scientists, be they British or not. In this regard, he had no hesitation in intervening with Napoleon to protect French scientists as well as their work during the French Revolution and Napoleonic Wars.

THE OFFICIAL 1812 PORTRAIT OF SIR JOSEPH BANKS AS PRESIDENT OF THE ROYAL SOCIETY. IT IS AN ETCHING BY LUIGI SCHIAVONETTI (1765-1810) AFTER THE ORIGINAL PAINTING BY THOMAS PHILLIPS (1770-1845). ALTHOUGH BANKS HIMSELF WAS NOT A *MEDAL* COLLECTOR, HIS SISTER SARAH SOPHIA BANKS WAS A COLLECTOR OF MANY THINGS, MEDALS INCLUDED. BANKS' INCLUSION IN THIS VOLUME REFLECTS BOTH THIS FACT AND HIS WIFE DOROTHEA'S ROLE IN BUILDING THE BRITISH MUSEUM'S COLLECTION OF COINS AND MEDALS THROUGH THE BANKS FAMILY'S GENEROSITY. IMAGE © TRUSTEES OF THE BRITISH MUSEUM.

PORTRAITS OF SIR JOSEPH AND DOROTHEA, LADY BANKS, CA. 1790. NOTE THE PICTURE OF THE SURFACE OF THE MOON BEING HELD BY SIR JOSEPH. BOTH PRINTS ARE STIPPLE ENGRAVINGS BY JOSEPH COLLYER (1748-1827) AFTER PAINTED PORTRAITS BY JOHN RUSSELL (1745-1806). COLLYER WAS LATER TO BE PORTRAIT ENGRAVER TO QUEEN CHARLOTTE. IMAGE © TRUSTEES OF THE BRITISH MUSEUM.

A SATIRICAL PRINT FROM SARAH SOPHIA BANKS' COLLECTION. THE TWO SIDES OF THE MEDALLION REPRESENT RESPECTIVELY 'BRITISH LIBERTY' AND 'FRENCH LIBERTY.' A REGAL BRITANNICA HOLDS THE STAFF AND CAP OF LIBERTY, THE MAGNA CARTA, AND THE SCALES OF JUSTICE. IN CONTRAST, THE 'FRENCH LIBERTY' MEDALLION PORTRAYS A RAGGED FIGURE TRAMPLING A DECAPITATED BODY WHILE HOLDING IN ONE HAND A TRIDENT ON WHICH A BLEEDING HEAD AND TWO HEARTS ARE IMPALED AND IN THE OTHER, A LONG DAGGER. WRITHING SERPENTS FORM HER HAIR AND GIRDLE WHILE BEHIND HER A BODY HANGS FROM A LAMP-BRACKET. THE PRINT REFLECTS THE INTENSITY OF FEELINGS ABOUT THE WAR BETWEEN BRITAIN AND FRANCE WHICH WAS RAGING AT THE TIME. IMAGE ©TRUSTEES OF THE BRITISH MUSEUM.

Sarah Sophia Banks

(1744-1818)

SARAH SOPHIA BANKS was the sister of Sir Joseph Banks,[402] who had gained prominence as the patron of Captain James Cook. She was in her own right, a serious, perhaps voracious collector, accumulating sizeable numbers of "...prints and printed ephemera, coins, medals and jetons,"[403] *cartes de visite*, etchings, and passports, as well as advertisements, political caricatures, playbills and bookplates. There seems to have been little that was not of interest to her. Never marrying, Sarah Banks was very close to her brother and sister-in-law Dorothea Banks, and assisted Sir Joseph in his numerous intellectual pursuits. She appears to have been a strong, energetic woman. Caygill provides a clear sense of her:

> [Sarah Banks]...is described as a dominant personality: She had a loud, even strident voice, was tall and imposing, and cut an unmistakable figure striding along the streets or through the parks, always accompanied by a servant carrying a long cane... [she] drove a four-in-hand with the skill and confidence of a man, and was skilled in archery and fishing.[404]

MISS SARAH SOPHIA BANKS. IMAGE © TRUSTEES OF THE BRITISH MUSEUM. UNFORTUNATELY, THERE ARE NO DETAILS AVAILABLE REGARDING THE MAKER OF THIS PORTRAIT.

Upon her death in 1818, the items in Sarah Banks' collections exceeded 20,000 in number. She left instructions for her collections to be conferred upon her brother, Sir Joseph Banks, and his wife Dorothea, her sister-in-law.[405] They immediately presented them to the British Museum, together with Ms. Banks' manuscript catalogue. The catalogue contains acquisition details, including prices, correspondence and papers. Later, the collection was divided between the British Library and the British Museum; the material deposited in the British Museum being further divided between the Department of Prints and Drawings and the Department of Coins and Medals. A separate bequest, consisting of some 2000 numismatic items, as well as her library, was presented to the Royal Mint Museum.

[402] Sir Joseph Banks was a collector of plants and animals, but apparently not of medals.

[403] *The E-Sylum*, vol. 14, no. 11, Mar. 13, 2011, article 7.

[404] M. Caygill (2014), *Creating a Great Museum: Early Collectors and the British Museum*, http: // www.lathom.com/course/21701728/session4.html.

[405] This material is identified on the British Museum collections database as 'presented by (D[onor]) DOROTHEA BANKS, with previous owner (PO), SARAH SOPHIA BANKS. In the Department of Coins and Medals, objects from Sarah Sophia Banks have tickets with the letters 'SSB.'

'AN OLD MAID ON A JOURNEY (1804).' A CARTOON BY JAMES GILLRAY.

THE SATIRE IN THIS PRINT IS SAID TO BE BOTH GENERAL AND PARTICULAR, AS THE ARTIST IS SUPPOSED TO HAVE PERSONIFIED IN HIS OLD MAIDS THE WELL KNOWN MISS BANKS, WHOSE COLLECTIONS HAVE ENRICHED THE BRITISH MUSEUM.

—T. Wright & R. H. Evans (1851), *Historical...Account of the Caricatures of James Gillray...*

Sarah Sophia Banks: Historical Commentary

In Soho-square, aged 74, Miss Sarah Sophia Banks, sister of the Right Hon. Sir Joseph Banks. She had been slightly indisposed for a short time, but was able a few days before her death to pay a visit with Lady Banks to the Princesses at Kew. Like her venerable brother, she was strongly animated with a zeal for science and the study of natural history, of which she had made even more a valuable collection. But her moral worth, even than her talents and knowledge, rendered her the object of esteem and regard to all who had the pleasure of being acquainted with her, and who from the rank and character of her brother, in addition to her own merits, constituted a very large circle of friends. By order of Sir Joseph Banks (an act of munificence that cannot be too highly praised) such of her collections of books and coins *at* the British Museum does not already possess, have been presented to that truly National Institution.

—Obituary, *The Gentleman's Magazine*, 1st series, 1818, pt. 11, p. 472.

§

BANKS, SARAH SOPHIA (1744-1818), only sister of Sir Joseph Banks, was born in 1744 and died on 27 Sept. 1818, at her brother's house in Soho Square, after a short illness. She had kindred tastes to her brother, and although debarred from such adventurous voyages as he undertook, she amassed a considerable collection of objects of natural history, books, and coins. Sir Joseph Banks presented her coins and engravings to the British Museum. The Abbé Mann, one of her brother's correspondents, presented her, in 1797, with a collection of German coins which she added to her collection (*Letters of Eminent Literary Men*, Carad. Soc. pp. 445-7).

—*DNB*, 1885-1900 ed., vol. 3, p. 133.

§

In 1818 Lady Banks (sister-in-law to Miss Banks) presented all such coins and medals belonging to the extensive cabinet of Miss S. S. Banks as were not previously in the Museum, including a collection of foreign coins of vast extent.

—*Penny Cyclopædia of the Society for the Diffusion of Useful Knowledge*, 1836, vol. 5, p. 453.

§

Sarah Sophia Banks, the only sister of Sir Joseph Banks, possessed similar tastes to her brother, and amassed a considerable number of books, coins, objects of natural history, etc. She died at her brother's house in Soho Square on the 27th of September 1818; and after her death a portion of her collections, consisting of sixty-six volumes of manuscripts, chiefly relating to heraldic matters, ceremonials, archery, etc., together with several printed books principally treating of chivalry, knighthood, etc., some of them enriched with her MS. notes, were presented to the library of the British Museum by Lady Banks, the wife of Sir Joseph. Several of the volumes were in very fine bindings.

—W. Y. Fletcher (2008). *English Book Collectors*, p. 274.

Matthew Young

(1771-1838)

• A Successful Early 19th century London Coin & Medal Dealer •

The son of Henry Young, a London coin and medal dealer, [W.] Matthew Young was a very active bidder at auction sales of the early 19th century, both for his business, and (apparently) for his own personal collection. His name appears among the successful bidders at almost every London auction of coins and medals in that period as well as at book auctions. He also acted for other bidders at auction. With a residence on Tavistock Street, Covent Garden, and his business initially located in Ludgate-street, then at 46, High Holborn, and afterwards on Tavistock Street, Young was well placed to attend the London auction sales. His obituary in the *Gentleman's Magazine* states:

> *These two last residences were the resort of the most eminent collectors, by whom he was highly esteemed, and will be sincerely regretted for his quiet, amiable manners, his honourable dealings, and his willingness and skill to assist them in their pleasing pursuits (1838, vol. III, p. 107).*

'W. Matthew Young,' an undated stipple etching on paper by an unknown artist. Image © Trustees of the British Museum.

Mr. Young purchased many lots for the British Museum, assisted *"Mess. Sotheby in forming the Catalogues of Coins submitted to their care for sale"* and also was involved in the manufacture and issuance of private tokens, a practice which he strongly encouraged. He contributed items to the British Museum, including, e.g., in 1829, dies executed by the Roettiers, together with a number of puncheons. He also appears to have published (or at least, reprinted) books on numismatics. His prominence in numismatics is indicated by his having been one of the founding members, in 1836, of the Numismatic Society of London (later the Royal Numismatic Society). At his death, the notice of that event in the *Proceedings* was highly laudatory, referring to him as being:

> *... equally well known for his zeal and ability as a collector, and for his high character for integrity and extensive operations, as a dealer in coins and medals (Proc. of the R.N.S., 1838/39, vol. I, p. 199).*

The auction catalogues for the sale of his library and numismatic material by Leigh & Sotheby refer to him as:

> *The highly notable and highly respected nineteenth century coin dealer.*

At his death, he left a remarkable library which went to auction in 1838 beginning on Nov. 26 and took four days. The sale catalogue contained 39 pages of book lots. The 'Remaining portion of the library of the late Mr. Matthew Young, Numismatist' was sold on November 14 through 29, 1842. His coins, medals, dies, etc. were sold over 10 days, beginning on February 25, 1839. The total number of items in these sales was an astounding 11,541 lots.

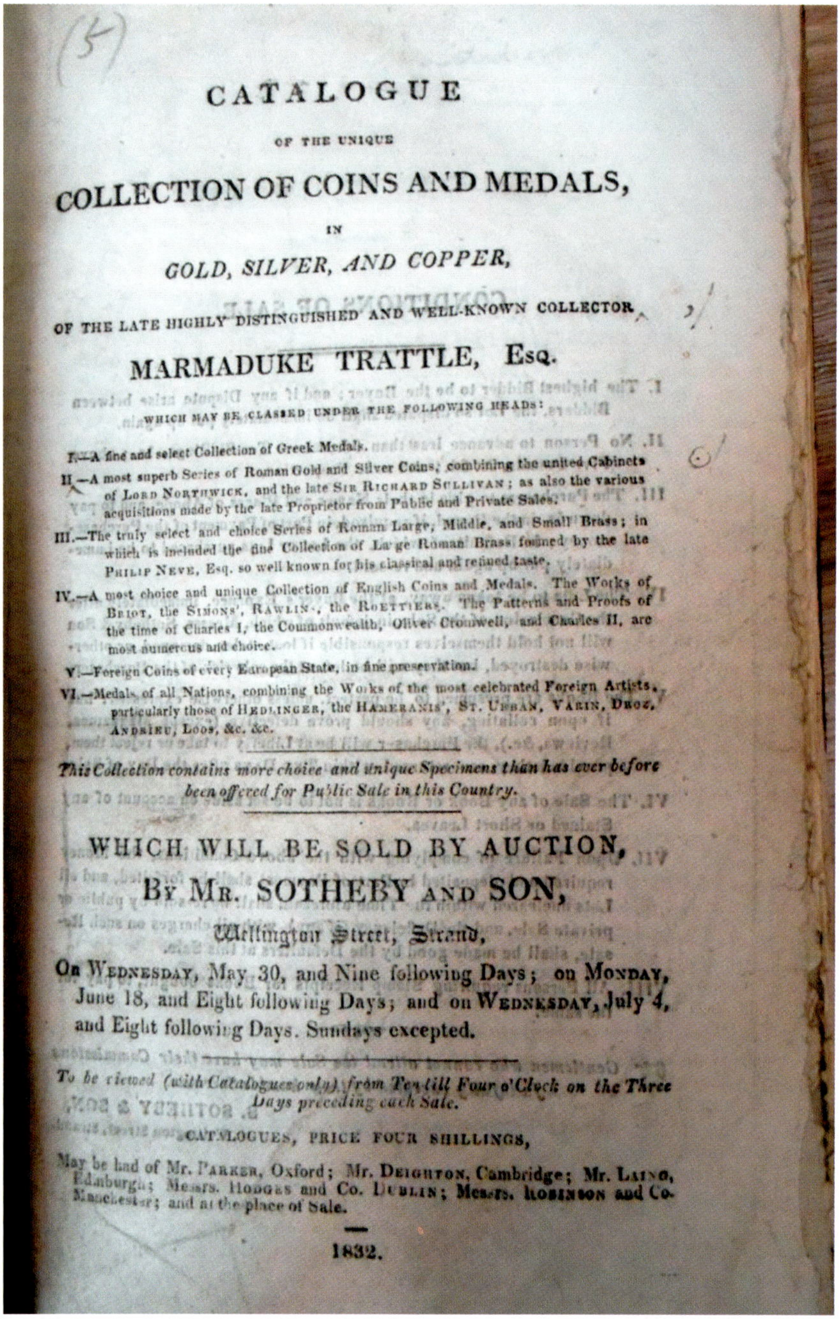

CATALOGUE

OF THE UNIQUE

COLLECTION OF COINS AND MEDALS,

IN

GOLD, SILVER, AND COPPER,

OF THE LATE HIGHLY DISTINGUISHED AND WELL-KNOWN COLLECTOR

MARMADUKE TRATTLE, Esq.

WHICH MAY BE CLASSED UNDER THE FOLLOWING HEADS:

I.—A fine and select Collection of Greek Medals.

II.—A most superb Series of Roman Gold and Silver Coins, combining the united Cabinets of Lord Northwick, and the late Sir Richard Sullivan; as also the various acquisitions made by the late Proprietor from Public and Private Sales.

III.—The truly select and choice Series of Roman Large, Middle, and Small Brass; in which is included the fine Collection of Large Roman Brass formed by the late Philip Neve, Esq. so well known for his classical and refined taste.

IV.—A most choice and unique Collection of English Coins and Medals. The Works of Briot, the Simons', Rawlins, the Roettiers. The Patterns and Proofs of the time of Charles I, the Commonwealth, Oliver Cromwell, and Charles II, are most numerous and choice.

V.—Foreign Coins of every European State, in fine preservation.

VI.—Medals of all Nations, combining the Works of the most celebrated Foreign Artists, particularly those of Hedlinger, the Hamerani's, St. Urban, Varin, Droz, Andrieu, Loos, &c. &c.

This Collection contains more choice and unique Specimens than has ever before been offered for Public Sale in this Country.

WHICH WILL BE SOLD BY AUCTION,

BY MR. SOTHEBY AND SON,

Wellington Street, Strand,

On Wednesday, May 30, and Nine following Days; on Monday, June 18, and Eight following Days; and on Wednesday, July 4, and Eight following Days. Sundays excepted.

To be viewed (with Catalogues only) from Ten till Four o'Clock on the Three Days preceding each Sale.

CATALOGUES, PRICE FOUR SHILLINGS,

May be had of Mr. Parker, Oxford; Mr. Deighton, Cambridge; Mr. Laing, Edinburgh; Messrs. Hodges and Co. Dublin; Messrs. Robinson and Co. Manchester; and at the place of Sale.

1832.

THE TITLE PAGE OF THE CATALOGUE FOR THE SALE OF MARMADUKE TRATTLE'S COLLECTION OF COINS AND MEDALS. THE SALE TOOK 28 DAYS IN MAY THROUGH JULY OF 1832. IMAGE COURTESY DEPT. OF COINS & MEDALS, BRITISH MUSEUM.

Marmaduke Trattle

(1751-1831)

MARMADUKE TRATTLE, ESQ.

"PORTRAIT OF MARMADUKE TRATTLE, ESQ., MODELLED FROM THE LIFE,—AN ENGRAVING OF WHICH WAS PREFIXED TO THE SALE CATALOGUE OF HIS COINS, AND MEDALS."[406]

THE ILLUSTRATION IS A STIPPLE ENGRAVING OF A MEDAL BY WILLIAM WYON. MARMADUKE TRATTLE WAS A MERCHANT TRADING AT BROAD STREET, LONDON WALL, FROM APPROXIMATELY 1777 UNTIL 1816. TRATTLE FORMED ONE OF THE GREAT 19TH CENTURY COLLECTIONS OF BRITISH MEDALS. IT WAS SOLD AT AUCTION BY MR. SOTHEBY AND SON BEGINNING ON MAY 30, 1832,[407] AND ACQUIRED BY THE BRITISH MUSEUM. IMAGE © TRUSTEES OF THE BRITISH MUSEUM. THE REVIEW OF THE SALE ON THE FOLLOWING PAGE APPEARED IN *THE GENTLEMAN'S MAGAZINE* OF *JULY 1832*. IMAGE © TRUSTEES OF THE BRITISH MUSEUM.

---

406 W. Carlisle & W. Wyon (1937). *A Memoir of the Life and Works of William Wyon,* privately printed, p. 204.

407 The title of the sale catalogue is: *A Catalogue of the Unique Collection of Coins and Medals, in Gold, Silver, and Copper of the Late Highly Distinguished and Well Known Collector, Marmaduke Trattle, Esq...which will be sold by auction by Mr Sotheby and Son [London, 1832]*. The advertisement stated that the collection contained:

> ...more choice and unique specimens than has ever before been offered for public sale in this Country.

Beginning on May 30, the sale covered a total of 28 days. The proceeds of the sale were £10,923 3*s* 3*d*.

As is sometimes the case today, individuals employed agents to bid for them at auctions. In a priced catalogue for the sale of Samuel Tyssen's collection in 1802, the notation "Miles for Trattle" appears before the listing of items to be sold. This notation appears again on pp. 118 and 119 of the catalogue

Historical Commentary on Marmaduke Trattle

Marmaduke Trattle, Esq. was born the 3rd of February, 1752, and was the only son of John Trattle, Esq. of Yarmouth, in, the Isle of Wight, and Mayor of that town about the year 1743. His mother was a Miss Langdale, a descendant of Sir Marmaduke Langdale, who commanded the left wing of King Charles's army at the battle of Naseby. Mr. Trattle commenced life as a West India merchant in London; which occupation he pursued with unsullied honour and integrity nearly to his death. He resided for fifty years in the Rectory-house of Allhallows, London Wall, where he died Sept. 26, 1831; and was buried at St. Michael Royal, Tower Hill, with the Langdale family. His residence was the focus of nearly all the numismatists of his age. His urbanity of manners, diversity of intelligence, and hospitality, made him a most valuable friend. Having acquired an ample fortune, which he devoted to his favourite pursuits, his collection of rare and valuable gems, natural history, library, and above all, his extensive cabinets of ancient and modern coins of all nations and of every age, caused him to be visited and valued by every lover of the refined arts. A portrait of Mr. Trattle has recently been engraved from a medallion, by Wyon.

> ***NOTICE***
>
> **SALE BY AUCTION**
>
> **The valuable and eminent collection of Antiquities, Gems, Enameled Portraits, Miniatures of celebrated Characters, a superbly sculptured marble Bust of Buonaparte, Foreign, Naval, and Military Orders, antique Cameo and Intaglio Rings, Jewelry, and Specimens of Natural History, &c.: the property of the late MARMADUKE TRATTLE, ESQ.—By Mr. HUGGART, on the Premises, at the Rectory House, London-Wall, close to Old Broad-street, This Day, at 11, by direction of the Executors.**
>
> —*The London Times*, November 18, 1831.

Mr. Trattle's Coins, &c.

A very rich collection of coins and medals, formed by the late Marmaduke Trattle, Esq. has been recently sold by Messrs. Sotheby in twenty-eight days sale. They may be classed under the following heads: I. Greek medals. II. A series of gold and silver coins, combining the united cabinets of Lord Northwick and the late Sir Richard Sullivan, with great additions. III. A series of Roman large, middle, and small brass, including the fine collection of large Roman brass formed by the late Philip Neve, Esq. IV. A rich collection of English coins and medals; the works of Briot, the Simons, Rawlins, and the Roettiers; with very numerous and choice patterns and proofs of the periods of Charles I. the Commonwealth, Oliver Cromwell, and Charles II. V. Foreign coins of every European state. VI. Medals of all nations.

The following were the most important articles:...

(Earlier coins have been omitted—au.)

English Medals in Silver.

Charles I. pattern probably for a Crown, by Briot. Obverse, the King bareheaded. Reverse, the King on horseback, 34*l.* 10s.

Commonwealth Half-Crown, by David Ramage, 35*l.* Shilling by Ramage, 38*l.* Blondeau's Half-Crown, inscribed on the edge "Truth and Peace," 27*l.* 10*s.* Oliver's Sixpence, 29*l.* 10s. The famous Petition Crown of Charles II. by Thomas Simon, the best ever sold at a public sale, bought by Mr. Young for 225*l.*

Charles II. Crown, the some as the last, in place of the Petition on the edge, " Reddite quæ Cæsaris," &c. 74*l.* 10*s.*,

Robert Devereux, Earl of Essex, 17l. 15s.

Ferdinand Lord Fairfax, 13*l.*

The small Medal in bronze on the Battle of Dunbar, 12*l.* 15*s.*

Lord Kimbolton, 7*l.* 7*s.*

Lord Inchinquin, Si. lit. Henry Scobel, 9*l.* 5s.

Bulstrode Whitelock, 23*l.* 10*s.*

The Half-Testoon of Mary, with her Portrait. This piece is unique and unpublished. Formerly in the collection of Philip Neve, Esq. 27*l.* 10*s.*

(Continued on p. 306)

61

ENGLISH MEDALS, IN SILVER (continued).

Buyer	Lot	Description	No.	£	s.	d.
Young	913	Charles II, reverse his father Charles 1, front faced in armour, *fine, and very rare*	1	1	13	"
Do.	914	On an Installation of the Order of the Garter, Plate 26, No. 5, 1671 and 1678	2	1	15	"
Do.	915	Two others, one as last, No. 26; the other represents St. George piercing the Dragon, "Salus populorum" reverse the Order suspended between four C's interlinked, crowned 1669, *very rare*	2	2	1	"
Do.	916	Another, on the same occasion, by *Roettier*, 29th May, 1671, when Charles XI of Sweden was made a Knight of the Garter	1	"	11	"
Do.	917	Charles II on his Embarking at Scheveling in 1660, Plate 27, No. 1	1	1	10	"
Do.	918	Charles II, reverse the Gods in council, "Nullum numen abest," Plate 27, No. 3, *very fine*	1	2	"	"
Do.	919	Charles II, reverse Jupiter destroying the giants, by *G. Bower, highly preserved*	1	3	12	"
Durrant	920	Charles II on his return to England, 29th May, 1660, Plate 28, No. 2, *a very fine and rare medal*	1	3	13	6
Young	921	Charles II, reverse Britannia helmetted, seated on a globe, "Invidior major," No. 3, *fine and rare*	1	1	5	"
Do.	922	Charles II, *the noble Medallion on the Restoration*, reverse "Felicitas Britannia, May 29, 1660," No. 4, *in beautiful preservation, and very rare*	1	8	8	"
Do.	923	Charles II on his Restoration, Plate 26, No. 4; and Plate 28, No. 5, and two of No. 6, rather different	4	1	15	"
Do.	924	Charles II on his Coronation, by *T. Simon*, No. 7, and one obverse three crowns, C.R.II. "Admit no partners, 1648;" reverse a Cupid with bow holding a laurel crown over an aged oak, from which a branch has just sprung up, *unpublished, if not unique*	1	1	13	"
Do.	925	Charles II on his Coronation, Plate 28, No. 8, the King's head and titles, reverse the King as a shepherd with his flock, "Dixit custodium, 23d April, 1661," inscribed on the edge, "Coronat. Pastore Quat. Ovile," *fine, and rare*	1	3	4	"

A page from the very rare sale catalogue of Marmaduke Trattle's collection of coins and medals at Sotheby's beginning on May 30, 1832. Matthew Young was the successful bidder on all but one lot on this page. His name is mentioned, *passim*, in numerous other medal related contexts during the period c.a. 1800-1840 (*q.v. p. 301*).

The principal purchasers were the British Museum, the Duke de Blacas, Baron Bollaud, Colonel Durant, Mr. Thomas, and Mr. Young. [408]

—*The Gentleman's Magazine*, July 1832, vol. 154 (pt. 2),pp. 64-65.

§

It was from the end of the first quarter of the last century, when Mr Sotheby sold the cabinet of Sir Mark Sykes, that the more modern lines of collecting may be said to have commenced. Marmaduke Trattle's extensive and splendid assemblage of English coins, however, was the earliest, perhaps, of first-class importance sold by the same firm, while in a pecuniary respect it proved, from the sum realized, one of the most remunerative and encouraging.

— H. Carew (1905). *The Coin Collector,* p. 23.

§§§§

AMÉDÉE DURAND AND ANTHONY DURAND

AMÉDÉE DURAND AND ANTHONY DURAND ARE TWO AUTHORS INFREQUENTLY DIRECTLY REFERENCED, BUT OFTEN PRESENT, ON THE FRINGES OF THE SUBJECT OF 19TH C. COMMEMORATIVE MEDALS.

AMÉDÉE DURAND (?-1828), A FRENCH SCULPTOR AND MEDAL ENGRAVER, IS PERHAPS BEST KNOWN FOR THE *SERIES NUMISMATICA UNIVERSALIS VIRORUM ILLUSTRIUM,* ISSUED BETWEEN 1818 AND 1846, A SERIES OF MEDALS CONTAINING THE PORTRAITS OF 'ILLUSTRIOUS INDIVIDUALS' OF ALL NATIONALITIES, INCLUDING ENGLISHMEN (E.G., WILLIAM SHAKESPEARE, FRANCIS BACON, OLIVER CROMWELL, JOSEPH ADDISON, JOHN MILTON, ETC.). THE NUMBER OF ORIGINAL MEDALS ISSUED IN THE SERIES EXCEEDED 150, AND WITH RESTRIKES AND VARIANTS, THE TOTAL NUMBER MAY HAVE EXCEEDED SEVERAL HUNDRED.

ANTHONY DURAND (1804-1873), WHO IS NOT KNOWN TO BE RELATED TO AMÉDÉE, AND WHO IS, IN FACT NOT MENTIONED IN THE LATTER'S VOLUME, WAS A NUMISMATIST, ARCHEOLOGIST AND DEDICATED COLLECTOR OF COINS AND MEDALS. ORIGINALLY INTERESTED IN ANCIENT NUMISMATICS, HE FOUND A NEW AVOCATION IN THE STUDY OF MEDALS RELATING TO THE FRENCH REVOLUTION OF 1789. ANTHONY IS THE AUTHOR OF *MÉDAILLES ET JETONS DES NUMISMATES,* PUBLISHED IN 1865. THIS FRENCH LANGUAGE WORK PROVIDES BRIEF BIOGRAPHICAL SKETCHES OF 285 17TH THROUGH MID-19TH CENTURY NUMISMATISTS AND COLLECTORS, INCLUDING SOME THIRTY-FIVE IN ENGLAND, OF WHOM COMMEMORATIVE MEDALS WERE STRUCK.

MEDALLIONS are medals of a larger size, and supposed to have been struck by the different emperors for their friends, or for foreign princes and ambassadors. That the smallness of the number of these, however, might not put to hazard the loss of the devices they bore, the Romans generally took care to stamp the subjects of them upon their ordinary coins. Medallions, in respect of other coins, resembled what modern medals, properly so speaking, are in respect to money, having had no current value, but merely an arbitrary one. Medallions are so scarce that no set can be made of them even with mixing the different metals.

—J. Elmes. (1826). *A General and Bibliographical Dictionary of the Fine Arts*..., pages unnumbered; found under 'Medals.' Cf. *Encyclopedia Britannica,* 1771 ed.vol. iii, p. 57, from which this quote was in large part taken by Elmes.

---

408 An auction catalogue has also survived for the sale of SAMUEL TYSSEN's collection in 1802 at Leigh, Sotheby & Son. The Tyssen catalogue contains annotations with the purchaser's names indicated for every lot. MR. TRATTLE acquired a number of lots, but did not attend every session, as some of his winning bids were executed by MR. MILES.

Surgeon-Major J. W. Fleming

'The Fleming Bequest'

(?-1877)

IN 1877 the widow of Surgeon-major J. W. Fleming, 4th Royal Irish Dragoon Guards, donated her late husband's collection of medals and portraits to the South Kensington Museum. The collection consisted of some 655 items, and among these were approximately 30 items which represented 17th century British medals. With only a few exceptions, all of the 17th century medals were either silver or gilded bronze electrotypes, most, however, of a very high quality of manufacture. The Victoria and Albert Museum possesses a 19th century manuscript handlist of the Fleming Bequest medals on which each item is clearly labeled as to whether it is an electrotype copy.

While it might be assumed that many of the electrotypes found in the 'Fleming Bequest" are from the series made at the order of the British Museum trustees in 1897,[409] the dates suggest that is not the case. Surgeon-major J. W. Fleming's widow had bequeathed the collection in 1877, some two decades before the official issuance of the British Museum electrotypes. Thus, there had to have been an earlier issue of a number of electrotype copies of these medals prior to 1877. Unfortunately, it was not possible to compare examples from each series in order to determine whether they are from the same manufacturing process.

Commentary on the Surg.-Maj. J. W. Fleming Collection

The "Fleming Bequest" was the gift of 655 medals, via his widow, of Surgeon-Major J. W. Fleming, F.R.C.S.E., 4th (Royal Irish) Dragoon Guards, in 1877. Dr J W Fleming, of Brighton, died a few days after sending them to his friend J. K. Ford, saying he wanted them to be presented to a public institution. Ford offered the collection of medals to the South Kensington Museum in May 1877, and the gift physically entered the Museum in January 1878. The collection includes military and commemorative medals, and decorations. There are military & naval portraits, historical medals commemorating battles, victories, treaties, and decorations, foreign and British. There is a mixture of original medals, and electrotype copies of medals. They range in date from the Spanish Armada to the Ashantee Campaign of 1874. All the war medals issued in the 19th century up to that date are represented.

—Dr. Melanie Vandenbrouck-Przybylski & Ms. Lucy Cullen, Dept. of Sculpture, Victoria & Albert Museum, personal communication, August 18, 2009.

§

---

409 In 1897, the British Museum prepared a series of electrotypes of medals in its collection, as described in the following notice:

> THE series of electrotypes of medals illustrating British History herein described has been presented by the Trustees of the British Museum, who receive annually by Parliamentary Vote a sum to be expended on reproductions of works of art in the British Museum for distribution among Local Museums (—Trustees of the British Museum. *Description of Electrotypes of British Historical Medals*, 1897).

The set consisted of 98 pieces, and the British Museum publication referenced here contains descriptions, in the style of *Medallic Illustrations*, for each of the original medals which were reproduced. The period covered by the medals listed range from two ca. 16th century medallic portraits of Henry VIII through an 1815 medal of the Duke of Wellington.

It is not clear over how long a period of time the series was issued, or how many sets were sold or otherwise found their way into other museum collections as intended, or into collectors' hands. Such sets are difficult to find, and the authors are not aware of any having come onto the market in recent decades; two sets were located, however, in the possession of private collectors.

It should be noted that SURGEON-MAJOR FLEMING wanted his medals to be presented to a public institution. He sent them to his friend J. K. FORD several days before his death, asking him to see that this was done. FORD offered the medals to the South Kensington Museum in May 1877, and the medals were physically received by the Museum in January 1878. The authors are much indebted to Dr. Melanie Vandenbrouck-Przybylski and Ms. Lucy Cullen for their assistance with our inquiries concerning the Fleming Bequest.

From the Twenty-fifth Report of the Science and Art Department, lately issued, we learn that...for the Art Collection at South Kensington...the most important gifts or bequests to the Art Collection were the series of military, civil, and historical medals and decorations belonging to the late Surgeon-major J. W. Fleming...

—*The Academy, A Weekly Review of Literature and Life*, 1878, vol. 14, p. 227.

§

Hart's *Annual Army List*..., 1869, vol. 30, p. 430, no. 67 states:

> Surgeon Major J. W. Fleming served in Ceylon during the rebellion of 1818. Also in the W. and N. W. Provinces of Bengal during the mutiny of 1857-58 (Medal).

§

Dr. Fleming also authored an illustrated catalogue on his collection: MEDALS, CLASPS, AND CROSSES, MILITARY AND NAVAL, IN THE COLLECTION OF J. W. FLEMING, F.R.C.S., SURGEON-MAJOR LATE 4TH DRAGOON GUARDS. The catalogue was described as being "for Private Circulation only," and the authors are only aware of the existence of three copies. The following reviews of this work appeared in 1871 and 1872:

§

Had we possessed any doubt as to whether this volume deserved our good word, the announcement that it was printed for "private circulation only" would have justified our passing it by in silence. But so far from this being the case, we think the author deserves great credit for his choice of a "hobby," in which he was doubtless guided by the esprit de corps, which is a characteristic of "the service," and scarcely less for the good feeling which induces him to print for the use and information of others interested in such trophies of heroism a Catalogue with illustrations—which, of course, add greatly to the value of such Catalogue—of the interesting memorials which he has succeeded in gathering together. The Catalogue is divided under the several heads of Military Medals; Medals to Auxiliary Forces; Medals to H. E. I. Company's Forces; Naval Medals: Medals, &c., from Foreign Sovereigns; Military and Naval Commemorative Medals; and Miscellaneous Medals. This will give a general idea of Mr. Fleming's collection; not the least interesting portion of which consists of a number of various medals not struck for general distribution, but for special presentation to individuals.

—*Notes and Queries,* 1871 (Nov. 4), 4th S. VIII, p. 388.

§

We have had the pleasure to receive from Surgeon-Major J. W. Fleming, late 4th Dragoon Guards, a privately printed brochure, entitled "Medals, Clasps, and Crosses, Military and Naval"—which is an illustrated catalogue of a large number of such objects in his collection. It commences chronologically with gold and silver medals presented by Elizabeth for service against the Spanish Armada, and it comprises numerous examples of such rewards from that time forward to the present day. Of particular interest is a silver medal, struck by order of Charles I. in 1643, for service in the forlorn-hope-a kind of prefigurement of the Victoria Cross—and the Commonwealth gold and silver medals for Dunbar, the first instance, it is stated, of general distribution to officers and men, as is now the practice. We commend to our readers' attention the fact, that, like other collectors, Mr. Fleming has his "wants." One of these is the medal given by Colonel Beckwith to Tom Plunkett, the rifleman, as lately told in our pages; (fn: April, 1871, part 3, p. 584) he would also like the Ceylon " forlorn-hope " medal, the Indian war medal, and half-a-score others, including the Victoria Cross. Can any of our readers oblige him? His address is 113, Marine Parade, Brighton.

—*Colburn's United Service Magazine and Naval and Military Journal*, 1871, vol. 45, p. 288.

§

Although this work bears in its title-page the words "private circulation only," we venture to break the seal of secrecy, and give it due honour in our columns for many and good reasons. First of all, it is a most creditable example of the manner in which many of our brethren, and more especially' those who are engaged in the service of the army and navy, despite of their hard routine duties, of the uncertain and fleeting character of their residence, and of the difficulty of carrying about libraries and collections from one military post to another, and of the temptations to frivolous amusements, yet continue to devote their leisure hours to some substantial branch of science, moral or physical. In the next place, although the book is marked "private," the demands of scholars, antiquarians, and historians must ere long compel it to be made public, as the unique authority on the subject it treats of; and, lastly, should anyone desire to get the book at present, we are pretty sure he could not, for it is not in the market, and not likely to be let go out of the hands of private possessors...

—*Medical Times & Gazette*, Jan 20, 1872, p. 81

§§§§

Sir Richard Tangye

(1833-1906)

Sir Richard Tangye's personal bookplate. Tangye was a most enthusiastic collector of Cromwellian artifacts. His collection of 'Cromwelliana' is now housed in the Museum of London. The bookplate suggests that this copy of *The Cromwellian Collection* is from Tangye's own library.[410]

BORN on a farm in Cornwall, Richard Tangye (1833-1906) might well have become a farmer himself. At the age of eight years, however, he broke his right arm, an injury that prevented him from engaging in manual labor. Sent for an education by his father, he became a pupil-teacher instructing younger children. Soon he had applied for and obtained a position at an engineering works in Birmingham where he was joined by his two brothers, both of whom were mechanics. In 1856, Tangye opened his own business as a hardware factor and commission agent and soon, joined once again by his two brothers, was manufacturing hardware, mechanical equipment, and hydraulic jacks. Success was enhanced by the adoption of his hydraulic jacks for use in the launching of the steamship Great Eastern, and the company branched out to include, in addition to hydraulic equipment, steam, diesel and electrically driven engines. Tangye was knighted in 1894.

[410] This photograph seems to be the same one appearing in the biography of Tangye by Reid, i.e., Stuart Johnson Reid (1908), *Sir Richard Tangye*. London: Duckworth.

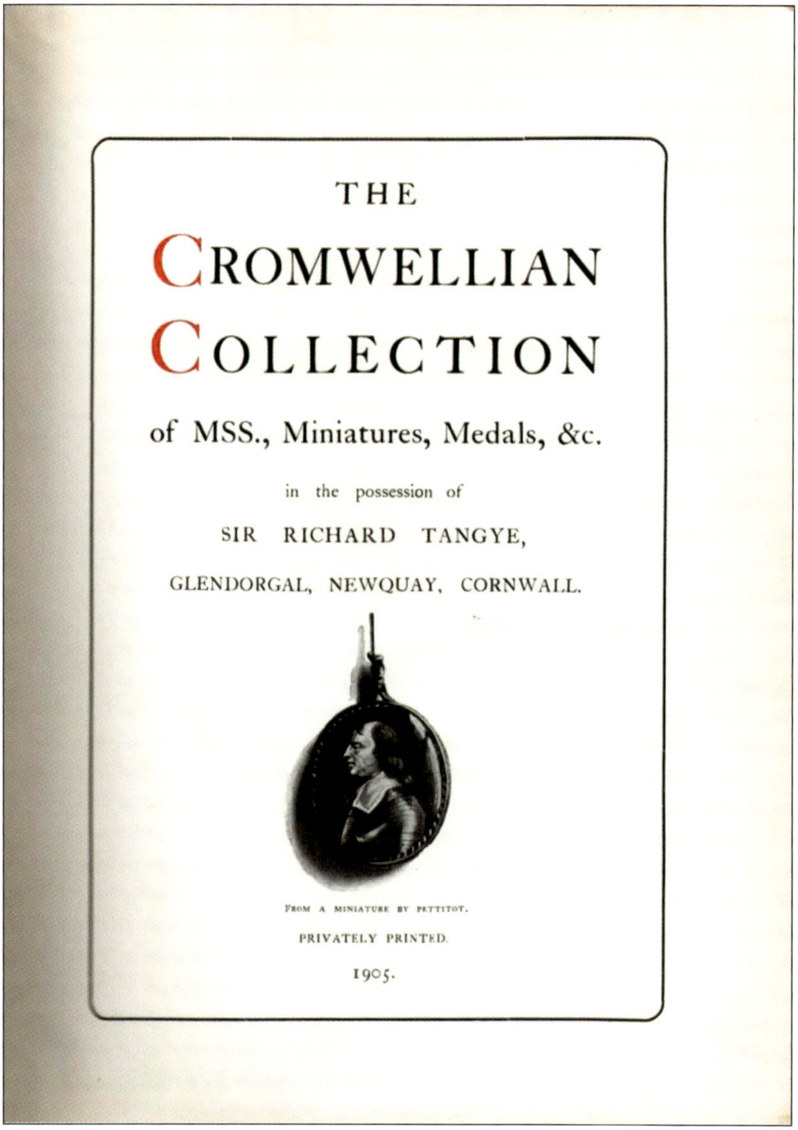

THE

CROMWELLIAN COLLECTION

of MSS., Miniatures, Medals, &c.

in the possession of

SIR RICHARD TANGYE,

GLENDORGAL, NEWQUAY, CORNWALL.

FROM A MINIATURE BY PETTITOT.

PRIVATELY PRINTED.

1905.

The title page of the catalogue of Sir Richard Tangye's collection (1905). Privately printed and somewhat ideosyncratically presented, the wealth of Cromwellian material it describes has probably never been duplicated in a single collection elsewhere.

Tangye was an enthusiastic collector of artifacts, manuscripts and memorabilia related to Oliver Cromwell. Financially capable of purchasing almost any item associated with Cromwell, regardless of cost, and collecting at a time when such items were still relatively inexpensive, he amassed a large number of them. Tangye's collection included coins, medals and medal dies, autograph letters, books, paintings, prints, and personal 'relics' of the Protector. This last category included such items as Oliver Cromwell's bible, coffin plate, death mask and funeral escutcheon. The Museum of London now houses this collection, it having been donated at the time of Tangye's death.[411] Perhaps the best description of Tangye and his collection is found in the biography by Reid:

> Probably it was the pages of Carlyle which first drew Richard Tangye into the ranks of Cromwell's whole-hearted, but, at the same time, not uncritical admirers....He eagerly read every book about him on which he could lay his hand, and when his own means became ample he began to collect medals, miniatures, pamphlets, and historical documents of the Commonwealth, and everything that seemed likely to elucidate the character of this extraordinary man.
>
> He began this task—if such a term is applicable to what was clearly a labour of love—as early as 1875, and as his enthusiasm became known nearly everything which was on the market, which in the least degree threw light on Cromwell's career, was offered to him...(p. 203).
>
> Apart from books, political tracts, and autograph letters, the Cromwell collection is surprisingly rich in commemorative medals of the Protector, and in coins minted during the Commonwealth. There are also many manuscripts...[as well as] several beautiful miniatures of Cromwell, John Hampden, John Lilburne, Prince Rupert, General Fleetwood, General Ireton, and many other celebrities of the period, and portraits in oil of Charles I. and Oliver Cromwell, and many rare prints. Perhaps the most interesting personal relic is Oliver Cromwell's watch, made at Worcester, a button from Oliver's coat, purloined when he was sitting in judgment on Charles...Amongst other interesting mementoes is the baton of Sir Thomas Fairfax, General of the Parliamentary forces, an ebony staff with silver head, bearing an inscription, and dated 1645, and the skull of Richard Brandon, the supposed executioner of Charles I,. But beyond all else, he valued Oliver Cromwell's Bible, with his own Signature on the fly-leaf (pp. 208-209).[412]

Tangye prepared two books—*The Two Protectors: Oliver and Richard Cromwell*[413] as well as a catalogue of his personal collection of *Cromwelliana: The Cromwellian Collection of Mss., Miniatures, Medals. &c. in the Possession of Sir Richard Tangye*.[414] Charles Harding Firth, in preparing his classic work, *The Letters and Speeches of Oliver Cromwell*, consulted Oliver Cromwell's original letters in Tangye's exhaustive collection.

[411] H. Chisum (ed.), *Encyclopedia Britannica*...(1911), vol. xxxi, p. 398; S. J. Reid, (1906). 'Death of Sir Richard Tangye.' New York Times, October [illegible], 1906. 'Sir Richard Tangye,' Wikipedia, the Free Encyclopedia.

[412] S. J. Reid, op cit..

[413] London: Partridge, 1899.

[414] Privately printed, 1905. This work being very scarce when compared to *The Two Protectors*. The bookplate which appears on the preceding page is from Tangye's personal copy of this work.

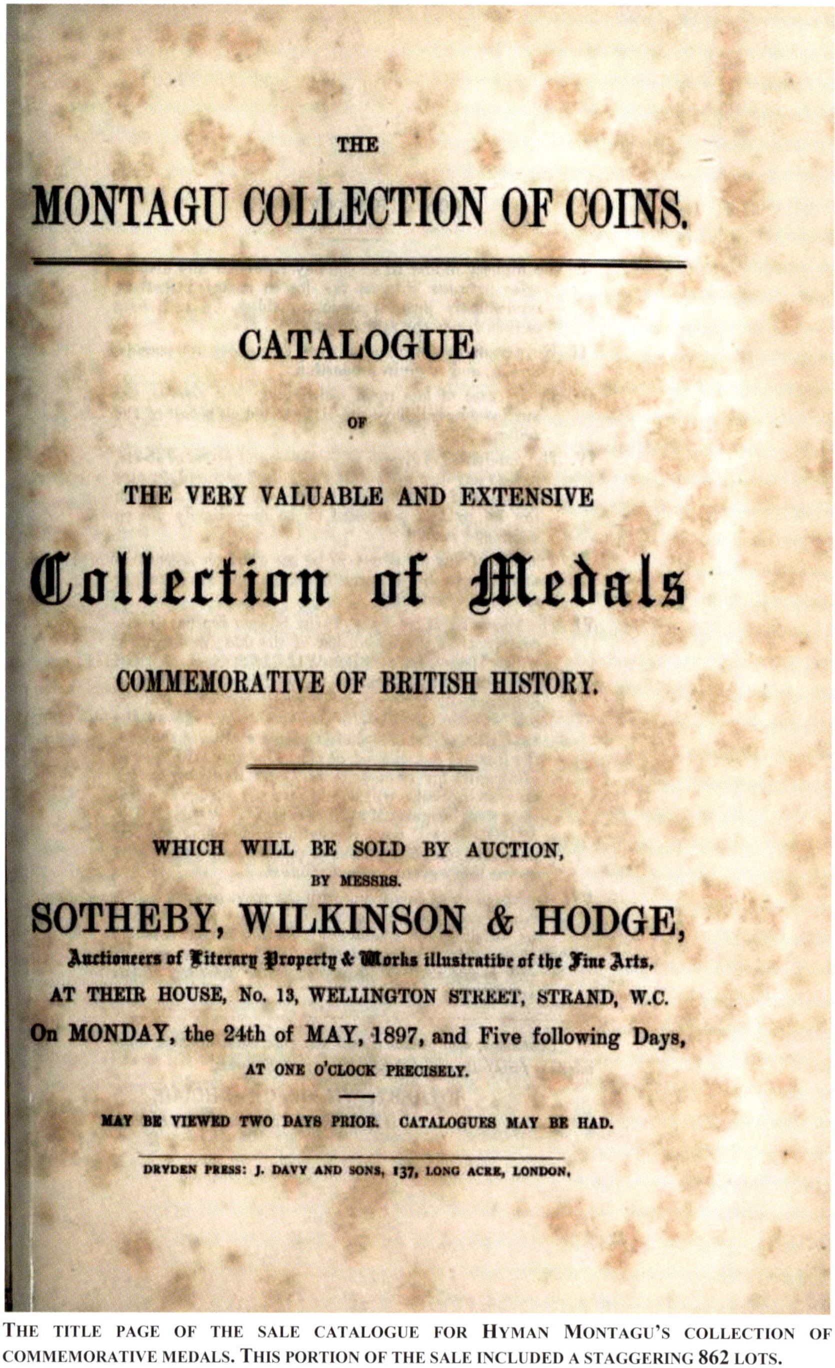

THE

MONTAGU COLLECTION OF COINS.

CATALOGUE

OF

THE VERY VALUABLE AND EXTENSIVE

Collection of Medals

COMMEMORATIVE OF BRITISH HISTORY.

WHICH WILL BE SOLD BY AUCTION,

BY MESSRS.

SOTHEBY, WILKINSON & HODGE,

Auctioneers of Literary Property & Works illustrative of the Fine Arts,

AT THEIR HOUSE, No. 13, WELLINGTON STREET, STRAND, W.C.

On MONDAY, the 24th of MAY, 1897, and Five following Days,

AT ONE O'CLOCK PRECISELY.

MAY BE VIEWED TWO DAYS PRIOR. CATALOGUES MAY BE HAD.

DRYDEN PRESS: J. DAVY AND SONS, 137, LONG ACRE, LONDON.

THE TITLE PAGE OF THE SALE CATALOGUE FOR HYMAN MONTAGU'S COLLECTION OF COMMEMORATIVE MEDALS. THIS PORTION OF THE SALE INCLUDED A STAGGERING 862 LOTS.

Hyman Montagu

(1844-1895)

HYMAN MONTAGU, whose father was named Samuel Moses, was born and educated at the City of London School and later took the name of Montagu. Having been articled to a firm of attorneys, Montagu passed his bar examinations with distinction and soon was recognized as an expert in bankruptcy law. He was a collector from his early years, first of beetles, and from 1878, of coins. Montagu also gained a reputation as an expert numismatist, and contributed to the knowledge of the science through lectures, and the authorship of articles and books. These achievements earned him election as a fellow of the Society of Antiquaries and vice-president of the Numismatic Society.

HYMAN MONTAGU, F.S.A. ALTHOUGH MONTAGU, LIKE MANY OTHER 'GREAT COLLECTORS,' COLLECTED BROADLY, INCLUDING ANCIENT GREEK, ROMAN, ANGLO-SAXON AND MODERN ENGLISH COINS, HIS COLLECTION INCLUDED 250 MEDALS RELATING TO THE CIVIL WAR, COMMONWEALTH AND RESTORATION PERIODS. IMAGE © TRUSTEES OF THE BRITISH MUSEUM.

Montagu's collecting interests included the British and English series, Greek coins, and Roman gold coins, this last group alone numbering some 1,800 items, as well as medals relating to British history. Among his publications, in addition to some 30 papers in the *Numismatic Chronicle*, were: *A Catalogue... of a Collection of Milled English Coins Dating from the Reign of George I. to that of Queen Victoria* (1890) and *The Copper, Tin, and Bronze Coinage, and Patterns for Coins of England from the Reign of Elizabeth to that of Queen Victoria* (1885-93). He also prepared the catalogue of coins for the Anglo-Jewish Historical Exhibition which was held in London in 1887, presented a valuable collection of coins to the British Museum, and served on the boards of Jewish charities.[415]

Montagu's collections were sold by Sotheby, Wilkinson & Hodge in a series of auctions beginning on November 18, 1895, the medals being sold in the last six sessions beginning on May 24, 1897. A description of Montagu's collection has recently been published elsewhere.[416]

[415] Obituary, *Jewish Chronicle and Jewish World*, Feb. 22, 1895; also in *The Jewish Encyclopedia* (1906); *Numismatic Chronicle*, 1895, pp. 23-24.

[416] Farey, R. 'Hyman Montagu (1844-1895).' *Coin News* (March 2013), vol. 50, no. 3, p. 38.

THE 'JUXON MEDAL,' THE FIVE-BROAD PIECE IN GOLD GIVEN BY CHARLES I TO BISHOP JUXON ON THE SCAFFOLD AND NOW IN THE BRITISH MUSEUM (38 MM., M.I.I 374/270, M.I.ILL XXXIII/21, PLATT I/278/A). IMAGE © TRUSTEES OF THE BRITISH MUSEUM. M.I.I INTERPRETS THE *REV.* INSCRIPTION AS 'KINGDOMS FLOURISH BY CONCORD.'

Exceptional interest has been taken in the sale during December of the large collection of rare coins belonging to the late Mr. Hyman Montagu, F.S.A. The most important item in the sale was that of the celebrated "Juxon Medal," which fetched the extraordinary sum of *£770*. The medal is really a pattern five broad piece in gold, and it possesses a double interest as being not merely one of the finest works of Thomas Rawlins, but also on account of its having been presented to Bishop Juxon by Charles I. on the scaffold just before his execution. From the bishop it passed in a direct line to his descendant, Mrs. Mary Gythens, who bequeathed "her gold medal of King Charles I." to James Commeline, a Fellow of St. John's College, Cambridge, who had married her daughter, Miss Gythens. The late Lieut.-Colonel John Drummond purchased the coin of a grandson of the Rev. James Commeline, and he in turn disposed of it to Mr. Till, the dealer, who sold it soon afterwards to Mr. Cuff. From the Cuff collection it has passed successively into the possession of Mr. Thomas Brown, for many years a partner in the firm of Longman and Co., the publishers, of Mr. Edward Wigan, of Mr. Samuel Addington, and, lastly, into the collection of Mr. Montagu. From these facts it will be seen that its pedigree and authenticity are irreproachable. It is in a perfect state of preservation, as may be seen from the accompanying illustration, and as a relic of Charles I. it is unquestionably of very high interest.

—*The Antiquary*, Jan., 1897, vol. xxxiii, p. 3.

THE MONTAGU SALE

THE TITLE PAGE FOR THE MONTAGU COLLECTION SALE CATALOGUE APPEARS ABOVE ON P. 312, AND TWO SAMPLE PAGES OF ILLUSTRATIONS FROM THE SALE APPEAR ON PAGES 315 AND 317. INCLUDED IN THE SALE WAS A SUBSET OF COINS FOR WHICH SOTHEBY'S HAD SOUGHT A SINGLE BUYER IN ORDER TO MAINTAIN THE COLLECTION INTACT. IN THE END, THE ITEMS WERE SOLD SINGLY. TO GIVE SOME IDEA OF THE SIZE OF THIS COLLECTION, THERE WERE 862 LOTS OF COMMEMORATIVE MEDALS ALONE OF WHICH APPROXIMATELY 250 COULD BE CONSIDERED TO BE RELATED TO THE ENGLISH CIVIL WAR. THESE INCLUDE (A) THE REIGN OF CHARLES I AND CIVIL WAR (LOTS 105-200), (B) COMMONWEALTH (LOTS 201-259), AND (C) CHARLES II PERIODS (LOTS 260-379). EXCLUDING LATER CHARLES II MEDALS, THERE WERE PERHAPS 150 EARLY RESTORATION ERA MEDALS, INCLUDING A NUMBER OF DUTCH NAVAL MEDALS (E.G., ADMIRAL TROMP, ETC.). THE PAGES ILLUSTRATED HERE CONTAIN AN EXTRAORDINARY PROPORTION OF VERY RARE GOLD MEDALS.

THE ITEMS ILLUSTRATED ON PLATE I FROM THE SALE CATALOGUE ARE: N$^{o.}$ 63. MAURICE, PRINCE OF ORANGE, ON HIS CAPTURE OF GRAVE, 1602, IN GOLD, M.I.I 180/182; 65. QUEEN ELIZABETH, IN COMMEMORATION OF HER SUCCESSFUL REIGN, 1602, IN SILVER, M.I.I 181/184; 79. HENRY, PRINCE OF WALES, 1612, IN GOLD, M.I.I 200/29; 131. SUPPRESSION OF THE SCOTTISH REBELLION, 1639, IN GOLD, M.I.I 283/92; 139. EARL OF ESSEX, GENERAL, 1642, M.I.I 296/114; 149. SIR RICHARD BROWN, 1644, IN SILVER, M.I.I 312/142; 157. BARON DE REEDE, 1645, IN SILVER, M.I.I 320/156; 162. ALBERT JOACHIM, AMBASSADOR EXTRAORDINARY; 204. M.I.I 324/162. OLIVER CROMWELL AS CAPTAIN-GENERAL, IN SILVER, 388/7; 215. NAVAL REWARD, 1653, IN GOLD, M.I.I 400/28.

PLATE I FROM THE CATALOGUE FOR THE SALE OF HYMAN MONTAGU'S COLLECTION. FOR THE LEGEND, SEE PREVIOUS PAGE. PAGE IMAGES COURTESY OF UNIVERSITY OF CALIFORNIA LIBRARIES AND INTERNET ARCHIVE.

Historical Commentary on Hyman Montagu

Next week will begin the sale of what is perhaps the finest collection of coins that has ever come under the hammer. It was formed by the late Hyman Montagu, who was not only a keen collector with a long purse, but also a profound numismatist, who delighted to annotate his treasures and to determine their provenance and pedigree. He used to buy up complete collections and newly found hoards, selecting only the rarest and best specimens for his own cabinet. His special interest was in the coinage of this country from the earliest times, though he also extended his favour to Greek and Roman gold. In the British and Anglo-Saxon series, no collection in private hands could rival his; and the same might be said of his English historical medals...The remainder of the collection will be disposed of at intervals during next year. If possible, the English medals will be sold *en bloc;* and it is noticeable that the Roman series is reserved for the Paris market.

—*The Academy*, Nov. 16, 1895, no. 1228, p.418.

§

The medals commemorative of British history collected by the late Mr. Hyman Montagu were dispersed by Messrs. Sotheby, Wilkinson & Hodge between the 24th and 29th ult... Charles, Prince of Wales, 1616, by the same, 24*l.* 5s.; Maurice, Prince of Orange, 1616, by the same, 38*l.*; The Synod of Dort, 1619, 35*l.*, and Earl of Essex, 1642, 37*l.*; Oliver Cromwell as Captain-General of the Army of the Parliament, 1650, gold, by T. Simon, 30*l.* 10s...; William II. of Orange and Admiral Van Tromp, 50*l.* Oliver Cromwell, on his elevation to the Protectorate, 1653, gold, by Simon, 70*l.*, and Peace between Great Britain and Holland, 1654, gold, 51*l.*

—*The Athenæum*, June 12, 1897, no. 3622, p.786.

§

Among the many heavy losses which during the past year the Society has sustained is that of Mr. Hyman Montagu, F.S.A., one of our Vice Presidents, who by his constant attendance at our meetings, his readiness to take part in our discussions, his numerous contributions to numismatic knowledge, and his uniform courtesy and consideration for others had endeared himself to all our members ...

From his early life he had been a collector, but principally in the direction of natural history, and as a young man his application to business as a solicitor left him but little leisure for other pursuits. He had, however, already an extensive collection of coins when he joined this Society in January, 1882. At that time he was paying attention principally to the British and English series, but in after years he by no means restricted himself to that series. His fine collection of Jewish coins exhibited at the Anglo Jewish Exhibition in 1887, and his Greek collection, with a part of which we made acquaintance in the *Numismatic Chronicle* for 1892, comprise numerous rare coins in splendid condition; while his cabinet of Roman gold coins, numbering some 1,800 pieces, is probably the finest that it has ever been the fortune of a private individual to form. His series of medals relating to English history is also, I believe, unique of its kind. *The secret of forming such collections is known but too few. The doing so involves, however, many somewhat rare personal qualifications—first, an intuitive knowledge of the value and importance of coins, strengthened by much reading and handling of the coins themselves; secondly, a confidence in one's own judgment; and, lastly, facilities for travel and the possession of ample pecuniary means to take advantage of any opportunity that may arise. These, and probably other, qualifications Mr. Montagu possessed*[417]...Of his papers in the *Chronicle*, amounting to nearly thirty in number, I need hardly append a list. They are all marked by great care and attention to detail, and by an acquaintance with the work of others. In addition to these, he published in 1885 *The Copper, Tin, and Bronze Coinage, and Patterns for Coins of England*, which has already reached a second edition, and is the standard work upon the subject. His premature decease took place on the 18th of February last after a short, but severe illness, at the age of fifty years.

—*The Numismatic Chronicle and Journal of the Numismatic Society*, 1895, vol. 15, pp. 23-24.

[417] Emphasis added by the authors.

Plate II from the catalogue for the Hyman Montagu sale. The illustrated medals [illegible] Oliver Cromwell, Protector [illegible]; [illegible] General Monk, 1660, silver, M.I.1 465/63; 288. Charles II, Coronation, 1661, silver, M.I.1 475/83; 299. Thomas Wriothesley, Earl of Southampton, 1664, silver, M.I.1 502/137; 304. Charles II, Honorary Naval Reward, 1665, silver, M.I.1 506/144; 349. Installation of John George Elector of Saxony as a Knight of the Garter, 1671, gold, M.I.1 548/205; 407. Landing of William of Orange at Torbay, 1688, gold, M.I.1. 639/65.

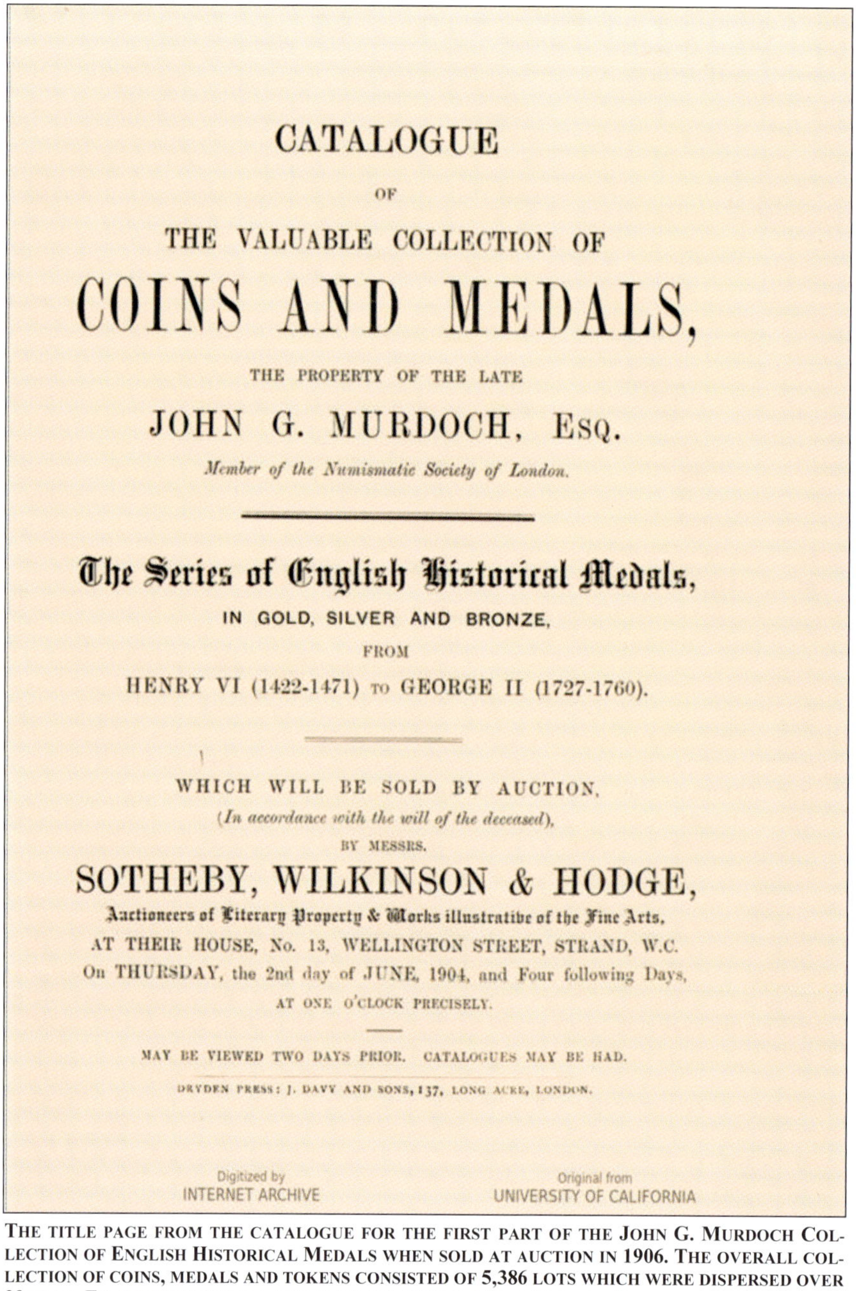

CATALOGUE

OF

THE VALUABLE COLLECTION OF

COINS AND MEDALS,

THE PROPERTY OF THE LATE

JOHN G. MURDOCH, ESQ.

Member of the Numismatic Society of London.

The Series of English Historical Medals,

IN GOLD, SILVER AND BRONZE,

FROM

HENRY VI (1422-1471) TO GEORGE II (1727-1760).

WHICH WILL BE SOLD BY AUCTION,

(In accordance with the will of the deceased),

BY MESSRS.

SOTHEBY, WILKINSON & HODGE,

Auctioneers of Literary Property & Works illustrative of the Fine Arts,

AT THEIR HOUSE, No. 13, WELLINGTON STREET, STRAND, W.C.

On THURSDAY, the 2nd day of JUNE, 1904, and Four following Days,

AT ONE O'CLOCK PRECISELY.

MAY BE VIEWED TWO DAYS PRIOR. CATALOGUES MAY BE HAD.

DRYDEN PRESS: J. DAVY AND SONS, 137, LONG ACRE, LONDON.

THE TITLE PAGE FROM THE CATALOGUE FOR THE FIRST PART OF THE JOHN G. MURDOCH COLLECTION OF ENGLISH HISTORICAL MEDALS WHEN SOLD AT AUCTION IN 1906. THE OVERALL COLLECTION OF COINS, MEDALS AND TOKENS CONSISTED OF 5,386 LOTS WHICH WERE DISPERSED OVER 39 DAYS. ENGLISH HISTORICAL MEDALS FROM HENRY VI TO GEORGE II CONSISTED OF 670 LOTS WHILE THOSE FROM GEORGE III TO VICTORIA TOTALED 414 LOTS, INCLUDING A FEW SCOTTISH COINS. IMAGE FROM THE UNIVERSITY OF CALIFORNIA, DIGITIZED BY INTERNET ARCHIVE.

John G. Murdoch

(1830-1902)

THE Murdoch collection of coins and medals was sold by Sotheby, Wilkinson & Hodge in a series of seven auctions in 1903-1904: These sales included ancient British, Anglo-Saxon and English coins (March 1903, June 1903, and March 1904); Scottish and Anglo-Gallic coins (May 1903); coins of the British colonies and dependencies, America and the European Continent (July 1903); and Ancient British, Anglo-Saxon and English coins (June 1904).

The Murdoch collection of English historical medals of Henry VI to George II was sold in a sale over six days (June 2-6, 1904). Although slightly smaller than the Montagu collection, it was one of the largest collections of such material to have come to auction in Britain. The sale contained over 670 lots overall, of which 657 were of medals; included were a total of 235 lots for Charles I (lots 53-146), Commonwealth (147-192) and Charles II (193-288) periods, respectively.

JOHN G. MURDOCH, WHO AMASSED A TRULY GREAT COLLECTION OF MEDALS OF THE ENGLISH CIVIL WAR, COMMONWEALTH AND RESTORATION PERIODS.

John G[loag] Murdoch was born in Huntingtower, Perthshire, and began his working life at age 13 as an apprentice block-cutter for the printing of patterns on cotton. When the introduction of newly developed machinery made his skills obsolete before he had completed his apprenticeship, he began a second apprenticeship learning the new machine printing technique. After working in this trade for several years, he sought advancement by joining a Glasgow-based family bible publisher. Having been successful in expanding the business to other cities in the north of England, he struck out on his own, opening a bible-printing firm in London, an enterprise which became highly successful. He soon expanded his business to include the publication and sale of reproductions of paintings of eminent contemporary artists. Murdoch's reproduction oleographs were lithographic prints using oil colors. These were first printed on plates given as gifts to purchasers of the bibles his firm produced; they became very popular and sold very well on their own. The next addition to Murdoch's product line was photograph albums and he soon was publishing and selling them in large numbers. Many of these albums incorporated a music box which played a tune when opened, and a new product line of music boxes soon followed. Once again, the popularity of one product line led to the development of another and Murdoch was soon selling larger music boxes, and then musical instruments of all kinds, including pianos and organs. This last was perhaps the product line, along with bibles, with which Murdoch is most often associated, although the company also sold prams, mangles and toys and more. Eventually he would have all these diverse enterprises plus a large chain of retail music and furniture stores. In [illegible], Murdoch stood for Parliament, but failed to gain election.[418]

[418] C. Smythe, http://www.colinsmythe.co.uk/cslinks/john_g_murdoch.htm.

PLATE V. FROM THE AUCTION CATALOGUE FOR THE 1906 SALE OF THE JOHN G. MURDOCH COLLECTION. THE MEDALS ILLUSTRATED ARE: N$^{O.}$ 64. DEATH OF THE EARL OF ESSEX (M.I.I 326/167, M.I.ILL XXXI/8); 105. SIR JOHN HOTHAM (M.I.I 313/144, M.I.ILL XXVII/7); 111. BARON DE REEDE (M.I.I 320/156, M.I.ILL XXVIII/4); 112. JOHN CAMPBELL, EARL OF LOUDOUN (M.I.I 321/157, M.I.ILL XXVIII/5); 114. LORD INCHIQUIN (M.I.I 324/161, M.I.ILL XXXVIII/1); 115. SIR SYDENHAM POINTZ (M.I.I 325/163, M.I.ILL XXVIII/12); 116. MANTEAU VAN DALEM (M.I.I AND M.I.ILL *no entry*); 147. HENRY SOBELL (M.I.I 384/2, M.I.ILL XXXIV/20); 176. SIR JAMES HARRINGTON (M.I.I 408/43, M.I.ILL XXXVII/6); 195. GENERAL GEORGE MONK (M.I.I 465/63, M.I.ILL XLIV/11); 224. SOLICITOR-GENERAL COOK[E] (M.I.I 469/70, M.I.ILL XLV/2); 229. LADY LANE (M.I.I 480/89, M.I.ILL XLVI/2); 239. EARL OF SOUTHAMPTON (M.I.I 502/137, M.I.ILL XLVIII/9).

Captain John Hamilton

IN mentioning collectors, I must not pass over Captain John Hamilton, of 26, Charles Street, St. James's, who, when I knew him, devoted himself entirely to the study of decorative and commemorative Medals. His well-known figure, in a semi-eastern costume, as he sat at his writing-table with a large cigar in his mouth, examining, perhaps, some new acquisition to his cabinet, will not be forgotten by his numismatic friends. His collection, which contained many brilliant and rare examples, was originally intended to be left to the Marquis of Dufferin; he changed his mind, seemingly, and they became the property of Mr. Saunders [sic], by purchase, who ultimately sold them by auction at Sotheby's.

—G. Tancred, Preface to Colonel Murray's Catalogue, in *Historical Record...,* 1891, p. 406.

§

•The Earl and Countess of Dufferin prize medals•

These medals were struck in 1873 by order of the Earl of Dufferin, at that time Governor-General of Canada, for general distribution as prizes during his term of office. It was executed by Messrs. Wyon under the direction of Captain John Hamilton, the well-known collector of historical medals and decorations, whose collection was sold in 1882, having passed after his death into the hands of Mr. James Sanders [sic].

—*Numismatic Chronicle,* 1890, 3rd series, vol. x, pp. 97-98.

CATALOGUE

OF THE

MEDALS OF SCOTLAND

FROM THE EARLIEST PERIOD TO THE PRESENT TIME

ARRANGED BY

R. W. COCHRAN-PATRICK OF WOODSIDE, M.P.

LL.D. GLAS., LL.B. CANTAB, B.A. EDIN., F.S.A., SEC. S.A. SCOT.

MEMBER OF THE NUM. SOC. OF LOND.

ETC. ETC. ETC.

EDINBURGH: DAVID DOUGLAS, CASTLE STREET

MDCCCLXXXIV.

THE TITLE PAGE OF R. W. COCHRAN-PATRICK'S WORK ON MEDALS. PUBLISHED IN 1884, THIS WAS THE FIRST ATTEMPT AT A CATALOGUE OF SCOTTISH HISTORICAL AND MISCELLANEOUS MEDALS. ONE REVIEWER, HOWEVER, FOUND THE MEDAL DESCRIPTIONS SCANTY, AND THE EXPLANATORY AND HISTORICAL NOTES INADEQUATE (ANON., *THE ANTHENÆUM*, JAN. 31, 1885, P. 156). ONE WONDERS IF THERE WAS A BACKGROUND STORY HERE, GIVEN COCHRAN-PATRICK'S PREEMINENT POSITIONS IN BOTH THE NUMISMATIC AND ACADEMIC WORLDS.

R. W. Cochran-Patrick

(1842-1897)

ROBERT WILLIAM COCHRAN-PATRICK authored a volume attempting to catalogue all the medals of Scotland, including historical medals as well as those of more local interest, such as agricultural tournament and sports medals. A collector himself, he built one of the great collections of Scottish medals. For the production of his work *Catalogue of the Medals of Scotland from the Earliest Period to the Present Time,* published in 1884, Cochran-Patrick also drew upon medals in the National Collection in Edinburgh as well as upon medals in private collections. The catalogue, of which 350 numbered copies were printed, only includes those medals having a Scottish association. It is 194 pages in length and has 36 plates. The illustrated medals are from the reigns of James I through George IV as well as "medals of the Stuart family, other than the reigning monarch." This last group includes medals of such figures as the duke of Albany (the son of Alexander, younger brother of 'James III'), the duke of Monmouth (Charles II's son), and the consorts of the kings of Scotland. Also included are chapters on 'medals of the Revolution of 1688 and the subsequent fortunes of the Stuart family,' 'medals relating to Scottish history,' and 'medals of illustrious Scottish persons,' and 'local and miscellaneous medals.'

Born in Ladyland in Ayrshire, Cochran-Patrick was educated at the University of Edinburgh and Trinity Hall, Cambridge. Following his education, he returned to Ladyland House and devoted his time to his archeological and numismatic interests. In addition to his *Catalogue of the Medals of Scotland...,* he also produced *Records of the Coinage of Scotland: From the Earliest Period to the Union* (2 vols., 1876) and several other works of a non-numismatic nature (e.g., *Medieval Scotland; Agriculture, Manufactures, Factories, Taxation, Revenue, Trade, Commerce, Weights and Measures,* 1892). Elected to Fellowship in the Society of Antiquaries of Scotland as well as the Society of Antiquaries of London, Cochran-Patrick represented North Ayrshire in the House of Commons from 1880 to 1885 and was permanent undersecretary for Scotland from 1887 to 1892. From 1882 to 1885 he was Dean of Faculties at Glasgow University.[419]

Historical Commentary on R. W. Cochran-Patrick

Mr. Robert W. Cochran Patrick, F.S.A., of Beith, in Ayrshire, was an old Member of the Society, having been elected in 1871, and was among the most distinguished Scottish numismatists of this century. His Records of the Coinage of Scotland, published in two volumes in 1876, was soon followed by Records of Mining in Scotland, which appeared in 1878, and the Catalogue of the Medals of Scotland, published in 1884. These four handsome quarto volumes are monuments of his learning, zeal, and industry; but besides producing these independent standard works, he was for many years a constant contributor to the pages of the Numismatic Chronicle. In the New Series there are no less than eighteen papers from his pen, all relating to the Scottish coinage, and several of them giving accounts of unpublished varieties. Of late years his communications have been fewer in number, but the last of these, published in 1888, constituted an important supplement to his work on Scottish medals. Besides being a first-rate numismatist and a good antiquary, Mr. Cochran Patrick played a not unimportant part in politics. In the days when Scottish Conservative M.P.s were far scarcer than at present, he sat for North Ayrshire, from 1880 to 1885. From 1887 to 1892 he was Under- Secretary for Scotland, and at the time of his death, which was sudden, on the 15th of March, 1897, he was Deputy- Chairman of the Scottish Fishery Board. He took an active part in all matters relating to his native county of Ayrshire, as well as in all that concerned Scottish antiquities, and at different times held the offices of Secretary and Vice-President of the Society of Antiquaries of Scotland. He died deeply regretted by many personal friends at the comparatively early age of fifty-five.

—*The Numismatic Chronicle and Journal of the Numismatic Society*, 3rd Series, vol. xvii, p. 26.

419 L. Brown (2003). A Discourse of Medals, *B.N.J*, vol. 73, p. 175.

PLATE 2 FROM COCHRAN-PATRICK'S *CATALOGUE OF THE MEDALS OF SCOTLAND*. THE MEDALS ILLUSTRATED ARE: N$^{o.}$ 1. JAMES VI, JETON (1588, M.I.I 150/123); 2. JAMES VI OF SCOTLAND, MEDAL (1590, COPY, M.I.I 158/137); 3. JAMES VI AND HIS QUEEN, MARRIAGE (1590, M.I.I 157/36); 4. JAMES VI, ATTEMPTED UNION OF ENGLAND AND SCOTLAND (1604, M.I.I 194/17); 5. JAMES VI, SCOTTISH CORONATION (M.I.I 265/59); 6. DITTO (M.I.I 266/60); 7. CHARLES I, RETURN FROM SCOTLAND, 1633 (M.I.I 266/62); 8. CHARLES I, SCOTTISH REBELLION (1639, M.I.I 282/90); 9. CHARLES II, CORONATION IN SCOTLAND (1651 M.I.I 394/18).

Plate 18 from Cochran-Patrick's *Medals of Scotland*..., illustrating medals of English Civil War personages: N$^{o.}$ 1. John Campbell, earl of Loudoun (M.I.i 321/157, M.I.Ill xxviii/5), 2. Sir Charles Seton, earl of Dunfermline (M.I.i 328/168, M.I.Ill xxviii/13); 3. Sir Charles Erskine of Alva (M.I.i 330/173, M.I.Ill xxix/5); 4. James Graham, marquess of M[illegible], M.I.Ill [illegible]; 5. John Maitland, duke of Lauderdale (M.I.i 328/169, M.I.Ill xxviii/18); and 6. another of Lauderdale (M.I.i 550/200, M.I.Ill [illegible])

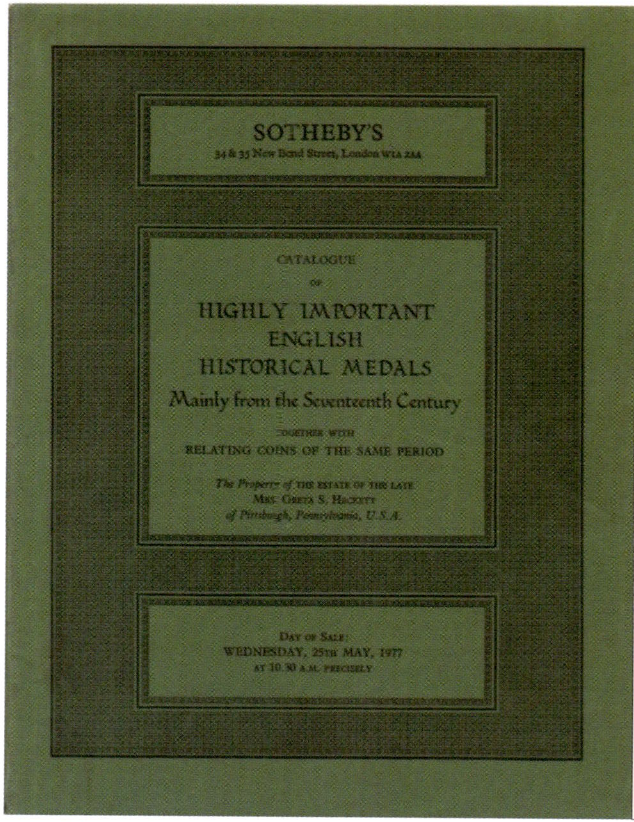

(Left) The cover of the catalogue for the sale of Mrs. Greta Heckett's collection of English historical medals at Sotheby's in 1977. *(Right)* Plate 8. Of the many rare items illustrated, items 102 and 103 are of particular interest, the catalogue entries for which respectively note: *[No. 102] excessively rare, apparently unpublished…The portrait of James I applied to this badge is similar to that on M.I.1 1/233/96, [and for no. 103]…almost certainly unique. Ex Phillip Spence Collection, 1 April 1947 (lot 314).*

Greta Heckett

(1899-1976)

MENTION needs to be made of the collection of "Highly Important English Historical Medals," sold by the estate of Greta Heckett, on May 25, 1977, at Sotheby Park Burnet (London). A total of four sales dispersed the collectibles in Mrs. Heckett's estate— her collections of miniatures included "a group of Stuart memorabilia…, as well as books on the subject," ancient coins, Renaissance medals and Continental coins. These sales included many rarities—the collection of Royalist badges and medals was, however, extraordinary. The catalogue stated that Mrs. Heckett's:

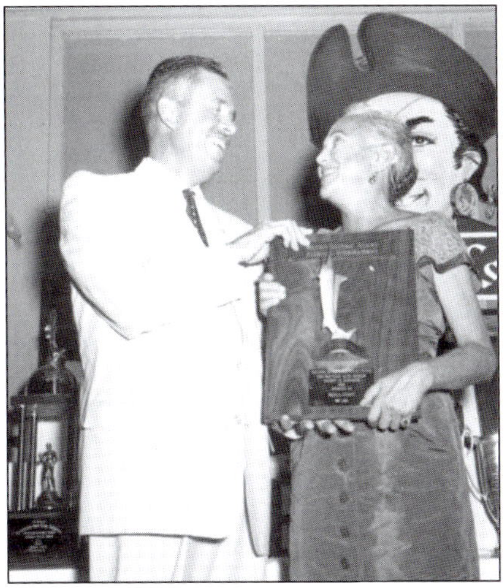

A RARE PICTURE OF MRS. HECKETT, HERE RECEIVING A PRIZE FOR SPORT FISHING IN MIAMI, FLORIDA. IMAGE COURTESY STATE ARCHIVES OF FLORIDA. PHOTOGRAPH BY FRANCIS P. JOHNSON.

> ...cabinet of seventeenth century medals is the most comprehensive to appear at public auction since the last war. A number of very rare pieces were bought for her at the Farquhar and O'Byrne sales but the variety and number of medals in this sale far exceeds those earlier two provenances. Similarly, Mrs Heckett was fortunate enough to be offered many medals straight from the collection of H. K. Hepburn-Wright and these purchases, together with those from Miss Helen Farquhar's sale in 1955, allowed her to assemble a formidable number of rarities, in addition to a surprising complete series of the more well-known badges and medals. Many of these were once considered to be relatively common but so few have come onto the market in recent years that it is as much of a pleasure to see them as it is to see the great rarities which accompany them. Amongst these rarer items Mrs Heckett was able to acquire several unpublished medals and more than one of them appears to be unique... the royalist badges, in particular lots 102 and 103, are equally significant and worthy of particular attention (—Sotheby Parke Bernet, foreword to the sale catalogue, March 1977).

LEGEND FOR PLATE 8 OF THE HECKETT SALE CATALOGUE

SEE FACING PAGE: ALL CHARLES I BADGES AND IN SILVER EXCEPT WHERE NOTED: N^O.^ 100. CHARLES I, UNCROWNED, *OBV. INSCRIPTION:* CAROLVS D G MAG BRI FR ET HIB RX, ROYAL ARMS; *REV.:* INCUSE CROWNED ROYAL ASRMS WITHIN GARTER (SIMILAR TO M.I.I 360/231, M.I.ILL XXXII/8, PLATT I/169/B); 102. CHARLES I, UNCROWNED, *REV.* WITH A PLAQUE OF JAMES I (SIMILAR TO M.I.I 215/231, M.I.ILL XXXII/8, PLATT I/177/A) WITH SMALL JAMES I BADGE SIMILAR TO M.I.I 233/96; 103. CHARLES I, UNCROWNED, *REV.* WITH INSCRIPTION *KING CHARLES DY'D / I FEARE MY GOD / I LOVE MY KING / I ABHORE A REBLE. JANUARY 30 1648* BELOW (*OBV.*: M.I.I 215; M.I.ILL XXXII/8,), *REV.* APPARENTLY UNIQUE (*CF.* PLATT I/178/B); 104. CHARLES I, CROWNED, IN SILVER-GILT, *REV.* ROYAL ARMS WITHIN GARTER LARGE CROWN ABOVE (M.I.I 360/232, M.I.ILL XXXII/10, PLATT I/162/C), 106. CHARLES I, SMALL BADGE (M.I.I 361/235, M.I.ILL XXXII/13, PLATT I/289/I); 109. CHARLES I, SMALL BADGE (M.I.I 362/238, M.I.ILL XXXII/16, PLATT I/289/M); 111. CUT OUT FROM MEDAL BY HEINRICH REITZ, POSSIBLY 19TH C (M.I.I 370/259, M.I.ILL XXX/10, PLATT I/221/A$_1$, SIMILAR); 112. PRINCE [illegible] FARQUHAR COLLECTION (M.I.I 372/[illegible], M.I.ILL [illegible], PLATT I/290/C), 113-120. LOCKETS IN SILVER (M.I.I 360/249, M.I.ILL [illegible], SEE PLATT I/292-295/A-F FOR SIMILAR PIECES); 121. COMMONWEALTH, DUNBAR MEDAL IN SILVER (M.I.I 392/14, M.I.ILL [illegible], PLATT [illegible], WITHOUT LOOP); 124. CHARLES II, CORONATION AT SCONE IN SILVER (M.I.I 394/18, M.I.ILL XXXV/8, PLATT II/124/A).

Plate 12 from the Heckett Collection sale: No. 211. Scottish Coronation, 1633, by Nicholas Briot (M.I.i 266/60, M.I.Ill xxii/2, Platt i/133/b); 212. The King's children (M.I.i 274/74, M.I.Ill xxii/15, Platt i/142/c); 213. Death of the earl of Essex (M.I.i 327/167, M.I.Ill xxviii/17, Platt 2/88/a); 214. Royalist badge (M.I.i 260/232, M.I.Ill xxxii/9, Platt i/161/a1); 215. Royalist badge (M.I.i 360/248, M.I.Ill, Platt i/290/c); 216. Naval Reward for captains (M.I.i 400/28, M.I.Ill xxxv/16, Platt i/335/c); 217. Charles II 'Restoration badge' (M.I.i 444/19, M.I.Ill i/xli/1, Platt ii/354/-); 218. Battle of Lowescroft (M.I.i 503/139, M.I.Ill xlviii/11).

'A Collection of British Historical Medals'

(March 16, 1989)

THE collection dispersed at this sale, as was the case for so many of the more recent sales of British historical medals, was assembled over a long period of time—35 years—by a collector, possibly a couple, with a broad interest in British history. The venue for the auction was Glendining's, the coin and medal auction house then affiliated with Phillips.[420] The sale was conducted in three parts—the first was held on March 16, 1989, and included some 388 medals covering the Tudor and subsequent reigns through the death of George II. The second auction, held on June 28, 1989, was of the foreign medals in the collection. The third sale, held on November 15, 1989, covered English medals from the beginning of the reign of George III in 1760. The catalogue for the first auction commented that while the collection did not match the Hyman Montagu collection in terms of:

> ...some of the rich and rare items it included, it has to be the most extensive one of its kind to be offered by sale by auction...

In addition to a large number of English Civil War medals and badges, the collection, included the medals of Sir Edmund Berry Godfrey, Archbishop Sancroft, the Queen Anne pieces of John Croker, and some Jacobite pieces. There was also an interesting series of 'restitutions' or forgeries of medals likely made by '— Stuart in the late 18th century,' although the catalogue errs in attributing them to James 'Athenian' Stuart.[421]

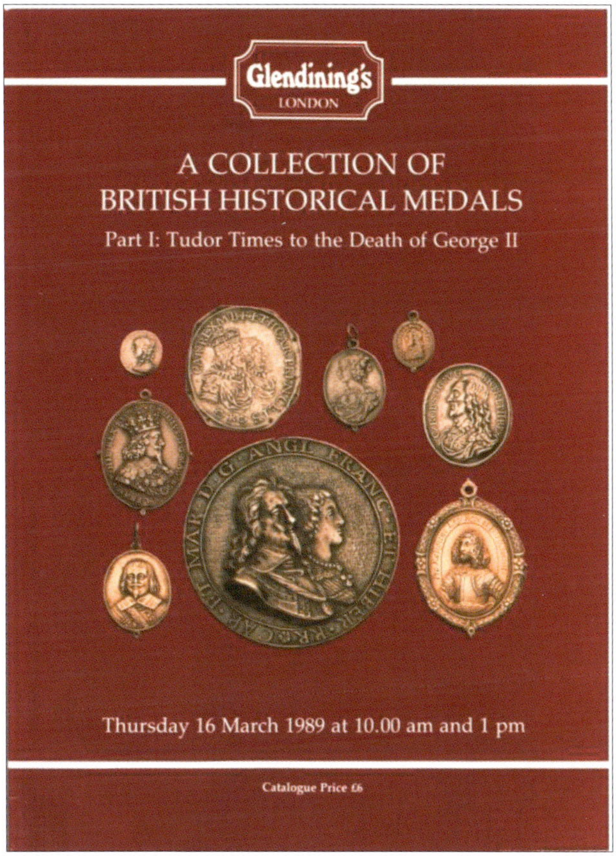

THE CATALOGUE FOR THIS EXTRAORDINARY COLLECTION, WHICH EXPLORED MANY MEDALLIC THEMES IN A DEPTH NOT OFTEN SEEN IN COLLECTIONS OF EARLY BRITISH HISTORICAL MEDALS. THE TWO PLATES ON THE FOLLOWING PAGES, IN PARTICULAR PLATE X, OF THE MEDALS ATTRIBUTED TO '— STUART,' ILLUSTRATE THIS POINT.

[420] Glendining's merged with Bonham's in October 2001.
[421] See pages 220-224 for more on '— Stuart.

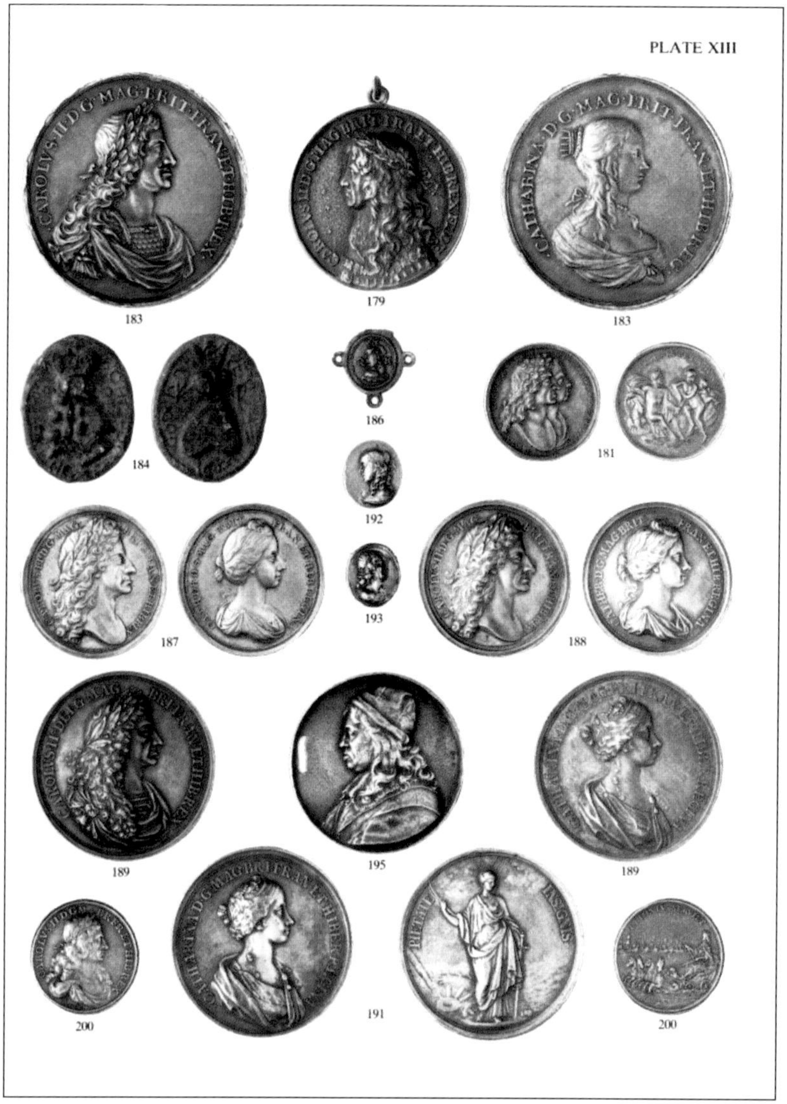

PLATE XIII, FROM THE GLENDINING'S SALE OF BRITISH HISTORICAL MEDALS ON MARCH 16, 1889. N$^{o.}$ 179. CORONATION OF CHARLES II AND QUEEN CATHERINE OF BRAGANZA ('IAM FLORESCIT') 1661, BY THOMAS RAWLINS (AN AFTERCAST, M.I.I 473/83, M.I.ILL XLV/13)[422]; 181. SMALL MARRIAGE MEDAL BY GEORGE BOWER (M.I.I 481/91, M.I.ILL XLVI/4); 183. MARRIAGE MEDAL, UNDATED, BY BOWER?, (M.I.I 482/94); 184. MARRIAGE BADGE BY ?, IN LEAD (NOT IN M.I. OR M.I.ILL); 186. SMALL UNIFACE BADGE OF CATHERINE, EX FARQUHAR COLL. (M.I.I NO ENTRY, M.I.ILL CLXXXII/12); 187. CHARLES II & CATHERINE (M.I.I 488/109, M.I.ILL XLVI/21); 188. ANOTHER, BY BOWER (M.I.I 489/110, M.I.ILL XLVI/22); 189. THE 'GOLDEN MEDAL' BY JOHN ROETTIER (M.I.I 489/111, M.I.ILL XLVII); 191. QUEEN CATHERINE AS 'ST. CATHERINE' (M.I.I 490/113, M.I.ILL XLVII); 192. SMALL UNIFACE PORTRAIT MEDAL OF QUEEN CATHERINE (M.I.I 492/117, M.I.ILL XLVII/6); 193. CLICHÉ MEDAL OF AN UNKNOWN GENTLEMAN (APPARENTLY UNRECORDED?); 195. A CONTEMORARY CAST MEDAL OF THOMAS WRIOTHSLEY BY THOMAS AND ABRAHAM SIMON (1664, M.I.I 502/17, M.I.ILL XLVIII/9, PLATT II/326/A); 200. A SMALL 'DOMINION OF THE SEA,' MEDAL BY T. SIMON 1665 (M.I.I 506/145 M.I.ILL XLIX/4).

---

422 This medal is particularly interesting in that, according to George Vertue, it was "to be the badge for a new intended Order of Knights of the Royal Oak" for those who had supported the Restoration.

PLATE X

Plate X, from the Glendining's sale. An extraordinary collection of late 18th or early 19th c. medals assumed to have been made by one man—'— Stuart.' The lot numbers and original medals they were intended to represent are: No. 139. Earl of Essex (M.I.i 312/141); 140. Sir Thomas (M.I.i 319/153); 141. John Campbell, earl of Loudon (M.I.i 321/157); 142. Albert Joachim (M.I.i 324/162); 143. Sir Sidenham Poyntz (M.I.i 325/163); 144. Charles, earl of Dunfermline (M.I.i 328/160); 145. Gen' Edward Rossiter (M.I.i 329/170); 146. Henry Scobell (M.I.i 384/65); 147. Gen' John Lambert (M.I.i 405/39, Platt ii/183/type E); 148. John Thurloe (M.I.i 406/40); 149. William Lenthall (M.I.i 407/42); 150. Elizabeth Cleypole (M.I.i [illegible]); 151. Thomas Wriothesley (M.I.i 502/107); 152. Abraham Simon (M.I.i 512/154); Thomas Simon (M.I.i 512/155); 153. Sir Edward Nicholas (M.I.i 546/202), the last ex Farquhar collection.

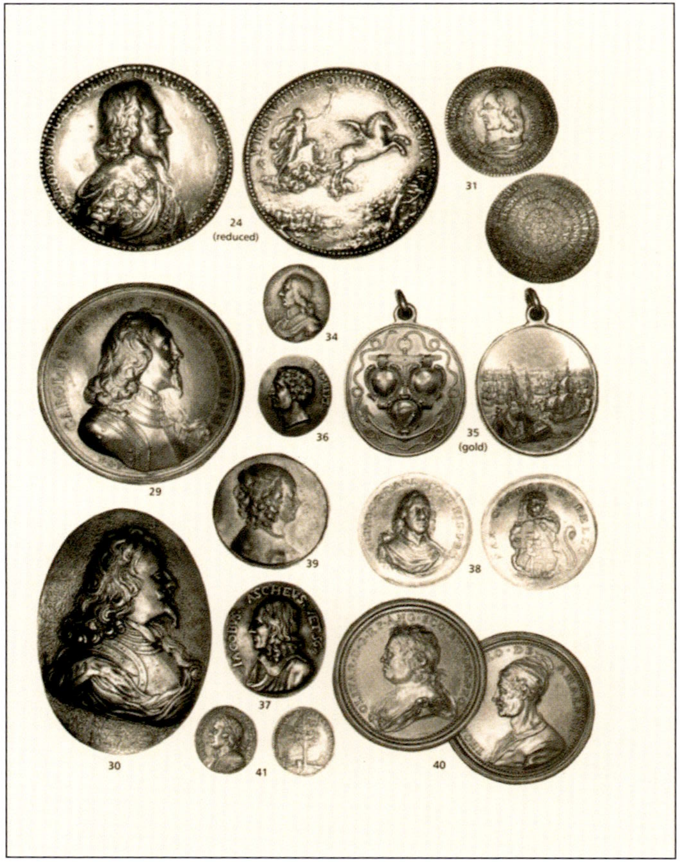

The Papillion Collection

Legend for (Unnumered)Plate

N$^{o.}$ **24.** Portrait medallion of Charles I by Claude Warin [Varin] "silvered?" (1642?, M.I.i 292/107, Platt I/241/b); **29.** Charles I memorial medal, undated, in ar (?) (M.I.i 346/199), and sold with a uniface trial striking of M.I.i 346/200, in Æ; **30.** Portrait medallion of Charles I by John O'Brisset,* 18th c.; **31.** Trial of John Lilburne, 1649 (in ar, M.I.i 385/3); **34.** Battle of Dunbar, Æ, (M.I.i 391/13, restrike of an unknown date); **35.** Naval Reward for captains,** 1653 (in gold, M.I.i 400/28); **36.** Gen. John Lambert (M.I.i 405/39), an 18th c. restitution in ar; **37.** James Ash, MP for Bath (M.I.i 422/—), an 18th c. restitution in ar; **38.** Cromwell, Lord Protector, 1653, two examples, ar and Æ (M.I.i 410/46); **39.** Death of Elizabeth Cleypole, 1658? (M.I.i 430/74), a contemporary cast in tin; **40.** Cromwell and Masaniello, 1658, Æ, (M.I.i 435/86).

*O'Brisset (fl. 1705-1727) is known for his medallic and other portrait work in pressed horn, and less frequently in silver. Working in London, he catered to English tastes, and speculation exists as to his nationality—Irish (i.e., O'Brisset) or French, possibly Huguenot (i.e., Aubrisset) in origin. See C. H. Read, *English work in impressed horn*, 1893, p. 25.

**Bonham's' catalogue entry is informative:

> Today there are four examples known in public collections and three (including this one) in private collections. Each of the privately owned examples have appeared at auction since the War, the first, [at] Glendenning's sale of 12 February, 1964 (Lot 10). The second ex. David F. Spink collection, at Spink Coin Auction 50, 6-7 March, 1986 (Lot 930), and this the third. This example is to be listed as PB1 [by Lessen, *B.N.J*, *67*, 48-72]. It is estimated that a further one or two specimens might also exist. Ex Greta S. Heckett (Lot 216 collection. almost certainly ex Hamilton-Smith (Lot 1004) Collection.

The fourth plate from the Papillion Collection sale catalogue. Several examples of rare English Civil War medals are represented—in particular nos. **24.** portrait medallion of Charles I by Claude Warin [Varin]; **35.** naval reward in gold for ship's captains; **36.** uniface portrait medals of General John Lambert; and **37.** James Ash, MP for Bath. the naval reward being exceedingly rare while the others should be considered very rare.

The 'Papillion Collection'

(Sale of March 25, 1998)

ON March 25, 1998, at Bonham's, Knightsbridge, a magnificent collection of 314 lots of British historical medals was sold. Owned by an American collector, it consisted of medals issued during the reigns of Henry VIII through Victoria. Included were 28 lots of medals issued during the reigns of James I, Charles I and the Commonwealth and 83 from the reigns of Charles II and James II. Additionally, another eight lots from the reigns of Elizabeth I through Charles II, presumably from other collections, were auctioned as part of the afternoon sale. The medals in the Papillion collection had been collected over an 18-year period beginning in the early 1970s through 1989. While not as massive a collection of 17th c. medals as those of the Morton & Eden and Christopher Foley sales which followed it, the medals herein as a whole are representative of the corpus of the period and this marks this collection as a significant one, as may be seen by the two pages of catalogue illustrations included here. Further, a number of medals from the same collection had been previously sold anonymously by Sotheby's in March 1989. There appeared to be, however, a higher than usual proportion of other than original strikings among this group of medals, a lamentable fact of 17th c. medals, in part resulting from the large demand for such medals during the late 18th early 19th and late 19th-early 20th centuries—two periods when medal collecting as a pastime may have been at particularly high points.

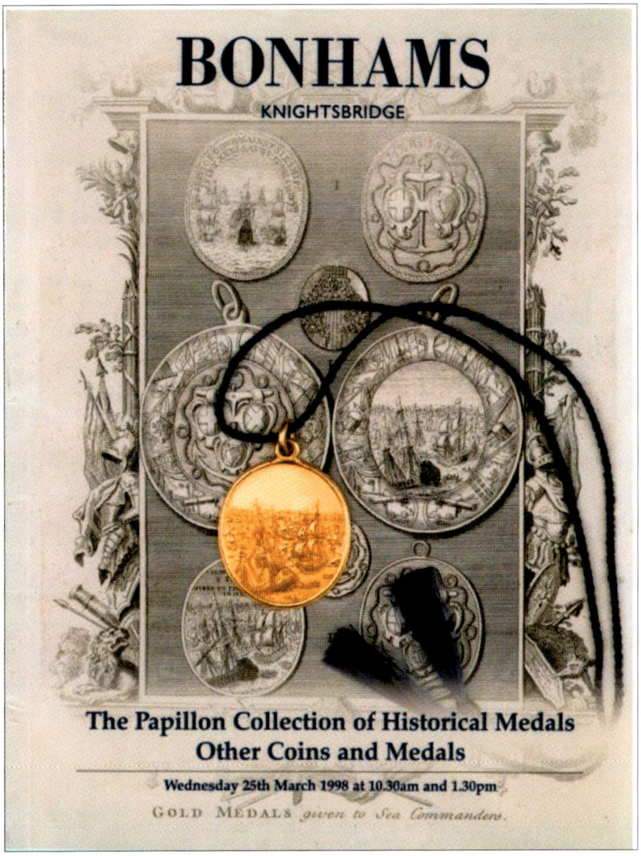

THE CATALOGUE FOR THE PAPILLON SALE AT SOTHEBY'S ON MARCH 25, 1998. OWNED BY AN AMERICAN COLLECTOR, IT WAS ASSEMBLED THROUGH PURCHASES FROM SPINK & SON, OR THROUGH THE FIRM'S AUSPICES. A PORTION OF THE COLLECTION HAD BEEN SOLD PREVIOUSLY, IN 1979, ALSO IN A LONDON AUCTION.

Several magnificent and very rare early English medals sold at Morton & Eden's sale of May 21, 2003. *Clockwise, from top:* John Kendal, 1480, in bronze, M.I.i 17/3; Charles I, a unique portrait medal in silver, the obverse attributed to Jean Warin, dated 1649, M.I.i 292/107; Military reward for the Battle of Edgehill, 1642, in silver-gilt, M.I.i 299/119, ex Helen Farquhar collection; Henry, Duke of Gloucester, ca. 1660, silver, M.I.Ill clxxxii/10; James I, Attempted Union of England and Scotland, 1604, in silver, M.I.i 194/17; James I, Ireland, 1605-1620?, reverse of the gold and enamel 'Ireland badge' which is shown on the facing page, M.I. no entry; *Center*: Lucy, Countess of Bedford, by N. Briot, 1625, M.I.i —, unique? Image © Morton & Eden, Ltd.

'An Important Collection of British Historical Medals'

(Sale of May 21, 2003)

AN outstanding collection of British historical medals, the property of a single collector, came under the hammer at Morton & Eden's sale of May 21, 2003. This sale arguably contained more early British medals of high average rarity, condition and interest than any auction since the Heckett Collection was dispersed in 1977. Offered without reserves, the sale attracted many bidders from both sides of the Atlantic, and resulted in keen competition in the auction room.

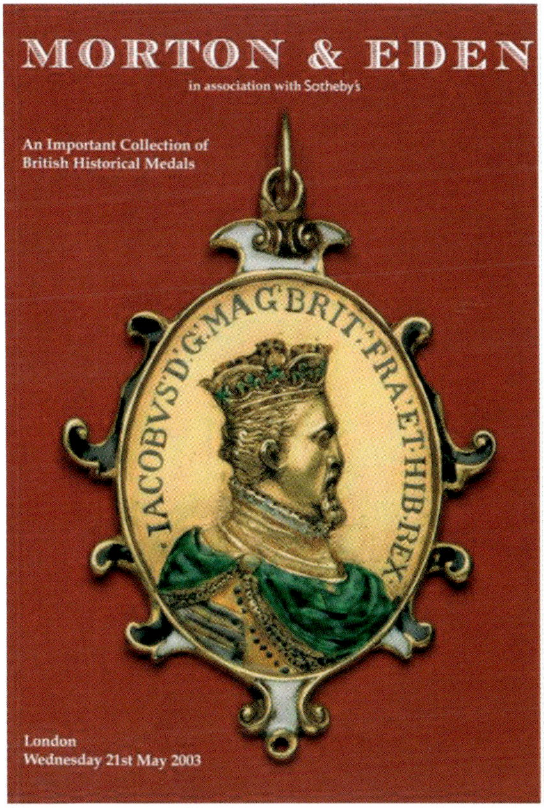

PICTURED ON THE COVER OF THE CATALOGUE FOR THIS SALE IS A JAMES I 'IRELAND BADGE' IN GOLD AND ENAMEL. THIS PIECE IS VERY MUCH IN THE 'GNADENPFENNIGE' STYLE PREVALENT IN THE GERMAN PRINCELY STATES BETWEEN THE 16TH AND 17TH CENTURIES, WITH A REVIVAL IN THE 19TH CENTURY, WHEN BOTH MEN AND WOMEN WORE SUCH MEDALS OF THEIR SOVEREIGN, USUALLY MOUNTED IN GOLD. IMAGE COURTESY OF MORTON & EDEN, LTD.

The medals illustrated on the facing page from the catalogue reflect both the rarity and excellent condition of the overwhelming majority of pieces in the sale and it is these factors, together with their sheer number, that made this such an important sale.[423] The John Kendal medal by Niccolò Fiorentino, dated 1480, is of particular interest to those familiar with the War of the Roses as Kendal was killed in 1485 fighting for King Richard III during the Battle of Boswell Field. This was the first medal to bear the image of an Englishman. The medal of Lucy, Duchess of Bedford, an early work by Nicholas Briot, ca. 1625, is believed to be unique. It was purchased by Christopher Eimer acting for the Fitzwilliam Museum. The very rare silver medal by Peter van Abeele of Henry, duke of Gloucester and youngest son of Charles I and Queen Henrietta Maria bears on the reverse the image of Henry's sister, Princess Mary, the princess royal. It was likely a memorial to both, having been created ca. 1660, the year in which they died. Overall, including buyer' premium, the sale brought £1,118,736.

423 This sale consisted of 385 lots, of which nearly 300 were dated pre-1700. Of course, with respect to numbers of items, no one could have foreseen the future sale of some 600 items, all dated pre-1700, at the dispersal of the Christopher Foley Collection held at Woolley & Wallis' rooms in October 2014. *See next entry.*

399. Charles II, Exile or Restoration gilt-silver badge, crowned bust right, hair long over lace collar, in incuse, CAROLVS SECVNDVS, *rev.*, in incuse, crowned Royal arms within Garter, C - R to either side of crown, 32.5 x 21.5mm (MI 440/9, illus.; pl. XL/14), integral suspension loop. *Very fine* £350-450

Provenance: Ex E. K. Barnsdale Collection, Spink, New York, 11 December, 2001 (lot 27, part).

400. Charles II, Exile or Restoration gilt-silver badge, crowned and draped bust left, hair long, *rev* [illegible] crowned Royal arms within Garter, wreath border [illegible] both sides, 19.5 x 15.5mm (MI 440/8, var.; pl. XL, 13 [illegible] *Suspension loops broken top and bottom, the gilding tooled, pleasing very fine* £250-35[illegible]

Medallic Illustrations records the badge from [illegible] example with the CAROLVS SECVNDVS legend.

Provenance: Bt. R. Falkiner, October, 2003.

401. Charles II, Exile or Restoration silver badge bust right, long hair falls over plain lace collar, [illegible] legend, CAROLVS SECONDVS, *rev.*, Royal arms [illegible] Garter, crowned, C - R to either side, 24.5 x 16.5mm [illegible] 441/11). *Casting flaw follows the line of the King's [illegible] good fine, scarce* £150-[illegible]

402. Charles II, Exile or Restoration silver badge bust right, long hair falls over plain lace collar, *rev* [illegible] arched crown, 23mm x 20.5mm (MI 442/12). *Ver*[illegible] *uneven colour, perhaps traces of original gilding* [illegible] *rare* £40[illegible]

Provenance: Baldwin's Auction, 3 May, 2011 (lot [illegible]

158

A PAGE FROM THE SALE CATALOGUE FOR THE FOLEY COLLECTION WHICH ILLUSTRATES FOUR OF THE TWENTY-FOUR SMALL BADGES OR LOCKETS, SEVEN OF WHICH WERE HEART-SHAPED, WHICH WERE INCLUDED IN THE SALE. THE ILLUSTRATED BADGES WERE LIKELY WORN BOTH CONCEALED AS PERSONAL SYMBOLS OF LOYALTY TO THE KING WHILE HE WAS IN EXILE, AND OPENLY, AFTER THE RESTORATION.

'The Christopher Foley, F.S.A., Collection of English Medals of the 15th-17th Centuries'

(Sale of October 16, 2014)

RECENTLY, a most extraordinary assemblage of 15th through 17th c. English medals came to auction with the sale of the Christopher Foley collection. Mr. Foley, an art dealer, had acquired over a quarter century nearly 600 medals, beginning with such early rarities as a 1547 Edward IV coronation medal in gold. The range of items was basically from the reigns of Henry VIII through George II. The auctioneers, Woolley & Wallis, Salisbury, gave much deserved praise to the collection when they commented in the catalogue:

> [A]s a personal collection, amassed in a systematic and scholarly way, it has perhaps never been equaled and certainly never surpassed in more than a hundred years.

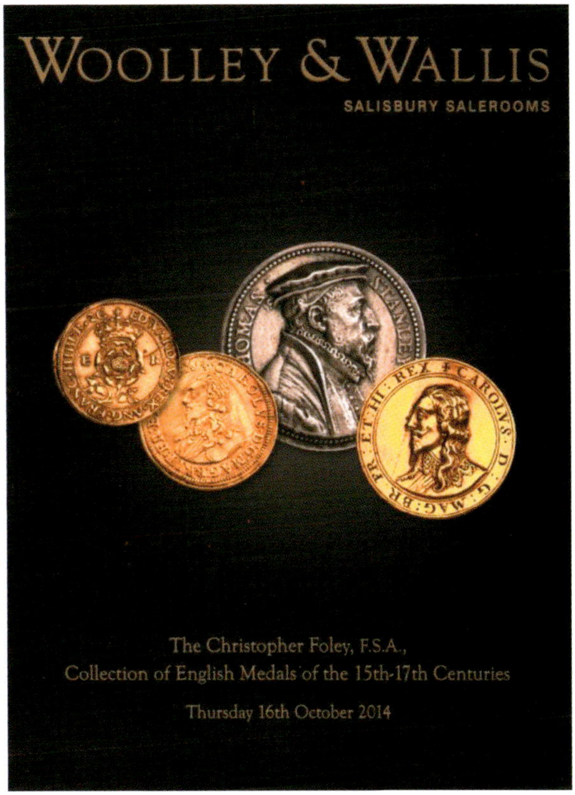

THE COVER OF THE CATALOGUE FOR THE RECENT SALE OF THE CHRISTOPHER FOLEY, F.S.A., COLLECTION OF 15TH THROUGH 17TH CENTURY ENGLISH MEDALS BY WOOLLEY & WALLIS.

Noticeably, the prices realized at the auction ranged from a modest £30 for a 1597 Dutch copper jeton to a very healthy £44,000 (without premium) for a gold naval reward medal for captains by Thomas Simon, dated 1653. This medal is only the fourth of 80 issued to have appeared at public auction. Mr. Foley seems to have been particularly interested in Simon de Passe's oval portrait medals, ca. 1616, of which there were ten in this sale. That these were attractive to collectors was evidenced by the prices they brought—an average hammer price of some £7,100— with lot 127, that of Elizabeth I, bringing £13,500. Only de Passe's medal of Richard Sackville, 3rd earl of Dorset, did not sell, perhaps because it is a poor example of de Passe's work when compared against the others. Overall, the sale brought £583,000, and once again demonstrated that rarity and quality were very much the variables driving prices. Although the Foley collection brought nearly 600 medals under the auctioneer's hammer, careful examination of the provenances laid out by the cataloguer, Daniel Fearon, and the present authors' own experience in following auctions over several decades, leads to the conclusion that, despite the large number of lots in this and Morton & Eden's 2013 sale, there are relatively few examples of pre-18th c. British medals in existence. Overall, most of these 'survivors' having appeared at auction at least once during the last century, and many of those having appeared more than once.

A wonderful grouping (ca. 1814) of late 18th-early 19th c. collectors and dealers seen at sales of rare prints, several of whom are mentioned in the present volume: William Richardson, Henry Constantine "Dog" Jennings, John Thane, Thomas Dodd, Alexander Beugo, John Scott, Robert Graves, James Caulfield, Robert Vernon and Anthony Molteno. The print is signed "Beugo Delt" [folioed by Beugo] and "Pub'd. by A[lexander] Beugo." Caulfield, Thane, and Jennings are known to have been collectors or otherwise associated with medals through authorship and/or publication of related material. Beugo (fl. 1801-1827) was a printseller in Maiden Lane. Image © Trustees of the British Museum.

Antiquaries, Chroniclers, Engravers, Printers Book- & Print-sellers

This section surveys a number of 17th through 19th century figures whom the present authors have encountered in their explorations of the literature associated with early medal collecting in Britain. ***Francis Perry*** *was the artist and engraver of ten of the plates which appeared in* ***Thomas Snelling's*** Thirty-three Plates of English Medals *and later, in* ***John Pinkerton's*** Medallic History of England. ***Richard Gouth*** *prepared the revised second edition of George Vertue's* Medals…of Thomas Simon…. ***John Thane*** *was directly involved in buying, selling and collecting medals, coins, books and prints as well as being a collector of these items himself. As for the* ***Rev. James Granger****, he represents the very popular pastime of print collecting in the 18th and early 19th centuries, when most of the personages in this section lived, being carried to [near?] irrationality.* ***James Caulfield****, another book and print seller contemporary to John Thane, and a publisher of albums to be used in 'grangerizing' books, was just too eccentric a character of the period to omit!* ***Martin Folkes****, an omnivorous collector, maintained a medal collection and serves as a contemporary example of an incidental collector of medals among other classes of items.*

Andrew Coltée Ducarel *initially employed Francis Perry to engrave plates illustrative of a "series of coins and medals…relative to the history of England…," an undertaking which eventually involved* ***Thomas Hollis*** *and the* ***Bowyer-Nichols family*** *of printer-publishers as well. These plates, including those prepared by Perry, evolved into the works attributed to Thomas Snelling and John Pinkerton. Two editions of this work were published by the Nichols family, who had earlier published George Vertue's* Medals…of Thomas Simon *and whose own* Literary Anecdotes *provides much useful information about medal collectors of the period.*

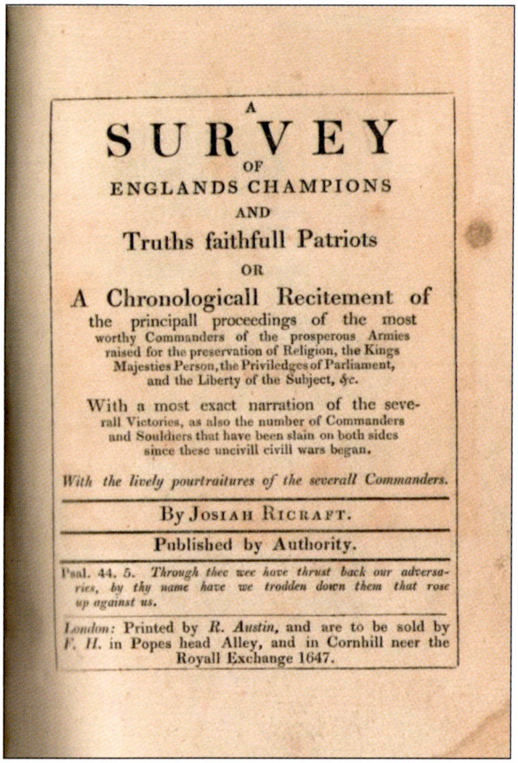

A

SURVEY

OF

ENGLANDS CHAMPIONS

AND

Truths faithfull Patriots

OR

A Chronologicall Recitement of

the principall proceedings of the most worthy Commanders of the prosperous Armies raised for the preservation of Religion, the Kings Majesties Person, the Priviledges of Parliament, and the Liberty of the Subject, &c.

With a most exact narration of the severall Victories, as also the number of Commanders and Souldiers that have been slain on both sides since these uncivill civill wars began.

With the lively pourtraitures of the severall Commanders.

By JOSIAH RICRAFT.

Published by Authority.

Psal. 44. 5. *Through thee wee have thrust back our adversaries, by thy name have we trodden down them that rose up against us.*

London: Printed by *R. Austin*, and are to be sold by *F. H.* in Popes head Alley, and in Cornhill neer the Royall Exchange 1647.

THE TITLE PAGE FROM THE 1830 REPRINT OF RICRAFT'S 1647 WORK. RICRAFT WAS 'MUCH RESPECTED AMONG THE PRESBYTERIANS' BUT WAS ALSO ACCUSED OF 'CORRESPONDENCE WITH ROYALISTS.' AT THE RESTORATION, RICRAFT RENOUNCED HIS PRESBYTERIANISM.

Thomas Hollis *maintained a lifelong interest in medals and championed medallic art and artisanship, working with James 'Athenian' Stuart and the Kirk and Pingo families.* ***Josiah Ricraft*** *and* ***Edward Hyde, 2nd earl of Clarendon****, have been included to provide the reader with a sense of authors whose works reflect the political and religious climate of the mid-17th century, as well as providing firsthand accounts of events of that time. Josiah Ricraft was a highly partisan and provocative writer who seems to have seen events through his own prism. Edward Hyde, earl of Clarendon, may be said to occupy the opposite pole in his having provided a detailed and, on balance, a very likely reasonably accurate detailed history of events in mid-17th century Britain. In hindsight, Ricraft was more closely associated with the religious and political upheavals of mid-17th century England than the collecting world and more likely would have been a better fit within the two volumes of our earlier work on the English Civil Wars. In a similar vein, Granger and Caulfield are more closely tied to book collecting than to medals. Nonetheless, all these personages informed the present authors' perspective for both this and their previous work by having provided a greater awareness of aspects of the political, collecting and literary cultures of the 17th through 19th centuries; thus they have been retained here. They also provided the authors with a great deal of enjoyment which they would like to share with their readers.*

Josiah Ricraft

(d. 1688)

·Chronicler·

JOSIAH RICRAFT (also Rycraft), a Presbyterian merchant, was the author of a number of books and tracts during the Civil War. His most frequently encountered volume is *A Survey of England's Champions...* (1647). Reprinted, with additions, as *The Civil Wars of England* (1649), the work was reissued in the early 19th century. According to *DNB*:

> [Josiah Ricraft,] author and merchant was probably [the] son of James Ricrafte, sailor, of Stepney, by his wife Grace... Josiah subsequently became a merchant of London, and a writer of much repute among the presbyterians. In 1640 he involved himself in the quarrel between John Goodwin and Thomas Edwards,[424] and was in consequence threatened by an apprentice called George Caudron with personal violence. The committee of both kingdoms accordingly issued, on 12 and 13 May 1645, orders for his protection. He was also accused of correspondence with the royalists. At the Restoration he renounced his Presbyterian principles...In 1679 he appears as a magistrate in the Middlesex county sessions rolls... (*DNB*, 1906, p. 268)

DNB listed the following as among Ricraft's publications:

> 1. A Looking Glass for the Anabaptists and the rest of the Separatists, wherein they may clearly behold a brief Refutation of a certain unlicensed scandalous Pamphlet entitled "The Remonstrance of the Anabaptists (1645); 2. The Peculiar Characters of the Oriental Languages and sundry others exactly

THE PORTRAIT OF JOSIAH RICRAFT WHICH APPEARS AS THE FRONTISPIECE OF HIS *SURVEY OF ENGLISH CHAMPIONS...* (1647, REPRINTED IN 1830). A LINE ENGRAVING BY WM. FAITHORNE, CA. 1665-1667.

[424] Ricraft, never one to avoid a public dispute, severely criticized another Presbyterian writer of the day, JOHN GOODWIN, for his "unchristian use" of language and style in his pamphlet *A Nosegay of rank-[illegible] John Goodwins Garden, gathered upon occasion of his late lying libell against Mr Thomas Edwards*. In the end, [illegible] Goodwin again, adding that:

> [illegible] glory and privilege of a Scold." (p. 10).

delineated for the benefit of all such as are studious in the Languages and the choice rareties thereof,' &c. (1645); 3. A perfect List of the many Victories obtained (through the Blessing of God) by the Parliament's Forces under the Command of his Excellency the Earl of Essex, &c. ... to the 14 June 1645 (1645); 4. A Nosegay of rank-smelling Flowers, such as grow in John Goodwins Garden, gathered upon occasion of his late lying libell against Mr. Thomas Edwards (1646): 5. A perfect List of the many Victories by God's Blessing upon the Parliamentary Forces under the Command of Sir Thomas Fairfax since 14 June 1645 to the present month of April (1646), 6. A perfect List of the many Victories, &c.,' as above,' up to 18 Aug. 1646 (1646); 7. A Survey of England's Champions and Truths, Faithfull Patriots, or a Chronologicall Recitement of the principall Proceedings of the most worthy Commanders of the prosperous Armies raised for the Preservation of Religion, the Kings Majesteys person (1647); and (8) A Funeral Elegy upon the most honoured upon Earth and now glorious in Heaven, his Excellency Robert Devereux, E. of Essex (1646).

DNB further noted that:

> *The Civil Warres of England briefly related from his Majestys first Setting-up his Standard 1641 to this present personal hopeful Treaty with the lively Effigies and Eulogies of the Chief Commanders,'* London, 1649, which is falsely said on the title-page to have been collected by John L. Leycester, consists of Ricraft's books, respectively numbered 3, 5, and 6 above, with the addition of twelve pages at the end containing ' a catalogue of the earls, lords, knights, &c., slain on the parliaments and kings side,' and one page by Leycester containing' the late proceedings of the army to this present' (September 1648). A portrait of Ricraft, engraved by W. Faithorne, is prefixed to his *'Oriental Characters' and 'Survey of England's Champions.*
>
> —"W. A. Shaw, *DNB*, 1896, pp. 268-269.

Historical Commentary on Josiah Ricraft

JOSIAH RICRAFT. *Fn*: It is generally thought this head was published as a frontispiece to 'England's Champions' of which there was but one edition, although it is sometimes seen with the name of Leicester as the author as well as that of Ricraft. I have had a copy with both titles; the book is extremely rare, and contains eighteen portraits of the parliament generals, very indifferently engraved, but bears a most extravagant price, seldom being to be had under twenty guineas. A much more valuable, and rare work by Vicars, author of the Parliamentary Chronicle, I have known to sell for upwards of thirty pounds, and which bears the title of "*England's Worthies under whom all the Civil and Bloudy warres since anno* 1645, *to anno* 1647, *are related. Wherein are described the several Batails, Encounters and Assaults of Cities, Townes and Castles at several times and places; so that the Reader may behold the time, yeare and event of every Battle, Skirmish and Assault, wherein London Apprentices had not the least share, &c. &c. &c.* with sixteen Portraits, among which are the following rare ones by Hollar, *Basil Fielding Earl of Denbigh, Henry Gray Earl of Stamford, Sir William Waller,* and others equally rare and valuable. The late Mr. Brand bought a copy at Newbury in 1786 for eighteen pence, which he cut up for his Granger. I bought the Fragments at the sale of his books made up by MS. in his hand writing [sic]

—J. Caulfield (1814).In *Calcographiana*..., p. 35, commenting on the portrait of Josiah Ricraft which appears as the frontispiece to *England's Champions*.

§

Mr. Wood, who styles [Ricraft] "a bigoted Presbyterian," informs us, that he was author of "a canting book," entitled, "A Survey of England's Champions, and Truth's faithful Patriots" &c. 1647, 8vo...This book, which has been mentioned before, has in it an account of twenty-one persons, who distinguished themselves in the civil war, with short encomiums in verse prefixed, and a head of each person. He also published a book of alphabets, entitled "The peculiar Characters of the Oriental Languages, and sundry others, exactly delineated, for the benefit of all such as are studious in the Languages and the choice Rarities thereof, and for the Advancement of Language Learning in these latter Days. Published by Josiah Ricraft, of London, merchant, and approved by the most, learned of the kingdom of England and other foreign Nations."

—J. Granger (1824). *A Biographical History of England*..., vol. iii, p. 149.

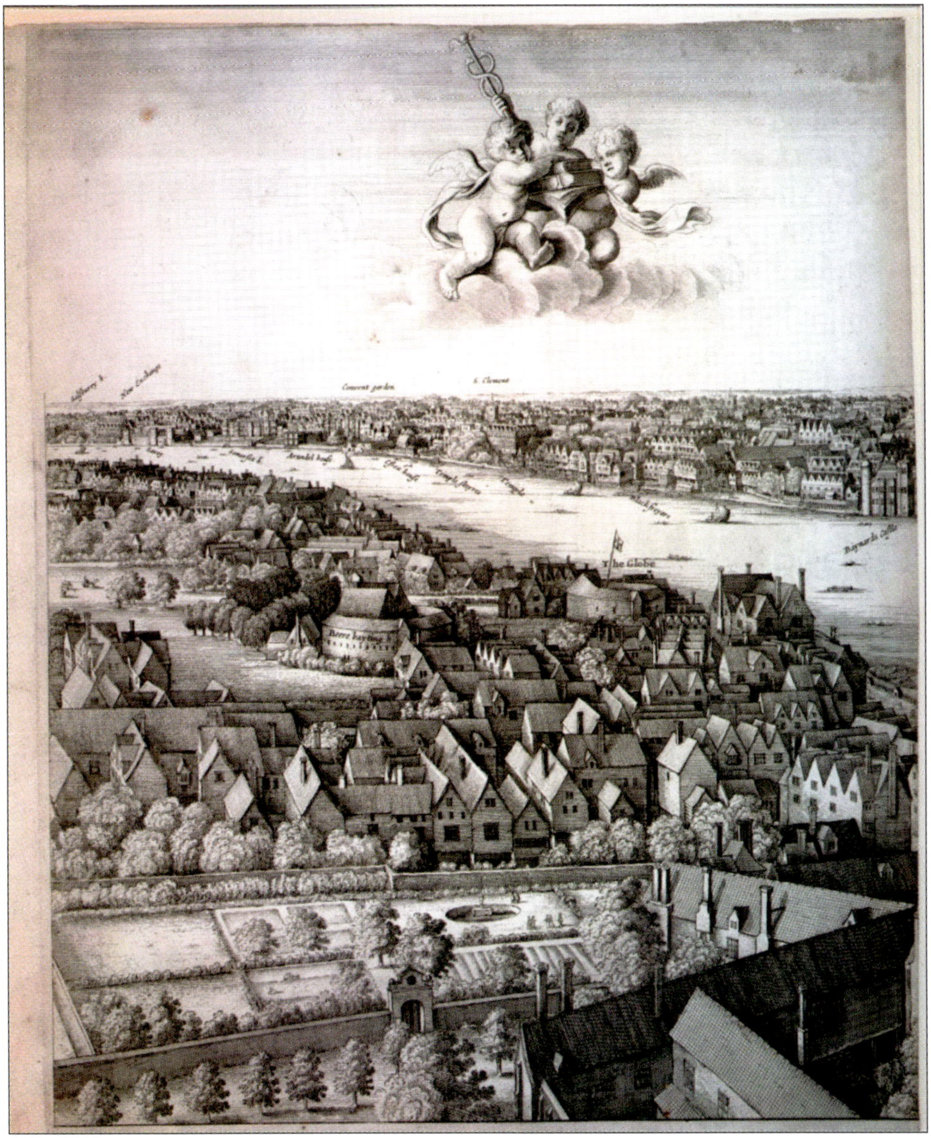

The second panel of nine of Wenceslaus Hollar's etching 'Long View of London,' showing a view from the south bank of the Thames, ca. 1647. This section shows the Globe theatre, although it is mislabeled as a bear-baiting ('Beere bayting') arena. Also, the theatre labeled the 'Globe' is actually the 'Swan.' This error reveals Hollar's use of Claes Jansz. Visscher's earlier panorama which contains the same error. Across the river is the Strand, with a number of the structures labeled. These include the Savoy Palace, Somerset House, Arundel House, Covent Garden, Essex House, St. Clement Danes and Blackfriars. Hollar also drew a pair of views of London and Westminster in 1666, showing the city before and after the Great Fire of 1666 (see p. 333, above). Note the three cherubs above, two holding books and the third, Mercury's staff. Mercury was the messenger of the gods and protector of commerce and merchants (as well as of liars and thieves). Image © Trustees of the British Museum (acc./reg. no 1864,0611.434).

Clarendon's work, first published in 1707, has been, since its publication, an important source of information about events and personages of the Civil War period which, along with the causes leading up to it in the 1630s and the early years of the Restoration period, occupied over three decades of the 17th century. The present authors often turned to it in the preparation of The English Civil Wars... *for a contemporaneous account of personages and events.*

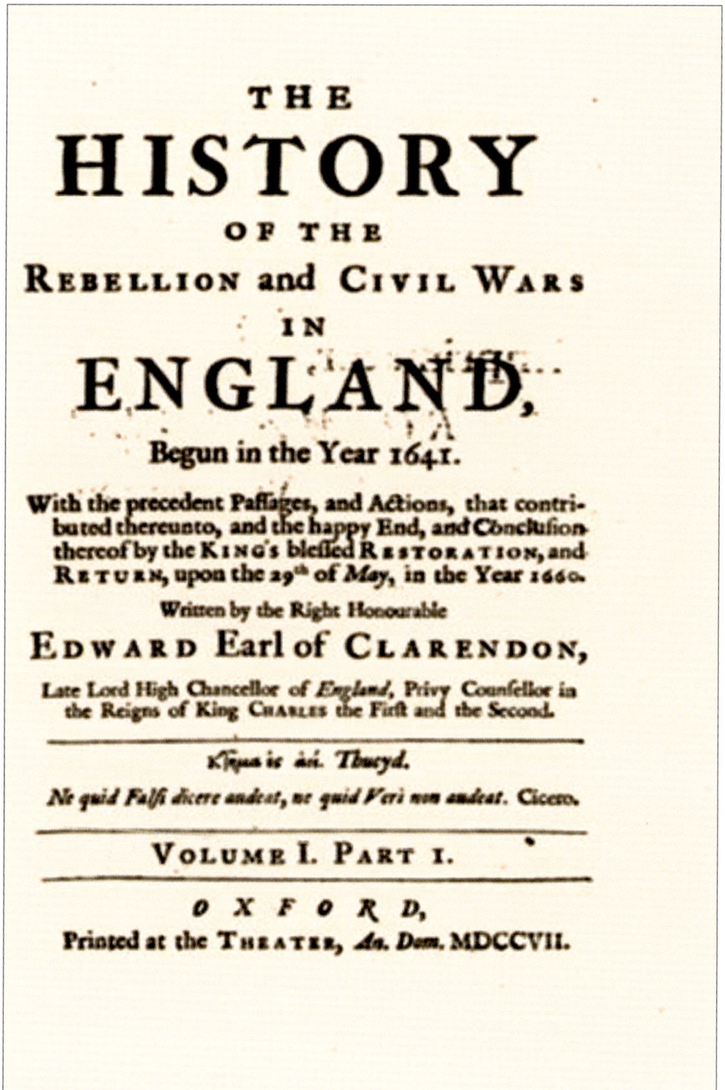
THE
HISTORY
OF THE
REBELLION and CIVIL WARS
IN
ENGLAND,
Begun in the Year 1641.
With the precedent Passages, and Actions, that contributed thereunto, and the happy End, and Conclusion thereof by the KING's blessed RESTORATION, and RETURN, upon the 29th of *May*, in the Year 1660.
Written by the Right Honourable
EDWARD Earl of CLARENDON,
Late Lord High Chancellor of *England*, Privy Counsellor in the Reigns of King CHARLES the First and the Second.

Κτῆμα ἐς ἀεί. *Thucyd.*

Ne quid Falsi dicere audeat, ne quid Veri non audeat. Cicero.

VOLUME I. PART I.

OXFORD,
Printed at the THEATER, *An. Dom.* MDCCVII.

THE TITLE PAGE OF THE FIRST VOLUME OF THE FIRST EDITION OF CLARENDON'S FAMOUS *HISTORY OF THE REBELLION...*, PUBLISHED IN 1707. IMAGE BY GOOGLE, A COPY OF THIS WORK IN THE STATE LIBRARY OF BAVARIA.

Edward Hyde

·Earl of Clarendon·

(1609-1674)

·Chronicler·

A biographical commentary on Edward Hyde Clarendon appears in *The English Civil Wars...*, vol. II.[425] An entry is included in this volume in recognition of his great work *The History of the Rebellion and Civil Wars in England* which provides a detailed narrative account of the events of mid-17th century Britain.

'EDWARD HYDE, 2ND EARL OF CLARENDON.' A WATER-COLORED ENGRAVING BY GEORGE P. HARDING, AFTER THE PAINTING BY SIR PETER LELY. THE ENGRAVING BY R. COOPER, EARLY 19TH C. IMAGE © TRUSTEES OF THE BRITISH MUSEUM.

...Clarendon relates that he 'indulged his palate very much, and even took some delight in eating and drinking well, but without any approach to luxury, and in truth rather discoursed like an epicure than was one.

—C.H. Firth, *DNB*, 1891 ed., vol. xxviii, p. 386, from *The Life*, vol. i, p. 72,

From 1641, Clarendon had served as an advisor to the future Charles II during the latter's exile in France. As guardian of the Prince of Wales in 1645, he had fled with prince Charles to Jersey. Although not close to the prince for the last years of the Civil War, he joined him in exile in 1652 and was made Lord Chancellor in 1658. During this time Hyde served as Charles' principal advisor. In 1660, upon Charles' return to England and assumption of the throne, Hyde was rewarded with a peerage. In 1661, he was created viscount and earl of Clarendon. During the Second Anglo-Dutch War (1665-1667), however, intrigues among Charles II's court advisors were very much directed against Clarendon. During this period, Hyde also had to face a growing disenchantment with his leadership by members of the Commons. This continuing campaign of schemes against him resulted in a loss of confidence in him on the part of the king. In 1667 he was impeached by the Commons and forced to flee England for France where he remained in exile until his death in 1674.

During 1646-1648, Hyde had begun *The History of the Rebellion and Civil Wars in England,* and following his exile in 1667, he was able to complete it despite his increasing debilitation due to gout. The first edition of *The History...* was published at Oxford in 1702-1704. Clarendon Press at Oxford was built with the proceeds of this monumental work. Given the immense size of the final set of volumes, one might speculate whether this work would have been completed had Clarendon not been exiled.

[425] J. J. Platt & A. K. Platt, *The English Civil Wars...*, op. cit., vol. 2, pp. 162-172

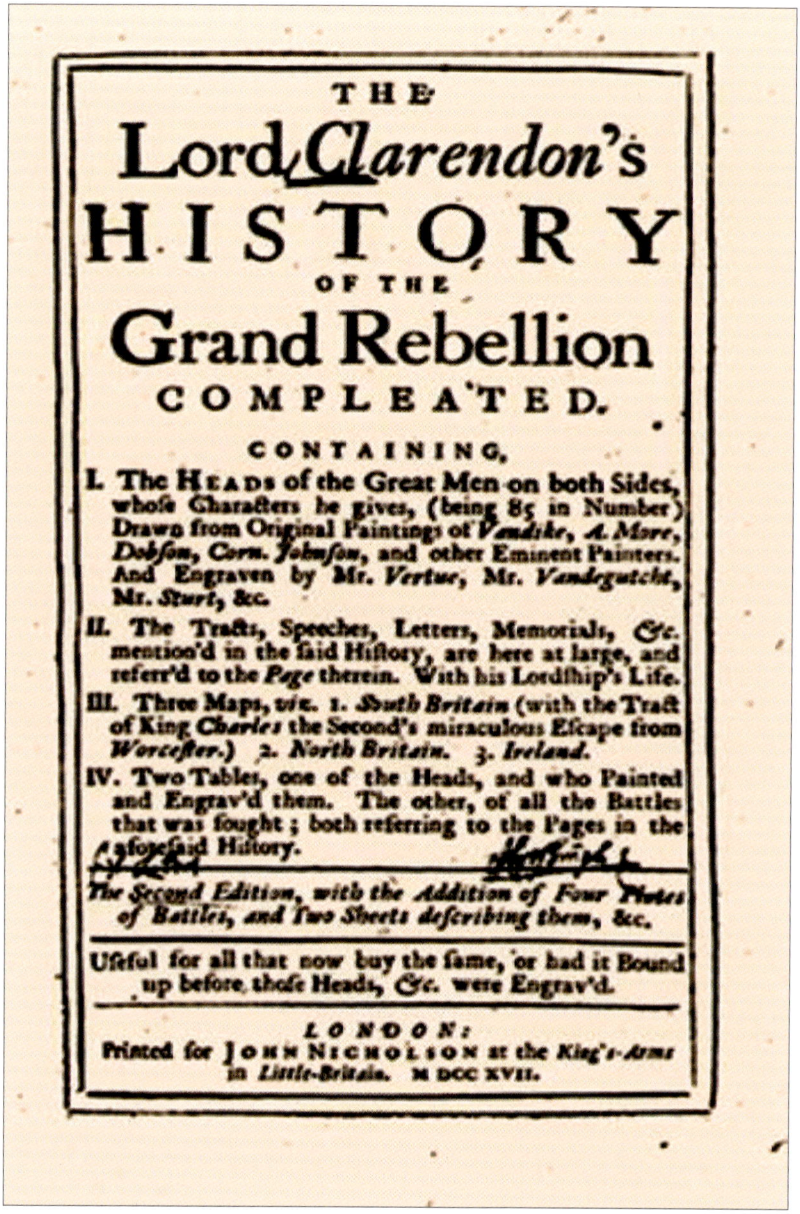

THE
Lord Clarendon's
HISTORY
OF THE
Grand Rebellion
COMPLEATED.

CONTAINING,

I. The HEADS of the Great Men on both Sides, whose Characters he gives, (being 85 in Number) Drawn from Original Paintings of *Vandike*, *A. More*, *Dobson*, *Corn. Johnson*, and other Eminent Painters. And Engraven by Mr. *Vertue*, Mr. *Vandegutcht*, Mr. *Sturt*, &c.

II. The Tracts, Speeches, Letters, Memorials, *&c.* mention'd in the said History, are here at large, and referr'd to the *Page* therein. With his Lordship's Life.

III. Three Maps, *viz.* 1. *South Britain* (with the Tract of King *Charles* the Second's miraculous Escape from *Worcester*.) 2. *North Britain*. 3. *Ireland*.

IV. Two Tables, one of the Heads, and who Painted and Engrav'd them. The other, of all the Battles that was fought; both referring to the Pages in the aforesaid History.

The Second Edition, with the Addition of Four Plates of Battles, and Two Sheets describing them, &c.

Useful for all that now buy the same, or had it Bound up before those Heads, *&c.* were Engrav'd.

LONDON:
Printed for JOHN NICHOLSON at the *King's-Arms* in *Little-Britain*. M DCC XVII.

THE TITLE PAGE OF THE SUPPLEMENT TO THE SECOND EDITION OF CLARENDON'S FAMOUS *HISTORY*..., PUBLISHED IN 1717. THIS VOLUME CONTAINS ILLUSTRATIONS, TRANSCRIPTS OF DOCUMENTS AND TABLES. NOTE THAT THIS EDITION WAS PRINTED BY JOHN NICHOLSON AND NOT BY THE OXFORD PRESS. IMAGE BY GOOGLE, COURTESY OF THE NEW YORK PUBLIC LIBRARY.

Historical Commentary on Clarendon and his *History...*

Lord Clarendon began the History of the Rebellion on the 18th of March 1645/6, in the island of Scilly; and continued it to the end of the seventh book, (with portions of the three following books,) during his subsequent residence in the island of Jersey, previously to the year 1648, as appears from the dates prefixed to those several portions as they were respectively entered upon, and finished; and that he did not proceed further until some years after his banishment, appears likewise from the same source of information. Indeed, before the completion of this History, it was "supposed by his family", (and the supposition seems to carry with it great probability,) that "seeing an unjust and cruel persecution prevail against him, he was induced to alter the original plan of his work, by writing the particular history of his own life, from his earliest days down to the time of his disgrace, as the most effectual means of vindicating his character;—but afterwards, on more mature thoughts, his great benevolence and public spirit prevailed on him to drop the defence of his own private character, and resume his original plan of the History of the Rebellion."

—B. Bandinel, *History of the Rebellion...*, "Advertisement to the edition of 1826," vol. i, pp. i-ii.

§

In the case of a man like Clarendon, the chief part of whose life was the making of history, and only a very secondary part the writing of it..., the making of history was far more than the writing of it; and the habits bred of action in a great scene and in a great crisis, the varied tasks which had been thrust upon him, the tragic significance of the long struggle that constituted his life, have, in combination with those literary interests that from first to last sweetened his toil, given to his style its special and inimitable characteristics... His *History of the Rebellion*—be it noted, the first history which our literature possesses from the hand of a great actor in the struggle it portrays—has something of the burden of an epic.

—H. Craik, (ed.). *English Prose*. 1894, vol. ii, pp. 389-391.

§

[*The History...*] is a composite narrative... some parts of it were written during the author's first exile...Some portions were designed merely to narrate the great events he had witnessed, others were originally intended to relate and vindicate his own career. At one time his narrative is based on documentary evidence which he had before his eyes whilst he wrote, at another time it rests solely on the treacherous foundation of his own memory. Thus the different parts of Clarendon's great work are of varying degrees of trustworthiness...

—C. H. Firth, *English Historical Review*, 1904, xix (lxxiv), pp. 26-54.

§

As an historian Lord Clarendon was unquestionably careless and inexact to a surprising degree, which may in some measure be excused by the necessity of writing very much from recollection; and he was a perpetual advocate and partisan of the Royal cause, though by no means of most of its supporters. But though his narration constantly betrays the bias of party, and cannot therefore be safely relied upon for our historical conclusions, his misrepresentations arise from the avowed partiality and intense concern he feels for the cause he is advocating, and not from any design to suppress or distort facts. His style is luxuriant and undisciplined, and his expression in the narrative parts of his history is diffuse and inaccurate; but his fervent loyalty and the warmth of his attachment to his political friends have infused a richness of eloquence into his delineations of character, which has perhaps never been surpassed in any language.

—A. T. Malkin, *A Gallery of Portraits*, 1835, vol. v, p. 34.

AT present I know of none who can show a better chosen set of medals than the Earle of Clarendon...

—[illegible] letter from John Evelyn to Samuel Pepys, referring to Lord Cornbury, Lord Clarendon's son, and dated August 12, 1680.
Evelyn, *Diary...*, 1906, vol. iii, p. 443.

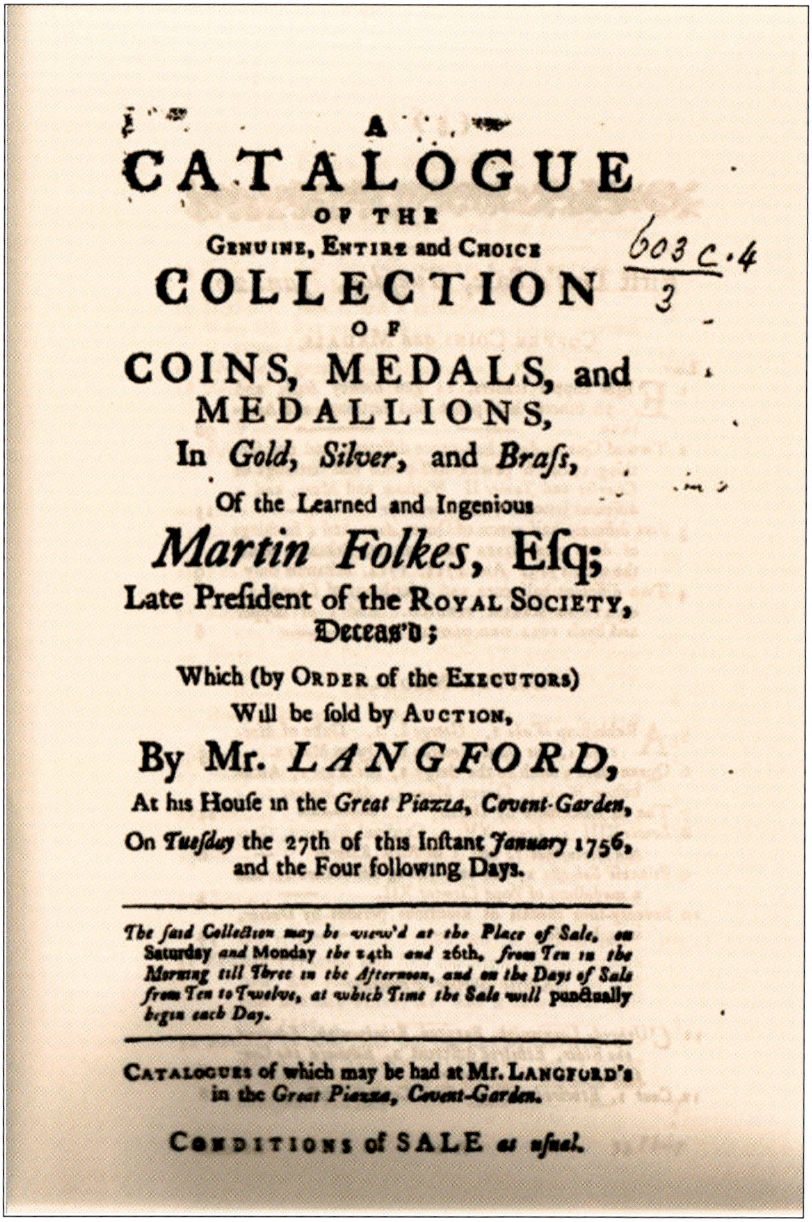

A
CATALOGUE
OF THE
GENUINE, ENTIRE and CHOICE
COLLECTION
OF
COINS, MEDALS, and
MEDALLIONS,
In *Gold*, *Silver*, and *Brass*,
Of the Learned and Ingenious
Martin Folkes, Esq;
Late President of the ROYAL SOCIETY,
Deceas'd;
Which (by ORDER of the EXECUTORS)
Will be sold by AUCTION,
By Mr. *LANGFORD*,
At his House in the *Great Piazza*, *Covent-Garden*,
On *Tuesday* the 27th of this Instant *January* 1756,
and the Four following Days.

The said Collection may be view'd at the Place of Sale, on Saturday *and* Monday *the* 24th *and* 26th, *from Ten in the Morning till Three in the Afternoon, and on the Days of Sale from Ten to Twelve, at which Time the Sale will* punctually *begin each Day.*

CATALOGUES of which may be had at Mr. LANGFORD's in the *Great Piazza*, *Covent-Garden*.

CONDITIONS of SALE *as usual.*

THE CATALOGUE FOR THE SALE OF MARTIN FOLKES' COLLECTION OF COINS, MEDALS AND MEDALLIONS AT LANGFORD'S BEGINNING ON JANUARY 27, 1756. THE SALE OF HIS SUBSTANTIAL LIBRARY BEGAN ON FEBRUARY 2, AND TOOK OVER 40 DAYS TO COMPLETE.

Martin Folkes

(1690-1754)

• Antiquary and Numismatist •

THE eldest son of a lawyer, Folkes attended the University of Saumur and Clare Hall, Cambridge, earning such accolades in mathematics that he was elected to the Royal Society at age 23 and to the Society of Antiquaries at age thirty. While vice-president under Sir Isaac Newton, he lost the competition for president of the Royal Society to Sir Hans Sloane, but succeeded him in 1741. He held the presidency until 1752 when he was forced to resign because of poor health. In 1742 Folkes had also been elected to membership in the French Academy. An antiquary and polymath, he published on such diverse subjects as numismatics, astronomy and metrology.[426] Among his publications on numismatic themes are *...the Weights and Values of Ancient Coins, the Trajan and Antonine Pillars at Rome* and *English Gold Coins from the 18th Year of King Edward III.* Folkes also was an avid collector, having interests in antiquarian books, paintings, prints, engraved gems, coins and medals as well as other items.

'MARTIN FOLKES,' A MEZZOPRINT MADE AND PUBLISHED CA. 1737 BY JOHN FABER THE YOUNGER (CA. 1684-1756) AFTER THE PAINTING BY JOHN VANDERBANK (1694-1739) ("J. VANDERBANK PINXT. 1736, / I. FABER FECIT 1737, / SOLD BY I FABER AT THE GOLDEN HEAD IN BLOOMSBURY SQUARE"). IMAGE © TRUSTEES OF THE BRITISH MUSEUM.

Folkes died from a 'paralytic attack' in 1754, at age 64. He was married at the time to Lucretia Bradshaw, an actress, who is described as having been 'deranged' and 'living in confinement' at the time of Folkes' death. After his death, his possessions were sold at auction by Samuel Baker at his house in York Street, Covent Garden beginning on February 2, 1756, and for the successive forty days. The number of sessions (40 covering 56 days), items (5,126 lots) and proceeds (£3,091) give some indication of the overall size of Folkes' collections.[427] Only a modest proportion of the sale lots, however, consisted of medals—Folkes' collection of "coins, medals and medallions" was sold over five days beginning on January 27, 1756, including a set of Dassier's *Medals of Illustrious Persons*,... "on four boards."

---

426 The science of measurement.

427 D. B. Haycock, 'Martin Folkes,' *ODNB* on-line, 2004 2013.

THE OBVERSES OF TWO MEDALS OF MARTIN FOLKES. (*LEFT*) JACQUES-ANTOINE DASSIER'S MEDAL IN BRONZE, FROM HIS SERIES ON FAMOUS CONTEMPORARIES RESIDING IN ENGLAND (CA. 1740, M.I.I 558/185, V.&A. ACC./REG. NO. A.11-1971, 52 MM.). (*RIGHT*) ANOTHER MEDAL, THIS A SILVER PROOF OF A BRONZE MEDAL SAID TO HAVE BEEN STRUCK AT THE ORDER OF THE POPE FOR PRESENTATION TO FOLKES DURING HIS VISIT TO ROME (CA. 1738 OR 1742, M.I.I 571/206, M.I.ILL CLXI/5, BRITISH MUSEUM ACC./REG. NO. M.8466, 36 MM.). IMAGES © VICTORIA AND ALBERT MUSEUM, LONDON AND © TRUSTEES OF THE BRITISH MUSEUM, RESPECTIVELY.

Historical Commentary on Martin Folkes

LOUIS FRANÇOIS ROUBILIAC'S ICONIC MARBLE BUST OF MARTIN FOLKES, CA. 1749. FOLKES WAS HELD IN HIGH ESTEEM IN BOTH BRITAIN AND OTHER COUNTRIES, AS EVIDENCED BY HIS HAVING BEEN ELECTED TO BOTH THE ROYAL AND FRENCH ACADEMIES. IMAGE © TRUSTEES OF THE BRITISH MUSEUM.

Folkes... formed a fine collection of books, prints, drawings, pictures, gems, coins, etc., a considerable portion of which he acquired during his travels in Italy and Germany. His library, which was very rich in works on natural history, coins, medals, inscriptions, and the fine arts, was sold by Samuel Baker, York Street, Covent Garden, on Monday, February the 2nd 1756, and forty following days. A catalogue, marked with the prices, is preserved in the Library of King George III. in the British Museum. A copy of the first Shakespeare folio fetched but three guineas. The sale of Folkes's prints and drawings occupied eight days, and that of his pictures, gems, coins, and mathematical instruments five days. Dibdin says that 'the MSS. of his own composition, not being quite perfect, were, to the great loss of the learned world, ordered by him to be destroyed.'

— W. Y. Fletcher (1902). *English Book Collectors*, p. 197.

Andrew Coltée Ducarel

(1713-1785)

·Antiquarian·

AN antiquary and librarian employed at Lambeth Palace from 1757, Ducarel achieved this post, which he held for 30 years, after having failed to be appointed sub-librarian at the British Museum in 1755. Among his published works were *A Series of above 200 Anglo-Gallic, or Norman and Aquitain Coins of the antient Kings of England* (1757) and *Histories of Lambeth Palace* (1785) and of *St. Catharine's Church* (1782). A fellow of both the Society of Antiquaries and the Royal Society, he died in 1785. Chalmers, in *The General Biographical Dictionary* (revised ed.), 1813 states:

> DUCAREL, an eminent English civilian and antiquary, was born in 1713 in Normandy; whence his father, who was descended from an ancient family at Caen in that province, came to England, soon after the birth of his second son James, and resided at Greenwich (p. 380).

Dr. Andrew Coltée Ducarel by Francis Perry. The frontispiece from his work on *Norman and Aquitain Coins...*, published in 1757.

As early as the 1740s, Ducarel had been organizing a set of plates on the coins and medals of England to be published by the Society of Antiquaries, of which he was a member. At least three different engravers worked on the plates; Martin Folkes (1690-1765), Francis Perry (fl. 1750-1765), and James Green (?-1768). Ducarel's involvement gives us further insight into how the plates, which were published first by Thomas Snelling, and then, with the involvement of John Pinkerton, came into existence:

> Dr. Ducarel had some view to forming a series of English medals, which, by admitting such as have been struck abroad relative to the history of this kingdom, he thought could be carried beyond the Conquest, provided the medals proved genuine. But when he engaged Francis Perry to engrave a series, of which the late Mr. Hollis gave the out line, he began no earlier than Henry VIII. and closed it with James I. in ten plates. Three supplemental ones were afterwards published of the same period. Mr. Hollis intended it should be more extensive, by taking in the Roman medals; he, however, assisted Perry in his own way. It was taken up by Mr. Snelling, who did not publish it in Mr. Hollis's life time.—Mr. Snelling's being a posthumous publication, there is no letter-press to ac-

> company his 33 plates, which reach from the conquest to 1742. It will be easily seen that the medals of the first five kings are by [Jean] Dassier.[428]

Blind in one eye and with limited vision in the other, Ducarel's poor eyesight likely inhibited his contributions to numismatics. Another reason may have been his personality. In this regard, Horace Walpole had less than high regard for Dr. Ducarel, as evidenced by this attributed comment which appears in *Walpoliana*:

> Dr. Ducarel was a poor creature. He was keeper of the library at Lambeth; and I wanted a copy of that limning there, which is prefixed to my Royal and Noble Authors. Applying to the Doctor, I found nothing but delays. I must purchase his works, and take some of his antiques at an exorbitant price, &c. Completely disgusted, I applied to the Archbishop himself, who immediately permitted a drawing to be taken.[429]

Nonetheless, as:

> ...his attachment to the study of English Antiquities formed his principal amusement...he amassed a significant collection of manuscripts...All these, with a good collection of coins and medals, he gave by his last will, to his nephew Gerard Gustavus, in the fond hope of their being preserved as *heir-looms* in his family. But they were all very soon consigned to the hammer of the auctioneer; and the greater part of the MSS. passed into the hands of Mr. Gough and Mr. Nichols.[430]

Historical Commentary on Dr. Ducarel

Such was the Doctor's assiduity in whatever he undertook, that, besides the fair copy of the index by him taken of all the Lambeth registers, and the general index which he made to them, he reserved for himself another, which at his sale became the property of Mr. Gough...After dinner, Mr. Gale [his friend], smoked his pipe; whilst Dr. Ducarel took notes, which he regularly transcribed, and which after his death were purchased by Mr. Gough. They constantly took with them Camden's Britannia, and a set of maps. In Vertue's plate of London-bridge chapel, the figure measuring is Dr. Ducarel, that standing is Mr. Samuel Gale.

—J. Nichols, *Literary Anecdotes*..., 1812, vol. vi, pp. 377, 395.

A medal is a piece of metal in the form of a coin, stamped with a figure or device on one or both sides to preserve either the portrait of some eminent person or to commemorate some important action or event.

—Trustees of the British Museum, *Description of Electrotypes of British Historical Medals*, 1897, p. 5.

---

[428] A. Chalmers (1813 ed.), *The General Biographical Dictionary,* p. 377; *Literary Anecdotes*..., 1812, vol. vi., pt i, pp. 384.

[429] H. Walpole (J. Pinkerton, ed.) (1800), *Walpoliana,* p. 52. London: Burnett, Wogan et al.

[430] *Literary Anecdotes*..., 1812, vol. vi., pt i, pp. 403-404. Ducarel's coins, pictures, and antiquities were sold by auction at Leigh & Sotheby's rooms on Nov. 30, 1785, and his books, manuscripts and prints on the following April 3. Upon the death of Nichols, those books in his collection which were formerly owned by Ducarel went to the British Museum Library. It appears that at least some of those purchased by Richard Gough have found their way into recent auctions.

> Andrew Coltee Ducarel, LL.D. of Doctors Commons, an indefatigable Antiquary. The sale of his library at Leigh's, for eight days, produced 987*l*. 1*s*. (—*The Gentleman's Magazine, and Historical Chronicle*, vol. 82, Part i, p. 516).

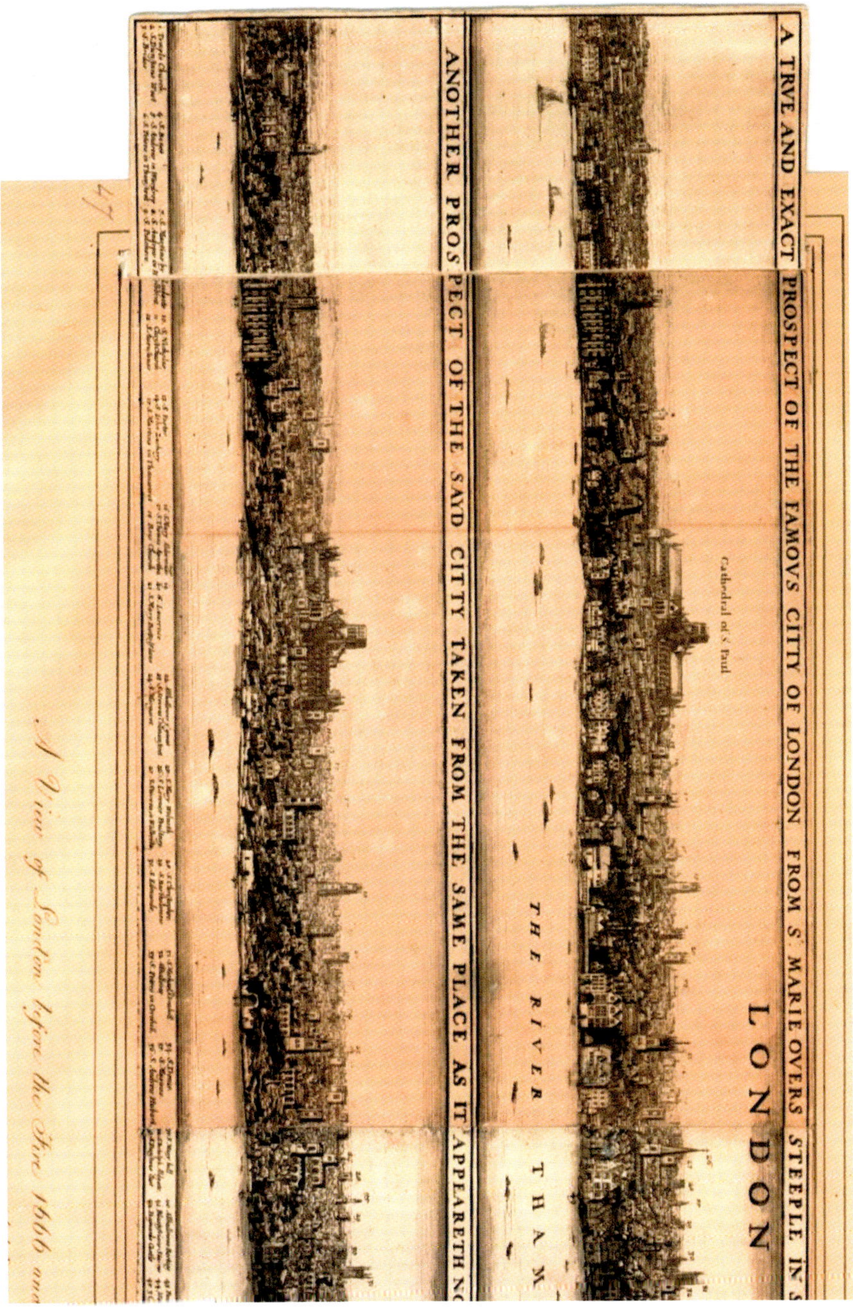

Wenceslaus Holler's Long Views of London Before and After the Great Fire of 1666

Or A True and Exact Prospect of the Famous City of London … Before the Fire [and] … After the Sad Calamitie and Destruction by Fire in the Yeare MDCLXVI. This work illustrates Hollar's exact [illegible] his work. The British Museum points out that this "1666 etching [is] printed from two plates on two sheets of paper [illegible] the centre." Image © Trustees of the British Museum (Acc./Reg. No. 1880,1113.1154-1155).

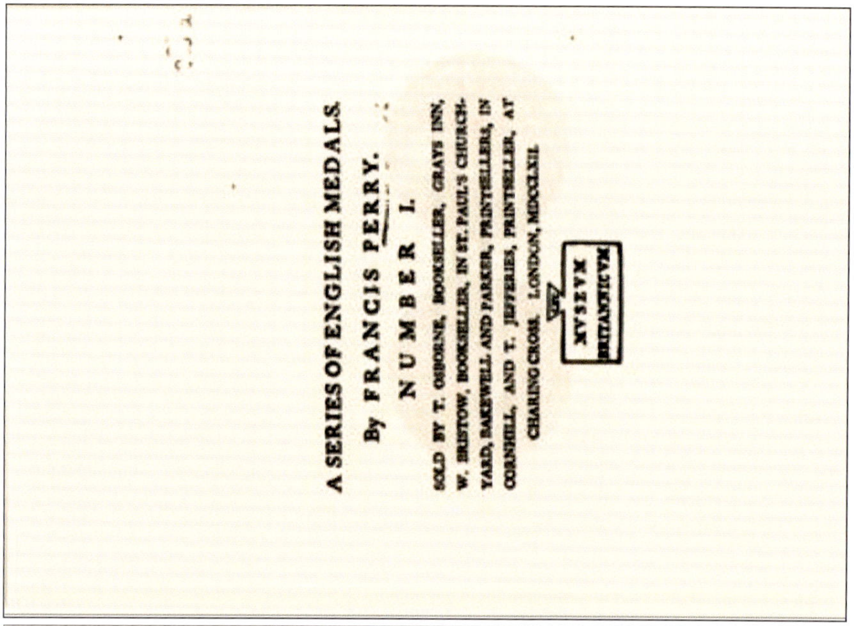

A SERIES OF ENGLISH MEDALS.

By FRANCIS PERRY.

NUMBER I.

SOLD BY T. OSBORNE, BOOKSELLER, GRAYS INN, W. BRISTOW, BOOKSELLER, IN ST. PAUL'S CHURCH-YARD, BAKEWELL AND PARKER, PRINTSELLERS, IN CORNHILL, AND T. JEFFERIES, PRINTSELLER, AT CHARING CROSS. LONDON, MDCCLXII.

MVSEVM BRITANNICVM

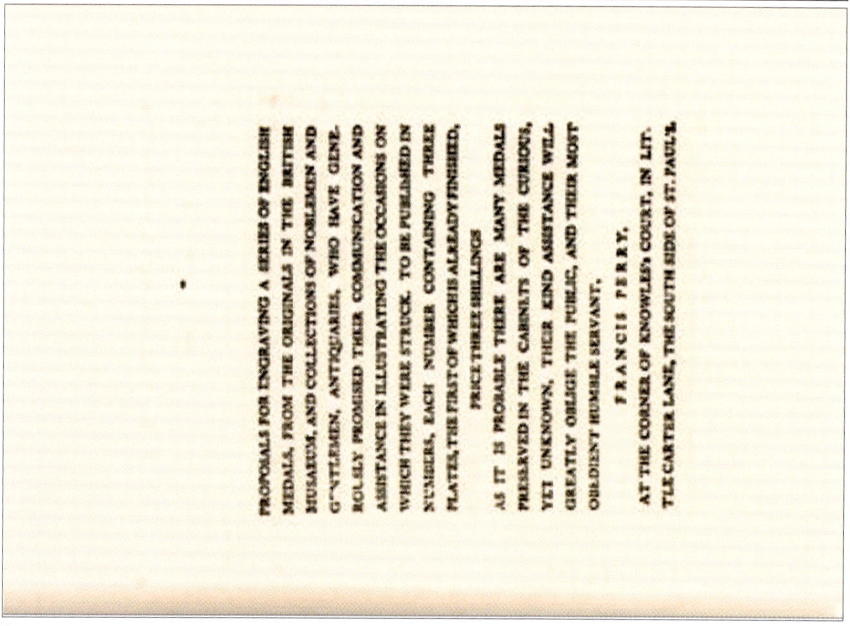

PROPOSALS FOR ENGRAVING A SERIES OF ENGLISH MEDALS, FROM THE ORIGINALS IN THE BRITISH MUSAEUM, AND COLLECTIONS OF NOBLEMEN AND GENTLEMEN, ANTIQUARIES, WHO HAVE GENEROUSLY PROMISED THEIR COMMUNICATION AND ASSISTANCE IN ILLUSTRATING THE OCCASIONS ON WHICH THEY WERE STRUCK. TO BE PUBLISHED IN NUMBERS, EACH NUMBER CONTAINING THREE PLATES, THE FIRST OF WHICH IS ALREADY FINISHED.

PRICE THREE SHILLINGS

AS IT IS PROBABLE THERE ARE MANY MEDALS PRESERVED IN THE CABINETS OF THE CURIOUS, YET UNKNOWN, THEIR KIND ASSISTANCE WILL GREATLY OBLIGE THE PUBLIC, AND THEIR MOST OBEDIENT HUMBLE SERVANT,

FRANCIS PERRY.

AT THE CORNER OF KNOWLES's COURT, IN LITTLE CARTER LANE, THE SOUTH SIDE OF ST. PAUL'S.

THE TITLE AND ADVERTISEMENT PAGES FROM 'NUMBER I' OF FRANCIS *PERRY'S A SERIES OF ENGLISH MEDALS*. HEREIN ARE CONTAINED THE BEGINNINGS OF WHAT WERE TO BECOME SOME OF THE PLATES WHICH FIRST APPEARED IN SNELLING'S *THIRTY-THREE PLATES OF ENGLISH MEDALS* (1776), AND THEN IN THE FOUR EDITIONS OF [JOHN PINKERTON'S] *MEDALLIC HISTORY OF ENGLAND* (1789, 1802, 1831, AND AN UNDATED EDITION).

Francis Perry

(fl. 1750-1765; d. ca. 1765)

·Artist & Engraver·

A ENGRAVER and illustrator of images of 17th and 18th c. English coins and medals, but one whose name is not so often known today, Francis Perry had studied painting under John Vanderbank and then Jonathan Richardson,[431] but apparently his studies did not prosper and he did not pursue this medium. Rather, he earned his living from employment as an engraver of topographical views and antiquities, particularly of churches and coins and medals prepared for magazines. Perry prepared the plates for Dr. Ducarel's *Anglo-Gallic, or Norman and Aquitain Coins...* (1757), including the etched portrait of Ducarel which appears as the frontispiece (*q.v. p. 353*), as well as illustrations of churches in London, Kent and York.[432]

Perry is perhaps best known to numismatists for his generally accurate and carefully detailed illustrations of coins and medals. His most important works, from a numismatic viewpoint, were *A Series of English Medals*[433] which first appeared in 1762 and *27 Plates of English Silver Coins.*[434] With respect to *A Series of English Medals (see illustration on facing page),* Perry had initially been engaged for this work by Dr. Ducarel, following an outline which had been provided by the deceased Mr. Hollis.[435] Although Hollis had wished to have the series start with Roman medals, Ducarel instructed Perry to begin with the reign of Henry VIII and end with James I—a total of ten plates. These plates, of course, are now known to have appeared in Thomas Snelling's *Thirty-three Plates of English Medals* (1776), and then in the four editions of *The Medallic History of England...*[436]

F. M. O'Donoghue, the author of Perry's entry in the *DNB,* notes that:

> Perry had the use of only one eye, and habitually etched on a white [back]ground, which facilitated his working by candlelight. Though painstaking and industrious, he could only earn a precarious living. He died on 3 Jan. 1765 (p. 31).[437]

Walpole, in *Literary Anecdotes*..., comments on Perry's passing, saying:

> Francis Perry, engraver, who had begun to engrave a set of English medals, and had published three or four numbers, died Jan. 3, 1765, in Carter's Lane, Doctor's Commons.[438]

---

[431] JOHN VANDERBANK (1694–1739), painter. Vertue, in *Anecdotes of Painting...* said of Vanderbank :

> Had he not been careless and extravagant...he might have made a greater figure than almost any painter this nation had produced; so bold and free was his pencil, and so masterly his drawing (1849 ed., vol. ii, p. 676).

JONATHAN RICHARDSON (the elder; 1665-1745), painter, great collector of drawings, and the author of *An Essay on the Theory of Painting* (1715), the work that is reputed to have inspired Joshua Reynolds to take up painting.

[432] *DNB*, 1896, vol. 45, p. 31; L. Binyon, *Catalogue of Drawings by British Artists*, 1902, vol. iii, p. 162n.

[433] Sold by T. Osborne, W. Bristow, Bakewell and Parker, and T. Jefferies. London. This work consists of three numbers without an overall title page for the series. There are also three additional (supplemental plates by J. Lodge), with an explanation.

[434] It is not clear that these plates were ever published under Perry's name; more likely they appeared in Snelling's works, which totaled eleven, including the posthumous volume on medals. Gough seems to have been satisfied with the evidence against Snelling regarding his improper use of the plates (*q.v. p. 57)*:

> What Snelling was to blame for is in having availed himself somewhat unhandsomely of the Society's unpublished Plates, though not continued beyond the reign of King George the Second (Gough, *Literary Anecdotes*, 1812, p. 586).

[435] *See entry for Dr. Ducarel, this volume, pp. 351-352.*

[436] The four editions of Pinkerton's *Medallic History* each had 40 plates, as opposed to 33 in the original edition by Snelling. The plates are signed 'Jno. Kirk,' 'Barlow,' 'Hall' or 'C. Hall' or 'Charles Hall.' Seventeen are unsigned. The identity of 'Barlow' is not clear (*q.v. Manville, 2005, p. 66*).

[437] *DNB*, 1896, vol. 45, p. 31.

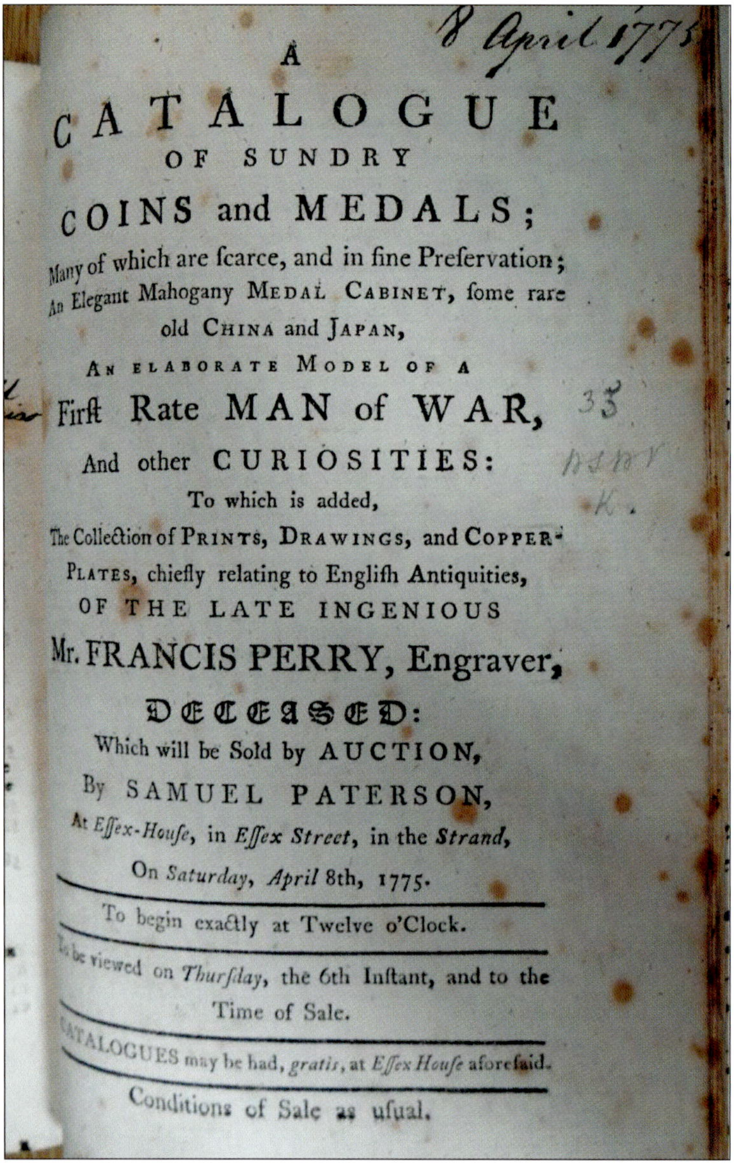

8 April 1775

A

CATALOGUE

OF SUNDRY

COINS and MEDALS;

Many of which are ſcarce, and in fine Preſervation;
An Elegant Mahogany MEDAL CABINET, ſome rare
old CHINA and JAPAN,
AN ELABORATE MODEL OF A
Firſt Rate MAN of WAR,
And other CURIOSITIES:
To which is added,
The Collection of PRINTS, DRAWINGS, and COPPER-PLATES, chiefly relating to Engliſh Antiquities,
OF THE LATE INGENIOUS
Mr. FRANCIS PERRY, Engraver,
DECEASED:
Which will be Sold by AUCTION,
By SAMUEL PATERSON,
At *Eſſex-Houſe*, in *Eſſex Street*, in the *Strand*,
On *Saturday*, *April* 8th, 1775.

To begin exactly at Twelve o'Clock.

To be viewed on *Thurſday*, the 6th Inſtant, and to the Time of Sale.

CATALOGUES may be had, *gratis*, at *Eſſex Houſe* aforeſaid.

Conditions of Sale as uſual.

THE TITLE PAGE TO THE AUCTION CATALOGUE FOR THE POSTHUMOUS SALE OF FRANCIS PERRY'S COINS, MEDALS, PRINTS, AND OTHER COLLECTIBLES. PERRY'S COLLECTION, BY COMPARISON WITH THOSE OF CONTEMPORARY COLLECTORS, REFLECTS HIS VERY MODEST MEANS AS A JOURNEYMAN ARTIST AND ENGRAVER. THE REASON FOR THE LATE DATE OF THE AUCTION, SOME TEN YEARS AFTER PERRY'S DEATH, IS NOT CLEAR, PARTICULARLY GIVEN THE MODEST NUMBER OF POSSESSIONS BROUGHT TO SALE. IMAGE COURTESY OF THE DEPT. OF COINS AND MEDALS, BRITISH MUSEUM.

[438] *Anecdotes of Painting in England*, 1879 ed., vol. i, p. 389.

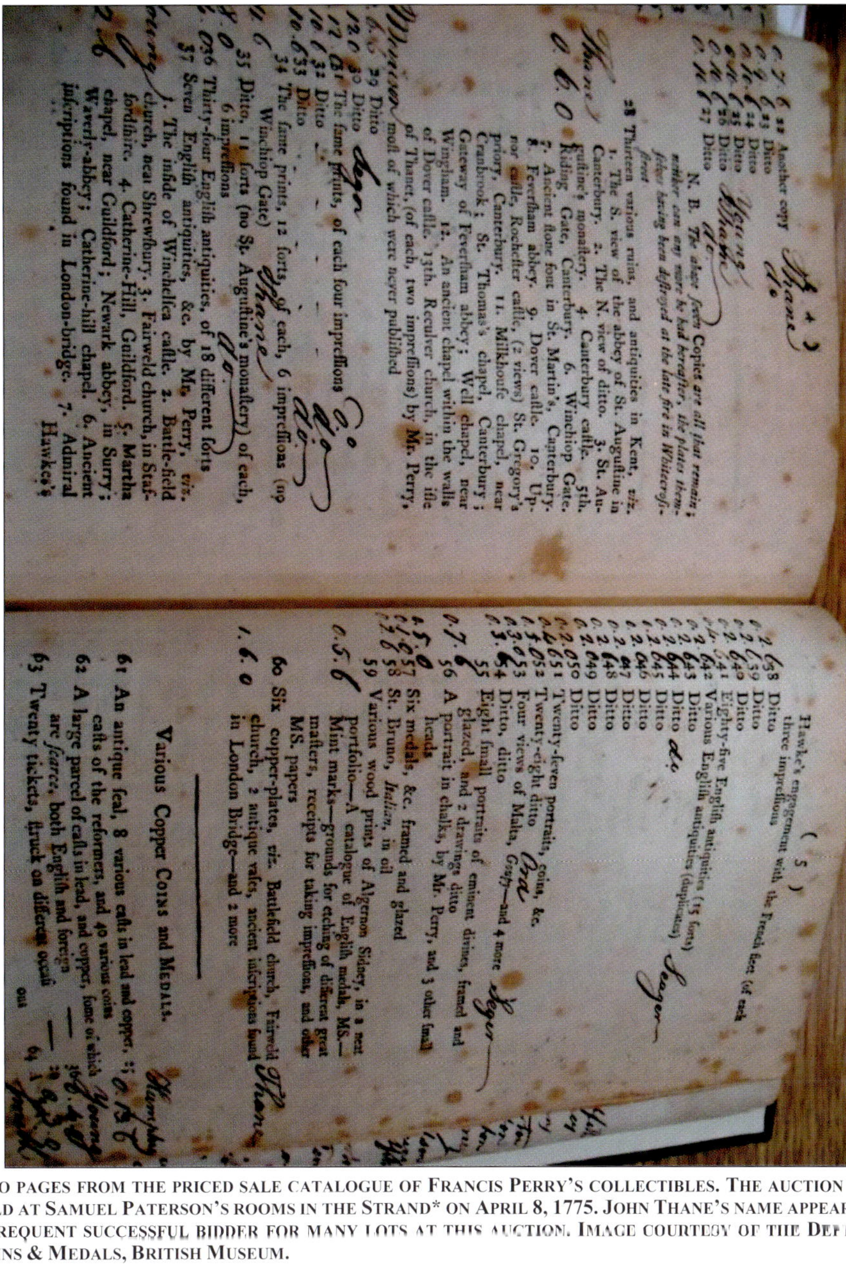

(5)

22 Another copy
23 Ditto
24 Ditto
25 Ditto
27 Ditto
N. B. *The above seven Copies are all that remain; neither can any more be had hereafter, the plates themselves having been destroyed at the late fire in Whitecross-street*
28 Thirteen various ruins, and antiquities in Kent, viz. 1. The S. view of the abbey of St. Augustine in Canterbury. 2. The N. view of ditto. 3. St. Augustine's monastery. 4. Canterbury castle. 5th. Riding Gate, Canterbury. 6. Winchiop Gate. 7. Ancient stone font in St. Martin's, Canterbury. 8. Feversham abbey. 9. Dover castle. 10. Upnor castle, Rochester castle, (2 views) St. Gregory's priory, Canterbury. 11. Milkhouse chapel, near Cranbrook; St. Thomas's chapel, Canterbury; Gateway of Feversham abbey; Well chapel, near Wingham. 12. An ancient chapel within the walls of Dover castle. 13th. Reculver church, in the isle of Thanet, (of each, two impressions) by Mr. Perry, most of which were never published
29 Ditto
30 Ditto
31 The same prints, of each four impressions
32 Ditto
33 Ditto
34 The same prints, 12 sorts, of each, 6 impressions (up Winchiop Gate)
35 Ditto, 11 sorts (no St. Augustine's monastery) of each, 6 impressions
36 Thirty-four English antiquities, of 18 different sorts
37 Seven English antiquities, &c. by Mr. Perry, viz. 1. The inside of Winchelsea castle. 2. Battle-field church, near Shrewsbury. 3. Fairweld church, in Staffordshire. 4. Catherine-Hill, Guildford. 5. Martha chapel, near Guildford; Newark abbey, in Surry; Waverly-abbey; Catherine-hill chapel. 6. Ancient inscriptions found in London-bridge. 7. Admiral Hawkes's Hawke's engagement with the French fleet (of each three impressions
38 Ditto
39 Ditto
40 Ditto
41 Eighty-five English antiquities
42 Various English antiquities (15 sorts) (duplicates)
43 Ditto
44 Ditto
45 Ditto
46 Ditto
47 Ditto
48 Ditto
49 Ditto
50 Ditto
51 Twenty-seven portraits, coins, &c.
52 Twenty-eight ditto
53 Four views of Malta, Gozo—and 4 more
54 Ditto, ditto
55 Eight small portraits of eminent divines, framed and glazed, and 2 drawings ditto
56 A portrait in chalks, by Mr. Perry, and 3 other small heads
57 Six medals, &c. framed and glazed
58 St. Bruno, *Italian*, in oil
59 Various wood prints of Algernon Sidney, in a neat portfolio—A catalogue of English medals, MS.—Mint marks—grounds for etching of different great masters, receipts for taking impressions, and other MS. papers
60 Six copper-plates, viz. Battlefield church, Fairweld church, 2 antique vases, ancient inscriptions found in London Bridge—and 2 more

Various Copper Coins and Medals.

61 An antique seal, 8 various casts in lead and copper, 35 [illegible]
62 A large parcel of casts in lead, and copper, some of which are *scarce*, both English and foreign
63 Twenty tickets, struck on different occasions

Two pages from the priced sale catalogue of Francis Perry's collectibles. The auction was held at Samuel Paterson's rooms in the Strand* on April 8, 1775. John Thane's name appears as a frequent successful bidder for many lots at this auction. Image courtesy of the Dept. of Coins & Medals, British Museum.

*Samuel Paterson (1728–1802) was a bookseller with premises in Durham Yard Strand, then an auctioneer who, from 1757, [illegible] commented in the *DNB* (Vol. 44, 1895): *He was an honest man [illegible] but constantly failed in business, as he always preferred reading to selling books. 'Perhaps we never had a bookseller who knew so much of the contents of books generally, and he was particularly well acquainted with our English [illegible]' ([illegible] Magazine [illegible]).*

'The Crown or Tryal-piece of Thomas Simon, magnified...'

An illustration (ca. 1762-1764) by Francis Perry of the 'Petition Crown' after Thomas Simon's original prototype coin. Image © Trustees of the British Museum. The legend reads:

(above) *The Crown, or Tryal-piece of Thomas Simon, magnified from that now in the possession of Thomas Hollis Esq. F.R.&A.SS. Round the edge is the underwritten petition.* (below) *Thomas Simon most humbly prays your Majesty to compare this his Tryal-Piece with the Dutch, and if more truly drawn and emboss'd, more gracefully order'd, and more accurately engraven, to relieve him.*

Historical Commentary on Francis Perry

[Francis Perry...born in Abingdon...] was a pupil of Vanderbank and Richardson, but showed very little aptitude for painting. He mainly engraved coins and medallions for the magazines of his time.

—*Benezit Dictionary of British Graphic Artists...*, 2012, vol. i, p. 206.

§

Mr. Thomas Hollis sent me the first number of Mr. Perry's English Medals, &c. which is curious.

—Letter from Dr. Ducarel to Mr. [Peter] Thomson dated August 16, 1762.
The Literary Anecdotes..., 1812, vol. v, p. 514.

§

[FRANCIS PERRY] was born at Abingdon in Berkshire, and was first placed as an apprentice to a hosier but having, as he thought, a turn for painting, his friends put him under one of the Vanderbanks, a good artist, but a man of dissipation. With him Perry learned very little, being chiefly employed in obtaining goods on credit, answering duns, or removing his cloaths from one lodging to another: sometimes he was sent to fetch coals in the table cloth, at other times in a sheet.

From Vanderbank, our artist went to Mr. Richardson; but not making any great progress, he was employed as clerk to a commissary, with whom he went down into Staffordshire, where he made drawings of the cathedral of Litchfield, which he afterwards etched from this time he commenced engraver, and worked for the magazines.

His best works are coins and medals, which he copied with great neatness and precision; we have also several portraits by him; and, among others, that of Dr. Ducarel in folio, placed at the title of his Anglo-Norman Antiquities.

He etched upon a white ground, by which means he was the better enabled to work by candle-light. He was an honest, industrious man, but could scarcely earn a subsistence...

— J. Strutt (1785). *Biographical Dictionary...an historical account of all the engravers...*, p. 221.

§

The following letter is of particular interest, once again illustrating the interaction of contemporary figures on the subject of 'medals.' Not only does this segment of a letter indicate the association of Horace Walpole to Dr Ducarel, but the subject of the letter is Francis Perry. In the next paragraph, Walpole complains of George Vertue's misidentification of an illustration of Henry VIII as Henry VII.

To Dr. Ducarel,

I am glad my books have at all amused you, and am much obliged to you for your notes and communications. ... After the medals I lent Mr. Perry, I have a little reason to take it ill, that he has entirely neglected me; he has published a number, and sent it to several persons, and never to me.(fn.: 'A series of English Medals, by Francis Perry, 4to. with thirteen plates.') wanted to see him too, because I know of two very curious medals, which I could borrow for him. He does not deserve it at my hands, but I will not defraud the public of any thing valuable; and therefore, if he will call on me any morning, but a Sunday or Monday, between eleven and twelve, I will speak to him of them.

—H. Walpole, letter to Dr. Ducarel, dated Feb. 24, 1762. In Walpole, H. (J. Wright, ed.), *The Letters of Horace Walpole, earl of Orford*, 1840, vol. iv, p. 212.

§

To the Editor,

Another subject that I would recommend to your consideration (and which, in My opinion, could not fail to be well received) is, a collection of English medals, to be continued occasionally. Such a work, was begun some years ago by Mr. Francis Perry, a very ingenious painter and engraver, who first learnt the rudiments of his art under Mr. Richardson...That gentleman, I have been told, met with great encouragement; but death put a period to his labours, before he had near compleated his plan.

It seems, however, to have been his misfortune not to have been sufficiently acquainted with history to investigate the subjects of his medals. Indeed, it is no easy task to ascertain the events to which many of them allude; yet, among your numerous readers, those that appear doubtful to one, may be explained by another; and by that means the curious may be gratified In a point that would give much satisfaction to many, and could be displeasing to none.

And now, Mr. Urban, having said thus much concerning an article which you seem willing to improve, and with regard to which you have desired the assistance of your correspondents, I have only to add, that, if you would think what I have suggested worthy your attention, a specimen or two will at least serve for variety, and, if not approved by your readers, can be of no great loss either to you or the public.

—An Old Customer

—*The Gentleman's Magazine, and Historical Chronicle,* 1778, vol. 48, pp. 246-247.

THE DEDICATION PAGE FROM THE *MEMOIRS OF THOMAS HOLLIS.* THOMAS BRAND, A POLITICAL RADICAL AND DISSENTER, WAS THE BENEFICIARY OF THOMAS HOLLIS' ESTATE WITH THE CONDITION THAT HE ADOPTED THE SURNAME HOLLIS. BRAND HAD BEEN THOMAS HOLLIS' FRIEND AND TRAVEL COMPANION. THE ETCHING IS BY GIOVANNI BATTISTA CIPRIANI R.A. (1727–1785), A FOUNDING MEMBER OF THE ROYAL ACADEMY.

Thomas Hollis[439]

(1720–1774)

· Collector, Bibliophile·and Philanthropist ·

As part of his preparation for a mercantile career, at 12 years of age Thomas Hollis was sent to Amsterdam to learn Dutch and French. After returning to England, his father, also named Thomas, died. Having inherited both his father's estate and that of his great uncle Thomas, it was decided that the young Thomas would study for and enter the law. Accordingly, he entered Lincoln's Inn, following which he embarked upon the 'grand tour,' as was then customary for wealthy young men, travelling for four years throughout the Continent. Accompanying him was his friend Thomas Brand, who would become his future heir.[440]

THOMAS HOLLIS, ESQ., AN ENGRAVED PORTRAIT BY WILLIAM BROMLEY (1769-1842). FROM THE *EUROPEAN MAGAZINE*, NOV. 1, 1788. THE FIGURE WOULD SEEM TO BE BRITANNIA STYLED AS MARIANNE, THE FRENCH ALLEGORICAL FIGURE OF LIBERTY AND REASON. IMAGE © TRUSTEES OF THE BRITISH MUSEUM.

Returning home in 1750, Hollis took up his further duties as a wealthy young gentleman of the time:

> He therefore entered upon what was to him the evidently congenial occupations of the dilettante and connoisseur and began collecting books and medals, as he says, "for the purpose of illustrating and upholding liberty, preserving the memory of its champions, to render tyranny and its abettors odious, to extend science and art, to keep alive the honour and estimation of their patrons and protectors, and to make the whole as useful as possible; abhorring all monopoly; and if it should be the fitness of things to propagate the same benevolent spirit to posterity....[441]

In part because of his political beliefs as a *Whig* as well as his idea of a young gentleman's duty, Hollis sought to obtain a seat in Parliament. As Clegg further comments, Hollis:

[439] This THOMAS HOLLIS (1720–1774) should not be confused with his grandfather THOMAS HOLLIS (d. 1735) or great uncle, THOMAS HOLLIS (1659-1731) both of whom were wealthy English merchants, collectors and benefactors of Harvard University. To confuse the issue further, THOMAS BRAND HOLLIS (1719–1804), born THOMAS BRAND, a radical and dissenter who had accompanied Hollis on his 'grand tour,' was required to add Hollis to his name by the terms of Thomas Hollis' will which left the younger man his estate.

[440] *DNB*, 1891 ed., vol. xxvii, p. 176.

[441] S. Clegg (1908). Thomas Hollis.... *The Bibliophile*, vol. 1 (1) p. 37.

> ...revolted at the methods of party management under the Pelham regime and found it quite impossible to obtain a seat without resorting to bribery.[442]

Finding his entry into politics and Parliament blocked, Hollis decided to disseminate his republican views by distributing large numbers of books and portraits to universities.[443] A man of strong views and modest habits, he achieved recognition in his lifetime as evidenced by his being elected to fellowship in both the Royal Society and the Society of Antiquaries. Yet Clegg, an early 20th century biographer, believed that Hollis' name and contributions as a collector and bibliophile had been relatively neglected compared to such contemporaries as Horace Walpole:

> The most typical name of the period is, perhaps, that of Horace Walpole, but his pretty wit as a writer, his social position and paradoxical career have won for him a pre-eminence and attention which by implication hardly does justice to other collectors of the time.
>
> Among these an honourable place is held by Thomas Hollis, with whom Walpole may not unfairly be compared. Both, as inheritors of ample fortunes were in the position to gratify their whims–(and alike they had many); both had the tastes and inclinations of the connoisseur and dilettante; and both professed the same political faith...Desirable works which existed only in ill-printed and unshapely editions, he had re-printed, and from the very laudable desire of rendering his gifts of books both beautiful and serviceable he had them put in bindings of capital quality...
>
> The stamps on Hollis's books, which were in several cases copied from coins or medals in his collection and for the rest part purposely designed by capable artists, were cut for him by the medallist Pingo.
>
> They include figures of Britannia, Liberty, the owl of Minerva, the caduceus of Mercury, the wand of Aesculapius; the cock, olive and palm branches, the cap of liberty and the pugio or Roman short sword.[444]

Aside from his interest in books and bindings, Hollis had an interest in medallic art:

> The stamps on Hollis's books, which were in several cases copied from coins or medals in his collection and for the rest part purposely designed by capable artists, were cut for him by the medallist Pingo.[445]

To some extent, this interest reflected his belief that the medals could be a medium which he could utilize and assist in his campaign to disseminate the spread of liberty. As was the case for his involvement in printing and bookbinding, Hollis took a very active role in promoting the medium itself. As O'Connell notes:

> The Society [of Arts's] encouragement of medal-making was led by Thomas Hollis, who also commissioned medals privately as part of a personal campaign to promote Whig ideals of civil and religious liberty by distributing medals, books and prints to individuals and libraries throughout the world. Hollis worked closely with James 'Athenian' Stuart and Giovanni Battista Cipriani as designers, and with the two leading medal-making families, the Pingos and the Kirks. Hollis's collections of coins and prints provided sources for images, and inscriptions were taken from classical texts.[446]

---

442 Ibid.

443 Among the portraits of political figures he distributed was that of Oliver Cromwell by SAMUEL COOPER which went to Sidney Sussex College.

444 Ibid. S. Clegg, 'Thomas Hollis....', op. cit., p. 38.

445 Ibid.

446 Ibid. O'Connell, S. (2003). *London 1753,* p. 189.

TENTH DAY. 297

Relative of the Possessor of the Blenheim Library, may come forth in due season, and with a due guerdon of praise.

150 A medallion of *Henry VIII.* with a *Latin, Greek,* and *Hebrew* inscription, in *Evelyn*, p. 89, 1 *oz.* 9 *pwt.* 12 *gr.* - - 8 18 6

151 A like medallion of *Edward VI.* not in *Evelyn*, 2 *oz.* 7 *pwt.* 22 *gr.* 12 15 0

ENGLISH GOLD MEDALS.

152 A medal of Queen *Elizabeth*, her head, inscription, *Quid nos sine Te*, reverse, a castle, QVID HOC SINE TE, not in *Evelyn*, 2 *pwt.* 17 *gr.* A medal of Prince *Henry*, *Evelyn*, p. 103, 7 *pwt.* 1 *gr.* 5 7 6

153 A medal of King *Charles I.* the King's head, and usual titles, reverse, arms of *Great Britain*, FLORENT. CONCORDIA REGNA. not in *Evelyn*. Inauguration medal of King *Charles I. Evelyn*, p. 104, 14 *pwt.* 6 *gr.* - - - - 3 4 0

154 Another medal of this King, reverse, city of *London*, SOL ORBEM REDIENS, SIC REX ILLVMINAT URBEM. *Evelyn*, p. 109. A small medal of this King. His head, and no inscription, 1 *oz.* 5 *pwt.* 2 *gr.* 6 16 0

155 Medal of Lord *Fairfax*, reverse, POST HÆC MELIORA. 1645. MERVISTI. *Evelyn*, p. 116, 6 *pwt.* 6 *gr.* - - - 1 10 0

156 Another of the same Lord: his face, but no inscription, reverse, as the last. It has a loop, 3 *pwt.* A thin plate, with a head, 19 *gr.* 1 6 0

157 A medal of *Oliver* on the victory at *Dunbar*. *Evelyn*, p. 117, 4 *pwt.* 9 *gr.* - - - - - - 9 0 0

158 A medallion on *Oliver's* death, struck by his son. *Evelyn*, p. 119, 2 *oz.* 4 *pwt.* 4 *gr.* - - - - 11 5 0

159 A medal on the same occasion, the face-side struck from the shilling dye, reverse, as the last, 11 *pwt.* 3 *gr.* - 3 14 0

160 A smaller on the same occasion, like the first, 4 *pwt.* 3 *gr.* 7 0 0

CHARLES II.

161 His inauguration medal at *Scoon*, not in *Evelyn*, 7 *pwt* 22 *gr.* Ditto in *England*, by *Simon*. *Evelyn*, p. 129, 7 *pwt.* 8 *gr.* - 3 11 0

162 A medallion by *Simon*. King's head laureated, with his titles, reverse, the Royal Oak and sun over it, JAM. FLORESCIT. 23 *Ap.* 1661, with a loop, 1 *oz.* 16 *pwt.* 20 *gr.* - - - 7 7 0

Q. Whether not designed for the Order of the Royal Oak? Not in *Evelyn*.

163 A fine medallion on the *Dutch War*, PRO. TALIBUS AVSIS. *Evelyn*, p. 137, 4 *oz.* 19 *pwt.* 18 *gr.* - - - 21 0 0

164 A medal of King *Charles* and Queen *Catharine*. *Ev.* 1 *oz.* 12 *pwt.* 19 *gr.* - - - - - - 6 17 6

165 The *Lucar's* Farthing, as commonly called, QVATVOR MARIA. VINDICO. struck in gold, 6 *pwt.* 2 *gr.* A small medal with the Prince's feathers, reverse, SI VIS OMNIA SVBJICERE, SVBJICE RATIONI, 2 *pwt.* 20 *gr.* - - - - 2 1 0

A PARTIAL LISTING OF [illegible] AUCTION [illegible] FOR THE MAY 14, [illegible], SALE AT SOTHEBY'S OF THOMAS HOLLIS' MEDALS. IMAGE FROM DIBDIN'S *BIBLIOGRAPHICAL DECAMERON*, 1817, VOL. 2, P. [illegible].

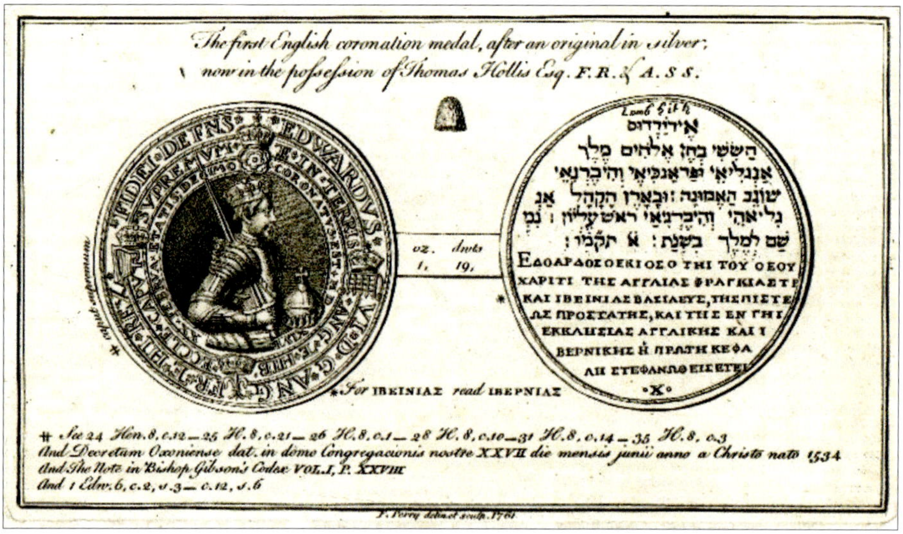

THE PROOF ILLUSTRATION OF THE MEDAL IN THOMAS HOLLIS' COLLECTION COMMEMORATING THE CORONATION OF EDWARD VI IN 1547. THE ENGRAVING IS SIGNED *F. PERRY DELIN ET SCULP, 1761*. PUBLICATION DETAILS ARE NOT KNOWN. AS THE TEXT INDICATES, THIS WAS THE FIRST ENGLISH CORONATION MEDAL. BRITISH MUSEUM ACC./REG. NO. Y,1.108, IMAGE © TRUSTEES OF THE BRITISH MUSEUM (*q.v. p. 25 for an illustration and details of this medal).*

Thomas Hollis was one of those individuals whose name keeps 'popping up' in connection with 17th century medals. Hollis employed '— Stuart' in preparing medals; he and James 'Athenian' Stuart were the medal committee of the Royal Society of Arts; the resulting medals being executed by the engraver Thomas Pingo (*q.v. p. 221*). Hollis, following up on a suggestion by Dr. Ducarel, also engaged Francis Perry to engrave the plates for "a series of English medals." These are the very plates which later appeared in Snelling's *Thirty-three Plates of English Medals* and Pinkerton's *Medallic History*... (*q.v. p. 361*).

After Hollis' death, his library was sold by Sotheby's on April 22-30, 1817, and his medal collection on May 14, 1817. The advertisement for the first sale was as follows:

> HOLLIS, Thomas (1720-1774), Thomas Brand HOLLIS (d. 1804), and John DISNEY (1746-1816) – *A Catalogue of the very Valuable and Highly Interesting United Libraries... to which is added, the Entire Collection of Prints.* London: Wright & Murphy for Sotheby's, 22 April 1817.

Christie's auctioneers, in their sale of a copy of this auction catalogue, on March 22 and 23, 2005, commented:

> This is principally the library of Thomas Hollis, "the republican" who left it, together with his fortune, to Thomas Brand who adopted the name Hollis; he in turn, bequeathed it to John Disney a Unitarian clergyman. The catalogue only occasionally indicates the Hollis provenance, but the books in red morocco were almost certainly bound for him.

Hollis' medal collection was sold separately, on May 14, 1817:

> A Catalogue of the very valuable and extensive Collection of Ancient & Modern Coins and Medals: collected by Thomas Hollis, Esq. and Thomas Brand Hollis, Esq. Sold by auction by Mr. Sotheby [on] May 14, 1817 and five following days (Sunday excepted).

A portion of the catalogue was reprinted in Dibdin, and that author's astonishment about the intense interest in collecting coins and medals at that time is evident in the following passage which preceded the inclusion of a page, with prices realized, in his essentially philosophical work:

> By way of illustrating what is above intended to be conveyed respecting the present rage for OLD ENGLISH COINS, let me subjoin...a few specimens from 'A Catalogue of the very valuable and extensive Collection of Ancient and Modern Coins and Medals, collected by Thomas Hollis Esq. and Thomas Brand Hollis, Esq. Sold by auction by Mr. Sotheby. May. 14, 1817." (Six days sale, 727 articles. Total amount 3223*l.* 15*s.* 6*d.*)[447]

A Letter from John Pinkerton to his Publisher

INHERITING from my father what was at that time a sufficient income for a man of very moderate wishes and pleasures, I published many books on antiquarian subjects, from mere love of the science; and which, far from yielding any emolument, intrenched on my little revenue. The occupations of literature do not furnish the best qualifications for conducting the pecuniary transactions of life, as I have been taught by experience...

—Letter from Pinkerton to Messrs. Longman & Co., London, April 5th, 1810. In D. Turner, *Literary Correspondence*, vol. ii, p. 393.

[447] T. F. Dibdin (1817). *The Bibliographical Decameron. or, Ten Days Pleasant Discourse upon Illuminated Manuscripts...*, vol. 3, p. 294.

The authors hope that the reader will forgive their digression in including this biography of Rev. James Granger. Although removed from the events of the Civil War period by well over a century and a half, his Biographical History *seemed to appear frequently in the literature in connection with details of many of the of 17th and early 18th figures who appear in this section. It was decided to grant the biography of Rev. Granger more space than the rather long footnote in which his 'system' was originally intended to be described—the entire story and the wide-spread adoption of his 'system' simply being so 'fantastical.'*

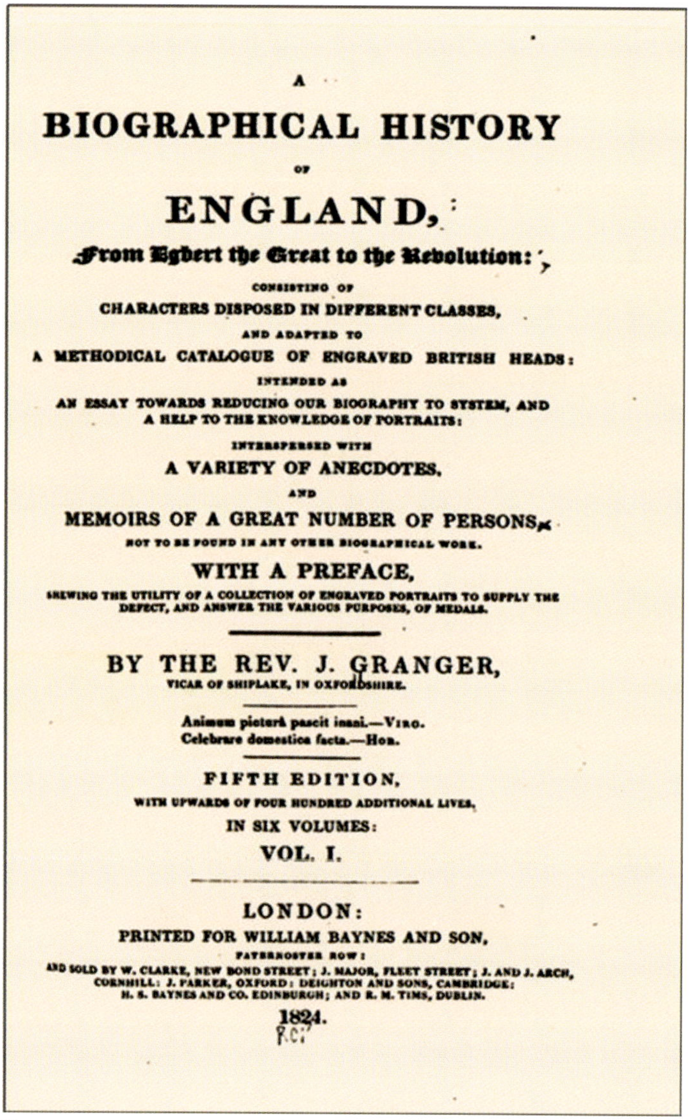
A

BIOGRAPHICAL HISTORY

OF

ENGLAND,

From Egbert the Great to the Revolution:

CONSISTING OF

CHARACTERS DISPOSED IN DIFFERENT CLASSES,

AND ADAPTED TO

A METHODICAL CATALOGUE OF ENGRAVED BRITISH HEADS:

INTENDED AS

AN ESSAY TOWARDS REDUCING OUR BIOGRAPHY TO SYSTEM, AND A HELP TO THE KNOWLEDGE OF PORTRAITS:

INTERSPERSED WITH

A VARIETY OF ANECDOTES,

AND

MEMOIRS OF A GREAT NUMBER OF PERSONS,

NOT TO BE FOUND IN ANY OTHER BIOGRAPHICAL WORK.

WITH A PREFACE,

SHEWING THE UTILITY OF A COLLECTION OF ENGRAVED PORTRAITS TO SUPPLY THE DEFECT, AND ANSWER THE VARIOUS PURPOSES, OF MEDALS.

BY THE REV. J. GRANGER,

VICAR OF SHIPLAKE, IN OXFORDSHIRE.

Animum picturâ pascit inani.—Virg.
Celebrare domestica facta.—Hor.

FIFTH EDITION,

WITH UPWARDS OF FOUR HUNDRED ADDITIONAL LIVES,

IN SIX VOLUMES:

VOL. I.

LONDON:

PRINTED FOR WILLIAM BAYNES AND SON,

PATERNOSTER ROW:

AND SOLD BY W. CLARKE, NEW BOND STREET; J. MAJOR, FLEET STREET; J. AND J. ARCH, CORNHILL: J. PARKER, OXFORD: DEIGHTON AND SONS, CAMBRIDGE: H. S. BAYNES AND CO. EDINBURGH; AND R. M. TIMS, DUBLIN.

1824.

THE TITLE PAGE FOR VOLUME I OF *A BIOGRAPHICAL HISTORY…* WHICH HAD GROWN TO A SIX-VOLUME EDITION BY 1824. IT IS DOUBTFUL THAT REV. GRANGER COULD HAVE FORESEEN THE LONGEVITY AND PERPETUAL NOTORIETY OF HIS 1769 CREATION. THE PAGES DELIBERATELY LEFT BLANK IN THIS VOLUME ALLOWED THE PLACEMENT OF PORTRAITS AS 'EXTRA ILLUSTRATIONS.' IMAGE DIGITIZED BY GOOGLE.

❧ Rev. James Granger ❧

(1723-1776)

·Biographer and Print Collector·

Rev. Granger was the author of: *'A Biographical History of England, from Egbert the Great to the Revolution, consisting of Characters dispersed in different Classes, and adapted to a Methodical Catalogue of Engraved British Heads. Intended as an Essay towards reducing our Biography to System, and a help to the knowledge of Portraits; with a variety of Anecdotes and Memoirs of a great number of persons not to be found in any other Biographical Work. With a preface, showing the utility of a collection of Engraved Portraits to supply the defect, and answer the various purposes of Medals.'*

THE REV. JAMES GRANGER, AN OIL ON COPPER PAINTING BY JOHN CORNISH (FL. 1751-1765). IMAGE © NATIONAL PORTRAIT GALLERY, LONDON.

THE Rev. James Granger, in his dedication to Horace Walpole in the fifth edition of his work: *A Biographical History of England: from Egbert the Great to the Revolution...* says:—

> ...I write neither' for fame nor bread; but have taken up the pen for the same reason that some of my brethren have laid it down, that is, only to amuse myself. I present you, Sir, with a numerous catalogue of the portraits of our countrymen, many of whom have made a considerable figure in the world. To this I have added SKETCHES of their characters. But I pretend to little more merit than the keeper of a muster-roll, who is by no means entitled to share the honours or rewards of brave and active soldiers, only for writing down their names.
>
> This singular book, which has been the employment of my leisure hours for several years of my life, will, doubtless, be numbered among my idlenesses, [sic] perhaps my weaknesses; but, I hope, never amongst my sins. The performance falls far short of my own expectation; I wish, Sir, it may, in any degree, answer yours. I was not sufficiently informed of my ignorance when I undertook it: like one walking in a fog, I fancied I saw it at a distance, when I was surrounded with it. The work, with all its defects, has afforded me much amusement, and not a little labour: the pleasure of writing resembles that of travelling; many delightful scenes present themselves on the road; but there are also objects to create disgust, and it is attended with languor and fatigue. However well-meant my poor endeavours may be, I do not expect to escape censure. To this I shall very patiently submit.[448]

And there it is—in 260 words, Granger both provides the rationale for his work, acknowledges the criticism of it, replies, and awaits his literary chastisement. And he does this in a letter to one of 18th c. England's luminaries (Horace Walpole)—'literary man,' art historian, and antiquarian

[448] J. Granger (1824). Dedication (to Horace Walpole). *Biographical History...*, (5th) ed., vol. i.

in one person. Is there more to say? Perhaps, given that Granger's name has spawned a verb—'grangerize'—associated with the vandalism of books. Granger, however, has been outdone by both those who have adopted his system and others who have attempted the same feat on their own.[449] Thomas comments on this fashionable pastime:

> In the eighteenth century, so-called catalogues of English Heads, and the likenesses in Granger's *Biographical Dictionary* intensified the passion for collecting portrait engravings as visual exemplars of the British past.[450]

Among the most well-known of these, Thomas lists Richard Bull, an MP from Cornwall, who collected a total of 14,500 portraits in his extra-illustrated copy of Granger.[451] John Pinkerton also emulated Granger, with his publication of *Iconographia Scotia or Portraits of Illustrious People of Scotland, with Biographical Notes* (1797) and *The Scottish Gallery, or Portraits of Eminent Persons of Scotland, with their Characters* (1799). Thomas Birch and Joseph Ames did much the same in their respective works, *The Heads of Illustrious Persons of Britain, on one hundred and eight copper-plates. Engraved by Mr Houbraken, and Mr Vertue. With their Lives and Characters...* (1743-1751) and *A Catalogue of English Heads: Or an Account of about Two Thousand Prints* (1748).

Yet, James Granger was not a likely candidate for long-lived notoriety. From Dorset, he attended, but did not graduate from Christ Church, Oxford University, and then entered religious life, gaining an appointment as vicar of Shiplake. It is entirely likely that few persons, if any, would have known his name today had he not had a hobby—portrait-collecting, which he attempted to 'systematize,' as stated in the subtitle of his work:

> ...consisting of characters dispersed in different classes, and adapted to a methodical catalogue of engraved British heads; intended as an essay towards reducing our biography to system, and a help to the knowledge of portraits...[452]

Clearly then, the concept underlying Granger's work was not out of step with other works of his times, some of which were likely fashioned after his *Biographical History...* What distinguishes Granger's *Biographical History* from the others was his provision of blank pages to be used by the reader for the purpose of inserting portraits, usually clipped from other works for the purpose of 'extra-illustration,' and it is that practice which has in large part brought down so much modern criticism upon him. In particular, the placement of blank pages in the volumes to facilitate this process literally licensed a defacement of other volumes. Given that most published works of the day had few illustrations, those which have survived to the present may be found at a minimum absent their frontispieces. Another outcome at the time was that the prices of already scarce illustrated books showed an immediate rise.

As is evident from the several letters between Granger and his publisher and reprinted in this volume, the first edition of his work, in two volumes, had modest initial success, although within

---

[449] 'Extra-illustration' in practice literally meant the excision of portraits and other illustrations from one book for insertion in another. This practice also extended to the cutting of signatures from letters and documents. Collector's books, both with images to excise or with space provided for insertion of extra-illustrations, were available for purchase. Some of James Caulfield's publications were intended to address this 'need.' *Portraits…of Remarkable Persons* (*q.v. p. 370*) was one such work.

[450] K. Thomas (2005). *Changing Conceptions of National Personality,* pp. 48-49.

[451] RICHARD BULL (1725-1805), MP for Newport, Cornwall (1756-1780), a friend of Horace Walpole and a serious collector of prints and books who seems to have been the first well-known 'extra-illustrator' of Granger's *History*. Bull's first two efforts resulted in an expansion of Granger's work to nineteen volumes and then to an additional sixteen volumes. Bull then turned his attention to Walpole's *Anecdotes of Painting in England*, which he later expanded with an additional fourteen volumes (K. Baetjer & J. Dobkin, 2010). In carrying out extra-illustration, Bull and his contemporaries appear to have driven up the prices of books containing illustrations.

[452] J. Granger (1779). *Biographical History…*, 3rd ed., vol. i, title page.

two years of publication it had reaped him £400 in income, a not inconsiderable sum. The work apparently struck a chord among the gentry and later volumes and new editions appeared in 1774, 1775, 1779, 1804, and 1824. Rev. Granger died in 1776 and thus did not live to see subsequent editions past that date. At the time of his death his own collection of engraved 'heads' or portraits exceeded 14,000, a number equal in size to Richard Bull's collection.[453] While the auction of the collection in 1778 was not hugely successful, this style of collecting was becoming fashionable as judged by both the increasing demand for his books and for collectable portraits and their increasing value at auction. The later editions of Granger's *Biographical History...* were prepared by the Rev. Mark Noble.[454]

Historical Commentary on Rev. James Granger

You will be concerned, my good Sir, for what I have this minute heard from his nephew, that poor Mr. Granger was seized at the communion table on Sunday with an apoplexy, and died yesterday morning at five. I have answered the letter with a word of advice about his MSS. that they may not fall into the hands of booksellers. He had been told by idle people so many gossiping stories, that it would hurt him and living persons, if all his collections were to be printed; for as he was incapable of telling an untruth himself, he suspected nobody else—too great goodness in a biographer.

—Horace Walpole, in a letter to William Cole, dated April 16, 1776.

§

The publication of Granger's work excited an eager competition for portraits, and unfortunately many of his disciples carried their zeal to the highly-censurable extreme of mutilating valuable works for the sake of the portraits which they contained:

> Previously to the publication of the first edition of this work in 1769, five shillings was considered a liberal price by collectors for any English portrait; until the late Lord Oxford, Sir William Musgrave, and Richard Bull, Esq. have declared to several persons still living, that the most valuable prints in their Collections were purchased by them at, or under, that sum. But on the appearance of Mr. Granger's work, the rage to illustrate it with portraits was so prevalent, that scarcely a copy of a book ornamented with portraits could be found in an unmutilated state; and books of this description rose in price to five times their original value..[Many works] have been freely plundered for the sake of their attractive embellishments.[455]

Rowe Mores, in his criticism upon Ames's Catalogue of English Heads, is loud in his complaint of these mutilators—often depredators:

> If this *gout* for prints and thieving continues, let private owners and public libraries look well to their books, for there will not remain a valuable book ungarbled by their connoiseuring villainy; for neither honesty nor oaths restrain them.

—A. Allibone (1899). *Dictionary of English Literature and British and American Authors to the Latter Half of the 19th C,* (unpaginated).

'[TO] GRANGERIZE'

(A verb, often used as a pejorative adjective.)

1. to illustrate (a book already printed) with engravings, prints, etc. by the addition of engravings, prints, etc. obtained elsewhere, often by clipping them from other books.
2. to damage (a book) by clipping such engravings, etc.

—*Webster's New World Dictionary*

---

[453] *Biographical Dictionary...*, 5th ed., 1824, vol. i, pp. ii-iii.

[454] The REV. MARK NOBLE (1754–1827) was the author of *Memoirs of the Protectoral House of Cromwell* (1784, 1787) and *The Lives of the English Regicides* (1798). Noble's further edition of Granger's work in 1806 incorporated materials from his own collection, as well as from Granger's books.

[455] J. Granger, Advertisement, *Biographical History...*, 5th ed., 1824, vol. i; pp. ii-iii.

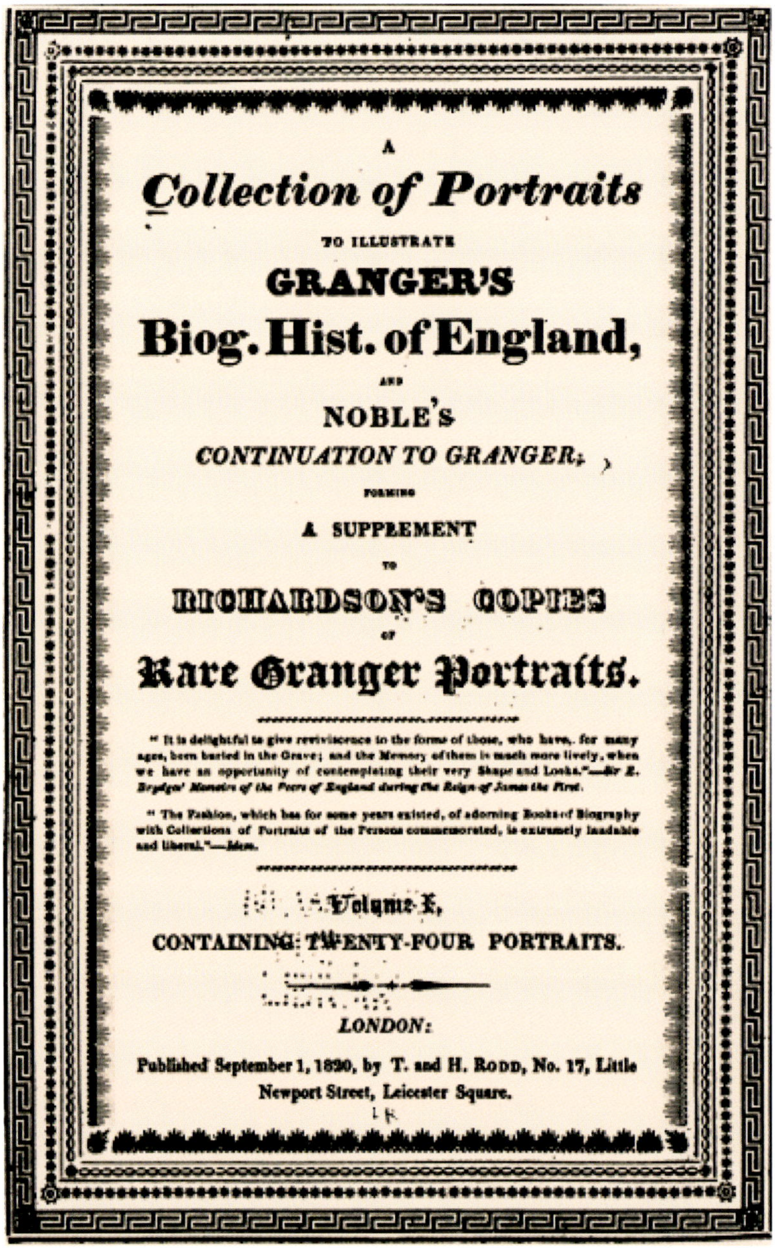
A

Collection of Portraits

TO ILLUSTRATE

GRANGER'S

Biog. Hist. of England,

AND

NOBLE's

CONTINUATION TO GRANGER;

FORMING

A SUPPLEMENT

TO

RICHARDSON'S COPIES

OF

Rare Granger Portraits.

" It is delightful to give reviviscence to the forms of those, who have, for many ages, been buried in the Grave; and the Memory of them is much more lively, when we have an opportunity of contemplating their very Shape and Looks."—*Sir E. Brydges' Memoirs of the Peers of England during the Reign of James the First.*

" The Fashion, which has for some years existed, of adorning Books of Biography with Collections of Portraits of the Persons commemorated, is extremely laudable and liberal."—*Idem.*

Volume I,

CONTAINING TWENTY-FOUR PORTRAITS.

LONDON:

Published September 1, 1820, by T. and H. RODD, No. 17, Little Newport Street, Leicester Square.

THE TITLE PAGE OF A *COLLECTION OF PORTRAITS* PUBLISHED IN 1820 AND SPECIFICALLY INTENDED FOR 'EXTRA-ILLUSTRATING' GRANGER'S *BIOGRAPHICAL HISTORY*... IMAGE DIGITIZED BY GOOGLE.

"GRANGERIZING"—TWO 19TH C. VIEWS

THE question, Which was the first instance of "extra-illustrating"? has not, I believe, been discussed in these pages. If we accept the expression as applying to any volume in which have been inserted drawings, engravings, maps, MS. notes, or additional matter of any kind, it is obviously probable that there are examples both recorded and existing before 1769...As Granger's biographer in the 'D.N.B.' indicates, the advance in the price of prints after the publication of the 'History' was remarkable, and their enhanced value explains the sale of Granger's first collection of portraits, largely the gifts of sympathetic antiquaries.

— A. Abrahams, *Notes and Queries*, 10th Series. vi (July 14, 1906), p. 23-24.

§

ONE of the notable features in the present bibliophilist *furia* is the revival or resuscitation of a certain obscure clergyman, whose one publication was destined, for nearly a century, to have an extraordinary influence. He succeeded in devising or inventing an altogether new taste, and in furnishing a number of idle persons with a mode of employing their spare time, and the cash which it was likely enough they could not so well spare. Many have bewailed the appearance of this cleric as one of the most disastrous events that have occurred in the realms of 'bookland,' akin to something like famine, plague, or conflagration in other departments. Others bless his memory, and have cheerfully consecrated their whole life to carrying out his doctrine. This person was, however, one of the most worthy, amiable men of his time, with a good deal of simplicity in his character, enjoying the friendship of persons of all conditions; modest withal, and with a certain attraction in his nature. He was, in short, the REVEREND JAMES GRANGER, and the science, pastime, or 'Art of Devastation,' which he introduced, is known now as 'Grangerising.'

To 'the general' this may not convey much, and Granger and his 'Grangerising' seem mysteriously obscure. About the middle of last century, when he attained his fame, at one bound, as it were, the amateurs of the day, including Mr. Walpole, had a passion for gathering what were called 'heads'—that is, engraved portraits of notable persons. These were of all kinds and merit; some...being fine works of art. But they were sought not for their artistic merits, but as representing some small celebrity, of whom it was unlikely that a portrait should be in existence. Often a 'head' was specially etched or engraved from some old picture to fill the blank. Many would form a collection of English nobles, or of the members of a particular noble family, or of a particular reign. The Duchess of Portland indulged in this hobby, and had a fine collection of 'heads'; but Mr. James West, Secretary to the Treasury, and President of the Royal Society, was most conspicuous in this line, having filled twenty-three folio volumes with 'heads,' which, on being 'dispersed' at his death, it took thirteen days to sell by auction. Still there was wanting system and direction for these labours. To the 'head' collector all was fish that came to his net; he had to stow them away in portfolios, and he felt that this was a rambling, incoherent mode of following the business. The Rev. Mr. Granger, however, conceived the happy idea which set all this to rights. What was wanted was a sort of gallery in which the pictures should be hung, or a narrative which they would illustrate, and where they could take their places in regular series. What could be better for such a purpose than A History of England...In such a programme [as proposed by Granger] the names of thousands and thousands of persons could be introduced. Here would be ranged kings, nobles, statesmen—in short, here was accommodation for the flotsam and jetsam lying unclassed and disordered in the portfolios. Granger further consulted the convenience of his patrons by issuing sets in quarto with every second page blank, so that gentlemen might insert their own ' heads' at the proper places.

It is really amazing to think what an influence this simple event—the publication of two small, 'lean' quartos—has had in the book world....It was received by the most learned and captious antiquarians with enthusiasm. Everyone was enchanted by the originality of the idea and the irresistible entertainment offered.

[Rev. Granger's] object, as we have seen, was to provide shelter for the loose detached prints which go knocking about the world. It was easy to arrange all the heads that were issued...But presently it was found that many of the most derivable ones belonged to books which they illustrated, and could be obtained nowhere else. With that the signal was given, and for over a century the work has gone on bravely of slaughtering, cutting up, and rifling many a noble tome for the sake of its prints. The ravaging that has obtained steadily for over a century is almost inconceivable. The finer and more stately the volume, the more likely it is to become a prey to this sort of spoiler. Once the prints have been rifled, the volume is felt to be a maimed and useless incumbrance; it becomes a cripple, as it were, and its fate is usually to be cast away or torn up. Worse than this, a whole 'set' is often destroyed for the sake of obtaining a print or two. There is surely something reckless and even savage in this process...

The Vicar of Shiplake, having all his own sins to bear, must not, however, be held accountable for this debased form of 'Grangerism' now in fashion. A gradual corruption has set in, and instead of merely securing illustrations and portraits suggested by the allusions in the text, every sort of scrap, cutting, document, &c., is now 'pasted in' and bound up. The copy has thus become a sort of hotch-potch or dust-bin into which everything is cast, and where nothing is refused....

...At last, while still dreaming of his ' heads' and meditating new ventures, he died suddenly and was 'Grangerised' himself, and 'inset' in the parish churchyard. On him there was written this inscription:—

To the Memory of the REVEREND JAMES GRANGER,

who on the Sunday after Easter, when the Sacrament is administered in the church of Shiplake, Oxfordshire, of which he was vicar, was seized with an apoplectic fit while at the Communion table there, after having gone through the duties of the desk and pulpit as usual, and notwithstanding every medical assistance died early the next morning, April 5, 1776...'

—Anon., *The Cornhill Magazine*, 1890 (Jan.-June), pp. 135-142.

§

A Series of Letters between Rev. Granger and his Publisher

(Including a final one to his friend Mr. William Musgrave)[456]

§

1. From the Rev. Granger to Mr. Thomas Davies (—Malcolm, p.15)

Shiplake, Dec 26, 1767

Honoured Sir,

I, by the last post, received a very kind letter from Mr. Walpole, written with so much elegance, that it would have given me great pleasure, if it had not at all related to myself. He speaks of as much as he has read of my work in higher terms than I ever expected; indeed, too much in my favour for me to repeat.

I intend, according to Mr. Walpole's advice, to alter the title of my book, which he says will greatly help its sale. He says, that he could wish I would entitle it, "A history of England, illustrated by Portraits and Characters." I presume, Sir, the following form would not be amiss, as it is explanatory of the work.

"A History of England, from Egbert the Great to the Revolution, illustrated by Portraits and Characters; intended as an essay towards reducing our biography to system, and containing a methodical catalogue of engraved English heads during the above period: with a preface, shewing their utility in answering the various purposes of medals."

I thought it expedient, Sir, to inform you of this alteration of the title, before you treaty with any bookseller in relation to the copy...

I am, &c., James Granger

§

2. From Mr. Davies to the Rev. Granger (—ibid. p. 27)

London, May 16, 1769

Dear Sir,

This day the 'Biographical History of England' is published! May it be a propitious day! I have all the reason in the world as yet to encourage you to proceed in your labours: *macte virtue.*

The Bishop of Gloucester [Dr. Warburton] has bought the book which he calls an odd one; this is praise from him, for, if he had not an intention to peruse it, he would have called it a sad book. I was honoured with a visit from him this day. A clergyman of distinguished learning and amiable virtues [Mr. Cracherode] praised your work very much. He, I am afraid, will wait for another edition; this he seems to be almost certain of...

I am, Dear Sir, & c., Thomas Davies

---

456 J. Granger & J. P. Malcolm (1805). *Letters [of the Rev.] James Granger...*

§

3. From Mr. Davies to the Rev. Granger (—ibid. p. 27)

London, July 11, 1769

Dear Sir,

...I have spared no pains to circulate your work; but we must not expect that a book of the price of two guineas will sell like a play or a political pamphlet. I am in great hopes it will come to a second edition, and I cannot say that I doubt it. By this time next year we shall be able to talk decisively of it. To tell you the real truth, no book has been more censured, nor more applauded; the number of approvers exceeds by much that of the censurers...

I am, Dear Sir, & c., Thomas Davies

§

4. From the Rev. Granger to Mr. William Musgrave[457]

Shiplake, March 13, 1770

Sir,

I lately took the liberty of troubling you with what, I fear, has been thought a very impertinent letter, in relation to a book of mine, entitled, 'A Biographical History of England,' in which I mentioned a second Edition as being likely soon to take place. It is indeed very true, that Mr. Davies the bookseller thought so but a few months since, and that he told me that he did not question but he must begin re-printing it within the year. But he is now assured that a second Edition is at a much greater distance, and tells me that a great number of copies remain unsold in his hands, and especially in the hands of the booksellers his subscribers. After all, he owns the book has been very well received, and has, with great generosity, promised to give me a gratuity of 50*l*. besides his present of 13 copies; to say nothing of smaller presents. He is very much afraid, that what I have said to you, Sir, and other gentlemen, in relation to a second Edition, may be circulated to his disadvantage, I therefore think it incumbent upon me to obviate any reports of that kind, as they will doubtless prejudice the sale of the book. Mr. Davies tells me that the additions and emendations will be printed by themselves. It has been falsely reported that I neglected to take an account of a *great number* of the Heads in Mr. West's Collection. Nothing is more certain than that I did not wilfully [sic] omit one that could with any propriety be introduced into my work. I am, Sir, with great respect,

Your most obedient humble servant,
James Granger.

> THANE...collected Snelling's tracts into a volume, and prefixed a general title to them...
>
> —*Literary Anecdotes of the 18th c.: Comprising Biographical Memoirs of Wm. Bowyer, Printer, F.S.A. and many of his Learned Friends*, 1812, vol. iii, pp. 417-418.

---

457 Presumably SIR WILLIAM MUSGRAVE (1735-1800), civil servant, antiquary and prominent print collector, had been the purchaser of RALPH THORESBY'S print collection. Musgrave's collection, together with the collections of HORACE WALPOLE and JAMES WEST, provided the material for JAMES GRANGER'S *Biographical History of England*. Musgrave introduced Granger to his fellow collectors Walpole and West and helped him in negotiations with Thomas Davies, the publisher. Musgrave's collection of prints numbered approximately 10,000. In 1799, Musgrave sold his portrait prints to WILLIAM RICHARDSON the auctioneer and print dealer. Upon Musgrave's death, the remainder of his collection was sold at auction in February and March 1800. The sale comprised approximately 10,000 prints in 3503 lots over 31 days ([illegible], 2014).

An engraving with etching of John Thane, ca. 1819, by John Ogborne (1755-1837), after William Redmore Bigg (1782-1846). From Thane, *British Autography And Portraits, A Collection of Fac-Similes [sic] of the Hand-Writing of Royal and Illustrious Persons, with their Authentic Portraits* (1838 ed.). This illustration is from the "Twenty-seven additional portraits... of which only 100 copies were made up." The background details of this illustration, the frontispiece to 'The Additional Plates,' are a treasure trove for today's medal collector to examine at leisure—consider the coin or medal in hand, the cabinets, of which one tray is on the table, the research library with gaps, presumably for the books in use, and the portrait visible on the piece in Thane's hand. Aside from the style of dress, the wig, and the absent computer, what are the differences between Thane and the modern collector?

John Thane

(1747/48?-1818)

· Print- and bookseller, Publisher, and Medallist ·

THANE, although not usually thought of as a medal collector, was one, and had a collection of both coins and medals. He did business at various London addresses, including his home.[458] Thane also possessed a specialist knowledge of pictures, coins and 'vertu.'

The British Museum describes him as having been a 'major dealer' in coins, drawings, prints, manuscripts and autographs and he was an occasional publisher of prints. Thane appears to have entered the print-selling trade after his marriage in 1770 to Mary Snelling, the daughter of Thomas Snelling (*q.v.*). Thane collected the works of Thomas Snelling and would cut up the volumes, usually for the illustrations, and dispose of the contents to major collectors, a not uncommon practice at that time.[459] Some idea of the nature of Thane's business may be gathered from the advertisement for his second catalogue for 1772:

> ...a curious collection of prints and drawings, both antient and modern: Consisting of fine historical prints and foreign portraits, by the following masters, viz. Israel van Meck Martin Schoon Albert Durer Lucas Van Leyden Michael Angelo Raphael Julio Romano Goltzius Nicolas de Bruin Carrache Rubens Van Dyck Jourdaens Poussin Rembrandt Worlidge Hollar...&c. &c. &c. likewise a large collection of English portraits, by Faithorne Marshall Pass Hollar Cross Payne Loggan White Blootling Vertue Vander Gucht, &c. &c. &c. a small collection of books of prints, and books of coins, medals, and antiquities: also, several antient and modern coins and medals of all sorts; which will begin to be sold on Friday, the first of May, 1772, for ready-money only. The lowest price in the catalogue, by John Thane, removed from Old Bond-street, to the corner of Gerrard-street in Princes-street, St. Ann's, Soho. Who gives the full value for any collection of prints, books, coins, and medals, &c. Catalogues to be had at the place of sale, and at Mr. Snelling's, bookseller, next the horn tavern, Fleet-street.

Similar catalogues appeared in 1773 (2) and 1774. The second catalogue for 1773 would seem to have had more emphasis on numismatic material, perhaps reflecting the disposal by Thane of Mr. West's collection[s]:

> ...a most curious and valuable collection of prints, drawings, books, books of prints: illuminated missals, antient manuscripts, deeds and rolls, coins, medals, and antiquities, and other curiosities, the whole collected with great care and expence, out of the cabinets of the late Mr. West, and others. The collection consists of the finest impressions of historical and other prints, both ancient and modern...The books are chiefly early printed, and on antiquities, coins, medals, &c. including several hundred scarce tracts and plays. Now on sale (for ready money only) by John Thane, the corner of Gerrard-Street, in Princes-Street, St. Ann's Soho, who will buy any collection or parcel of prints, books, coins, medals, &c. Catalogues to be had at sixpence each, at the place of sale, and at Mr. Hooper's, printseller, No. 25, Ludgate-Hill.[460]

---

[458] These include Old Bond-street (?-?), 24 Gerrard Street in Princes-street, St. Ann's, Soho (1772-1775) from where he issued catalogues; 159 Strand (1779); Rupert Street; 28 Haymarket (1781-1792; this was a second shop, opened with the print-seller ANTHONY TORRE, likely selling 'modern' stipple engraved prints); Spur Street, Leicester Square (1795-1798); 36 New Lisle Street (?). At the time of his death, Thane appeared to be living at the Spur Street, Leicester Fields address.

[459] *DNB*, 1898, vol. 56, p.107; T. Clayton & A. McConnell, *ODNB, on-line*, 2013. (*see* 'grangerizing,' *this vol., pp. 367-373).*

[460] Mr. West's sale appears to have been successful, for Horace Walpole wrote to Rev, Cole:

> At Mr. West's sale, I got literally nothing. his prints sold for the frantic sum of 1495*l.* 10*s.* 0*d* Your and my good friend Mr. Gulston threw away above 200*l.* there (Feb. 18, 1773). (and again, later) ... books are selling outrageously. His family will make a fortune by what he collected from stalls and Morefields. But I must not blame the virtuosi, having surpassed them. (April 7, 1773).
>
> —G. Montagu, *Personal Correspondence of Horace Walpole,* 1837 ed., vol. iii, pp. 60, 62.

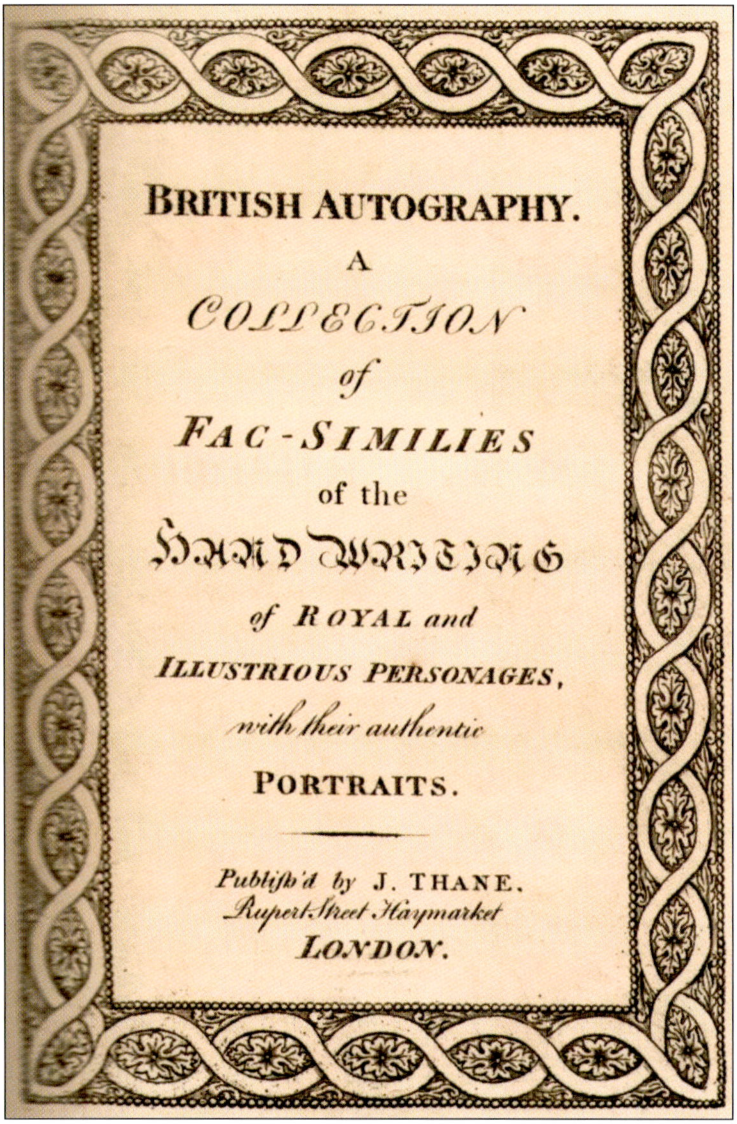

BRITISH AUTOGRAPHY.

A

COLLECTION

of

FAC-SIMILIES

of the

HAND WRITING

of ROYAL and

ILLUSTRIOUS PERSONAGES,

with their authentic

PORTRAITS.

Publish'd by J. THANE.
Rupert Street Haymarket
LONDON.

THE TITLE PAGE FROM VOL. 1 (4 QUARTO VOLS. IN 3) OF THE 2ND EDITION OF *BRITISH AUTOGRAPHY*… (1838). A HANDWRITTEN NOTE (CA. 19TH C.), IS BOUND INTO THE AUTHORS' COPY:

> The coppers of this work were sold in 1838, and the purchaser (Mr. Daniel, Bookseller, Mortimer St.) re-issued the work without altering the date; and also published "Twenty-seven Additional Portraits with the Autographs never before published" London 1839 4to. consisting of title, list of 27 portraits. 3 sheets of fac-similes, portrait of Mr. Thane & letter-press, 66 pp. of which additions only 100 copies were made up [sic]." (Lownes, W. T., *The Bibliographer's Manual of English Literature*..., London, vol. 5, 1865, p. 2658). *See explanatory note, this volume, p. 379.*

“Abraham Cowley, *From an Original by* Sir Peter Lely.” A sample illustrated page from another undated edition, most likely 1820, of John Thane’s *British Autography*. The copperplate engravings are the same as in the 1838 edition with the exception of the red decorative borders and background tint seen here. Many copies of this edition have been broken up for the sale of individu al portraits

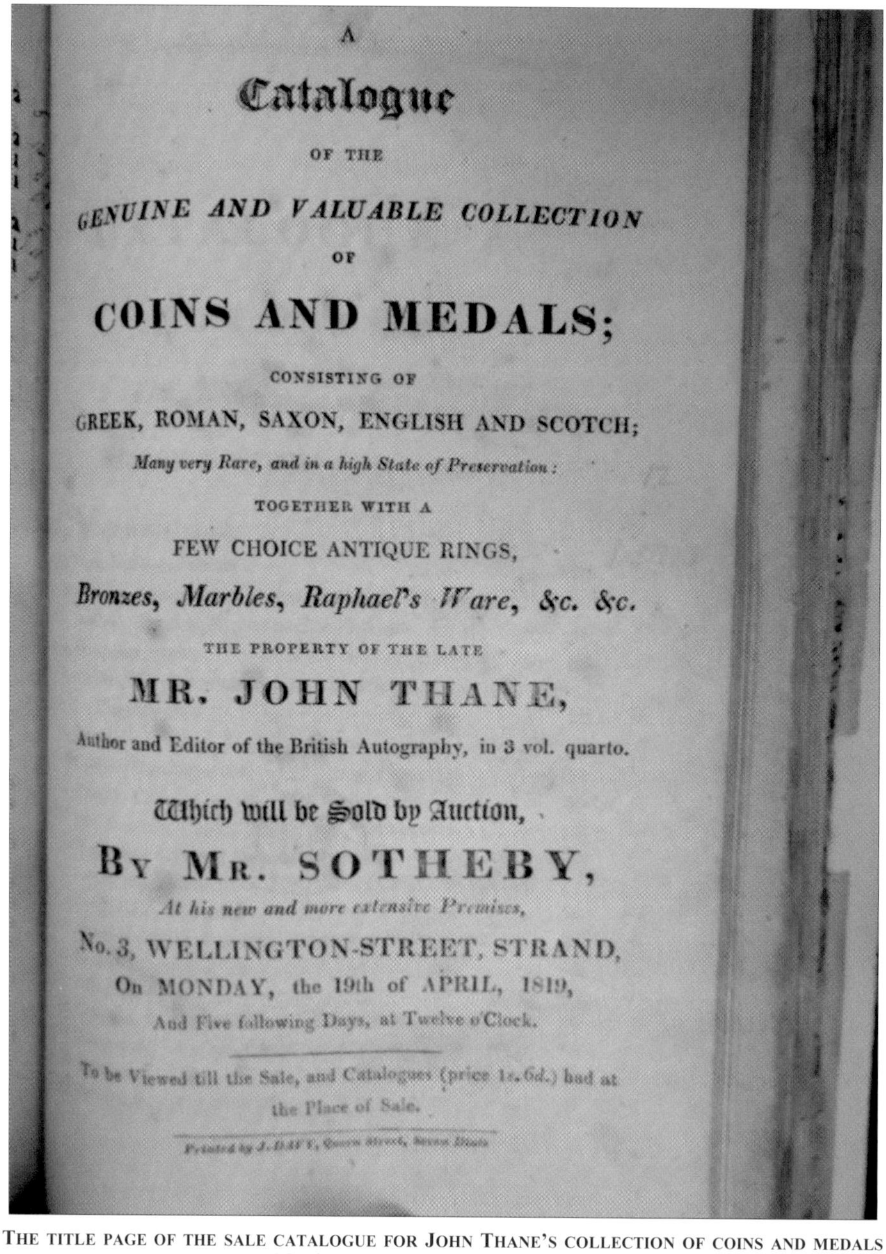

A

Catalogue

OF THE

GENUINE AND VALUABLE COLLECTION

OF

COINS AND MEDALS;

CONSISTING OF

GREEK, ROMAN, SAXON, ENGLISH AND SCOTCH;

Many very Rare, and in a high State of Preservation:

TOGETHER WITH A

FEW CHOICE ANTIQUE RINGS,

Bronzes, Marbles, Raphael's Ware, &c. &c.

THE PROPERTY OF THE LATE

MR. JOHN THANE,

Author and Editor of the British Autography, in 3 vol. quarto.

Which will be Sold by Auction,

BY MR. SOTHEBY,

At his new and more extensive Premises,

No. 3, WELLINGTON-STREET, STRAND,

On MONDAY, the 19th of APRIL, 1819,

And Five following Days, at Twelve o'Clock.

To be Viewed till the Sale, and Catalogues (price 1s. 6d.) had at the Place of Sale.

Printed by J. DAVY, Queen Street, Seven Dials

THE TITLE PAGE OF THE SALE CATALOGUE FOR JOHN THANE'S COLLECTION OF COINS AND MEDALS THAT WAS SOLD AT AUCTION BY MR. SOTHEBY IN SIX SESSIONS BEGINNING ON APRIL 19, 1819. THE SALE CONSISTED OF ANCIENT GREEK AND ROMAN COINS AS WELL AS GERMAN, SAXON AND ENGLISH COINS. ENGLISH MEDALS IN VARIOUS METALS ACCOUNTED FOR APPROXIMATELY TWENTY PERCENT OF THE NEARLY 700 LOTS. THE TOTAL MADE BY THIS PART OF THE SALE WAS £967. IMAGE COURTESY OF THE DEPT. OF COINS & MEDALS, BRITISH MUSEUM.

Historical Commentary on John Thane

John Thane, the celebrated collector of Soho...

—Comment in *Notes and Queries, a Medium of Intercommunication for Literary Men, General Readers, etc*..., 11th Ser., vol. iii, (Jan.-June, 1911).

§

Edward Thane, a descendent, reported the following:

I have been in touch with Essex Records Office and have gleaned more information on John Thane, I suspected he might have been married twice because [I] found reference to a John Thane marrying Mary Lord Snelling 25 November 1770, now John was in partnership with a Thomas Snelling (1712-1773) he was a well known Numismatist who published three major works on English coins, 1762-6. I have found the Christening details for Mary Lord Snelling and sure enough Thomas Snelling was her father and Elizabeth was her mother. In Charles Stuart Thane's (1857-1878) version of the family tree he stated that John Thane was married in Bocking, Essex, as I stated earlier. I contacted the Essex Records Office yesterday and they came up with the following information: John Thane, widower of St Anns Soho, Middlesex and Elizabeth Seamer Flack of this parish spinster married by licence, 1 January 1776. Both signed the register, Elizabeth spelt her middle name as Seymour, The witnesses were a William Flack, an Ann Flack[?] and an Ellen Amey.

—Posted on the 'Thane Family' internet site, in an e-mail from Edward Thane, dated June 3, 2004.

§

The Earl of Oxford began the first collection in England, which afterwards came in part to Mr. West, and on his death was dispersed by the rude hand of the auctioneer— Mr. Nickolls [sic] was the next regular Collector of English heads; and his collection, which was formed from Moorfields and ?, and consequently was not first-rate, consisted of about 3000 heads, four volumes in folio, and six in quarto, neatly let-in; which furnished Mr. Ames with his valuable catalogue; and came soon after the death of Mr. Nickolls into the library of Dr. Fothergill, who purchased it for eighty guineas. Mr. Granger, in his Preface, had said Mr. West bought the ten volumes; but, on the better information of Dr. Ducarel, corrected himself in his Supplement, p. 2.

On Dr. Fothergill's death the entire collection of portraits was sold to Mr. John Thane, print-seller and medalist, in Rupert-street, Soho, for one hundred and fifty pounds, who cut up the volumes and disposed of the contents to the principal collectors of British portraits at that time; *viz.* Mr. Bull, Mr. Crachcrode, Mr. Gulstone, Sir Janus Lake, Mr. Blackburne of Lancashire, and Mr. Bindley. Dr. Fothergill purchased likewise a pretty large-collection of tracts, which Mr. Nickolls had picked up in his pursuit of heads, written by those of his own persuasion from their first appearance; which the benevolent possessor informed the Editor of these Anecdotes, in 1780, he then intended to leave to the Meeting to which he then belonged, in Peter's-court, Westminster. Besides these collections, Mr. Nickolls had several views by great masters; some of which fell also into the hands of Dr. Fothergill. The Catalogue of Mr. Nickolls's Library, in his own hand-writing (including 132 volumes of tracts in folio, quarto, and octavo), was in the possession of Mr. Tutet.—For a considerable part of the information respecting Mr. Nickolls I was indebted to Dr. Fothergill, who died (before the former edition was published) Dec. 5, 1760; and of whom some account shall be given in a future page.—Anthony Wood, in his account of Elias Ashmole, tells us, "In his library I saw a large thick paper book, near a yard long, containing on every side of the leaf one, two, or more pictures or faces of eminent persons of England, and elsewhere, printed from copper cuts pasted on them, which Mr. Ashmole had with great curiosity collected...

—J. Nichols, *Literary Anecdotes*..., vol. ii, p. 160.

Note to Accompany Thane's *British Autography*... (See pp. 376 and 377, above).

Thane was the editor/author of *British Autography: A Collection of the Facsimiles of the Handwriting of Royal and Illustrious Personages, with their Authentic Portraits*, published in London in 3 volumes in 1793. The title page of the 2nd edition (illustrated on p. 376), dated 1818, was published by Edward Danielle, London with a frontispiece consisting of an engraved portrait of Thane by John Ogborne (1755-1837), after a portrait by William Redmore Bigg (1755-1828).

(31)

544	Charles I. and his Queen. *a chasing without a reverse*	1 / 2 ·
545	Charles I. on the Fishery, *finely chased by Stewart*	1 / 2 ·
546	Charles I. *reverse* the Seven-headed Monster on his Death, *fine* — — —	1 / 0
547	Charles I. *inscribed* " Successor veres utriusque; *reverse* a Hammer and Anvil " Inexpugnabile, 1648, *chased* — — —	1 · 15 ·
548	Charles I. on his Death — —	3 · 10 6
549	Charles I. small oval medals to his memory, *one gold*	3 / 7 ·
550	A richly chased imitation of the medal, engraved by Thomas Simon, presented to Admiral Blake, by Oliver Cromwell — — —	1 6 2 6
551	A fine cast of the same, *gilt* — —	1 2 3
552	Oliver, *reverse*; Fairfax, *another small reverse*, the Olive Tree, *both restored by chasing* . —	2 · 17 ·
553	Oliver, a small oval medal, his head without a reverse, by T. Simon, and a cast — —	2 / 3 ·
554	Oliver, *reverse* a Lion supporting the Arms of the Commonwealth, *finely repaired*, and another on his Death, *by Dassier* — — —	2 / 6 ·
555	Oliver, *reverse* the House of Parliament, on the battle at Dunbar, *by T. Simon, fine* — —	1 2 9 ·
556	Oliver, *reverse* an Olive Tree, " Non Deficient, Olivia, Sep. 3, 1558, *fine and scarce* — —	1 2 10 ·
557	Ferdinand Lord Fairfax, in a rich border, *chased by Stewart* — — —	1 / 10 ·
558	The Earl of Essex and Thomas Lord Southampton, *restored* — — —	2 · 15 ·
559	The same gilt — — —	2 · 0 6
560	Sir T. Fairfax, Earl of Essex, and a chased medal	3 · 7 6
561	The Earl of Essex on his Death, *by T. Simon, well preserved and rare* — — —	1 · 10 6
562	General Monk, Lenthal the Speaker, *both restored*	2 · 16 ·
563	General Monk, *a cast gilt*, Dorcas Babason, *chased*	2 · 10 6
564	Cleypole and his Wife, Ann Cleypole daughter of Oliver Cromwell, *restored* — —	2 · 12 ·

The priced auction catalogue pages for the sale of John Thane's medals at Mr. Sotheby's sale. The sale included 76 lots of Englsh medals in silver (132 medals) and 23 lots in bronze (246 medals). The greater part of the sale, as might be expected for the estate of a dealer in prints, consisted of works on paper. Image digitized by Google.

. 17	565	Cleypole 2. Ann Cleypole 1. *chased* — —	3
1 11 6	566	Henry Cromwell, and two unknown — —	3
. 15	567	John Milton, *by Dassier, fine* — —	1
1 14	568	Sir Franis Bacon, *by Dassier, fine* — —	1
2 2	569	Charles II. "Magnalia Dei" on his Coronation, &c.	3
1 6	570	Charles II. *reverse* the Royal Oak, one a cast —	2
. 16	571	Charles II. and Queen Catherine, 1670, *reverse* the Globe, *fine* — — —	3
1 10	572	Charles II. and his Queen, *fine* — —	3
. 10	573	Jettons, Charles II. *reverse* his Queen; another, a Lion, &c. — — —	3
1 13	574	Lucy, Dutchess of Portsmouth, *reverse* Cupid on a Globe, "Ommia Vincit." *fine and rare* —	1

Sixth Day's Sale.

ENGLISH MEDALS in BRONZE.

	LOT.		
. 10 6	575	POETS, without reverses, twelve of them are pewter	27
1 5	576	Queen Mary, in a frame, and various rare Medals in Pewter, &c. — — —	21
4	577	Medallions without reverses of Henry VIII. 5, one an oval, has the King and Prince Arthur. A fine Cast of the Coronation Medal of Edward VI. —	7
1 0	578	Elizabeth of York, Queen to Henry VII. 1. Queen Elizabeth, 3. *Mary Queen of Scotland, by J. Primaue in Pewter*, Robert Earl of Leicester, &c.	11
3 11	579	Elizabeth of York, Queen Elizabeth, Mary Queen of Scotland, Robert Earl of Leicester, Jettons of Philip, Mary, &c. — — —	20

After examining this listing of medals, one wonders to what extent these medals were from Thane's personal collection rather than from the inventory for his business. Image digitized by Google.

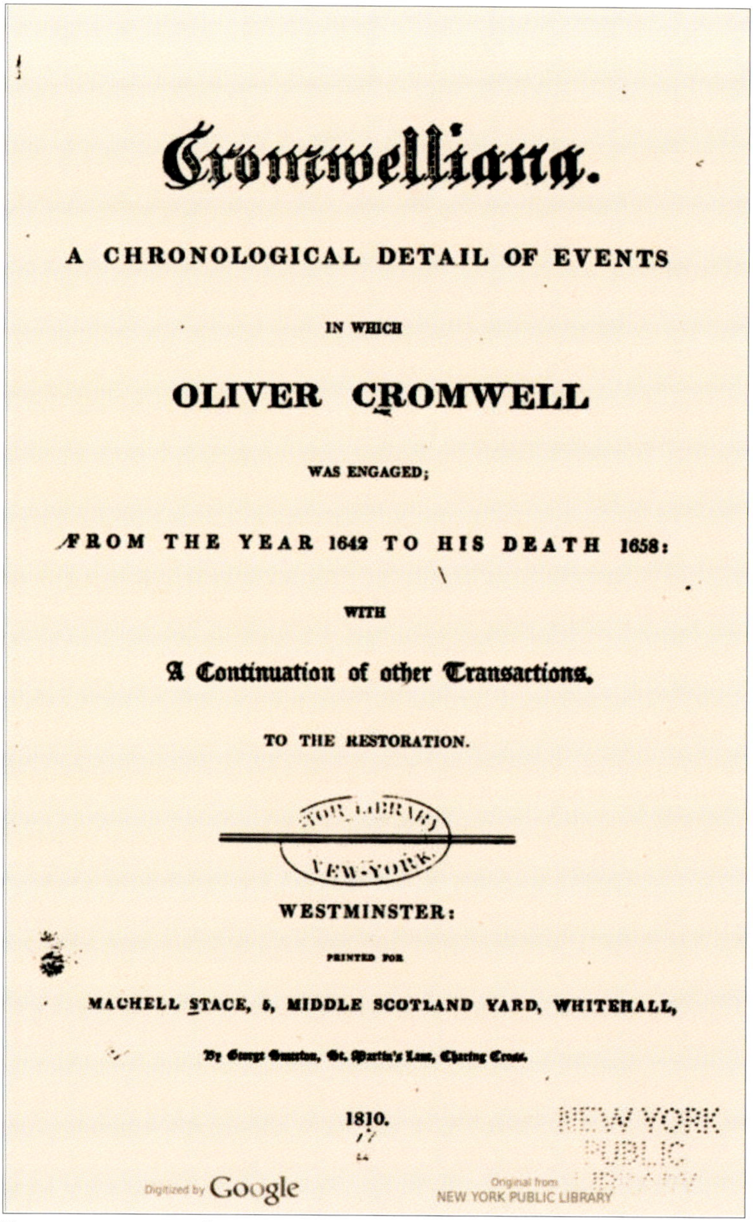

Cromwelliana.

A CHRONOLOGICAL DETAIL OF EVENTS

IN WHICH

OLIVER CROMWELL

WAS ENGAGED;

FROM THE YEAR 1642 TO HIS DEATH 1658:

WITH

A Continuation of other Transactions,

TO THE RESTORATION.

WESTMINSTER:

PRINTED FOR

MACHELL STACE, 5, MIDDLE SCOTLAND YARD, WHITEHALL,

By George Smeeton, St. Martin's Lane, Charing Cross.

1810.

THE TITLE PAGE OF *CROMWELLIANA*, PUBLISHED IN 1810, WITH A TOTAL OF SIX ENGRAVED PLATES, INCLUDING THE FRONTISPIECE. AN 'EXTRA-ILLUSTRATED' COPY (*SEE EARLIER ENTRY FOR REV, GRANGER*), WITH 84 ADDITIONAL ENGRAVED PLATES, WAS SOLD AT BONHAM'S ON JUNE 22, 2011 (LOT 1209). IMAGE DIGITIZED BY GOOGLE.

James Caulfield

(1764-1826)

·Collector, Author and Book and Print-seller·

CAULFIELD is the author of a number of illustrated biographical works of personages of the late 18th-early 19th centuries. His early volumes include *Portraits, Memoirs, and Characters of Remarkable Persons* (1790), *The Oxford Cabinet* (1797), which incorporated engravings and anecdotes from the notes of Aubrey's *'Anecdotes of Extraordinary Persons'* and other manuscripts at the Ashmolean Museum[461] and *The New Wonderful Museum* (1802). His later works include *Portraits, Memoirs, & characters of Remarkable Persons...* (1813), *Cromwelliana* (1810), *Chalcographimania* and *Calcographiana*[462] (both 1814), *The High Court Of Justice; Comprising Memoirs of the Principal Persons Who Sat in Judgment on King Charles the First, and Signed His Death-Warrant...* (1820), among others. Caulfield also edited the six volumes of the fifth edition of Granger's *Biographical History of England* (1824). The popularity and notoriety of Caulfield's works in part derived from the notoriety of his subjects:

> Caulfield's 'remarkable characters' are persons famous for their eccentricity, immorality, dishonesty, and so forth. The publication of Granger's 'Biographical History of England' in 1769 had given a marked impetus to the taste for engraved portraits. In the advertisement Caulfield announces: 'Of the twelve different classes of engraved portraits arranged by the late ingenious Mr. Granger, there is not one so difficult to perfect, with original prints, as that which relates to persons of the lowest description.[462A]

JAMES CAULFIELD, BOOK & PRINT-SELLER. A (SOMEWHAT FOXED) STIPPLE AND ETCHED ENGRAVING BY ROBERT COOPER (1795-1836) AFTER A PORTRAIT BY HENRY WALTON (1746-1813). IT APPEARED AS THE FRONTISPIECE FOR *CALCOGRAPHIANA* (1814).

---

[461] Aubrey, J. (ed.) (1798). *The Oxford cabinet, consisting of engravings from original pictures, in the Ashmolean Museum, and other public and private collections; with biographical anecdotes, by John Aubrey, F.R.S. and other celebrated writers.* London printed for James Caulfield.

[462] These two works offer some 'flavor' of the often less than ethical behavior exhibited by Caulfield. In *Chalcographimania*, published under the pseudonym 'Satiricus Sculptor,' he repeats malicious gossip about personages in his world—artists, collectors and print dealers. In *Calcographiana*, which appeared in the same year, Caulfield offers 'upon [his] oath' a denial of any association with the former work.

[462A] J. H. R. TEDDER, *B.N.J.*, 1887, vol. 9, p. 330; Tedder's biographical sketch of Caulfield is drawn from the obituary by GEORGE SMEETON (1800-1828; printer and biographical collector) that appears on p. 385.

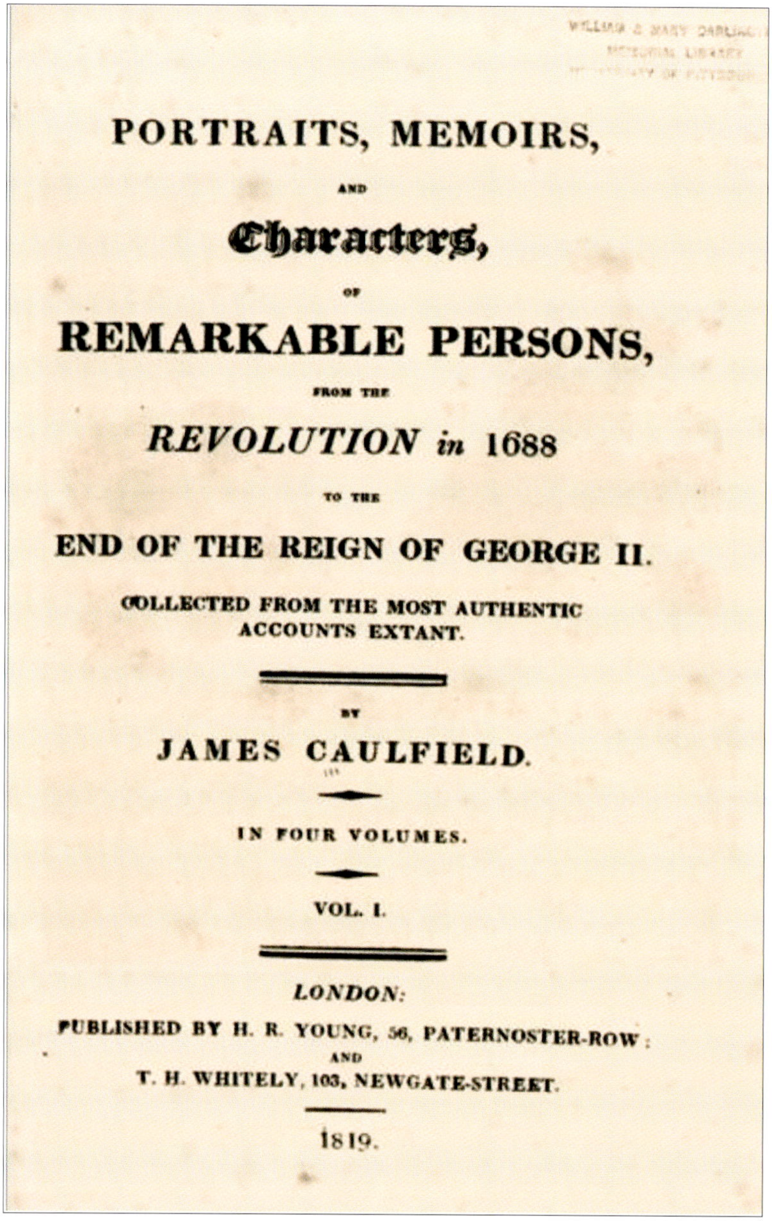

PORTRAITS, MEMOIRS,

AND

Characters,

OF

REMARKABLE PERSONS,

FROM THE

REVOLUTION in 1688

TO THE

END OF THE REIGN OF GEORGE II.

COLLECTED FROM THE MOST AUTHENTIC ACCOUNTS EXTANT.

BY

JAMES CAULFIELD.

IN FOUR VOLUMES.

VOL. I.

LONDON:

PUBLISHED BY H. R. YOUNG, 56, PATERNOSTER-ROW; AND T. H. WHITELY, 103, NEWGATE-STREET.

1819.

Never one to miss an opportunity to "excite public curiosity," Caulfield published this volume which contained illustrations of "persons…of peculiar notoriety, particularly such as have not been restrained by the laws…or influenced by the common obligations of society" (*Portraits…*, vol. i, p. 1). The popularity of this work is reflected in the fact that while the 1794-1795 edition had contained sixty plates and 214 pages of biographical material in two volumes, the 1813 edition had been expanded to 109 plates and 292 pages of text contained in four volumes. Image by Google.

In his biography, Tedder offers this assessment of Caulfield:

> Caulfield had a good memory. His knowledge of English history and biography was minute and extensive, while his acquaintance with engraved British portraits was unequalled by any person of his time. His liberality in imparting his information, and even the mysterious secrets of the trade, was viewed with great jealousy by his rivals. The numerous works written and edited by him usually attain a high standard of excellence. He was always fond of attending places of amusement, and at one time was conspicuous for neatness of dress. With advancing years Caulfield took to drink, became neglectful of his appearance, and troublesome in his social relations.[463]

Historical Commentary on James Caulfield

[Caulfield's] father was a music-engraver, and he intended his son James for the same business, but he having contracted a scorbutic afflection [sic] in his eyes, which rendered the sight extremely limited, the idea was relinquished. When about eight years old, his father went with him to Cambridge for the benefit of his health; and while there, he became acquainted with Mr. Christopher Sharpe, the celebrated print collector and turner. This gentleman was so delighted with the enthusiasm of his young friend, with regard to engravings, that he took every pains [sic] to satisfy his enquiries as to the different works of art; and at his departure, presented him with the sum of five pounds, and a collection of prints, among them being many of his own etchings. This laid the foundation of young Caulfield's knowledge and love of engravings;— highly delighted with his new treasures, he appropriated all the pocket-money which his father allowed him, in purchasing additional portraits; and in a short time he possessed a tolerable collection...At length, in 1780, his father opened a small shop for him in Old Round-court, Strand; and here he was honoured with the patronage of Dr. Johnson, Mr. Cosway the Royal Academician, and many other eminent men...and being very expert, earned a sufficiency of money to enable him to open a larger shop in Castle-street, Leicester square. Here he published the first Number of his popular work, "The Lives and Portraits of Remarkable Persons...

...[W]e now come to the close of the life of this highly-gifted man, who, with a mind well stored with historical and biographical lore, and a memory astonishingly retentive, possessed unquestionably the greatest knowledge of the rarity of engraved British portraits of any man of his time; and no person was more liberal and kind in honestly giving his opinion relative to prints than he was; but his generosity gained him many enemies in the trade, who blamed him for being too explicit, wishing him to keep his opinions to himself...

—*The Gentleman's Magazine*, 1826, pt. i. pp. 569-570 by G[eorge] S[meeton], Caulfield's friend and printer; *cf.* Nichols' *Illustrations*, vol. i, 441.

[463] Ibid. p. 329.

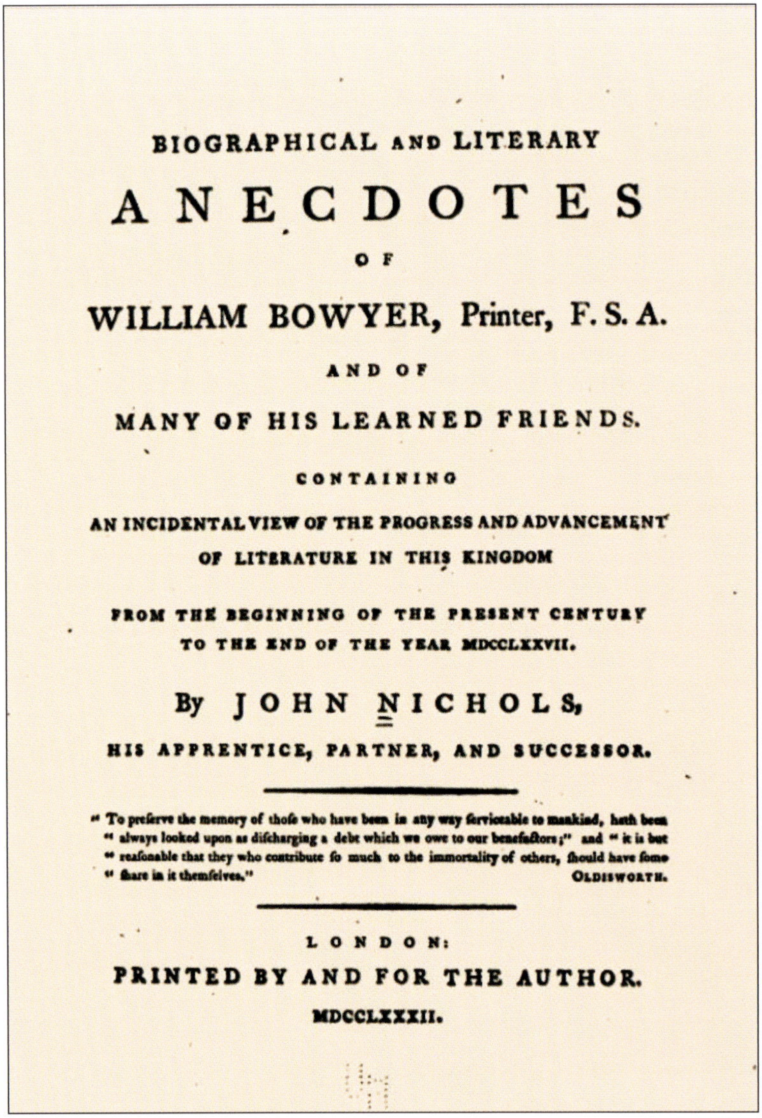

BIOGRAPHICAL AND LITERARY

ANECDOTES

OF

WILLIAM BOWYER, Printer, F. S. A.

AND OF

MANY OF HIS LEARNED FRIENDS.

CONTAINING

AN INCIDENTAL VIEW OF THE PROGRESS AND ADVANCEMENT
OF LITERATURE IN THIS KINGDOM

FROM THE BEGINNING OF THE PRESENT CENTURY
TO THE END OF THE YEAR MDCCLXXVII.

By JOHN NICHOLS,

HIS APPRENTICE, PARTNER, AND SUCCESSOR.

"To preferve the memory of thofe who have been in any way ferviceable to mankind, hath been "always looked upon as difcharging a debt which we owe to our benefactors;" and "it is but "reafonable that they who contribute fo much to the immortality of others, fhould have fome "fhare in it themfelves."

OLDISWORTH.

LONDON:

PRINTED BY AND FOR THE AUTHOR.

MDCCLXXXII.

THE FIRST OF THE NICHOLS-BOWYER PUBLICATIONS, THIS VOLUME PRECEDED THE *LITERARY ANECDOTES…* IT WAS ORIGINALLY ASSEMBLED AND PUBLISHED BY JOHN NICHOLS* IN A BRIEFER FORMAT IN 1777 ON THE DEATH OF WILLIAM BOWYER (THE YOUNGER), BUT IT GREW INTO THIS LATER EDITION (1782). *LITERARY ANECDOTES* PROVIDES A VALUABLE ANECDOTAL HISTORY OF BRITISH LITERARY AND SOCIAL LIFE OF THE 18TH CENTURY. IMAGE DIGITIZED BY GOOGLE.

*JOHN NICHOLS (1745-1826), AN APPRENTICE AND THEN PARTNER IN THE BOWYER PRINTING BUSINESS, BEGAN A LITERARY TRADITION THAT WAS TO BE CARRIED ON BY HIS SON JOHN BOWER NICHOLS AND GRANDSON JOHN GOUTH NICHOLS (*Q.V. BELOW*). THEIR ESSAYS PROVIDE A WINDOW INTO THE 18TH AND 19TH C. WORLD OF LETTERS IN LONDON.

The Bowyer & Nichols Families

•William Bowyer, the Elder•

(1663-1737)

•Printer•

WILLIAM BOWYER was a major figure in the London printing world of the late 17th and early 18th centuries, a time when the writing and printing of books was assuming an increasing role in the British intellectual world. After the Restoration, memoirs were also assuming a significant part of published literature. Bowyer's importance is based on the central role he played in this world as an established printer. Apprenticed in 1679 to Miles Flesher, a London printer, in 1686 the elder Bowyer became a freeman of the Worshipful Company of Stationers, and a liveryman in 1700. In the latter year he was also appointed as one of the twenty printers permitted by the Star Chamber. In 1712/13, his establishment was destroyed by fire in one of London's periodic 'great' conflagrations, but he was soon back in business, first at other printer's establishments and then at his shop in Whitefriars through the support provided by his friends and fellow liverymen.[464]

With the assistance of his son, also named William Bowyer ("the younger," 1699-1777; *see following entry*), the two Bowyers printed some 5,000 works by over 1,000 authors for some 500 customers (e.g., booksellers, institutions, etc.) and delivered books to more than 1,500 individuals.

WILLIAM BOWYER, THE ELDER. AN ETCHING AND ENGRAVING MADE BY JAMES BASIRE THE YOUNGER (1769-1822) AND PUBLISHED BY JOHN NICHOLS (BOWYER'S GRANDSON) IN 1812. WHEN PUBLISHED IT WAS INSCRIBED: "FROM AN ORIGINAL PAINTING AT STATIONERS HALL. 1812." IMAGE © TRUSTEES OF THE BRITISH MUSEUM.

ADVERTISEMENT.

THE NINTH VOLUME OF "LITERARY ANECDOTES" IS PRESENTED TO THE PUBLICK, WITH A CONFIDENCE ARISING FROM THE EXTRAORDINARY INDULGENCE WITH WHICH THE FORMER VOLUMES HAVE BEEN RECEIVED. NOTHING BUT THAT RECEPTION COULD HAVE INDUCED ME TO PERSEVERE IN RESEARCHES ATTENDED WITH ANXIOUS SOLICITUDE AND CONSIDERABLE PERSONAL LABOUR.☛

—J. Nichols, *Literary Anecdotes*…, 1812, p. iii.

[464] *DNB*, 1886 ed., vol. vi, p. 83.

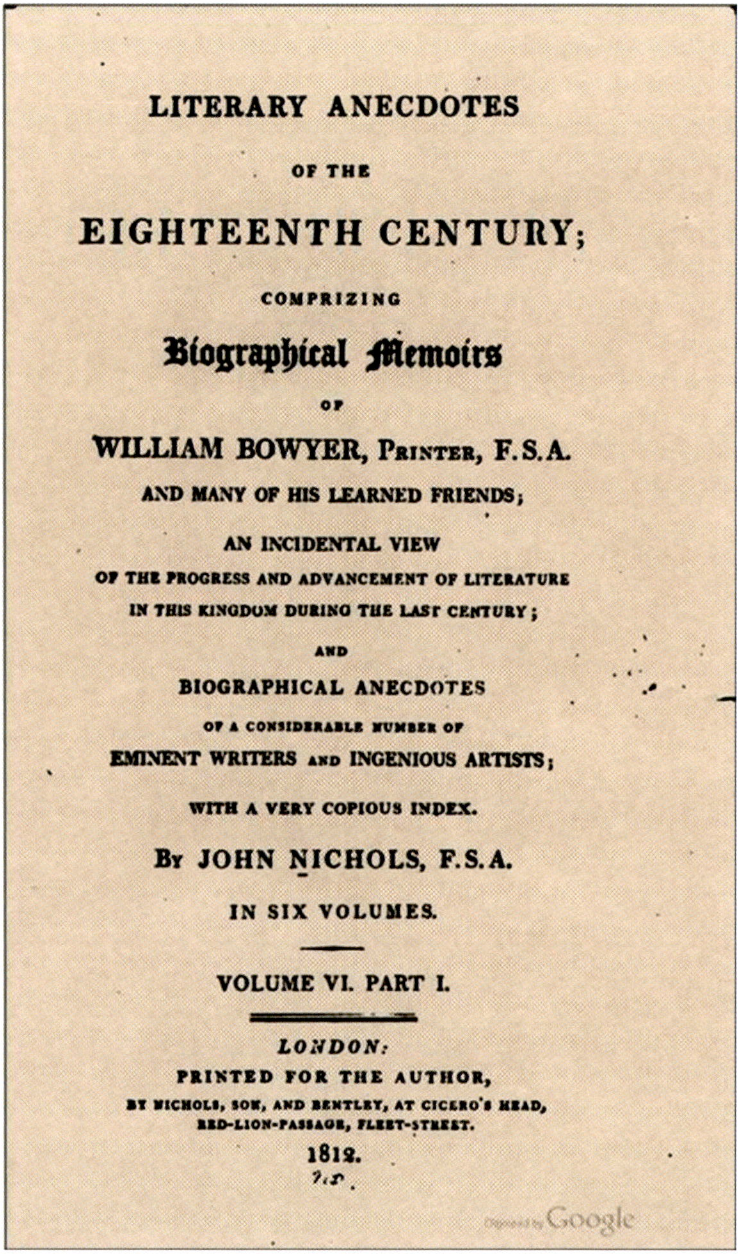

LITERARY ANECDOTES

OF THE

EIGHTEENTH CENTURY;

COMPRIZING

Biographical Memoirs

OF

WILLIAM BOWYER, Printer, F.S.A.

AND MANY OF HIS LEARNED FRIENDS;

AN INCIDENTAL VIEW

OF THE PROGRESS AND ADVANCEMENT OF LITERATURE

IN THIS KINGDOM DURING THE LAST CENTURY;

AND

BIOGRAPHICAL ANECDOTES

OF A CONSIDERABLE NUMBER OF

EMINENT WRITERS AND INGENIOUS ARTISTS;

WITH A VERY COPIOUS INDEX.

By JOHN NICHOLS, F.S.A.

IN SIX VOLUMES.

VOLUME VI. PART I.

LONDON:

PRINTED FOR THE AUTHOR,

BY NICHOLS, SON, AND BENTLEY, AT CICERO'S HEAD,

RED-LION-PASSAGE, FLEET-STREET.

1812.

The title page of volume vi, part i, of John Nichols' *Literary Anecdotes...* (1812). Based on a large collection of material from correspondents, as well as historical and literary 'odds and ends,' this collection, published in 1812-1815, eventually reached nine volumes in size. Image courtesy New York Public Library, digitized by Google.

William Bowyer, the Younger

(1699-1777)

·Printer & Author·

THE Bowyers, father and son, kept detailed records of the books they printed, including their physical characteristics and production details—e.g., paper, type style, print runs, and corrections. Given the central role of the Bowyers in the book trade of their time, the existence of these records provides an important source of knowledge on both major and minor figures of the London literary world of his time, and the printers and booksellers that they frequented. In many cases, the Bowyers' journals, together with those of the Nichols, provide what is perhaps the primary gateway through which one can enter the literary and book-publishing world of their time.

WILLIAM BOWYER THE YOUNGER, 'THE LEARNED PRINTER', AN ETCHING AND ENGRAVING BY JAMES BASIRE II, AND THE FRONTISPIECE TO BOWYER'S *CONJECTURAL EMENDATIONS* (1812). THE BRITISH MUSEUM NOTED THAT THE PHOENIX SYMBOLIZES THE ASSISTANCE PROVIDED TO THE BOWYER FAMILY BY BOOK-SELLERS FOLLOWING THE 1713 FIRE WHICH DESTROYED HIS SHOP. IMAGE © TRUSTEES OF THE BRITISH MUSEUM.

Known as 'the learned printer,' the younger Bowyer was educated at St. John's College, Cambridge, and in 1722, at age 23, became corrector of the press and a partner in his father's business. Success built on success, with appointment as printer of votes of the House of Commons in 1729, printer to the Society of Antiquaries, and election as a fellow, in 1736 and 1737 respectively. In 1738, he was admitted as a liveryman to the Stationers' Company (being advanced to master in 1771), in 1761 appointed printer to the Royal Society, and in 1767 printer of journals of the House of Commons and of the rolls of the House of Lords. He contributed to many of the books he published, as well as authoring his own works, including a Greek edition of the New Testament. Left unfinished at his death was a reprint of the *Domesday Book*. A bust of the younger Bowyer and a portrait of the elder Bowyer reside in the hall of the Stationers' Company, of which he was a benefactor.[465]

IN 1753 [William Bowyer] printed "Medals, Coins, Great Seals, impressions from the elaborate Works of Thomas Simon, Chief Engraver of the Mint to King Charles the First, to the Commonwealth, the Lord Protector Cromwell, and in the Reign of King Charles the Second, to MDCLXV. By George Vertue," 4to. A new and improved edition of this Work, with a valuable Appendix by Mr. Gough, and two additional plates finely engraved by Basire, was printed, by the Compiler of these "Anecdotes," in 1780; and a copy of the Work, with Notes by Mr. Gough, has been transmitted to the Bodleian Library.

—J. Nichols, *Literary Anecdotes*, 1812, vol. 2, pp. 246-262.

[465] Ibid. *DNB*, 1886 ed., vol. vi, p. 93.

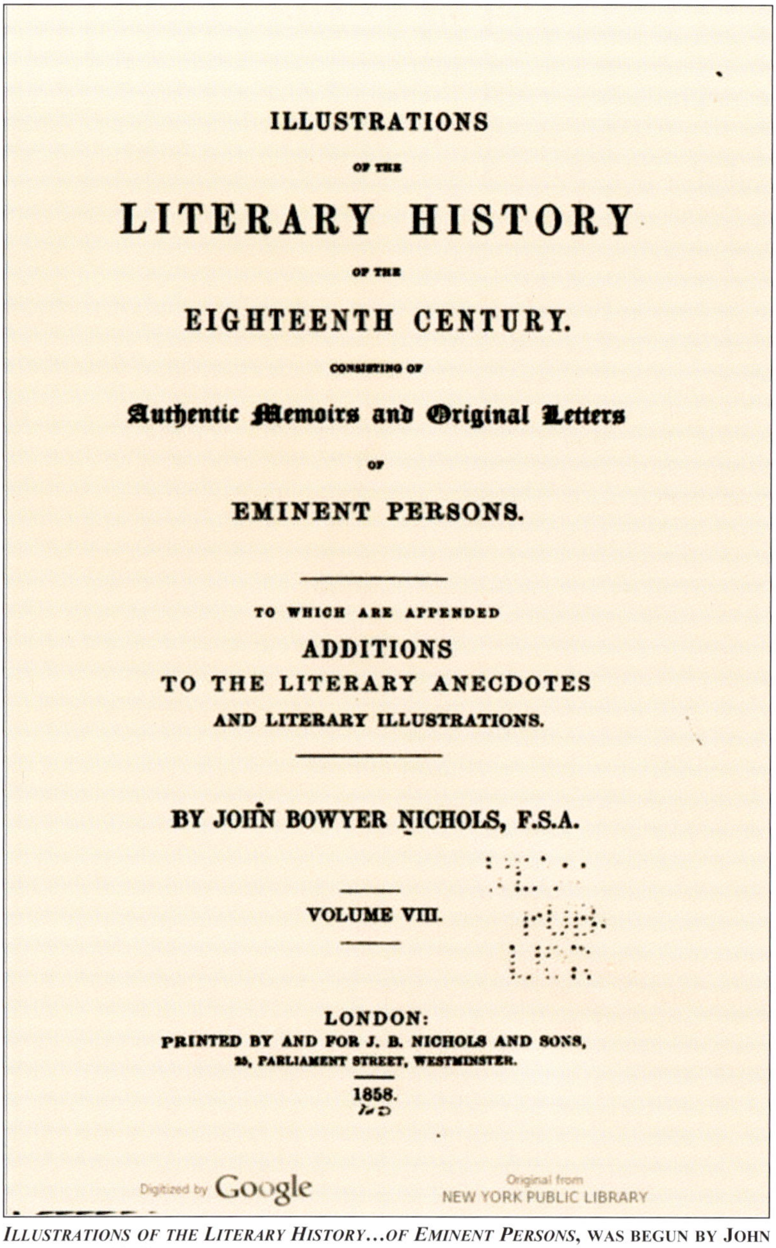

ILLUSTRATIONS

OF THE

LITERARY HISTORY

OF THE

EIGHTEENTH CENTURY.

CONSISTING OF

Authentic Memoirs and Original Letters

OF

EMINENT PERSONS.

TO WHICH ARE APPENDED

ADDITIONS

TO THE LITERARY ANECDOTES

AND LITERARY ILLUSTRATIONS.

BY JOHN BOWYER NICHOLS, F.S.A.

VOLUME VIII.

LONDON:

PRINTED BY AND FOR J. B. NICHOLS AND SONS,

25, PARLIAMENT STREET, WESTMINSTER.

1858.

Illustrations of the Literary History…of Eminent Persons, was begun by John Nichols in 1817 and completed after his death by John Bowyer Nichols. It provides a broad range of useful information on the authors, publishers and printers (the latter two often being the same person) and booksellers of the period. Image courtesy New York Public Library, digitized by Google.

•John Nichols•

(1745-1826)

· Printer, Author & Publisher ·

INITIALLY intended by his parents for a naval career, these plans evaporated upon the death of his uncle, a naval officer, and in 1757 the twelve year old Nichols was then apprenticed to William Bowyer the Younger. Working as a compositor under Bowyer, a thoughtful and erudite man, Nichols received what amounted to "a very fair classical training under his auspices." Soon, the young man was writing verse, and by age eighteen had published poems and prose essays. In 1766, Nichols was made a partner in the family business by Bowyer, and with the removal of the business from Whitefriars to Red Lion Passage, Fleet Street in 1774, the two printer-writers collaborated in editing Middleton and Meerman's *The Origin of Printing...*[466] This was followed by the editing by Nichols of some of Jonathan Swift's works, as well as other volumes, the authors of which:

> ...had already been attracted by the young man's antiquarian tastes.[467]

Upon William Bowyer's death in 1777, Nichols was made an executor and was a benefactor of his personal estate. An insight into Nichols' character was his building of a monument to Bowyer at Leyton. In 1778 Nichols and a col-

JOHN NICHOLS, WHO HAD BEGUN HIS CAREER AS AN APPRENTICE TO WILLIAM BOWYER THE YOUNGER, FORMALIZED THE RECORDS, ANECDOTES, AND DETAILS CONCERNING THE AUTHORS AND LITERARY FIGURES WITH WHOM THE BOWYERS HAD DEALT. HE ASSEMBLED THEM IN A SERIES OF VOLUMES CONTAINING BOTH PERSONAL OBSERVATIONS AND OUTRIGHT GOSSIP. HIS MEMOIRS ARE BASED ON HIS PERSONAL INTERACTIONS WITH, AND OBSERVATIONS OF, THESE PERSONAGES. THE INFORMATION COLLECTED BY NICHOLS ULTIMATELY RESULTED IN A WORK WHICH GREATLY EXPANDED THAT OF THE BOWYERS AND WHICH, IN SOME CASES, ALSO PROVIDED A SOMEWHAT DIFFERENT PERSPECTIVE. ILLUSTRATION FROM *LITERARY ANECDOTES...*, 1812 ED., VOL. III, FRONTISPIECE.

---

466 Regarding this work:

> In 1735 [DR. CONYERS MIDDLETON] published, "A Dissertation concerning the Origin of Printing in England; shewing, that it was first introduced and practised by our countryman, William Caxton, at Westminster; and not, as is commonly believed, by a foreign printer, at Oxford;" an hypothesis has been since ably controverted in Bowyer and Nichols's "Origin of Printing," 1776 (—*A New General Biography...*, vol. x, p. 132).

467 The biographies of the BOWYERS and NICHOLS families are, to a great extent, based on those appearing in: *DNB*, 1895, vol. xli, pp. 2-8; *DNB*, 1909 ed., vol. xiv, pp. 117-453, and *The Encyclopædia Britannica: A Dictionary of Arts, Sciences, Literature and General Information*, 1911, 11th ed.

league, David Henry, undertook management of the *Gentleman's Magazine*, both as publisher and contributor. Ever a prolific literary man, he jointly authored and published *A Collection of Royal and Noble Wills...* (1780), *Select Collection of Miscellaneous Poems* (four volumes in 1780, followed by four more in 1782), the *Bibliotheca Topographica Britannica* (eight vols.), completed in 1790, as well as a total of ten volumes of 'Miscellaneous Antiquities' (1791-1800).

Nichols maintained a seemingly inexhaustible literary output throughout his lifetime. He contributed to and published, among other works, *Biographical Anecdotes of Mr. Hogarth, and a Catalogue of his Works, with occasional Remarks* (1781), *The Genuine Works of William Hogarth* (three vols., 1808-1817), *Biographical and Literary Anecdotes of William Bowyer, Printer, F.S.A., and of many of his learned friends...*, the predecessor of his most important work on the same subject.[468] *DNB* quotes Horace Walpole as commenting on this work:

> 'I scarce ever saw a book so correct as Mr. Nichols's *Life of Mr. Bowyer*. I wish it deserved the pains he has bestowed on it every way, and that he would not dub so many men *great*. I have known several of his heroes, who were very *little* men' (*Letters*, viii. 259).[469]

From 1779, he had been engaged in preparing *The Works of the Rev. Jonathan Swift, D.D., arranged by Thomas Sheridan, with Notes, Historical and Critical. A new edition, in nineteen volumes, corrected and revised by John Nichols, F.S.A.* (1801). A great success, this work was reprinted in 1803 and 1808. Among other works published or printed for a publisher, are Pinkerton's *Select Scottish Ballads*... (1783), and Pinkerton's reworking of Thomas Snelling's *Thirty-three Plates of English Medals* (as *The Medallic History of England...*, 1790 ed.). The correspondence between Pinkerton and Nichols appears in print in *Literary Anecdotes*.

Nichols received a number of honors during his lifetime, having been elected a fellow of the Society of Antiquaries, London, and an honorary member of the Societies of Antiquaries at both Edinburgh and Perth. In 1804, he was elected a master of the Stationers' Company, which he appears to have considered one of his greatest honors. He numbered among his close friends Sir Joseph Banks, Edward Gibbon, and Dr. Samuel Johnson.

Nichols retired from his business in 1804. In February 1808, fire destroyed the business, resulting in an uncovered loss of over £10,000 and the stock of books stored there. This did not prevent Nichols from rebuilding and continuing his writing, editing and involvement in further publication. His literary involvement after retirement included Fuller's *History of the Worthies of England* (1840), *Literary Anecdotes of the Eighteenth Century* (nine vols., an expansion of his earlier work, 1812-1816). A supplementary work, *Illustrations of the Literary History of the Eighteenth Century*, in six volumes, appeared between 1817 and 1831, the last two posthumously. Nichols' son John Bowyer Nichols published an additional two volumes, primarily correspondence, in 1848 and 1858. Not surprisingly for a man with such wide interests, Nichols had a great collection of manuscripts and antiquities of other antiquaries. These were sold by auction at Sotheby's on April 16-19, 1828, bringing over £9500.

Nichols died on November 26, 1826, and was buried in the parish church of his home in Highbury Place. He had been married twice; first to Anne, daughter of William Cradock, and two years later, following her death, he married Martha, daughter of William Green of Hinckley, Leicestershire. His one surviving son, by his second marriage, was John Bowyer Nichols. He had a total of six daughters, but Martha died in 1788 at age thirty-three, following the birth of a child.

---

[468] The first version of this work appeared in 1777 as a brief memoir of WILLIAM BOWYER THE YOUNGER. It eventually grew into the voluminous *Anecdotes of William Bowyer and his Literary Friends* (1782, etc.):

> As his materials accumulated, he compiled a sort of anecdotal literary history of the century, based on a large collection of important letters (*Encyclopedia Britannica*, 11th ed., 1911, vol. 19, p. 656).

This work in turn grew into *The Literary Anecdotes of the 18th Century* (1812-1816).

[469] *The Letters of Horace Walpole*, 1840, vol. vi, p. 176.

John Bowyer Nichols

(1779-1863)

·Printer, Author and Publisher·

JOHN Bowyer Nichols, the eldest son of John Nichols, was born at Red Lion Passage, Fleet Street, London. He grew up with his maternal grandfather at Hinckley, Leicestershire, and was educated at St. Paul's School, London, leaving, however, in 1796 to join his father in the printing business.

JOHN BOWER NICHOLS, FROM HIS MEMOIRS..., REPRINTED FROM *THE GENTLEMAN'S MAGAZINE* OF MARCH 1864.

John Bowyer Nichols wrote for and edited *The Gentleman's Magazine,* becoming its sole proprietor in 1833. He briefly sold the magazine, and then repurchased it, later selling it again. Carrying on the family business, now renamed 'J. Nichols, Son, & Bentley,' he maintained offices at the Cicero's Head, Red Lion Passage, Fleet Street, as well as at 25 Parliament Street, Westminster; the latter address becoming the sole business location because of its proximity to Parliament for which he continued to print bills and proceedings. He was also appointed, although briefly, as printer to the corporation of the City of London. Continuing the family literary tradition, he also wrote profusely. With Richard Gough, he prepared a biography of the bookseller John Dunton (1816), who had provided material for the *Literary Anecdotes*. Nichols' final literary work was the completion of *Illustrations of the Literary History of the Eighteenth Century* (vol. vii, 1848, and vol. viii, 1856), the follow-up to *The Literary Anecdotes* which his father John Nichols had written. Like his father, despite the loss of his sight, John Bowyer Nichols was active to the end of his life. He was a member of the recently founded Athenaeum Club, the Numismatic Society, and a fellow of the Society of Antiquaries, among others. He was married twice and the father of fourteen children, of whom seven survived.

> WHEN a man has laid in a fund of knowledge, in any branch, from Books or other means of attainment, it is not to be wondered that the itch for scribbling seizes him.
>
> —John Bower Nichols, *Literary Anecdotes*..., 1812, vol. vi, p. 619.

John Gough Nichols

(1806-1873)

·Printer, Author and Publisher·

JOHN Gough Nichols, the eldest son of John Bowyer Nichols, aside from his involvement in the family printing business, was the successor to the Nichols tradition of distinguished scholarship and antiquarianism. He was born, as was his father, at the family house in Red Lion Passage, Fleet Street. He was named Gough after his godfather, Richard Gough, his father's friend and collaborator. He received private tutoring and for a period had attended school with Benjamin Disraeli.

'JOHN GOUGH NICHOLS, E^{SQ}., F.S.A. IN HIS 60TH YEAR' (1866). THE FRONTISPIECE IS FROM "*THE MEMOIR OF JOHN GOUGH NICHOLS* BY ROBERT CRADDOCK NICHOLS (1874).

As a younger man, he displayed the same aptitudes and interests as his father and grandfather:

> ...he kept antiquarian journals and copied inscriptions and epitaphs. He went with his father to the meetings of the Royal Society and Society of Antiquaries, and corresponded with the author of the *Curiosities of Literature*...[470]

In 1824 he entered the family business, working in the counting-house of the printing firm. While His first literary work was assisting his grandfather in the completion of *Progresses, Processions, and Magnificent Festivities of King James the First,* which he was to finish and edit in 1828, after the latter's death. Again, like his father and grandfather before him, he edited and wrote articles for the *Gentleman's Magazine,* was elected as a fellow of the Society of Antiquaries (1835), and then became printer for this Society. His deep involvement in the *Gentleman's Magazine* during the most productive years of his life is reflected in the following comment with respect to the Camden Society, of which he was a founder:

> 'The Athenæum says (22 Nov. 1873), 'There is scarcely a volume among the long series which does not bear more or less marks of his revision.'[471]

In 1856, ill health compelled Nichols to resign from the editorship of the *Gentleman's Magazine*, and he transferred ownership to John Henry Parker for a nominal sum. This allowed Nichols to complete a volume on *The Literary Remains of Edward VI*, meanwhile supervising work on other projects, including editing the new publication *Herald and Genealogist*, which first appeared in 1862. According to *DNB*, Nichols':

---

470 *DNB*, 1909, vol. xiv, pp. 447-453.

471 *DNB*, 1895, vol. xli, p. 7. The words "of upward of a hundred" were added in the notice of JOHN GOUTH NICHOLS' death which appeared in The *Proceedings of the Massachusetts Historical Society*, 1875, vol. 13, p. 124. The actual number was a not insignificant eighty-six. Nichols prepared a *Descriptive Catalogue*, initially in 1862, and a revised edition in 1872.

> ...love of obituary-writing caused him to found the short-lived *Register and Magazine of Biography* in 1869.

Nichols' son, John Bruce Nichols, joined the family firm at age 30. In 1868, Leonard Charles Wyon struck a medal of Nichols and his wife commemorating their silver wedding anniversary. Nichols died in 1873 at age 67, leaving his wife, one son and two daughters. In 1874, earl Stanhope eulogized Nichols in an address at the meeting of the Society of Antiquaries:

> Nichols was the third in succession, and not the last, of a family which has added to the unblemished record of a great printing business a hereditary devotion to the same class of learned studies [sic]. The following list of separate publications, particularly those issued by the Camden Society and the Roxburghe Club, include many valuable contributions to the materials of English history and topography. His heraldic and genealogical researches are of great importance. As president of the Society of Antiquaries, Earl Stanhope testified to the loss of Nichols as making 'a void which it is no exaggeration to call irreparable as regards the particular line of inquiry to which he devoted himself.'[472]

'JOHN GOUGH NICHOLS AND HIS WIFE LUCY LEWIS ON THEIR SILVER ANNIVERSARY.' A BRONZE PORTRAIT MEDAL BY W. WYON, 1868. THE IMAGE FROM R. C. GOUTH'S *MEMOIR OF JOHN GOUGH NICHOLS*, 1874, P. 25.

> THE "Literary Anecdotes" are now finished; but, as has been suggested in a former Advertisement, another Work is in the press, which (I will not attempt to disguise) is in reality, to those who choose so to consider it, a CONTINUATION of the former, though under a different Title, and an entirely independent Publication. Two Volumes of the new Work are actually in the press, under the title of "Illustrations of Literature;" consisting of Biographical Memoirs and Original Letters of Eminent Persons who flourished in the Eighteenth Century—principally from materials supplied by various Friends, who are themselves among the brightest Ornaments of Literature.
>
> JOHN NICHOLS, Feb. 14, 1816.
>
> —*Literary Anecdotes of the Eighteenth Century*..., 1816, vol. vii, pt. 2, p. 492.

[472] *DNB*, 1909, vol. xiv, p. 452.

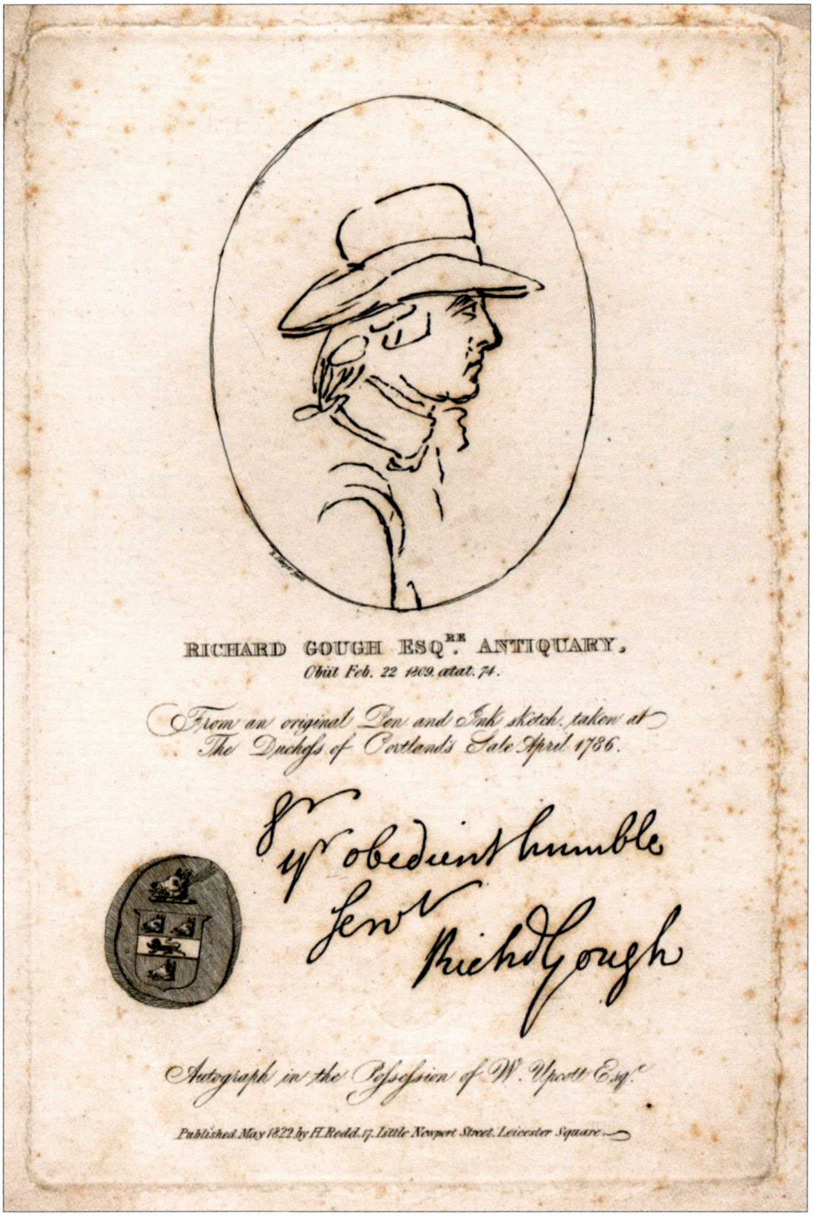

RICHARD GOUTH (1735-1809), ANTIQUARY. AN ENGRAVING (1822) BY R. SAWYER (FL. 1820-1830) AFTER AN UNKNOWN ARTIST. THE PAGE LAYOUT IS IN THE STYLE USED BY JOHN THANE IN HIS *BRITISH AUTOGRAPHY AND PORTRAITS* (1ST ED., 1793), BUT THE PAGE DOES NOT APPEAR IN THE 1793 AND 1819 EDITIONS. IMAGE © NATIONAL PORTRAIT GALLERY, LONDON.

Richard Gough[473]

(1735–1809)

·Antiquary·

THE son of Harry Gough (1681–1751), merchant, MP and director of the East India Company, Richard Gough learned Latin and Greek at an early age from a succession of learned tutors. Precocious, the young Richard had his first book published when he was just twelve years of age—*The History of the Bible: Translated from the French* (1747). This was followed by two more works, one of which—*Atlas Renovatus: or Geography Modernized* (1751)—foreshadowed his life-long interest in geography. Although these early works were published privately by his mother, [474] this work soon came to the attention of John Nichols, who became a life-long friend and who regularly published articles, correspondence and reviews by Gough in the *Gentleman's Magazine*. Shy and awkward, Gouth was not entirely comfortable when in school at Cambridge and left without taking a degree.[475] Bypassing the customary 'grand tour' of the Continent, he traveled throughout England, collecting information for a new edition of Camden's *Britannia*. In 1767, at age 32, Gough was elected to the Society of Antiquaries of which he later was a director, and from 1775 he was a fellow of the Royal Society.

A true antiquary, Gouth conducted research and published extensively. Happily for him, he did not have to carry out his extensive research and writing in order to make a living, as he would have been hard-pressed to subsist on his income from it. Luckily, however, his parents had left him with a substantial estate and income. His most important work was *British Topography* (1768, 2 vols., 1780) and his revision of *Camden's Britannia* (1768, 3 vols., 1789, 1806), and *Sepulchral Monuments of Great Britain...* (3 vols., 1796-1799). Most relevant to the present work, Gouth undertook the revision of George Vertue's *Medals, Coins, and Great Seals of Thomas Simon* which then appeared in a revised larger second edition in 1780. Rarely, if ever, is he given credit for this last work.

At his death in 1809, Gouth's collections of "prints, drawings, coins, medals, and other antiquities" were sold at auction while his topological collections, comprising an astonishing 3,700 volumes, went to the Bodleian Library.[476] There they were placed near the work of Dodsworth and other notables in the 'Antiquaries' Closet' adjacent to the Picture Gallery. Apparently miffed at not having been appointed a trustee of the British Museum, and unable to come to an agreement with respect to his access to a proposed donation of the copper-plate engravings for *Sepulchral Monuments*, Gouth omitted the Museum as a beneficiary of his collections. [477]

On Richard Gough and Vertue's *Medals of...Thomas Simon...*

GOUGH'S edition of Vertue's book, published in 1780, contains some interesting additions connected with Simon's life and works, as well as plates of some seals and medals which had escaped the researches of Vertue, and had been unnoticed by any other writer.

—B. Nightingale Notices of Thomas Simon, *Numismatic Circular,* 1842, p. 212.

---

[473] RICHARD GOUTH does not appear to have been related to JOHN GOUTH NICHOLS other than as a friend and collaborator of JOHN BOWYER NICHOLS and godfather to JOHN GOUTH NICHOLS.

[474] R. H. Sweet, *ODNB on line*, 2004-14.

[475] Although Gouth was apparently shy and retiring, one is somewhat taken aback by Horace Walpole's description of him as "a Bore," particularly as other writers have stated otherwise, noting:

> ...his good company..., his lively conversation, his humour, and his generosity in sharing and communicating knowledge (Sweet, *ODNB*).

[476] *Literary Anecdotes*..., vol. xxii, p. 180.

[477] Sweet, ibid. When sold at auction, the balance of Gouth's library brought £3552 and in 1810 the sale of his prints, drawings, coins and medals realized £517.

BIBLIOGRAPHY

To avoid repetition, some citations of works or online sources appearing in the footnotes, in particular D.N.B. *and the* Oxford D.N.B.*, are not repeated in this bibliography.*

Addison, J. (1837). *The Works of Joseph Addison*. New York: Harper Bros (3 vols.).

Aitken, G. A. (ed.) (1899). *The Tatler*. London: Duckworth (4 vols.).

Allen, D. (1938-1939). Thomas Simon's Sketchbook. *The Walpole Society*, vol. 27, pp. 13-53 + plates.

Anon. (1826). *Gentleman's Magazine*, Obituary of John Pinkerton, Esq., vol. XCVI, pt. I, pp. 462-472.

Arbuthnott, C. (2006). 'The life of James 'Athenian' Stuart, 1713-1788,' in Soros, S.W. (ed.). *James "Athenian' Stuart: The Rediscovery of Antiquity*. New Haven: Yale University Press. Pp. 59-101.

Aymonino, A. (2012). The Musæum of the 1st Duchess of Northumberland 1716-1776) at Northumberland Houser in London: An Introduction. In Bracken, S., Galdy, A. M. & Turpin (eds.). *Women Patrons and Collectors*. Newcastle upon Tyne: Cambridge Scholars Publishing, pp. 101-120.

Baetjer, K., & Dobkin, J. (2010). Mr. Devis and Mr. Bull. *Metropolitan Museum Journal*, v. 45, 203-209.

Banks, J. (1962). *The Endeavour Journal of Joseph Banks, 25 August 1768-12 July 1771.* (2 vols.).

Barclay, C. & Syson, L. A Medal Die Rediscovered: A New Work by Nicholas Hilliard. *The Medal*, 1993 (spring), no. 22, pp. 3-11.

Beaufoy, G. B. H... (1853). *A Descriptive Catalogue of the London Traders, Tavern, and Coffee-House Tokens Current in the Seventeenth Century*. London: Printed for its members, Corporation of London.

Bell, R. (ed.). (1854). *Poetical Works of Edmund Waller.* London: Charles Griffin, fn. p. 226.

Besly, E. (2003). The Coinage of the Stuarts. *J. British Numismatic Society*, vol. 73 pp. 120-27.

Binyon, L. (1902). *Catalogue of Drawings by British Artists and artists of Foreign Origin working in Great Britain*. London: British Museum.

Blackburn, M. A. S. Biographical entry for Edward Hawkins, *Oxford DNB*, on line (2004-2005).

Boizard (*also* Boisard), J. (1692). *Traité Des Monoyes, De Leurs Circonstances & Dépendances*. Paris: La Veuve de J. B. Coignard & J. B. Coignard. Further editions appeared in 1711, 1714 and 1723.

Bowyer, W. ('the Younger,'1699-1777) (1774). *The origin of printing. In two essays: I. The substance of Dr. Middleton's Dissertation on the origin of printing in England. II. Mr. Meerman's Account of the first invention of the art. ; An appendix is annexed, 1. On the first-printed Greek books. 2. On the first-printed Hebrew books... 3. On the early polyglots.* London: Printed for W. Bowyer & J. Nichols, at Cicero's Head, Red Lion Passage, Fleet-Street.

Bray, W. (ed.) (1819), *Memoirs, Illustrative of the Life and Writings of John Evelyn, Esq., F.S.A... comprising his Diary, from the Year 1641 to 1705-6, and a Selection of his Familiar Letters. To which is subjoined, the Private Correspondence between King Charles I. and His Secretary of State, Sir Edward Nicholas... London: H. Colburn,* 2nd ed., vol. ii, pp. 240-241.

Bray, W. (ed.) (1871), *Memoirs of John Evelyn, Esq., F.S.A. comprising his Diary, from 1641 to 1705-6, and a Selection of his Familiar Letters.* London: F. Warne and Co.

Bray, W. (H. B. Wheatley, ed.) (1906). *Diary of John Evelyn.* London: Bickers & Son. 4 vols.

Brears, P. C. D. (1989). A Museum Visitor in Stuart England. *Journal of the History of Collections*, vol. 2, 213-224.

British Museum Trustees. (A. W. Pollard, ed.) (1915). *List of Catalogues of English Book Sales,* 1676-1900. pp. ix-x.

Brown, L. (1980). *A Catalogue of British Historical Medals 1760 - 1960. Vol I. The Accession of George III to the Death of William IV.* London: Seaby.

Brown, L. (2003). A Discourse of Medals. *British Numismatic Journal*, vol. 73, pp. 175-185.

Bruce-Chwatt, L. J. (April 1983). George Bate—Cromwell's Devious Physician. *Journal of the Royal College of Physicians of London*, vol. 17 No. 2. pp.

Buchanan, J. L. (1804). *A Defence of the Scots Highlanders, in General; and Some Learned Characters in General…* London: J. Egerton, W. Stewart, & W. Richardson.

Buchanan, W. W. (2003). William Hunter (1718–1783), *Rheumatology*, vol 42, 1260-1261,

Burgess, J. & R. Piles (1754). *The lives of the most Eminent Modern Painters, who have lived since, or were omitted by Mons. De Piles*. London: T. Payne.

Bury, S. (ed.) (2012). *Benezit Dictionary of British Graphic Artists and Illustrators* Oxford: University Press.

Camden, W. (1722). *Britannia or a Chorographical Description of GREAT BRITAIN and IRELAND, Together with the Adjacent Islands. Written in Latin by WILLIAM CAMDEN And Translated into English, with Additions and Improvements. Revised, Digested, and Published, with Large Additions, by EDMUND GIBSON*. London (2nd ed.). Printed by Mary Matthews, for Awnshan Churchill, and sold by William Taylor, in Pater-Noster-Row.

Carlisle, W. & Wyon, W. (1937). *A Memoir of the Life and Works of William Wyon*, privately printed, p. 204.

Carlton, C. (1972). *Going to the Wars: The Experience of the English Civil Wars 1638-1651*. London: Rutledge.

Caygill, M. M. & J. Cherry (eds.) (1997). *A. W. Franks: Nineteenth-Century Collecting and the British Museum*. London: British Museum.

Caygill, M. M. (2006). "Creating a Great Museum: Early Collectors and The British Museum." www.fathom.com/course/21701728/session2.html (12. IX. 2006).

Challis, C. E. (1992). *A New History of the Royal Mint*. Cambridge: Cambridge University Press.

Chisum, H. (ed.). *Encyclopedia Britannica…* (1911), vol. xxxi, p. 398.

Christie, Manson & Woods Ltd. (14 July 1987). *Important English Drawings and Watercolours*. Lots 14-29. (The catalogue for the sale at which Thomas Simon's notebooks, sketches of coins and medals and seals and historically significant documents were sold. Among the documents was Oliver Crowell's letter to the Committee of the Army, asking that his effigy not be used for the obverse design of the Dunbar medal).

Clegg, S. (1908) Thomas Hollis, Book-lover, Politician and Philanthropist. *The Bibliophile*, vol. i (i), pp. 37-40.

Cochran-Patrick, R. W. (1876). *Records of the Coinage of Scotland: From the Earliest Period to the Union*. Edinburgh: Edmonston & Douglas.

Cochran-Patrick, R. W. (1884). *Catalogue of the Medals of Scotland: From the Earliest Period to the Present Time*. Edinburgh: David Douglas.

Constable, A. & R. P. Gillies, et al., (Stoddard, R. H., ed.) (1876). *Personal Reminiscences by Constable and Gilles*. New York: Scribner, Armstrong.

Constable, T. (1873). *Archibald Constable and his Literary Correspondence* [by his son, T. Constable]. New York: Scribner, Armstrong.

Copp, A. E., A. (May-August 1902). On Portrait Medals or Plaques by Simon van de Passe and Michel Le Blonde. *The Connoisseur*, vol. iii, pp. 80-82.

Couper, S. (2008). "John Pinkerton," *ODNB*, online.

Cowley, A (A. Pritchard, ed.) (1973). *The Civil War*. Toronto: University of Toronto Press.

D. N. B. (1885-1900). *Dictionary of National Biography*. First ed., vols. 1-63 + Supplements and Index.

D. N. B. (1908-1909). *Dictionary of National Biography*. Second ed., vols. 1-22 + 3 supplementary volumes.

Davies, M. (1716). Of Medals and Writings and Writers thereon. In *Athenae Britannicae: or, A Critical History of the Oxford and Cambridge Writers and Writings*… (Part III), London. pp. 73-112.

Dawson, E. P. & W. R. Uphill, (eds.) (1995). *Who Was Who in Egyptology*. 3rd Revised Edition. London: Egypt Exploration Society.

Desmond, R. (1995). *Kew: The History of the Royal Botanic Gardens*. London: Harvill Press.

Diblin, T.F. (1817). *The Bibliographical Decameron: or, Ten Days Pleasant Discourse upon Illuminated Manuscripts…*, (vol. 3). Printed for the author by W. Bulmer & Co.

Dugdale, W. (W. Hamper ed.) (1827). *The Life, Diary and Correspondence of Sir William Dugdale, Knight…with an Appendix*... London: Harding, Lepard, & Co.

Durand, Anthony. (1865). *Médailles et Jetons des Numismates*. Geneva: George & Cherbuliez.

Eames, J. A. (1826). *General and Bibliographical Dictionary of the Fine Arts*... London: Thomas Tegg.

Eimer, C, (1998). *The Pingo Family & Medal Making in 18th Century Britain*. London: The British Art Medal Trust.

Eimer, C. (2006). Stuart and the Design and Making of Medals. In S. W. Soros (ed.). *James "Athenian' Stuart: The Rediscovery of Antiquity*. New Haven: Yale University Press pp. 494-512.

Eimer, C. (2010). *British Commemorative Medals and their Values*. London: Spink (2nd ed.).

Eisler, W. (2010). *Lustrous Images from the Enlightenment: Medals of the Dassiers of Geneva*. Milano: Skira.

Encyclopaedia Britannica: A Dictionary of Arts, Sciences, Literature and General Information, 1911 ed., 11th ed.

Evelyn J. (E. W. Harcourt, ed.). (1888). *Life of Mrs. Godolphin*. London: Sampson Low, Marston, Searle & Rivington.

Farquhar, H. (1908). Nicholas Hilliard, Embosser of Medals of Gold. *Numismatic Circular*, 8, 324-356.

Farquhar, H. (1909). Portraiture of our Stuart Monarchs on Their Coins and Medals. Part I. *British Numismatic Journal*, vol. v, pp. 147-172+illustr.

Farquhar, H. (1910). Portraiture of our Stuart Monarchs on Their Coins and Medals. Part II: James II. *British Numismatic Journal,* vol, vi., pp 213-262+illustr.

Farquhar, H. (1911). Portraiture of our Stuart Monarchs on Their Coins and Medals. Part III: William and Mary. *British Numismatic Journal,* vol. vii. pp 199-267+illustr.

Farquhar, H. (1912). Portraiture of our Stuart Monarchs on Their Coins and Medals. Part IV: William III. *British Numismatic Journal,* vol. viii. pp 209-273+illustr.

Farquhar, H. (1913). Portraiture of our Stuart Monarchs on Their Coins and Medals. Part V: William III.—*continued. British Numismatic Journal,* vol. ix. pp 201-266+illustr.

Farquhar, H. (1914). Nicholas Briot and the Civil War. *Numismatic Chronicle*, vol. xiv, series iv, pp. 169-235.

Farquhar, H. (1914). Portraiture of our Stuart Monarchs on Their Coins and Medals. Part VI: Anne. *British Numismatic Journal,* vol. x. pp 227-294+illustr.

Farquhar, H. (1916). Portraiture of our Stuart Monarchs on Their Coins and Medals. Part VII: Anne. *British Numismatic Journal,* vol. xi. pp 219-287+illustr.

Farquhar, H. (1917). *Portraiture of* our *Stuart Monarchs on Their Coins and Medals; Reprinted from the British Numismatic Journal*, in seven parts. London: London: Harrison and Sons.

Fearon, D. (1984), *Spink's Catalogue of British Commemorative Medals 1558 to the Present Day with Valuations.* Exeter: Webb & Bower.

Ferguson, W. (1998). *The Identity of the Scottish Nation: An Historic Quest*, Edinburgh: Edinburgh University Press.

Firth, C. H. (1904). History of the Rebellion: Part ii.—The 'Life' of Himself. *English Historical Review*, vol. xix (lxxiv), pp. 26-54.

Fletcher, W. Y. (1902). *English Book Collectors*. London: Kegan Paul, Trench, Trűber.

Forrer, L. (1907, 1987 reprint). *Biographical Dictionary of Medallists: Biographical Dictionary of Medallists: Coin, Gem, and Seal Engravers, Mint-Masters, &C., Ancient and Modern, with References to their Works B.C. 500-A.D. 1900*. London: Baldwin (8 vols.).

Franks, A. W. & Howell, E. R. J. G. (1908). *Franks Bequest: Catalogue of British and American Book Plates Bequeathed to the Trustees of the British Museum*. London: British Museum & Longman, Quaritch, etc.

Franks, A. W. (1885). Preface. *Medallic Illustrations of Great Britain and Ireland to the Death of George II*, London: British Museum (pp. v-viii).

Gamez, L. R. (1988). "And Art Reflected Images to Art:" Addison's Use of Numismatics in "Cato." *Modern Philology*, vol. 85, pp. 256-264.

Gay-Ambrose, J. (1997). Horace Walpole, Fourth Earl of Orford. In Lindsey, A. *Index of English Literary Manuscripts*. London: Mansell Publishing vol. iii, part 2, pp. 235-254.

Gillies, R. P. (1851). *Memoirs of a Literary Veteran Including Sketches and Anecdotes of the most Distinguished Literary Characters from 1794-1849*. London, R. Bentley.

Glendenning's (April 25, 1955). *Catalogue of the Important Collection of English Coins, Commemorative Medals and Badges of the Reign of Charles I in Gold, Silver, and Copper, and other English Coins and Medals: The property of a deceased Lady Collector, and sold by order of the Executors*. London: Glendenning. (n.b.: The "deceased Lady Collector' is Ms. Helen Farquhar).

Granger, J. [1769 (2 vols.), 1774 (2 vols. + supplement), 1775 (2nd ed., 4 vols.), 1779 (3rd ed., 4 vols.), 1804 (4th ed., 4 vols.), 1824, 5th ed., with 400 additional lives)]. *A Biographical History of England: from Egbert the Great to the revolution: consisting of characters disposed in different classes, and adapted to a methodical catalogue of engraved British heads: intended as an essay towards reducing our biography to system, and a help to the knowledge of portraits: interspersed with a variety of anecdotes, and memoirs of a great number of persons not to be found in any other Biographical work. With a preface, showing the utility of a collection of Engraved Portraits to supply the defect, and answer the various purposes of Medals.* London: Richardson, Darton & Harvey, & W. Baynes. (n.b.: Mark Noble edited a posthumous '*Continuation,' i.e., 1688 to the end of the reign of George I* (1806, London: Rodd, 3 vols.).

Granger, J., & Malcolm, J. P. (ed.) (1805). *Letters between the Rev. James Granger... and many of the most eminent literary men of his time: Composing a copious history and illustration of his Biographical history of England. With miscellanies, and notes of tours in France, Holland, and Spain, by the same gentleman*. London: Longman, Hurst, Rees, and Orme.

Grant, M. H. Catalogue of British Medals since 1760. *B.N.J.*, 1936-37, vol. 22, pp. 269-293; 1938-39, vol. 23, pp.

119-152; 1939-40, vol. 23, pp. 321-362; 1940-41, vol. 23, pp. 449-480.

Graves, R. E. (ed.) (1886). *Bryan's Dictionary of Painters and Engravers: Biographical and Critical.* London: G. Bell and Sons (2 vols.).

Griffiths, A. (1996). *Landmarks in Print Collecting: Connoisseurs and Donors at the British Museum since 1753.* London: British Museum Press. (pp. 21-29).

Grueber, H. A. (1881). *A Guide to the English Medals Exhibited in the King's Library.* London: Trustees of the British Museum.

Grueber, H. A. (1904-1911; 1979). *Medallic Illustrations of the History of Great Britain and Ireland.* London: Trustees of the British Museum. Reprinted in 1979 in one vol. by Seaby Productions Ltd.

Guppy, H. (Dec., 1902). 'The Booksellers of London Bridge.' *Library Association Record.* vol. iv, no. 12, pp. 626-627.

Guthrie, N. (2012). 'Johnson's Touch-piece and the 'Charge of Fame:' Personal and Public Aspects of the Medal in Eighteenth-century Britain. In J. C. D. Clark & H. Erskine-Hill, *The Politics of Samuel Johnson.* Hampshire: Palgrave/MacMillan, pp. 90-111.

Harris, W. (1772, 2nd ed.). *An Historical and Critical Account of the Life of Oliver Cromwell...After the manner of Mr. Bayle....* London: Printed for W. Strahan, T. Becket and Co., and T. Cadell, in the Strand; and S. Bladon, in Pater-noster-Row (sic).

Hawkins, E., Franks, A. W. & Grueber, H. A. (1885). *Medallic Illustrations of the History of Great Britain and Ireland to the Death of George II.* London: Trustees of the British Museum (2 vols.). Reprinted by Spink & Son Ltd. (1969) (2 vols.).

Henfrey H. W. (1877). *Numismata Cromwelliana: or, the Medallic History of Oliver Cromwell, Illustrated by his Coins, Medals, and Seals.* London: J. R. Smith.

Henfrey, H. W. (1870). *A Guide to the Study and Arrangement of English Coins.* London: George Bell & Sons.

Highfill, P. H., Burnim, K. A. & Langhans, E. A. (1982). *Biographical Dictionary of Actors, Actresses, Musicians, Dancers, Managers, and other Stage Personnel in London, 1660-1800.* Carbondale: Southern Illinois University Press.

Hill, C. P. (1988). *Who's Who in Stuart Britain: 1603-1714.* London: Shepheard-Walwyn.

Hill, G. F. (1920). *Medals of the Renaissance.* Oxford: Clarendon Press.

Hill, G. F. & Pollard, G. (1967). *Renaissance Medals at the National Gallery of Art. London: Phaidon Press.*

Hilton, J. (1885). *Chronograms Continued.* London: Elliot Stock, Paternoster Row.

Hobbes, J. R. (1849) *The picture collector's manual, being a dictionary of painters, containing fifteen hundred more names than in any other work, vol.* 1 (Painters). London: T. & W. Boone.

Howe, G, Gambier, E. R. J. & Franks, A. W. (1908). *Franks Bequest. Catalogue of British and American Book Plates Bequeathed to the Trustees of the British Museum by Sir Augustus Wollaston Franks.* British Museum: Department of Prints and Drawings (3 vols.).

Hunter, J., Rev. (1830). *The Diary and Correspondence of Ralph Thoresby, F.R.S.* London: Colburn and Bentley. (2 vols.).

Hurd, R. (ed.) (1811). *The Works of the Right Honourable Joseph Addison. New ed. with Notes by Richard Hurd.* London: T. Cadell and W. Davies (6 vols.).

Hustvedt, S. H. & Ballard (1916). *Criticism in Scandinavia and Great Britain during the Eighteenth Century.* New York: The American-Scandinavian Foundation. Pp. 252-253.

Jones, M. (1979). *The Art of the Medal.* London: British Museum Press.

Jones, M. (1982, 1988). *Catalogue of French Medals in the British Museum, 1600-1672.* London: British Museum Press (2 vols.).

Jones, M. (1983). The Technique of Simon Van de Passe Reconsidered, *Numismatic Chronicle*, 143, 227-230.

Jones, M. (1985). The Medal Collection of the British Museum. *The Medal*, no. 6, pp. 8-11.

Keynes, G. (1968). *John Evelyn: A Study in Bibliophily with a Bibliography of His Writings.* Oxford: Clarendon Press.

Langford, P. 'Walpole, Horatio (Horace),' *O. D. N. B.*, 2004-2006.

Latham, R. C. (2001). *The Diary of Samuel Pepys*, vol. x, *Companion.* Berkeley: University of California Press.

Lewis, W. S. *Yale Edition of Horace Walpole's Correspondence,* vol. 16, New Haven CT.: Yale.

Lindsay, A. (1997). *Index of English Literary Manuscripts: vol. 3: 1700-1800*, London: Mansell (Cassell). Part 2.

Lowndes, W. T. (H. G. Bohn, ed.) (1865). *The Bibliographer's Manual of English Literature: An Account of Rare, Curious, and Useful Books, Published In or Relating to Great Britain and Ireland, from the Invention of Print-*

ing; With Bibliographical and Critical Notices, Collations of the Rarer Articles, and the Prices at Which They Have Been Sold in The Present Century. London: Bell & Daldy (6 vols.).

Lustig, I. S. & Pottle, F. A. (eds.) (1986). *Boswell: The English Experiment, 1785-1789.* New York & London: William Heinemann & McGraw-Hill.

MacGregor, A. (ed.). (1994). *Sir Hans Sloane: Collector, Scientist, Antiquary.* London: British Museum Press/ Alistair McAlpine.

Malkin, A. T. (1835). *The Gallery of Portraits: With Memoirs.* Vol. v. London: Charles Knight.

Manville, H. E. (1993). *Numismatic Guide to British & Irish Periodicals, 1731-1991.* (*Encyclopedia of British Numismatics.* Vol. II, part 1). London: Baldwin/Spink.

Manville, H. E. (2005). *Numismatic Guide to British & Irish Printed Books, 1600-2004.* (*Encyclopedia of British Numismatics.* Vol. III). London: Spink.

Manville, H. E. (2014). *Dictionary of English Numismatic Terms*. London: Spink.

Matthew, H. C. G. 'Henry William Henfrey' *Oxford D.N.B., on line* (2004-2005).

Mayo, J. H. (1897). *Medals and Decorations of the British Army and Navy.* Westminster: Archibald Constable (2 vols.).

Middleton, C. (1735). *A Dissertation concerning the Origin of Printing in England Shewing, that it was first introduced and practised by our countryman William Caxton....* Cambridge.

Mitchiner, M. (1998). *Jetons, Medalets and Tokens: Vol. 3. British Isles circa 1558-1830.* London: Hawkins/Spink.

Montagu, G. (ed.) (1837). *Personal Correspondence of Horace Walpole*. London: Coburn. (3 vols.).

Myrone, M. George Vertue, *Oxford D.N.B.*, on line (2004-2005).

Nathanson, A. J. (1975). *Thomas 'Simon.' O. D. N. B. (online).*

Nathanson, A. J. (1975). Thomas *Simon, His Life and Work 1618-1665*; London: Seaby.

Newman, P. R. (2006), *Atlas of the English Civil War*. London: Routledge.

Nichols, J. & Bentley, S. (1812; 1815). *Literary Anecdotes of the Eighteenth Century: Comprising Biographical Memoirs of William Bowyer, Printer, F.S.A. and Many of His Learned Friends; an Incidental View of the Progress and Advancement of Literature in this Kingdom During the Last Century; and Biographical Anecdotes of a considerable number of Eminent Writers and Ingenious Artists.* London: Nichols, Son, and Bentley, at Cicero's Head, Red-Lion-Passage, Fleet-Street.

Nichols, J. (1828). *The Progresses, Processions, and Magnificent Festivities of King James the First: His Royal Consort, Family, and Court.* London: J. B. Nichols (4 vols.).

Nichols, J. (1848). *Illustrations of the Literary History of the Eighteenth Century: Consisting of Authentic Memoirs and Original Letters of Eminent Persons; and Intended as a Sequel to the Literary Anecdotes*. London: J.B. Nichols and Sons.

Nichols, J., (1743). *Original Letters and Papers of State Addressed to Oliver Cromwell; concerning the Affairs of Great Britain. From the Year MDCXLIX to MDCLVIII. Found among the Political Collections of Mr. John Milton. Now first published from the Originals.* London: William Bowyer, and sold by John Whiston Bookseller, at Boyle's Head in Fleet Street.

Nichols, R. C. (1874). *Memoir of the late John Gouth Nichols, F.S.A., F. R. G. S.* Westminster: Privately published.

Nightingale, B. (1842). Notices of Thomas Simon, *Numismatic Chronicle.* vol. iv (old series), pp. 211-232.

Noble, M. (1806). *biographical History of England, from the Revolution to the end of George I's reign : being a continuation of J. Granger's work: consisting of characters disposed in different classes; and adapted to a methodical catalogue of engraved British heads; interspersed with a variety of anecdotes, and memoirs of a great number of persons. The materials being supplied by the manuscripts left by Granger, and the collections of the editor, Mark Noble* (vol. 1) London: W. Richardson.

Numismatic Society (1882). Proceedings. *Numismatic Chronicle*, 3rd ser., vol. ii, pp. 21-22.

O'Connell, S. (2003). *London 1753.* London: British Museum Press.

Packard, F. R. (1922). Guy Patin and the Medical Profession in Paris in the Seventeenth Century (part ii). *Annals of Medical History,* vol. iv (3), pp. 215-240.

Parkes Weber, F. (1894). Medals and Medallions of the Nineteenth Century, Relating to England, by Foreign Artists. *Numismatic Chronicle*, Ser. 3, vols. xiii–xiv.

Pearce, S. & Arnold, K. (2000). *The Collector's Voice: Critical Readings in the Practice of Collecting.* Aldershot, Hampshire: Ashgate.

Pepys, S. (Wheatley, H. B., et al.). (1893). *The Diary of Samuel Pepys M.A. F.R.S.* London: Geo. Bell & Sons.

Petty, W. (1672, 1691, 1769, 1970). *The Political Anatomy of Ireland: With the Establishment for that Kingdom when the late Duke of Ormond was Lord Lieutenant; Taken from the Records. To which is added Verbum Sapienti; or an Account of the Wealth and Expences of England, and the Method of raising Taxes in the most Equal manner ... / By Sir William Petty, late Fellow of the Royal Society, and Surveyor-General of the Kingdom of Ireland.* London: Printed by Boulter Grierson (1769 ed.). Shannon: Reprinted by the Irish University Press (1970 ed.).

Pfister, J. G. (1852-53). Memoir of Johann Crocker, Chief Engraver and Medallist of the English Mint during the Reigns of Queen Anne and the Kings George I and II. *Numismatic Circular*, vol. 15, pp. 67-73.

Pickup, D. (1990). Edward Hawkins and Medallic Illustrations. *The Medal.* No. 16 (spring), pp. 48-52.

Pincott, A. (2004). The Book Tickets of Sarah Sophia Banks, *The Bookplate Journal*. Vol.2, No.1 (March), pages 3-30.

Pinkerton, J. (1790). *The Medallic History of England to the Revolution, with Forty Plates.* London: Printed for Edwards and Sons, Pall Mall; and Faulder, in New Bond Street.

Pinkerton, J. (1802). *Medallic History of England, Illustrated by Forty Plates.* London: Printed, at the Oriental Press, by Wilson and Co., Wild Court, Lincoln's Inn Fields; for E. Harding, No. 98, Pall-Mall; and J. Scott, St. Martin's Court, Leicester-Fields.

Pinkerton, J. (1831). *384 Medals of England, Engraved on Forty Plates.* London: Printed for J. B. Nichols & Son, 25, Parliament-Street.

Pinkerton, J. (undated). *The Medals of England, Consisting of 384 Specimens Engraved on Forty Plates.* London: Nichols & Son, 25 Parliament Street.

Pinkerton, J. [1784 (1 vol.), 1789 (2 vols.), 1808 ed. (2 vols.)]. *An Essay on Medals.* London: James Dodsley in Pall-Mall.

Platt, J. J. & Platt, A.K. (2013). *The English Civil War: Medals, Historical Commentary and Personalities.* London: Spink.

Pollard, J. G. (2007). *Renaissance Medals. (Vol. 2: France, Germany, the Netherlands, and England).* Washington: National Gallery of Art, & Oxford: Oxford University Press.

Porritt, A. (1967). *Matthew Young and his Numismatic Correspondents a Century and a Half Ago: With a Glimpse at the First London Numismatic Society*. Newcastle upon Tyne: Corbitt & Hunter, Ltd.

Price, F. G. H. (ed.). *A Handbook of London Bankers: With Some Account of their Predecessors the Early Goldsmiths*. London: Leadenhall Press.

Rashleigh, J. (1850-51). A Brief Notice of the Bute Collection of Medals and Coins. *Numismatic Chronicle and Journal of the Numismatic Society*, vol. 13, pp. 4-7.

Read, C. H. (1893). English Work in Impressed Horn. *The Portfolio: An Artistic Periodical*, vol. xxiv, pp. 23-35.

Reid, S. A. (1908). *Sir Richard Tangye*. London: Duckworth.

Ricraft, J. (1647, reprinted 1830). *A survey of England's champions and truths faithfull patriots, or, A Chronological recitement of the principall proceedings of the most worthy commanders of the prosperous armies raised for the preservation of religion, the Kings Majesties Person, the Privileges of Parliament, and the liberty of the subject, etc. , with a most exact narration of the several victories, as also the number of commanders and soldiers that have been slain on both sides since these uncivill civill wars began…* London: Printed by R. Austin.

Ritson, J. (Frank. J., ed.) (1784, reprinted 1883). *The Letters of Joseph Ritson, edited chiefly from original in the possession of his nephew [J. Frank]. To which is prefixed a memoir of the author by Sir Harris Nicolas, K.C.M.G.* London: Pickering (2 vols.).

Robbins, C. (Jul., 1950). The Strenuous Whig: Thomas Hollis of Lincoln's Inn. *William and Mary Quarterly*. Third Series, vol. 7, no. 3 pp. 406-453.

Rondot, M. Natalie (1884). *Les Sculpteurs de Lyon de Quatorzième au Dix-huitième Siecle.* Lyon: Impri- merie de Pitrat Ainè.

Ruding, R. (1840). *Annals of the Coinage of Great Britain and its Dependencies.* London: John Heane, 81 Strand (3rd ed., 3 vols.).

Sandwich, earl of (1937). *British and Foreign Medals Relating to Naval and Maritime Affairs*. Greenwich: National Maritime Museum.

Sharp, T. (1825). *The Life of John Sharp, D.D., Lord Archbishop of York: To which are Added, Select, Original and Copies of Original Papers…* vol. i, London: C. & J. Rivington (Two vols.).

Smith, M. M. (1992). *Index of English Literary Manuscripts* (1700-1800), vol. iii, part 2 (p. 243).

Society of Gentlemen in Scotland. (1771). *Encyclopaedia Britannica, or, A Dictionary of Arts and Sciences Compiled Upon a New Plan.* (1st ed.). Edinburgh: Printed for A. Bell and C. Macfarquhar, and sold by Colin Macfarquhar, at his Printing-office, Nicholson-street.

Soros, S. W. (ed.). (2006). *James "Athenian' Stuart, 1713-1788, The Rediscovery of Antiquity*. New Haven: Yale University Press.

Sotheby's (14 December 1993). *The Fairfax Library and Archive: The Property of the Lord and Lady Fairfax.* London: Sotheby's.

Sotheby's (1925). *Catalogue of a Selected Portion of the Library at Sprotborough Hall, Doncaster. The Property of the Rt. Hon. Lord Cromwell*. London: Sotheby & Co.

Sotheby's [Auction Catalogue, Dec. 3, 1980]. *European Historical Medals from the Collection of His Grace the Duke of Northumberland...Removed from Alnwick Castle*. London: Sotheby's.

Sotheby's [Auction Catalogue, June 17, 1981]. *European Historical Medals from the Collection of His Grace the Duke of Northumberland (final portion)...Removed from Alnwick Castle*. London: Sotheby's.

Southey, C. C. (ed., 1850, 1855). *Life & Correspondence of the late Robert Southey, in six volumes, edited by his Son*. London: Longman, Brown, Green & Longmans.

Southgate, Rev. R. (1795). *Museum Southgatianum, Being a Catalogue of the Valuable Collection of Books, Coins, Medals, and Natural History, by Rev. Richard Southgate, A. B., F.A.S., Rector of Warsop, in Nottinghamshire, one of the librarians of the British Museum; and near thirty years Curate of St: Giles's in the Field to Which Is prefixed Memoirs of his Life.* London: Printed for Leigh and Sotheby, Covent-Garden (Price Five Shillings in boards).

Stewart, I. (1981). Two Centuries of Scottish Numismatics, In A. S. Bell, *The Scottish Antiquarian Tradition, Essays to Mark the Bicentenary of the Society of Antiquaries of Scotland and its Museum, 1780-1980.* Edinburgh: John Donald, pp. 227-265.

Stewartby, (Lord) (1996). Scottish Coin Collectors, *British Numismatic Journal*, vol. 66, pp. 87-112.

Stoddard, R. H. (ed., 1876). *Personal Reminiscences by Constable & Gillies*. New York: Scribner & Armstrong.

Stouraiti, A. (2014). Collecting the past: Greek Antiquaries and Archeological Knowledge in the Venetian Empire. In, Tziovas, D. (ed.). *Re-imagining the Past: Antiquity and Modern Greek Culture*. Oxford: Oxford University Press (pp. 27-46).

Strong, R. (1975). *Nicholas Hilliard*. London: Michael Joseph Ltd./Folio Press.

Strutt, J. (1785). *Biographical dictionary; containing an historical account of all the engravers, from the earliest period of the art of engraving to the present time: and a short list of their most esteemed with the cyphers, monograms, and particular marks, used by each master, accurately copied from the originals, and properly explained. To which is prefixed, an essay on the rise and progress of the art of engraving, both on copper and on wood. With several curious specimens of the performances of the most ancient artists, vol. ii,* London: printed by J. Davis, for Robert Faulder, New Bond Street.

Syson, L. The Legacy of Edward Hawkins: Franks as Numismatist. In M. Caygill and J. Cherry (eds.) (1997). *A. W. Franks: Nineteenth-Century Collecting and the British Museum. London: British Museum.* (pp. 296-307).

Taffs, H. W. (1952/54). Obituary: Miss Helen Farquhar, F. R. Hist. S. *British Numismatic Journal,* vol. 27, pp.101-03.

Tancred, G. (1891). *Historical Record of Medals and Honorary Distinctions Conferred on the British Navy, Army & Auxiliary Forces: From the Earliest Period.* London: Spink.

Tangye, R. (1905). *The Cromwellian Collection: Miniatures, Medals &c in the Possession of Sir Richard Tangye.* Glendorgal, Newquay, Cornwall: Privately printed.

Thompson, G. S. (1937, 1965). *Life in a Noble Household: 1641-1700*. London: Jonathan Cape.

Thompson, R. H. (1969). The Dies of Thomas Spence (1750-1814). *British Numismatic Journal*, vol. 38, 126-162.

Thompson, R. H. (2004-2005). Biographical entry for Thomas Snelling, *Oxford DNB, on line*.

Thoyras, Paul Rapin de (1724-1727). *History of England,* vols. I-X. London: John James and Paul Knapton.

Till, W. (1838). *An Essay on the Roman Denaris and English Silver Penny*. London: Longman, Orme, Brown, etc. (2nd ed.).

Trustees of the British Museum. (1915). *List of Catalogues of English Book Sales 1676-1900 Now in the British Museum.* British Museum: Longmans & Co, etc. Pp. ix-x.

Tucker, J. T. & Winstock, L.S. (eds.). (1972). *The English Civil War: A Military Handbook.* London: Arms & Armour Press.

Turner, D. (1830). *The Literary Correspondence of John Pinkerton, Esq. Now first printed from the originals in the possession of Dawson Turner, Esq., M.A., F.R.S.* London: Colburn & Bentley (2 vols.).

Walker, A. (2012). A. Macgregor & M. Hunter (eds.). *From Books to Bezoars: Sir Hans Sloane and his Collections.* London: British Library.

Walker, J. (1953). The Early History of the Department of Coins and Medals, *British Museum Quarterly,* vol. 18, No. 3 (Sept.), pp. 76-80.

Walpole Society, (1968). *Vertue Notebooks, vol. 18.* Printed for the Walpole Society by John Johnson at the University Press. London: Wm Dawson Ltd.

Walpole, H. & Vertue, G. (1888). (R. N. Wornum, ed.). *Anecdotes of painting in England; with some account of the principal artists. With additions by the Rev. James Dallaway, and Vertue's catalogue of engravers who have been born or have resided in England. A new edition, revised, with additional notes by Ralph N. Wornum*. London: Swan, Sonnenschein, Lavrey, Paternoster Square. (3 vols.).

Walpole, H. (1871 ed.), *Anecdotes of Painting in England.* London: A. Murray.

Walpole, H. (J. Wright, ed.) (1840). *The letters of Horace Walpole, Earl of Orford: including numerous letters now first published from the original manuscripts.* (6 vols.), vol. iv, 1759-1764. London: Richard Bentley, New Burlington St., London.

Warburton, E. (ed.) (1852). *Memoirs of Horace Walpole and His Contemporaries: Including Numerous Original Letters, Chiefly from Strawberry Hill.* London: Colburn.

Ward, A. W. (1875). *A History of English Dramatic Literature to the Death of Queen Anne.* London: Macmillan, 2 vols.

Watkins, L.-M. (ed.) (1822). *Anecdotes, Biographical Sketches and Memoirs. London:* F. C. & J. Rivington, Waterloo Place and St. Paul's Churchyard (2 vols.).

Weber, F. P. (1893). Medals and medallions of the nineteenth century, relating to England, by foreign artists. (part 1). *The Numismatic Chronicle and Journal.* Vol. 13 (3rd series), pp. 286-335.

Whetmore, S. A. H. (1960-61). Further Notes on Thomas Simon, *B.N.J.*, vol. 30, pp. 159-173.

Williamson, G. C. (1904). *Bryan's Dictionary of Painters and Engravers*, New York: Macmillan, vol. 4, p. 104.

Wilson, D. M. (1984). *The Forgotten Collector: Augustus Wollaston Franks of the British Museum*. New York: Thames & Hudson.

Wilson, David M. Biographical entry for Sir (Augustus) Wollaston Franks, *Oxford D.N.B.*, on line (2004-2005).

Wilson, H. (1842). *Wonderful Characters: Comprising Memoirs and Anecdotes of the Most Remarkable Persons, of Every Age and Nation.* London: J. Barr.

Wood, E. H. H. (1972). *'Letters to an Antiquary': The Literary Correspondence of G. J. Thorkelin* (1752-1829). Ph.D. thesis, University of Edinburgh.

Woolf, D. R. (2003). *The Social Circulation of the Past: English Historical Culture, 1500-1730.* Oxford: University Press.

Wright, T. & Evans, R. H. (1851). *Account of the Caricatures of James Gillray, Comprising a Political and Humorous History of the Latter Part of the Reign of George The Third.* London: Henry G. Bohn, York Street, Covent Garden.

Wroth, W. (1909). Thomas Simon; *D.N.B.*, vol. xxviii, 265-267.

'The Progress of selling Books by Catalogues'
By Richard Gough, Esq. 1788

IF the *circulation* of Books be a mark of a learned age, no method has been thought of better adapted to that purpose, than by making what are commonly called *Sale* CATALOGUES of them. These are of two sorts; by *auction* and by *hand.* The practice has now obtained considerable above a century.

—*Gentleman's Magazine*, 1788, vol. lviii, p. 1066.

Index

Note: An entry in bold type denotes a section on the subject, including footnotes; an entry in italics, a footnote; material within a section is not indexed further.

A

Abeele, van, Pieter **122-124**, 335
Acheson, John 119
Acker, van, Nicholas 164
Acker, van, Prudence 164
Addington, Samuel 314
Addison, Joseph 2, 5, *5*, *6*, *26*, **26-30**, 64, 165
Adolfszoon, Christoph[er] **124-125**
Albemarle, duke of, 204, 251 *See also* Geo. Monck
Alençon, J. 3
Allen, Derek *150*, 152, 172, *172*, 174, *174*, *181*, 182, *183*, *187*, 191
Allen, Martin xiii
Allibone, A. 369
Ames, Joseph 50, 368, 369, 379
Amey, Ellen 379
Ancient Scottish Poems 63
Andrew, W. J. 108
Anglo Jewish Exhibition 313, 316
Anglo-Dutch Wars (medal) 124, 125, 345
Anne of Austria 195
Anne, princess of Denmark, later queen of England 90, 120, 204, 211, 212, 252, 253, 329
Anthony, Charles **118-121**, 139
Anthony, Derick[e] *119*, 121
Antiquaries, Society of, 33, *34*, 36, 41, 42, 44, 57, 85, 87, 90, 91, 92, 93, 94, *145*, 226, 290, 313, 323, 349, 351, 362, 389, 392, 393, 394, 395, 397
Antiquaries, Society of, Scotland 323
Arbuthnott, C. 226, *226*
Archer, A. 285
Archer, John, 164
Ash, James 220, 332
Ashbrook, Lord 168
Ashmole, Elias 24, 238, 240, *249*, 379
Ashmolean Museum xxxi, *21*
Attwood, P, 209, *209*
Aymonino, A. *264*
Aytoun, William 61

B

Baetjer, K. *368*
Baker & Leigh 236. *See also* Sotheby's
Baker, M. *215*, 349, 350, 253, 236
Baker, Samuel, Baker's 253, 349, 350
Baldwin, A. H. & Co. xiii, 107, 111, 118, 119, 120, 122, 124, 126, 137, 146, 179, 216, 220, 223, 260, *262*
Ball, John, MP 88
Bandinel, B. 347
Banks, Lady Dorothea 288, 297, 298, 299, *299,* 300*,* 301
Banks, Sarah Sophia, 236, **299-301**
Banks, Sir Joseph 236, 270, 289, 294, **296-298,** 299, 300, 301 392
Barberini (collection) 273
Baseggio, Lorenzo 3, *3*
Basire, James, II 33, 226, 387, 389
Bastie, de la, — 3
Bathloe, William iv
Bateson, D. *286*
Batten, Sir W. 243
Beattie, Dr. James 61, *61*
Beauclerc, Lady Diana *66*
Beaufoy, H. B. H. 155, 156
Beauhin, Jean 131
Becken, Elizabeth Brown 68
Beckford, William 230
Beckwith, W. H., Col. 308
Bedford, Lucy, Duchess of 335, 335
Bédoyère, de la, Guy *17*
Bennet, H. *61*, 63
Bentinck, Margaret Cavendish, Duchess of Portland 257
Bentley, Dr. J. 16, 240
Bentley, S. 247, 277, 280, 295, 393
Berninck, Jan 196
Berti, Pompeo *3*
Besly, Edward 110, *110*, *111*
Beugo, Alexander 338
Bigg, William Redmore 374, 379
Bindley, Mr. 379
Binyon, L. *355*
Biographical Dictionary of Medallists. See Forrer, L.
Biographical History of England See Rev. James Granger
Birch, Diana *111*
Birch, Samuel 91
Birch, Thomas 368
Bird, Mr. 289
Bishop, Richard *111*
Blacas, de, duke Pierre Louis Jean Casimir 306
Blackburn, M. A. S. xiii, *87*
Blackburne, Mr. 379
Blagge, Margaret 17
Blaise Gentot 33
Blake, Anne 142
Blake, Robert, Adm. 142, 221
Blake, William 142
Blondeau, Peter (Pierre) 109, 110, *110,* 134, **158-165**, 183, 184, 185, 203, 304
Blurton, R. T. 218
Bodicoat, Edward 294
Bodley, Sir Thomas 143, 144, 224
Boizard (or Boisard), Jean 162
Bollaud, Baron 306
Bolles, Sir Robert and Lady 150, *150*, 154
Bon, Nicolò 8
Bonham's 111, *329*, **332-333**, 382
Bonomi, Joseph 81
Bootle, Robert 263
Bordier, Pierre (Peter) **192-196**
Boswell, James 272
Boudot, Jean 3
Boulton, Matthew *216*
Bower[s], George 204, 206-208, 330
Bowyer, William, the Elder (1663-1737) **387**
Bowyer, William, the Younger (1699-1777) 41, 44, 57, 373 **389**
Bowyer[s] and Nichols families xii, **386-395**
Brabazon, Dorcas (medal) 43, *182*
Bradshaw, John 14, *14*
Bradshaw, Lucretia 349
Braganza, Catherine of 201, 202, 200, 330, 331

Brand, Thomas, *see* Hollis, Thomas Brand
Brandon, Richard 311
Brandon, Robert 115, *115*
Bray, William *13, 14, 15, 16, 21,* 24, *172,* 241
Braybrooke, Lord 20
Bridgeman, Mrs. Katherine 263
Briot, Didier *131*
Briot, François *131*
Briot, Isaac *131*
Briot, Nicholas 95, 105, 107, 109, 127, **130-137**, 149, 153, 159, 161, 163, 181, *181*, 182, 189, 191, 304, 334, 335
Bristol Taken (medal) 55, 149, *150,* 154,
Bristow, Whiston 246, *355*
British Autography... 12, 177, 374, 376, 377, 379, 396
British Commemorative Medals and their Values xiv, 110, 111
British Historical Medals, see Brown, Laurence
British Historical Medals, A Collection of, **328-331**
British Historical Medals, An Important Collection of, **334-335**
British Museum iv, xii, xiii, xv, 5, 7, 19, 26, 41, 51, 64, 66, 76, 85-103, 105, 107, 112, 128, 129, 132, 133, 134, 135, 140, 141, 142, 144, 146, 147, 150, 153, 155, 156, 157, 159, 163, 165, 166, 168, 169, 170, 173, 174, 176, 177, 178, 179, 183, 186, 187, 193, 194, 197, 198, 199, 201, 202, 203, 206, 207, 209, 210, 212, 216, 218, 222, 224, 225, 226, 227, 229, 230, 230, 231, 233, 234, 236, 237, 238, 239, 240, 241, 244, 247, 250, 251, 252, 257, 258, 259, 262, 264, 265, 270, 273, 274, 276, 277, 279, 278, 281, 288, 289, 295, 296, 297, 298, 299, 299, 300, 301, 302, 303, 306, 307, 313,314, 338, *345*, 349, 350, 351, 352, *352*, 353, 356, 357, 358, 361, 364, 375, 378, 387, 389, 397
Bromley, William 361
Brown, Laurence *50*, 111, 141, *221*, 228, 233, *323*
Browne, Mary *See* Evelyn, Mary
Browne, Mr. *145*
Browne, Sir Richard (medal) 14, 262, 314
Browne, Thomas 314
Brucher, Antoine *131*
Bryan, M. 44
Bryan's Dictionary, 195
'Bryatt, Nicholas,' 134.
Brydges, Samuel Egerton, *152*, 272
Buchan, earl of *see* Erskine, David Steuart (*sic*)
Buchanan, Rev. John Lane 67, *67*, 72, *139*
Buchanan, W. W. 277
Buckingham, duke(s) of 35, 65, 140, *190*, 219.
Bull, Richard MP 368, *368*, 369, 379
Burch, Edward 274, 277
Burch, Henry Jacob 288, 294
Burgess, Henrietta Maria. *Also see* Pinkerton, Henrietta Maria (née Burgess) 67
Burgess, James *194*
Burgess, Thomas 67
Burgundy, Margaret of 103
Bushell, Thomas 154
Butler, James 164

C

Cadogan, Elizabeth 252
Caldecott, Thomas 3, *4*
Calvert, Cecil, 2nd Lord Baltimore 155
Camden Society 394, 395
Camden, lord 228
Camden, William 219, *219,* 249, *249*, *397*
Campbell, John, 2nd duke of Argyll *251*
Campbell, John, earl of Loudoun (medal) 177, 320, 325 331,
Cardonell, de, Adam 164
Carew, H. 306, 241
Carey, Margaret (medal) 142, 143
Carey, Peter (medal) *182*
Carey, Thomas (medal) 142,143
Carlton, Charles 14, *14*
Carlyle, Thomas 84, 134, *190*, 191, 311
Caroline, queen 35, *36*, 37, 212, 215, 216
Carter, Mary 33
Carter, T. C. 109
Carteret, Sir G. 164
Cartwright, J. J. 82, 164
Catherine II, queen of Russia 101
Catherine of Braganza. *See Braganza, Catherine of*
Caudron, George 341
Caulfield, James *81*, 338, 342, **382-385**
Cavendish, Lady Margaret, duchess of Newcastle and Tyne 257
Cavino, Giovanni 107
Caxton, William *391*, 412
Caygill, M., *xvi*, 94, 299, *299*
Cellini, Benvenuto 159
Chaffinch, William 35, *35*
Challis, C. E. *132*, *133,* 134, *134*, 199, *199*
Chalmers, Alexander 56, 58, 241, 351, *352*
Charles I, coronation. *See Coronation medals*
Charles I, king of England viii, 10, 17, 20, 21, 26, 35, *35*, 36, 39, 41, 42, 55, 65, 70, 84, 101, 103, 106, 107, 110, 111, 119, 122, **126-128**, 130, 131, 132, 133, 134, 135, 136, 137, 139, 141, 142, 145, 146, 148, 149, *150*, 151, 152, 153, *153*, 154, *154*, 156, 158, 166, 167, 182, 183, 189, *190*, 193, *193*, 196, 200, 217, 219, 200, 236, 237, *237*, 238, 239, 240, 241, 262, 265, 304, 308, 311, 314, 319, 324, 325, 327, 332, 333, 334, 335, 345, 383, 389
Charles II, king of England 15, 17, 20, 24, 35, 39, 73, 95, 103, 109, *110*, 122, 123, 124, 134, 137, 150, *150*, 152, 153, 154, *154*, 156, 159, 163, 167, 168, 172, 180, *180*, 183, 184, *184*, 185, 186, 189, 191, 198, 199, *199*, 201, 202, 203, 204, 206, 207, 208, 209, 219, 238, 240, 262, 265, 304, 306, 314, 317, 319, 323, 324, 327, 328, 330, 333, 336, 345, 358, 389
Charles Louis, Elector Palatine 154
Charles Stuart Thane 379
Charles, prince of Wales viii, 119, *111*, 138, 139, 141, 151, 153, 193, 239, 241, 316, 327, 345
Charlotte of Hesse Cassel, Electress Palatine 155
Charlotte, queen of England 228, 275, 298

Cheke, Sir John 107
Cherry, J. xvi, *88*, *91*, *93*, 94,
Chisum, H. 311
Cholmondeley family 272
Christiana, queen of Sweden, 171, 174, 175, 176, *181*
Cipriani, Giovanni Battista 360, 362
Clapinson, M. *4*
Clarendon, Edward Hyde xii, *20*, 21, *33*, 65, 167, 168, *182*, *33*, **344-347**
Claypole (or Cleypole), Elizabeth (medal) 106, 178, 229, *182*, 331
Clayton, T. *375*
Clegg, S. 362, *362*
Clements, L. 107
Cleypole, Elizabeth. *See* Claypole, Elizabeth
Cochran-Patrick, R. W. **322-325**
Cock, Christopher 257, *257*, 262
Cole, Rev. William 369, *375*
Colebrook, Mr. 57
Coleridge, Samuel Taylor *61*
Collyer, Joseph 298
Combe, Dr. Charles 72, 76, 85, 277, 280
Combe, Taylor 76, 85, 87, 90
Comenius, Johannes Amos 343
Commeline, James 314
Conduit, Mr. 217
Constable, Archibald 73,
Constable, T. *68*
Constantine I ('the Great') x
Constantine, Henry 338
Cook, Capt. James 297, 299
Cook, Sir Robert 14
Cook[e], John, solicitor-general (medal) 320
Cooper, Anthony Ashley 207
Cooper, Robert 345, 383
Cooper, Samuel *362*
Cooper Walker, Joseph. *See* Walker, Joseph Cooper
Copland, George 178
Cornbury, Lord 347
Corney, B. 121
Corns, C. 241
Coronation medal(s), 130, 131, 132, 137, *150*, 154, 184, 204, 207, 244, 306, 317, 324, 327, 328, 330, 337, 364
Cotton, Sir Robert Bruce 219, *257*
Couper, S. *63*, 66, *66*, 67, *67*, *68*
Cowley, Abraham 377
Cracherode, Clayton Mordaunt 273, 372
Cradock, William 392
Craig, J. *119*
Craik, H. 347
Crisp, Nicholas 226
Crofts, Thomas 275
Croker, John (Johannes) 204, **211-212**, 217, 329
Crompton, George 181
Cromwell, Henry 108, 172, **178**
Cromwell, Oliver 14, 17, 19, 22, 39, 42, 65, **81-84**, 103, 110, *112*, 123, *123*, 134, 155, 158, 159, 162, *162*, 163, 164, 168, 172, 182, 183, 189, 190, *190*, 191, *191*, 194, 203, 212, *212*, 216, 217, 221, 228, 229, 232, 244, *244*, 262, 304, 309, 310, 311, 314, 316, 317, *362*, 389
Cromwell, Richard 39, 262, 311
Cromwell, Thomas, earl of Essex *112*
Cromwell, William 178
Cuff, Mr. 314
Cullen, Lucy 113, 307, *307*
Cunningham, Peter 81, *240*
Curll, E. 3, *3*, *5*

D

D'Ewes, Sir Simonds 237, 238
D'Israeli, Benjamin 241
Dahl, Michael 258, 257
Dalem, van, Manteau 320, *172*, 175
Danfrie, Philippe 131
Daniel, Mr. 376
Danielle, Edward 379
Dassier, Domaine 215, 215
Dassier, Jacques-Antoine ('James Anthony') 215, 216, 229, 251, 349, 350, 352
Dassier, Jean ('John') xiii, 56, 81, 101, **214-218**, 229, 251, 349, 350, 352
Davenport, C. 196
David Steuart (sic) Erskine, 11th earl of Buchan 66, 67, *67*
Davies, Myles 27, *27*
Davies, Thomas 372, 373, *373*
DeBure, Guillaume-François 3
Dekesel, C. E. *20*
Des Pieces Obsidionales et de Nécessité. *See* Duby, Pierre xii, 58
Desborough, John, col. 172, 178
Dialogues upon the Usefulness of Ancient Medals 27, 29
Dibdin, 350, 365
Dickinson, W. 26
Dimsdale, Dr. Thomas, the elder, 283
Dimsdale, Dr. Thomas, the younger **283-284,** 289
Dixon, Matthew 17
Dobkin, J. *347*
Dodd, Thomas 338
Dodsley, Robert 59, 64, 152
Dodsworth, Roger 249, *249*, 397
—Dominion of the Sea (medal) (1630; 1639) 131, 135, 150, 154, 186, 330
Doort, van der, Abraham, *35*, *36*, 241
Dorset, earl of. *See* Sackville, Richard
Douce, Mr. Francis 18, 64
Draper, William 17
Drummond, John, Lieut.-col. 314
Duby, Pierre (Peter) xi, xii, **58**
Ducarel, Rev. Andrew Coltée 56, *56*, 57, 247, *247*, **351-352**, 355, *355*, 358, 359, 364, 379
Dufferin, marquis of 321
Dufour, Jean-Baptiste 147
Dunfermline, earl of *172*, 325, 331
Dupré, Guillaume 131, 143, *143*
Durand, Amédée xiv, 28, 53, 251, 277, 289, 308
Durand, Anthony 53, 306
Durant, Col. 306
Dürer, Albrecht 273
Dutens, Louis 264, *264*

E

Eden Upton Eddis, 89
Eden, R. A. 90
Eden, T. *See* Morton & Eden, Ltd.
Edward III 19, 101, 103, 349
Edward IV 103
Edward VI 25, 103, 107, 119, 269, 364, 394
Edwards & Sons 71, 75, 77, 270, *270*
Edwards, Thomas 50, 341, 342
Edwards, W. C. 71
Eimer, Christopher xiv, 48, 110, 111, 114, 116, 118, 119, 120, 122, 123, 124,

125, 126, 128, 166, 177, 207, 211, 212, 216, *225*, 226, *226*, 251, 335
Eisler, W. *215*
Elizabeth I, queen of England 13, 95, 115, *119*, 120, *131*, 138, 140, 141, 159, 333, 337
Elizabeth II, queen of England 157
Elizabeth, Lady Wardlaw *61*
Elizabeth, princess Palatine 138
Elizabeth, Princess Palatine 140
Elmes, J. A. xiv, 156, 191, 218
England, History of 215
English Civil Wars...See J.J. Platt & A. K. Platt
Erskine, David Steuart (sic), 11th earl of Buchan 66, 67, *67*, 72
Erskine, Sir Charles of Alva (medal) *172*, 325
Erskine-Hill, H. 6, *27*, 28
Essay on Medals 5, 7, 10, 19, 46, 59, 60, 62, 63, 64, *64*, *65*, 69, 71, *72*, 79, *79*. *Also see* Pinkerton, John
Essex, earl of, 40, 106, 110, *112,* 262, 304, 314, 316, 320, 328, 331, 342
Evans, R. H. 300
Evans, Sir Thomas 272
Evans, William 288, 294
Evelyn, Glanvill 14
Evelyn, John xii, **12-24**, 34, 39, 109, 119, 136, 150, 151, 153, 154, 155, 165, 171, *172*, 189, 203, 204, 236, 238, 240, 241, 247, 261, 262, 347
Evelyn, Mary (née Browne) 14, 17
Evelyn, Susanna 17

F

Fairfax 'Jewel' 112, **192-195**
Fairfax, Ferdinando 110, 304
Fairfax, Thomas 81, 84, 110, 112, 184, 185, 192, 194, *194*, 195, 221, 247, 249, *249*, 262, 304, 311, 342
Fanshaw, Sir Thomas 24, 219
Farquhar, Helen & Farquhar collection **104-108**, 109, 110, 136, 142, 146, 175, 188, 236, 327, 330, 331
Fearon, Daniel xiii, 111, 117, 337
Felton, John *190, 191*
Ferdinand, prince of Bavaria 145
Ferguson, W. *68, 69*, 73
Fiorentino, Niccolò 335
Firth, C. H. 311, 347
Fitzwilliam Museum xiii, 40, 41, *41*, 114, 177, 223, 335
Flack, Ann [?] 379
Flack, Elizabeth Seamer 379
Flack, William 379
Fleetwood, Adolphus Jacobus 164,
Fleetwood, George *88,* 164, 178
Fleetwood, Gustavus Miles164
Fleming, Surg.-maj. J. W. 236, **307-308**
Flesher, Miles 387
Fletcher, W. Y. 245, 273, 301, 350
Foley, Christopher, Collection 117, 120, 220, 232, *335*, **336-337**
Folkes, Sir Martin xi, 26, *26*, 57, 164, 165, 263, **348-350**, 351
Fontijn, Claire 9, *9*
Ford, J. K. 307, *307*
Ford, Mr., Ford's auction rooms 36, 44
Forgotten Collector. See Syson, L.
Forlorn Hope (medal) 105, 110, 111, *111*, 112, *112,* 149, *150, 151,* 153
Forrer, L. 109, 123, *123*, 125, *125, 127,* 131, *131*, 134, *134*, 139, 140, *140, 143, 145,* 149, *149,* 151, *151*, 152, *162, 163*, 175, 188, *188*, 189, 199, 215, *215*, *216*, 200, 209, *209*, 215, 215, 216, 221, 221, 229
Foster, J. J. *117*
Fothergill, Dr. 379
Fountaine, Sir Andrew 217
Franks, Frederica 191
Franks, Sir Augustus W. xiv, 88, 89, 90, **91-97**, *99*, 142, 230, 277
Frederick, count Palatine 138
Frederick, prince of Wales viii
Frederick, prince Palatine 138
Fuller, T. 392
Fuller, W. 24

G

Gale, Roger 3, *3*, 4, *4*
Gale, Samuel 352
Gallet, George 3
Garrick, David 228, 233
Gatteaux, Jacques-Édouard Gay-Ambrose, xx, 147
Gauci, Maxim viii, 89
General Biographical Dictionary 56, 58, 121, 239, 351, *352*
Gentleman's Magazine 19, *41*, 50, *50*, 56, *61*, 62, 73, *50*, *61*, *62, 63, 64, 68*,121, 229, 249, 300, 301, 303, 304, 306, 385, 392, 393, 397
George I, king of England 33, 211, 252, 313
George II, 87, 89, 95, 97, *97*, 99, *99*, 175, 212, 215, 216, 228, 252, 253, 318, 319, 329, 337
George III, 25, 99, 179, 209, 210, 216, 228, 329, *237*, 236, 269, 275, 318, 350
George IV, 179, 210, 216, 236, 318, 323
Gesvre, de, Louis Potier 131
Gibbon, Edward 63, *66*, 68, *68*, 69, 72, 392
Gilford, Dr. Andrew 57
Gillray, James 300
Gilpin, Rev. William 44, 59
Glendining's 104, 108, 1878, 223, *236*, *329*, 330, 331
Gloucester, duke and duchess of 228, 233, 334, 335, 372
'Gnadenpfennige' style of medal 335
Godolphin, Mrs. (see Blagge, Margaret)
Goodwin, John 341, *341*, 342
Goorle, Abraham van. *See* Gorlæus, Abraham
Gordon, L. L. 111
Goræus, *See* Gorlæus, Abraham
Gorlæus, Abraham 238, 239, 240, 241
Gorton, J. 58
Gough, Harry 397
Gough, Richard *34*, 41, *41*, 57, 352, *352*, *355*, 389, 393, 394, **396-397**
Granby, marquis of 228
Granger, Rev. James, viii, *34, 145,* 189, 209, 249, 342, **366-373**, 379, 383,
Grangerize, Grangerizing *145*, 368, 369, **371-373,** 375
Grant, Col. M. H. *99*
Graves, R. E. *195*
Graves, Robert 338
Green, James 57, 351
Green, M.A.E. *184*
Green, William 392

Greene, Edward 110, 181, *181*
Griffin, Charles 202
Grueber, Herbert A. xiv, 87, 89, 90, 94, **95-103**, 125, *125,* 134, 167, *167*
Gruter, (Pierre de?), 21
Gucht, van der, Gerard 375
Guerdain, Dr. Aaron 160
Guide to the Exhibition of English Coins 96
Gulstone, Mr. 379
Gustavus, Gerard 352
Guthrie, W. 3, 6, 27, *27,* 28, *28*
Gythens, Mrs. Mary 314

H

Hadley, S. 229, *229*
Halley, Edmond *251*
Hamilton, duke of 65, 219
Hamilton, James, 2nd viscount Claneboye 251
Hamilton, John, Capt. 321
Hamilton, W. R. 165
Hamilton-Smith, G. 332
Hammon, Stephen 164
Hammond, Robert 178
Hamper, William *294*
Handley, S. *200*, 229, *229*
Hands, Rev. A. W. 4, 4, 24
Hanmer, Sir Thomas 219
Harding, George P. 345
Harding, Sylvester 60
Hardouin, Jean *10*
Harley, Edward, 2nd earl of Oxford viii, **257-263**
Harley, Henrietta, née Cavendish Holles, 257
Harley, Robert 257
Harrington, Sir James (medal) *182,* 320
Harrison & Sons, 105
Harrison, Thomas 178
Hastings, Lord 192
Hawkins, Edward xiv, **86-90**, *91*, 92, *92*, 93, 94, **97-100**, 134, 144, 163, 173, 187, 203, 206, 210, 215*, 220,* 236, 251
Hawkins, Eliza 90
Haycock, D. B. *349*
Hayls, John 243
Hayward, John *111*
Hazilrig, Lord Arthur 178
Head, B. V. 96
Heal, Sir Ambrose 230, *230,* **231**
Heath, Sir Robert 55, 106
Hebrat, Jean 196
Heckett, Mrs. Greta **326-328**, 335
Heiress of Strathern, or, *The Rash Marriage. See* Pinkerton, John
Henfrey, Arthur 81
Henfrey, Elizabeth Anne 81
Henfrey, Henry **80-84**, 110, 159, *159*, *160*, *162, 163*, 164, 237, 238, 240,
Henrietta Maria, queen 110, **126-128**, 139, 149*, 150,* 151*,* 152*, 153*, 166, 196, 202, 335
Henry IV, of France *143*
Henry VI 175, 318, 319
Henry VII 103, 107, 359
Henry VIII 25, 56, 95, 103, 105, 107, *112,* 240, 269, *270*, 287, 294, 333, 337, 351, 355, 359
Henry, prince of Wales 65, 119, 139, 219, 237-241, 314
Heron, Mary 61
Heron, Robert 61, *61*, 63, *63*, 72
Hewson, John, col. 178
Highfill, P. H., Jr. *211*
Hill, C. P. *13*
Hill, Sir George F. 25, 136, 143, *143,* 151, *151*, 191
Hilliard, Nicholas 105, **114-117**, 119, 139
Hilliard, Richard *115*
History of Medals, Introduction to the 7, 10. *See* Patin, Charles
Hodsoll 289, *289,* 290*, 294, 294, 295*
Hogarth, William 26, 392
Holbein, Hans 35, 92
Hollar, Wenceslaus iii, iv, xv, 7, **31**, 35, 129, 157, 169, 191, 259, 342, 353, 375
Holles, William 119
Hollis, Thomas 56, *56,* 178*,* 221*, 221,* 225, 226, 351, 355, 358, **360-365**
Hollis, Thomas Brand **360-365**
Hopwood, William 60
Hotham, Sir John (medal) 43
Houbraken, Jacobus 34, *34*
Howard, Mr. [Robert?], controller of the mint 242
Howard, Philip 145
Howard, Thomas, 21st earl of Arundel iv, 24, 31, 65
Howard. Mr., controller of the mint 242
Huggart, Mr. 304
Hunter, Dr. John & Hunter prize medals 249, **276**
Hunter, Dr. William & collection 50, *50,* 56, 65, *65*, 85, 117, 219, 236, **274-277**, 281; prize medals 274, 276
Hunter, Rev. J. 249
Hunwick, Christopher 265
Hurd, R. 2
Hustvedt, S.B. 62, *62, 63*

I

Inchiquin, lord. *See* O'Brien, Murrough
Introduction to the Science of Medals xi, **45-46**, 65
Ireland (badge) 335
Ireland 56, 150, 163, 178
Ireland, Samuel 26, *26*
Ireton, Henry 19, 43

J

James I of England 24, 56, 109, 114, 115, 116, 117, 118, 119, 120, 121, 138, 139, 140, 141, 190, *190,* 236, 240, 241, 287, 323, 326, 327, 333, 334, 335, 351, 355
James II *3,* 33, 35, *35*, 37, 109, 140, *200*, 204, 207, 209, 210, 240
James III *See* Monmouth, duke of
James IV of Scotland 103
James VI of Scotland 120
Jenner, Edward, 276
Jennings, David xi, **45-46**, 51, 65, 136
Jennings, Henry Constantine 338
'Jewels' 111, 112, 114
Joachim, Albert 43, 179, 314, 331
Jobert, Louis xi, xii, *xii*, **2-7**, 10, 19, 24, 30, 69, 121
John George, elector of Saxony
Johnson, Dr. Samuel *27*, *61,* 90, 272, 385, 392
Johnson, Francis P. 327
Jones, Indigo 282
Jones, Mark 143, *143*
Jones, Michael, lieut.-gen. 178
Joslin, Edward C. 111
Juxon, Bishop William 149, (medal) 55, 137, 314

K

Keary, Charles F. 96, *96*
Kendal, Sir John (medal) 93, 103, 248, 334, 335
Keynes, G. 20, *20*
Kirk, Catherine 229
Kirk, James 230

Kirk, John 226, **228-233**, 362
Kneller, Sir Godfrey 33, 170, 242, 252
Knowledge of Medals 3, 4, 5, 6, 45, 46, 121
Knyvet, Sir Thomas 119
Kolbe, G. F. 53, *53*

L

La Science des Médailles xi, xii, 3, 4, 5
Lake, Sir Janus 379
Lambert, John, major-gen'l. 162, 178, 331, 332
Lambert's 'jewel' 109
Langdale, Miss 304
Langdale, Sir Marmaduke 304
Langerack, Joh. Artnold 3
Langford, Abraham, Langford's 36, 44, 51, 52, 253, *257*, *269*, 272, *272*, 348
Laud, Archbishop 20, 55, 65, 137, 154, *154*, *182*, 219
Lauderdale, duke of *172*, 176, 204, 205, 244, 325
Lawrence, Sir Thomas 283, *283*
Leigh, George *See* Sotheby's
Leigh, Sotheby &Son. *See* Sotheby's
Lely, Sir Peter 203, 331, 345, 377
Lenthall, William 178, 331
Lessen, M. xiii, 110, *111*
Lewis W. S. & Wallace, A. D. 41, *66*, 69, 218. *Also see Horace Walpole's Correspondence*
Leyden, van, Lucas 375
Lilburne, John (medal) *190*, *191*, *244*, 311, 332
Lindsay, A. 273
Literary Anecdotes ii, *3*, 33, *33*, 41, *41*, 56, 57, 140, 277, 280, 281, *289*, 295, 345, 352, *352*, 355, *355*, 358, 373, 379, 386, 387, 388, 389, 391, 392, *392*, 393, 395
Literary Correspondence… *61*, *62*, *65*, *66*, *67*, *68*, 71, 72, *79*, *270*, 365
Litherland, Andrew *111*
Lockhart, William 178
Lodge, E. *272*
London, Long View xv, 129, 353
Long, W. H. *See War Medals of the British Army, 1650-1891.*
Lort, Michael *41*
Loudoun, earl of 106, *172*, 177, 320, 325,
Louis XIII of France 127, 131, *143*, 145, 171, 176
Louis XIV of France *12*, *143*, 193, 195, 196, 204, 209, 216
Louis, Charles I, Elector of the Palatine 155
Lownes, W. T. 376
Lucas, Louis 3
Lustig, I. S. 272
Lyte 'jewel' 114
Lyttleton, Edward, 1st baron 190, *190*

M

MacPhail, Neil 274, 276
Malcolm, J. P. 372, *372*
Malkin, A. T. 167, 168, 347
Manchester, earl of, 110
Mann, Abbé 300
Marbre-Cramoisy, Francoise 3, 3
Maria Theresa, queen 195
Maria, Infanta of Spain 138
Markham, Sir Clements Robert 192
Marrian, J. 216
Marten, Henry 190, *190*, *191*,
Mary, princess royal 335
Mary, queen of England 24, *88*, 107, 204, 207, *211*, 304
Maunder, S. 58
Maxentius x
Maxfield, V. A. x
Mayo, J. H. 109 132, *132*, 151, *151*, 192
McConnell, A. *375*
McCullough, J. E. 51
McMillan, Andreas 276
Mead, Dr. Richard 218, **253-256**
Mead, Rev. Matthew 253
Meck, van, Israel 375
Medallic History of England xii, 49, 55, 60, **71-78, 80-82,** 220, 270, *270*, 286, 293, *295*, 354, *355*. *Also see* Pinkerton, John
Medallic Illustrations 'The Plates' **100-103**
Medallic Illustrations… xiv, 87, 90, 94, 95, 96, **97-99,** 105, 109
Medals, Coins, Great-Seals… of Thomas Simon xiii, 19, 34, 35, **38-44,** 164, 172, 173, 175, 176, 181, 189, 389, 397
Mestrelle, Eloye 159
Middleton, Dr. Conyers 391, *391*
Miles, Richard 27, 69, 289, 306, *306*
Millington, Mr. 112
Milton, John 290
Mitchiner, M. *Jetons, Medalets, and Tokens…* 111, *111*, 230
Molesworth, Walter & John 28
Molteno, Anthony viii, 338
Monk *or* Monck[e] gen'l George (medal) 155, 178, *182*, 251, 262
Monk *or* Monck, Christopher 251
Monmouth, duke of 195, 207, 209, 323
Monnaie du Moulin 127
Montagu, Hyman x, 146, **312-317**, 329, *375*
Montagu, Mr. 243
Montague, Edward (medal) *182*
More, Sir Thomas *112*
Mores, Rowe 369
Morosini, Pietro 8
Morrison, Mr. *145*
Morton & Eden xiii, 111, 127, 130, 138, 146, **334-335,** 337
Morton, James xiii, 111.
Moulyn, De Lewis 164
Müller, O. *Also known as* Wouter Müller 123, *123*
Murdoch, John G. 146, 172, 175, **318-320**
Murray, J., col. 164, 321
Murray, Sir David 240
Murray, Thomas 252
Musgrave, Sir William 369, 372, 373, *373*
Myron, M. *269*

N

Nanteuil, Robert 12, *12*, 15, 196
Nathanson, A. J. 109, 110, 149, *149*, *161*, *162*, *163*, *181*, *182*, *183*, 184, *184*, *186*, 188
Newton, Sir Isaac *26*, 30, 212, 217, 252, 253, 349
Nichol, George *66*
Nicholas, Mr. 42
Nichols family **386-395**
Nichols, Anne 392
Nichols, John Bowyer 390, 392, **393**, 394
Nichols, John Bruce 395
Nichols, John Gough 346, **394-395**

Nichols, John ii, *33*, 125, 277, 280, *289*, 295, 352, *352*, 379, 385, 386, 387, 388, 389, 390, **391-392,** 393, 395, 397
Nicholson, John 346
Nightingale, B. 34, *34*, 59, *149, 181, 187*
Noble Numismatics (Australia) xiii, 118, 139, 185, 200
Noble, Rev. Mark 178, *178*, 369, *369*
Nonesuch House, Old xv
Northumberland. *See* Percy, Sir Hugh, 1st duke of
Northwick, Lord 289, 304
Numismata Britannica 44, 86, 87, 88, *88*, 90, *97*
Numismata Cromwelliana **80-84**
Numismata: A Discourse of Medals (Evelyn) xii, 12, 13, 16, **18-24**, 130, 189, 238, 239, 240*, 261, 262, 295*
Numismatic Chronicle 34, 81, *81*, 90, 94, 105, 141, *143*, *144, 149,* 165, *181, 187,* 237, *237*, 241, *313*, 316, 323

O

O'Brien, Murrough (Lord Inchiquin) (medal) 176, 221, 270, 320, *172*
O'Connell, S. 362, *362*
O'Donoghue, F. M. 355
O'Flaherty, P. 72, *72, 79*
Ogborne, John 374, 379
Old Customer, An 359
Old Scottish Ballads 63
Oliver, Alexandre 127
Oliver, René 127
Olivier, Aubin (or Aubry) 145
Olivier, Pierre 145
On Tudor and Stuart Coins and Medals **105-108**
Orange, Prince Maurice of 314, 316
Orange, Prince William of (later King William III of England 123, 125, 207, 210, 317, 314, 316, 88, 97, 99, 125
Orange, Princess Mary of 123
Ormerod, G. 87
Ormond, duke of 204, 240
Osborne, Thomas 257, *355*
Ottoboni, Cardinal 273

P

Papillon collection, sale **332-333**
Parker, John Henry 394
Parkes Weber, 143, *143, 144*
Parkhurst, Sir William 55, 110, *150,* 154*, 154,* 181
Pasch, James 220
Passe, de Crispijn (the elder) 139
Passe, van de Crispijn (the younger) 139, 140
Passe, van de, Magdalena 139
Passe, van de, Simon **138-141**, 337
Passe, van de, Willem 139
Paterson, Samuel 357
Patin, Charles xi, xii, 7, **8-11**, 19, 24, 147
Paton, George 72
Pavia x
Peace of Breda 124, 205, 243, 265
Peace or War (medal), 133, *150, 154*
Peacock, J. 241
Pembroke, Lord (& collection) 197, 263, 282
Pen, Sir W. 243
Pennington, Mr. 178
Pepys, Samuel *3*, 15, 16, *16*, 17, 20, 24, 164, 203, *211*, **242-245**, 347
Percy, Elizabeth, 1st duchess of Northumberland **264-265**
Percy, Sir Hugh, 1st duke of Northumberland **264-265**
Perry, Francis xii, xiii, 55, *55*, 56, *56*, 57, 351, **354-359**, 364
Person, Algernon *181*
Peters, Hugh 238, 240, 241
Petitot, Jean (John) **192-196**
Phillips, Thomas 297
Pingo Family, The (Eimer) *226*
Pingo, Benjamin, *221*
Pingo, John *221*
Pingo, Lewis 216
Pingo, Thomas 48, 49, 50, 56, 221, *221*, 224, 225, 226, 362, 364
Pinkerton, Ann 67
Pinkerton, Elizabeth (née Elizabeth Brown Becken) 68
Pinkerton, Henrietta Maria (née Burgess) 67
Pinkerton, John xii, 5, *5*, 7, 10, 19, 41, 46, 49, 50, 53, 55, **59-79**, 87, 109, *131*, 179, 204, 218, 219, 220, 236, 238, 270, *270*, *279*, 280, 286, 293, 351, [illegible], [illegible], 333, [illegible], 364, 365, 368
Planta, Mr. 270
Plates, The. See Medallic Illustrations…
Platt, J. J., & Platt A. K *xi*, xiv, 19, 40, 83, 93, *93*, 95, *123*, *126*, 132, 133, 135, 139, 146, 149, *149*, 151, 153*, 153, 154,* 166, 168, 172, 176, 177, 178, *179*, 182, *182*, 183, 184, 185, 190, 192, 199, 200, 205, 217, 223, 229, 248, 250, *275*, 314, 225, 328, 330, 331, 327
Plessis, Armand Jean du (*See* Cardinal Richelieu)
Plot, Dr. Robert 21*, 21*
Plunkett, Tom 308
Pollard, A. W. 112
Pollard, John Graham xiii, *143*, 151, *151*, 168
Pope, Alexander 28, 30, *251*
Pope, William *172*
Porden, William 61, *62*
Porta, della, Guglielmo 208
Porter, Endymion 145
Portraiture of our Stuart Monarchs on their Coins and Medals 105, *172*, 175
Pottle, F. A. *272*
Pride, Thomas, col., 'Pride's Purge'238
Prideaux, John 143, *143*
Puisne, le Huard 196
Pulteney, William, 1st earl of Bath *251*
Pym, John *191*

Q

Quarterman Publications 100

R

Ramsay, Allan 275
Rapson, E. J. 96
Rashleigh, Mr. 289
Rawle, G. 49, 48
Rawlins, Thomas 24, 95*,* 108, **148-156**, *182*, 183, 184, 199, 263, 271, 304, 314, 330
Rawlinson, Bishop Richard 263
Rebellion, History of 33, **345-347**
Rebellion, The 152, *152*, 153
Recollections of Paris 67, 68
Record, James 177
Reede, de, John, Baron 43, 172, 314, 320
Regnier, Pierre **126-128**, 145
Reid, S. J. *309*, 311,*311*
Reitz, Heinrich, the Younger **166-168**
Rembrandt, Harmenszoon van Rijn 371, 375

Revett, Nicholas 224, 225, 226, 227
Reynolds, Sir Joshua 264, 277, *355*
Richard III 335
Richardson, Jonathan, the elder viii, 32, 33, 355, *355*, 358, 359
Richardson, William 338, *373*
Richeletin, Pierre, 196
Richelieu, Cardinal 146, 147
Richmond, duchess of **202-205**
Ricovrati, L'Accademia dei 9
Ricraft, Josiah xii, **340-342**
Roettier[s] brothers *110*, 164, 184, 185, 199, 207, 212, 215, 244, 304
Roettier[s], James 199, 200, 204
Roettier[s], John (Jan) 184, 185, 186, **198-205**, 215, 243
Roettier[s], Joseph 184, 199, 200, 204, 219
Roettier[s], Norbert 24, 199, 200, 204, 215
Roettier[s], Philip 199,
Rogat, Emile 28
Rogers, William 3
Rollin & Feuardent x, 98
Rondot, Natalis 143, 144, *144*
Ronsard, de, Pierre 15
Rosenhein, Max 107
Roubiliac, Louis François 350
Roxburghe Club 395
Royal Collections, **236-241**
Royal Numismatic Society 96, 105, 107, 108
Royal Numismatic Society and Journal 165, 301
Royal Society 17, *26*, *34*, 46, 81, 87, 90, 93 *145*, 208, 226, 251, 252, 253, 275, 296, 297, 349, 351, 362, 364, 389, 394, 397
Royal Society of Arts 196, *221*, 225, 226, 229, 364
Ruding, Rev. Rogers 164
Rupert of the Rhine, prince 149, 198, 311, 374
Ruyter, de, Michael 125
Rymer, Thomas *131*, 136

S

Sacchetti collection 273
Sackville, Richard, 3rd earl of Dorset 337
Saltus, John Sanford, medal 105, *107*
Sandwich, earl of 164, 198
Savage, John 20, *20*
Sawyer, R. 396
Scala, della, Cesare *136*, 219, 238, 239
Scaliger, Joseph (*Also known as Cesare della Scala*).
Schiavonetti, Luigi 297
Schoon, Martin 375
Schuppen, van, Pierre 194
Scobell, Henry (medal) *182*, 331
Scotland xx
Scott, James (Duke of Monmouth) (medal) 207, 209
Scott, John 338
Scott, Patrick xiii
Scott, Sir Walter 63, *68*, 69, 73
Scott, Sir Wm. (Lord Stowell 68)
Scottish Rebellion, Suppression of (medal) 181, 314
Scroop, Adrian 178
Seaby's 111
Seaman, Dr. Lazarus 112
Selden, John 219, 241
Select Scottish Ballads (Pinkerton, John) 61, *62*
Select Tragic Ballads (Pinkerton, John) 61
Severus, Alexander 273
Shaftesbury, earl of 204, 207
Sharpe, Christopher 385
Sheridan, Thomas 392
Silvecane, de, Constant 143
Silver Coins of England 88, 90
Simmons, Samuel Foart 277
Simon Beal[e] (medal) 55, *150*
Simon, Abraham 103, 108, 110, 159, **170-179,** 180, 181, 181, *183*, 187, 188, 189, 191, 205, 221, 222, 223, 225, 250, 270, 330, 331
Simon, Ann (daughter) 187
Simon, Ann (mother) 171, 181
Simon, Elizabeth (daughter) 187
Simon, Elizabeth (wife) 187
Simon, Hibberd (daughter)187
Simon, Peter (Pierre) 181
Simon, Samuel 187
Simon, Thomas xii, 19, 34, *34*, 35, **38-44**, 82, 84, 95, 103, 105, 109, *109*, 110, *110*, 134, 136, *145*, 149, 150, 151, 152, 152, 158, 159, 162, 163, 164, 165, 171, 172, 173, 174, 175, 176, 178, **180-191**, 185, 194, 199, *199*, 203, 204, *211*, *212*, 216, 221, 222, 223, 225, 250, 261, 262, 270, 304, 316, 330, 337, 358, 389, 397
Simon, William 187
Simpkin, Brian *111*
Sketchbook, Thomas Simon's 191, *181*, 187, *187*
Slingsby (*also* Slingesby), Sir Henry (medal) *150*, 244, *244*, 245
Sloane, Hans 146, 154, 174, 202, 204, **250-252**, *257*, 349
Sloane-Stanley, auction 146
Smeeton, George *383*
Smeltzing, Jan (Johannes) **209-210**
Smeltzing, Martin 209
Smith, George Hamilton 236
Smyth, C. *319*
Snelling, Mary Lord 373, 375, 379
Snelling, Thomas vii, xiii, 19, 44, **47-57,** 60, 69, *69,* 70, 71, 72, *72,* 78, 109, 164, 218, 236, *270*, *279*, 289, *295*, 351, 354, 355, *355*, 364, 373, 373, 375, 379,
Solly, Edward 290, *290*, 294, **295**
Somers, Lord 33
Sotheby, Sotheby's, Sotheby Park Burnet etc. 85, 111, 142, 171, 175, *221*, 236, *294*, 301, *303*, *306*, 336, 265, *265*, 273, 278, 279, 280, *280*, 281, 283, 285, 288, 289, 291, 294, *294*, 295, 301, 303, *303*, 304, 305, 306, *306*, 313, 314, 316, 319, 321, 327, 333, , , *352*, 363, 364, 365, 378, 380, 392
Sotheby, Wilkinson & Hodge. *See* Sotheby's
Southampton, earl of (medal) 317, 320, *182*
Southey, Robert *61, 62*
Southgate, Rev. Richard 64, 85, **278-281**, 289, 290, 294
Spanheim, Friedrich (?) 21
Speed, John 219
Spelman, Sir John, Judge 294
Spink, S. M. 107
Spink, Spink & Son *xi*, *xiii*, *53*, *93*, 97, 99, 111, 126, *131*, 133, 137, 149, 154, 179, 184, *186*, 220, 228, 289, *294*, 330
St. John, Oliver 178
St. John's College 314, 389
St. Martin-in-the-Fields, 117
Stace, Machell *81*

Stanhope, earl 395
Stanley, Sarah 252
Staunton, Sir William *294*, *295*
Steele, Richard *5*
Stevenson, Mr. (of Norwich) viii
Stewart, Frances. *See* Richmond, duchess of
Stewart, Ian 78, 96, 404
Stewartby, Lord 283
Stirling, Sir Walter 289
Stoker, D. 257
Strutt, J. 358
'—Stuart,' — xiv, 43, 173, 179, *181*, 187, 188, **220-223**, 225, 329, 331, 364
Stuart Coins and Medals **105-106**, 107, 108, *173*, 323
Stuart Monarchs, 105, *172*. *Also see* Farquhar, Helen
Stuart, earl of Traquair (medal) 131
Stuart, I. 404
Stuart, James 'Athenian' 179, *221*, **224-228**, 362, 364
Stuart, James 200
Stuart, John, earl of Traquair 131
Stuarts, house of, 66, 88, 105, 107, 108, 109, 155, 175, 200, 210, 241, 323, 327
Swaine, John 12, *12*
Sweet, R. H. *397*
Swift, Dean *212*
Swift, Jonathon 391, 392
Sykes, Sir Mark 306
Symond(s), Mr. *See* Simon, Thomas.
Symonds, H. D. 60
Syson, Luke xiii, 88, *88*, 89, *89*, *92*, *93*, 94

T

T[affs], H. W. 108
Tancred, G. 109, 189, 321
Tangye, Sir Richard, Tangye collection 236, **309-311**
Tanner, John Sigismund 212, *212*
Tassie, James 71, 277
Taylor, Charles 271, 277
Taylor, W. B. S. 204
Tedder, J. H. R. *383*, 385
Thane, Edward 379
Thane, John 12, 27, 49, 50, 51, 56, 177, 216, 289, 338, 357, **374-380**, 396, 397
Thesaurus numismatum e musæo Caroli Patini 8, 10, 11
Thirty Three Plates of English Medals xii, xiv, 47, 49, 50, *50*, **53-57**, 60, 69, 70-72, 77-78, 89, 218, *295*, 354, 355, *355*, 364,
Thomas, Thomas **284-287**
Thomason, Sir Edward, 216, *216*
Thompson, R. H. 49, 50
Thomson, Peter 358
Thomson, Thomas 73
Thoresby, John 247
Thoresby, Ralph 192, 194, *194*, **246-249**, *373*
Thorkelin, G. J. *67*
Thoyras, de, Paul Rapin, *History of England…* 215
Thurloe, John (medal) *182*, 222, 223, 331
Ticinum x
Till, William 69, 314, 271
Tillotson, Archbishop John 33
Tompion, J. 196
Tooke, Benjamin 16, 20, *20*, 21
Toriesen, Peter Aucher. *See* Duby, Pierre
Torre, Anthony *375*
Toutin, Jean 193
Tradescant, John (elder) *249*
Tradescant, John (younger) *249*
Traquair, earl of. *See* Stuart, John
Trattle, Marmaduke 173, 289, **302-306**
Trezzo, da, Jacopo Nizolo 107, 146
Triphook, Robert 62
Turner, Dawson, *61*, *62*, *65*, *66*, *67*, *68*, *69*, 71, 72, *79*, 365
Turner, Martha (?), Mrs. 164
Turquet, de, Sir T. Mayern[e] 193
Tutet, Mark Cephas 57, 379
Tyssen, Samuel 108, 236, 279, *279*, 280, 281, **288-295**, *306*

U

Urban, Sylvanus 121, 359

V

Vaillant, — 219,
Vandenbrouck-Przybylski, Dr. Melanie 307, *307*
Vanderbank, John 349, 355, *355*, 358,
Vaughan, Robert 95
Vaux, W. S. W. 89, 93, 97
Verney, Margaret 15
Vernon, Robert 338
Vertue, George ii, iv, viii, xii, 19, 31, **32-44**, 109, 110, 119, *35, 36, 39,* 85, 136, *145*, 164, 170, 171, 172, 173, 174, 175, 176, 177, 178, 180, 181, *181*, 188, 189, 190, *193*, 215, *220*, 236, *247*, 257, *258*, *259*, 261, 263, 267, 268, 269, *269*, 273, *330*, 352, *355*, 359, 368, 375, 389, 397, 398
Vertue, Margaret 15, 35, 36
Victoria and Albert Museum xiii, *17*, 93, 115, 117, 141, 208, 236, 350
Victoria Cross 308
Victoria, Queen 313, 333
Villiers, Barbara, duchess of Cleveland, 204, 250
Villiers, George, marquess of Buckingham 35, 65, 140
Visscher ,Claes Jansz. xv, 353
Voss (*also known as* Vossius), Gerhard Johann Ernie 136, *136*

W

Wade, Edward 110, 181, 182
Wade, William (medal) 149, 150, *150*
Waldegrave, earl of 269, 272
Wales, National Museum of 111
Walker, Joseph Cooper 65, *65*, *68*
Walker, Mr. 227
Walker, Obadiah **3-7**
Walker, Robert 13
Waller, Edmund 201, 202
Waller, Sir William (medal) 110, 178, 342
Walpole, Catherine 267
Walpole, Horatio, earl of Orford viii, 16, *21*, 24, 34, 35, *35*, 36, 37, 41, 44, 63, *64*, 66, *66*, *68*, 69, *69*, 72, *72*, 119, *119*, 121, 136, 147, 152, 154, 171, *187*, 192, 193, *194*, 196, 199, *199*, 202, *215*, *217*, 218, 238, 240, 247, 263, **265-273**, 275, 352, *352*, 355, 359, 362, 367, *367*, *368*, 369, 371, 372, *373*, *375*, 392, *392*, *397*
Walpole, Mary 272
Walpole, Sir Robert 267
Walton, Henry 383
War Medals of the British Army, 1650-1891 109
Warburton, E. 372

Ward, A. W. 153
Ward, Dr. John 57
Wardlaw, Lady Elizabeth *61*
Warin (Varin), Claude **142-144**
Warin, (Varin) Jean 127, 143, 144, **145-147**
Warwick, earl of 134, 178
Watkins, Josiah
Watkins, L. M. 272
Welch, Sir Robert (medal) 110, 149, *150*
West, Mr. James 34, *34*, 56, 145, *145*, 371, 373, *373*, 375, *375*, 379
Westminster Hall (by Hollar) 157
Wheatley, H. B. *243*
Whetmore, H. *186, 187*
White, Mr. 375
White, Robert 242, 245
White, William 21, 294
Whiteaves, Mr. 168
Whitelock[e], Bulstrode *182,* 221, 238, 241, 304
Wigan, Edward 314
Wilkes, John 228
William III (William of Orange, later) king of England 88, 97, 99, 123, 125, 204, 207, *211*, 316,
Williamson, G. C. *193*
Wilson and Co. 77
Wilson, D. M. *92*
Wood, Anthony 379
Wood, E. H. *67*, 68, *68*
Wood, Mr. (the critic) 342
Wood, Mr. (the engraver) 57
Woodburn, Samuel, 283, *283*
Woolf, D. R. 7, 84
Woolley & Wallis xiii, 111, 117, 120, 220, 232, *335*, 337
Wornum, R.N. 193, *194,* 196
Wray, Edward 150
Wren, Christopher 17
Wright, C. J. *373*
Wright, J. 359
Wright, T. 300
Wriothesley, Sir Thomas 270, 317, 331
Wroth, W. 50, *50*, 96, *151*
Wyon, Leonard Charles 395
Wyon, Thomas 164
Wyon, William 303, *303*, 304

Y

York, duke of 33, 141, 164, 172, 198, 204, 244
Yorke, James 156
Young, Henry 56, 263
Young, Matthew 51, 168, 202, 203, 289, 301, 304, 305, 306
Young, Patrick, librarian to Chas. I 237, 238, 240

AND for as moche, says he, as in the wrytyng of the same my penne is worn, myn hande wery & not stedfast, myn eyen dimed with overmoche lokyng on the whit paper.

—William Caxton (ca. 1422-1491), in the epilogue to his translation of Raoul Lefèvre's *The Recuyell of the Historyes of Troye* (ca. 1463-1464), the first book printed in English (ca. 1473).